D1540428

The ENCYCLOPEDIA of FLOWER GARDENING & LANDSCAPING

TIME LIFE® BOOKS

Alexandria, Virginia

CHAPTER ONE

Garden Design

There is much more to designing a flower garden than selecting your favorite plants and putting them in the ground. Before you touch your trowel, you must ask yourself how you intend to use the garden, how you would like it to look, and—most important—you must get to know the property itself.

The Berkeley, California, garden at left strikes a fine balance between style and practicality, demonstrating how plants and landscape elements can work together to create a cohesive design. The lush plantings of pink-flowered fleabane, spiky lavender, and the common garden pole-bean lead the eye upward to take in the wood trellis and the garden gate. The trellis serves as both a boundary and a backdrop for the plants, while the gate's window breaks the horizontal line and offers a glimpse of what lies beyond. In the foreground, a sundial reinforces the geometric design of the garden's structural elements.

On the following pages you'll learn how to create your own design—one that makes the most of your property and fulfills your fondest dreams for a garden of beautiful blooms.

Planning for Outdoor Living

In summer, a climbing rose scrambles up an arched trellis gateway in this Connecticut garden, drawing the eye also to the tall stand of globe thistles and deep orange Asiatic lilies surrounded by a sweep of English lavender. The fine foliage of Artemisia and Dianthus adds texture and cooling shades of green to the scene. In winter (inset), the underlying plant framework of the garden emerges, including the hedge of evergreen eastern hemlocks that marks the border.

Your garden should make as important a contribution to your home life as your house, and its design deserves the same careful attention given your interior decor. Like your house, the garden can be a source of pleasure and relaxation. It can express your interests and tastes. And by projecting beauty and interest to the passing public, it can be an asset to your community.

To design such a space successfully, follow the steps that landscape architects do. First, ask yourself some questions to determine your wants and expectations for a garden. Next, take a discerning look at your property. Then, assess the potential for improvement—what can be upgraded, what should be replaced, what is fine just as it is. Finally, decide on a style *(pages 12-15)*. At that point you are ready to plan—first the hardscape (terraces, walkways, and the like), then the plant choices and the planting arrangement.

Executing a good garden design takes time. A garden will evolve as it matures, changing character as plants grow taller and broader. While this is going on, your needs and interests may change as well. At some point you may have to hire a professional for difficult jobs such as earth grading or tree removal. You might also need to implement your design in stages so you don't break your budget. Fortunately, the design process does not have to be rushed. You can give yourself plenty of time to make the right choices. Begin by asking a basic question:

What Is a Garden?

A garden is fundamentally a humanized outdoor space, an idealized form of the natural landscape. The term *garden* can sometimes mean a discrete planting, such as a perennial border or a vegetable patch. At other times it can refer to an entire property as the object of a comprehensive garden design.

A garden can occupy various locations in relation to the house. It can be on a remote part of the property, as might be typical of a vegetable or cutting garden. Or it can be adjacent to the house—a kind of outdoor room. And, of course, it can encompass all the grounds, including the house itself.

In practice, most properties are made up of more than one garden, each in its own space, according to its use. The individual gardens are then linked into a whole by a unifying network of pathways and sightlines.

Rewards of a Good Design

By linking all parts of your property with the house, a well-designed garden will increase your living space. Various areas will become cherished parts of daily life as places to entertain, play, or relax in comfort and safety. The sense of security afforded you by your house will extend to the surrounding property.

The character of your neighborhood can be a starting point for design decisions. You may want to block a sightline to a neighbor's property or frame a distant view. The style of your house and the history of your area are other possible cues. To complement a 19th-century southern farmhouse, for example, a dooryard flower garden surrounded by a white picket fence, with a stone path leading from fence to door, might be just right. Or you may be influenced by the local ecology, choosing plants to either attract or repel wildlife.

But your garden could also be designed to satisfy less tangible impulses—to create a mood, conjure up memories, or express certain ideals. You might be inspired by the soft feel of pine needles underfoot or the fluttering of swarms of butterflies on a butterfly bush. Such ideas can be the beginning of a highly satisfying garden plan.

Deciding What You Want

Your first step is to assemble a wish list of attributes for your garden. For most people, the top priority is year-round interest. It is a good idea to study your site first in winter to get the clearest idea of its structural framework—the hardscape, made up of imposed features such as walks and fences; and the softscape, composed of trees, shrubs, and ornamental grasses. Another important criterion for most gardeners is conservation—of energy, money, and natural resources. This means devising a plan that minimizes mowing, watering, fertilizing, weeding, and pruning, and choosing plants that have proved themselves.

Although the design of your house will directly affect the design of your garden, you should also consider the garden's effect on the house. Shade trees, for example, can reduce the cost of cooling your house. On the other hand, some plants can be destructive and should be grown away from the house. A wisteria vine, for example, can pull down your gutters. And tree limbs overhanging your roof can come crashing down in a storm.

Consult the other members of the family who will be using the garden. What kind of play area will the children want? Do you want a cook's garden with fruits, vegetables, and herbs? Also con-

sider the kinds of pets you have and what their impact may be on a garden.

If you have particular horticultural interests, look for suitable places to realize them—a stony slope for a rock garden, a soggy area for a bog garden, a south- or east-facing wall for an attached greenhouse. The site itself will suggest intriguing possibilities to add to your wish list.

Assessing Your Property

The next step is to make an informal survey of your property. Eventually, you will need to make detailed sketches and keep a record of your ob-

The metal wall sculpture at the rear of this elegant circular terrace garden in New Orleans provides a dramatic focal point that beckons a visitor. Twin pillars topped with geraniums, as well as the potted palms at the entrance, frame the view and strengthen the axis.

servations *(page 11),* but at this stage you should only be taking an overall look at the site.

Start beyond its boundaries. From here you will see the public face of your property. Walk or drive past and try to look at the site with the eyes of someone encountering it for the first time. Is the house open to view or shrouded by trees? Is the entryway welcoming or obscured by shrubs? What kind of impression does the garden make, and is it harmonious with the architecture of the house?

Ask your neighbors for permission to walk your boundary line from their side, and look at your house from their point of view. From here you'll see what privacy screening you may want or need. Then go inside your house and look out each window and door. From this vantage you'll see opportunities to feature certain sightlines. Inspecting the grounds from upstairs windows is particularly revealing of patterns that are not otherwise apparent. Areas visible from important viewpoints such as a picture window in the living room or the window over the kitchen sink are obvious spots for a garden.

The view from a door might reveal a destination—an inviting, sun-dappled bench, for example—and the passage toward it should begin with a comfortable transition space to the outdoors, such as a wide landing with a pathway leading to a patio or to another part of the garden. You might decide that it is worth enlarging a window or replacing a small door with wider French doors to give the house better views to the garden.

Developing Focal Points

As you explore the views on your property, you will discover eye-catching spots you may wish to feature. These will be the focal points on which to base your garden design.

Focal points occur wherever sightlines intersect. They usually lie within the property but sometimes occur beyond it. In the front of the house, for instance, the focal point is the entranceway, where the strong vertical lines of the front door meet the horizontal of the threshold. In a landscape, a focal point will exist where the curve of a path disappears around a row of shrubs or the corner of a house. It could also be an imposing feature beyond your boundaries—a graceful tree or a pond, perhaps.

The sightline leading to a focal point is known as an axis, and your garden may have more than one. An axis creates movement in the garden, inviting the eye to follow it to the focal point. Together, axes unify the design by linking the viewer to all its parts. These links can be strengthened in several ways. First, a focal point itself will become more prominent if an object or a plant is placed there, or if it is framed or enclosed. Also, an axis will be accentuated if a pathway is built along it and the line enhanced with plantings. For instance, the focal point of a view from a patio might be a small flower bed. Adding a flagstone walk from the patio to the bed and framing the view with a pair of vertical shrubs or an arched trellis will create a unified arrangement.

Moving through the Garden

Just as you surveyed your property from the vantage points of the street and the house, you should also stroll through the garden itself to find existing or potential focal points. These will become stopping places and the sightlines leading to them will become pathways.

You can best create this delightful effect by establishing a series of spaces, or rooms, that are either open or closed, beginning with the enclosed space of the house, moving away from the house, and then back again. For example, a network of axes might start from the living room, conveying the visitor through sliding glass doors to the deck, then across a lawn to an intimate shade garden with a hammock under a tree, then over to a sunny, open vegetable garden, and finally back to an herb garden beside the kitchen door.

A garden subdivided into such separate rooms, each with its own character, is both inherently interesting and functional. As in a house, each space has its own purpose: A sunny corner near a hedge might be a retreat; the open lawn, a playing field; the patio, a place for dining alfresco.

How you or your visitors move through the garden—the route you take and what you see along the way—will affect your experience of it. You can determine whether someone strides along quickly or lingers to admire the view. For instance, a walk along a narrow, winding path bordered with interesting flowers is likely to be slower than one along a straight, wide path crossing a lawn. Gates at transition points and steps built into a sloping path also affect the pace of your walk, forcing you to slow down and take in the scene.

Finally, it is the stopping places—a deck, patio, walled courtyard, clearing, or shady bench overlooking a view—that lend a garden a feeling of shelter and restfulness. Be sure to have several such stops on your garden journey, and keep them separate and discreet so that they are a pleasure to rediscover each time you arrive.

Highlighting a Property's Strengths and Weaknesses

On a property-survey plat serving as a base map, the homeowner has used red ink to indicate existing plantings and record notes on topography, views to emphasize or screen, and possible drainage problems. The assessment reveals minimum landscaping but plenty of potential for an outstanding garden on this nearly one acre property. Two obvious problems demand attention: The overgrown woods to the south and west take up considerable space and loom over the house to such an extent that it is not even necessary to mark on the map the oppressive shade they cast. Another target for major redesign is the steep slope in the eastern corner, planted with randomly scattered trees.

Although the gravel paths in this Los Angeles garden are its "official" walkways, stepping-stones interplanted with sweet alyssum allow for the human tendency to create shortcuts.

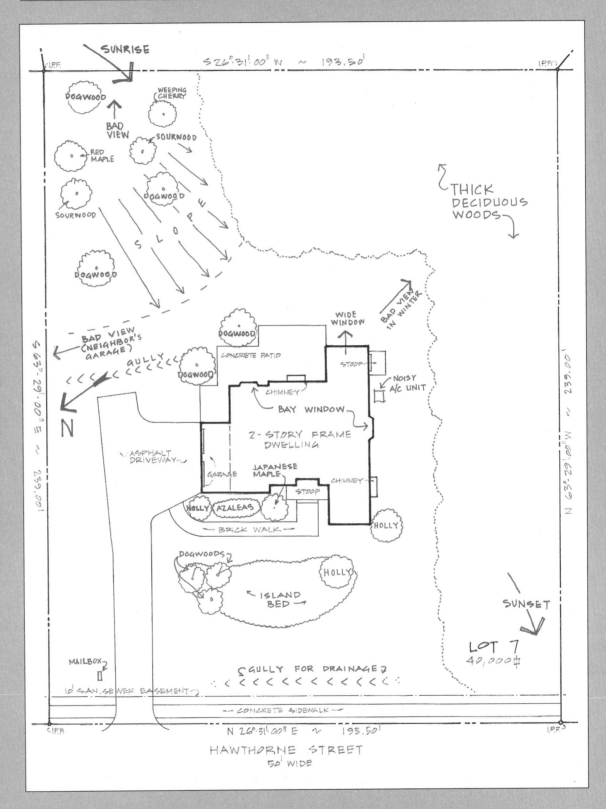

Garden Styles

A garden may have a certain character or style, just as houses do. Styles have historical associations, but they are also influenced by regional cultures and growing conditions. Your first consideration should be to keep the style of your garden in harmony with that of your house. Next, take into account climate, soil, and the lay of the land. In fact, many popular garden styles have developed over the years specifically to address regional environmental conditions.

But the style you choose should not be the result of practical considerations alone. It should reflect your taste, your sense of beauty, and your desires. Thus you might decide to have one style of garden in the front yard—a formal one, perhaps—and a totally different look for the side or back yard, where you entertain or where your children play. The garden types described here are only an indication of the range of possibilities.

Formal and Informal Gardens

A house with a strong classical design calls for the strong axes and crisply defined focal points of a formal garden. Building materials such as brick or stone block look appropriate in a formal setting. Formal gardens are boldly geometric in structure. Straight lines, simple curves, precise angles, and sharp edges all contribute to a formal feeling. Symmetrical pairings mirroring each other and framing a central feature—such as two roses pruned into standards flanking a garden sculpture; carpet planting of a single type of plant; and ornate pruning are all elements of a formal design.

Despite this rigidity, formal gardens come in great variety and include rose and herb gardens, flower beds arranged like mosaics, water gardens that reflect the sky in yet another kind of symmetry, and walled vegetable gardens called potagers. Their strong ground plans are easy to read, and they retain a presence even in winter's landscape.

If you like the formal look but only up to a point, you can soften the formal geometry with a cascade of wisteria or a climbing rose on a wall or with a naturalistic planting of herbaceous perennials that billows over a border's straight edge. This softening of the formal style became the basis for the traditional English cottage garden, typically a charming, informal tangle of annual and peren-nial blossoms set within a well-defined space.

During Colonial times, American houses had cottage or dooryard gardens that were similar to their English-cottage counterparts, with a profusion of flowering plants blooming in beguiling disarray on either side of the front door and along the front of the house. Today, a more structured version of the dooryard garden has become the most popular American landscape style—an informal garden with a somewhat loose, natural appearance featuring irregular or compound curves. But this is not laissez faire gardening. The style calls for crisply defined beds forming a strong ground pattern. Planting arrangements, though not usually symmetrical, are carefully balanced. Brick, stone, and concrete effects borrowed from the house are built into paths and walls.

The axes and focal points in an informal garden are subtler and the patterns less regular than in a formal arrangement. They may exist naturally on your land, needing only a little emphasis from you to bring them out. Or a focal point might be implied by making a clearing in a line of trees, and the axis leading to it may be no more than an irregularly spaced line of shrubs.

In addition, the mechanism for framing a focal point by bracketing it will be more naturalistic than in a formal garden. For example, rather than balancing two identical clipped shrubs on either side of a focal point, you might achieve an informal balance with a small conifer and a clump of soft foliage to one side and a large rock on the other. The two masses may be equivalent in visual weight, but their textures and forms are quite different.

Japanese-Inspired Gardens

The Japanese-style garden blends some of the principles of formal design—strong, clean lines, for example—with the asymmetry of the informal garden. Each element is carefully chosen to achieve an exquisite effect—a rock is placed just so, a tree is sited to weep over a pool and be reflected in the water, the sinuous motion of a stream is captured in the flowing bends of a path.

The plants and building materials in a Japanese garden reflect a fine attention to detail and are generally kept to a small scale. The emphasis is on the texture and form of plant foliage, rock, and wood, with occasional splashes of flower color.

Enclosed by a low hedge of Japanese holly, this Atlanta, Georgia, parterre—four rectangular beds laid out in a carpetlike pattern—lends a formal accent to the stone steps leading up to the back garden. Wall germander outlines the central beds, which are filled with red wax begonias surrounding a pot of trained ivy.

Regional Gardens

Regional garden designs reflect local climate and growing conditions. They incorporate native plants best suited to that environment and include structural elements, such as walls and water features, that temper the effects of the weather.

Desert gardens thrive in extremes of drought and heat. A desert is not hot all year round, but it is dry, with annual rainfall of less than 10 inches. Plants grow low to the ground, and trees are spaced widely to conserve water. A desert garden follows that model, using plants like prickly pear, ocotillo, and spiky yucca. Trees such as carob, acacia, and common olive have deep taproots to reach underground water, and cast cooling shade. High courtyard walls and sun-screening trellises help moderate the heat and glare.

Mediterranean gardens are a variation on the desert garden. Originating in the arid climate of Spain, North Africa, and the eastern Mediterranean, they have transplanted easily to California and the American Southwest. Suited to contemporary, stucco, or Spanish-style houses, these gardens nestle in the shelter of a courtyard or atrium. The plantings can be lush, featuring exotically colored and scented tropical trees such as citrus, banana, and palm, all surrounding a central fountain. Vines such as jasmine and bougainvillea climb the garden's walls, and ferns, hibiscus, oleander, and bird-of-paradise grow in pots and raised beds.

Landscape Plants for Specific Styles

FORMAL

TREES
Acer
(maple)
Cedrus
(cedar)
Cupressus sempervirens
(Italian cypress)
Fagus sylvatica
(European beech)
Magnolia
(magnolia)
Picea
(spruce)
Quercus
(oak)

SHRUBS
Berberis thunbergii
(Japanese barberry)
Ilex crenata
(Japanese holly)
Ilex vomitoria
(yaupon)
Prunus laurocerasus
(cherry laurel)
Rosa hybrids
(hybrid roses)
Taxus baccata
(English yew)

VINES
Rosa
(climbing hybrid rose)
Wisteria
(wisteria)

GROUND COVERS
Calluna vulgaris
(heather)
Hosta
(plantain lily)

INFORMAL

TREES
Acer rubrum
(red maple)
Acer saccharum
(sugar maple)

SHRUBS
Euonymus alata
(winged spindle tree)
Lagerstroemia indica
(crape myrtle)
Rhododendron
(rhododendron)
Rosa rugosa
(rugosa rose)
Syringa
(lilac)

JAPANESE

TREES
Acer palmatum
(Japanese maple)
Malus floribunda
(Japanese flowering crab apple)
Pinus densiflora
(Japanese red pine)

SHRUBS
Chaenomeles
(flowering quince)
Juniperus
(juniper)
Pieris japonica
(lily-of-the-valley bush)
Pinus mugo
(dwarf mountain pine)

VINES
Wisteria floribunda
(Japanese wisteria)

GROUND COVERS
Liriope muscari
(big blue lilyturf)

Acer rubrum
(red maple)

Woodland Gardens

Wherever it might appear, a woodland garden consists of the same two elements: a number of large trees to create an overhead canopy, and a succession of underlayers—smaller trees, shrubs, and ground-level plants like wildflowers, ferns, and mosses. To create a successful design, reduce the natural abundance of a woodland to a few simple elements. Build in a clearing to let in light for the less shade-tolerant plants and to bring about a contrast of light and dark. But make sure a few saplings are interspersed among the older trees to ensure successive generations of shade trees. Then make

a path through the garden to take you from place to place and to keep visitors from trampling delicate plants. If you choose plants that produce berries and flowers to create a habitat for wildlife, after a time you will develop a self-sustaining environment that requires little further effort.

Meadow and Prairie Gardens

While woodland gardens provide a shady oasis, wildflower meadow and prairie gardens are open, sunny, and alive with color and texture. They also are more precarious, requiring periodic mowing to prevent unwanted saplings from taking over and to allow desirable seedlings to become established. These gardens work especially well as transition areas between the more structured part of the garden and the openness of the surrounding countryside. Plant mixtures for meadows and prairies will vary according to soil and rainfall, but all will require full sun. You can purchase seed mixes suited to your area from seed companies. These mixes will include annual and perennial wildflowers, such as daisies, sundrops, butterfly weed, and Texas bluebonnet. The annuals should reseed themselves after the first year. Also included will be native bunch grasses like switch grass, big bluestem, and little bluestem. Bulbs planted in broad swaths also naturalize well in a wild meadow.

A North Carolina garden sets the simplicity of the Japanese style within a Western border and lawn. Plants indigenous to Japan, such as red laceleaf Japanese maple, multicolored Houttuynia cordata, and two varieties of Japanese cedar, harmonize beautifully. The shape of the pyramidal rock, for example, is echoed in the smaller cedar 'Bandai-Sugi'.

Pathways and Pavings

The path in this New Hampshire garden is paved with long rectangular stones set in a zigzag pattern; within the frame they create are multicolored cobblestones and round and diamond-shaped concrete slabs. Simple plantings, including a compact Rhododendron 'Ramapo' and an arborvitae hedge, line one side of the path; yellow shrubby cinquefoil spills in from the other.

Paths and walkways create physical links between one place and another. In working them into your garden plans, keep in mind that no matter where they go or what they are made of, walkways should be compatible with the style of your house and with your landscape.

Start by deciding where you want the walkways to begin and end. Stroll around your property, examining its dimensions and contours. Do your design ideas lend themselves to pathways that follow a straight line, as in a formal garden? Or are meandering routes more appropriate, paths that induce the visitor to stop here and there along the way?

Take plenty of time in your exploratory walk through the garden, following natural routes from place to place. Once you've chosen the likeliest lines for your paths to follow, wait for a good heavy rain to come along, and then go out and check drainage patterns along and adjacent to these lines. Improperly positioned walkways can act like dams, exacerbating drainage problems.

In general, heavily traveled walkways, such as those leading to the house from the front sidewalk or the driveway, should be formal in design and constructed from hard, durable materials like concrete, brick, unglazed tile, or stone. They should follow straight lines and right angles or simple curves, and their edges should be well defined. For safety's sake, all walkways should present smooth but nonslick surfaces, and, ideally, they should be wide enough—4 to 5 feet across—for two people to walk abreast comfortably.

Informal Paths

Informal styles are usually chosen for less traveled paths, such as those leading into and through the garden, and can be constructed with softer paving materials. Such paths often have a meandering quality, but they can take any form you want them to. Merely setting out stone slabs in an irregular pattern through your garden will create a simple walkway and add visual interest. A winding gravel path with wood rounds set into the gravel at intervals would not only be aesthetically pleasing

but would also encourage a leisurely stroll. Informal paths are usually narrower than main walkways—from 2½ to 3 feet wide—but should still be wide enough for you to traverse comfortably with garden equipment. For an even more informal look, you can soften the effect of paving materials by letting plantings spill over onto them. Place small mound-forming plants like moss, thyme, or alyssum around paving stones to add texture, beauty, and softness to the surface.

Selecting Pavement Styles

The mood a hardscape material contributes to your overall design is a major consideration in choosing it. But equally important are such practical matters as cost and ease of installation and maintenance. If you don't have a lot of time to devote to plant care, you may want to invest in an intricate paving pattern or a mosaic tile that will act as a focal point, and then put in plants and ground covers that virtually look after themselves. If, on the other hand, you have considerable time for gardening, select a simple garden paving material and offset it with glorious flower borders.

Weather is another practical matter to consider. Some paving materials are more susceptible than others to damage by frost or hot, baking sun. And some, such as smooth concrete, tile, wood, brick, and stone, can be slippery when wet.

When you've worked out the practical questions, it's time to consider aesthetics. First look at the style and colors of your house and at the colors and textures of your present plantings. Decide how you want your pathways to fit in with them.

The gray stones of this Berkeley, California, pathway take a backseat to the Dianthus 'Rose Bowl', thrift, and Dalmatian bellflower that grow between them. Geraniums and Santa Barbara daisies offer a profusion of blooms, while spotted dead nettle, lamb's ears, and Siberian iris add texture and lushness.

Making a Natural Fieldstone Pathway

Using only a shovel, you can build an informal pathway of natural fieldstone. This material, an unquarried stone, fits in well with rustic, naturalistic landscape designs. The one drawback is that the stones are heavy, so it's best to have your local stone yard or quarry deliver them and deposit them beside the site of the pathway.

Choose randomly sized stones that are flat on top and large enough to tread upon comfortably. Then experiment with different arrangements, mapping out a route that is underlain by firm soil. Working along the route, but before you have begun digging, set the larger stones in place to get the general shape of the path. Then fill in the gaps with smaller stones. Leave a natural stepping distance between large stones laid in a line—about 18 inches. If your path is curved, set a large stone at the points where the path bends, to serve as stopping areas. Vary the size of the stones, and try to match shapes of adjoining stones so that their sides align fairly well.

To set a steppingstone path of large, widely spaced stones, dig a hole for each stone, add a little builder's sand or stone dust (available where you buy the fieldstone), and position the stone in the hole. Adjust the material underneath the stone and replace the soil around it until the stone is firm and stable. For a path of closely set stones, follow the directions below for laying the stones in a trench.

1. Before you dig your trench, *do a practice run by laying the stones down in a pattern that's both comfortable to walk on and aesthetically pleasing. Once you have settled on a workable path, dig a trench 5 to 6 inches deep and spread a 3-inch-deep bed of builder's sand or stone dust over it. Then lay the stones in place, aligning their irregular sides as much as possible.*

2. When the stones are set in the trench, *fill the spaces between them with soil. To keep the stones from tilting or wobbling, make sure at least two-thirds of the thickness of each is encased firmly in the soil. Then wet the soil with a fine spray of water. If the soil settles, add more. The surface of the stones should stand slightly higher than ground level. Plant grass or a ground cover between the stones or sweep builder's sand between them (left).*

Paving Materials

The possibilities for paving are almost limitless. Your choices range from such hard materials as brick, concrete, flagstone, fieldstone, granite, tile, and wood to softer materials, including loose aggregates such as gravel, cobbles, crushed rock, woodchips, or bark chips. And, of course, you can combine hard and soft materials very successfully.

Stone works especially well in naturalistic settings; you can find it in many sizes and in both regular and random shapes. In making a choice, remember that different types of stone vary in durability, slipperiness, and resistance to frost damage. Tiles—both terra-cotta and the more durable high-fired types—though relatively expensive are highly decorative, conveying a feeling of elegance. Tile is a poor choice, however, in climates where cycles of freezing and thawing occur, because wide cold-weather temperature fluctuations can cause it to crack. Remember, too, that in the rain, glazed tiles are slipperier than unglazed types.

Wood is a versatile paving material and conveys a warmth difficult to achieve with a harder material such as concrete. Woods that can be left to weather naturally, such as red cedar, cypress, and redwood, can be especially attractive. Although easy to install and fairly inexpensive, wood pavings will eventually decompose. You can extend their life somewhat by installing them in a way that allows for ventilation on the underside.

Loose Aggregates

Gravel is a popular choice among loose-aggregate paving materials. Inexpensive and easy to install, it is especially useful in spots where a less porous paving might create or worsen a drainage problem. Some maintenance is required, however. You'll need to rake gravel periodically, because it gets squeezed out of place when walked on. Your pathway will also require an edging to keep the migrating gravel from spilling over onto plantings.

Gravel tends to refract and absorb light, which can help soften the appearance of the entire garden. Remember, though, that gravel may look a bit boring when used exclusively, so plan to interrupt the line of a simple gravel path by introducing other paving materials at random, such as stone pavers or wood rounds.

The same holds true for other visually neutral materials, such as woodchips. It is best to combine them with other, more intricate-looking pavers. And no matter what type of loose-aggregate material you use, be sure to place layers of newspaper under it to help control weeds.

Patterns and Textures

As you plan your walkways, consider the roles that color, pattern, and texture play in the appearance of your garden. Simple, neutral paving works best with complex planting schemes. If your garden is filled with flowers, for example, brick might clash with red, pink, or orange blooms. Consider using gravel or flagstone and save brick for areas where the focus is on evergreens or foliage.

You can use pattern and texture in paving to convey various moods. Woodchips used together with steps created from landscape timbers, for example, lend a quiet, woodland feel. Wood planks set in a base of gravel give a more dynamic feeling—the mixture of textures, patterns, and materials keeps the eye moving.

Straight lines that run away from a particular viewpoint intensify a sense of direction and depth, whereas lines that cross the field of vision create a sense of breadth. Patterns that have a static quality—regular, symmetrical shapes such as squares, circles, and hexagons, for example—can help create a restful effect. Use them in places where you might want guests to linger. If you do choose a static arrangement, pay attention to the size of your paving units. A broad expanse of small units can create a fussy or dull appearance.

Edgings

There are several good reasons for bordering your pathways with some sort of hard edging. First, if you pave a path with a soft material such as gravel, bark, or woodchips, you will need some sort of edging to contain the material and prevent it from spreading out onto the surrounding ground and thinning out on the path until bare earth shows through. Second, if the path cuts across the lawn, edging will serve the dual purpose of keeping the turf grass within bounds and providing a hard surface for the wheels of your lawn mower as you mow the edge of the lawn.

You will find a variety of edgings at home stores. Brick can be set on edge or on end, for example. You can also buy stone or concrete pavers or concrete sections designed to be set end to end. For rustic or woodsy landscapes, pressure-treated 4-by-4 or 6-by-6 timbers and uncut stone work well.

Paving with Brick

Brick comes in many colors, shapes, and textures, and adds warmth and interest to virtually any landscape. It can be arranged in a variety of different patterns and looks equally appropriate in formal and informal settings. It is also durable and easy to work with.

In selecting a specific brick, first consider your climate. Where frost occurs, look for brick designated SX, which means it will resist the effects of freezing and thawing. Then select a brick texture: Some have smooth, sleek surfaces and sharp edges, whereas others are more porous, with rounded edges.

The way in which you lay the brick can create moods. A running pattern—used alone, as shown below, or in combination with a stacked bond pattern—conveys fluidity and movement. By contrast, a basket-weave pattern gives a feeling of containment.

STACKED BOND

HERRINGBONE

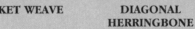

BASKET WEAVE **DIAGONAL HERRINGBONE** **RUNNING AND STACKED BOND**

Defining the Path with Plants

Plantings along a pathway can elicit different feelings or moods depending on the plants used. For example, parallel rows of dwarf fruit trees along a path would create a formal processional way, whereas tall, dense evergreen shrubs might, in time, produce a tunnel-like effect.

Plants define and reinforce the garden structure. When choosing plants for pathways consider height, width, and growth habit. In the La Jolla, California, garden above, a stone stairway is edged with clumps of low-growing perennials. The variety of plants and the way they creep onto the stones emphasize the informal woodland feel of the design.

A uniform border of low shrubs or perennials along a curved path, as shown here, mimics the vegetation lining a fast-running stream and reinforces linear movement along the pathway. A colonnade of trees or tall shrubs along the same path would give the illusion of enclosing the path with a physical barrier and thus even more strongly direct the eye along its length to a destination in the distance.

To deemphasize a pathway— say, a driveway—you can soften its straight lines by edging it with plants that will spill onto the surface. You could also widen the path at certain points and install plantings, creating stopping places. Trees or shrubs clustered in the bends of a curved path, like the pooling of water in the bend of a stream, also create visual interest along the length of the walkway.

Accessories for
the Garden

Decorative elements such as containers, statuary, benches, and sundials can help you create a garden that's more than just a pretty collection of plants. Thoughtfully selected and placed, outdoor decorative pieces can create a focal point, complement foliage and flowers, define boundaries, provide smooth transitions between plantings, and increase the area available for cultivation. Before you select your garden decorations, make sure you know your garden well, and let its size, style, and purpose guide you. Classical statues look appropriately imposing in a formal garden with well-defined beds; a stone frog hiding under parsley sprigs might better suit a kitchen garden.

Culinary plantings of thyme, oregano, fennel, sage, tarragon, and mint share space with ornamental daisies, pinks, heliotrope, and alyssum in a trio of terra-cotta containers at the edge of a brick patio.

Container Gardening

Containers, a favorite of the city gardener with limited space for cultivation, come in many shapes, sizes, and materials. Filled with annuals or perennials, they can go almost anywhere to brighten an existing plant bed or to extend your growing area on patios, decks, balconies, sidewalks, and even walls. People confined to wheelchairs or those for whom bending and kneeling are difficult may find containers a pleasing gardening alternative to

Making a Log Planter

A fallen tree trunk can be recycled into a distinctive wooden planter that will hold a mixture of perennials and annuals. First, dig out the center of the log to a depth of about a foot, then cut a V-shaped groove from the center opening out to one end of the log; this will provide drainage. Fill the hole with an appropriate soil mix, then plant easy-care varieties such as begonias, hostas, impatiens, or bulbs.

Place one or more logs around a patio or along a garden path; or place your log planter in a less structured setting. Set several small boulders around the log to stabilize it and help it blend with its setting.

working in the ground. Containers can also become garden focal points or accents if they have a striking shape or texture.

Be sure to choose containers that will suit their contents. If you want to highlight your plantings, simple containers are best. If, on the other hand, you wish to feature a lovely pot, choose a simpler plant. And if an outdoor container is to hold perennials, be sure it is large enough to keep freezing temperatures from reaching the roots.

Choosing Containers

Pick a container that is the correct size and weight for your plant and your purposes. If you are hanging plants from a ceiling or wall, lightweight plastic planters or a wire-and-moss arrangement may be best. Heavier trees and shrubs need to be based in sturdy tubs or barrels so that they are not blown over by a strong wind. And always locate your containers where they're not too difficult to reach for watering.

Anything from a wheelbarrow to an old sink can be turned into a container for plants. Most of the containers available commercially are made of terra cotta, wood, plastic, cast stone, or concrete or fiberglass molded to look like stone.

Terra cotta works well in both formal and informal settings, and its neutral color harmonizes with almost any color of flower or foliage. But it may not stand up to repeated freezing and thawing, and glazed terra cotta is even less resistant to fluctuating hot and cold temperatures.

Wood containers, such as barrels or tubs, are unaffected by frost and can be treated to resist rot. They look better in casual settings and, because they are available in large sizes, are often used for permanent plantings such as ornamental fruit trees, juniper trees, and some varieties of cypress, azalea, and rhododendron. Small wooden boxes are attractive underneath windows, on porch or deck railings, or along the perimeter of a patio. You can paint them for added visual interest.

Because plastic and composite containers start to look shabby relatively quickly, it's best to limit their use to annuals. Petunias, impatiens, geraniums, and snapdragons will flourish in a plastic container hung from the porch ceiling. Plastic is

Vinca 'Little Bright Eyes', Cleome 'Royal Queen', Zinnia elegans 'Bouquet White', and Artemisia schmidtiana 'Silver Dust' surround this New Jersey garden's sundial in summer. In winter, the absence of flowers will bring out its elegant form even more strongly.

available in a variety of colors. Green and other neutral colors are a safe bet with any planting; white containers quickly show scratches and dirt.

Cast stone and concrete containers are appropriate for both formal and informal gardens. They resist damage from rain, snow, and freezing temperatures. Plan the placement of a large stone container carefully—once it is filled it will be difficult to move. Some fiberglass containers look like stone but are much lighter.

Decorative Details

Garden ornaments can make a garden uniquely your own. Adornments help set a garden's tone, be it whimsical, understated, formal, practical, or sentimental. An ornament might be a focal point, or you might tuck one in an out-of-the-way corner to be come upon unexpectedly.

Heavy stone objects like urns look best in a formal garden with well-defined paths. In this sort of setting you might use an obelisk or a sundial on a pedestal as a centerpiece. A fragrant herb garden would be a prime location for a conical beehive shape; small stone sculptures of dogs, cats, frogs, rabbits, turtles, or gnomes are popular additions to a woodland garden.

Ornaments of all sorts are available in gardening stores and through catalogs, but if you're creative, you can turn almost anything into a garden decoration. Birdbaths and old birdcages are an inviting touch. Or if an old weather vane or lantern appeals to you, try it out. After all, it's your garden.

Seating

Before you choose seating for your garden, consider these questions: Will a seat at a given location serve as a brief rest spot, an afternoon lounging retreat, or a vantage point from which to view a certain portion of the landscape? Will the seating be permanent, or will you want to shift it as the sunlight fades and the seasons change?

A bench or chair for the garden is more than just a place to sit; it can be used as a decoration as well. Various kinds of seats are available in a range of sizes, materials, and colors. The challenge is to make sure that your seat, bench, or swing harmonizes with its surroundings. A formal scrolled-iron bench, for example, may look out of place among plant containers created from rusted milk pails and weathered wine cases.

In formal gardens, stone benches might be used to define boundaries between cultivated

beds; they can also work in tandem with such stone ornaments as statues, vases, and urns to contribute to the stately tone of such gardens.

You might also place a bench at the end of a path, grass alley, or arbor to provide a visual focal point and a convenient resting place after a stroll in the garden. Cast-iron furniture looks at home in a formal setting, while rustic twig furniture adds a homey touch to a more informal garden. Wicker and rattan contribute an exotic flavor to many settings; they will survive longer if they are somewhat protected from the elements.

Traditionally, garden furniture has been green, white, or black. White contrasts most sharply with the surrounding foliage; green blends more smoothly with the varied tints of leaves, bushes, and grasses; and black is the most stately. But many colorful alternatives are now available.

The owner of this Los Angeles garden, not Mother Nature, provided the large flat-topped stone on which to sit and enjoy the scenery. Set atop flagstones among plumes of rose fountain grass, feather grass, and drifts of sweet alyssum, the stone seat also provides a visual transition between the two plant groupings.

Composing with Color

You can ensure maximum year-round interest in your garden by weaving threads of seasonal color throughout its beds and borders. The first step is to sketch out color ideas on paper, so that when you are ready to plant you will be able to create a sense of unity throughout the garden. Your personal preferences will guide you in your initial choice of colors. You may lean toward hues from the warm end of the spectrum, such as red, orange, and yellow, rather than the cool end, which includes the greens, blues, and violets. Perhaps you prefer delicate tints over strong shades, and harmonious blendings over bright contrasts. Before you make any final decisions, however, there are a number of other things you must consider.

Color, Light, and Mood

How colors appear in your garden will depend on two factors—whether a planting is located in sun or shade and the way light changes from morning to night and through the seasons. Pastels stand out in the soft light of early morning or evening, for example, and fairly glimmer in the shade, but their pale presence is lost in bright midday sun, where strong, bright colors like reds and oranges do best. Colors that glow warmly in autumn light, such as bronze or purple, may look drab on hazy summer days or in the cold glare of winter.

One way to plan for successful seasonal colors is to observe the hues nature reveals over time. Spring is a symphony of pastel-blooming trees, shrubs, and bulbs, followed by deeper tints of blue, yellow, and pink as summer gets under way. Late summer is dominated by highly saturated colors—vibrant yellow, Day-Glo orange, hot red, deep pink, fuchsia, and violet. By contrast, fall is cloaked in muted shades of gold, bronze, rust, plum, and purple.

Certain color groupings will create different moods in the garden. Try planting pink, purple, or blue pastels interspersed with neutral whites and grays for a cooling and soothing effect. A garden theme mixing the neutral colors with various shades of green will create a cool retreat in the heat of summer. To add a little warmth, introduce soft creams and buttery yellows to the mix.

If you want a more vibrant atmosphere, choose strong yellows, golds, oranges, and reds. But use red with care; it is the most dominant color in the spectrum and can be overpowering. A backdrop of dark green foliage can tone down even the brightest reds, but a bright green background will make the reds pop out even more.

Color and Space

Through creative placement of colors, you can define spaces and change perspectives in a garden design. Cool colors lengthen distances, warm colors make them appear closer. Your choice of color groupings, therefore, should be based on the perspective you want to achieve.

Setting the landscape afire with its glowing orange-red fall foliage, a katsura tree (Cercidiphyllum japonicum) stands out from the subtler lime-yellow coloring of Hydrangea anomala ssp. petiolaris (climbing hydrangea) and Idesia polycarpa (iigiri tree).

Anchored by a Colorado blue spruce, drifts of Zinnia elegans 'Sun Red', orange Helichrysum bracteatum 'Bright Bikini' (strawflower), pink Phlox maculata 'Alpha' (wild sweet William), and yellow Lilium 'Citronella' put on a dazzling summer show. In the foreground, a broad green drift of Sedum spectabile 'Brilliant' (showy stonecrop) completes the planting.

When planning beds and borders close to the house, consider how you can accentuate or complement the color of the roof, sides, or trim with foliage and flowers. Also, select herbaceous plants with colors that will tie in with those of adjacent small shrubs, ground covers, and larger plantings. This way, you will maintain a unified color theme.

You can also choose flower colors to attract butterflies and hummingbirds, which favor strong pinks, reds, yellows, and oranges. (Hummingbirds prefer tubular flowers; butterflies, flat and cup-shaped flowers.) To reduce the potentially overwhelming visual impact of these bright colors, use white flowers or dark green, gray, and variegated foliage to separate vivid pinks and reds from equally intense yellows and oranges.

Color from Bulbs and Annuals

To color your landscape from late winter into fall, be sure to include masses of small- and large-flowering bulbs in your design. Select different varieties that bloom simultaneously or those whose bloom times coincide with those of other flowering plants. For example, create a pleasing contrast by teaming up spring-blooming yellow tulips with blue forget-me-nots or with deep blue grape hyacinths. Or, for a harmonious combination, plant purple pansies next to pale lavender crocuses.

Many summer- and fall-flowering bulbs, such as lilies, dahlias, and begonias, bloom for several weeks and will brighten your beds and borders with a rich tapestry of hues ranging from deep pink to brick red, from apricot to bronze. For a blooming sequence that lasts from late winter through fall, plant a sunny border with a mixture of bulbs and perennials—daffodils, Siberian irises, flowering onion, peonies, daylilies, dahlias, rudbeckias, perennial phlox, asters, and chrysanthemums.

Because of their long bloom periods, which can span three seasons, annual bedding plants are good additions to planting schemes that focus on color. Choose their colors carefully, though, so that they will continue to complement the perennials and bulbs in the bed. You can also plant annuals to cover bare spots in the early years of a garden and to fill gaps between shrubs and trees.

Color in the Shade

Areas dominated by trees and shrubs are typically shady, and many varieties of annuals, perennials, and bulbs can brighten these shadowy spots. Begin with late-winter and early-spring bulbs that bloom before deciduous trees leaf out to block the sun. Snowdrops, crocuses, squill, Grecian windflowers, and daffodils are early bloomers that will naturalize into colorful masses.

For the rest of the growing season, fill spaces that receive partial or dappled shade with brightly colored, long-lasting, shade-tolerant perennials such as astilbe, foxglove, spurge, cardinal flower, alumroot, Virginia bluebells, monarda, St.-John's-wort, and red valerian *(Centranthus ruber)*. The most reliable annual for a shady nook is *Impatiens wallerana* (busy Lizzie). If you'd like to draw attention to a planting of dark green shrubs, illuminate them with a grouping of white or pastel flowers, such as impatiens, columbine, lily of the valley, primrose, and bleeding heart.

Foliage Plants

Flowering plants bring a rainbow of colors to a border or bed, but herbaceous foliage plants also have their place. By no means confined to green, the foliage colors of these plants range all over the rest of the spectrum. Used in contrast with the blooms surrounding them, they can turn a merely pleasing border into a visual feast.

The texture of the foliage, which can vary from fine to coarse, also plays a major role. When foliage plants of different texture and shape are planted next to each other, for example, they add a dramatic dimension to the design. Ferns are a good example of plants with fine and feathery foliage. The leaves range in color from dark green to bright green, but one, *Athyrium nipponicum* 'Pictum', is dramatically edged in silver. Other fine, feathery-leaved plants include astilbe, *Artemisia* x 'Powis Castle', goatsbeard, *Perovskia* (Russian sage), yarrow, and *Dicentra eximia* 'Luxuriant'.

A good combination for a shade garden is to plant ferns beside smooth-leaved hostas. Depending on the variety, hosta leaves may be small and narrow or large and flat; tinted with blue, cream, yellow, chartreuse, or dark green; variegated with spots and stripes, or one intense solid color.

Other winning texture combinations include furry silver-gray lamb's ears planted with spiky gray-green lavender or green *Santolina*; the large, glossy, purple leaves of *Heuchera micrantha* 'Palace Purple' with the fragile, feathery leaves of achillea; the thick, vertical, sword-shaped leaves of *Yucca filamentosa* with the small, rounded leaves of *Sempervivum* (houseleek); and the narrow, stiff leaves of ornamental grasses with the low-growing lacy foliage of *Astilbe chinensis* 'Pumila'.

In this Ashton, Maryland, garden, the home-owner has used a sequence of green tones—with pink roses as a foil—to draw a visitor toward the archway and into what she calls a "fairy garden" of silvery foliage beyond. The yellow-leaved Japanese barberries, which thrive in shady areas and poor, dry soils, marry beautifully with the mauve 'Belle de Crecy' rose and the pink 'Aloha' climbers.

Finalizing Your Plan

When you are ready to commit your final planting plan to paper, you'll need to keep in mind how large each plant you choose will grow and how far and how fast it will spread. It takes about 3 years for most herbaceous perennials to spread into drifts, and 5 years for many shrubs to reach maturity. Depending on the growth rate of trees (slow, moderate, or fast) it can take anywhere from 8 to 20 years for them to reach significant size. You'll need to consider whether the trees you have in mind will eventually branch out so broadly that they'll turn your sunny garden into a shady one.

If you're planting slow-growing trees and shrubs, it's important to select a combination of evergreen and deciduous species that will continue to complement each other at maturity. Careful planning in the beginning will save you from the unpleasant and possibly expensive task of removing major plantings after several years of growth because they are crowding each other or simply no longer look good together.

Spacing shrubs to allow for future growth need not leave your garden looking bare and uninteresting during its first few years. To create fullness, you can interplant with perennials, annuals, and filler bulbs, such as tulips, hyacinths, or lilies. And once the shrubs start spreading, it's a simple matter to relocate the herbaceous plants as needed.

Planning for Seasonal Interest

To create a garden that provides four seasons of interest, you will need a mixture of plants that includes some that are visually appealing throughout the year and others that bloom in different months. Before you break ground, your paper plan should indicate which plants produce long-lasting foliage or flowers and which overlap their blooming cycles.

Perhaps the surest way to formulate a successful year-round planting plan is to superimpose on your base map a different tissue overlay for each season. Indicate on each overlay which features—bloom color, leaf texture, distinctive bark, berries, and the like—will be prominent at which locations during that season.

Noting life cycles of flowers, trees, and shrubs will allow you to group plants to advantage. For

In this Connecticut garden, tulips and dafodils share a bed with perennials that will help disguise the bulbs' fading foliage. At the far end, a scarlet Japanese maple contrasts pleasantly with the pastel purple blossoms of a Higan cherry, while a backdrop of rhododendrons provides year-round greenery and the promise of summer flowers.

Tracking the Growth of a New Garden

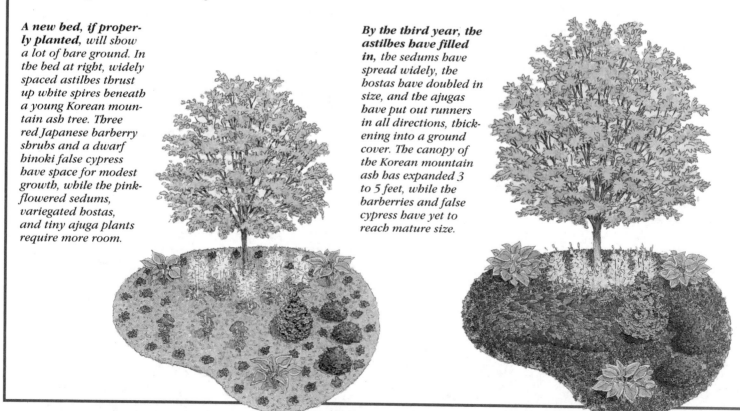

A new bed, if properly planted, will show a lot of bare ground. In the bed at right, widely spaced astilbes thrust up white spires beneath a young Korean mountain ash tree. Three red Japanese barberry shrubs and a dwarf hinoki false cypress have space for modest growth, while the pink-flowered sedums, variegated hostas, and tiny ajuga plants require more room.

By the third year, the astilbes have filled in, the sedums have spread widely, the hostas have doubled in size, and the ajugas have put out runners in all directions, thickening into a ground cover. The canopy of the Korean mountain ash has expanded 3 to 5 feet, while the barberries and false cypress have yet to reach mature size.

The bed has attained a pleasing fullness by the fifth year. While the shrubs show steady but compact growth, the mountain ash continues to expand at 2 feet or so a year, toward its maximum size of 40 feet tall with a canopy 25 feet wide. The astilbes, sedums, and hostas require little maintenance or division, meaning that this bed need not be disturbed for many years to come.

example, when daffodils have finished blooming, you will want their withering leaves out of view. The best way to accomplish this is to grow them in the midst of colorful foliage or tall swaths of annual or perennial flowers, which will come into full growth just as the bulb foliage begins to fade.

And although annuals have a life cycle of just a few months, they create a continuous flow of color from late spring to summer's end. Some, such as impatiens, scarlet sage, pot marigold, zinnia, cleome, cosmos, and zonal geranium, keep on producing blooms until they are killed by a hard frost. Overlapping with these warm-weather favorites are late-summer perennials, which also carry their colorful flowers until nipped by cold temperatures.

You can plan for even more fall color by choosing deciduous shrubs and trees with leaves that take on intensely brilliant hues and by planting perennials such as asters, *Sedum* x 'Autumn Joy' (stonecrop), goldenrod, *Chrysanthemum* x *morifolium* (florist's chrysanthemum), Japanese anemone, *Caryopteris* (bluebeard), *Colchicum autumnale* (autumn crocus), *Colchicum speciosum* 'Album' (showy autumn crocus), Rosa Meidiland varieties, and ornamental grasses.

29

Brightening Winter Months

In the winter, when trees and shrubs have dropped their fiery leaves, you can still enjoy ample color in the various shades of evergreen foliage, tree and shrub bark, berries, dried grasses, and the seed heads of some perennials and shrubs. The bark of certain deciduous trees, such as birch, eastern sycamore, and *Stewartia pseudocamellia* (Japanese stewartia), and the shiny leaves of holly, bull bay, and ivy will delight your eye after most herbaceous plants have gone dormant for the winter.

By late winter, small-bulb shoots are already pushing their way out of the soil. The delicate snowdrops are among the first to bloom, quickly followed by crocuses and other small bulbs and by the blossoming of shrubs such as witch hazel, forsythia, and *Prunus mume* (Japanese flowering apricot). From then on there is no stopping the show of spring-flowering squill, hyacinths, daffodils, and tulips. And if you have planned carefully, you can enjoy the sequential blooms of rhododendron species, flowering cherries, magnolias, dogwoods, lilacs, viburnums, and a host of other blooms that creep over the ground, wind their tendrils up fences, and blossom overhead.

Putting in the Plants

Begin with the largest trees, which involve the greatest amount of digging and the most extensive trampling on surrounding soil. Because cultivated soil is easily compacted, don't till any soil for planting smaller shrubs and herbaceous plants until you are sure you no longer have any need to walk on it. After the large trees are in, add medium-sized shrubs and trees. Follow this stage by planting small decorative specimens, dwarf shrubs, perennials, vines, and ground covers and other filler plants, such as bulbs, annuals, and herbs.

When planting small shrubs, place them in groups of two, three, or even five if space allows. If they are slow growing, shrubs can be sited fairly close together to form a mass that makes a strong impression; you can also plant them farther apart at regular intervals to impart rhythm and continuity to a bed or border. Perennials look better when they are planted close to one another in groups of three or five; but if the plants are young, leave ample room between them. Annuals are more effective when planted in drifts or massed along the edges of a border. It doesn't matter if they crowd one another. Avoid planting flowers singly at random intervals, where their impact would be lost.

In this East Hampton, New York, garden, low-growing bird's-nest spruce, bloodleaf Japanese maple, and variegated hinoki false cypress (far right) furnish year-round interest. The ground-hugging lady's-mantle combined with the large ribbed leaves of hosta, the tall spires of foxtail lily, and the lacy heads of hydrangea contribute more seasonal texture. 'Just Joey' roses, 'Johnson's Blue' geraniums, and other perennials provide weeks of color.

Bringing It All Together

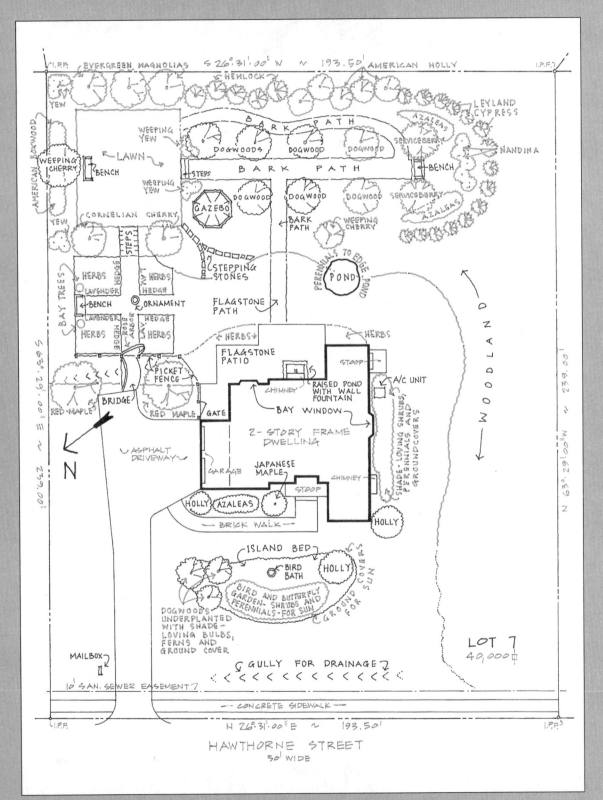

The final phase of this sample garden design is to impose a planting plan on the property map. The map now shows in black ink the regrading and transplanting to be done, and the installation of hardscape elements—such as a brick path and a flagstone patio—the gardener has chosen. Using green ink, she has laid out an ambitious project that will probably take several years to complete. Included are a screen of ornamental trees along the rear property line, a foliage cul-de-sac in the south corner, a lawn framed by shrubs and ornamental trees on the new terrace in the east corner, a formal herb garden, a mixed shade border on the southwest side of the house, and a bird-and-butterfly garden in the existing bed at the front of the house.

CHAPTER TWO

Annuals and Biennials

When it comes to spectacular flower color, annuals can't be topped. From the simplest display in a window box to the most lavish design in a formal garden, this plant group—which includes biennials, with their two-year lifespan—dress up any space. The flowers of annuals can also be depended upon to hold their color long after they have been picked, making them perfect for indoor arrangements. And many annuals boast a heady fragrance—another feature that makes them welcome both in the garden and in the home.

Because they are easy to grow and easy to replace, annuals allow you to experiment with designs as no other garden plants can. In the Pennsylvania yard at right, for example, the gardener has created stunning circular beds of pink, red, and white 'Elfin Mix' impatiens, partnered with perennial rose pink astilbe. Whether you choose old favorites like impatiens or some of the lesser-known but equally lovely plants described here, you'll be amazed at the versatility of annuals.

How Annuals Grow

Simply put, gardeners love annuals for their flowers. While perennials and shrubs may produce beautiful blossoms, they last only a few weeks, and thoughtful gardeners choose such plants at least as much for their form and foliage as for any other consideration. But for the pure glory of flowers—for a riot of color that lasts from spring through frost—annuals are the way to go.

In the first place, for sheer variety they are unbeatable. Annuals span the rainbow in terms of color, from the bluest blues to the brightest scarlets. As for plant form, they grow in bushy mounds, creep along the ground, cascade down a wall, climb a fence, or tower from the back of a border. And the size and shape of their flowers and foliage vary enormously. Indeed, the different cultivated varieties number in the thousands, and each year hybridizers produce still more.

Add to these virtues the fact that annuals are exceedingly easy to care for. With uncomplicated, shallow root systems, they are dependable performers that require little in the way of nutrients, space, and maintenance. And they grow at a rambunctious rate, racing to maturity and flowering in a matter of weeks—and gratifying the most impatient gardener with a prolific and long-lasting display. If they are simply given the right amount of sun, they usually grow readily from seed and are not terribly fussy about soil conditions. Even in less than perfect surroundings, annuals rarely let you down, adapting to many adverse conditions, including drought and extreme heat.

A final virtue is their economy. Of all the flowers your garden can display, annuals give you the biggest return on your investment. You can purchase young annuals from your local garden center at reasonable cost, or you can grow them from seed for next to nothing. As a bonus, many varieties reseed, so you may see them return year after year on their own.

What Is an Annual?

Strictly speaking, a true annual is a plant that completes its entire life cycle—from seed germination through flowering, setting seed, and death—in just one season *(opposite)*. Garden petunias, zinnias, and marigolds are just a few popular favorites that are true annuals. From a practical standpoint, however, an annual is any plant that is going to flower for only a single season or year in your garden, regardless of its potential for greater longevity. The definition of *annual,* then, expands to include biennials and tender perennials.

A typical biennial, left to its own devices, usually requires two growing seasons to complete its life cycle. Sprouting from seed and producing a leafy rosette in the first year, it then flowers in the second year, sets seed, and dies. Biennials can be started in the open garden in late spring or seeded in flats and moved to the garden in late summer or early fall for blooms the next spring. By getting seeds started early indoors, though, you can give some biennials enough of a head start that they'll flower late in the first season.

The deep carmine-orange hues and open faces of Calendula officinalis (pot marigold) are a perfect companion for the star-shaped blue flowers of Borago officinalis (borage). Borage's blossoms last only a single day but are quickly replaced by new blooms. Both flowers are hardy annuals that can be directly seeded into the ground as soon as it is workable in the spring.

Life Cycles of Garden Flowers

FIRST YEAR: *Spring*

FIRST YEAR: *Summer*

FIRST YEAR: *Fall*

Annuals

An annual, such as the impatiens shown here, sprouts from a seed in the spring, sending a few delicate roots below ground and some tender green shoots above (far left). By early summer, the plant has grown fuller and begun to blossom. It blooms with increasing vigor and fullness, reaching its peak in late summer (left, center). With the fall, its roots, stems, and flowers begin to wither (left), and by winter the plant will have died.

FIRST YEAR: *Summer*

SECOND YEAR: *Late Spring*

SECOND YEAR: *Fall*

Biennials

In nature, a typical biennial usually has two distinct growing seasons. The first year the seed will germinate in the spring, then develop roots and foliage, usually in the form of a rosette. During the summer the plant will continue to grow (far left), but won't produce flowers unless it has had an early start indoors. During the fall and winter, it ceases its growth and becomes dormant. Early in the second spring, the plant resumes growing, and flowers appear by late spring (left, center). In midsummer it will set seed and wither; by fall it will have died (left).

FIRST YEAR: *Spring*

FIRST YEAR: *Summer*

FIRST YEAR: *Winter*

SECOND YEAR: *Summer*

Perennials

Unless it is too tender to survive the winter, a perennial goes through a cycle of growth that repeats each year, as illustrated by the daylily shown above. Sprouting from seed in the spring, the plant develops roots and foliage (above, left), and may flower as well during the first summer (above, second from left); by winter the foliage has died back and the roots have gone dormant (above, second from right). The following spring the plant reawakens, and during the summer and into the fall both roots and foliage renew their growth while the plant blossoms (above, right). As subsequent seasons pass, the plant will repeat the process, producing more roots, foliage, and flowers.

Whether a biennial can complete its cycle in one season depends on the variety and your area's climate. Most foxgloves, for example, take up to 300 days to flower and set seed, and in cooler climates must overwinter. If you plant biennial seedlings in their permanent home and plan for blooms the next spring, make sure the variety is hardy enough for your zone *(see zone map and frost date maps, pages 270-271)*. If it's not, overwinter the young plants in a cold frame.

Tender perennials—which include the popular wax begonias—may live out several seasons in semitropical climates. But these plants don't have hardy roots that can tolerate the winter cold of more northerly zones and so they die with the frost. Since they flower in their first season, tender perennials are treated as annuals in most climates.

Hardy, Half-Hardy, and Tender

When discussing perennials and shrubs, hardiness refers to a plant's ability to survive degrees of winter cold, usually in terms of geographical zones.

When applied to annuals, on the other hand, *hardy* and *tender* instead signify the minimum temperature required for the seeds of a variety to germinate. With annuals, the terms also indicate their frost tolerance once a plant is in the ground.

Hardy annuals are those whose seeds can withstand temperatures below freezing (32°F)—and in fact may even require such frigid conditions to break dormancy and sprout. Moreover, once they germinate, hardy annuals easily weather any number of late-winter and early-spring freezes and thaws. If seeded directly outdoors, they are typically sown as soon as the soil can be worked in the spring or a couple of weeks past the first frost in fall. As mature plants, hardy annuals are able to tolerate hard frosts. Ornamental cabbage, for example, effortlessly stands up to cold temperatures and is a favorite in the winter garden, its colorful foliage offering a sparkling dash of purple or white against the usual backdrop of evergreens.

Tender annuals originate in tropical climates, and to flourish they require equally warm conditions. These annuals can't be sown outdoors—or transplanted—until all danger of frost has passed and the soil has warmed completely. A few

months later, they will usually die at the first indication of a fall frost. The popular New Guinea impatiens, the purple-podded vine *Dolichos lablab* (hyacinth bean), and the heavenly scented *Nicotiana alata* (jasmine tobacco) are examples of tender annuals that cannot survive a blast of cold.

A third group—half-hardy annuals—is a catch-all class composed of annuals that fall anywhere between the two extremes; some tolerate a surprising number of frosts, others just a few. Typically, half-hardy annuals can be sown or transplanted to the garden after the last spring frost even if the soil has not thoroughly warmed. Half-hardy seedlings willingly accept the extended periods of cold and damp that often accompany mid- to late-spring weather—but they aren't immune to hard freezes. In semitropical areas of the Deep South and in southern California, where frosts rarely occur, half-hardy annuals can be seeded outdoors in the fall for a late-winter or early-spring flowering season. The encyclopedia section on annuals at the back of this volume *(pages 273-301)* indicates the hardiness of each plant listed.

Selecting Your Annuals

Each year, hundreds of new flower varieties are introduced as plant breeders and seed companies seek to improve the color, size, drought tolerance, and pest or disease resistance of those already in existence. Seed catalogs offer a wealth for you to choose from, and the selection can change significantly from year to year as new cultivars become available. For this reason, you may not be able to find, for example, the variety of *Ageratum houstonianum* that you loved last year—but rest assured that there's a new one to delight you just as much, if not more.

When choosing the seeds and young plants you'll be putting into your garden, you'll want to take into account your climate and the conditions of the site. Such considerations as sun, shade, and length of growing season—all of which are covered in this chapter—will affect how well your annuals grow and flower. Use the encyclopedia as a guide to finding those plants that you like and that match your particular climatic conditions before venturing to the garden center or placing your catalog order. The encyclopedia is also a handy reference for determining the best way to get the annuals into the ground. You'll find instructions for the various planting methods—sowing seeds indoors and out, and transplanting seedlings—in Chapter 7, on pages 214-217.

Combining Plants

Among the many reasons to grow annuals—length of bloom period, ease of care, minimal expense—perhaps the most compelling is that you can choose from an enormous variety of colors. During their short life spans, annuals produce seed so rapidly that hybridizers have been able to tinker with them endlessly, introducing new colors far more quickly than is possible with other types of plants.

The temporary nature of annuals also allows you to experiment with compositions and color schemes that are more daring than any you might be willing to undertake with your more permanent plantings. You can let your imagination run wild with the lavish selection of annuals that are available for your garden.

The Mixed Border

Annuals bring a vitality to the mixed border. If your garden is newly planted, their colors and shapes can supply eye-catching contrasts and harmonies during the time it takes for perennials and shrubs to fill out and mature. For example, soft pink *Diascia barberae* and a pale blue cultivar of *Lobelia erinus* contrast soothingly with the large, lustrous dark green leaves of Oregon grape or the simple blue-green to gray-green foliage of *Daphne mezereum*. Tall pink *Cleome hasslerana* can supply height at the back of the border and pull the composition together by repeating tints of pink.

If it's bold color you like, try yellow and crim-

'Raspberry Rose' and 'Jolly Joker' pansies and pink and peach 'Oregon Rainbow' Iceland poppies brighten the front of this mixed border in Oregon. Pink and creamy white spires of Digitalis purpurea 'Excelsior' and ruby blooms of 'Red Charm' peony are shaded by a backdrop of white, yellow, and salmon azaleas.

Blazing red Salvia splendens 'Hot Shot' sizzles around 'Ultra White Madness' petunias, deep purple Salvia farinacea 'Rhea', and the coarse foliage of rose daphne (upper right), igniting this Pacific Northwest garden with hot color.

son 'Double Madame Butterfly' snapdragons with a smattering of 'Giant Double Mixed' zinnias in red, scarlet, orange, and golden yellow. Low-growing clusters of white *Iberis umbellata* nestled among the fiery hues will help temper them.

Other annuals combine marvelous color with a flower shape so distinctive that they are worthy of a spot in the most prominent border. Perfectly at home among showy perennials are the jewel-like red-orange blooms of *Emilia javanica*, which look like miniature paintbrushes atop wiry 2-foot stems; the quill-petaled, urn-shaped rose red flowers of *Cirsium japonicum*, which hover 2 feet above dark green spiny leaves; and the enormous sunburst-shaped pink, lavender, or white flower clusters of cleome, which float on 3- to 4-foot stems. When designing with such striking flowers, plant each species together in large groups, weaving in drifts of gray-leaved plants such as *Stachys byzantina* (lamb's ears), *Artemisia, Senecio,* and *Santolina* to soften the color scheme.

Some annuals with distinctive blooms have forms that are equally elegant. Consider *Lavatera trimestris* (rose mallow), which grows 3 feet tall and wide. Its densely branching stems, large cup-shaped pink or white flowers, and lower leaves that resemble those of a maple blend in effortlessly with border regulars such as iris, fluffy lady's-mantle, cabbagy bergenia, and old-fashioned shrub roses. In a border with big, downy, early-summer-blooming peonies, rose mallow can carry the flower show from midsummer to early fall.

Annuals that have sparse foliage are at their best when mated with plants that have abundant leaves. Stiff stands of easy-to-grow *Verbena bonariensis,* with its pale lilac-colored flat-topped blooms, pair well with lemon yellow daylilies, whose slender, arching leaves mask the strong but spindly stems of the verbena. The verbena offers summer color long after the perennial's petals have dropped. Simply pull up the stalks of the daylilies once they turn dry and brown, and leave the foliage intact to provide a green backdrop for the verbena.

The Annual Border

Simple borders composed of only a few judiciously chosen flowering plants often have the greatest impact. *Cuphea ignea,* an eye-catcher whose

abundant scarlet cigar-shaped flowers have black-and-white tips resembling cigar ash, forms a compact foot-high mat of color; place it before soaring red-blooming cannas with their curled wide-bladed leaves to create a pleasing contrast in form and a harmony of color. An ideal backdrop for this marriage would be a yellow-green hedge of *Philadelphus coronarius* 'Aureus' (mock orange) or tall, woody layers of fast-growing green-leaved *Spiraea prunifolia* (bridal wreath).

For a tall border with a tropical effect, try combining gold, yellow, and apricot cannas with the 5-foot stems of *Abelmoschus manihot* (sunset hibiscus), a Brazilian native whose large, fragile-looking flowers come in shades of pale to buttery yellow with maroon centers. To create a striking border in limited space, pair the red-plumed form of *Celosia cristata* (feather amaranth) with deep yellow marigolds and golden-hued calendulas. In back of the combination plant a fountain of *Miscanthus sinensis* 'Zebrinus', a perennial ornamental grass whose 5- to 6-foot-tall arching, straplike leaves display horizontal bands of creamy yellow and green.

Color Massing

Probably the easiest way to make the most of annual color is to plant a solid mass of a single variety that has especially striking blossoms. Choose an area of your yard that you want to highlight, and plant enough of the annual variety to make a bold statement. Because dramatic shocks of color dominate the area in which they're placed, resist the temptation to repeat the bold planting all around your property—or else the sheer numbers of the one color will overwhelm the viewer and lose its impact.

No matter how stunning the hue of an individual bloom, however, a stretch of unbroken color tends to tire the eye. Masses of color look best in out-of-the-way settings seen briefly and from a distance. The far corner of your backyard or the side wall of your garage is ideal; a mass of color in such removed, even remote, locations comes as a pleasant surprise when the viewer's eye discovers it. And you can extend the pleasure for months by

Four beds filled with pansies—yellow 'Crown Cream', peach, red, and pink 'Imperial Antique Shades', and purple 'Blue Perfection' —square off at the intersection of paths in a Virginia garden. Perennial orange 'Harvest Moon' Oriental poppies rise above the symmetrical arrangement.

Low-growing orange and russet nasturtiums and white candytuft edge an Oregon bed layered with red and pink zinnias and deep gold marigolds and capped by radiant yellow sunflowers. The hedge runs along the edge of the yard, hiding a busy road from view.

changing the planting as the growing season progresses—replacing an expanse of fading summer-blooming purple petunias, for instance, with the fall flowers of lemon yellow chrysanthemums.

Design Bedding

Compact, profusely blooming annuals are ideal for decorative plantings called design beds, where the creative range is limited only by the gardener's imagination. These plantings can be simple, composed of, say, deep yellow *Rudbeckia hirta* 'Double Gold' blooming behind neat, squat mounds of pink, white, and red 'Prince', 'Princess', and 'Gaiety' *Dianthus chinensis,* all planted in a free-form island in your lawn. Or the beds can be formal, tracing strict geometric lines or neatly defined shapes.

If you prefer the ornate, try fashioning a circle bed divided into four equal pie-like slices of color by flagstone paving. Within the structured bed, plant scarlet geraniums in opposite quadrants and bright blue petunias in the other two; soften them

How to Keep Annuals Blooming All Season Long

Once an annual has formed seeds, its life cycle is over and the plant stops producing flowers. For this reason, you'll need to prune off spent flowers before they go to seed if you want your annuals to bloom continuously through the season. In addition, cutting back plants that have become tall and scraggly encourages new, leafy growth. Pruned stems usually form new flower buds within 2 to 3 weeks.

Cut main stems just above a leaf or pair of leaves *(above, left)*. The joint where the leaf or leaves emerge from the stem is the place from which side shoots will grow. Make a clean cut with pruning shears, removing about one-third or more of the stem. This will stimulate branching and the production of new flowers *(above, right)*.

Salvia, zinnias, and most annuals with daisylike blooms take readily to this degree of pruning. Trailing and soft-stemmed annuals such as nasturtiums, petunias, portulaca, and sweet alyssum that have grown shabby-looking benefit from a more drastic treatment that removes all but a few inches of leafy stem. For annuals with decorative seedpods such as love-in-a-mist and those whose seed you plan to collect, stop cutting back at least 2 months before the first fall frost to give them time to mature.

by ringing the perimeter of the bed with the bronzy-leaved 'Early Splendor' cultivar of *Amaranthus tricolor* and by planting an outermost rim of silver *Senecio cineraria* (dusty-miller).

The fancier the bed's design, the more formal its appearance. Beds in the shapes of rectangles, circles, and half-moons can be any size that suits your property, but for a large-scale bed, avoid the overused combination of a solid block of one color edged with another color. A mass of blue ageratum skirted with pink wax begonias or yellow marigolds is rescued from the realm of the ordinary when clusters of other varieties that grow or can be trimmed to the same uniform height are interspersed among the rim plantings. Hybrid petunias in violet, blue, and yellow are easy-care annuals that respond well to trimming in such a design.

When planting an edging or a row in a formal design, situate your annuals so that you achieve a lush, unbroken line. Planted single file or on a straight grid, the row will be pocked with unsightly holes. Instead, arrange the plants in a zigzag, or for wider perimeters, position them in slanted, overlapping rows three, four, or five plants deep.

Less formal bedding designs reflect the planting patterns of a border: bands of color interwoven throughout the groupings of plants. A delightful annual bed for a somewhat dry spot in your yard might combine two popular annuals—yellow and white snapdragon and cream and peach-colored common nasturtium—with the lesser-known *Linaria maroccana* (Moroccan toadflax), whose blooms resemble small snapdragons, and lacy-leaved *Foeniculum vulgare* 'Purpureum' (bronze fennel). Choose white and yellow toadflax and group it near a mass of the snapdragons for a contrast in scale; repeat the pairing as space allows, placing the taller fennel in the middle of the bed and letting the nasturtiums wander throughout.

Multicolored Annuals

Among the most interesting annuals are those that display contrasting colors on a single bloom in zoned, striped, and spotted patterns. Pansies, for example, have been bred to produce symmetrical blotches, with as many as three colors on one flower. Some petunias have bicolored designs in red, purple, blue-violet, or pink with white stripes that look like the spokes of a wheel. The beautiful funnel-shaped flowers of *Salpiglossis sinuata* (painted tongue) carry velvety swatches of purple, red, and brown with overtones of white, yellow, and pink, with prominent veining in dark, contrasting shades. The dianthus tribe, includ-

ing sweet William and *D. chinensis* (China pink), comprises virtually all types of variegation. In one prevalent type, called picotee, petals sport a thin outer margin in a color that contrasts with the rest of the blossom. Impatiens, wax begonia, and *Nicotiana alata* hybrids are just a few of the many annuals that can have picotee markings.

An ideal plant to blend with multicolored flowers is *Cynoglossum amabile* (Chinese forget-me-not), renowned for its exquisite clear blue color. For early-spring display in Zones 7 through 10, sow Chinese forget-me-nots in late summer and early fall with creamy yellow, dusty pink, and purplish many-toned blooms of 'Imperial Antique Shades' pansies. Add the delicate pastels of the multicolored *Papaver rhoeas* 'Mother of Pearl' (corn poppy); each bloom boasts shades of gray, lilac, peach, and palest pink that blend together like a parfait. For summer bloom in cooler areas, sow Chinese forget-me-nots in early spring with hybrid verbena 'Peaches and Cream' and apricot, peach, lavender, and salmon *Clarkia amoena* (farewell-to-spring), which features speckled and picotee markings.

Annuals with Multicolored Blooms

Abelmoschus spp.
(abelmoschus)
Agrostemma githago
(corn cockle)
Alcea rosea
(hollyhock)
Antirrhinum majus
(snapdragon)
Arctotis stoechadifolia
(African daisy)
Callistephus chinensis
(China aster)
Chrysanthemum carinatum
(chrysanthemum)
Clarkia amoena
(farewell-to-spring)
Cosmos bipinnatus
(cosmos)
Dahlia hybrids
(dahlia)
Dianthus barbatus
(sweet William)
Dianthus chinensis
(China pink)
Digitalis spp.
(foxglove)
Gazania rigens
(treasure flower)
Impatiens spp.
(impatiens)
Layia platyglossa
(tidytips)
Linaria maroccana
(Moroccan toadflax)
Lobelia erinus
(lobelia)
Mimulus x hybridus
(monkey flower)
Mirabilis jalapa
(four-o'clock)
Nemesia strumosa
(nemesia)
Nemophila menziesii 'Pennie Black'
(baby-blue-eyes)
Papaver rhoeas
(corn poppy)
Pelargonium spp.
(geranium)
Petunia x hybrida
(petunia)
Rudbeckia hirta 'Gloriosa Daisy'
(gloriosa daisy)
Salpiglossis sinuata
(painted tongue)
Tropaeolum spp.
(nasturtium)
Viola spp.
(pansy)

Note: The abbreviation "spp." stands for the plural of "species"; where used in lists it means that many, but not all, of the species in a genus meet the criterion of the list.

Alcea rosea (hollyhock)

Heat-Tolerant Annuals

Annuals are unequaled when it comes to landscaping around paved driveways, brick paths, stone terraces, concrete walls, and a variety of other hard or rocky surfaces, known collectively as hardscapes. Hardscapes pose special challenges to plants growing close to them. For one thing, they absorb and radiate heat: On a sunny summer day a blacktopped driveway or stuccoed wall can significantly raise the temperature in the immediate area, so anything planted nearby must be reliably heat tolerant. Also, soil that is close to buildings or pavement may contain high levels of minerals deposited by water that has first washed over these surfaces. And driveways are sources of chemical pollution in the form of oily runoff and vehicle exhaust fumes.

Fortunately, there are many heat-loving, poor-soil-tolerant annuals that flourish unfazed in these locales. In addition, the microclimates created by hardscapes can even make it possible for you to grow more kinds of plants than would otherwise be possible under the normal conditions on your property. The warm environment created by a stone patio with a southern exposure, for example, might allow tender annuals to do well in a region where summers are short and cool.

Choosing the Right Plants

When planning any garden, you'll get the best results if you consider the conditions of the site and choose plants that are best suited to them. This is especially so of hardscape locations, which may be dramatically affected by patterns of light and shade, heat, and traffic. Start by noting how many hours of sunlight the site receives. Be aware that the amount may vary widely from one spot to the next because vertical hardscapes such as walls and buildings can block light, forming pools of shade in the midst of sun. Bear in mind, too, that the heat given off by pavement or other hardscape surfaces will cause the surrounding soil to dry out faster than normal, and that walls can keep rainfall from reaching ground adjacent to them. Plan on watering plants in these areas more often, and for added insurance, use annuals that are especially drought resistant. A thick layer of mulch will also help keep the soil cool and moist. For plants that will prefer the conditions around your hardscapes, check the Plant Selection Guide on pages 62-67

Flowering undaunted through a sultry Virginia summer, purple blooms of verbena overflow their raised planter. The dry heat produced by the bricks enclosing the bed is increased by a brick sidewalk beneath. But with regular watering the verbena—descended from plants native to the Americas—is thriving.

Sweet alyssum, purple pansies, silver dusty-miller, and white geraniums fill the beds of this California garden in the spring. The alyssum guards the pansies from contact with heat-retaining gravel and also softens the straight lines and sharp corners created by the bricks. Pink geraniums make a grand focal point in the stone planter.

and the encyclopedia section on pages 273-301.

Last, look at the size and use patterns of walkways and driveways. Broad paths and lightly used hardscapes have the room to accommodate annuals that sprawl over their borders. On the other hand, narrow, heavily trafficked hardscapes—the paths to back or side doors, for instance—are best edged with upright plants that won't spill onto the walkway and get trampled. Varieties of *Tagetes* (marigold), *Begonia* (wax begonia), and *Senecio* (dusty-miller) are just a few candidates for tight situations. The list at right features plants with both neat, vertical habits and more relaxed attitudes.

Dressing Up Your Hardscapes

Bare hardscapes seem to cry out for the beauty and vitality annuals can bring. Grow the plants in beds and borders along patios, terraces, and wooden decks. If space is narrow, try planting a mixed-color variety of a bushy annual such as *Salvia splendens* (sage) or *Zinnia elegans* (common zinnia) that will grow 8 to 12 inches tall. If you have room for a wide swath of color, place low-growing, compact plants such as *Gazania* species and *Ageratum houstonianum* (flossflower) along the edges of the hardscape and larger accent plants—*Zinnia angustifolia* (narrowleaf zinnia) or *Kochia scoparia* (burning bush), for example—behind them.

You need not restrict the beauty to the perimeter of your hardscape. For a weed-inhibiting carpet of blossoms in the midst of a sunny patio where foot traffic is light, plant *Portulaca grandiflora* (moss rose) and *Lobularia maritima* (sweet alyssum) between the pavers. Just remove any grass or weeds, and then fill the spaces with a fast-draining soil that contains 1 part gardener's sand for every 2 parts topsoil. Sow seeds in the soil or set out seedlings, and water lightly. And in your search for hardscape plants, don't overlook herbs. Many, such as basil and sweet marjoram, will like the hot,

Plants for Hardscapes

UPRIGHT

***Abelmoschus* spp.**
(abelmoschus)
Ageratum houstonianum
(flossflower)
Antirrhinum majus
(snapdragon)
Arctotis stoechadifolia
(African daisy)
Begonia* x *semperflorens-cultorum
(wax begonia)
Calendula officinalis
(pot marigold)
Canna* x *generalis
(canna lily)
Catharanthus roseus
(Madagascar periwinkle)
***Cosmos* spp.**
(cosmos)
***Dimorphotheca* spp.**
(Cape marigold)
Foeniculum vulgare
(fennel)
***Gazania* spp.**
(gazania)
Kochia scoparia
(burning bush)
Ocimum basilicum
(basil)
***Salvia* spp.**
(sage)
Senecio cineraria
(dusty-miller)
***Tagetes* spp.**
(marigold)
***Zinnia* spp.**
(zinnia)

SPRAWLING

Brachycome iberidifolia
(Swan River daisy)
Browallia speciosa
(browallia)
Celosia cristata
(celosia)
Dyssodia tenuiloba
(Dahlberg daisy)
Gaillardia pulchella
(Indian blanket)
Gypsophila elegans
(baby's-breath)
***Impatiens* spp.**
(impatiens)
Lobelia erinus
(lobelia)
Lobularia maritima
(sweet alyssum)
Pelargonium peltatum
(ivy-leaved geranium)
Petunia* x *hybrida
(petunia)
Portulaca grandiflora
(moss rose)
***Tropaeolum* spp.**
(nasturtium)
***Verbena* spp.**
(verbena)

Note: The abbreviation "spp." stands for the plural of "species"; where used in lists it means that many, but not all, of the species in a genus meet the criterion of the list.

dry microclimate furnished by sunny hardscapes.

On sloping terrain alongside a flight of stone or concrete steps, plant annuals that are naturally sprawling. They will drape gracefully on the incline, whereas more-upright species will tend to lean uphill or downhill in their efforts to resist gravity. Raised flower beds with sides of brick or other stonework are also pretty when dressed with these trailing plants to soften their edges.

If a wall runs beside your driveway, patio, or walk, with a narrow strip of land separating the two hard surfaces, try planting *Cobaea scandens* (cup-and-saucer vine) or *Ipomoea* species (morning glory) along the wall's base. These robust climbers should form a lavish upper growth in a short period of time. (See pages 54-55 for instructions on training vines up a wall or other structure.)

Like other hardscapes, a rock garden creates a special microclimate since its stones absorb heat and block precipitation and wind. Rocks also help maintain moisture in the soil below them by shading it from the sun—and by returning water to the soil at night as humidity condenses on their cool surfaces and seeps into the ground. For these reasons, well-chosen plants in rock gardens often require little maintenance.

In general, the most appealing rock gardens include a combination of small, mounded plants and sprawlers that can be trained over the edges of the rocks, brightening the surfaces with their flowers and foliage. Petite flowering annuals are well suited to the task because their small roots adapt to the confined spaces between stones and to the shallow soil on rocky outcrops. Also, they are ideal for providing color and interest in the hot season, when many perennials rest.

Spreading *Phlox drummondii* (annual phlox), brightly colored *Brachycome iberidifolia* (Swan River daisy), and dwarf varieties of *Cheiranthus cheiri* (English wallflower) are just a few annuals that thrive in sunny rock gardens. If your site is partially shaded, try snapdragon-like *Collinsia heterophylla* (Chinese houses) or delicate *Exacum affine* (German violet). The lee side of a partially

Nestled between pavers on a southern Pennsylvania patio, Portulaca grandiflora (moss rose) self-sows from year to year. Blooms stay open through the day, providing maximum beauty in a cheerful mix of bright colors that hug the ground at heights of about 6 inches. The flowers do tend to attract bees, so barefooted visitors should beware.

shaded rock may be moist and chilly enough to let cool-loving *Iberis* species (candytuft) and *Nemophila menziesii* (baby-blue-eyes) bloom all summer long.

If you have a natural rocky area on your property, try planting it with annual wildflowers that are native to your locale or from regions with comparable climates. Natives often self-sow, and they also blend well with the other aspects of the landscape where they evolved. Talk to your local Cooperative Extension Service or check catalogs that sell seeds and young plants specifically for your region to find the right annual wildflowers for your rock garden.

To plant rock-garden annuals, create pockets of well-draining soil, using 2 parts topsoil to 1 part gardener's sand. If the site is partially shaded and you're installing plants that prefer fertile soil, add 1 part compost or leaf mold and 1 part peat moss to the mix as well. Either sow seeds or transplant seedlings into the spaces. Once the seedlings are a few inches high, spread a mulch of shredded bark around them to keep the soil cool and moist.

Heat-loving annuals in this Connecticut garden add a touch of softness to the stone surfaces in this walled garden niche. Red-violet Petunia integrifolia surrounds the base of the center sculpture, while tall white Nicotiana alata, which self-sows from year to year, lightens and brightens the entire space.

Petite yellow Dahlberg daisies, open-faced Gaillardia aristata 'Burgundy', spiky Salvia coccinea 'Lady in Red', and orange California poppies flourish through the summer in the rocky Missouri garden at left. The limestone chunks bordering the raised bed prevent rainwater from draining through the soil too quickly.

47

Creating a Cutting Garden

This cottage garden in New York supplies an abundance of flowers—mostly annuals—for cutting. Pink and cream snapdragons bloom in the foreground, while yellow everlastings, pink and orange dahlias, and rose thistle populate the rear. Red and pale violet globe amaranth blooms behind a mound of baby's-breath, and the central path is bordered by 'Indigo Spires' salvia and 'Pink Perfection' lilies.

One of the great pleasures of growing annuals is having a steady supply of fresh-cut flowers. Annuals make ideal cut flowers because the more you cut them, the more blooms they produce. If you grow many different varieties you'll have a large collection of colors and fragrances from which to choose, whether you're arranging fresh flowers in a vase or drying the blooms, foliage, and seedpods for year-round bouquets.

Annuals with strong stems and a long vase life—such as those listed on page 51—are ideal for cutting and happen to look magnificent in all manner of beds and borders. For example, the airy, branching stems and delicate starlike blossoms of *Gypsophila elegans* (annual baby's-breath) perform beautifully with early single peonies, creamy white marigold cultivars, and the bright golden spheres of the shrub *Kerria japonica* 'Pleniflora' (globeflower kerria)—both in your garden and in a vase.

Survey your garden and note those places where you can tuck in a half-dozen or more lemon yellow snapdragons and *Eustoma grandiflorum* (prairie gentian), with its sprays of flowers in purple, shell pink, or white. Another combination to brighten up your garden or any room in your house is ethereal blue *Cynoglossum amabile* (Chinese forget-me-not) nestled among cheerful summer blooms of apricot nasturtium, peach-colored calendula, blush pink clarkia, and a creamy verbena. And in a cottage garden just outside your kitchen door, an informal group of pink and white foxglove and blue larkspur towering above clouds of *Nigella damascena* (love-in-a-mist) and *Centaurea cyanus* (bachelor's-button) can supply blooms for dramatic indoor decoration.

A Working Garden

A purely utilitarian garden, where appearance is secondary to the production of flowers for cutting, can be of any size. Allow at least 1 square foot of

Annual Grasses Worth Admiring

When planning flower beds and cutting gardens, don't overlook the charms provided by annual ornamental grasses. Their stunning flowers and seed heads not only add unique interest to sunny beds and borders but also make exquisite dried bouquets. And a few have beautiful foliage as well; *Zea mays* var. *japonica* (variegated corn), with its glorious yellow, white, and pink straplike leaves, is one of the most colorful members of the grass family.

In the backyard of the Oregon property shown here, nodding, oatlike seed heads of *Briza maxima* (quaking grass) have been planted to form a shimmering bed of pale green punctuated by a smattering of deep rose pink poppy mallow; they tremble appealingly both in the garden and in a vase. Another grass, *Coix lacryma-jobi* (Job's-tears), produces hard, oval, pearly white seeds dusted bluish gray or black that for centuries have been used as beads for necklaces and rosaries. This grass may be of only passing interest in the garden but is a true novelty in dried arrangements.

For edging, both *Agrostis nebulosa* (cloud grass), with delicate spikelets floating over short clumps of foliage, and *Lamarckia aurea* (goldentop), whose panicles are a silver-green color, spill over paths and walkways. Because of their delicate constitutions, these grasses need resowing in midsummer.

If you long for drama in the garden, you can count on the mammoth, bristly plumes of *Pennisetum villosum* (feathertop grass). But beware: They shatter easily when dry. Use them in fresh-cut arrangements, discarding the plumes before they dry to avoid a mess. Also a knockout in the garden is *Setaria italica* (foxtail millet), whose drooping seed pods, unlike those of feathertop, seem to last forever when dried. Shiny and black-seeded, the panicles of robust *Sorghum bicolor* var. *technicum* (black sorghum) quickly spruce up the background of any bed or border. And 4-foot-tall, dense yellow-green stands of *Triticum turgidum* (bearded wheat) and *T. aestivum* (common wheat), though not usually grown in ornamental gardens, bring clean lines and an almost sculptural look to a contemporary planting and are spectacular crowded into winter bouquets.

Divided by straw-mulched paths for the gardener's easy access, orderly rows of Celosia cristata 'Red Chief' and 'Apricot Brandy', assorted basils, red and lavender globe amaranth, and Lonas annua (yellow ageratum) stand primed for cutting in a New Jersey field (left). Later in the season, harvested blooms of red cockscomb, globe amaranth in colors of red, lavender, and deep rose pink, yellow ageratum, and fragrant greenish bundles of Artemisia annua 'Sweet Annie' hang to dry from the rafters of a barn near the garden (below).

space in full sun for each plant—and more for exhibition-size flowers such as 'Cactus Hybrid' dahlias and large sunflower cultivars. Locate the garden near a water source, and consider placing it near low hedges or walls that don't block the sun to help protect your flowers from wind and rain.

For the greatest number of blooms in the least amount of space, grow your annuals in wide, orderly rows laid out east to west for maximum sun exposure. Position the shortest plants in the southernmost row to prevent their being shaded by taller ones. Wide rows of one type of plant also cut down on weeds and provide neighboring plants with root and stem support. Separate these long rows with wide grassy strips or mulched paths to make the garden convenient for watering, weeding, pruning, and harvesting blooms.

Harvesting Flowers

Select flowers that are halfway to three-quarters open and in perfect condition, and cut them early in the morning after a cool night, when they are plump with moisture. Two exceptions to this rule

are marigolds and zinnias, which should be gathered during the warmest part of the day, as their stems draw up water best when warm. Using clean, sharp scissors, cut the stems at a slant, then place them in a bucket of tepid, clean water to which you've added a few drops of chlorine bleach. A water temperature of 100° to 120°F allows most annuals to drink up the maximum amount.

Cut flowers benefit from a period of conditioning before they are displayed indoors. Remove any foliage that will be underwater, and sink the stems into a bucket of warm—preferably distilled—water up to the lowest set of remaining leaves. Keep them in a cool, dark place such as a basement for at least 6 hours. Commercial preservative solutions to extend vase life can be added to the water; follow package directions. Or use a homemade solution of 1 tablespoon corn syrup and 10 drops of chlorine bleach to 1 quart of water.

When cut, a few annuals—including poppies, dahlias, and Mexican sunflowers—ooze a milky fluid that fouls water and clogs the cut ends of other flower stems. Before you condition them, sear their stems by placing them in hot, almost boiling water until the sap stops seeping out, or hold the

cut end of each stem over a candle flame briefly until the flow of sap ceases.

Annuals for Drying

Bouquets and wreaths of dried flowers last almost indefinitely. Not all flowers that make gorgeous fresh bouquets look good dried, however, so it's best to know which ones to work with *(list, right)*. As a rule, dark red or deep purple blossoms tend to turn an unattractive black when dry, and some white flowers turn a dingy brown.

Flowers displaying the brighter hues of the color spectrum generally retain their color the best. For example, 'Pink Tassels' celosia, light green *Moluccella laevis* (bells of Ireland), and golden *Lonas annua* (yellow ageratum) remain pretty and fresh looking when dried properly.

Among the best annuals for drying are those composed of tiny flowers surrounded by leaflike

structures called bracts that arise from the stem and encase the flowerhead. Known as everlastings, these flowers—which include *Helichrysum bracteatum* (strawflower), *Xeranthemum annuum* (immortelle), and *Limonium* (sea lavender)—retain their original form and color when dried.

In addition to flowers, the seed heads of some annuals look splendid in dried displays and wreaths. Most annual grasses dry well, as do the coin-shaped, milky satin seedpods of *Lunaria annua* (honesty), the bronzy round pods of *Scabiosa stellata* (paper moon, sweet scabious), and the split, curling fruits of *Proboscidea louisianica* (common devil's-claw).

Flowers for drying should be cut as they begin to open, on a dry, sunny day after the dew has evaporated. Keep in mind that dry flowers lose half of their original bulk, so gather twice as many for your dry arrangements as for your fresh ones. Sort through the harvest and select unblemished flowers with the most pleasing shapes and colors.

Strip the leaves and bundle the stems without tangling them, fastening the bunches about 1 inch from the stem tips with a rubber band, which will continue to hold the bundle securely together as the stems dry and shrink. Suspend the flowers upside down in a dark, dry, well-ventilated space—perhaps an attic or a garden shed. If you live in a warm, humid climate, make smaller bunches than usual and allow a longer drying time. Your flowers are ready for arranging when the stems are brittle and break with a crisp snap. Depending on the fleshiness of the stems, the size of the bundles, and the humidity level, this should take from several days to 2 weeks.

Annuals for Cutting and Drying

FLOWERS WITH A LONG VASE LIFE
Ammi majus
(bishop's flower)
Antirrhinum majus
(snapdragon)
Calendula officinalis
(pot marigold)
Callistephus chinensis
(China aster)
Centaurea cyanus
(bachelor's-button)
Centaurea moschata
(sweet-sultan)
Consolida ambigua
(rocket larkspur)
Cosmos bipinnatus
(cosmos)
Dahlia hybrids
(dahlia)
Eustoma grandiflorum
(prairie gentian)
Tithonia rotundifolia
(Mexican sunflower)

ANNUALS FOR DRYING
Amaranthus cruentus
(prince's-feather)
Asclepias fruticosa
(gomphocarpus)
Briza maxima
(quaking grass)
Celosia cristata
(celosia)
Gomphrena globosa
(globe amaranth)
Helichrysum bracteatum
(everlasting, strawflower)
Limonium sinuatum
(notchleaf statice)
Lunaria annua
(honesty)
Moluccella laevis
(bells of Ireland)
Scabiosa stellata
(paper moon, sweet scabious)
Xeranthemum annuum
(everlasting, immortelle)

Annual Vines

Annual vines—including those tropical perennials grown as annuals—contribute a lot more than mere good looks to your garden. They can camouflage unsightly fences or walls, accent pleasing architecture, or frame a view, for example, all the while adding color, texture, and height to your garden design. You can also press them into service to provide shade or to form a windbreak or privacy screen, and if planted on sloping terrain as a ground cover, they'll help prevent erosion.

The Virtues of Vines

The glory of many annual vines is their spectacular or unusual flowers. The impact of fully open 'Heavenly Blue' morning glories massed on a fence is hard to beat for drama, but there are other vines with intricate and subtle blooms that have a beauty all their own. For example, *Cobaea scandens* produces white or purplish red cup-shaped blossoms with contrasting green calyxes, giving rise to its common name, cup-and-saucer vine.

There is more beauty to annual vines than their flowers, however. Certain climbers are distinguished by exceptional foliage: The leaves of *Ipomoea quamoclit* (cypress vine) split into thin, frondlike segments that flutter in the breeze; the dark purple stems of *Dolichos lablab* (hyacinth bean) boast purple-tinted heart-shaped leaves; and *Tropaeolum peregrinum* (canary creeper) produces elegant five-lobed leaves reminiscent of the fig plant.

Some vines also offer pretty fruits or useful produce. Varieties of the genus *Cucurbita*, for example, yield edible squash and interestingly shaped ornamental gourds that can be dried for decoration *(page 54)*. Though they aren't typically grown as vines, other squashes, melons, and gourds can be coaxed to climb to great effect if the support is strong enough to bear their weight.

For gardeners who would like to attract a variety of wildlife to their property, vines create a hospitable habitat for all sorts of creatures. Birds appreciate the sheltered perches that vines offer, as well as the banquet of insects that live among the stems. Hummingbirds, bees, and butterflies are drawn to the nectar and pollen of flowering vines. And squirrels and chipmunks love dense vines such as hyacinth-bean and clematis for their potential as aerial highways and jungle gyms.

The owner of the Oregon garden at right planted Tropaeolum majus (common nasturtium) across the front of this border for several purposes: The plants not only provide cheerful red and orange blooms and bold round leaves, they also hide spent bulb foliage and even camouflage an unsightly tree stump.

As darkness descends on a September evening in this Virginia garden, the scented white blooms of Ipomoea alba (moonflower) begin to unfurl. Cords attached to the walls of the house support the fast-growing vine, whose bright green heart-shaped leaves give it daytime interest as well.

Annual Vines

***Cardiospermum
balicacabum***
(balloon vine)

Cobaea scandens
(cup-and-saucer vine)

Cucumis melo
(pomegranate melon)

Cucurbita ficifolia
(Malabar gourd)

***Cucurbita maxima
'Turbaniformis'***
(Turk's-cap squash)

***Cucurbita pepo* var.
*ovifera***
(pumpkin gourd)

Dolichos lablab
(hyacinth bean)

Humulus japonicus
(Japanese hopvine)

Ipomoea alba
(moonflower)

Ipomoea purpurea
(common morning glory)

Lagenaria siceraria
(calabash gourd)

Mina lobata
(crimson starglory)

Phaseolus coccineus
(scarlet runner bean)

***Rhodochiton
atrosanguineum***
(purple bell vine)

Thunbergia alata
(black-eyed Susan vine)

***Tropaeolum* spp.**
(nasturtium)

*Note: The abbreviation "spp."
stands for the plural of
"species"; where used in lists
it means that many, but not
all, of the species in a genus
meet the criterion of the list.*

Selecting and Starting Vines

When you're choosing a vining plant, you'll want to consider not only its flowers, foliage, or fruit but also its ultimate height. Depending on the species, annual vines grow from about 6 feet to upward of 30 feet per season. Make sure the species you select has the growth potential to fill the space you have in mind. If you're trying to blanket an old shed, for example, consider 15-foot morning glories or Japanese hopvines, whereas a chain-link fence will require only 6-foot nasturtium vines. The encyclopedia section that begins on page 273 can help you select a suitable species.

Follow seed-packet guidelines on spacing, and plant a sufficient number to ensure that your plants will be close enough together to form a uniform cover yet have enough root room to flourish. Always plant on the windward side of any support, so that prevailing breezes will blow the vines toward the support, not away from it.

For a long season of bloom, most annual vines should be started from seed in late winter and then transplanted outdoors in spring. Some varieties, however, including morning glories, nasturtiums, and sweet peas, should be sown in the ground outdoors after the last frost. Instructions for growing sweet peas, which require a little extra care, are given on page 56. Nearly all annual vines do best where they receive at least half a day's sun. Less than this, and the plants grow grudgingly and may not flower at all.

Vines as Screens

Once they start to grow, your annual vines will take off quickly. Many species grow 20 feet long, leaf out, and come into bud in a matter of weeks. This makes them ideal to plant as screens against sun, wind, or unattractive views. Left to their own devices, vines tend to flower mostly among top growth, leaving several feet of leggy stem exposed at their base. To force better distribution of the blooms, fasten young vine shoots horizontally along supports such as trellises and fences when they begin to grow; this encourages them to form low, lateral shoots that will flower. See pages 54-55 for illustrated instructions on training vines.

Vines can easily transform a small townhouse garden or a narrow side yard by capitalizing on vertical space. Train them up a simple rot-resistant wood post or a freestanding arch or pergola to add overhead interest to your garden. Vines grown on a wood-framed arbor will provide summer shade

Growing and Using Gourds

Gourd species, including the *Cucurbita pepo* shown here, are renowned for their useful or decorative fruits. Thanks to their bold foliage, they also make good screening plants when trained up a sturdy trellis—and even do well on overhead arbors.

Because gourds need a long season for their fruit to mature, you should start seeds indoors *(pages 214-215)* a month before your garden soil is warm enough for tender annuals. Plant the seedlings outdoors in full sun, allowing plenty of room for vigorous growth, and fertilize lightly with low-nitrogen compounds. Trimming the main stem to 10 feet will encourage the growth of fruiting lateral stems. When the tendrils beside the stems are brown, cut the fruits off, leaving a short stem on the fruit.

Cure gourds on screens or slats in any dry place, turning them weekly until they feel light and their skins are hard. This may take up to 4 months. Dried gourds can be varnished, painted, or even carved for decoration.

over a deck or patio, then die back after frost to let the winter sunshine in. To clothe an exterior wall in summer blooms, install a trellis of wood or metal tubing about 3 inches away from the wall and plant the climbers along its base.

If you're placing a screen across open space, you will need to provide adequate support for the vines. Start with a sturdy, well-built frame of wood or metal and sink the legs of the structure at least 2 feet into the ground—deeper in regions of deep frost so that it won't be heaved up by the freezing and thawing of the ground. Indulge in diagonal or free-form trellis designs, square latticework, or a wide range of other shapes you can find or build. For a swag effect, suspend sturdy chains between posts and train vines up the posts and then along the chains, tying them loosely at 4-inch intervals. Always set your supports in place before you plant the vines; otherwise you may damage the roots or any new growth.

Vines with dense foliage, such as hyacinth bean, are the best choice for totally concealing an unat-

Training Vines

Annual vines use various strategies for climbing, as shown at right, but the planting and maintenance needs for the different types are much the same. First, sow seeds or plant seedlings as close as possible to their support. If you're training them up a solid fence or wall, attach a lath trellis, wires, or other plants such as wisteria or roses that the vines can twine around. Tie the stems loosely to the support to hold them in place *(far right)*, and pinch back the most vigorous stems by several inches to encourage full, bushy growth. For best results with all flowering vines, water deeply and feed them a low-nitrogen fertilizer.

Many vines, including Ipomoea species (morning glory) (above), climb by twining around another object. If this object has a slippery surface, wind a strip of cloth or string around it to give the vine a place to grip. Guide growing stems to the support and poke them gently around it in the direction they tend to move until they begin to wrap on their own. To cover a trellis, arrange growing tips along the framework, and tie the stems to it as they lengthen.

tractive wall or view. *Phaseolus coccineus* (scarlet runner bean) also makes a tough yet beautiful screen, as do common vegetable pole or runner beans, which develop thick, attractive foliage and white flowers—as well as a tasty crop. Species with sparser leaf growth, such as canary creeper, soften a wall or veil a view without covering it completely.

Other Uses for Vines

Just as you use annuals in mixed beds and borders to maintain color and interest all through the season, interplant annual vines among your perennial climbers. Morning glories or moonflower vines make good companions for wall-climbing ivy and Virginia creeper. In most zones, annual vines bloom from midsummer to frost; pair them with early-flowering clematis, tall or climbing roses, or spring-flowering bushes and specimen trees so the vines can take over when the other blossoms fade.

To mingle annual climbers with a shrub or tree, sow seeds or transplant seedlings beside the specimen plant and draw the growing vine stems up over their companion as the season progresses. Pull the vines off again at summer's end to display the shrub's autumn color or winter fruits. You can use the same tactic to add color accents to a natural (not clipped) evergreen hedge. Plant scarlet runner beans, cup-and-saucer vines, or *Mina lobata* (crimson starglory) beside forsythia or holly, for example, to cover the dull green summer bushes with flowers.

When planting a vine next to mature perennials, shrubs, or trees, prepare an ample hole for the vine's roots but take care not to disturb those of the other plant. The vine will have to compete with the established plant's root system for nutrients, so fertilize it with a commercial slow-release formula, taking care not to overfertilize and burn the tender tissue. When choosing a vine for this purpose, be sure to match the scale of the vine to its host plant: A fine-foliaged companion like *Genista hispanica* (broom) makes a good partner for delicate *Thunbergia alata* (black-eyed Susan vine), but it will take a vine with a more commanding presence, such as hyacinth bean, to show up nicely against a bold-foliaged witch hazel.

A number of annual vines make splendid ground covers, particularly trailing types such as *Tropaeolum majus* (common nasturtium), *Cucurbita* species (gourds), and *Pelargonium peltatum* (ivy-leaved geranium). Planted in a dry, sunny spot, nasturtium spreads and sprawls rapidly. Ivy-leaved geranium is noted for its reliable, constant bloom and its vigor in colonizing. You can also set annual vines among established perennial ground covers to increase the area's visual interest.

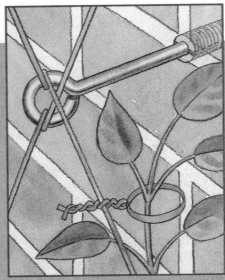

Special plant features called tendrils hold vines such as Cobaea scandens (cup-and-saucer vine) (above) to their supports. Give these grabbers something slender to climb, since the coiling tendrils can't get around thick poles or slats. Tie the young stems to their supports; as soon as tendrils form the vine will hold itself on. To control the shape of the vine, arrange the stem along the path you want it to follow, and tie it in place until the tendrils secure it.

Sprawling vines such as Tropaeolum species (nasturtium) (above) don't grip their supports as they climb but simply grow long, flexible stems that scramble over neighboring objects. These sprawlers can be woven through the lattice of a trellis or the spaces in a chain-link fence or spread out to ramble across the ground, a low bush, or a rock. When using such vines as ground cover, plant them thickly and trim rampant growth as necessary to keep them in bounds.

Fasten vine stems to their supports with cloth strips, twist ties from the grocery store, or special plant twine from garden centers. Begin tying the stems when they are still short so that the plant will be held from the bottom up as it grows and will not sag; tie each stem loosely to allow room for it to thicken as the plant matures. Check the ties occasionally during the season; they should be firm enough to hold the vine in place without cutting into the stems.

Growing Sweet Peas

With its rich honey scent and blooms shaped like frilly sunbonnets, *Lathyrus odoratus*—the climbing sweet pea *(left)*—has been a favorite of gardeners in climates with cool nighttime temperatures for more than two centuries. Most fragrant are the old-fashioned purple, blue, crimson, and rose pink strains that haven't been bred for larger blooms. Because sweet peas need a sunny spot but cool, moist soil, these 6-foot tendril-bearing vines do best with the special treatment described below.

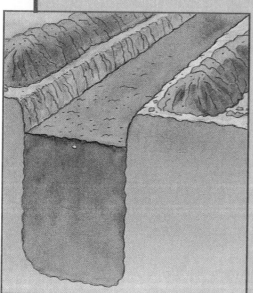

1. Dig a long, narrow trench 1 foot wide and 2 feet deep, keeping the sides vertical. Fill the trench to within 4 inches of the top with a nutrient-rich mixture of 2 parts well-rotted cow manure or compost, 2 parts loam, and 1 part coarse sand, and add a sprinkling of ground limestone.

2. Soak the seeds in water overnight; then, in fall in warm climates and in very early spring in cooler areas, push the seeds ½ inch into the soil, 6 inches apart. When the seedlings are 2 inches tall, add ½ inch of soil around the stems to support the plants (above). Continue backfilling around the stems at the rate of ½ inch of soil for each 2 inches of plant growth until the trench is filled nearly to ground level.

3. Provide support for the climbing plants using, for example, tepees of bamboo canes (above). Keep the plants well watered, and remove spent flowers to ensure continued bloom. Because sweet peas are heavy feeders that take a lion's share of nutrients out of the soil, don't plant them in the same spot in the garden 2 years in a row.

Planting in Containers

Thanks to their shallow roots, vigorous growth, and prolific blooms, annuals are perfect for planting in containers. They are an inexpensive way to add a dash of fast color to a dull spot, and indeed, most annuals seem to take on a new character when they're planted in an attractive pot or box and given a place where their beauty can be enjoyed up close.

Annuals in containers are extremely versatile. In addition to accenting any corner of your outdoor living space, they are the ideal solution when growing space is limited. And since they aren't planted in the ground, they can live indoors at either end of the gardening season or be moved in temporarily during bad weather to keep them healthy and prolong their display.

Your annuals will thrive in almost any type of container as long as it has a hole at the bottom for drainage. Experienced container gardeners prefer large, deep containers for annuals because they al-low for a more diverse planting and don't need to be watered as often as small or shallow pots.

When choosing your containers, take into consideration where they'll be spending most of their time. Plastic pots hold moisture better than clay ones and, if placed in shadier spots, should be monitored to make sure the soil doesn't stay too wet. Pots and boxes made of clay, which is porous, provide good air circulation and drainage—and for this very reason need to be watered frequently so that the soil doesn't dry out. Use them anywhere, but check the soil daily if they receive full sun. Wooden tubs provide superior protection from both heat and cold and will do well anywhere; they'll need to be replaced eventually, though, because they rot. And if you want to use a copper pot, plant your annuals in another container placed inside the copper one, since most plants find the metal poisonous.

Single containers can add sparkle to any num-

A large clay pot of pink Swan River daisies anchors the many fragrant container plants lining these porch steps in Washington State. The casual yet artful display stars an intriguing array of geraniums—including the cultivars 'Persian Queen', with chartreuse foliage and magenta flowers, 'Wilhelm Langguth', with variegated leaves, and 'Lady Plymouth', a scented variety. The grouping is accented by the white-throated blue flowers of Nolana and the tiny purple blossoms of heliotrope.

Annuals for Containers

Agrostemma githago
(corn cockle)
Antirrhinum majus
(snapdragon)
Brassica oleracea
(ornamental cabbage)
Calendula officinalis
(pot marigold)
Celosia cristata
(celosia)
Centaurea cyanus
(bachelor's-button)
Chrysanthemum coronarium
(crown daisy)
Clarkia amoena
(farewell-to-spring)
Coleus x hybridus
(coleus)
Convolvulus tricolor
(dwarf morning glory)
Helianthus annuus
(sunflower)
Lavatera trimestris
(tree mallow)
Limonium sinuatum
(sea lavender)
Linaria maroccana
(Moroccan toadflax)
Matthiola incana
(common stock)
Mimulus x hybridus
(monkey flower)
Nemophila menziesii
(baby-blue-eyes)
Nigella damascena
(love-in-a-mist)
Omphalodes linifolia
(navelwort)
Papaver rhoeas
(corn poppy)
Pelargonium spp.
(geranium)
Phacelia campanularia
(harebell phacelia)
Phlox drummondii
(annual phlox)
Reseda odorata
(mignonette)
Salpiglossis sinuata
(painted tongue)
Torenia fournieri
(blue torenia)
Viola x wittrockiana
(common pansy)
Zinnia elegans
(common zinnia)

Note: The abbreviation "spp." stands for the plural of "species"; where used in lists it means that many, but not all, of the species in a genus meet the criterion of the list.

Spikes of Pennisetum setaceum (fountain grass) arch over low-growing Setcreasea pallida (purple-heart) in this late-summer container planting in Maryland (left). A nearby pot of herbs helps brighten the gray deck.

ber of spots around your property. A large, elegant pot on your front step or a rustic one at the mailbox will both brighten and distinguish your home. Even a container placed among your bed or border plantings will add interest and dimension.

A container that isn't itself impressive can be brought to life with plantings of trailing annuals, whose flowers and leaves will cover the sides. Sweet alyssum, baby-blue-eyes, or portulaca, with their draping foliage, will hide a homely concrete block, for instance. On the other hand, a pretty pot might be filled exclusively with an upright variety to highlight the container as well as its occupants.

Some of the most beautiful arrangements combine different annuals with a variety of habits, colors, and foliage interest. Mix various flowering plants—some trailing and some tall and spiked—with light- and dark-colored foliage such as pale dusty-miller and purple-toned basil in sunny spots, or pair them with multihued coleus and polka-dot plants in partial shade. Annual grasses, including red or purple *Pennisetum* (fountain grass), provide a nice change from commoner flowers and are especially suitable in contemporary settings. Even a vegetable or two, like a purple eggplant or a red pepper, can add drama near summer's end.

When choosing your plants, match their size at maturity with the scale of the pot. An upright plant shouldn't rise more than about one and a half to two times the height of the container, or the overall look will be top-heavy. Also, consider your annuals' growth habits: Those that are especially dense and bushy, such as wax begonias and impatiens, are best grown by themselves rather than with other species if your container is small.

For visual impact in large spaces, arrange several containers together. Try combining contrasting flower colors, placing a tub of golden *Calendula officinalis* (pot marigold) next to deep blue *Centaurea cyanus* (bachelor's-button), for example. Or simply cluster pots blooming with assorted varieties of marigolds or geraniums. Usually, three or four medium-sized containers look better than a large tub surrounded by small pots.

Hanging Baskets

Your container annuals need not be confined to the floor. In fact, nothing shows off a trailing or spreading annual like a basket suspended from above eye level. Hanging plants do need a little more care than those in other containers. Because they are meant to be seen from the bottom as well as the top, they require more grooming to stay attractive. And because hanging plants are exposed to air on all sides, they dry out faster than other plants. In particular, moss-lined wire baskets *(pages 60-61),* which have no solid sides to hold moisture, need a great deal of water and should be placed in a spot out of the harsh sun.

Planting and Caring for Container Plants

Before you plant your annuals in a container, decide on the arrangement if you're using an array of varieties. The tallest plants should go in the center or the back, the trailers around the rim, and the medium-sized bushy and upright annuals in between. Be sure the plants you've chosen all prefer similar light and soil conditions.

Your pot should be at least 8 inches deep. Place a layer of rocks, gravel, or pottery shards in the bottom to keep the drainage holes clear of soil. Then fill the container to within 2 inches of the top with a potting-soil mix from a gardening cen-

Annuals and perennials combined create an impression of movement in this Portland, Oregon, container garden. Annuals include yellow Bidens, tall yellow Verbascum, silvery-green-leaved Helichrysum petiolare, and red and fuchsia cosmos. Perennials Astrantia major, with white flowers, and spiky Phormium tenax complete the display.

Tuberous Begonias

Tuberous begonias *(Begonia* x *tuberhybrida)* have an upright or a trailing habit, simple or compound blooms, and come in every color but blue. And although many gardeners treat them as potted annuals, these summer favorites are actually tender bulbs.

Start the tubers indoors in flats several weeks before the last frost date. When the shoots are 3 inches tall, move them to containers filled with a commercial potting-soil mix. Space three or four tubers concave side up in the container, 2 to 3 inches apart, with the top of the tuber at the soil line. For a hanging basket, choose a cascading form. Upright begonias, like the bright red varieties at left, are better suited to pots on the ground.

Tuberous begonias prefer partial to full shade and cool and moist, but not soggy, soil. Keep them well fertilized and watered throughout the season for maximum bloom.

Making a Moss-Lined Basket

A moss-lined hanging basket is typically fashioned of a simple wire frame and lined with sphagnum moss, both purchased from a garden center. This simple container will display lush foliage and colorful blossoms from all sides. Water the basket every day to maintain a fresh and vibrant show of blooms.

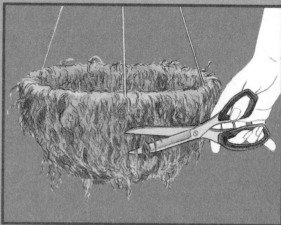

1. Soak the moss in water to make it pliable; squeeze out the excess moisture. Place it in a basket frame (above) and press it into an even 1-inch layer, adding or removing moss as necessary.

2. Cover up any wire showing on the outside of the basket by pressing additional moss around it (above, left). Next, attach the wire hanger, hang the basket, and trim any dangling moss with scissors to achieve a neat but natural appearance (above). In a separate bucket, mix enough commercial potting-soil mix to fill the basket, adding a few handfuls of peat moss to retain moisture. Cover the bottom of the basket with some of the soil mixture.

Hanging under a leafy arbor, a moss-lined wire basket overflows with hot pink Impatiens wallerana and dangling blooms of tender perennial fuchsia. Both plants prefer the partial shade and humid atmosphere of their Seattle home.

ter or nursery or with a homemade version. A soil composed of equal parts topsoil, compost, and vermiculite will do nicely.

Plant healthy young annuals that you've purchased or grown from seed. Remove the plants from their cell packs or pots, and gently spread apart the bottom of the rootball. Using a small trowel, dig a hole slightly bigger than the roots and position the annual, distributing its roots evenly in the space. Fill the hole with soil, pressing it firmly in place. Group plants closer together than you would in an outdoor garden. Water the container, and cover the soil with a bark mulch or sphagnum moss to help hold in moisture.

Sun, wind, and drought can be the mortal enemies of containers because they dry them out quickly. Infrequent watering can kill your potted plants outright, and irregular watering will stress them, leaving them vulnerable to pests and diseases. To protect outdoor container plants that dry out quickly, water them daily—more often during the height of summer—and move them to sheltered locations during very hot weather. When watering, wet the soil thoroughly and avoid wetting the leaves, which can invite disease.

Although frequent watering is essential, it tends to leach nutrients out of the soil. Keep your plants supplied with vital minerals by feeding them regularly with a commercial liquid fertilizer that contains an equal balance of potassium, phosphorus, and nitrogen. Too much nitrogen will encourage leafy growth at the expense of blooms. If you water several times a week, use the fertilizer at half strength and apply it every 2 weeks or so.

3. Use a pencil to poke a hole through the moss near the bottom of the basket. *Remove a seedling from its cell pack and insert it through the hole (below), firming the moss around it on the outside. Repeat to make a row around the basket, then cover the roots with soil. Continue planting in rows to within 2 inches of the top of the basket. Then plant a few seedlings at the top of the basket (bottom), and water.*

Planting in Window Boxes

A window box of annuals pleases the eye from both inside and outside the house. Geraniums are a favorite for window boxes, but you may want to experiment with combinations of unusual varieties of flowers and foliage to enliven a picture that may be growing overly familiar.

In attaching boxes to your windows, keep in mind that they are heavy. Mount them securely with bolts or brackets, and check them yearly to make sure the hardware hasn't weakened by rusting. Also note that if your boxes hang inside the drip line of the house, they may not get much rainfall. This, along with drying winds and the warmth from the house, means they will need diligent watering, although a mulch of shredded bark will help retain some moisture. On the plus side, the extra heat allows early planting in spring and extends the fall blooming season.

Rosy pink petunias flank this container garden, which hangs from a fence in a seaside Delaware town. Planted in a commercially available "hay basket," the garden also features white African daisies, trailing yellow Bidens, and blue Salvia farinacea 'Victoria'.

Organized by flower or foliage color, this chart provides information needed to select species and varieties that will thrive in the particular conditions of your garden. For additional information on select annuals and biennials, refer to the encyclopedia section that begins on page 273.

WHITE

Species	ANNUAL	BIENNIAL	TENDER PERENNIAL	RICH, LOAMY	AVERAGE	POOR	FULL SUN	PARTIAL SHADE	SHADE	UNDER 12 INCHES	1 TO 3 FEET	OVER 3 FEET	VINE OR CREEPER	SPRING	EARLY SUMMER	LATE SUMMER	FALL	FLOWERS	FOLIAGE	FRAGRANCE	FRUIT/SEEDS	CUT FLOWERS	DRIED FLOWERS	CONTAINERS	DROUGHT	HEAT	COASTAL CONDITIONS
AGERATUM HOUSTONIANUM 'SUMMER SNOW'			✓				✓	✓		✓					✓	✓	✓	✓	✓								
AMMI MAJUS	✓		✓				✓	✓			✓				✓	✓		✓				✓	✓				
AMMOBIUM ALATUM			✓		✓		✓				✓				✓	✓		✓	✓			✓	✓				
ANTIRRHINUM MAJUS 'WHITE SONNET'			✓	✓			✓	✓			✓				✓	✓	✓	✓				✓					
ASCLEPIAS FRUTICOSA			✓	✓			✓					✓			✓	✓	✓	✓			✓	✓				✓	
BROWALLIA SPECIOSA 'SILVER BELLS'			✓	✓				✓	✓		✓				✓	✓		✓						✓			
COBAEA SCANDENS 'ALBA'			✓	✓			✓						✓		✓	✓	✓	✓									
COSMOS BIPINNATUS 'SONATA WHITE'	✓				✓		✓	✓			✓				✓	✓	✓	✓				✓					
CREPIS RUBRA 'ALBA'	✓				✓	✓	✓	✓							✓	✓		✓								✓	✓
DATURA METEL	✓		✓				✓	✓			✓				✓	✓		✓		✓							
DAUCUS CAROTA VAR. CAROTA		✓		✓	✓		✓				✓			✓	✓			✓				✓	✓		✓		
DIGITALIS PURPUREA 'ALBA'		✓	✓					✓			✓				✓			✓									
EUPHORBIA MARGINATA	✓				✓		✓				✓					✓		✓	✓						✓		
HELIANTHUS ANNUUS 'ITALIAN WHITE'	✓		✓				✓					✓			✓	✓	✓	✓				✓			✓	✓	
IBERIS AMARA	✓				✓		✓			✓					✓	✓		✓		✓		✓	✓				
IBERIS ODORATA	✓			✓			✓			✓					✓	✓	✓	✓		✓		✓					
IMPATIENS GLANDULIFERA	✓		✓					✓	✓			✓			✓			✓		✓							
IPOMOEA ALBA			✓	✓			✓						✓		✓	✓	✓	✓	✓							✓	
LAGENARIA SICERARIA	✓		✓				✓						✓		✓	✓		✓			✓			✓			
LAGURUS OVATUS 'NANUS'	✓				✓		✓			✓					✓	✓		✓	✓			✓	✓			✓	
LAVATERA TRIMESTRIS 'MONT BLANC'	✓				✓		✓				✓				✓	✓		✓				✓			✓		
LUNARIA ANNUA 'ALBA'		✓		✓	✓	✓	✓	✓			✓			✓				✓					✓	✓	✓		
NICOTIANA SYLVESTRIS	✓		✓				✓	✓				✓			✓	✓	✓	✓		✓							
OMPHALODES LINIFOLIA	✓		✓				✓	✓	✓						✓	✓	✓	✓				✓					
PAPAVER SOMNIFERUM 'WHITE CLOUD'	✓				✓		✓	✓			✓			✓	✓			✓				✓					
RESEDA ODORATA	✓				✓		✓	✓		✓	✓				✓	✓	✓	✓		✓				✓			
SCABIOSA STELLATA 'PING-PONG'	✓		✓				✓				✓				✓	✓		✓				✓	✓				
SENECIO CINERARIA			✓	✓	✓	✓	✓	✓		✓						✓			✓						✓	✓	

Column groups: **PLANT TYPE** · **SOIL** · **LIGHT** · **HEIGHT** · **BLOOM SEASON** · **NOTED FOR** · **SPECIAL USES** · **TOLERATES**

Color	Plant	ANNUAL	BIENNIAL	TENDER PERENNIAL	RICH, LOAMY	AVERAGE	POOR	FULL SUN	PARTIAL SHADE	SHADE	UNDER 12 INCHES	1 TO 3 FEET	OVER 3 FEET	VINE OR CREEPER	SPRING	EARLY SUMMER	LATE SUMMER	FALL	FLOWERS	FOLIAGE	FRAGRANCE	FRUIT/SEEDS	CUT FLOWERS	DRIED FLOWERS	CONTAINERS	DROUGHT	HEAT	COASTAL CONDITIONS
YELLOW	CARTHAMUS TINCTORIUS	✓				✓		✓				✓				✓	✓		✓				✓	✓				
	CELSIA CRETICA		✓		✓	✓		✓				✓				✓	✓		✓		✓							
	DYSSODIA TENUILOBA	✓		✓	✓	✓		✓			✓					✓	✓	✓	✓							✓	✓	✓
	ESCHSCHOLZIA CAESPITOSA	✓			✓	✓	✓	✓			✓					✓	✓		✓	✓						✓		
	GAZANIA LINEARIS			✓	✓	✓		✓			✓					✓	✓		✓						✓	✓		✓
	HELIANTHUS ANNUUS 'TEDDY BEAR'	✓		✓				✓				✓				✓	✓	✓	✓							✓	✓	
	HIBISCUS TRIONUM			✓	✓			✓	✓		✓					✓	✓	✓	✓							✓	✓	
	LAYIA PLATYGLOSSA	✓			✓			✓			✓				✓	✓			✓							✓		
	LONAS ANNUA	✓			✓	✓		✓			✓	✓				✓	✓		✓					✓	✓			
	MENTZELIA DECAPETALA		✓		✓	✓		✓				✓				✓	✓		✓							✓	✓	✓
	MENTZELIA LAEVICAULIS		✓	✓	✓	✓		✓					✓			✓	✓		✓							✓	✓	✓
	OENOTHERA BIENNIS		✓		✓	✓	✓	✓	✓			✓				✓	✓	✓	✓								✓	
	OENOTHERA ERYTHROSEPALA 'TINA JAMES'		✓		✓	✓		✓				✓				✓	✓	✓	✓								✓	
	RUDBECKIA HIRTA 'DOUBLE GOLD'	✓	✓	✓	✓	✓	✓	✓	✓			✓				✓	✓		✓					✓			✓		
	SANVITALIA PROCUMBENS 'GOLD BRAID'	✓			✓	✓	✓	✓			✓					✓	✓	✓	✓							✓	✓	✓
	TAGETES ERECTA 'PRIMROSE LADY'	✓		✓	✓			✓				✓				✓	✓	✓	✓					✓		✓	✓	
	TROPAEOLUM PEREGRINUM	✓				✓	✓	✓						✓		✓	✓	✓	✓									
	VERBASCUM BOMBYCIFERUM 'SILVER LINING'		✓		✓	✓		✓				✓				✓	✓		✓	✓								
ORANGE	CARTHAMUS TINCTORIUS 'LASTING ORANGE'	✓				✓		✓				✓				✓	✓							✓	✓			
	ERYSIMUM PEROFSKIANUM		✓	✓				✓	✓		✓	✓			✓	✓			✓		✓		✓					
	ESCHSCHOLZIA CALIFORNICA 'AURANTIACA'			✓	✓	✓	✓	✓				✓			✓	✓	✓	✓								✓		
	IPOMOEA QUAMOCLIT	✓			✓	✓		✓						✓		✓	✓	✓	✓							✓		
	MINA LOBATA			✓	✓			✓	✓					✓		✓	✓	✓	✓									
	SANVITALIA PROCUMBENS 'MANDARIN ORANGE'	✓			✓	✓		✓			✓					✓	✓	✓	✓							✓	✓	✓
	TITHONIA ROTUNDIFOLIA 'GOLDFINGER'	✓			✓	✓	✓	✓				✓				✓	✓		✓					✓			✓		
	ZINNIA ANGUSTIFOLIA	✓			✓	✓	✓	✓				✓				✓	✓		✓							✓	✓	
RED	ADONIS AESTIVALIS	✓			✓			✓	✓			✓			✓				✓	✓								✓
	AMARANTHUS CAUDATUS	✓			✓	✓	✓	✓					✓			✓	✓	✓	✓	✓				✓	✓			
	ASCLEPIAS CURASSAVICA			✓	✓	✓		✓				✓	✓			✓	✓	✓	✓			✓						
	ATRIPLEX HORTENSIS 'RUBRA'	✓		✓				✓					✓			✓				✓			✓					✓
	CAPSICUM ANNUUM 'HOLIDAY CHEER'			✓	✓			✓			✓					✓	✓					✓	✓			✓		
	CLEOME HASSLERANA 'CHERRY QUEEN'	✓			✓	✓		✓	✓			✓			✓	✓	✓	✓	✓					✓			✓	

Table: Plant selection guide (page 64). Columns grouped under PLANT TYPE, SOIL, LIGHT, HEIGHT, BLOOM SEASON, NOTED FOR, SPECIAL USES, TOLERATES.

Color	Plant	Annual	Biennial	Tender Perennial	Rich, Loamy	Average	Poor	Full Sun	Partial Shade	Shade	Under 12 Inches	1 to 3 Feet	Over 3 Feet	Vine or Creeper	Spring	Early Summer	Late Summer	Fall	Flowers	Foliage	Fragrance	Fruit/Seeds	Cut Flowers	Dried Flowers	Containers	Drought	Heat	Coastal Conditions
RED	CUPHEA IGNEA			✔	✔	✔	✔	✔	✔		✔					✔	✔		✔						✔		✔	
RED	ECHIUM WILDPRETII		✔				✔	✔				✔				✔	✔		✔	✔								
RED	FOENICULUM VULGARE 'PURPUREUM'			✔	✔	✔	✔	✔				✔				✔			✔	✔			✔				✔	
RED	HIBISCUS ACETOSELLA 'RED SHIELD'			✔	✔			✔	✔			✔					✔			✔					✔		✔	
RED	IPOMOEA NIL 'SCARLETT O'HARA'	✔			✔	✔		✔						✔		✔	✔	✔	✔								✔	
RED	PHASEOLUS COCCINEUS			✔	✔			✔						✔	✔	✔			✔			✔	✔					
RED	RICINUS COMMUNIS 'CARMENCITA'			✔	✔			✔					✔			✔	✔	✔		✔							✔	
RED	SALVIA COCCINEA 'LADY IN RED'			✔	✔	✔		✔	✔		✔					✔	✔	✔	✔						✔			
RED	ZINNIA ELEGANS 'BIG RED'	✔			✔	✔		✔				✔				✔	✔	✔	✔				✔				✔	
PINK	CATHARANTHUS ROSEUS 'TROPICANA'			✔	✔			✔	✔		✔					✔	✔	✔	✔						✔		✔	
PINK	CELOSIA CRISTATA 'PINK TASSELS'	✔				✔		✔				✔				✔	✔		✔				✔	✔		✔	✔	
PINK	CIRSIUM JAPONICUM		✔		✔	✔	✔	✔	✔			✔				✔	✔		✔				✔	✔				
PINK	CLEOME HASSLERANA 'PINK QUEEN'	✔			✔	✔		✔	✔				✔			✔	✔	✔			✔						✔	
PINK	COSMOS BIPINNATUS 'VERSAILLES PINK'	✔				✔		✔	✔							✔	✔		✔				✔					
PINK	CREPIS RUBRA	✔				✔	✔	✔			✔	✔				✔	✔		✔							✔		✔
PINK	DAHLIA HYBRIDS 'AUDACITY'		✔	✔		✔		✔				✔				✔	✔		✔				✔					
PINK	DIASCIA BARBERAE 'PINK QUEEN'	✔				✔		✔			✔					✔	✔	✔	✔									
PINK	DIGITALIS PURPUREA 'GIANT SHIRLEY'		✔		✔				✔			✔				✔			✔									
PINK	LAVATERA TRIMESTRIS 'SILVER CUP'	✔				✔		✔				✔				✔	✔		✔				✔			✔		
PINK	MATTHIOLA BICORNIS	✔						✔	✔		✔					✔	✔		✔		✔		✔		✔			
PINK	PAPAVER SOMNIFERUM 'PINK CHIFFON'	✔				✔		✔	✔			✔				✔	✔		✔				✔					
PINK	PELARGONIUM X HORTORUM 'FRECKLES'		✔	✔				✔			✔					✔	✔	✔	✔	✔					✔			
PINK	PETUNIA X HYBRIDA 'FANTASY PINK MORN'	✔						✔			✔					✔	✔	✔							✔			
PINK	SILENE ARMERIA	✔	✔		✔	✔		✔			✔					✔	✔				✔							
PINK	SILENE PENDULA	✔			✔	✔		✔	✔		✔					✔	✔								✔			
PINK	VERBENA X HYBRIDA 'SILVER ANN'	✔				✔		✔			✔					✔	✔	✔							✔			
PURPLE	ANTIRRHINUM MAJUS 'BLACK PRINCE'			✔	✔			✔	✔			✔				✔	✔	✔					✔					
PURPLE	CLARKIA CONCINNA	✔			✔	✔		✔	✔			✔			✔	✔			✔									
PURPLE	COBAEA SCANDENS			✔		✔								✔		✔	✔	✔	✔									
PURPLE	CYNARA CARDUNCULUS			✔	✔			✔					✔			✔	✔	✔	✔				✔	✔				
PURPLE	DOLICHOS LABLAB			✔	✔			✔						✔		✔	✔		✔	✔	✔	✔					✔	
PURPLE	EUSTOMA GRANDIFLORUM		✔		✔			✔			✔					✔		✔					✔		✔	✔	✔	

Plant selection guide — checkmarks (✓) indicate applicable characteristics.

	Plant	PLANT TYPE			SOIL			LIGHT			HEIGHT				BLOOM SEASON				NOTED FOR				SPECIAL USES			TOLERATES		
		ANNUAL	BIENNIAL	TENDER PERENNIAL	RICH, LOAMY	AVERAGE	POOR	FULL SUN	PARTIAL SHADE	SHADE	UNDER 12 INCHES	1 TO 3 FEET	OVER 3 FEET	VINE OR CREEPER	SPRING	EARLY SUMMER	LATE SUMMER	FALL	FLOWERS	FOLIAGE	FRAGRANCE	FRUIT/SEEDS	CUT FLOWERS	DRIED FLOWERS	CONTAINERS	DROUGHT	HEAT	COASTAL CONDITIONS
PURPLE	HELIOTROPIUM ARBORESCENS			✓	✓			✓	✓		✓					✓	✓		✓		✓				✓	✓		
	OCIMUM BASILICUM 'DARK OPAL'	✓			✓	✓		✓				✓				✓	✓	✓	✓	✓					✓			
	ONOPORDUM ACANTHIUM	✓	✓			✓	✓	✓					✓		✓	✓			✓	✓						✓	✓	
	ORTHOCARPUS PURPURASCENS	✓				✓	✓	✓			✓					✓			✓								✓	
	PENNISETUM SETACEUM 'RUBRUM'			✓		✓		✓				✓	✓			✓	✓	✓		✓			✓	✓				
	PERILLA FRUTESCENS VAR. CRISPA	✓				✓	✓	✓	✓			✓					✓			✓								
	PETUNIA X HYBRIDA 'HEAVENLY LAVENDER'	✓		✓				✓		✓						✓	✓	✓	✓						✓			
	RHODOCHITON ATROSANGUINEUM			✓	✓			✓						✓	✓	✓	✓	✓	✓								✓	
	SALVIA SPLENDENS 'LASER PURPLE'			✓	✓	✓		✓	✓		✓					✓	✓	✓	✓						✓			
	SILYBUM MARIANUM	✓	✓			✓	✓					✓				✓			✓	✓					✓			
	VERBENA BONARIENSIS			✓	✓			✓					✓		✓	✓	✓	✓	✓				✓					
BLUE	AGERATUM HOUSTONIANUM 'BLUE HORIZON'	✓		✓				✓			✓					✓	✓	✓	✓				✓					
	BORAGO OFFICINALIS	✓				✓		✓	✓		✓					✓	✓	✓	✓				✓			✓		
	BROWALLIA SPECIOSA 'BLUE BELLS'			✓	✓	✓			✓	✓	✓	✓				✓	✓		✓						✓			
	CALLISTEPHUS CHINENSIS 'BLUE SKIES'	✓		✓				✓	✓			✓				✓	✓	✓										
	CONSOLIDA AMBIGUA 'IMPERIAL BLUE BELL'	✓		✓				✓	✓				✓			✓			✓				✓					
	CYNOGLOSSUM AMABILE		✓		✓	✓	✓	✓	✓			✓				✓	✓	✓	✓				✓					
	EXACUM AFFINE		✓	✓					✓	✓	✓	✓				✓	✓	✓	✓		✓				✓		✓	
	LOBELIA ERINUS	✓		✓	✓			✓	✓							✓	✓	✓	✓						✓			
	MYOSOTIS SYLVATICA 'VICTORIA BLUE'	✓	✓					✓	✓						✓	✓			✓									
	NEMOPHILA MENZIESII	✓		✓				✓	✓		✓					✓	✓		✓									
	OXYPETALUM CAERULEUM			✓	✓			✓				✓			✓	✓	✓	✓	✓							✓	✓	
	PHACELIA CAMPANULARIA	✓			✓	✓		✓			✓	✓				✓			✓								✓	
	SALVIA FARINACEA 'VICTORIA'			✓	✓	✓		✓	✓			✓				✓	✓	✓	✓						✓			
	SCABIOSA STELLATA	✓		✓				✓				✓				✓	✓		✓				✓	✓				
GREEN	BRIZA MAXIMA	✓				✓		✓				✓			✓	✓			✓	✓		✓	✓	✓				
	CARDIOSPERMUM HALICACABUM			✓		✓		✓						✓	✓	✓			✓		✓					✓	✓	
	FOENICULUM VULGARE			✓	✓	✓	✓	✓					✓			✓		✓	✓	✓			✓			✓		
	HUMULUS JAPONICUS			✓	✓									✓		✓				✓							✓	
	MOLUCELLA LAEVIS	✓				✓		✓				✓				✓	✓						✓	✓				
	NICOTIANA LANGSDORFFII	✓		✓				✓	✓			✓				✓	✓		✓									
	RICINUS COMMUNIS			✓	✓			✓					✓			✓			✓	✓							✓	

	Annual	Biennial	Tender Perennial	Rich, Loamy	Average	Poor	Full Sun	Partial Shade	Shade	Under 12 Inches	1 to 3 Feet	Over 3 Feet	Vine or Creeper	Spring	Early Summer	Late Summer	Fall	Flowers	Foliage	Fragrance	Fruit/Seeds	Cut Flowers	Dried Flowers	Containers	Drought	Heat	Coastal Conditions
SETARIA ITALICA	✔			✔			✔				✔	✔			✔	✔	✔	✔	✔			✔	✔				
TAGETES FILIFOLIA	✔		✔	✔	✔		✔			✔					✔				✔					✔	✔		
ABELMOSCHUS MANIHOT 'GOLDEN BOWL'			✔	✔			✔	✔			✔				✔			✔	✔							✔	
AMARANTHUS TRICOLOR	✔				✔	✔	✔			✔	✔				✔	✔			✔							✔	✔
ARCTOTIS STOECHADIFOLIA			✔		✔	✔	✔				✔				✔	✔	✔	✔				✔				✔	✔
BRASSICA OLERACEA 'COLOR UP'		✔	✔				✔			✔	✔								✔					✔			
CHRYSANTHEMUM CARINATUM	✔			✔			✔	✔			✔				✔	✔	✔	✔				✔					
CLARKIA AMOENA	✔				✔	✔	✔				✔				✔	✔		✔				✔					
COLEUS X HYBRIDUS			✔	✔				✔			✔				✔	✔			✔					✔			
COLLINSIA HETEROPHYLLA	✔			✔				✔			✔				✔	✔	✔	✔				✔					
CONVOLVULUS TRICOLOR 'ROYAL ENSIGN'	✔			✔			✔				✔				✔	✔	✔							✔	✔	✔	
CUCUMIS MELO	✔		✔				✔						✔		✔		✔			✔	✔						
CUCURBITA MAXIMA 'TURBANIFORMIS'	✔		✔	✔			✔						✔		✔						✔					✔	
DAHLIA HYBRIDS 'MICKEY'			✔	✔			✔				✔				✔	✔		✔				✔					
DIGITALIS FERRUGINEA		✔		✔				✔				✔			✔			✔									
DIMORPHOTHECA PLUVIALIS	✔			✔	✔	✔	✔							✔	✔	✔	✔								✔	✔	
GAILLARDIA PULCHELLA	✔			✔	✔	✔	✔				✔				✔	✔	✔					✔			✔	✔	✔
GAZANIA RIGENS 'SUNSHINE'			✔	✔	✔	✔	✔			✔					✔	✔	✔							✔	✔		✔
KOCHIA SCOPARIA 'ACAPULCO SILVER'	✔			✔	✔		✔				✔				✔		✔		✔					✔			
LIMONIUM SUWOROWII	✔			✔			✔			✔	✔				✔	✔	✔					✔	✔	✔			✔
LINARIA MAROCCANA 'FAIRY BOUQUET'	✔			✔			✔	✔		✔					✔	✔		✔						✔			
RUDBECKIA HIRTA 'GLORIOSA DAISY'	✔	✔	✔	✔	✔	✔	✔	✔			✔				✔	✔		✔				✔		✔			
SALVIA FARINACEA 'STRATA'			✔	✔	✔		✔				✔				✔	✔	✔	✔				✔	✔	✔			
THUNBERGIA ALATA			✔	✔			✔	✔					✔		✔	✔								✔			
TORENIA FOURNIERI	✔			✔				✔	✔	✔					✔	✔								✔			
VIOLA RAFINESQUII	✔			✔			✔	✔		✔				✔	✔			✔						✔			
VIOLA TRICOLOR	✔			✔			✔	✔		✔				✔	✔			✔		✔				✔			
ZEA MAYS VAR. JAPONICA	✔			✔			✔					✔			✔				✔		✔						
ZINNIA HAAGEANA 'PERSIAN CARPET'	✔			✔			✔				✔				✔	✔	✔	✔				✔				✔	
AGROSTEMMA GITHAGO	✔			✔	✔	✔	✔				✔				✔	✔						✔			✔		
ALCEA ROSEA 'PINAFORE MIXED'		✔		✔			✔					✔			✔	✔	✔										
BEGONIA 'PIZZAZZ MIXED'			✔	✔			✔	✔	✔					✔	✔	✔	✔	✔	✔					✔			

PLANT TYPE · **SOIL** · **LIGHT** · **HEIGHT** · **BLOOM SEASON** · **NOTED FOR** · **SPECIAL USES** · **TOLERATES**

MULTI- AND BICOLORED

MIXED

MIXED

	Annual	Biennial	Tender Perennial	Rich, Loamy	Average	Poor	Full Sun	Partial Shade	Shade	Under 12 Inches	1 to 3 Feet	Over 3 Feet	Vine or Creeper	Spring	Early Summer	Late Summer	Fall	Flowers	Foliage	Fragrance	Fruit/Seeds	Cut Flowers	Dried Flowers	Containers	Drought	Heat	Coastal Conditions
	PLANT TYPE			**SOIL**			**LIGHT**			**HEIGHT**				**BLOOM SEASON**				**NOTED FOR**				**SPECIAL USES**			**TOLERATES**		
BRACHYCOME IBERIDIFOLIA	✓		✓				✓			✓	✓				✓	✓		✓						✓			
CALENDULA OFFICINALIS 'BON BON'	✓		✓				✓				✓				✓	✓		✓				✓		✓			
CAMPANULA MEDIUM 'CALYCANTHEMA'		✓	✓				✓	✓		✓	✓				✓	✓		✓				✓					
CANNA X GENERALIS			✓	✓			✓				✓	✓			✓	✓	✓	✓						✓			
CENTAUREA CYANUS	✓				✓		✓				✓				✓	✓	✓	✓				✓	✓				
CHEIRANTHUS CHEIRI			✓	✓			✓			✓	✓			✓				✓		✓							✓
COREOPSIS TINCTORIA	✓				✓		✓				✓				✓	✓	✓	✓				✓			✓	✓	
DIANTHUS BARBATUS		✓	✓				✓	✓		✓	✓			✓	✓			✓				✓					
EMILIA JAVANICA	✓			✓	✓	✓	✓				✓				✓	✓		✓				✓	✓		✓	✓	✓
GOMPHRENA GLOBOSA	✓				✓		✓			✓	✓				✓	✓	✓	✓				✓	✓	✓		✓	
GYPSOPHILA ELEGANS	✓				✓		✓				✓			✓	✓	✓	✓	✓				✓	✓				
HELICHRYSUM BRACTEATUM			✓	✓	✓	✓	✓				✓				✓	✓	✓	✓				✓	✓		✓		
IMPATIENS GLANDULIFERA	✓		✓					✓	✓		✓				✓	✓	✓	✓									
IMPATIENS WALLERANA	✓		✓					✓	✓	✓	✓				✓	✓	✓	✓						✓			
LATHYRUS ODORATUS 'BIJOU MIXED'	✓		✓				✓	✓		✓				✓	✓			✓		✓							
LATHYRUS ODORATUS 'ROYAL FAMILY'	✓		✓				✓	✓					✓	✓	✓			✓		✓							
LIMONIUM SINUATUM	✓			✓	✓		✓				✓				✓	✓		✓				✓	✓		✓		✓
LOBULARIA MARITIMA			✓		✓		✓	✓		✓				✓	✓	✓	✓	✓		✓				✓			
MATTHIOLA INCANA		✓	✓				✓	✓			✓			✓	✓			✓		✓		✓		✓			
MIMULUS X HYBRIDUS			✓	✓			✓	✓	✓	✓					✓	✓		✓						✓			
MIRABILIS JALAPA			✓	✓	✓		✓	✓			✓				✓	✓	✓	✓				✓				✓	
NEMESIA STRUMOSA 'CARNIVAL MIXED'	✓		✓				✓	✓		✓					✓	✓	✓	✓									
NICOTIANA ALATA 'NIKKI'	✓		✓				✓	✓			✓				✓	✓		✓		✓							
NIGELLA DAMASCENA	✓				✓		✓				✓				✓	✓		✓			✓	✓	✓				
PELARGONIUM PELTATUM			✓	✓			✓						✓		✓	✓	✓	✓	✓					✓			
PHLOX DRUMMONDII 'TWINKLE' SERIES	✓				✓	✓	✓			✓					✓	✓		✓									
PORTULACA GRANDIFLORA 'SUNDANCE'	✓				✓	✓	✓			✓					✓	✓	✓	✓	✓						✓	✓	✓
PROBOSCIDEA LOUISIANICA	✓				✓	✓	✓				✓				✓			✓			✓		✓				
SALPIGLOSSIS SINUATA 'BOLERO'	✓		✓				✓				✓				✓	✓		✓						✓			
SCHIZANTHUS PINNATUS	✓		✓				✓	✓				✓			✓	✓		✓						✓	✓		
TROPAEOLUM MINUS 'ALASKA MIXED'	✓				✓	✓	✓			✓					✓	✓	✓	✓	✓					✓			
XERANTHEMUM ANNUUM	✓		✓	✓	✓	✓	✓				✓				✓	✓	✓					✓	✓				

Perennials

Perennials have become the favorite flowers of American gardeners. Valued for their beauty, variety, and vitality, these herbaceous plants live at least 3 years and usually much longer. In an age when leisure time is a precious commodity, home gardeners are increasingly turning to perennials to create gardens that provide lovely views year round and require little in the way of maintenance.

Like all gardens, the successful perennial garden is the product of a well-conceived plan that takes into account climate, site, the gardener's personal tastes, and basic design principles. Such planning is evident in the Santa Monica, California, garden pictured here, where spikes of foxglove and delphinium rise from the center of a bed of perennials that includes lavender, verbena, catmint, and salvia. The splendid island bed is supplemented with bulbs and annuals to produce 10 months of bloom each year.

Many perennial garden styles are detailed on the following pages, along with guidance on how to plan for four-season interest. With an understanding of basic design principles and a little imagination, you can create a unique perennial garden of your own.

The Many Styles of Perennial Gardens

This Pennsylvania garden uses the symmetry of an arbor to impose formality on its plantings of dark violet Salvia x superba, pale violet Nepeta, pink Dianthus deltoides, and blue oatgrass. The bench provides an eye-level focal point against the backdrop of the towering hedge.

As you search for an appropriate style for your perennial garden, the possibilities will be almost endless. You might wish to recreate all or part of a garden fondly remembered from childhood, or one seen on a memorable vacation. Your inspiration might come from a fictional garden in a favorite novel, or from a particular time in history: perhaps the plantation gardens of the South, the wildflower meadows of Texas, the mission gardens of California, or the prairie landscapes of the Midwest. Or your model garden could have a horticultural theme—a rock garden, a cutting garden, and a shade garden are examples.

Be careful not to design a garden that will be too difficult for you to construct, plant, and take care of. A 200-foot double border—one that flanks both sides of a walkway or driveway—on an English country estate is magnificent to see, but it takes hundreds of hours, great professional expertise, and a lot of money to install the border and maintain it in peak condition. Similarly, a serene Japanese garden you may once have admired most likely required major earth working, backbreaking placement of stones, and meticulous pruning of trees and shrubs to achieve its stylistic simplicity and grace.

Garden Ideas to Borrow

Countless gardeners before you have wrestled with making gardens, and their successes—the re-

sults of their hard work and imaginations—are evident in the pages of gardening books and magazines. These are great resources when it comes time to plan your own garden. You can also look for ideas in the gardens of friends and neighbors, and in public gardens, which are useful to study because they give a true measure of how well specific plants will grow in your area.

Use these gardens for inspiration—to borrow an idea or two or mix and match a few plant combinations—but resist the urge to copy them plant for plant. Tempting as it might be to simply duplicate a planting that appeals to you, even if you were to succeed at recreating one of these elaborate productions, you would rob your garden of its own character and deprive yourself of the satisfaction of creating something unique.

Nor is it necessary to recreate a whole landscape to capture its essence. Some pairings of columbine and Solomon's-seal in your own shady corner might be just enough to remind you of the plantings along a woodland path. Likewise, a single mature lavender plant in a terra-cotta contain-er placed just so on the patio might be all that is necessary to conjure up the appealing look of an entrance to a French country inn.

Choosing Your Design Framework

One thing you will want to decide on from looking at other gardens is your design framework—whether you prefer your garden to be formal or informal, or a mixture of both. These are loose concepts; what is formal to you might seem quite relaxed or even chaotic to a neighbor. Clearly, however, some gardens are laid out in a more architectural and orderly manner than others.

Within both formal and informal design frameworks, you can choose from a number of different garden styles. Perennials will have a major role regardless of the style you select. They form such a rich and diverse family of plants that they can fit comfortably into virtually any planting scheme.

The mossy path curving through this informal shade garden evokes a woodland scene. Framed by a blanket of mondo grass, the path meanders through a thicket of white foamflower, and, in the foreground, purple phlox and a variegated variety of Solomon's-seal.

The daisies, delphiniums, poppies, and snapdragons of this garden are grouped tightly in a color plan of blues, pinks, and whites, with yellow added as an accent. Such a jumble of plants in rich, vibrant colors is the essence of the cottage garden style.

Perennials for a Cutting Garden

Achillea
(yarrow)
Allium
(flowering onion)
Aster
(aster)
Campanula
(bellflower)
Chrysanthemum
(chrysanthemum)
Coreopsis
(tickseed)
Delphinium
(delphinium)
Digitalis
(foxglove)
Echinacea
(purple coneflower)
Echinops
(globe thistle)
Eryngium
(sea holly)
Gaillardia

(blanket flower)
Gypsophelia
(baby's-breath)
Heliopsis
(false sunflower)
Iris
(iris)
Lavandula
(lavender)
Liatris
(gay-feather)
Paeonia
(peony)
Phlox
(phlox)
Rudbeckia
(phlox)
Solidago
(goldenrod)
Thalictrum
(meadow rue)
Veronica
(speedwell)

Formal Gardens

Generally, the mark of a formal garden is the straight line—in its paths, pools, borders, hedges, and even in the way a view is directed along an axis, or sightline. In the most formal gardens, spaces are crafted into open-air rooms by the use of walls or hedgerows. Often, columns of marble, stone, wood, or even living trees are used to suggest walls. In classical gardens, the formality is reinforced through symmetry, with one side of the garden mirroring the other.

Most such elements would overpower the typical suburban garden, of course, but it is possible to have formality on a more intimate scale. You might put in a small knot garden—so called for its knotlike shape—where you arrange the beds in a balanced geometric pattern with, perhaps, brick walkways in between the plantings. The beds in a knot garden can be curved or have squared corners, and are usually edged in miniature boxwood. However, some gardeners in warmer climates outline the edges of the beds with perennials and herbs, including lavender, germander, and rose-

The same general color scheme and some of the same plants used in the cottage garden at left appear in this perenni-al border in Atlanta, Georgia. However, this garden's neat edging of brick and the layers of plants rising against a vertical backdrop—the clipped hedge—give it a more elegant and formal aspect.

mary, instead of using the evergreen shrubs.

You might choose to adopt an even more subdued level of formality, using a patio's straight edge as the boundary of your garden, for example, or choosing to plant perennials in borders instead of in beds with a freer form. A simple curve with a fixed radius can lend a formal air to a border in a way that a winding curve will not.

Without changing the outlines of a rectangular garden plot, you can either enhance or soften its air of formality by your choice of plantings. If you prefer the less formal, plant the garden's straight borders with perennials of different colors and with a relaxed form that will creep over the edges of the border. On the other hand, if order and regularity are to your liking, you could lay out a neat pathway through the plot with a mass planting on both sides of a graceful perennial like *Nepeta* (catmint) or a showy one like peony.

Informal Gardens

Curving lines and asymmetry are the key characteristics of the informal garden. The landscape is no less crafted than in a formal garden, but the borders, if there are borders, might take a rambling course alongside a lawn. Often, the plantings are in beds rather than borders, the walkways are curved rather than straight, and trees and shrubs are located randomly and pruned only for their health, not to conform to a particular shape.

Cottage Gardens

One of the most popular and enduring styles is the cottage garden, whose air of rustic domesticity may be a better match for a suburban property than would a grand, classically formal garden. The cottage garden's origins lie in the old-fashioned villages of England, where the occupants of small thatched- or tile-roofed cottages filled their gardens with annuals and perennials. These were species plants—not today's highly developed cultivars and hybrids, which usually cannot reproduce themselves faithfully from seed. The old plants set seed freely, however, perpetuating themselves and producing a riot of color amid a rambling growth of foliage—and, best of all, requiring little care from the owner.

In the late 19th and early 20th centuries, some of England's leading gardeners developed a style based on the cottage garden but refined to a high level of sophistication. They took pains to design herbaceous borders that would bloom in rolling

waves of color throughout the summer months.

The American cottage garden so in favor now lies somewhere between its two predecessors. Crafting color schemes and choosing plants for their foliage, form, and ease of care—as well as their flowers—are more important to today's gardeners than to those who tended the appealing but unruly tangle of plants dominating the early dooryard gardens. Even so, today's standards are not as rigid or demanding as those that produced the refined English border. The variety of plants to choose from is different, too, with a greater reliance on hardy perennials that are distinctly American, such as daylilies and rudbeckias.

Cutting Gardens

Nothing announces serious gardeners—or a serious love of flowers—more than choosing to grow a cutting garden. There, plants are raised for the sole purpose of producing beautiful blooms for indoor arrangements. Although the cutting garden is less common in the American landscape than other garden styles, it deserves a second look.

Again, perennials are an ideal ingredient, especially long-stemmed plants like delphinium, solidago, and iris. Most will not rebloom, as cut annuals do, but they will present an array of flowers across the growing season if enough different kinds are planted.

Traditionally, the cutting garden occupies its own bed or beds away from the main garden; plants grow in well-spaced rows, allowing the gardener to reach them easily. Even a small area, about 10 by 10 feet, will yield hundreds of blooms in a season. But if space is at a premium, you can grow flowers for cutting in between plants in the vegetable plot or within display beds and borders.

Perennial Borders and Beds

The two most common ways to display perennials are in a border or a bed. The border typically forms the edge of a garden space and lies next to a vertical element—a wall of the house, a fence, or a hedge, for example.

The width of the border can vary, but it is an important factor in choosing plants. In a conventional border, the rule of thumb is that no plant should be taller than one-half the width of the space. If

your border is a thin strip of ground between a wall and a sidewalk, for example, the scale of the perennials you place there must be modest—perhaps a row of petite plants such as candytuft, threadleaf coreopsis, or ajuga.

One advantage of the border garden is that its vertical element offers a handsome backdrop for the flowers. A white fence or wall, for instance, spotlights the color and form of the plants growing in front of it. Be careful, though, of color clashes, particularly against red brick walls, where bold red or orange blooms might be jarring.

A flower bed doesn't have the visual anchor that is inherent in a border; it often takes the form of a free-floating island. But the bed does valuable service: It can direct views across a lawn, and spotlight such landscape features as decks, patios, and swimming pools. Also, a bed might be the only place on your property where you can grow perennials in the full sun that most require.

There are pitfalls to watch out for, however, in deciding to create island beds. Islands must be made large enough to hold their own in an overall design. Even at that they might need the added visual weight of some shrubs or small trees in order not to be overshadowed by imposing elements—such as the house—that are nearby.

Both borders and beds, if they are broad enough, will need maintenance paths—narrow, hidden trails that give you access to plants without the risk of your stepping on them or compacting their soil. In a bed, you might create a path from woodchips or river stones that, from a distance, is hidden by plant foliage. In a border, your path might run between the back of the plantings and the wall or hedge backdrop. Apart from the access it affords you, the path will also improve air circulation among the plants and prevent lingering dampness that might cause fungal infections.

Borders and beds also benefit from edging, especially if the adjacent ground is a lawn. Brick, stone, or concrete pavers laid just 6 to 12 inches wide will keep the lawn mower away from the plants and keep the plants from smothering the grass as they flop forward. Edging also acts as a unifying element for the whole plant display.

A handsome fence adds strength and completeness to this border, which includes pale yellow Achillea 'Moonshine' (foreground), reddish Alstroemeria, and tall, lilac-colored Verbena bonariensis. Without such backdrops, which define the plants' shapes and highlight their colors, some borders might lose their visual impact and become harder to see.

Choosing the Right Plants

Selecting plants to fit your garden style is the most challenging and rewarding aspect of perennial gardening. The complexities of selecting perennials for their bloom colors, their shapes, and their foliage and textures can appear overwhelming, but by taking a systematic approach and learning all you can about the plants and how they might look in your garden, you can become a master.

The whole idea of composing with herbaceous plants can be a new one for many home gardeners. In the past, gardeners were able to find beauty in only a limited range of old-fashioned species of such perennials as daylilies, hostas, peonies, bearded iris, and phlox. Shrub borders were old favorites, as were foundation plantings of broad-leafed evergreens and a well-trimmed lawn. Color was achieved by planting a few perennials, some spring-blooming bulbs, flowering trees, shrubs, and, especially, beds of bright, cheery annuals.

An Explosion of Perennial Choices

In recent years, gardeners have found in mail-order catalogs and local nurseries alike a sumptuous and sometimes bewildering array of perennials. At the same time, a distinct type of perennial garden

A drift of Echinacea purpurea, the purple coneflower, shows up nicely against a backdrop of unfinished fenceboards (right). Lending a different character to the species is a cultivar called E. purpurea 'Alba', or white purple coneflower (above), which can be used in a color scheme where purple would clash. Echinacea purpurea is one of many enduring species that have been bred to produce new colors.

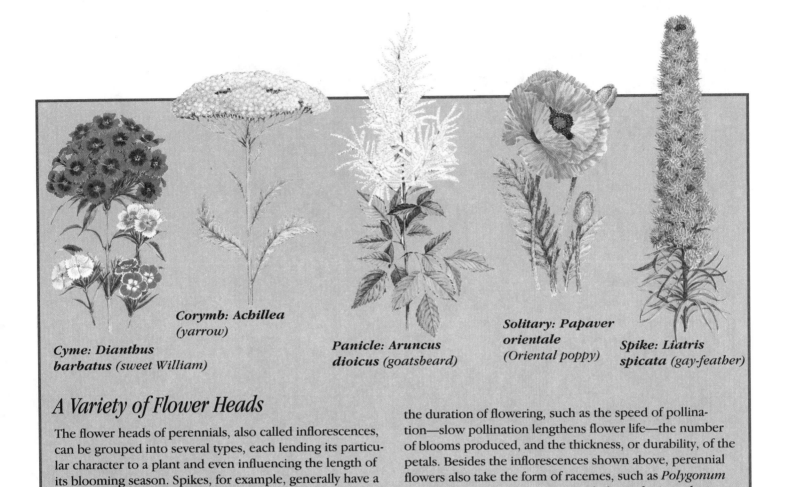

Corymb: Achillea *(yarrow)*

Cyme: Dianthus barbatus *(sweet William)*

Panicle: Aruncus dioicus *(goatsbeard)*

Solitary: Papaver orientale *(Oriental poppy)*

Spike: Liatris spicata *(gay-feather)*

A Variety of Flower Heads

The flower heads of perennials, also called inflorescences, can be grouped into several types, each lending its particular character to a plant and even influencing the length of its blooming season. Spikes, for example, generally have a long season, as the tiny individual flowers open in sequence from bottom to top. Other factors also influence the duration of flowering, such as the speed of pollination—slow pollination lengthens flower life—the number of blooms produced, and the thickness, or durability, of the petals. Besides the inflorescences shown above, perennial flowers also take the form of racemes, such as *Polygonum bistorta* 'Superba' *(page 328)*; umbels, *Asclepias tuberosa (page 306)*; and heads, *Echinacea purpurea (page 314)*.

plant, the ornamental grass, has gone from being a relative unknown in the garden to a sought-after addition to any planting, particularly given the development of many fine cultivars.

The enduring popularity of perennials has changed the face of the American garden. In an age when people want beauty and color in their garden but have little time to nurture it, well-chosen perennials provide ready solutions. Diverse and versatile, perennials can be used in any setting but are particularly well suited to looser, more natural landscape styles. They are also tougher in their ability to withstand climatic extremes and troublesome pests and diseases.

If you do not have a ready source of free perennials from gardening friends or relatives eager to divide mature plants, or if you can't take advantage of low-cost perennials from garden-club plant sales, your initial investment in perennials can be high. But with your expenditure comes the chance to create landscapes full of color and vitality using plants that require relatively little care. You'll also save the money you would spend on replacing annuals year after year, and in a fairly short period of time you'll have mature plants from which to propagate new ones.

Choosing Perennials for Color

The most important task perennials perform in the garden is enlivening the landscape with color. It is this decorative factor that places the well-designed perennial bed or border at the heart of any garden plan.

If you consciously choose a color scheme for a part or all of your perennial garden, it is best to start not with a specific plant in mind but with a particular color or colors. Once you decide on an all-white garden, say, or a grouping of soft yellows, white, and blue, you can select plants that will fall into those color bands and bloom throughout the growing season *(for information on perennials organized by color, see the Plant Selection Guide that begins on page 90)*. Interplanting foliage perennials that echo the selected hues—silvery foliage plants in an all-white garden, for in-

Mixing and Matching Colors

In the planting at left, the gardener has used the neutral gray foliage of Stachys byzantina to link the harmonious colors of Veronica 'True Blue' and the pink-flowered cranesbill Geranium x oxonianum 'Claridge Druce'.

Red, yellow, and blue are the primary colors on the color wheel. When equal amounts of two primary colors are mixed, secondary colors—orange, green, and violet—result. A primary color mixed with an adjacent secondary hue creates a third level of colors. Colors said to be harmonious share a portion of color; contrasting colors do not.

stance—or provide a buffer of green between potentially clashing colors, will help tie the entire arrangement together.

One color is virtually unavoidable in the garden—green. But green comes in many different shades and tints. (Shades are colors darkened by black, such as deep purple from violet; tints are colors that have been lightened by white, such as pink from red.) The careful selection of the right quality of green will enhance your color scheme. For example, the mauve-pink *Dianthus plumarius* 'Agatha' blends well with its own blue-green foliage but would jar disagreeably when paired with the yellow-green fringes of *Hosta fortunei*

'Aureo-marginata'. Successful pairing of colors is made much simpler if you understand the basics of the color wheel.

Using the Color Wheel

Different versions of the color wheel have been devised over the years, some reflecting the great scientific lengths to which color theory has been taken. However, most gardeners rely on the simple, standard version that starts with the three primary colors— red, yellow, and blue.

An equal mix of two primary colors produces one of the three secondary colors; hence orange is a mix of yellow and red and lies between them on the wheel, violet appears between red and blue, and green between blue and yellow. Mixing primary colors with their adjacent secondary colors yields the further gradations yellow-orange,

Coming from opposite sides of the color wheel, the rich blue of Nepeta mussinii and the pale yellow, umbrella-shaped blossoms of Achillea 'Moonshine' demonstrate the striking combinations that are possible with the use of contrasting colors (right).

The robust blooms of the popular daylily Hemerocallis 'Bejeweled' team with the dainty pink flowers of Achillea 'Rose Beauty' to produce a striking monochromatic effect (below).

red-orange, red-violet, blue-violet, blue-green, and yellow-green.

Conventional wisdom holds that the most pleasing color combinations are either contrasting, meaning that they stand directly opposite each other on the color wheel, or harmonious, found next to each other on the wheel and sharing a common pigment. A contrasting color combination might be blue and orange, violet and yellow, or red and green. Harmonious pairings include green and yellow-green, red-orange and orange, or blue-violet and blue.

Tints and shades, as well as blends of different colors—mauve, for example, which combines red and violet—add more variables. So do such elements as the amount and strength of the light the plants receive (pastels show up better in low light, bright colors look better in full sun), how well the the flower's petals reflect light, and the tendency for light colors to seem to come forward toward the viewer's eye and for dark colors to recede.

Clearly, with all these considerations to be taken into account, it is easy to become bogged down in the complexities of color. The best course is to use the color wheel to follow the basic rules of composing contrasting and harmonious color groupings but to let your garden plants, your eye, and your taste have the final say. If you occasionally create combinations that simply don't work well together, you won't be the first gardener to make a misstep. Always remember, it is easy to move perennials from one spot in the garden to another if you have to.

The robust, coarse-veined leaves of Hosta sieboldiana create a bold contrast in size and texture when placed next to the delicate foliage of Saxifraga stolonifera (strawberry saxifrage). Texture can provide visual interest for a garden well after the flowers have faded.

Marrying Cool and Hot Colors

Besides combining plants for harmony or contrast, it is generally considered preferable to group cool colors such as violets, blues, and off-whites together. Such combinations work particularly well in those areas that receive filtered light or partial shade, where there will be no glaring sun to wash out the lighter hues. Within this family of cool colors you can use yellows or reds to create accents, but for a better blending consider a red leaning toward violet rather than toward orange, and yellows that are lemon and pastel, not the pure and brilliant yellow of some achilleas or euphorbias, for example.

A garden of hot colors—reds, oranges, and pure yellows—works best in beds or borders that receive full sun. Here, you can have fun with fiery-colored varieties of such plants as geums, poppies, daylilies, kniphofias, and gaillardias. Be careful with rich colors such as magenta, blue-violet, or purple, however; they sometimes create a strident note in a bed or border unless they are somehow tempered. One way to handle such dominant colors is to isolate them in a separate bed where their brilliance will not overshadow more subdued

colors. If you lack the space for this, try planting them in partial shade (if they are suited for these conditions), which will reduce their impact. When viewed in shadows, colors that were once overpowering or garish will softly glow.

Foliage is an another important component of color in the perennial garden. It might not present itself as vividly as flowers, but it lasts much longer. A color scheme of reds, purples, and grays, for instance, might be constructed of the gray foliage of artemisia and one of the purple-leafed varieties of heuchera with coral red flowers. For a color combination of violet, yellow-green, and gray, you might plant *Stachys byzantina* (lamb's ears) between *Alchemilla mollis* (lady's-mantle), lavender, and euphorbia. Note that gray is of immense value in the perennial garden: It calms the colors around it and, as a neutral, ties them together.

Planning for Texture and Mass

Plant foliage not only contributes color, it also gives the garden texture and mass. Many perennials are grown principally for their foliage, among them hostas, artemisia, lamb's ears, epimedium, santolina, and lamium. A number of others—ajuga, lady's-mantle, and Solomon's-seal, for exam-

ple—produce foliage at least as valuable as their flowers. Even such prominent flowering plants as Japanese and Siberian iris, ligularia, acanthus, and blackberry lily accompany their blooms with a display of handsome leaves.

The fineness or coarseness of the leaves gives a plant its texture. Just as light colors advance to the eye and dark hues recede, a coarse-textured plant leaps forward into view and a fine-textured one retreats. With careful attention to the placement of fine-textured plants, for example, you can create an illusion of depth in a small garden.

More to the point, you can add interest to your garden through the thoughtful positioning of plants of varying textures. A coarse-leafed plant like ligularia would have greater visual impact set against the fine foliage of veronica than if it were next to an equally big-leafed plant like hosta.

If a plant's character comes from its leaf and flower texture, then its overall shape, or mass, dictates its stature. Mature miscanthus grass, for example, though it is fine in texture, may grow 6 feet high and 4 feet across—the size of a large shrub. Wild ginger, on the other hand, though it has coarse foliage, grows only a few inches high.

Just as you should think about associations of different colors and textures in planning your garden, you should also consider mass. For example, a flowering mound of phlox will look more imposing when given space to show off than when it is surrounded by other perennials of similar bulk.

Putting It All Together

With all these components in mind, it is time to put your planting ideas down on paper. Assemble those ideas first according to the colors, textures, and shapes you have decided on and then select the plants to produce them. For a long border or bed, it is best to work in short sections, mindful that the most pleasing designs have some unifying element, such as a repeated pattern of color, a progression of color, or a recurring plant.

The perennial garden should present itself in layers—tall plants at the back, medium ones in the middle, and smaller ones up front. There are exceptions, of course: You might plant a tall perennial like macleaya at the front of a border to serve as an accent at a strategic spot. In island beds, which are viewed from all sides, the layering generally moves from the center outward in all direc-

The gentle undulation of this California perennial border is achieved by combining plants of similar mass. A fan of Iris 'Victoria Falls' and the compact mounds of deep purple Spanish lavender, spiky English lavender, and fleabane, a member of the daisy genus Erigeron, echo the shapes of the background shrubs and provide a transition to the creeping thyme in the foreground.

Perennials That Attract Butterflies

Asclepias tuberosa (butterfly weed)
Butterflies: swallowtail, sulfur, gray hairstreak, spring azure, great spangled fritillary, question mark, monarch
Aster spp.
Butterflies: sulfur, painted lady, American painted lady, red admiral, buckeye, viceroy, Milbert's tortoiseshell
Centaurea spp. (knapweed)
Butterflies: American painted lady, common checkered skipper
Coreopsis spp. (tickseed)
Butterflies: sulfur, buckeye, monarch
Echinacea purpurea (purple coneflower)
Butterfly: great spangled fritillary
Malva spp. (mallow)
Butterflies: painted lady, American painted lady, red admiral, monarch
Rudbeckia hirta (black-eyed Susan)
Butterfly: great spangled fritillary
Sedum spectabile (stonecrop)
Butterflies: comma, Milbert's tortoiseshell, monarch, mourning cloak, painted lady, red admiral

Note: The abbreviation "spp." stands for the plural of "species"; where used in lists it means that many, but not all, of the species in a genus meet the criterion of the list.

Perennials That Attract Hummingbirds

Aquilegia spp.
(columbine)
Heuchera sanguinea
(coral bells)
Lobelia cardinalis
(cardinal flower)
Lupinus 'Russell Hybrids'
(lupine)
Monarda didyma
(bee balm)

Monarch butterfly (left, top) and mourning cloak (below) on Sedum spectabile

tions. And in a garden to be seen from within the house as well as outside, you would not want tall plants blocking the view of the rest of the flowers.

It is best to plant in odd numbers—threes, fives, sevens—so that identical plants are not rigidly grouped and can flow easily into and among the others. You can give structure to a bed through the regular and rhythmic placement of bulkier perennials or drifts of plants, and then fill in gaps with buffers like gray-leafed neutrals or other foliage plants. By limiting the types of plants and planting individuals en masse, you will achieve a garden with less variety in color but with a simple, strong, and effective design.

Finally, as you combine plants consider scale. A bear's-breech, with its tall flower spikes and coarse leaves, would be a minor accent in a long border; next to a patio, however, it would dominate the scene. Within the confines of a small garden in the city or in the suburbs, or in the small subgardens of larger properties, it is usually best to limit the use of large-scale plants.

Buying Your Perennials

Whether you are purchasing perennials to fill a new bed or add to an established plot, you'll want to look for two things: the healthiest plants possible and a wide assortment from which to choose.

Fragrant Perennials

Artemisia absinthium
(common wormwood)
Clematis heracleifolia 'Davidiana'
(tube clematis)
Clematis recta 'Mandshurica'
(ground clematis)
Dianthus barbatus
(sweet William)
Dianthus gratianopolitanus
(cheddar pinks)
Dianthus plumarius
(cottage pinks)
Dictamnus albus
(gas plant)
Geranium endressii 'Wargrave Pink'
(cranesbill)
Hemerocallis citrina and specific hybrids, including H. 'Becky Lynn', 'Betty Woods', and 'Janet Gayle'
(daylilies)
Hemerocallis flava
(lemon daylily)
Hosta plantaginea
(fragrant plantain lily)
Iris graminea

'Plum Tart'
(plum-scented iris)
Lavandula angustifolia
(English lavender)
Lupinus arboreus
(tree lupine)
Monarda didyma
(bee balm)
Nepeta cataria
(catmint)
Oenothera biennis
(evening primrose)
Oenothera caespitosa
(tufted evening primrose)
Oenothera odorata
(twisted evening primrose)
Paeonia lactiflora
(Chinese peony)
Polygonatum odoratum
(fragrant Solomon's-seal)
Polygonum polystachyum
(spiked knotweed)
Primula veris
(cowslip)
Saponaria officinalis
(bouncing Bet)
Viola odorata
(sweet violet)

Selecting Healthy Plants

If you decide to purchase your perennials locally, look for robust plants that reflect good care. In general, choose plants that are compact and bushy with bright-colored foliage (far left); if the plants are not yet in bloom, so much the better—their first spurt of energy will be spent on sending out strong roots. Tall, spindly plants with scant, pale foliage (left) may be badly root-bound or perhaps were grown in poor light. While these plants can usually be nursed back to full health, perennials that show signs of disease or insect infestation should definitely be avoided.

You can purchase plants locally at nurseries or garden centers, or buy them from mail-order catalogs. While plants are probably even available at your local supermarket or hardware store, it is generally wise to deal with a reputable grower.

Local Sources for Plants

At local nurseries or garden centers, you can shop for the best prices, widest selections, and healthiest specimens. Unlike mail-order nurseries, which may list plants for your hardiness zone that are actually borderline cases where you live (*see endsheets for USDA zone map*), local nurseries will only carry plants that are hardy in your region. At local shops, moreover, the plants will already be growing in containers, and will thus be larger and better established than the dormant plants sent out through the mail. And local nurseries and garden centers will be glad to answer any questions that may come up and give you gardening tips about the plants you purchase.

Ordering Plants by Mail

Large-scale and specialty nurseries that ship to customers over a broad area are likely to offer a wider choice of plant varieties than most local operations are able to do, including the very latest cultivars and hybrids—and often at lower prices.

Mail-order nurseries typically ship your order to arrive at the proper planting time in your part of the country, but it is probably best to specify a delivery date. Most mail-order perennials are shipped in a dormant, bare-root state to save postage. Once the plants arrive, look them over carefully; if you find evidence of disease or damage, return them immediately for a refund. Put healthy plants into the ground right away, if possible. But if you must delay planting for a few days, rewrap them and keep the roots moist until you are ready to plant. If planting is delayed more than 2 weeks, use the technique described on page 203 to temporarily put the plants in the ground—a process known as heeling in.

Perennials That Resist Pests and Diseases

Achillea
(yarrow)
Amsonia
(bluestar)
Anchusa
(bugloss)
Anemone x *hybrida*
(Japanese anemone)
Artemisia
(wormwood)
Asclepias tuberosa
(butterfly weed)
Astilbe
(astilbe, false spirea)
Aurinia
(basket-of-gold)
Boltonia
(boltonia)
Brunnera macrophylla
(Siberian bugloss)
Coreopsis
(tickseed)
Dianthus
(pinks)
Dicentra
(bleeding heart)

Echinacea
(purple coneflower)
Echinops
(globe thistle)
Eupatorium
(boneset)
Geranium
(cranesbill)
Hemerocallis
(daylily)
Heuchera sanguinea
(coral bells)
Iberis
(candytuft)
Iris cristata
(crested iris)
Iris sibirica
(Siberian iris)
Liatris
(gay-feather)
Limonium
(sea lavender)
Nepeta
(catmint)
Oenothera
(sundrop)

Papaver
(poppy)
Phlox divaricata
(wild blue phlox)
Phlox stolonifera
(creeping phlox)
Physostegia
(false dragonhead)
Polygonatum
(Solomon's-seal)
Rudbeckia
(coneflower)
Sedum
(stonecrop)
Trollius
(globeflower)
Verbena canadensis
(rose verbena)
Veronica
(speedwell)
Note: The plants listed here are naturally disease and pest resistant. But almost all perennials will be problem free if properly planted and maintained.

Selecting Perennials for a Long Season of Bloom

Traditionally, the perennial border in an English cottage garden was viewed as the centerpiece of a lovely, but relatively short-lived, display of flowers. Because English summers are warm but not hot, the blooms would unfurl in a delightful progression of eye-catching blocks of color, emerging at one spot while other flowers were fading elsewhere. By late August, the show was over.

As American gardeners have turned to perennials in recent years, they have brought a very different quality to their gardens. First, the perennial garden is not just a summer garden but a place where interest can be found year round if you know where to look for it. Second, the growth cycles of plants, individually and as a group, are so dramatic in a garden planted heavily with perennials that the look of the property is constantly changing, taking on a whole new character from month to month. No longer a ho-hum, green sweep of lawn and woody evergreens, the garden has become a vibrant and dynamic landscape.

There have always been peak moments in a perennial garden, of course, such as when bearded irises bloom alongside foxgloves, columbines, campanula, and dianthus. But by choosing from a broader range of plants and observing some of nature's more subtle decorating touches, American gardeners have discovered a type of ornamental

Drifts of spring tulips brighten the bare spaces of this small backyard garden in the weeks before perennials and grasses begin to stir. Blue Brunnera macrophylla at the base of the sweet bay magnolia tree will reseed after flowering. Behind the magnolia, the purple flowers of Camassia, a bulb, tower over Christmas fern.

gardening that is visually rich and long-lasting.

These qualities can be seen in the three photographs taken of the same garden during different seasons that appear on pages 84-86. In spring, there is an openness to the narrow townhouse backyard that will not be seen again until winter, and then only in a completely different form. Spring-blooming bulbs carry the garden through this early stage, with trees and fences providing a framework, and decorative pots and garden sculpture serving as focal points. Even when the garden is in this relatively bare state, there is a sense of the lushness and visual layering of plants to come.

In summer, the promise of the spring is fulfilled, and the garden is transformed into an entirely different landscape: Grasses, ground covers, and a wide array of foliage textures and colors tangle together in a well-crafted jungle. Shades of green dominate the property, the hues changing in subtle ways as the sun backlights some areas and shines directly on others.

After the first frost, in late fall and early winter, some of the openness of the spring returns, but the grasses and perennials remain a firm presence. They take on colors associated with the cooler seasons—harmonious blends of gold, tan, and ivory. The garden's heavy reliance on stands of tall grasses might not be to everyone's taste, but the design demonstrates what is possible if you are open to the beauty of form and color as well as the exuberance of blooms.

Orchestrating Seasonal Moods

Visually, the perennial garden alternates between periods of intense, glorious growth and color and times when it is quiet, seeming to gather its strength for the next burst of blooms. The secret to creating a garden that is satisfying to look at year round is to include plants that provide interest

Summer plantings produce a lush medley of texture, with delicate annuals providing color beside the steps, and the spikes of Acanthus hungaricus lending an accent in the middle ground. A sweep of grasses—Calamagrostis acutiflora 'Stricta' (center) and Miscanthus floridulus (right)—add to the jungle-like feel of the garden.

After the first hard frost of late fall, the winter garden belongs to the ornamental grasses. Gone are summer's exuberant greens, replaced by the bronze, copper, and tan of the winter landscape. The smaller grasses struggle to maintain their form and eventually are cut down. The giant Miscanthus floridulus, which cascaded like a fountain in summer, is stiffened upright by the frosts of autumn.

during the periods between peaks of color. Some of these also extend the blooming period both early in the growing season and toward its end.

Much of the country experiences winter frosts that kill off the top growth of herbaceous perennials for the season. Even after the freeze, though, the dead and dried forms of many perennial leaves, flower heads, and seeds are interesting to look at, especially when dusted with frost or light snow or wearing a sparkling glaze of ice. Sedums, echinops, rudbeckia, and achillea are known for their winter appeal; see the list opposite for more perennials that will enhance the garden in winter.

By treating these plants and others as you would ornamental grasses and not cutting them back until midwinter or later, you can prolong their value. Of course, these freeze-dried plants may be too untidy for some tastes, and some gardeners may feel that the garden—and its owner—deserve a winter vacation. But only by experimenting and experiencing the impact of these

plants in winter will you know for sure if the look is right for you and your garden.

If you happen to live in the milder climates of the Deep South, the Southwest, or southern California, you can have garden color and growth year round. Perennials do well in these parts of the United States, although without periods of winter dormancy the plants tend to be shorter lived than they would be farther north.

Cold-Blooming Hellebores

For those who like to have some active plants while the rest of the garden is hibernating for the winter, the hellebores—members of the buttercup family—occupy a class of their own.

Four species are grown widely in America, including two with particularly beautiful foliage. The first is the vein-leafed Corsican hellebore, *Helleborus argutifolius* var. *corsicus,* with clusters of

Perennials for a Winter Garden

WINTER FLOWERS:

Helleborus foetidus
(stinking hellebore)
Helleborus niger
(Christmas rose)
Helleborus orientalis
(Lenten rose)

WINTER FOLIAGE:

Acanthus mollis
(bear's-breech)
Ajuga reptans
(bugleweed cultivars)
Artemisia spp.
(wormwood)
Arum italicum
(Italian arum)
Dianthus spp.
(pinks)
*Festuca ovina
'Glauca'*
(sheep's fescue)
Lavandula angustifolia
(English lavender)
Macleaya cordata
(plume poppy)
Saxifraga stolonlifera
(strawberry geranium)

Saxifraga x *urbium*
(London pride)
Stachys byzantina
(lamb's ears)

OTHER ORNAMENTS:
(dried flower heads,
stems, and pods)

*Calamagrostis
acutiflora 'Stricta'*
(feather reed grass)
Miscanthus floridulus
(giant miscanthus)
Miscanthus sinensis
(eulalia)
*Miscanthus sinensis
'Gracillimus'*
(maiden grass)
*Pennisetum
alopecuroides*
(fountain grass)
Sedum spp.
(stonecrop)

*Note: The abbreviation
"spp." stands for the plural
of "species"; where used in
lists it means that many, but
not all, of the species in a
genus meet the criterion of
the list.*

nodding, apple green flowers that become yellow at their centers; the second is what is commonly known as the stinking hellebore, *Helleborus foetidus*. In spite of its unfortunate name (which refers to the scent of its root, not its flower), the stinking hellebore is a lovely plant bearing pale green flowers and handsome leaflets shaped like slender arrowheads. A third species, the Christmas rose, *Helleborus niger,* blooms the earliest, as its name suggests, with showy flowers that open white and grow pink as they mature.

The best-loved hellebore is the Lenten rose, *Helleborus orientalis.* It is the least fussy and most reliable of the group and within a few seasons after planting forms large colonies. The blooms emerge in late winter or early spring and last for weeks. Flower color varies with hybrid and age, and includes pale green, white, maroon, and pink. Hardy to Zones 3 and 4, the leaves of the hellebores remain evergreen to 10° F.

The late-winter garden has a number of other stalwart perennials, most of them—including Italian arum, lamb's ears, ajuga, and the wild gingers—of value for their foliage. Evergreen in many areas, these plants hold the garden fort until early spring arrives with the glorious, much anticipated explosion of spring-blooming plants.

The end of the growing season is not the end of the show for such perennials as Rudbeckia (coneflower), which produces daisy-like flowers from summer into fall (left), and Miscanthus sinensis (eulalia grass), whose golden fronds cast a glow in the winter garden (below).

Early Spring
to Summer Bloomers

Many early-season perennials brighten the floor of the garden—*Iberis* (candytuft), *Phlox divaricata* (wild blue phlox), *Allium* (flowering onion), aubrieta, and the small blue-leafed grass *Festuca*. Ajuga is thought of as a foliage ground cover, but several varieties offer a stunning haze of blue and violet flower spikes in midspring. They pair nicely with yellow miniature daffodils.

A few weeks later, when the perennial garden has gone from the cool freshness of midspring to the soft warmth of early summer, it reaches its glorious peak with the showiest flowers of the year—the Japanese and bearded irises, the oriental poppy, and, of course, the opulent blooms of the herbaceous peony. But it is in the withering heat of summer that you will find tougher workhorses to sustain color, plants like daylilies, butterfly weed, macleaya, gypsophila, rudbeckia, coreopsis, hollyhock, perovskia, penstemon, echinacea, and, in warmer regions, cosmos, verbena, and California poppy.

This is also the time when the many species of ornamental grasses, which have been growing slowly through the spring, announce their presence with decorative wands of flower heads that catch the slightest summer breeze.

The Arrival of the
Ornamental Grasses

The ornamental grasses come in many distinct forms and sizes. If properly placed in the garden, they will flourish with a minimum of fuss and a maximum of visual interest. There are cool-season species well suited to northern gardens (although most will do fine in a shelter area and with some watering in the South) and warm-season types that begin their growth cycle later and save their best displays for the fall and winter.

Small grasses suited for the front of the border include the delicate blue-green *Festuca ovina* 'Glauca'; sea oats, *Chasmanthium latifolium*, with its curious wafer-thin seed heads resembling barley; and Japanese blood grass, *Imperata cylindrica* 'Red Baron', whose thick, spiky blades turn bright red in autumn.

Other grasses grow to the size of a small shrub—about 3 feet high and 3 feet in diameter. These include the many cultivars of fountain grass,

Pennisetum alopecuroides, with their arching wands of flower heads; the upright and sophisticated-looking feather reed grass, *Calamagrostis acutiflora* 'Stricta'; and flame grass, *Miscanthus sinensis* 'Purpurascens'.

The giants of the grass world, often growing 6 feet or taller, make good back-of-the-border plants, accents, and screens. These include giant Chinese silver grass, *Miscanthus floridulus*; Ravenna grass, *Erianthus ravennae*; and the old-fashioned pampas grass, *Cortaderia selloana*.

Planting for Early
and Late Color

Another approach to extending the bloom season in the garden is to select cultivars that have been bred to be early or late flowering within the plant's natural bloom cycle. With columbine, for example, you could have weeks of bloom by planting a range of varieties. Other candidates include astilbe, lavender, iris, and one of the most flexible perennials around, the daylily.

Many gardeners also sustain color by using other classes of plants, such as shrubs for border structure and annuals as fill-ins. *Caryopteris,* an aromatic shrub, produces a cloud of blue flowers in the high summer. *Buddleia davidii,* the butterfly bush, has long-lasting flower spikes in a range of colors, including white, blue, and purple. The rose of Sharon is another good summer-flowering shrub that fits into the perennial border. But be careful to choose a variety that won't self-seed, or you may find yourself fighting an avid spreader.

The choice of annuals is vast. Some of the most successful are nicotiana (which offers the bonus of being heavily fragrant at night), zinnias, marigolds, impatiens, petunias, cleome, and cosmos. (For more on annuals, see Chapter 2, pages 32-67.)

In late summer, a number of perennials come into bloom, freshening the garden after the hot months. They include cultivars of the fragrant plantain lily, *Hosta plantaginea;* veronicastrum, with its spiky racemes of tiny flowers; Joe-Pye weed, and the asterlike boltonia. Many bearded iris varieties rebloom with as much vigor as in the late spring, and the Japanese anemone is an excellent late-season plant, blooming for weeks. Other summer-flowering perennials that keep blooming valiantly into fall include the stately acanthus, cheerful daisy-like coreopsis, old-fashioned dianthus, and the fragrant spires of salvia.

The Autumn Perennial Garden

In areas of the country that experience the change of seasons, autumn is an extraordinary time in the garden. The light is clear but low, casting a glow over the changing foliage color of trees and shrubs. But as summer's soft days shorten into fall, the flower border in your garden may look somewhat bedraggled. With some care and planning, however, your garden will continue to reward you with bouquets of color.

In northern zones, where forests and wood lots are fiery with color, consider planting flowers that will pair up well with the surrounding trees and shrubs. The reds, bronzes, golds, and soft oranges of chrysanthemums, for example, create beautiful, harmonious fall color combinations. Other perennials to consider are the many stunning species of aster, the flowering sedums, and such autumn-flowering salvias as the leggy blue sage, *Salvia azurea* var. *grandiflora.*

Perennials for Drying

Some perennials, such as those listed below, will dry naturally in airy, dry, dark rooms and will retain their beauty long after drying. Others, however, including peonies, hellebore, and dianthus, must be buried in a desiccant such as fine-textured sand or silica gel to keep their color and form while drying. For correct harvesting times and drying techniques, consult local garden clubs or specialty books.

Achillea **spp.**
(yarrow, particularly 'Coronation Gold', 'Moonshine', and other golden types)
Achillea filipendulina
(fernleaf yarrow, white forms only)
Achillea ptarmica
(sneezewort)
Allium **spp.**
(ornamental onion, chives)
Anaphalis **spp.**
(pearly everlasting)
Artemisia lactiflora
(white mugwort)
Artemisia ludoviciana
(white mugwort)
Astilbe **spp.**
(astilbe)
Delphinium
(delphinium)

Echinops ritro
(globe thistle)
Eryngium **spp.**
(sea holly)
Gypsophila paniculata
(baby's-breath)
Lavandula angustifolia
(lavender)
Liatris spicata
(gay-feather)
Limonium latifolium
(sea lavender)
Stachys byzantina
(lamb's ears)

Note: The abbreviation "spp." stands for the plural of "species"; where used in lists it means that many, but not all, of the species in a genus meet the criterion of the list.

Yarrow, Lamb's Ears, Sea Lavender (left to right)

Plant Selection Guide for Perennials

Organized by flower color, this chart provides information needed to select species and varieties that will thrive in the particular conditions of your garden. For additional information on select perennials, refer to the encyclopedia section that begins on page 302.

WHITE

	Zone 3	Zone 4	Zone 5	Zone 6	Zone 7	Zone 8	Zone 9	Zone 10	Zone 11	Sandy	Loam	Dry	Well-Drained	Moist	Full Sun	Shade	Spring	Summer	Fall	Winter	Under 2 ft.	2-3 ft.	Over 3 ft.	Long Bloom Season	Fragrance	Distinctive Foliage	Cut Flowers
ACONITUM NAPELLUS 'SNOW WHITE'	✓	✓	✓	✓	✓	✓					✓		✓	✓	✓		✓	✓					✓	✓			
AGAPANTHUS ORIENTALIS 'ALBIDUS'				✓	✓	✓					✓		✓	✓	✓			✓					✓				
ANAPHALIS TRIPLINERVIS	✓	✓	✓	✓	✓	✓	✓				✓		✓	✓	✓			✓	✓		✓						✓
ANEMONE X HYBRIDA 'HONORINE JOBERT'			✓	✓	✓						✓		✓		✓	✓		✓	✓			✓					
ARABIS CAUCASICA 'SNOW CAP'	✓	✓	✓							✓			✓		✓		✓				✓				✓		
ARENARIA MONTANA		✓	✓	✓	✓								✓	✓	✓	✓	✓				✓						
ARTEMISIA LACTIFLORA		✓	✓	✓	✓					✓	✓		✓		✓			✓	✓				✓			✓	
ARUNCUS DIOICUS	✓	✓	✓	✓	✓	✓					✓			✓		✓		✓					✓			✓	
ASTILBE JAPONICA 'DEUTSCHLAND'		✓	✓	✓	✓						✓			✓		✓		✓				✓				✓	
BOLTONIA ASTEROIDES 'SNOWBANK'	✓	✓	✓	✓	✓								✓	✓	✓			✓	✓				✓				✓
CAMPANULA PERSICIFOLIA 'ALBA'	✓	✓	✓	✓							✓		✓		✓	✓		✓				✓					
CHRYSANTHEMUM NIPPONICUM			✓	✓	✓	✓					✓		✓		✓	✓			✓		✓						✓
CHRYSANTHEMUM X SUPERBUM 'ALASKA'		✓	✓	✓	✓	✓					✓		✓		✓	✓		✓	✓			✓			✓		✓
CIMICIFUGA RAMOSA	✓	✓	✓	✓	✓						✓			✓		✓		✓					✓		✓	✓	
CRAMBE CORDIFOLIA		✓	✓	✓	✓						✓		✓		✓			✓					✓		✓		✓
DICENTRA EXIMIA 'ALBA'	✓	✓	✓	✓	✓	✓							✓	✓	✓	✓	✓	✓			✓					✓	
FILIPENDULA ULMARIA	✓	✓	✓	✓	✓	✓					✓			✓		✓		✓					✓		✓	✓	✓
GILLENIA TRIFOLIATA		✓	✓	✓	✓						✓		✓	✓		✓	✓	✓				✓					
GYPSOPHILA PANICULATA 'PERFECTA'		✓	✓	✓	✓	✓					✓		✓	✓	✓			✓				✓					
HELLEBORUS NIGER		✓	✓	✓	✓	✓					✓		✓		✓	✓			✓	✓	✓						
HEUCHERA SANGUINEA 'SNOWFLAKES'		✓	✓	✓	✓	✓					✓		✓	✓	✓	✓		✓			✓					✓	
HOSTA PLANTAGINEA	✓	✓	✓	✓	✓	✓					✓			✓		✓		✓				✓			✓	✓	
IBERIS SEMPERVIRENS 'LITTLE GEM'		✓	✓	✓	✓	✓					✓		✓	✓	✓	✓	✓				✓					✓	
IRIS 'CINDY'		✓	✓	✓	✓	✓						✓		✓	✓		✓						✓				✓
IRIS SIBIRICA 'WHITE SWIRL'		✓	✓	✓	✓	✓	✓				✓		✓		✓		✓						✓				✓
LIATRIS SCARIOSA 'WHITE SPIRES'	✓	✓	✓	✓	✓	✓	✓		✓		✓		✓	✓	✓			✓	✓			✓					✓
LUPINUS RUSSELL HYBRID 'WHITE'	✓	✓	✓								✓		✓	✓	✓			✓					✓		✓		
LYSIMACHIA CLETHROIDES		✓	✓	✓	✓	✓					✓			✓	✓	✓			✓			✓				✓	

Table — Perennials by color (continued). Columns grouped as: **ZONES** (Zone 3–11), **SOIL** (Sandy, Loam, Dry, Well-Drained, Moist), **LIGHT** (Full Sun, Shade), **BLOOMING SEASON** (Spring, Summer, Fall, Winter), **PLANT HEIGHT** (Under 2 ft., 2–3 ft., Over 3 ft.), **NOTED FOR** (Long Bloom Season, Fragrance, Distinctive Foliage, Cut Flowers).

Color	Plant	Z3	Z4	Z5	Z6	Z7	Z8	Z9	Z10	Z11	Sandy	Loam	Dry	Well-Drained	Moist	Full Sun	Shade	Spring	Summer	Fall	Winter	Under 2 ft.	2–3 ft.	Over 3 ft.	Long Bloom Season	Fragrance	Distinctive Foliage	Cut Flowers
WHITE	MACLEAYA CORDATA		✓	✓	✓	✓	✓					✓		✓	✓	✓		✓						✓			✓	✓
WHITE	PAEONIA LACTIFLORA 'KRINKLED WHITE'	✓	✓	✓	✓	✓						✓		✓		✓	✓	✓					✓			✓	✓	✓
WHITE	PENNISETUM CAUDATUM			✓	✓	✓	✓					✓		✓		✓			✓	✓				✓			✓	
WHITE	PHLOX MACULATA 'MISS LINGARD'		✓	✓	✓	✓	✓					✓		✓	✓	✓			✓	✓			✓				✓	
WHITE	RODGERSIA PODOPHYLLA			✓	✓	✓	✓					✓		✓	✓	✓	✓	✓						✓			✓	
WHITE	ROMNEYA COULTERI					✓	✓	✓	✓				✓	✓		✓			✓					✓				✓
WHITE	SILENE 'ROBIN'S WHITE BREAST'		✓	✓	✓	✓	✓				✓			✓		✓	✓	✓	✓	✓		✓				✓	✓	
WHITE	SMILACINA RACEMOSA		✓	✓	✓	✓						✓			✓		✓	✓	✓			✓				✓	✓	
WHITE	TRICYRTIS HIRTA		✓	✓	✓	✓	✓					✓			✓		✓		✓	✓		✓	✓					
WHITE	VERBASCUM CHAIXII 'ALBUM'			✓	✓	✓	✓				✓		✓	✓	✓	✓			✓				✓				✓	
WHITE	VERONICA SPICATA 'ICICLE'		✓	✓	✓	✓	✓					✓		✓		✓			✓			✓				✓		✓
YELLOW	ACHILLEA FILIPENDULINA 'CORONATION GOLD'		✓	✓	✓	✓							✓	✓		✓			✓				✓				✓	✓
YELLOW	ALCHEMILLA MOLLIS	✓	✓	✓	✓	✓						✓		✓	✓	✓	✓	✓	✓			✓					✓	✓
YELLOW	ANTHEMIS TINCTORIA	✓	✓	✓	✓								✓	✓		✓			✓	✓		✓			✓	✓		✓
YELLOW	AQUILEGIA CHRYSANTHA		✓	✓	✓	✓						✓		✓	✓	✓	✓	✓					✓					
YELLOW	AURINIA SAXATILIS			✓	✓	✓	✓	✓			✓			✓		✓		✓	✓			✓					✓	
YELLOW	CENTAUREA MACROCEPHALA	✓	✓	✓	✓	✓						✓		✓		✓			✓	✓				✓				✓
YELLOW	COREOPSIS GRANDIFLORA 'SUNRAY'		✓	✓	✓	✓	✓					✓		✓		✓			✓	✓		✓						✓
YELLOW	COREOPSIS VERTICILLATA		✓	✓	✓	✓	✓						✓	✓		✓			✓	✓			✓		✓			✓
YELLOW	DIGITALIS GRANDIFLORA		✓	✓	✓	✓						✓		✓	✓	✓	✓		✓				✓					
YELLOW	DORONICUM 'MISS MASON'		✓	✓	✓							✓			✓	✓	✓	✓				✓						
YELLOW	GAILLARDIA X GRANDIFLORA 'YELLOW QUEEN'	✓	✓	✓	✓	✓					✓			✓		✓			✓	✓			✓		✓			✓
YELLOW	HELENIUM AUTUMNALE 'BUTTERPAT'	✓	✓	✓	✓							✓			✓	✓			✓	✓			✓		✓			✓
YELLOW	HELIANTHUS ANGUSTIFOLIUS			✓	✓	✓	✓					✓			✓	✓				✓				✓				✓
YELLOW	HELIANTHUS X MULTIFLORUS 'FLORE PENO'		✓	✓	✓	✓	✓					✓		✓	✓	✓			✓	✓				✓				✓
YELLOW	HELIOPSIS HELIANTHOIDES SCABRA 'KARAT'		✓	✓	✓	✓	✓					✓		✓		✓			✓	✓				✓				✓
YELLOW	HEMEROCALLIS 'HYPERION'	✓	✓	✓	✓	✓	✓	✓				✓		✓		✓	✓		✓	✓				✓		✓		
YELLOW	HEMEROCALLIS 'STELLA DE ORO'	✓	✓	✓	✓	✓	✓	✓				✓		✓		✓	✓		✓	✓		✓			✓			
YELLOW	INULA ENSIFOLIA		✓	✓	✓	✓	✓							✓		✓	✓		✓			✓						
YELLOW	IRIS PSEUDACORUS			✓	✓	✓	✓								✓	✓	✓	✓	✓					✓			✓	
YELLOW	LIGULARIA DENTATA 'DESDEMONA'			✓	✓	✓	✓								✓	✓	✓		✓					✓			✓	
YELLOW	LINUM FLAVUM			✓	✓	✓	✓				✓			✓		✓	✓		✓			✓						

	ZONES									SOIL					LIGHT		BLOOMING SEASON				PLANT HEIGHT			NOTED FOR			
	Zone 3	Zone 4	Zone 5	Zone 6	Zone 7	Zone 8	Zone 9	Zone 10	Zone 11	Sandy	Loam	Dry	Well-Drained	Moist	Full Sun	Shade	Spring	Summer	Fall	Winter	Under 2 ft	2-3 ft	Over 3 ft	Long Bloom Season	Fragrance	Distinctive Foliage	Cut Flowers
YELLOW																											
LYSIMACHIA PUNCTATA		✓	✓	✓	✓						✓		✓	✓	✓	✓	✓	✓				✓					
OENOTHERA FRUITICOSA		✓	✓	✓	✓	✓					✓		✓		✓			✓			✓				✓		
PAEONIA MLOKOSEWITSCHII			✓	✓	✓						✓		✓		✓	✓	✓				✓				✓	✓	✓
PRIMULA AURICULA	✓	✓	✓	✓	✓						✓			✓	✓	✓	✓				✓				✓		
RANUNCULUS REPENS		✓	✓	✓	✓	✓					✓		✓	✓	✓		✓				✓						
RUDBECKIA FULGIDA 'GOLDSTURM'		✓	✓	✓	✓	✓					✓		✓		✓			✓	✓			✓		✓			✓
SEDUM AIZOON		✓	✓	✓	✓	✓	✓	✓					✓		✓	✓		✓			✓					✓	
SOLIDAGO 'PETER PAN'	✓	✓	✓										✓		✓	✓		✓	✓			✓					✓
THALICTRUM MINUS		✓	✓	✓	✓								✓	✓	✓	✓		✓				✓				✓	
TROLLIUS EUROPAEUS		✓	✓	✓	✓								✓	✓	✓	✓	✓				✓			✓			✓
VERBASCUM CHAIXII		✓	✓	✓	✓					✓			✓		✓			✓				✓					
ORANGE																											
ANTHEMIS SANCTI-JOHANNIS		✓	✓	✓						✓	✓		✓		✓			✓	✓			✓		✓			
ASCLEPIAS TUBEROSA	✓	✓	✓	✓	✓	✓							✓		✓			✓				✓					✓
BELAMCANDA CHINENSIS			✓	✓	✓	✓							✓	✓	✓			✓				✓					✓
CROCOSMIA MASONIORUM			✓	✓	✓	✓				✓			✓		✓	✓		✓				✓					✓
GEUM QUELLYON 'MRS. BRADSHAW'			✓	✓	✓						✓		✓		✓	✓	✓	✓			✓						
HEMEROCALLIS FULVA	✓	✓	✓	✓	✓	✓	✓						✓		✓	✓		✓					✓			✓	
INULA ROYLEANA		✓	✓	✓									✓		✓	✓		✓				✓					
LYCHNIS ARKWRIGHTII			✓	✓	✓						✓		✓		✓	✓		✓			✓						
PAPAVER ORIENTALE 'GLOWING EMBERS'	✓	✓	✓	✓	✓	✓	✓						✓		✓	✓	✓					✓					
PHLOX PANICULATA		✓	✓	✓	✓	✓	✓						✓		✓			✓				✓					
POTENTILLA NEPALENSIS 'ROXANA'		✓	✓	✓							✓		✓		✓			✓			✓						
SEDUM KAMTSCHATICUM	✓	✓	✓	✓	✓								✓		✓			✓			✓					✓	
TROLLIUS LEDEBOURII 'GOLDEN QUEEN'		✓	✓	✓	✓								✓	✓	✓	✓	✓					✓					✓
RED																											
ACHILLEA MILLEFOLIUM 'FIRE KING'		✓	✓	✓	✓					✓	✓		✓		✓			✓			✓						✓
ARMERIA ALLIACEA 'BEE'S RUBY'	✓	✓	✓	✓	✓	✓				✓			✓		✓		✓	✓			✓						
ASTILBE 'FANAL'		✓	✓	✓	✓						✓			✓		✓		✓			✓					✓	
CENTRANTHUS RUBER 'ATROCOCCINEUS'		✓	✓	✓	✓	✓						✓	✓		✓			✓				✓					✓
DIANTHUS DELTOIDES 'BRILLIANT'		✓	✓	✓									✓	✓	✓	✓	✓	✓			✓						
EPIMEDIUM X RUBRUM		✓	✓	✓	✓								✓	✓	✓	✓	✓				✓					✓	
GAILLARDIA X GRANDIFLORA 'BURGUNDY'	✓	✓	✓	✓	✓	✓							✓		✓			✓	✓			✓					✓
HELENIUM AUTUMNALE 'CRIMSON BEAUTY'	✓	✓	✓	✓	✓	✓					✓		✓		✓			✓	✓				✓	✓			✓

Table — Perennials by color (RED and PINK)

Plant	Zone 3	Zone 4	Zone 5	Zone 6	Zone 7	Zone 8	Zone 9	Zone 10	Zone 11	Sandy	Loam	Dry	Well-drained	Moist	Full Sun	Shade	Spring	Summer	Fall	Winter	Under 2 ft.	2-3 ft.	Over 3 ft.	Long Bloom Season	Fragrance	Distinctive Foliage	Cut Flowers
RED																											
HEMEROCALLIS 'AUTUMN RED'	✓	✓	✓	✓	✓	✓	✓						✓		✓			✓	✓			✓					
HEUCHERA SANGUINEA 'RED SPANGLES'		✓	✓	✓	✓	✓					✓		✓	✓	✓	✓		✓			✓					✓	
HIBISCUS 'LORD BALTIMORE'			✓	✓	✓	✓	✓				✓		✓	✓	✓			✓				✓	✓				
IRIS 'ALREADY'		✓	✓	✓	✓	✓					✓		✓		✓		✓					✓					
LOBELIA CARDINALIS	✓	✓	✓	✓	✓	✓					✓			✓	✓			✓	✓			✓					
LUPINUS RUSSELL HYBRID 'CARMINE'	✓	✓	✓	✓							✓		✓	✓	✓			✓				✓				✓	
MISCANTHUS SINENSIS 'GRACILLIMUS'			✓	✓	✓	✓	✓						✓		✓				✓	✓			✓			✓	
MONARDA DIDYMA 'CAMBRIDGE SCARLET'		✓	✓	✓	✓	✓							✓	✓	✓			✓				✓			✓		
PAEONIA TENUIFOLIA			✓	✓	✓						✓		✓		✓		✓					✓			✓	✓	
PAPAVER ORIENTALE 'BEAUTY OF LIVERMORE'	✓	✓	✓	✓	✓	✓							✓	✓	✓	✓	✓					✓					
PENSTEMON BARBATUS 'PRAIRIE FIRE'			✓	✓	✓	✓	✓						✓		✓			✓				✓					✓
PHORMIUM TENAX 'VARIEGATUM'							✓	✓			✓		✓		✓			✓					✓			✓	
POTENTILLA ATROSANGUINEA		✓	✓	✓	✓					✓			✓	✓	✓	✓		✓			✓						
PRIMULA JAPONICA 'MILLER'S CRIMSON'			✓	✓	✓						✓			✓		✓	✓	✓			✓						
SEDUM MAXIMUM 'ATROPURPUREUM'		✓	✓	✓	✓	✓	✓						✓		✓			✓				✓				✓	
SEDUM SPURIUM 'DRAGON'S BLOOD'	✓	✓	✓	✓	✓	✓							✓		✓			✓			✓					✓	
VERBENA PERUVIANA					✓	✓							✓		✓			✓	✓		✓			✓			
VERONICA SPICATA 'RED FOX'		✓	✓	✓	✓								✓		✓			✓			✓			✓			
PINK																											
ACANTHUS MOLLIS 'LATIFOLIUS'					✓	✓	✓						✓		✓			✓					✓			✓	
ANEMONE X HYBRIDA 'SEPTEMBER CHARM'			✓	✓	✓						✓		✓		✓	✓		✓	✓			✓					
ARMERIA MARITIMA 'LAUCHEANA'		✓	✓	✓	✓					✓			✓		✓		✓				✓						
ASCLEPIAS INCARNATA	✓	✓	✓	✓	✓	✓				✓			✓		✓			✓	✓			✓			✓		
ASTILBE CHINENSIS 'PUMILA'			✓	✓	✓						✓			✓		✓		✓			✓					✓	
ASTRANTIA MAJOR 'ROSEA'		✓	✓	✓	✓	✓					✓			✓	✓			✓				✓					✓
BEGONIA GRANDIS			✓	✓	✓						✓				✓	✓		✓	✓		✓					✓	
CALAMAGROSTIS ACUTIFLORA 'STRICTA'		✓	✓	✓	✓								✓		✓			✓	✓	✓			✓			✓	
CENTAUREA DEALBATA		✓	✓	✓	✓								✓		✓		✓	✓				✓					✓
CHRYSANTHEMUM MORIFOLIUM 'PINK DAISY'			✓	✓	✓	✓	✓			✓			✓		✓			✓	✓		✓						✓
COREOPSIS ROSEA			✓	✓	✓	✓	✓						✓	✓	✓			✓			✓						
DICENTRA EXIMIA	✓	✓	✓	✓	✓									✓		✓	✓	✓			✓					✓	
DICENTRA SPECTABLIS	✓	✓	✓	✓	✓									✓		✓	✓	✓				✓				✓	
ECHINACEA PURPUREA 'THE KING'	✓	✓	✓	✓	✓	✓	✓						✓		✓	✓		✓					✓				✓

	ZONES									SOIL					LIGHT		BLOOMING SEASON				PLANT HEIGHT			NOTED FOR			
	ZONE 3	ZONE 4	ZONE 5	ZONE 6	ZONE 7	ZONE 8	ZONE 9	ZONE 10	ZONE 11	SANDY	LOAM	DRY	WELL-DRAINED	MOIST	FULL SUN	SHADE	SPRING	SUMMER	FALL	WINTER	UNDER 2 FT.	2-3 FT.	OVER 3 FT.	LONG BLOOM SEASON	FRAGRANCE	DISTINCTIVE FOLIAGE	CUT FLOWERS
PINK																											
ERIGERON SPECIOSUS 'FOERSTER'S LIEBLING'	✓	✓	✓	✓	✓	✓							✓		✓			✓				✓					✓
EUPATORIUM FISTULOSUM	✓	✓	✓	✓	✓	✓	✓						✓	✓	✓	✓		✓	✓				✓				
FILIPENDULA RUBRA 'VENUSTA'	✓	✓	✓	✓	✓	✓	✓				✓			✓	✓			✓					✓				✓
GERANIUM CINEREUM		✓	✓	✓	✓								✓	✓	✓	✓	✓				✓			✓		✓	
GERANIUM DALMATICUM		✓	✓	✓	✓								✓	✓	✓	✓		✓			✓						
HEMEROCALLIS 'COUNTRY CLUB'	✓	✓	✓	✓	✓	✓	✓						✓	✓	✓	✓		✓			✓						
HEUCHERA SANGUINEA 'CHATTERBOX'		✓	✓	✓	✓						✓		✓		✓	✓		✓			✓			✓			
HIBISCUS 'LADY BALTIMORE'		✓	✓	✓	✓	✓					✓			✓	✓			✓					✓				
IRIS ENSATA 'PINK LADY'		✓	✓	✓	✓	✓					✓		✓	✓	✓			✓				✓					✓
MALVA MOSCHATA 'ROSEA'		✓	✓	✓	✓					✓	✓			✓	✓			✓	✓			✓		✓			
PAEONIA LACTIFLORA 'LOTUS BLOOM'	✓	✓	✓	✓	✓						✓		✓		✓	✓			✓			✓			✓	✓	✓
PAPAVER ORIENTALE 'MRS. PERRY'	✓	✓	✓	✓	✓	✓							✓		✓	✓	✓	✓				✓					
PHYSOSTEGIA VIRGINIANA 'VIVID'		✓	✓	✓	✓	✓				✓	✓		✓	✓	✓	✓		✓	✓		✓						✓
PLATYCODON GRANDIFLORUS 'SHELL PINK'		✓	✓	✓	✓	✓					✓		✓		✓			✓				✓					
POLYGONUM AFFINE		✓	✓	✓							✓		✓	✓	✓	✓		✓			✓					✓	
SAPONARIA OCYMOIDES		✓	✓	✓	✓	✓							✓		✓		✓	✓			✓						
SEDUM 'AUTUMN JOY'	✓	✓	✓	✓	✓	✓	✓	✓					✓		✓			✓	✓	✓		✓		✓		✓	
SIDALCEA MALVIFLORA 'ELSIE HEUGH'		✓	✓	✓	✓								✓	✓	✓			✓				✓					✓
VERONICASTRUM VIRGINICUM 'ROSEUM'		✓	✓	✓	✓	✓					✓		✓		✓			✓					✓	✓			
PURPLE																											
AJUGA REPTANS	✓	✓	✓	✓	✓						✓		✓		✓	✓	✓									✓	
ALLIUM CHRISTOPHII		✓	✓	✓	✓						✓		✓		✓			✓				✓					✓
ALLIUM GIGANTEUM			✓	✓	✓	✓					✓		✓		✓	✓		✓					✓				✓
ASTER NOVAE-ANGLIAE 'PURPLE DOME'		✓	✓	✓							✓		✓	✓	✓				✓		✓						✓
DELPHINIUM 'BLACK KNIGHT'	✓	✓	✓	✓	✓								✓		✓			✓					✓				
DICTAMNUS ALBUS 'PURPUREUS'	✓	✓	✓	✓	✓	✓					✓		✓		✓	✓	✓	✓				✓			✓		
ERIGERON SPECIOSUS 'AZURE FAIRY'	✓	✓	✓	✓	✓						✓		✓		✓			✓				✓		✓			✓
EUPATORIUM COELESTINUM			✓	✓	✓	✓	✓						✓	✓	✓			✓	✓		✓			✓			✓
IRIS ENSATA 'ROYAL BANNER'			✓	✓	✓	✓	✓				✓		✓	✓	✓			✓				✓					✓
IRIS SIBIRICA 'HARPSWELL HAZE'		✓	✓	✓	✓	✓	✓				✓		✓	✓	✓	✓		✓					✓				✓
LAVANDULA ANGUSTIFOLIA 'HIDCOTE'		✓	✓	✓	✓	✓							✓		✓			✓			✓				✓	✓	
LIATRIS SCARIOSA 'SEPTEMBER GLORY'		✓	✓	✓	✓	✓	✓			✓			✓		✓	✓		✓	✓				✓				✓
LIMONIUM LATIFOLIUM 'VIOLETTA'		✓	✓	✓	✓	✓	✓						✓		✓			✓				✓					✓

		ZONES									SOIL					LIGHT		BLOOMING SEASON				PLANT HEIGHT			NOTED FOR			
		Zone 3	Zone 4	Zone 5	Zone 6	Zone 7	Zone 8	Zone 9	Zone 10	Zone 11	Sandy	Loam	Dry	Well-Drained	Moist	Full Sun	Shade	Spring	Summer	Fall	Winter	Under 2 Ft.	2-3 Ft.	Over 3 Ft.	Long Bloom Season	Fragrance	Distinctive Foliage	Cut Flowers
PURPLE	SALVIA X SUPERBA			✔	✔	✔	✔	✔	✔			✔		✔		✔		✔	✔				✔					
	STACHYS MACRANTHA		✔	✔	✔	✔	✔					✔			✔	✔	✔	✔	✔			✔						
	THALICTRUM DELAVAYI			✔	✔	✔	✔					✔		✔	✔	✔	✔		✔					✔				✔
	THALICTRUM ROCHEBRUNIANUM			✔	✔	✔						✔		✔	✔	✔	✔		✔					✔				
	VERBENA BONARIENSIS					✔	✔							✔		✔			✔	✔				✔			✔	
	VIOLA CORNUTA 'LORD NELSON'			✔	✔	✔	✔					✔			✔	✔	✔	✔	✔	✔		✔			✔	✔		
BLUE	ACONITUM CARMICHAELII	✔	✔	✔	✔							✔			✔	✔	✔			✔				✔	✔	✔		
	AGAPANTHUS AFRICANUS					✔	✔	✔				✔		✔	✔	✔			✔				✔					
	AMSONIA CILIATA				✔	✔	✔	✔				✔		✔	✔	✔	✔	✔	✔				✔				✔	
	ANCHUSA AZUREA	✔	✔	✔	✔							✔			✔	✔			✔					✔	✔			
	AQUILEGIA FLABELLATA	✔	✔	✔								✔		✔	✔	✔		✔				✔					✔	
	ASTER X FRIKARTII			✔	✔	✔	✔					✔		✔	✔	✔			✔	✔			✔					
	BAPTISIA AUSTRALIS	✔	✔	✔	✔	✔	✔							✔		✔		✔						✔			✔	✔
	BRUNNERA MACROPHYLLA		✔	✔	✔	✔						✔			✔	✔	✔	✔			✔						✔	
	CAMPANULA CARPATICA 'BLAUE CLIPS'	✔	✔	✔	✔							✔		✔		✔	✔	✔	✔			✔						
	CERATOSTIGMA PLUMBAGINOIDES			✔	✔	✔	✔							✔		✔	✔		✔			✔						
	CLEMATIS HERACLEIFOLIA 'DAVIDIANA'			✔	✔	✔	✔					✔		✔	✔	✔			✔				✔			✔		
	DELPHINIUM X BELLADONNA 'BELLAMOSUM'	✔	✔	✔	✔	✔						✔		✔	✔	✔			✔					✔				✔
	ECHINOPS RITRO 'TAPLOW BLUE'	✔	✔	✔	✔	✔	✔					✔		✔	✔	✔			✔					✔				✔
	ERYNGIUM ALPINUM			✔	✔	✔	✔				✔		✔		✔		✔			✔				✔				✔
	GERANIUM 'JOHNSON'S BLUE'		✔	✔	✔	✔								✔	✔	✔	✔	✔	✔			✔					✔	
	LINUM PERENNE			✔	✔	✔	✔				✔			✔		✔		✔	✔	✔		✔					✔	
	LOBELIA SIPHILITICA		✔	✔	✔	✔						✔			✔	✔	✔		✔				✔					
	NEPETA X FAASSENII		✔	✔	✔	✔	✔							✔		✔			✔			✔				✔	✔	
	PEROVSKIA ATRIPLICIFOLIA			✔	✔	✔	✔	✔						✔		✔			✔					✔		✔	✔	
	PHLOX STOLONIFERA 'BLUE RIDGE'			✔	✔	✔						✔		✔	✔	✔	✔	✔				✔						
	PLATYCODON GRANDIFLORUS 'MARIESII'		✔	✔	✔	✔	✔					✔		✔	✔	✔			✔			✔				✔		
	PULMONARIA LONGIFOLIA 'ROY DAVIDSON'		✔	✔	✔	✔						✔			✔	✔	✔	✔				✔					✔	
	SALVIA FARINACEA 'BLUE BEDDER'					✔	✔	✔				✔		✔		✔			✔	✔		✔					✔	
	SCABIOSA CAUCASICA 'FAMA'		✔	✔	✔	✔	✔					✔		✔		✔			✔			✔			✔			✔
	STOKESIA LAEVIS 'BLUE DANUBE'			✔	✔	✔	✔	✔			✔			✔		✔			✔			✔			✔			✔
	VERONICA 'SUNNY BORDER BLUE'		✔	✔	✔	✔	✔					✔		✔		✔			✔	✔		✔			✔			

Bulbs

Bulbs usher in the garden's first colors in spring, paint the summer landscape, and bring fall to a brilliant conclusion. Beyond the familiar favorites of tulips, daffodils, crocuses, and irises are a great and varied family of lesser-known but equally beautiful bulbs that flower throughout the growing season. And best of all, bulbs that are properly planted maintain themselves with a minimum of care.

Whether occupying a bed of their own or sharing one with other types of flowers, as in the Virginia garden at left, bulbs make for a colorful scene. Here, tulips and jonquils join with daisylike doronicums to form a pool of golden yellow on an April morning. The rich violet-blue of grape hyacinths offers a pretty contrast to the yellow hues and picks up the lavender-pink of a nearby azalea. The emerging foliage of bee balm, a frost-tinged silver-gray, cools the scene.

Bulbs lend themselves to every planting scheme from the regimental trim of a formal bed to the lush jumble of a woodland garden to the cozy confines of a window box. This chapter will show you how to choose the best bulbs for your garden and create the most spectacular displays in all of these settings.

Bulb Basics

Flowering bulbs were probably the earliest ornamental plants to be grown. More than 3,500 years ago the Minoans on Crete cultivated *Lilium candidum* (Madonna lily) as a garden flower, and valued *Crocus sativus* (saffron) for its yellow pistil used in cooking. Today, many bulbs are grown for the distinctive shape, color, and scent of their flowers. Others, such as onions, garlic, carrots, potatoes, and celery, are more appreciated as edibles.

Bulb flowers have evolved to accommodate the insects and birds that pollinate them. They have assumed myriad forms and colors, and they range vastly in size, from a crocus less than 4 inches tall to *Dahlia imperialis* at a towering 20 feet.

Ninety percent of the bulbs we grow for flowers belong to just six genera: *Lilium, Iris, Tulipa, Hyacinthus, Narcissus,* and *Gladiolus.* But within these six are hundreds of species and thousands of varieties. And gardeners also have an array of other bulb genera from which to choose. In mail-order catalogs these plants are often called miscellaneous or specialty bulbs. Regardless of their varying physical characteristics, however, all bulbs have one thing in common—unique food-storage systems that ensure their survival and distinguish them from all other plants.

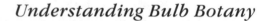

Understanding Bulb Botany

Garden bulbs are descendants of tough perennials that grew in areas with long periods of drought or cold. They adapted by evolving underground storehouses in which to conserve food and moisture for difficult times.

This makes bulbs particularly useful as garden plants, because they come with a ready-made food supply. When light and temperature conditions become favorable, bulbs grow rapidly. As the plants expand to full size and come into bloom, they deplete those food and moisture reserves. But for the rest of their time in leaf they are busy building up the next year's provisions, using photosynthesis to convert water and nutrients into stored energy for growth and other life processes.

Among the broad category of plants known as bulbs, four distinct types of storage systems evolved: true bulbs, corms, tubers, and rhizomes *(right).* Each type has a characteristic appearance and growth cycle *(pages 100-101),* and understanding the way they function is essential to cultivating these plants successfully. Equally important is a knowledge of where in the world given varieties of bulbs originated.

Native Habitats of Bulbs

A key to raising bulbs is understanding the growing conditions that drove their evolutionary devel-

Flourishing at the base of a tree in the Pacific Northwest, a patch of Iris reticulata emerges in early spring. This hardy species returns year after year if given the right conditions.

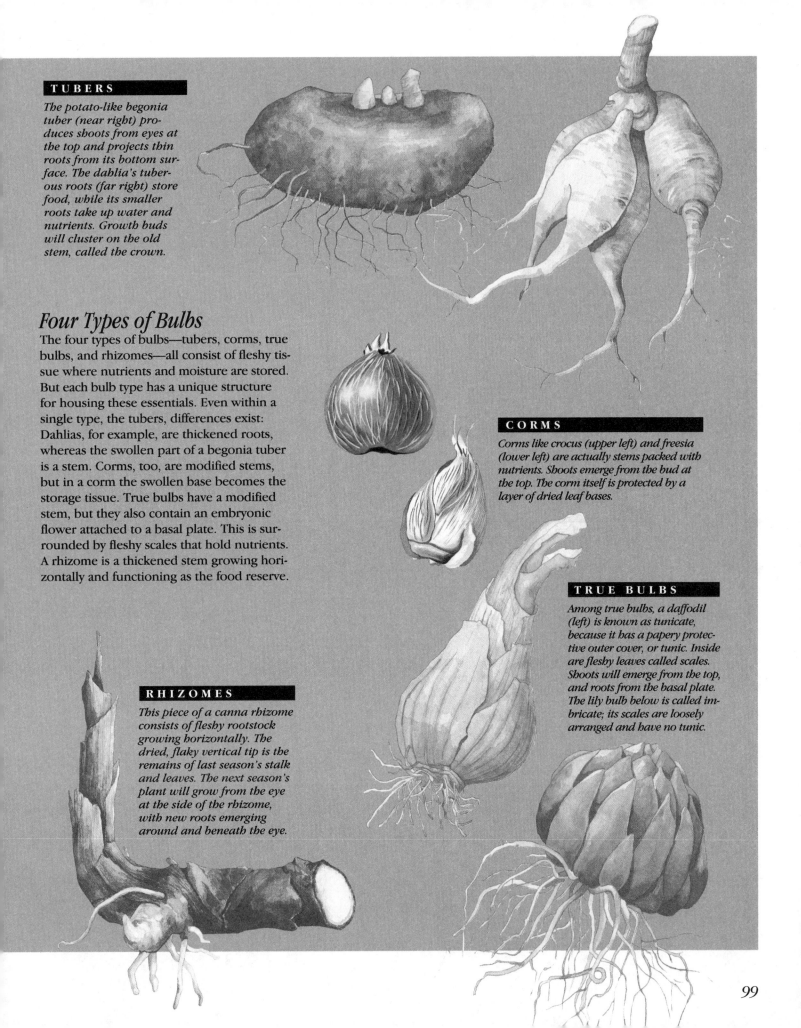

TUBERS

The potato-like begonia tuber (near right) produces shoots from eyes at the top and projects thin roots from its bottom surface. The dahlia's tuberous roots (far right) store food, while its smaller roots take up water and nutrients. Growth buds will cluster on the old stem, called the crown.

Four Types of Bulbs

The four types of bulbs—tubers, corms, true bulbs, and rhizomes—all consist of fleshy tissue where nutrients and moisture are stored. But each bulb type has a unique structure for housing these essentials. Even within a single type, the tubers, differences exist: Dahlias, for example, are thickened roots, whereas the swollen part of a begonia tuber is a stem. Corms, too, are modified stems, but in a corm the swollen base becomes the storage tissue. True bulbs have a modified stem, but they also contain an embryonic flower attached to a basal plate. This is surrounded by fleshy scales that hold nutrients. A rhizome is a thickened stem growing horizontally and functioning as the food reserve.

CORMS

Corms like crocus (upper left) and freesia (lower left) are actually stems packed with nutrients. Shoots emerge from the bud at the top. The corm itself is protected by a layer of dried leaf bases.

TRUE BULBS

Among true bulbs, a daffodil (left) is known as tunicate, because it has a papery protective outer cover, or tunic. Inside are fleshy leaves called scales. Shoots will emerge from the top, and roots from the basal plate. The lily bulb below is called imbricate; its scales are loosely arranged and have no tunic.

RHIZOMES

This piece of a canna rhizome consists of fleshy rootstock growing horizontally. The dried, flaky vertical tip is the remains of last season's stalk and leaves. The next season's plant will grow from the eye at the side of the rhizome, with new roots emerging around and beneath the eye.

opment. Most of the winter-hardy bulbs we grow today, for example, come from regions having hot, dry summers and cool, wet winters, such as California and the Mediterranean. Crocus, tulip, daffodil, hyacinth, and iris thrive in these conditions.

Another group comes from areas of steamy summers and dry winters, such as are found in areas of South America and Africa. These plants make up a group called tender bulbs—canna, freesia, amaryllis, agapanthus, dahlia, hippeastrum, and the showier gladiolus—which cannot tolerate freezing temperatures.

A third type comes from temperate areas of northern Asia and North America, where there is periodic rainfall. The tender bulb lycoris and some hardy lilies are of Asian origin. Some fritillaries, lilies, and anemones—all hardy bulbs—are natives of the United States.

Despite having come from such diverse parts of the world, many bulbs have proved able to perennialize—to come back and bloom year after year—in the United States. Even frost-tender bulbs such as agapanthus, canna, and dahlia have managed to make themselves at home in the warmer areas of the country. And where summers are warm but winters are frosty, a gardener can still enjoy tender bulbs from one year to the next. You simply have to lift the bulbs from the ground when they go dormant and overwinter them indoors—or grow the tender beauties in containers indoors or in a greenhouse.

The Growth Cycles of Bulbs

The roots and shoots of true bulbs, such as this narcissus, start to grow in autumn, slow down in winter, and lengthen rapidly in the spring when the soil warms up. As buds emerge and the blooms open, the bulb begins to divide. Though the flowers soon fade, the foliage persists, capturing light for photosynthesis. Before the foliage dies and the plant goes dormant, seed pods develop at the base of the flower where it meets the stem (far right). The narcissus's primary means of reproduction, however, are daughter bulbs that develop from the original. Lilies grow daughter bulbs too, as well as tiny bulblets, which emerge around the base of the bulb and the crown of the plant, and even smaller bulbils, found in the axils of the plant's leaves.

TRUE BULB: NARCISSUS

A corm, such as this crocus, begins its growth cycle in early spring, as soon as the ground thaws. It sends down roots, and shoots emerge from the apical bud at its top. As it grows and flowers, the corm is depleted. Then, as the plant gathers nourishment for the next season, a new corm develops on the top of the dying original (third from left). But before the plant goes dormant, additional reproductive units—miniature corms called cormels—form between the old corm and the new one (far right).

CORM: CROCUS

Creating the Right Conditions

To encourage your bulbs to perennialize, it is important to recreate as closely as possible their native habitat. Almost all bulbs prefer well-drained soil; they are susceptible to rot if they remain constantly wet, especially during dormant periods. *Galanthus* (snowdrop), narcissus, scilla, lily, and *Trillium* (wake-robin) tolerate summer rains; iris crocus, tulip, colchicum, and some fritillaries prefer dry conditions. Native woodland bulbs perform best if their soil is rich with organic matter and conditions are somewhat dry.

Gardeners in the Deep South (Zones 9 and 10) who wish to grow such hardy bulbs as crocus, hyacinth, snowdrop, scilla, tulip, and narcissus face an uphill battle: Hardy bulbs require a period of chilling before they can bloom in the spring. In the cold northern zones Mother Nature takes care of this requirement. But in the warm zones chilling must be accomplished artificially, by taking the bulbs out of the ground and refrigerating them over the winter. If you are unsure about the cultural needs of your bulbs, check the Plant Selection Guide at the end of this chapter *(pages 120-125)* and the encyclopedia section that begins on page 355 for complete growing information.

Rhizomes, such as this canna, send new roots downward in the summer and produce leafy flower stalks from growth buds that emerged the previous year. At the same time, new growth buds emerge on the fleshy rootstock, which grows continuously as its older portions become increasingly tough and fibrous and lose their ability to produce new buds. By the time the foliage has died back (far right), the new growth buds are poised to produce flowers once the next growing season comes around.

RHIZOME: CANNA

Unlike other bulbs, a begonia tuber is not consumed, broken up, or worn out by the effort of producing flowers and foliage. Sending out shoots from its growth buds and roots from its base (near right), it does become partially depleted. But then, as it takes up nutrients during the remainder of the season, it is replenished and develops new buds. The tuberous roots of a dahlia, on the other hand, are completely spent in the work of producing a flowering stem. Its reproductive strategy, aside from making seeds, is to grow new tuberous roots alongside the old ones.

TUBER: BEGONIA

Selecting Your Bulbs

When you shop for bulbs, you'll find them almost everywhere you look, from local hardware stores to grocery stores to garden centers and nurseries. You can also order them from one of the many mail-order catalogs that feature a range of beautiful and often unusual specimens. But because quality is key to any plant's performance, you should shop where the healthiest bulbs are sold.

You'll find a better selection of bulbs if you shop for them as soon as they arrive in the stores. Hardy spring- and summer-flowering bulbs are sold in late summer, tender summer-flowering bulbs are sold in spring, and fall-flowering bulbs reach the stores in mid- to late summer. If you order from catalogs, the bulbs will be shipped to you at the best planting times for your area.

What to Look For

Bulbs are sold by size, which is measured in centimeters of circumference. "Topsize" bulbs are generally the biggest of a species or class and are the most expensive. The larger the bulb, the more reserve food energy it contains, enabling it to produce more and bigger flowers. "Midsize" bulbs, also called premium, are considered a better buy for some bulbs; they cost less than topsize, and though they produce only one flower the first year, they'll send up multiple flowers the following year. Small bulbs (sometimes called planting stock) are at the lowest end of the scale. Their performance will be spotty, and they may have a short life span.

Narcissus bulbs are measured according to the number of growing points, or noses, that they have. The largest bulbs, called DN-1, have three to five noses, DN-2 bulbs have two noses, and healthy DN-3s—also called rounds—have one nose *(right)*. Size is also a factor when selecting tuber varieties such as caladiums and dahlias. The largest tubers have been maturing for a number of years and have several eyes. For this reason, they cost significantly more than small and midsize tubers, which have one or two eyes. Topsize caladium tubers will produce more than 20 leaves—even more if you break off the biggest eye with a gentle push of the thumb. The tuber then sends up leaves from other growing points.

But for some bulbs, bigger does not always mean better. Tulip bulbs that are larger than 14 centimeters often produce deformed flowers. And over-size bulbs may have been treated with nitrogen, which can weaken their cellular structure, making them more vulnerable to disease.

In addition to size, consider these factors when making your selections:

• A healthy bulb is plump and firm; the bottom—the area from which the roots will grow—should be hard. A soft, withered bulb has been stored too long and has dried out, or it is diseased.

• The bulb should be dormant and show no premature growth of roots and shoots.

• There should be no damage to the base of the bulb or the growth tips and minimal scars and bruises on the rest of the bulb. However, a split or flaking brown tunic—the bulb's papery outer skin—is normal. If a bulb has lost most of its tunic but shows no signs of disease or damage, it will likely perform well.

• When buying from garden centers, look for bulbs that are sold in mesh bags or boxes; loose bulbs in open bins may be damaged by excessive handling and jostling.

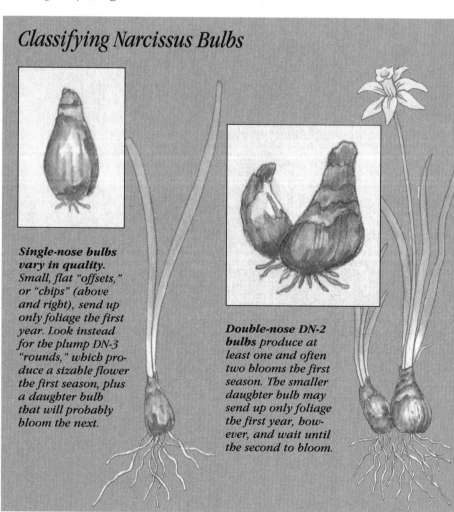

Classifying Narcissus Bulbs

Single-nose bulbs vary in quality. Small, flat "offsets," or "chips" (above and right), send up only foliage the first year. Look instead for the plump DN-3 "rounds," which produce a sizable flower the first season, plus a daughter bulb that will probably bloom the next.

Double-nose DN-2 bulbs produce at least one and often two blooms the first season. The smaller daughter bulb may send up only foliage the first year, however, and wait until the second to bloom.

• Most reliable bulb specialists offer large to medium sizes only, depending on the bulb variety. When many bulbs are offered for a low price, expect to receive very small, immature bulbs that may not bloom for years.

• Select a suitable bulb species for your climate. The Plant Selection Guide at the end of this chapter *(pages 120-125)* or the encyclopedia section that begins on page 335 will suggest which bulbs are likely to grow best in your region.

Holding Bulbs for Planting

If you aren't planting your bulbs as soon as you get them home, hardy spring bloomers can be kept in any place where the temperature doesn't rise above 60° F. Place them in open trays or loosely folded paper bags. Summer- and fall-blooming bulbs can be stored in a closed plastic bag with wood shavings, peat, vermiculite, or a combination of these; place the bulbs in a cool, dry, well-ventilated area. Try to get your bulbs in the ground as soon as planting conditions are right, to avoid tissue deterioration and dehydration.

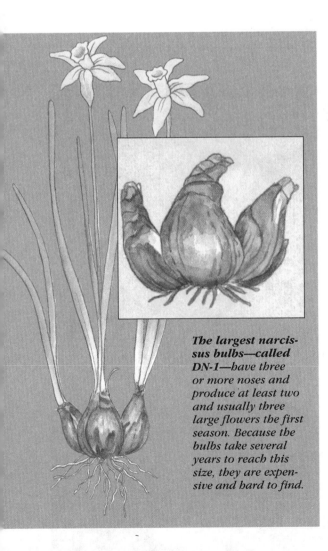

The largest narcissus bulbs—called DN-1—have three or more noses and produce at least two and usually three large flowers the first season. Because the bulbs take several years to reach this size, they are expensive and hard to find.

Delicate blue bells of Muscari (grape hyacinth) and roselike Ranunculus asiaticus (Persian buttercup) make ideal early spring companions in a warm climate, where the ranunculus can stay in the ground all year. Hardy only to Zone 7, ranunculus tubers are available from garden centers and specialty catalogs in spring, while the more cold-tolerant muscari bulbs appear in stores in time for fall planting.

Designing with Bulbs

Gardeners today use bulbs with abandon, incorporating them into traditional beds and borders *(pages 108-111)* and using them as colorful accents in combination with other plants. Bulbs shine in these settings. Yet there is something undeniably satisfying about all-bulb groupings, with their rich, simultaneous burst of color—especially in spring, when the rest of the garden is just beginning to stir. With such unlimited design choices, it's often a good idea to create a plan on paper first, to help you see how you might include bulbs in your garden; the first chapter of this book *(pages 4-31)* explains how to map out such plantings.

The Elements of Design

Just as certain homes lend themselves to particular styles of gardens—a Federal-style brick house, for instance, with its elements of balance and symmetry, seems an apt setting for a formal garden—certain plants lend themselves to particular styles of planting. The garden surrounding such a house would likely have tidy beds of uniform plantings, outlined in straight edges and simple curves. The

bulbs chosen would have simple, strong forms and compact blooms, and they would be closely grouped to create the effect of a stunning carpet of color. Tulips, hyacinths, and daffodils, placed in upright, soldierly formations and edged with annuals, make good formal plantings.

Since different types of bulbs bloom at different times you can highlight certain parts of the formal garden as the seasons progress. For example, in the early spring you can brighten the entrance to the front door and the path leading to it with a mass planting of early-blooming crocuses. As the weather warms up, shift attention to a pool or a slope edged with a bank of blooming lilies and allium or perhaps to a shady bench flanked by groupings of caladium and calla lilies. On a shady terrace, arrange large pots of colorful begonias.

The grounds around a simple frame house might be planted in mixed drifts of bulbs that would multiply over the years. Such an informal approach is characterized by irregular curves and asymmetrical shapes. A cluster of lilies, for example, might be balanced by a dwarf conifer on one side and a stand of low-growing blue fescue grass on the other.

The star-burst shape of spiky Eryngium (sea holly) beautifully echoes the open trumpet form of 'Golden Pixie' lilies. Strengthening the combination is the contrast between the lily's golden yellow color and the sea holly's lavender-blue.

An informal garden plan could also include naturalized plantings—drifts of robust species able to spread on their own from year to year *(pages 112-115)*. Such plantings might be started at the edge of a lawn, along a woodland floor, or around trees or shrubs. A rock garden made of randomly spaced stones set into a hillside also expresses a natural, informal look when planted with bulbs. Depending on the space, you could plant delicate-looking bulbs, such as scillas or allium, or larger bulbs such as daffodils or tulips *(pages 116-117)*. Just be sure to keep the planting in scale; you don't want the tall bulbs to dwarf the small ones.

Of course, your garden style may also combine some formal and informal elements. Deliberate contrast can be effective—a jewel-like formal bed, say, next to a naturalized woodland shade garden. But keep proportions in mind; plant large plants in large places, small plants where they can be isolated and featured.

Choosing Bulbs for Color

Deciding on a color scheme will help organize your choice of bulbs. Bulbs come in nearly every color you could want, from whites and the palest tints to the richest, most saturated hues. For vivid, energetic arrangements well-suited to a formal garden style, select plants in contrasting colors, such as yellow and violet, orange and blue-violet, or red and yellow. To create a more relaxed and peaceful mood, appropriate for an informal garden, consider harmonious color combinations such as blue-violet and mauve or shades of plum and rose. Remember, however, that these are guidelines, not hard and fast rules. If your heart is set on a particular color scheme, give it a try; your garden should reflect your tastes and your imagination. And part of the beauty of bulbs is that they can be lifted and moved easily.

Bulbs can contribute color to your garden as accent plants or in broad swaths. For example, a small group of *Allium giganteum,* with large purple globes on 4-foot stems, would highlight the foliage of a nearby planting of *Heuchera* 'Palace Purple' (alumroot) and the flowers of blooming *Lavandula* (lavender). But if you plant the allium in large bands among ornamental grasses and the rich yellow flowers of a few *Achillea* 'Coronation Gold' (yarrow), the contrast in colors and the scale of the planting will make the allium stand out from the other plants.

It is generally best to cluster like colors together and to group the clusters next to each other to make patterns. An exception might be when you combine different colors of the same type of bulb—a spring bed of *Anemone blanda* (Greek anemone) in blue, white, and pink, for example, can be quite cheery.

White-flowered bulbs such as tulips can be quite striking when planted as part of an all-white garden, especially when paired with the creamy-edged leaves of *Hosta* 'Northern Halo' and other silvery foliage plants. They are also useful to break up overly dominant color patterns or subdue strident colors. Plan for about a fourth of your bulbs at any given time to be white: crocus, narcissus, or tulip in spring; lily or dahlia in summer. In a shady location, the natural light-reflecting qualities of white flowers attract the eye and brighten shadowy curves and corners. In fact, whites and pale shades show up best in shady locations and at twilight.

Yellow is another color that makes a beautiful accent. A proportion of one yellow bloom to about three violet or blue ones creates a vivid combination. Green, a steady presence in the garden, forms a bridge between the two colors. Yellow also harmonizes with orange, a tricky hue to weave into a color scheme.

Texture and Form

Although color is a bulb's dominant attribute, the texture and overall shape of the plant can also add to the garden design. To begin with, there can be enormous variations in flower heads. Parrot tulips, for example, have developed ragged-edged petals that are wildly mottled in color. Lilies exhibit a wide range of trumpet shapes. Other lilylike flowers, such as the *Gloriosa superba,* have a lacy, airy quality.

Bulbs yield some of the largest and tallest of all flowers,

Polianthes tuberosa 'Dangerous Pleasures' (tuberose)

Scented Bulbs

Amaryllis belladonna
(belladonna lily)
Convallaria majalis
(lily of the valley)
Crinum americanum
(swamp lily)
Crocus biflorus
(Scotch crocus)
Crocus imperati
(crocus)
Cyclamen
(Persian violet)
Eucharis
(Amazon lily)
Freesia
(freesia)
Galanthus
(snowdrop)
Gladiolus calianthus
(gladiolus)
Hyacinthus
(hyacinth)
Hymenocallis
(spider lily)
Iris
(iris)
Leucojum vernum
(spring snowflake)
Lilium
(lily)
Lycoris squamigera
(magic lily)
Muscari
(grape hyacinth)
Narcissus
(daffodil)
Pancratium
(sea daffodil)
Polianthes tuberosa
(tuberose)
Puschkinia scilloides
(striped squill)
Scilla
(squill)
Sternbergia lutea
(winter daffodil)
Trillium
(wake-robin)
Tulipa
(tulip)

such as the 9-inch-wide "dinner-plate" dahlia and the equally extraordinary *Eremurus himalaicus* (Himalayan desert-candle), with a flowering stalk reaching as high as 9 feet. These giants never fail to make an impression. On the other hand, the miniature detailing of a *Cyclamen coum* or the dangling bells of a *Fritillaria meleagris* require a close inspection for the viewer to fully appreciate their delicate form.

Decorative Foliage

A few bulbs are grown solely for their interesting foliage. Notable is the caladium, whose heart-shaped leaves are speckled and striped in pink, red, lavender, and white. A common houseplant, caladium is frost-tender but will do well in a shady, moist spot in the garden. The gigantic elephant's ear, or *Colocasia esculenta,* also thrives in shady and damp conditions.

Many flowering bulbs also have attractive foliage, which gives the plants interest after their blooms fade. Some cannas, for example, have purplish leaves, and the foliage of *Canna* x *generalis* 'Pretoria' has startling green-and-gold variegation. Several small tulip cultivars—'Red Riding Hood', 'Cape Cod', and 'Oriental Splendor', to name a few—have red-striped leaves. And *Tulipa aucheriana* has wavy-edged leaves that radiate from its short stem.

The foliage of flowering bulbs such as arum, oxalis, and cyclamen, when planted in masses, makes a beautiful ground cover. And in Zones 8 to 10, agapanthus, clivia, and canna foliage is evergreen, preserving their position in the garden throughout the year.

For most bulbs, however, foliage is viewed as the price a gardener must pay to enjoy the beauty of the flower. It takes some ingenuity to deal with the sprawl of daffodil foliage or the withering of allium or hyacinth leaves. With careful planning, though, you can take advantage of the emerging foliage of perennials to disguise the bulbs' progressively unsightly leaves. Ferns, for example, come into leaf just as snowdrops, crocuses, and winter aconites are fading. *Astilbe* (false spirea), *Epimedium* (bishop's hat), *Paeonia* (peony), and Siberian iris are also good camouflage.

A Bulb for Every Season

Once you have settled on the bulbs and colors you like, select for bloom season. The flowering glory of most bulbs is brief—2 to 3 weeks. The Plant Selection Guide on pages 120-125 will help you pick bulbs that bloom when you want them to and in the colors and shapes you prefer. Happily, many bulbs of the same genus bloom at different times. So if you love tulips, you can extend their presence in the garden for months by planting early-spring-blooming species tulips, followed by Triumph and Darwin tulips, which flower in mid-spring, and finishing with single and double late varieties, which will carry you into summer.

The Bewitchment of Scent

The scents exuded by bulb flowers range from lemony to musky to honey-sweet. Scent evolved to attract pollinators, and the fragrance emitted by some lilies and narcissus may seem overpowering to human noses. By contrast, you will have to get down on hands and knees to enjoy the perfume of small spring bulbs such as crocuses and snowdrops. Most fragrant bulb flowers come in white, pale pink, mauve, or yellow, and their petals are waxy, like those of hyacinth, tuberose, and lily. To get the most enjoyment from scented bulbs, plant them in a border close to where you walk, near the front entrance to your house, near a deck or patio or outside your kitchen window.

Practical Considerations

Any garden design has to take into account the growing requirements of plants. With a few exceptions, bulbs prefer soil with a more or less neutral pH of about 7.0, and good drainage. Generally, spring bloomers such as daffodils require a dry period in the summer, when they are dormant. Cyclamen, trout lily, and other woodland bulbs need protection from hot summer sun. Plants that evolved in mountain meadows—crocuses and tulips are examples—can tolerate a good baking.

Meeting these requirements is made easier by the use of companion plants. Shrubs and perennials not only conceal the long spindly stems of tall bulb plants such as lilies—and, of course, help hide withering bulb foliage after flowering—but their roots also take up excess moisture in the soil. And later, when the bulbs are dormant, perennials shade the ground and moderate soil temperature.

You'll want to bring all these variables together when you create the detailed map of your garden design *(page 31)*. For example, a hard-to-mow slope might be just the place for a rock garden or a drift of naturalized bulbs. A diagram also helps you keep track of where your bulbs are planted.

Showy deep blue Agapanthus 'Bressingham Blue' (African Lily) stands out in bold contrast to golden mounds of orange coneflower, slender trumpets of Cape fuchsia, and lemon yellow daylilies in this Washington State garden. Vigorous summer-flowering tubers, the African lilies bloom throughout the season.

Bulbs in the Bed and Border

Beds and borders are the building blocks of most garden designs. These self-contained plantings give the garden its shape and character, and afford the gardener an opportunity to combine plants in myriad ways, using color, form, and texture for maximum effect. The strong hues of flowering bulbs have an immediate and vivid impact in such a setting. Indeed, many of the more formal bulbs that produce uniform shapes and colors, such as tulip, iris, narcissus, and hyacinth, look most at home in a bedding display.

Use a bed or border to position plants where they can best be appreciated—along a walkway or near an entrance, around a pool or patio or a garden bench. They are a versatile way of organizing your plants for viewing, presenting lovely vistas from afar or up close.

Cultivating a Bed or Border

Beds and borders also allow you to group your plants according to their growing requirements. They are the part of the garden where you can most easily focus your cultivation efforts to improve soil texture and fertility specifically for the plants you have chosen.

Bulb experts agree that the most important factor for success in growing bulbs is your soil's drainage. The soil must allow water to percolate away from the bulbs, but it also must contain enough compost or other organic matter to hold nutrients and to retain sufficient moisture to keep the bulbs from drying out completely. In a bed or border you can prepare the soil to meet those needs and thus protect your sometimes considerable investment in growing stock.

Serving a Purpose

Although they share a common purpose in the garden, beds and borders accomplish it slightly differently. A border forms the edge of a garden space and usually lies along a vertical element—a fence, a hedge, or a wall. The vertical element serves as a backdrop to set off the plants, which are typically laid out with the tallest at the back and the shortest in front and are generally viewed from the front only. A bed, on the other hand, is often a freestanding area visible from all sides. It can be geometric or irregular in shape and surrounded by lawn, ground cover, or even gravel.

A bed must be in proportion to the space around it—neither so small that it fades from view at a modest distance nor so large that it overpowers its surroundings. On a small lot, you can give a bed of limited size more visual weight by adding shrubs or small trees, or by mounding earth to form a raised bed (left). The height of the plants should be proportional to the width of the plot. As a general guideline, no plant should be taller than one-half the width of the space. And when designing either a bed or a border, be sure to give yourself enough room to move around the plantings to perform routine maintenance chores.

Formal Beds and Borders

Bulbs in massed plantings make spectacular formal designs. Expect to plant the bulbs rather densely in a formal bed—inches apart—and to think of the planting as a one-season affair, good for drawing attention to an area for a short period of time. Try, for example, a spring bed of clusters

---

TIPS FROM THE PROS

Making a Mounded Bed

One way to make your bulb bed more visible from a distance is to create a gentle hillock or mound. The extra elevation adds dimensional interest and increases the color impact you will get from plants of similar height—for example, a grouping of tulips and daffodils. In addition, the eye will naturally be carried to the top of the mound, where you can place a special feature—a dwarf shrub with an interesting shape, perhaps, or a large ornamental rock.

Besides its decorative appeal, a mounded or raised bed is an ideal location for bulbs because you can easily mix up your own soil recipe on the site to ensure that it will have good drainage.

To make a raised bed, pile topsoil at least a foot high, so there will be enough to envelop completely the roots of your plants. A few artfully arranged rocks will help keep the soil in place until the plants can establish a root system. Depending on your preference for a formal or an informal arrangement, the raised bed can be centered within an available space on your property or given an off-center position. Orient the slope of the bed to the point from which you will view it.

A line of nodding 'Ice Follies' daffodils leads to a cascading white wisteria in this formal San Francisco garden. Extending the white theme, creamy tulips and a snowy azalea glow against dark masonry walls.

The flowing curves of this informal early-spring border burst with colorful naturalized bulbs, including crown imperial, emerging scilla, and a variety of daffodils. Interspersed are ivory and purple pansies and primulas to fill in the bare spots.

of pink, red, and yellow tulips, surrounded by an edging of vivid blue grape hyacinths. Other good edging plants include pansies, impatiens, rock cress, candytuft, primroses, coleus, or ornamental kale. Forget-me-nots are a traditional foundation plant for bulb displays, creating a misty blue haze through which the bulbs grow.

You might want to experiment with a single-color scheme. For an all-white spring garden, plant *Crocus vernus* 'Snowstorm', *Narcissus* 'Thalia' and 'Mount Hood', *Hyacinthus orientalis* 'L'innocence', *Anemone blanda* 'White Splendor', *Leucojum aestivum,* and *Tulipa* 'Ivory Floridale' and 'White Dream'.

A summer bed could have clusters of red or yellow canna with a central group of red and yellow gladiolus, surrounded by mixed dahlias. For accents, try marigold, petunia, lobelia, and alyssum.

Informal Plantings

In contrast to the uniformity of a formal bed, an informal planting should offer some surprises. Give it an irregular, asymmetrical shape, and choose a wider variety of plants.

Consider, for example, creating dramatic pairings of bulbs with trees and shrubs. Blue-flowered bulbs such as scilla, muscari, and chionodoxa can create a beautiful effect when clustered in a ring around the base of a white-barked birch or small

flowering cherry. Bulbs also combine well with spring-blooming shrubs—witch hazel and forsythia are two excellent examples.

Certain shrubs benefit from a screen of plants around their bare stems. For example, a hedge of lilacs, such as *Syringa* x *chinensis,* looks better with a skirt of bulbs and ferns at the beginning of the year. A succession of early-spring bulbs such as snowflakes and snowdrops, followed by crocuses and winter aconites, will finish blooming just as the dark red and pale green fronds of the maidenhair fern and the royal fern begin unfurling at the base of the lilacs. The ferns will then fill out to mask the bulbs' dying foliage.

Pastel tulips in an informal bed or border can pick up the pale blue of a *Wisteria* or lilac or the pink of spirea. Position them in front of glossy green *Ilex* (holly) or the deep maroon foliage of *Berberis thunbergii* 'Rose Glow' (barberry), and the tulips will shine. Dark purple tulips pair well with the burgundy in a cut-leaf *Acer palmatum* (Japanese maple). Their waxy blooms create a stimulating contrast with the lacy maple foliage.

Similarly, bold, waxy hyacinth flowers contrast with the fine, delicate blossoms of arabis, goldentuft, and myosotis. While hyacinths are at their best massed in a formal bed, they can serve as a good accent dotted among other plants, and their perfume is a bonus.

A specimen tree or shrub anchoring a bed can be accented with a group of bulbs. The number of bulbs should vary with the mature size of the variety chosen—a dozen daffodils, tulips, or hyacinths, for example; half a dozen large fritillaries, lilies, or galtonias; or minor bulbs in groups of three to four dozen.

Going for a Large Effect

Whether your bedding plot is formal or informal, you can strengthen its impact by choosing bulbs for height. The white-veined green leaves of an elephant's ear, for example, would contrast dramatically with the spiky foliage of a yucca or with an upright temple juniper. Or place an immense *Dahlia imperialis* next to a mass of burgundy-leaved cannas and a vining gloriosa lily.

Lilies are generally tall plants with long, relatively bare stems. They combine well with plants that rise to conceal those stems. Low grasses work well, as do dwarf conifers. For example, plant copper-colored *Lilium* x *dalhansonii* with blue-gray *Pinus flexilis* 'Glauca Pendula' (limber pine). The purple bells of a 'Betty Corning' clematis climbing over such a pair would make a stunning display.

Other tall bulb plants include *Fritillaria imperialis, Camassia, Cardiocrinum giganteum,* the tender *Watsonia,* and the giant *Canna iridiflora*—all of which grow to more than 4 feet tall in the right conditions.

Managing Bulb Foliage

Since bulb leaves should not be cut back until they are withered and brown, you'll need various planting strategies to hide them as they decline. Daffodils, for example, develop a floppy habit, especially as their foliage yellows in the sun. Plant them with hostas, daylilies, peonies, leopard's-bane, astilbe, ferns, and grasses—perennials that emerge in time to hide the homely daffodil leaves. Or put them at the base of flowering shrubs or

Towering Lilium 'Golden Splendor' and the smaller white 'Gypsy' shine among the pastel pink of filipendula and the blue of campanula in this Oregon garden. Clipped box bushes anchor the corner of the bed.

Orange-trumpeted Asiatic hybrid lilies and purple-petaled columbine burst from a rock-edged bed in Idaho. Plum-colored oxalis climbs between the stones.

among ground covers such as ivy, vinca, or low-growing cotoneaster, allowing you to tuck the daffodil leaves out of sight.

Crocus foliage is shorter and thus not so troublesome, getting conveniently lost among low ground covers such as vinca, sedum, bugleweed, euonymus, ivy, and carpet junipers. Do not plant crocuses with pachysandra, however; it will smother the bulbs and cause them not to return.

Another way to hide withering bulb foliage is to plant annuals such as pansy, iberis, and *Lobularia maritima* (alyssum) among the bulbs just before the latter start to grow. Since the roots of annuals are shallow, the growing bulbs will find a way through them. The annuals will remain in flower through the summer, attracting attention away from the withering bulb leaves.

The foliage of certain autumn-flowering bulbs appears in the spring, long before the flowers arrive, and can be a nuisance if you have not planned for it in your garden design. Fall-blooming crocus and cyclamen have tidy, decorative leaves that add interest to the scene, but the foliage of the belladonna lily and colchicum is broad and floppy and should be tucked unobtrusively among other plants, such as hostas, in the spring.

Bulbs for Specific Conditions

MOIST SOIL
Caladium
(angel-wings)
Camassia quamash
(camassia)
Canna
(canna)
Convallaria majalis
(lily of the valley)
Eranthis hyemalis
(winter aconite)
Erythronium americanum
(dogtooth violet)
Fritillaria meleagris
(checkered lily)
Lilium superbum
(Turk's-cap lily)
Narcissus cyclamineus
(daffodil)

SHADE
Achimenes
(magic flower)
Anemone blanda
(Greek anemone)
Arum italicum
(painted arum)
Begonia
(begonia)
Clivia miniata
(Natal lily)
Convallaria majalis
(lily of the valley)
Crocus tomasinianus
(crocus)
Cyclamen
(Persian violet)
Erythronium americanum
(dogtooth violet)
Eucharis grandiflora
(Amazon lily)
Fritillaria
(fritillary)
Galanthus
(snowdrop)
Hyacinthoides hispanica
(Spanish bluebell)
Iris xiphioides
(English iris)
Leucojum aestivum
(summer snowflake)
Lilium candidum
(Madonna lily)
Lycoris squamigera
(magic lily)
Muscari
(grape hyacinth)
Oxalis spp.
(shamrock)
Zantedeschia
(calla lily)
Zephyranthes
(zephyr lily)

Note: The abbreviation "spp." stands for the plural of "species"; where used in lists it means that many, but not all, of the species in a genus meet the criterion of the list.

Naturalized Bulb Plantings

Naturalized plantings take advantage of the ability of some bulbs to multiply and spread on their own from year to year. By integrating bulbs into an existing environment, whether woodland or meadow or even in the midst of a ground cover such as ajuga or periwinkle, you can imitate nature with a planting that appears spontaneous and unplanned. Naturalized plantings are well suited to spots that are difficult to cultivate, such as areas of dry shade under trees, hard-to-mow banks, or spots that are rocky or wet.

Most woodland bulbs that naturalize well don't require full sun, flourishing instead in the bright pale sunlight of early spring and the dappled shade of the summer woods. Many other bulbs can be naturalized in a meadow or grassy area.

One of the charms of naturalized plantings is the reward they bring you in return for very little effort. You need only make sure the ground is well fertilized at the time of planting, especially for woodland bulbs, which must compete with shrubs and trees for water and nutrients. But after the initial work is done, these bulbs can be left alone.

Species bulbs are the best candidates for naturalizing because they spread by seed or underground by natural division, forming new plants year by year. However, some hybrid bulbs—daffodils, for example—do not self-seed. Although technically perennial, hybrid bulbs generally do not grow beyond the original clump and can only be spread by lifting and division.

To be effective, a naturalized planting should be compatible with the existing environment. In making plans for such a planting, study the landscape to determine its natural contours. Imagine water flowing across the area. This is how seeds might naturally be carried. Think of the way seeds tend to collect in pockets, such as among roots at the base of a tree. If you are planting on an embankment, take into account what the undersides of various plants look like, as these will be visible from the foot of the slope. In a meadow, imagine how the natural undulation of the ground will cause plants to spread or bunch.

In a Woodland Setting

Woodland plantings must be carried out on a fairly grand scale, or the result will look skimpy. Use trees and shrubs as the backbone of the landscape, and then put in enough of a given bulb to make a strong visible impact. Small woodland bulbs such as scilla, glory-of-the-snow, or snowdrops, for example, need to be laid down in large quantities—perhaps 100 or more bulbs per planting—in order to make an effective display.

Naturalized plantings create a stronger visual impact if different bulb varieties are not mixed. If you are planting two different species of daffodils, for example, keep them in separate clusters and blend them together gently, feathering the two into each other where the edges of the plantings touch. In an open meadow, create broad swaths of single types of bulbs in simple curved or spiral patterns. Remember that there are few straight lines to be found in nature.

Early spring brings a spectacular display to this planting of Spanish bluebells in a grove of rhododendrons. The dappled light filtering through the trees adds to the charm of this simple, naturalized woodland garden.

Naturalizing in Early Spring

Among the first spring bloomers—appearing in late winter—are snowdrops and winter aconite. Spring snowflake, similar to the snowdrop but with a smaller flower, blooms a few weeks later.

Many varieties of hardy cyclamen bloom in springtime. Cyclamen is one of the few bulbs that grow well beneath evergreen trees, and the plant's delicate appearance belies its vigorous self-seeding habit. Spring-blooming *Cyclamen hederifolium* is the most free-flowering species. It does well in woodlands, preferring moist, well-drained soil.

Crocus is a good candidate for naturalizing on a lawn. By the time the grass is ready for its first spring mowing, crocuses will have stored enough nutrients and moisture to meet their needs for the next year's growth, and their foliage can be cut down. *Crocus tomasinianus,* spread by seed and by cormels, multiplies easily in a naturalized setting. And unlike other crocus species, it has the added virtue of being unappealing as a food for squirrels and other animal pests such as voles.

Another spring bloomer is *Scilla siberica,* whose drooping, bright blue flowers look good under shrubs and with other bulbs, such as early daffodil cultivars. Chionodoxa is another early blue-flowered bulb. It needs to be planted in quantity initially in order to make a good show, but it soon spreads readily. Early-blooming *Anemone nemorosa,* with its pretty, fernlike foliage, produces 1-inch white flowers faintly tinged with pink.

Midspring Naturalizers

Among the next wave of spring bloomers is *Hyacinthoides non-scripta.* This blue-flowered bulb

Protecting Endangered Wild Bulbs

The destruction of habitat around the world, combined with the removal of bulbs from the wild by unscrupulous plant collectors, now threatens bulbs that were once abundant in nature, such as the trout lily above, with extinction. In an effort to reduce the damage caused by such acts, an international trade convention limits the export of galanthus, cyclamen, and sternbergia bulbs from their countries of origin. You can help prevent the loss of these irreplaceable plants by insisting on knowing where the wildflower bulbs you purchase come from and buying only those labeled "nursery propagated." Finally, never dig up plants from the wild.

prefers light shade during bloom time and makes a beautiful display in wooded areas. It grows 18 to 20 inches tall and spreads rapidly by seed and bulb division. In a moist area, summer snowflake naturalizes easily. This bulb resembles spring snowflake but has larger flowers and grows to 18 inches tall.

Daffodils—which usually require full sun—nevertheless have a long tradition of being naturalized in woodland settings. Where the trees are deciduous, enough sun filters through bare branches to reach the foliage in the spring. And by the time the trees have leafed out, blocking sun and moisture, the bulbs have become dormant.

Not every daffodil cultivar fills the bill, however. Good candidates include the small cyclamineus daffodils, such as early-blooming 'February Gold',

and 'Jetfire', which blooms later in spring. South of Zone 9, paper-whites multiply in shady woodland. In Zones 3 to 6, most trumpet, large-cupped, and double daffodils perform extremely well in a naturalized setting.

Another traditional use for daffodils is to plant them in orchards or unmowed meadows, where the foliage can remain undisturbed. As with other bulbs of the amaryllis family, daffodil foliage is poisonous, so deer, voles, and squirrels who might be attracted by fruit trees or other plants will avoid eating the daffodils.

Tulips tend to be thought of as bulbs for beds and borders. But some growers are developing hybrid tulips that perennialize successfully in areas similar to the tulip's native habitat, Asia and the eastern Mediterranean. In the United States, this means roughly Zones 6 to 8, where the summers are dry and the soil drains well. Try the Darwin hybrids 'Golden Apeldorn' or 'Jewel of Spring', or the lily-flowering tulip 'West Point'. In American

Native North American Bulbs

Native North American wildflower bulbs are well suited to the home garden, where they will thrive in conditions that approximate those of their natural environment. The Pacific Northwest native *Camassia quamash*, shown here blooming alongside red sorrel in an Oregon meadow, bears blue or white flowers and thrives in wet meadows and near streams. This plant was once used as a food source by native Americans, who cooked the bulbs.

Although not as large or showy as their hybridized foreign cousins, many North American woodland bulbs can make charming contributions to naturalized plantings. Bulbs such as *Arisaema triphyllum* (jack-in-the-pulpit), *Dicentra cucullaria* (Dutchman's-breeches), *Erythronium americanum* (trout lily), and *Sanguinaria canadensis* (bloodroot) have an intrinsic beauty that can seem exotic when compared with the simple forms of tulips, daffodils, and hyacinths.

Claytonia virginica (spring-beauty), with its narrow, spoon-shaped leaves and small pink flowers, seems delicate, but it has a robust habit and spreads quickly in woodlands and open thickets. *Uvularia* (great merry-bells) and *Polygonatum* (Solomon's-seal) are easy to grow.

prairie lands of the Dakotas and eastern Colorado, species tulips such as *Tulipa tarda, T. humilis,* and *T. linifolia* can be planted in meadows and left on their own to spread.

Summer and Fall Bloomers

A good summertime naturalizer is *Allium cernuum,* a member of the ornamental onion family that is native to the Allegheny Mountains and other parts of the eastern United States. It has light pink flowers and grows from 8 to 18 inches tall. This bulb also does well in rock gardens.

Two members of the lily family—*Lilium canadense* and *L. superbum*—are native to North America and naturalize well here. *L. canadense* grows wild, usually in shady areas, from Nova Scotia to Alabama, and produces yellow flowers dotted with red. It can reach a height of 6 feet. *L. superbum* has orange flowers with deep maroon centers. It too can tolerate some shade and can grow as high as 5 feet. Both *L. canadense* and *L. superbum* can be naturalized into a wet meadow or the edge of a woodland.

Autumn-flowering bulbs such as crocus and *Cyclamen hederifolium* tend to be small, modest bloomers that need to be planted in large groups to make a good show. Of the several autumn-flowering species crocuses, the blue-flowered *C. speciosus* is one of the easiest to grow. This crocus blooms in early fall and spreads rapidly by seed and natural division. It can be naturalized in lawns and grassy areas, where it soon runs rampant.

Colchicum autumnale is so eager to bloom that it will flower without even being planted, so put these bulbs in the ground as soon as possible. The pink, lilac, or white blooms appear on leafless stems; the foliage that grows in early spring begins to die down in summer and must be left undisturbed over the winter. Colchicum seeds are spread by ants, which are attracted to the seeds' sweet coating. The plants prefer sun and will form good-size clumps.

Naturalizing Bulbs

Many bulbs will take hold and spread rapidly in almost any location—under trees, on a slope, in a meadow, or on a lawn—as long as they are planted in well-drained soil. Left to grow undisturbed, they'll self-seed, multiply underground, and return in greater numbers year after year.

When choosing a site for naturalizing, consider your bulbs' decaying foliage. Small bulbs with low foliage—such as crocus, snowdrop, glory-of-the-snow, snowflake, and dwarf iris—are well suited for planting in a lawn at the front of the house. They bloom early in the season, and by the time the grass needs mowing their foliage is spent. Set your mower at 4 inches for the first few clippings; the blades will ride over short bulb foliage without cutting it, and the grass will conceal it as it dries.

Many of these same small bulbs—along with windflower, wood hyacinth, winter aconite, and spring and fall cyclamens—also naturalize well under deciduous trees. In a damp area of the garden where no other bulb will grow, *Fritillaria meleagris* will thrive, and in full sun, grape hyacinth, camassia, and ornamental onion are particularly vigorous spreaders.

Naturalize larger bulbs such as narcissus at the back or side of the house rather than in front. These bulbs also do nicely in a meadow or an orchard, where the longer grasses and emerging wildflowers help disguise the decaying foliage. Some of the best narcissus cultivars for naturalizing include 'Peeping Tom', 'Jack Snipe', 'Minnow', 'Ice Follies', 'Tête-à-Tête', 'Fortune', 'February Gold', 'Carlton', 'Mount Hood', and 'Birma'.

To make your bulb plantings look natural, scatter them over the ground and plant them where they land. Holes should be 6 to 7 inches deep for narcissus and 3 to 4 inches deep for smaller bulbs. On a lawn or other grassy environment where the soil is not compacted, use a hand-held hollow bulb planter or a trowel to dig individual holes. Some garden centers and catalogs also offer a "naturalizing tool" for planting bulbs in a lawn; it can be used from a standing position. Or, to limit the number of holes you must bore through the sod, cut away 8-inch squares of turf with a spade or an edger, loosen the soil below, and arrange the bulbs in a random pattern on the soil. Dig holes accordingly, plant the bulbs, and replace the sod. Repeat this technique until all of your bulbs have been put in the ground.

Bulbs with Ground Covers

Flowering bulbs add seasonal beauty to evergreen ground covers and vines. Try planting crocus, squill, grape hyacinth, and daffodils among ground covers under deciduous trees for bright spring color before the tree leafs out. The ground covers not only set off the blooms but will help hide wilting bulb foliage When making these combinations, however, be sure to consider the mature heights of the plants. A smaller bulb like crocus would be lost amid tall, thick pachysandra; try daffodils instead.

Bulbs for the Rock Garden

A rock garden reproduces on a small scale the growing conditions of the mountain plants known as alpines. These tough little plants can thrive in pockets of gritty soil sandwiched among rocks in wind-scoured heights.

Located on a terraced slope or in a natural outcrop, a rock garden is a sheltered environment that provides plants with a variety of microclimates. Those areas shaded by the rocks are shadowy and cool, while those in full sun are warm and sheltered. The rocks protect the plants from wind, keep their roots cool, and channel water to them. In winter the rocks absorb the sun's heat by day and release it at night, moderating root-damaging temperature fluctuations in the soil. And adding a coarse gravel mulch helps keep the plants' crowns and leaves from rotting.

Tailoring the Soil for Bulbs

Alpines are usually planted in a mixture of garden soil, sand or grit, and leaf mold. Additional coarse grit will create the pockets of quick-draining soil favored year-round by iris, crocus, narcissus, oxalis, and tulip. To mature well, iris, calochortus, and brodiaea plants need rapid drainage in summer. By adding more humus to the mixture, you can give erythronium, cyclamen, and anemone the moisture-retentive soil they need. You can also apply water and food as needed. For example, anemone and colchicum like extra water in summer; erythronium and fritillaria need extra fertilizer.

Nestling such early-spring bloomers as *Iris reticulata,* species tulips, and crocus against rocks will give them shelter and warmth. The periods of shade the rocks provide will give cyclamen, fritillary, galanthus, oxalis, and scilla a needed respite from the summer sun.

Showcasing Smaller Bulbs

A rock garden has just the right scale for those smaller bulbs that might get lost at ground level among larger plants. The rocks help set off the plants. For instance, elevated in a terraced rock garden and silhouetted against dark stones, the pale blue, purple-veined petals of *Crocus speciosus* stand out. And because the plants are elevated, the scents of species tulip, crocus, narcissus, iris,

Species Tulips: Tiny but Tough

Species tulips like these *Tulipa bakeri* 'Lilac Wonder' naturalize easily in a sunny spot. Natives of the Mediterranean, they bloom very early in spring in Zones 5 to 7; *T. clusiana* even grows in Zone 9. With multiple flowers on each stem, species tulips look best in an uncrowded position in a rock garden. They combine well with other bulbs that bloom at the same time—*Pulsatilla vulgaris, Adonis vernalis,* or bulbous iris. Evergreen dwarf shrubs, such as *Ilex crenata* (Japanese holly), *Chamaecyparis obtusa* (Hinoki false cypress), and *Arctostaphylos uva-ursi* (bearberry), also make good companions.

and grape hyacinth more easily reach your nose. Rock gardens for hardy spring and summer bulbs like *Allium cyaneum* and *Lilium cernuum* can be as small as 3 square feet. A larger garden would be appropriate for ixia, freesia, romulea, brodiaea, babiana, or bletilla. They generally grow from 12 inches to 18 inches high.

Bulbs for the Mixed Rock Garden

Bulbs combine handily in rock gardens with dwarf shrubs and perennials, which discreetly cover the

The nodding bells of Hyacinthoides hispanica seem to splash their way gaily past the mossy rocks in an Oregon garden in April. Bright pink arabis flows through a crevice alongside.

spots left bare when the bulbs go dormant. Low-growing, mat-forming herbs such as thyme, mint, and oregano protect the bulbs from splashing mud. They also provide ground-covering greenery for colchicum or *Cyclamen hederifolium,* which bloom without foliage in the fall.

Look for drought-tolerant plants that like good drainage. Dwarf evergreens and other small shrubs such as heather, daphne, dwarf cotoneaster, ground-cover azalea, and blue spruce offer excellent possibilities for combinations with bulbs. The bulbs' upright form rising through these sprawling plants makes an interesting contrast.

Finally, choose companion perennials for color: pinks and white from saxifrage, arabis, phlox, primula, and pink; blues and lavender from bellflower, gentian, and mint; yellow and orange from dwarf aster and chrysanthemum in the fall. The silver-blue foliage of blue fescue is a good foil for brightly colored bulbs. In a shady, damp spot, plant small astilbe, fern, and hosta.

Planting in Containers

Growing bulbs outdoors in pots offers advantages over growing the same plants in the ground and also allows you to raise varieties you otherwise couldn't consider. In containers, you can control how much sun or shade a plant receives, the soil mix you use, and the soil's drainage. You can move pots around the garden to give your bulbs optimal growing conditions, place them to brighten balconies or patios, and bring them up close so you can enjoy their blooms and fragrance.

You can grow tender bulbs during the warm months and keep them going strong through the winter by bringing them indoors. Shade lovers can come out of the summer sun, and bulbs that like quick drainage and extra-gritty soil can be satisfied as well. And when they are potted up they are protected from rodents and other pests.

To avoid unsightly bulb foliage, you can pothole bulbs in the garden, digging them into the ground, container and all. When the bulbs go dormant, remove them to a discreet location to complete their growth cycle.

Choosing the Container

Certain plants seem especially suited to particular pots. Narcissus are at home in a wooden box or woven basket. Formal-looking *Lilium regale* belongs in a glazed Chinese pot or stone urn. Diminutive snowdrops or crocuses are the right size for a bonsai pot. Be sure the pot has at least one drainage hole and that you can plant the bulb at the proper depth. There should be as much space under the bulb as the depth of soil above it.

All pots have pros and cons. Plastic and glazed pots retain moisture well but heat up in warm weather, possibly damaging fragile roots. Clay pots "breathe," allowing for good air circulation and good drainage, but they require more frequent watering. Large wooden tubs are superior insulators against heat and cold, but they are cumbersome to move and will eventually rot.

Combining Plants

Bulbs take up very little space and combine well in pots with each other and with other container plants. Annuals have very shallow roots that won't compete with those of bulbs, and thus make es-

pecially good companions. In spring, pair tiny hoop-petticoat daffodils with the taller scented jonquils. Rim the pot or window box with trailing variegated ivy, periwinkle, or sweet alyssum. Or pair blue scilla or grape hyacinth with white pansies in a hanging basket or window box. In summer, smaller cultivars of lilies or cannas in a pot create a tropical atmosphere. Gladiolus, dahlia, agapanthus, allium, and calla lily all are available in dwarf sizes. For colorful foliage, mix them with caladium or fern. Begonias, a favorite of most gardeners, make superb hanging-pot plants under the shade of a porch. Or try oxalis in a hanging pot or a sunny window box.

Asiatic hybrid lilies in white, yellow, and pink have been positioned in this Connecticut garden to pick up the white of potted pansies at their feet and the pink of nearby foxglove.

Coping with Cold Weather

Few bulbs, no matter how hardy, can survive a very cold winter in an outdoor container. The pot may freeze through before the bulb has established a root system, or a shallowly planted bulb may be heaved clear of the soil by repeated freezing and thawing.

To avoid these hazards, you can plant small pots in the fall, moisten them, and set them in a protected place so they remain cool and grow roots but do not freeze. For large planters or window boxes that can't be moved into shelter, start the bulbs in cell packs—small plastic starter pots—in late fall. Cover them with 8 inches of pine needles or leaves in a cool mulch pile in a north-facing location. Here they can stay evenly cold without freezing for as long as 16 weeks. As soon as the danger of hard frost has passed, you can pot them up, arranging them in combinations with small perennials or half-hardy annuals.

To design an outdoor container of summer bloomers, use one of two methods, depending on the types of bulbs chosen. Achimenes, begonia, caladium, calla lily, and canna need a warm (70°F) start indoors before they go outside. Plant them in cell packs indoors in early spring, about 30 days before the spring frost-free date. Then plant them in pots when the danger of frost has passed. Acidanthera, dahlia, and gladiolus can be planted directly into pots outdoors after the last frost.

To make an irrigation tube, use duct tape to close off one end of a length of 1½-inch PVC pipe, and drill ¼-inch holes randomly at 1-inch intervals from top to bottom. Fill in soil around the tube and even with its top edge. Plant two or three bulbs about 3 inches deep in each opening of the pot, grouping them more thickly at the top so their foliage will conceal the tube's opening.

Planting a Pot of Spring Bloomers

Tiny Tulipa bakeri and 'Little Gem' daffodils are ideal for planting in a tall strawberry pot. Prepare the pot in the fall, using a commercial growing mix or one you mix up yourself (try equal parts loam, compost, and vermiculite) and an irrigation tube to evenly distribute water through the pot. Then submerge the entire container in a cool mulch pile until after the last hard frost, when it can be put in a sunny spot to begin growing.

Plant Selection Guide for Bulbs

Organized by flower color, this chart provides information needed to select species and varieties that will thrive in the particular conditions of your garden. For additional information on select bulbs, refer to the encyclopedia section that begins on page 335.

WHITE

Species	Zone 3	Zone 4	Zone 5	Zone 6	Zone 7	Zone 8	Zone 9	Zone 10	Zone 11	Sandy	Well-Drained	Moist	Full Sun	Partial Shade	Shade	Spring	Summer	Fall	Winter	Under 1 Foot	1-3 Feet	Over 3 Feet	Naturalizing	Forcing	Container Plant	Fragrance	Cut Flowers
ACHIMENES TUBIFLORA							✓	✓			✓	✓		✓	✓	✓					✓				✓		
AGAPANTHUS AFRICANUS 'ALBA'						✓	✓	✓			✓	✓	✓	✓			✓				✓				✓		✓
ANEMONE CORONARIA 'THE BRIDE'			✓	✓	✓	✓					✓	✓	✓			✓				✓					✓	✓	✓
ARISAEMA SIKOKIANUM		✓	✓	✓	✓	✓						✓	✓	✓	✓	✓				✓							
ARUM ITALICUM 'MARMORATUM'		✓	✓	✓	✓	✓						✓		✓	✓	✓				✓			✓				
BLETILLA STRIATA 'ALBA'			✓	✓	✓	✓					✓	✓		✓			✓				✓				✓		
BRIMEURA AMETHYSTINA 'ALBA'		✓	✓	✓	✓	✓	✓					✓		✓		✓				✓					✓	✓	✓
CAMASSIA LEICHTLINII 'SEMIPLENA'		✓	✓	✓	✓	✓					✓	✓	✓	✓		✓					✓		✓	✓			
CARDIOCRINUM GIGANTEUM			✓	✓	✓						✓	✓		✓			✓					✓				✓	
CHIONODOXA LUCILIAE 'ALBA'	✓	✓	✓	✓	✓	✓					✓	✓	✓			✓				✓			✓	✓			
CONVALLARIA MAJALIS 'FLORE PLENA'	✓	✓	✓	✓								✓		✓	✓	✓				✓			✓	✓		✓	✓
CRINUM ASIATICUM				✓	✓	✓	✓				✓	✓	✓				✓					✓			✓	✓	
DAHLIA X 'BAMBINO WHITE'					✓	✓	✓				✓	✓	✓				✓	✓			✓						✓
EREMURUS HIMALAICUS		✓	✓	✓	✓	✓				✓	✓		✓			✓	✓					✓					✓
ERYTHRONIUM DENS-CANIS 'CHARMER'	✓	✓	✓	✓	✓						✓	✓		✓	✓	✓				✓							
EUCHARIS AMAZONICA						✓	✓	✓			✓	✓		✓	✓				✓		✓				✓	✓	✓
EUCOMIS COMOSA					✓	✓	✓	✓			✓	✓	✓	✓			✓				✓				✓		✓
GALANTHUS ELWESII		✓	✓	✓	✓						✓	✓	✓	✓					✓	✓			✓	✓			
GALTONIA CANDICANS			✓	✓	✓	✓	✓				✓	✓	✓				✓					✓				✓	✓
GLADIOLUS CALLIANTHUS 'MURIALAE'				✓	✓	✓	✓	✓			✓		✓				✓				✓					✓	✓
HAEMANTHUS ALBIFLOS						✓	✓	✓			✓	✓	✓	✓	✓			✓			✓				✓		
HIPPEASTRUM X 'DOUBLE RECORD'						✓	✓	✓			✓		✓			✓					✓			✓			
HYACINTHOIDES HISPANICA 'WHITE TRIUMPHATOR'			✓	✓	✓	✓					✓	✓	✓			✓					✓		✓	✓			
HYACINTHUS ORIENTALIS 'SNOW WHITE'			✓	✓	✓	✓					✓	✓	✓			✓				✓				✓		✓	✓
HYMENOCALLIS X FESTALIS						✓	✓	✓			✓		✓	✓			✓				✓					✓	✓
LEUCOCORYNE IXIOIDES						✓	✓	✓			✓		✓			✓					✓					✓	✓
LEUCOJUM AESTIVUM		✓	✓	✓	✓	✓	✓				✓	✓	✓	✓		✓					✓		✓			✓	✓
LILIUM REGALE	✓	✓	✓	✓	✓	✓					✓		✓				✓					✓				✓	✓

	ZONES									SOIL			LIGHT			BLOOMING SEASON				PLANT HEIGHT			NOTED FOR				
	ZONE 3	ZONE 4	ZONE 5	ZONE 6	ZONE 7	ZONE 8	ZONE 9	ZONE 10	ZONE 11	SANDY	WELL-DRAINED	MOIST	FULL SUN	PARTIAL SHADE	SHADE	SPRING	SUMMER	FALL	WINTER	UNDER 1 FOOT	1-3 FEET	OVER 3 FEET	NATURALIZING	FORCING	CONTAINER PLANT	FRAGRANCE	CUT FLOWERS
WHITE																											
LYCORIS ALBIFLORA				✓	✓	✓	✓				✓	✓	✓	✓				✓			✓					✓	✓
MUSCARI BOTRYOIDES 'ALBUM'		✓	✓	✓	✓	✓	✓			✓	✓		✓	✓		✓				✓			✓	✓		✓	✓
NARCISSUS X 'MOUNT HOOD'	✓	✓	✓	✓	✓	✓	✓				✓		✓	✓	✓	✓					✓		✓	✓		✓	✓
ORNITHOGALUM ARABICUM					✓	✓	✓				✓	✓	✓	✓		✓					✓				✓	✓	
OXALIS TRIANGULARIS SSP. PAPILIONACEA			✓	✓	✓	✓						✓	✓	✓			✓			✓					✓		
PANCRATIUM MARITIMUM					✓	✓	✓	✓		✓	✓		✓				✓	✓			✓					✓	
POLIANTHES TUBEROSA 'THE PEARL'					✓	✓				✓	✓	✓	✓				✓	✓			✓						✓
SCILLA SIBERICA 'ALBA'	✓	✓	✓	✓	✓	✓					✓	✓	✓	✓	✓	✓				✓			✓	✓			
TIGRIDIA PAVONIA 'ALBA'				✓	✓	✓	✓				✓	✓	✓				✓				✓						
TRITELEIA HYACINTHINA			✓	✓	✓					✓	✓		✓				✓	✓			✓	✓					✓
TULIPA X 'WHITE TRIUMPHATOR'		✓	✓	✓	✓	✓				✓	✓		✓			✓					✓			✓			✓
URGINEA MARITIMA					✓	✓	✓			✓	✓		✓					✓			✓						
WATSONIA X 'MRS. BULLARD'S WHITE'					✓	✓	✓				✓	✓	✓				✓				✓	✓					✓
ZANTEDESCHIA AETHIOPICA 'PERLE VON STUTTGART'					✓	✓	✓			✓	✓	✓	✓	✓		✓	✓			✓	✓				✓	✓	✓
ZEPHYRANTHES CANDIDA					✓	✓	✓			✓	✓		✓				✓	✓		✓					✓	✓	
YELLOW																											
ALLIUM MOLY 'JEANNINE'	✓	✓	✓	✓	✓	✓					✓	✓	✓	✓			✓			✓							✓
BEGONIA X TUBERHYBRIDA					✓	✓					✓	✓		✓	✓		✓	✓		✓					✓		
CANNA X GENERALIS 'PRETORIA'					✓	✓	✓	✓			✓	✓	✓				✓					✓					
CHLIDANTHUS FRAGRANS					✓	✓	✓				✓	✓	✓				✓			✓					✓	✓	✓
CLIVIA MINIATA 'AUREA'					✓	✓	✓				✓	✓		✓	✓	✓	✓			✓					✓	✓	
CROCOSMIA X CROCOSMIIFLORA 'CITRONELLA'				✓	✓	✓	✓				✓	✓	✓				✓	✓			✓	✓	✓				✓
CROCUS ANGUSTIFOLIUS 'MINOR'	✓	✓	✓	✓	✓	✓					✓		✓	✓		✓				✓			✓	✓			
ERANTHIS HYEMALIS		✓	✓	✓							✓	✓	✓	✓		✓			✓	✓			✓				
EREMURUS STENOPHYLLUS		✓	✓	✓	✓					✓	✓		✓			✓	✓					✓					✓
ERYTHRONIUM X 'CITRONELLA'	✓	✓	✓	✓	✓						✓	✓		✓	✓	✓				✓			✓				
GLADIOLUS X 'NOVA LUX'					✓	✓	✓				✓		✓				✓	✓			✓				✓	✓	✓
HYACINTHUS ORIENTALIS 'CITY OF HAARLEM'			✓	✓	✓	✓	✓				✓	✓	✓			✓				✓					✓	✓	✓
IRIS DANFORDIAE			✓	✓	✓	✓				✓	✓		✓			✓				✓						✓	
LILIUM X 'CONNECTICUT KING'	✓	✓	✓	✓	✓	✓	✓				✓		✓	✓			✓					✓					✓
LYCORIS AUREA					✓	✓	✓			✓	✓	✓	✓	✓			✓	✓			✓						✓
NARCISSUS 'DUTCH MASTER'	✓	✓	✓	✓	✓	✓	✓	✓			✓		✓	✓	✓	✓					✓		✓	✓			✓
NARCISSUS JONQUILLA	✓	✓	✓	✓	✓	✓	✓				✓		✓	✓	✓	✓				✓						✓	✓

	ZONES									SOIL			LIGHT			BLOOMING SEASON				PLANT HEIGHT			NOTED FOR				
	Zone 3	Zone 4	Zone 5	Zone 6	Zone 7	Zone 8	Zone 9	Zone 10	Zone 11	Sandy	Well-Drained	Moist	Full Sun	Partial Shade	Shade	Spring	Summer	Fall	Winter	Under 1 Foot	1-3 Feet	Over 3 Feet	Naturalizing	Forcing	Container Plant	Fragrance	Cut Flowers
YELLOW																											
RANUNCULUS 'TECOLOTE GIANTS'						✔	✔	✔		✔	✔					✔					✔				✔		✔
STERNBERGIA LUTEA			✔	✔	✔	✔	✔			✔	✔		✔					✔		✔			✔				
TIGRIDIA PAVONIA 'AUREA'				✔	✔	✔					✔	✔	✔				✔				✔		✔				
TULIPA BATALINII		✔	✔	✔	✔	✔					✔		✔			✔				✔				✔			✔
URGINEA MARITIMA					✔	✔	✔			✔	✔		✔					✔			✔				✔		
ZANTEDESCHIA X 'SOLFATARE'						✔	✔				✔	✔	✔				✔	✔			✔		✔		✔	✔	✔
ZEPHYRANTHES SULPHUREA						✔	✔	✔		✔	✔		✔					✔		✔					✔	✔	
ORANGE																											
ACHIMENES HETEROPHYLLA							✔	✔		✔	✔			✔	✔	✔				✔					✔		
BEGONIA X TUBERHYBRIDA							✔	✔		✔	✔			✔	✔		✔	✔		✔					✔		
BELAMCANDA CHINENSIS			✔	✔	✔	✔	✔	✔		✔		✔	✔			✔					✔				✔		
CANNA X GENERALIS 'PFITZER'S CHINESE CORAL'					✔	✔	✔				✔	✔	✔				✔				✔				✔		
CANNA X GENERALIS 'STADT FELLBACH'					✔	✔	✔	✔			✔	✔	✔				✔				✔						
CROCOSMIA X CROCOSMIIFLORA 'EMILY McKENZIE'					✔	✔	✔				✔	✔	✔				✔	✔			✔	✔			✔		
DAHLIA X 'ORANGE JULIUS'						✔	✔	✔		✔	✔	✔					✔	✔			✔						✔
SANDERSONIA AURANTIACA						✔	✔	✔	✔	✔	✔		✔				✔				✔						✔
TRITONIA CROCATA				✔	✔	✔				✔	✔		✔			✔	✔				✔						✔
TULIPA 'PRINCESS IRENE'		✔	✔	✔	✔	✔					✔		✔			✔				✔			✔				
WATSONIA X 'DAZZLE'					✔	✔	✔			✔	✔		✔			✔	✔				✔	✔					✔
RED																											
AMARYLLIS BELLADONNA 'CAPE TOWN'						✔	✔	✔		✔	✔	✔	✔					✔		✔				✔	✔	✔	
ANEMONE CORONARIA X 'HOLLANDIA'	✔	✔	✔	✔	✔	✔	✔			✔	✔		✔			✔				✔				✔	✔		✔
BEGONIA X TUBERHYBRIDA						✔	✔			✔	✔			✔	✔		✔	✔		✔					✔		
CANNA X GENERALIS 'BRANDYWINE'					✔	✔	✔	✔			✔	✔	✔				✔				✔						
CLIVA MINIATA 'FLAME'					✔	✔	✔	✔		✔	✔		✔		✔	✔	✔			✔					✔	✔	
COLCHICUM GIGANTEUM		✔	✔	✔	✔	✔	✔				✔		✔					✔	✔	✔			✔	✔			
CRINUM MOOREI					✔	✔	✔	✔		✔	✔	✔	✔				✔				✔	✔			✔	✔	
CROCOSMIA MASONIORUM					✔	✔	✔	✔		✔	✔		✔				✔	✔			✔	✔		✔			✔
CYCLAMEN GRAECUM				✔	✔	✔				✔	✔		✔		✔	✔			✔		✔			✔	✔	✔	
DAHLIA X 'JUANITA'						✔	✔	✔		✔	✔	✔					✔	✔			✔						✔
FRITILLARIA IMPERIALIS 'RUBRA MAXIMA'	✔	✔	✔	✔	✔					✔	✔		✔	✔		✔					✔	✔			✔		
GLADIOLUS COMMUNIS SSP. BYZANTINUS			✔	✔	✔	✔	✔	✔		✔		✔				✔				✔				✔			✔
HAEMANTHUS COCCINEUS						✔	✔	✔		✔	✔	✔	✔				✔	✔			✔					✔	
HIPPEASTRUM X 'RED LION'						✔	✔	✔	✔	✔	✔		✔			✔		✔		✔				✔	✔		

Plant characteristics table. Column groups: **ZONES** (Zone 3–Zone 11), **SOIL** (Sandy, Well-Drained, Moist), **LIGHT** (Full Sun, Partial Shade, Shade), **BLOOMING SEASON** (Spring, Summer, Fall, Winter), **PLANT HEIGHT** (Under 1 Foot, 1-3 Feet, Over 3 Feet), **NOTED FOR** (Naturalizing, Forcing, Container Plant, Fragrance, Cut Flowers).

RED

Plant	Z3	Z4	Z5	Z6	Z7	Z8	Z9	Z10	Z11	Sandy	Well-Drained	Moist	Full Sun	Partial Shade	Shade	Spring	Summer	Fall	Winter	Under 1 ft	1-3 ft	Over 3 ft	Naturalizing	Forcing	Container	Fragrance	Cut Flowers
HYACINTHUS ORIENTALIS 'HOLLYHOCK'		✓	✓	✓	✓	✓					✓		✓			✓				✓				✓		✓	✓
LILIUM PUMILUM	✓	✓	✓	✓	✓	✓					✓		✓				✓				✓						✓
LYCORIS RADIATA				✓	✓	✓	✓			✓	✓	✓	✓			✓		✓			✓						✓
NERINE SARNIENSIS 'CHERRY RIPE'				✓	✓	✓	✓	✓		✓	✓	✓	✓					✓			✓				✓		
RANUNCULUS 'TECOLOTE GIANTS'				✓	✓	✓	✓	✓		✓	✓	✓	✓			✓					✓				✓		✓
SCHIZOSTYLIS COCCINEA 'MAJOR'			✓	✓	✓	✓	✓				✓	✓	✓					✓			✓						
SPREKELIA FORMOSISSIMA				✓	✓	✓	✓	✓		✓	✓		✓				✓				✓						
TULIPA X 'PARADE'		✓	✓	✓	✓	✓					✓		✓			✓					✓			✓			✓
VALLOTA SPECIOSA							✓	✓	✓		✓	✓	✓				✓	✓			✓						✓

PINK

Plant	Z3	Z4	Z5	Z6	Z7	Z8	Z9	Z10	Z11	Sandy	Well-Drained	Moist	Full Sun	Partial Shade	Shade	Spring	Summer	Fall	Winter	Under 1 ft	1-3 ft	Over 3 ft	Naturalizing	Forcing	Container	Fragrance	Cut Flowers
ACHIMENES 'FASHIONABLE PINK'								✓	✓		✓	✓		✓	✓		✓				✓						
ALLIUM CERNUUM	✓	✓	✓	✓	✓	✓	✓				✓	✓	✓	✓			✓				✓						✓
AMARYLLIS BELLADONNA						✓	✓	✓		✓	✓	✓	✓					✓			✓			✓		✓	✓
ANEMONE BLANDA 'PINK STAR'	✓	✓	✓	✓	✓	✓					✓	✓	✓	✓		✓	✓			✓			✓	✓			✓
BEGONIA X TUBERHYBRIDA					✓	✓					✓	✓		✓	✓		✓	✓		✓					✓		
COLCHICUM AUTUMNALE		✓	✓	✓	✓	✓	✓				✓		✓					✓	✓	✓			✓				
CONVALLARIA MAJALIS 'ROSEA'	✓	✓	✓	✓	✓							✓		✓	✓	✓				✓			✓	✓		✓	✓
X CRINODONNA						✓	✓	✓			✓	✓	✓				✓			✓					✓	✓	
CYCLAMEN CILICIUM				✓	✓	✓	✓				✓	✓		✓		✓		✓	✓	✓					✓		
DAHLIA X 'CURLY QUE'					✓	✓	✓				✓	✓	✓				✓	✓				✓					✓
FREESIA X 'ROSE MARIE'					✓	✓	✓	✓		✓		✓					✓		✓		✓					✓	✓
HYACINTHOIDES HISPANICA 'ROSE QUEEN'		✓	✓	✓	✓	✓					✓	✓	✓		✓						✓		✓	✓			
HYACINTHUS ORIENTALIS 'PINK PEARL'		✓	✓	✓	✓	✓					✓	✓	✓			✓				✓				✓		✓	✓
LILIUM X 'CASA ROSA'				✓	✓	✓	✓				✓		✓				✓					✓				✓	
NERINE UNDULATA 'CRISPA'					✓	✓	✓	✓		✓	✓	✓	✓					✓			✓				✓		
OXALIS ADENOPHYLLA			✓	✓	✓	✓	✓				✓		✓				✓			✓				✓	✓		
RHODOHYPOXIS BAURII				✓	✓	✓	✓	✓		✓	✓		✓				✓			✓				✓	✓		
SCHIZOSTYLIS COCCINEA 'MRS. HEGARTY'			✓	✓	✓	✓	✓				✓	✓						✓			✓					✓	✓
SCILLA SCILLOIDES			✓	✓	✓	✓	✓			✓	✓	✓	✓	✓			✓				✓		✓	✓			
TRITONIA CROCATA 'PINK SENSATION'					✓	✓	✓	✓			✓	✓					✓	✓			✓						✓
TULIPA X 'ANGELIQUE'		✓	✓	✓	✓	✓					✓		✓			✓					✓			✓			✓
WATSONIA X 'PINK OPAL'					✓	✓	✓				✓		✓				✓	✓			✓			✓			✓
ZANTEDESCHIA X 'PINK PERSUASION'					✓	✓	✓			✓	✓	✓	✓				✓	✓			✓			✓	✓	✓	✓

Table — Bulb characteristics chart (PURPLE and BLUE)

	Z3	Z4	Z5	Z6	Z7	Z8	Z9	Z10	Z11	Sandy	Well-Drained	Moist	Full Sun	Partial Shade	Shade	Spring	Summer	Fall	Winter	Under 1 Foot	1-3 Feet	Over 3 Feet	Naturalizing	Forcing	Container Plant	Fragrance	Cut Flowers
PURPLE																											
ALLIUM AFLATUNENSE	✓	✓	✓	✓	✓	✓					✓		✓	✓		✓					✓						✓
ALLIUM X 'PURPLE SENSATION'	✓	✓	✓	✓	✓	✓					✓	✓	✓	✓		✓					✓						✓
BABIANA STRICTA 'PURPLE SENSATION'						✓	✓	✓	✓		✓		✓			✓					✓					✓	✓
BULBOCODIUM VERNUM	✓	✓	✓	✓	✓	✓				✓	✓		✓			✓			✓	✓							
CALOCHORTUS SPLENDENS			✓	✓	✓	✓	✓			✓	✓		✓				✓				✓				✓		✓
COLCHICUM AGRIPPINUM		✓	✓	✓	✓	✓	✓				✓		✓					✓		✓			✓	✓			
CORYDALIS SOLIDA			✓	✓	✓	✓					✓	✓		✓		✓				✓			✓				
CROCUS SEROTINUS SSP. CLUSII	✓	✓	✓	✓	✓						✓		✓			✓				✓			✓	✓		✓	
CROCUS SIEBERI 'HUBERT EDELSTEIN'	✓	✓	✓	✓	✓						✓		✓			✓				✓			✓				
FRITILLARIA PERSICA	✓	✓	✓	✓	✓	✓				✓	✓		✓				✓				✓		✓				
IRIS X HOLLANDICA 'PURPLE SENSATION'			✓	✓	✓	✓				✓	✓		✓				✓				✓		✓				✓
LIATRIS SPICATA	✓	✓	✓	✓	✓	✓	✓	✓		✓	✓	✓					✓					✓					✓
TULIPA BAKERI 'LILAC WONDER'		✓	✓	✓	✓	✓					✓		✓			✓				✓				✓			✓
BLUE																											
ACHIMENES X 'INDIA'							✓	✓		✓	✓			✓	✓		✓				✓				✓		
AGAPANTHUS X 'PETER PAN'							✓	✓	✓		✓	✓	✓	✓			✓				✓				✓		
ALLIUM CAERULEUM	✓	✓	✓	✓	✓	✓					✓	✓	✓			✓					✓						✓
ANEMONE BLANDA 'BLUE STAR'	✓	✓	✓	✓	✓	✓					✓	✓	✓	✓		✓				✓			✓	✓			
CAMASSIA SCILLOIDES	✓	✓	✓	✓	✓	✓					✓	✓	✓	✓		✓					✓		✓				
CHIONODOXA SARDENSIS	✓	✓	✓	✓	✓	✓					✓	✓	✓			✓				✓			✓	✓			
CROCUS SPECIOSUS 'ARTABIR'	✓	✓	✓	✓	✓						✓		✓					✓		✓			✓		✓		
DICHELOSTEMMA CONGESTUM		✓	✓	✓						✓	✓		✓			✓					✓				✓		✓
FREESIA 'ROMANY'					✓	✓	✓	✓		✓	✓		✓			✓			✓		✓					✓	✓
HYACINTHOIDES HISPANICA 'DANUBE'		✓	✓	✓	✓						✓	✓		✓		✓					✓		✓	✓			
HYACINTHUS ORIENTALIS 'BLUE MAGIC'		✓	✓	✓	✓						✓	✓		✓		✓				✓				✓		✓	✓
IPHEION UNIFLORUM 'WISLEY BLUE'		✓	✓	✓	✓	✓	✓			✓	✓		✓	✓		✓				✓			✓	✓	✓	✓	
IRIS X HOLLANDICA 'BLUE MAGIC'			✓	✓	✓	✓				✓	✓		✓				✓				✓						✓
IXIOLIRION TATARICUM				✓	✓	✓	✓			✓	✓		✓			✓	✓				✓					✓	✓
MERTENSIA PULMONARIODES	✓	✓	✓	✓	✓	✓					✓	✓	✓	✓		✓					✓		✓				
MUSCARI ARMENIACUM 'BLUE SPIKE'	✓	✓	✓	✓	✓	✓					✓	✓	✓			✓				✓			✓	✓	✓		
PUSCHKINIA SCILLOIDES VAR. LIBANOTICA	✓	✓	✓	✓	✓	✓					✓	✓	✓			✓				✓			✓				
SCILLA LITARDIEREI			✓	✓	✓	✓	✓				✓	✓	✓	✓		✓				✓			✓	✓			
TRITELEIA TUBERGENII 'QUEEN FABIOLA'				✓	✓	✓	✓			✓	✓		✓			✓	✓				✓						✓

MULTICOLORED

Plant	Zone 3	Zone 4	Zone 5	Zone 6	Zone 7	Zone 8	Zone 9	Zone 10	Zone 11	Sandy	Well-Drained	Moist	Full Sun	Partial Shade	Shade	Spring	Summer	Fall	Winter	Under 1 Foot	1-3 Feet	Over 3 Feet	Naturalizing	Forcing	Container Plant	Fragrance	Cut Flowers
ACHIMENES LONGIFLORA								✓	✓		✓	✓	✓	✓	✓	✓				✓					✓		
ALSTROEMERIA AUREA			✓	✓	✓	✓	✓	✓	✓		✓	✓	✓				✓				✓				✓		✓
ALSTROEMERIA LIGTU HYBRIDS			✓	✓	✓	✓	✓	✓			✓	✓	✓				✓				✓				✓		✓
BEGONIA X TUBERHYBRIDA							✓	✓			✓	✓		✓	✓		✓	✓			✓				✓		
BELLEVALIA PYCNANTHA			✓	✓	✓	✓	✓				✓		✓			✓				✓			✓		✓		
CALADIUM 'FANNIE MUNSON'							✓	✓			✓	✓		✓	✓		✓				✓				✓		
CALADIUM 'WHITE CHRISTMAS'							✓	✓			✓	✓		✓	✓		✓				✓				✓		
CALOCHORTUS VENUSTUS			✓	✓	✓	✓	✓			✓	✓		✓	✓			✓				✓				✓		✓
CANNA X GENERALIS 'ROSAMUND COLE'					✓	✓	✓	✓				✓	✓				✓					✓					
CROCUS SIEBERI SSP. SUBLIMIS 'TRICOLOR'	✓	✓	✓	✓	✓	✓					✓		✓			✓				✓			✓	✓	✓		
CROCUS VERNUS 'PICKWICK'	✓	✓	✓	✓	✓	✓					✓		✓			✓				✓			✓	✓			
DAHLIA X 'MICKEY'						✓	✓	✓			✓	✓	✓				✓	✓			✓						✓
FREESIA X 'BALLERINA'							✓	✓	✓	✓	✓		✓						✓	✓				✓		✓	✓
FRITILLARIA MELEAGRIS	✓	✓	✓	✓	✓	✓					✓	✓	✓	✓		✓				✓	✓						
GLADIOLUS 'PRISCILLA'				✓	✓	✓	✓				✓		✓				✓	✓			✓			✓			✓
GLORIOSA SUPERBA							✓	✓			✓	✓	✓	✓			✓				✓						✓
HABRANTHUS ROBUSTUS							✓	✓	✓		✓	✓	✓				✓	✓		✓							
HERMODACTYLUS TUBEROSUS				✓	✓	✓	✓				✓	✓	✓			✓					✓					✓	✓
HIPPEASTRUM X 'PICOTE'							✓	✓		✓	✓	✓	✓						✓	✓	✓			✓	✓		
INCARVILLEA DELAVAYI				✓	✓	✓					✓	✓	✓				✓				✓						
IRIS RETICULATA 'CANTAB'			✓	✓	✓	✓					✓	✓	✓			✓				✓				✓		✓	✓
IRIS RETICULATA 'SPRING TIME'			✓	✓	✓	✓					✓	✓	✓			✓				✓				✓		✓	✓
IXIA X 'BLUEBIRD'					✓	✓	✓				✓		✓			✓	✓			✓				✓	✓		✓
LACHENALIA BULBIFERUM							✓	✓		✓	✓	✓	✓			✓				✓							✓
LILIUM SPECIOSUM 'UCHIDA'		✓	✓	✓	✓	✓					✓		✓				✓					✓				✓	✓
NARCISSUS POETICUS	✓	✓	✓	✓	✓	✓	✓				✓		✓	✓	✓	✓					✓		✓	✓	✓		✓
NECTAROSCORDUM SICULUM				✓	✓	✓	✓				✓	✓	✓			✓						✓					
RANUNCULUS 'TECOLOTE GIANTS'						✓	✓	✓	✓	✓	✓	✓	✓			✓					✓				✓		✓
SAUROMATUM VENOSUM							✓	✓			✓	✓	✓	✓					✓						✓		
SPARAXIS TRICOLOR					✓	✓	✓				✓	✓	✓			✓	✓			✓					✓	✓	✓
TULIPA X 'FLAMING PARROT'		✓	✓	✓	✓	✓					✓		✓			✓					✓				✓		✓
VELTHEIMIA BRACTEATA							✓	✓	✓	✓	✓	✓	✓					✓	✓		✓				✓		

CHAPTER FIVE

Roses

The rose is, without question, the world's favorite flower. Praised by ancient Greek poets, buried with the pharaohs in Egypt, glorified in Roman festivals, and celebrated in every way by other cultures of antiquity from the Persians to the Chinese, roses have captivated hearts and imaginations for thousands of years. And over the millennia this most beloved of blooms has been cultivated and crossbred so extensively that the number of varieties is now far beyond counting.

With such an abundance, there is a rose for every gardener, for any garden. Many gardeners avoid roses, believing they require too much time and nurturing, but in fact there are hundreds that perform beautifully with little fuss—including the 'Baronne Prévost', 'Blush Noisette', and 'Madame Isaac Pereire' gracing a stone wall in the South Carolina garden at right. The truth is that nearly any rose will flourish as long as the climate and other basic conditions are to its liking. Finding the right place in your garden for what is often called the queen of flowers involves understanding the versatility of roses. By choosing wisely from the many types of roses profiled in this chapter, you'll be rewarded with a magnificent show of blooms.

The Features of a Rose

A rose is *not* just a rose. Rather, roses are a huge clan whose members vary widely in flower color, fragrance, size, and form; plant height and habit; and foliage texture and hue. Most have thorns or prickles, but a few don't. Many flower for months, while others produce one spectacular burst of blooms each year. Some put on a winter show with colorful ripe fruits, and a few grow a mossy coat on their buds—indeed, the list of individual quirks is nearly endless. How the *Rosa* population came to be so diverse is a story that begins in antiquity and will likely continue for as long as gardeners grow what one poet called the queen of flowers.

A Cast of Thousands

In the beginning—tens of millions of years ago—there were what are now called species roses. These wild roses are the ancestors of all the varieties available today, which number into the thou-

sands. Wind and insects transferred the pollen of one type of rose to another, creating entirely new varieties through natural crossing. Other new roses have come into being through spontaneous mutation; these roses, called sports, are different in some way—usually flower color, number of petals, or plant habit—from their parent.

However, the vast majority of today's roses are not the work of nature but of human hands. For centuries, in painstaking efforts to combine the best traits of various roses, botanists, horticulturists, and passionate gardeners have been crossing—or hybridizing—different varieties in a ceaseless quest for ever greater beauty.

All hybrids and their sports can be grouped into two general categories—old garden roses and modern roses—according to when they first appeared. The dividing line is the year 1867, the official date of introduction of the first modern rose. Called the hybrid tea, it set a new standard of beauty for roses and is the one most people envi-

FOUR FLOWER FORMS
As illustrated below, single blooms produce one open layer of 5 to 8 petals. Semidoubles also open wide, framing the flower's center with two layers of overlapping petals ranging in number from 8 or 9 petals to as many as 25. Double blooms have 21 to 50 petals that unfold from a pointed bud, and very double blooms seem to burst with anywhere from 50 to 200 petals.

Single   *Semidouble*   *Double*   *Very Double*

SPREADING
These roses have long, leafy canes that grow horizontally over the ground; the plant is much wider than its typical height of 1 to 3 feet.

UPRIGHT
Sometimes called bushes, roses with upright habits have canes that sprout few leaves but produce large blooms at the tips. Taller than they are wide, they usually reach a height of between 3 and 6 feet.

sion when they think of a rose. Unfortunately, some rose varieties—including most hybrid teas—are too tender for very cold climates, are vulnerable to an array of pests and diseases, or need substantial amounts of pruning and other care. Lovely as they are, these plants have given all roses a reputation for being difficult to grow. And yet there are many healthy, hardy, and even low-maintenance beauties as well, including species roses, several antique types, and a number of modern ones that defy trouble while representing the rose family in all its gorgeous variety.

The Blooms

Roses bloom in a rainbow of colors—all shades of pink, red, white, yellow, and orange, and exotic hues of apricot and mauve. But color is not the only distinguishing feature of the rose: The bloom itself can also take a number of forms. Depending on how many petals they have, how the petals open, and how much they reveal of the pistils and stamens at the center of the flower, rose blossoms are categorized as single, semidouble, double, or very double *(opposite)*.

The season when the flowers start blooming and how long the bloom season lasts also vary from rose to rose. Some produce one flush in spring or summer that lasts for a few weeks, then rest until the following year. Others, called repeating or remontant roses, can put out flowers continually from spring or summer through fall, or in a succession of waves with respites in between.

Growth Habits in Roses

Although the bloom is what the word *rose* usually calls to mind, roses are, of course, complete plants—woody shrubs that, like their flowers, also come in many shapes and sizes. They can restrict themselves to several inches in height or grow stems, called canes, as long as 50 feet. Their habits, as illustrated below, include spreading ground covers, upright and full bushes and shrubs, treelike "standards," and vertical climbing roses. Miniatures, a group of modern roses, don't have a distinct habit; rather, they can be round or upright or even climbing—habits found in their larger relatives, but on a smaller scale.

CLIMBING
Most very long caned roses, classified as either stiff-caned "climbers" or more pliable "ramblers," grow from 8 to 25 feet or more and should be secured to a fence, trellis, wall, or other support.

FULL
Graceful with leafy, arching canes, these shrubby roses are handsome even when they are not in bloom. They can be as wide as they are tall, although larger plants—reaching up to 10 feet or so—don't achieve a girth equal to their height.

STANDARD
Not the work of nature, standards are roses whose buds are grafted by plant growers onto a separate, leafless trunk to imitate the habit of a tree. The leafy, blooming rose has either a lollipop shape or a loose, cascading one, depending on the variety.

The Wild Species Roses

Long before there were gardens and gardeners, there were roses. These wild roses—about 200 distinct species of the genus *Rosa*—evolved throughout the Northern Hemisphere, and over thousands of years each has become as unique as its place of origin. Many grow rampantly, while others stay small and neat; some are at home in extreme cold, and others thrive in hot climates, sandy soil, or swamps. Even their fragrances are individually sweet, spicy, or earthy. What defines species roses is their ability to reproduce true versions of themselves from self-pollinated seed that ripens in fruits known as hips. Hybrids, by contrast, don't breed true from self-pollinated seed.

Besides their reproductive ability, perhaps the only other feature shared by most wild roses is flowers that are single in form. These cheerfully open-faced blooms usually range from pale pink to deep purplish red. *R. rugosa,* which is exceptionally hardy and nearly impervious to most diseases, and *R. eglanteria,* known as the sweetbrier or eglantine rose, are two of the most popular. Some wild roses differ from the majority by being white or yellow, and a handful have sported to semidouble or double-bloomed forms. *R. banksiae banksiae* and *R. banksiae lutea,* for example, are beautiful white and yellow double-bloom forms of *R. banksiae.* Rugosa roses include the original dark pink species and its sports *R. rugosa alba,* whose blooms are white, and *R. rugosa rubra,* whose mauve flowers are larger than its relatives'.

Rugosas begin blooming in spring and produce

Rosa rugosa, grown as a hedge, separates a trim lawn from the wooded area behind it on this Washington State property. Deep pink petals surrounding a creamy center bloom repeatedly throughout the season, offering months of pleasing contrast with the bright green foliage.

their blossoms continually into fall. But most species roses, like most other flowering shrubs, bloom just once during the season, putting on a display that can last up to several weeks. Species from warmer climates tend to bloom earlier than those native to regions where frequent spring frosts can damage a plant in flower. *R. banksiae*, from the temperate regions of China, blooms in early spring, for example; the eglantine rose, from Europe, flowers before midsummer; and North American *R. carolina* generally blooms anywhere between early summer and late summer.

Although wild roses typically don't produce blossoms through the entire growing season, they often make up for the lack of blooms with interesting foliage. *R. rugosa*'s rounded foliage is a lustrous medium green with the appearance of textured leather, while the soft green leaves of *R. spinosissima*—a small, hardy bush known as the Scotch rose—are daintily edged, giving the leaves a lacelike quality. The foliage of many species also turns attractive colors in the fall. *R. virginiana* takes on shades of scarlet, orange, and yellow, whereas the mountain rose, *R. woodsii,* and *R. gymnocarpa* from the American West turn red-orange and bright yellow. European *R. glauca* doesn't wait until fall to produce colorful foliage; the red tint of its leaves deepens during the growing season, becoming a smoky purple by autumn.

Stamina and Vigor

Despite their differences, all species roses share a certain air of wildness: They simply look as though they can take care of themselves—and they can. In the process of adapting over millennia to their environments, these roses became completely self-reliant, needing no chemicals to ward off disease and pests, no protection from winter cold, no fertilizer or watering or soil amendments—in short, no gardener's help.

Known as the eglantine or sweetbrier rose, R. eglanteria produces charming five-petaled blooms amid glossy apple-scented foliage (below). An ideal hedge rose, it is 8 or more feet tall, has a bushy habit, and has thorny canes to discourage intruders.

The Troubled Legacy of *Rosa foetida*

Species roses are generally the most resilient plants in the genus, and the wild Iranian rose *R. foetida* is no exception. Having learned to survive in the hot, dry climate of its native land, this rose can stand up to anything that harsh sun and whipping winds can dish out. However, because *R. foetida* was never forced to defend itself against the most common rose disease—the fungus black spot, which thrives in moist conditions—it never developed a resistance to it.

The solution is not as simple as banning *R. foetida* from your garden, though. Its blooms are a rich golden color—a trait that was rare and highly prized during the 19th century, when rose breeders were frantically crossing species and hybrids in a quest for new colors, among other qualities. In 1893 a French breeder named Joseph Pernet-Ducher produced a brilliant yellow rose using *R. foetida persiana*, a double-flowered form of the species. He named his prize 'Soleil d'Or'—sun of gold. 'Soleil d'Or' was then used to breed 'Rayon d'Or', the first yellow hybrid tea.

As might be expected, other hybridizers seized upon Pernet-Ducher's creations. The result was a revolution in the spectrum of modern roses: Most of today's yellow, orange, salmon, apricot, and flaming red-orange roses owe their brilliance to *R. foetida*. Unfortunately, along with their beautiful color, most of them—especially hybrid teas—inherited *R. foetida*'s vulnerability to black spot. If you live anywhere but the driest climate and you want healthy roses without the help of chemical fungicides, your best bet is to choose a rose without *R. foetida* in its ancestry. But if your heart is set on a yellow rose, experts suggest an unusually resistant hybrid tea called 'Elina', the miniature 'Rise 'n' Shine', a medium yellow climber named 'Golden Showers', or the shrubby 'Sunsprite'.

Rosa foetida persiana

With such independence, wild roses make gloriously easy-care additions to your landscape, doing the work of hiding the chain-link fence or standing sentinel at the far reaches of the yard where a hose won't reach. Most grow so large that they require more room than a bed or border has to offer. *R. rugosa,* which reaches a height of at least 8 feet and tolerates temperatures as low as -40° F, can serve as a thick hedge where space allows, spreading quickly into wide colonies by putting out new shoots from its roots. The super-long canes of *R. banksiae,* extending more than 25 feet, can be used to drape a shed or other structure you want to dress up with little fuss. And dense, 8-foot-high thickets of pink *R. palustris* do especially well in wet areas, where other roses fail—a trait that earned it the nickname swamp rose.

Native Roses

A number of species grow freely in North America because they originated here. If you'd like to grow roses in a wildflower garden, large natives such as *R. palustris* and the Virginia rose, *R. virginiana,* are perfectly suited. And although most species are amply sized, there are a few natives that are so compact and refined you can put them in a formal border. One of the loveliest of these, dark pink *R. carolina* (the pasture rose), usually grows to a height of only 3 feet. *R. carolina* looks fragile and sounds as if it might be a tender plant from the South, but its native range—the area it spans in the wild—stretches all the way from Nova Scotia west to Minnesota and south to Texas and Florida.

At home as far north as southern Ontario, pink-flowered *R. setigera* is the only North American native climber, with canes growing more than 16 feet. You can train it up a support or let it grow horizontally as a low-maintenance ground cover. Another native that has spread widely throughout the United States and Canada is *R. nitida,* a short, dainty shrub that produces deep pink blooms and, in the fall, crimson foliage. The state flower of Georgia, *R. laevigata*—also called the Cherokee rose—is actually from China but has established itself so thoroughly in the southern United States that most people think of its charming, floppy white spring flowers as native wildflowers.

New Roses from Wild Blood

Nonnative species like the Cherokee rose that thrive and spread without assistance are said by experts to have naturalized. Species roses some-

times come from environments so trying that when they take root in more hospitable conditions they don't simply naturalize but run rampant. Notorious among these is *R. multiflora,* from the poor mountain soils of Japan and Korea. This species can take over your landscape and should be avoided, but its boundless energy has been put to good use by rose hybridizers, who have used it in the breeding of most ramblers and a number of other modern varieties.

R. multiflora is also used as a rootstock. Rose growers often graft the buds of one rose onto the roots of another, combining the beauty of the former with the vigor or stamina of the latter. Multiflora is one of the most popular rootstocks, supporting plants that are less aggressive than it is but that are quick to grow and reach maturity.

This species is not the only one with qualities that appeal to hybridizers. In the early 20th century, Dr. William Van Fleet produced climbers using the vigorous, disease-resistant Asian *R.*

wichuraiana; the most famous of his cultivated varieties bears his own name: 'Dr. W. Van Fleet'. And in 1952, German hybridizer Wilhelm Kordes created a new species by crossing *R. wichuraiana* with resilient *R. rugosa.* The resulting *R. kordesii* has been used by a number of breeders to parent a group of exceptionally healthy and hardy modern hybrids called kordesii shrubs. The cold-hardy Explorer series from Canada, for example, includes some particularly sturdy kordesiis bearing the names of famous explorers, including 'Champlain' and 'John Cabot'.

At Iowa State University, plant scientist Griffith Buck has used the petite, bristly *R. arkansana* and a Siberian species to breed a series of Dr. Buck roses, which can take extreme temperature changes. The Arkansas rose, whose range stretches from Texas to Canada, has also been used by horticulturists in Canada to breed Parkland (Morden) roses, which are prized for their hardiness, resistance to disease, and long bloom periods.

The 2-inch-wide pink blooms of North American native R. carolina—the pasture rose—can be seen in clusters as well as one to a stem on this bush in New York. The hardy plant waits until late spring or early summer, long after the danger of frost is past, to put on its floral show. In fall, the foliage glows a warm orange and yellow.

Antique Roses

In the 17th century, Dutch and Flemish artists painted roses with what appear to be impossibly opulent, heavy-headed blooms. Such flowers were not figments of the imagination but realistic re-creations of the most popular rose varieties cultivated at the time. These are the European antique roses, early hybrids whose luxuriant blossoms differ noticeably from both free-spirited species roses and the elegantly tight-budded modern varieties that would begin to emerge in the 1860s.

The antique roses, also known as old garden roses, are among the most fragrant of all roses; some of the most redolent are listed below. Exceptionally large bloomed, many antique roses have their petals arranged in whorls—a pattern known as quartering—and their full, sometimes cupped shape lends them an old-fashioned look that sits well on the graceful shrubs. If nostalgia, beauty, and perfume are not reason enough to grow them, antique roses are also less demanding and less fragile than many of the modern varieties.

Antique roses are divided into several groups, or classifications, on the basis of their ancestry. In the family of European old garden roses, the most ancient is the gallica, which was cultivated by the Greeks and Romans for its beauty, perfume, and medicinal qualities. Noted for their exceptional cold and heat tolerance, disease resistance, and lack of prickles, gallica shrubs typically grow 3 to 5 feet tall and sprout dark green foliage. The flowers, in shades of palest pink to mauve, range from single to very double. Most are semidouble, however, including the first known gallica, dark pink 'Apothecary's Rose', and its striped sport 'Rosa Mundi'.

Gallicas figure in the ancestry of the exotically scented damasks, which are also hardy and fuss free. Unlike gallicas, though, damasks have thorny canes, and the shrubs are taller—usually 5 to 6 feet, with gray-green, sometimes downy foliage. Their semidouble to very double flowers bloom in clusters, mostly in shades of clear pink, and erupt only once each summer—except for 'Autumn Damask', a renegade whose blossoms repeat in the fall.

Fairer still are the albas; this class of antique roses blooms in shades of pale pink and pink-tinged white. Usually 4 to 6 feet tall, upright in habit, tough, and hardy, albas are among the easiest roses to grow because they are supremely tolerant of less than ideal conditions, including shade.

A fourth class, the centifolias, were once believed by rose fanciers to have a heritage as old as the gallicas, but 20th-century plant scientists have determined that most were developed by Dutch hybridizers in the 1600s. Centifolias are open, thorny shrubs that need a sunny site in the garden to keep their foliage free of fungal disease. They make up for this shortcoming, though, by producing of some of the roundest and largest very double flowers in all of rosedom, earning them the nickname cabbage roses. The flower color spectrum of these roses is broad, ranging from white to crimson to mauve. As the fragrant blooms open,

Highly Scented Antique Roses

'Alba Semi-plena'
'Baronne Prévost'
'Boule de Neige'
'Camaieux'
'Cardinal de Richelieu'
'Catherine Mermet'
'Celestial'
'Celsiana'
'Communis'
'Complicata'
'Duchesse de Brabant'
'Fantin-Latour'
'Félicité Parmentier'
'Ispahan'
'Königin
   von Dänemark'
'Lamarque'
'La Reine Victoria'
'Louise Odier'
'Madame Alfred
   Carrière'
'Madame Hardy'
'Madame Isaac
   Pereire'
'Madame Plantier'
'Maman Cochet'
'Marchesa Boccella'
'Mrs. B. R. Cant'

'Nastarana'
'Paul Neyron'
'Petite de Hollande'
'Reine des Violettes'
'Rêve d'Or'
'Rosa Mundi'
'Rose de Rescht'
'Sombreuil'
'Souvenir
   de la Malmaison'
'Tuscany'
'Variegata di Bologna'
'Zéphirine Drouhin'

'Fantin-Latour'

Deep pink very double blossoms of the bourbon 'Louise Odier' add an old-world flair to this Colorado garden in early summer. Pale yellow 'Windrush', a hardy modern rose; the leggy magenta herb Hesperis matronalis; and petite white blooms of Campanula latifolia 'Alba' surround the old rose centerpiece.

Hips: The Fruit of the Rose

If the blooms of certain roses are allowed to fade on the plant and lose their petals, fleshy fruits called hips will form. As they ripen and color, the hips produce a vivid show in fall and winter that's almost as delightful as the flowers in summer. Generally, the roses that set hips are most likely to have single or semidouble blooms. This is because flowers with fewer petals have an easier time self-pollinating—the first step in hip formation. Species roses and the single and semidouble gallicas, albas, and damasks have some of the most beautiful hips, whereas most centifolias, which are dense with petals, don't set them at all.

Hips are as varied as the roses that produce them. Some are round like the red globes of 'Apothecary's Rose', some are pear shaped, such as those of 'Alba Semi-plena', and some—like those of *R. moschata*—appear in sprays of tiny fruits. Their colors range from the bright orange of the gallica 'Complicata' to the glorious crimson of *R. rugosa (above)* to deep wine and black. This lovely late-season treat also occurs on some modern roses, including many hybrid rugosa shrubs. A number of moss roses set hips as well, and when they do the fruits are usually covered with the same moss that cloaks the buds. The large red hips of *R. laevigata* are bristly, and the oval fruits of the eglantine rose are abundant and especially long-lasting, asserting their bright red color throughout the winter.

Rose hips are edible as well as beautiful—and a rich source of nutrition. During World War II, for example, when citrus fruits were scarce in Britain, rose hips were found to have a vitamin C content 400 percent greater than that of oranges. In 1941 over 200 tons of the bitter red fruit of the country's ubiquitous *Rosa canina* were collected and made into syrup for civilian and military consumption.

they change from cup shaped to flat, finally revealing a button eye.

In the late 1600s, a centifolia sport was discovered with a curious feature that gave rise to a new class: the mosses. This sport had a unique coating on its buds and stems that looked like moss but was actually a layer of soft, enlarged glands that released a sticky, fragrant substance when touched. 'Communis', as the rose is known, has mossy buds that open to intensely sweet, rich pink quartered blossoms. Damask roses produced moss sports as well, and in the 1800s other varieties were bred.

Repeat-Blooming Varieties

In the Orient, where the tradition of gardens is far older than in the West, roses have probably been cultivated for longer than 5,000 years. As trade between Europe and Asia grew in the 18th century, it was not long before roses from the East reached the gardens of the West. This happened in the final years of the 1700s, when a few hybrids of *R. chinensis* were smuggled into England from China.

Shorter than other shrub roses and bearing single or, at most, double blossoms, the China roses weren't as hardy as their European counterparts. However, they possessed a trait that most European roses lacked: the ability to bloom not once but continuously throughout the season. As might be expected, rose enthusiasts immediately began mating the new arrivals, including 'Old Blush', with the European roses and spawning thousands of new varieties—and several new classifications.

Around 1800, repeat-blooming portland roses, named for England's Duchess of Portland, emerged in France. Though small in stature for an antique rose—only 3 to 4 feet tall—portland shrubs are neat and round, bearing semidouble to very double flowers in a range of colors. The original 'Duchess of Portland' has a semidouble red bloom, while the later 'Rose du Roi' has double blooms that are a bright red-shaded violet.

The French also introduced the bourbons, a class of everbloomers that combine the China imports with damasks. Taller than portlands and laxer in habit, most bourbon shrubs reach a height of 5 to 6 feet. Some have sported climbers, such as the 12-foot 'Queen of Bourbons'. All bear large, cupped flowers that bloom into the fall, perfuming the air. Deep pink 'Madame Isaac Pereire' is perhaps the most powerfully fragrant of all roses.

Tea roses, so named for their scent of fresh tea leaves, also trace their roots to China. Probably a cross between small, neat *R. chinensis* and a large evergreen species, *R. gigantea,* the original tea was shipped to Europe in the early 19th century and used to breed repeat bloomers endowed with its refined foliage and long canes. 'Sombreuil', a very double white climbing tea, reaches 8 feet or more. Although 'Sombreuil' is a little hardier than others of its class, tea roses are generally tender plants that fare best in the gardens of the South.

On the other side of the Atlantic, John Champneys, a plantation owner in South Carolina, created a new rose in the early 1800s by crossing a China variety with a form of the musk-scented species *R. moschata.* Noisettes, as the class came to be called, produce clusters of roses on canes that stretch to 15 feet or so, making them ideal for training on arbors and walls. 'Madame Alfred Carrière', a very double pale pink rose, climbs to 20 feet. Not particularly hardy, noisettes decrease in vigor the farther north they are grown, but they thrive in southern gardens and require little pruning.

Between 1840 and 1900, hybridizers engaged in a riot of pollen exchange using all of the European and new classes, creating thousands of antique roses whose genealogy was more complicated and confused than ever before. Most of the results were repeat bloomers called hybrid perpetuals. These roses were bred for huge, fragrant, upward-facing blooms that would win prizes in floral competitions. Unfortunately, breeders tended to neglect the habit and appearance of the shrub in favor of its flower, and as a result many hybrid perpetuals failed to catch on with gardeners. Most of these roses are no longer available. However, some hybrid perpetuals did inherit a pleasing habit along with a large bloom, and they are still grown today. 'Paul Neyron' shrubs, for example, are neat, sturdy, and disease resistant, producing intensely fragrant, rich pink, very double flowers that can measure an astounding 7 inches across.

Found Roses

Remnants of the old rose revolution are continually being discovered, growing unattended in fields, gardens, parks, cemeteries, and other public and private places on both sides of the Atlantic. Orphaned, without records or memory of their lineage, these plants are called found or mystery roses and given unofficial names while horticulturists attempt to identify them. As beautiful as their pedigreed counterparts, these nameless, persevering old roses come in all possible colors and habits. Many are propagated by specialty growers for sale through mail-order catalogs and are exceptionally reliable, having survived for what may be a century with no one's loving care.

Roses with Attractive Hips

'Alba Semi-plena'
'Altissimo'
'Ballerina'
'Belle Poitevine'
'Blanc Double
    de Coubert'
'Bonica'
'Buff Beauty'
'Carefree Beauty'
'Complicata'
'Delicata'
'Dortmund'
'Frau Dagmar
    Hartopp'
'Hansa'
'Max Graf'
'Nastarana'
'Old Blush'
'Penelope'
R. eglanteria
R. glauca
'Rosa Mundi'
R. palustris
R. rugosa alba
R. rugosa rubra
'Rugosa Magnifica'
'Will Scarlet'

Modern Roses

Eighteen sixty-seven was a watershed year in rosedom. It was then that a French hybridizer named Jean-Baptiste Guillot discovered growing in his experimental beds a rose that was a cross between an antique tea and a hybrid perpetual. This flower was so different from antique varieties that it not only established a new classification but also ushered in the modern era of rose breeding. That rose, 'La France', is officially recognized as the first hybrid tea.

Since that time, as plant science has grown increasingly sophisticated, other classes have made their debuts, and each of these modern types exemplifies some combination of the finest qualities of habit, hardiness, health, and beauty from all members of the genus *Rosa*. And yet, the first of the modern age still remains America's most popular rose.

Pink cups of 'Simplicity'—a vigorous floribunda with a full, relaxed habit—bloom freely among yellow and lilac irises, white Hesperis matronalis, indigo spikes of annual larkspur, pink phlox, and cheerful purple-eyed pansies in this informal garden on the Connecticut seashore.

Hybrid Teas

Unlike the plump buds of antique roses that open wide in maturity, the hybrid tea is at its peak in lean youth, the pointed bud of its semidouble or double bloom only partly unfurled. The rose blends the best features of its ancestors: From the bred-to-show hybrid perpetual it inherited superb large flowers, and from the tea parent came refined form and foliage and long, straight stems for cutting. China rose traits contributed by both parents gave the hybrid tea flowers that were everblooming.

With the introduction in the 1890s of vivid yellow blooms *(page 132),* the color spectrum—once mainly pink, white, and rosy red—gained a whole new dimension. Rose breeders envisioned vibrant new colors coupled with elegant flower

form. Their goal was to develop the ultimate display flower: a single large, perfect bloom borne at the top of a long, straight stem. Indeed, hybrid teas—many of which are listed on page 140—are ideal for cutting and showing off in arrangements.

In striving for the perfect bloom, however, breeders continued to pay little mind to how the overall plant looked or fared in the garden. Many varieties of these long-stemmed beauties—which number in the thousands—grow on bushes that lack the grace of the European old garden roses, a minor quibble if your desire is to display the showy blooms indoors. They also tend to be short on the admirable sturdiness of species roses and require more of the care and maintenance tasks outlined in Chapter 8 of this book.

Hybrid teas aren't as renowned for fragrance as the intoxicating old gallicas and damasks, but there are several that exude wonderful perfumes. A number in the class have even received the very selective James Alexander Gambel Award for Fragrant Roses, named for an English rose lover who donated funds in 1961 to encourage and reward

Musk Roses, Old and New

Like cousins many times removed, *Rosa moschata*—the original musk rose—and a group of modern shrub roses known as hybrid musks, which got their name primarily because of a rich, musky dimension to their scent, are only distantly related. *R. moschata*, a species that probably originated in southern Europe, appears in plant texts from 16th- and 17th-century England. These old sources describe the rose as a climber growing to 10 or 12 feet, with small, neat leaves, and either single or double flowers with the scent of musk. The texts also state that the rose flowers in late summer to autumn. The hybrid musks, for their part, are the progeny of teas, Chinas, hybrid teas, noisettes, and a couple of ramblers, all of which were crossed by an English priest at the beginning of the 20th century. Only the noisette part of their legacy contains *R. moschata* blood.

Hybrid musks are versatile garden shrubs that come in a variety of habits. Some, such as the upright and mannerly pink-flowered 'Erfurt' *(below)*, are dense and useful as hedging, while others are weeping shrubs or climbers. Apricot-colored 'Clytemnestra', for example, has long canes that can be trained on a support. Prolific bloomers in other shades of white to pink to scarlet, hybrid musks put out voluminous clusters of single or semidouble flowers in spring and fall, with scattered flowers in between. Best of all, they are somewhat shade tolerant and highly resistant to fungus diseases.

Sometime, probably in the late 18th century, a rampant summer-flowering rose was misidentified as the musk rose, and the error was perpetuated for over a century. But the true species has since been identified with the help of the old sources, and today both the old musk rose and a number of the misleadingly named hybrid musks are available for the garden. Although they have little in common, what they do share is an uncommon earthy-sweet perfume.

'Chrysler Imperial'

the introduction of scented roses. These hybrid tea winners include 'Crimson Glory', deep red 'Chrysler Imperial', rich yellow 'Sutter's Gold', two-toned red-and-white 'Double Delight', scarlet-orange 'Fragrant Cloud', multicolored 'Granada', and satiny pink 'Tiffany'.

The Next Generations

Following close on the heels of the hybrid tea was another of Guillot's creations, the polyanthas. Meaning "many-flowered," polyanthas are the offspring of a dwarf China rose and *R. multiflora,* a genetic commingling that produced clusters of small, everblooming double flowers on low, compact bushes. 'Cécile Brunner', for example, erupts in clusters of small, beautifully shaped pink blooms from spring to fall on billowing 4-foot shrubs.

Polyanthas are quite hardy, but their flowers are tiny compared with those of the hybrid teas. In an effort to combine the best qualities of the two classes, breeders in Denmark began crossing polyanthas with large-flowered hybrid teas, which are generally too tender to be grown successfully in the unforgiving Scandinavian climate. The result of the

Danes' efforts, and the efforts of hybridizers who followed them, was the floribundas.

Floribundas have fuller habits, enabling them to serve gracefully in landscaping, and they continually produce clusters of medium-sized flowers over a long season. The blooms can be single, semidouble, or double. 'Escapade', for instance, has a mauve-and-white semidouble blossom; ruffly dark pink 'Betty Prior' is a single; and the white blooms of 'Iceberg' are double and open flat.

Inevitably, hybrid teas and floribundas were crossed, thereby spawning, in 1954, the grandiflora class. Like the floribundas, grandifloras bear flowers in clusters rather than one to a stem, but they have the size and formal shape of hybrid tea blooms and grow on longer canes. Grandiflora shrubs, most of which are about as hardy as hybrid teas, can grow over 6 feet tall. The first grandiflora, 'Queen Elizabeth', sets an almost impossible standard in beauty: It produces abundant sprays of long-stemmed cotton-candy pink blooms on a vigorous shrub that can grow 10 feet tall. Prune it to 6 feet, however, to show it to best advantage.

Miniature and Climbing Varieties

If your bed or border isn't large enough to accommodate 6-foot bushes, or if you garden in containers on a patio or balcony, you can take advantage of the many beautiful roses that come in small sizes. Most of these plants, classified as miniatures, range from a few inches in height to just over 2 feet. All boast handsome small-scale foliage and flowers that come in a wide variety of shapes and colors.

In short, miniatures do all the things that other roses do. 'Popcorn', for example, has semidouble 1-inch white blooms centered on golden "kernels"; these profuse blossoms are borne on upright 15-inch bushes. The 24-inch 'Paper Doll' covers itself with high-centered hybrid-tea-like blossoms in pale salmon; 'Mossy Gem', with magenta pompoms, is a diminutive version of a moss rose; and 'Jeanne Lajoie', with pretty pink double blooms, is a miniature climber that exceeds 4 feet in height.

Climbing roses, both large and miniature, are simply those that have the long canes needed to

Roses for Cold Climates

'Belle Poitevine'	'Jens Munk'
'Blanc Double	'John Cabot'
de Coubert'	'John Franklin'
'Celestial'	'Linda Campbell'
'Champlain'	'Madame Plantier'
'Delicata'	'Nearly Wild'
'Dortmund'	R. rugosa alba
'F. J. Grootendorst'	R. rugosa rubra
'Frau Dagmar	'Roseraie de l'Hay'
Hartopp'	'Rugosa Magnifica'
'Great Maiden's Blush'	'The Fairy'
'Hansa'	'Thérèse Bugnet'
'Henry Hudson'	'William Baffin'

'William Baffin'

make a vertical display on a wall or freestanding support. It's not unusual for a bush or shrub rose in any of several classes to have a climbing sport, often identified by the abbreviation "Cl." The polyanthas 'Pinkie', 'Cécile Brunner', and 'The Fairy' all have long-caned forms, as do the China rose 'Old Blush' and the hybrid teas 'Peace' and 'Crimson Glory'. Such roses are like their parents in hardiness and disease resistance as well as in flower color and form.

Many long-caned varieties are not sported versions of their bushy parents but individuals in their own right. Those in the class officially termed climbers, or large-flowered climbers, are usually everblooming, producing an array of flowers ranging from the blood red singles of 'Altissimo' to the lemony double blooms of 'Golden Showers'. Classed separately from large-flowered climbers are ramblers, which, like pink 'Tausendschön', usually have *R. wichuraiana* and *R. multiflora* in their blood. Rambling roses bloom in clusters once per season, and their canes grow faster and are thinner and more supple than those of their climber cousins.

The Catchall Class: Modern Shrubs

Many of the most recent modern roses, which often have elaborately mixed parentage, can't easily be grouped into one class or another and are simply termed modern shrubs. Their flowers come in all forms and in all colors of the rose rainbow, and the plants can be low growing, upright, full, or even short climbers. What many have in common is foliage and habits so attractive that they warrant a place in the garden even when the shrub is not in bloom.

A number of modern shrubs mingle *R. rugosa* with polyanthas, teas, and other classes, even other rose species. These roses, collectively termed hybrid rugosas, are more refined than their namesake species, and yet many retain its iron constitution. 'Frau Dagmar Hartopp', for example, is a handsome, compact 3-foot shrub with clove-scented pink flowers that enjoys exceptional disease resistance. 'Agnes' bears yellow very double blooms on upright 4- to 6-foot bushes that are extremely winter hardy. Like other modern shrubs, including hybrid musks *(page 139)*, hybrid rugosas need minimal pruning.

In Great Britain, the hybridizer David Austin has bred dozens of modern shrub varieties—known unofficially as English roses—specifically to capture the fragrant, lush, delicately colored blooms of old European garden roses in a repeat-blooming bush. Among the best known are 'Graham Thomas', a large bush with yellow double flowers, and 'Heritage', whose cupped blooms are the palest of pinks with a citrus scent. Both have proven themselves reliable bloomers and healthy in cooler regions on the American side of the Atlantic.

Where the emphasis in breeding the English roses has been on combining old garden charm with modern hybrid vigor and bloom, Meidiland roses from the House of Meilland in France have been bred for low maintenance above all else. Their blossoms are relatively small, but they repeat bloom, and the shrubs are exceptionally hardy and require little or no pruning.

The foliage on the Meidiland roses is also extremely disease resistant, which is one of the qualities that hybridizers rank high on their list of desired qualities in the newest roses. In Germany, hybridizer Werner Noack spent many years developing 'Flower Carpet', which is nearly disease-proof, before its North American introduction in 1995. A low, bushy shrub, 'Flower Carpet' also puts on a very long floral show, blooming for 5 to 10 months, depending upon climate.

For gardeners in cold climates, species and old European varieties have always been excellent choices because of their hardiness. Joining the list in the modern era are the Dr. Buck roses, the Canadian Explorers and Parklands, and the kordesiis—all of them bred specifically to cope with extremes in temperature.

Selecting the Best Roses for Your Garden

When selecting roses for your garden, a little research at the outset may prevent many pounds of chemical cure and a great deal of frustration later on. Informing yourself about which plants will do best in your particular climate and conditions makes all the difference between a garden full of beautiful, healthy roses and one in which they have to struggle to survive.

First, eliminate those roses that are obviously not suited to your climate. If you live in a region where winter temperatures dip below -10° F, you're limited to species, antique, and modern shrubs bred specifically for cold climates. If you garden in the hot South, the Chinas, teas, and noisettes will perform beautifully. Although they produce flowers most abundantly when the daytime temperature is between 70° and 80° F, these roses continue to bloom in midsummer heat.

In the Midwest, where cold winters alternate with hot summers, you'll need a rose that tolerates both extremes. Consider a once-blooming rose, such as a European antique, which will give you a magnificent show in early summer before the heat arrives—soaring temperatures tend to stifle the flowering of most everbloomers. But if a repeat bloomer is your desire, choose a hardy modern shrub; some floribundas, grandifloras, and hybrid teas will also do well as long as they are protected through the winter *(page 241)*.

In cold regions you may want to purchase roses that are growing on their own roots instead of on grafted ones, because own-root roses survive harsh winters better. When canes of grafted roses die back during extreme cold, you may get new growth only from the rootstock and not from the rose variety you purchased the plant for. In Florida and other areas where plants never go dormant, roses grown on the roots of *R. fortuniana* do especially well.

In the Pacific Northwest, where the rust fungus is a particular problem, avoid rugosas and their hybrids. Elsewhere, though, rugosas are practically immune to diseases, and they perform especially well in the sandy soil and salt spray of the northeastern Atlantic region. Hybrid musks are also noteworthy for their disease resistance. The chart on page 144, which lists general characteristics for each rose classification, can help you see at a glance which types may work best for you.

Function and Maintenance

After you've crossed the obviously wrong off your list, consider how you plan to use your roses. If you're growing them for cut flowers, try hybrid teas, floribundas, and grandifloras. Many of the old garden varieties and David Austin's modern shrubs also produce blooms that are stunning in arrangements. If you're choosing roses to serve specific landscaping functions, such as lining a driveway or blanketing a slope, look for those whose heights and habits are most likely to do the job before you factor in flower color, form, and fragrance.

Next, consider your own habits. If you find puttering around plants relaxing, and you have the time to prune, fertilize, and perform other needed tasks, then you can confidently choose hybrid teas, floribundas, and grandifloras, or a climber or standard—all of which need more pruning than other types. If, on the other hand, your time is limited, you'll be happier with species and antique varieties or low-maintenance modern shrubs.

National and Local Resources

The surest way to choose a rose that's right for you is to see which ones are growing well in your area. Nothing beats local experience and information, and with roses there is a wealth of such information available. Public gardens that feature roses can be found just about anywhere in the country. By visiting them you'll get a good idea of the varieties that are likely to thrive in your yard.

More than 100 of the United States' largest public gardens show new roses that have been judged exceptional by the All-America Rose Selections (AARS), a nonprofit association of professional rose producers and hybridizers. AARS judges at many U.S. locations evaluate new hybrids from around the world for 2 years, testing their vigor, growth habit, disease resistance, foliage, flower production and form, and fragrance. A small percentage are officially designated "AARS winners"—look for them when you're buying your plants.

Another invaluable resource is the American Rose Society (ARS), composed of 360 local rose

Rose Classifications

Gallica

Damask

Centifolia

Hybrid Tea

Floribunda

Species

China

Tea

Noisette

Hybrid Perpetual

Shrub

Miniature

SPECIES   Fragrant, once-flowering, usually single blooms are often pink but may be white, red, or yellow. Plants are vigorous; many are hardy and disease resistant. Height and habit vary widely.

Antique Roses

GALLICAS   Scented blush, pink, or mauve single, semidouble, or double flowers bloom once per season on 3- to 5-foot shrubs. Upright plants are disease resistant and extremely hardy.

   DAMASKS   Extremely fragrant blooms are semidouble or double, pink or white; all but 'Autumn Damask' are once-blooming. Very hardy, shrubby plants are 5 to 6 feet tall and generally disease resistant.

   ALBAS   White or pink, fragrant, single to double flowers bloom once per season in clusters on vigorous, upright 5- to 8-foot shrubs with bluish foliage. Plants are very hardy and moderately disease resistant.

CENTIFOLIAS   Clusters of intensely fragrant, very double flowers bloom once per season, in white to deep pink. Most plants are 4 to 6 feet tall and hardy, but may be susceptible to fungal disease.

MOSSES   A mosslike growth covers parts of the plant. Fragrant, double or very double flowers are white to deep mauve or red; most bloom once per season. Plants can be susceptible to disease and vary in height, habit, and hardiness.

CHINAS   Small single or double flowers repeat bloom in a wide range of colors that darken with age. These mostly 3- to 4-foot plants need little pruning and are fairly disease resistant; some are tender.

PORTLANDS   Compact, round shrubs up to 4 feet tall produce waves of fragrant, very double flowers in pinks or reds. Plants are not particularly hardy or vigorous; disease resistance varies.

BOURBONS   Fragrant semidouble to very double flowers are white, pink, red, or purplish, and repeat on vigorous and somewhat hardy shrubs. Some are climbers. Plants are more susceptible than other old garden roses to black spot.

TEAS   Foliage and flowers are tea scented; elegantly shaped semidouble or double repeating blooms come in many delicate colors. Plants can be climbers or shrubs; vigor and disease resistance varies; most are tender.

NOISETTES   Repeating large flowers come in many colors and forms. Plants are vigorous climbers—in warm climates only—and resistant to diseases.

HYBRID PERPETUALS   Large, fragrant, double or very double white, pink, or maroon flowers usually repeat. Vigorous bushes can grow to 7 feet. Hardiness varies; disease resistance depends on climate.

Modern Roses

HYBRID TEAS   Mostly semidouble or double elegantly shaped flowers repeat bloom in a wide range of colors on upright, formal bushes. Fragrance varies. Most plants are susceptible to disease; hardiness varies.

POLYANTHAS   Small, clustering flowers are usually double, come in many colors, and repeat; fragrance is slight. Plants are hardy, compact, and disease resistant.

   FLORIBUNDAS   Repeating blooms grow in clusters, are single to double, and come in all colors. Plants are generally shrubby and vigorous, but some are susceptible to disease. Hardiness varies.

   GRANDIFLORAS   Large, generously repeating blooms cluster on upright canes that grow more than 6 feet tall; they have the elegant form and wide range of colors of hybrid teas. Hardiness varies; some plants have good disease resistance.

MINIATURES   First bred for containers, this class includes small-scale versions of other classes. Plants usually grow to about 2 feet, although climbers can reach 8 feet. Hardiness and disease resistance vary.

CLIMBERS   Flowers in all colors, forms, and fragrances are mostly repeat blooming; canes are stiff and grow up to 50 feet. This broad class includes large-flowered hybrids and climbing sports of other classes. Vigor, hardiness, and disease resistance vary.

RAMBLERS   Long canes on vigorous plants are more pliable than climbers' and have many lateral shoots. Flowers usually bloom once per season in clusters and come in many colors. Hardiness and disease resistance vary.

SHRUBS   Flowers bloom in all colors and forms on attractive leafy plants in a range of habits and heights. Most are everblooming, disease resistant, hardy, and easy to care for. Hybrid musks, hybrid rugosas, and kordesii roses are all groups of modern shrubs.

Top-Rated Roses

The roses in this list have received ARS ratings in the "outstanding" range, 9 and above. Those with an asterisk are AARS winners as well.

'Altissimo'	*'Minnie Pearl'*
'Ausburn'	*'Monsieur Tillier'*
'Ballerina'	*'Olympiad'* *
'Bonica' *	*'Pierrine'*
'Dainty Bess'	*'Plum Dandy'*
'Dortmund'	*'Pristine'*
'Europeana' *	*'Queen Elizabeth'* *
'Henry Hudson'	*'Rainbow's End'*
'Immensee'	*'Rise 'n' Shine'*
'Jean Kenneally'	*R. rugosa alba*
'Jeanne Lajoie'	*'Sexy Rexy'*
'Kingig'	*'Snow Bride'*
'Koricole'	*'Starina'*
'Madame Hardy'	*'Touch of Class'* *
'Magic Carrousel'	*'William Baffin'*

'Queen Elizabeth' with clematis

societies around the United States, with tens of thousands of members. Besides providing assistance and encouragement to its membership, the ARS has a Consulting Rosarians program available to anyone who wants to grow roses. Even if you aren't a member, one of these consultants, an expert rose grower in your region, will try to answer your questions and help troubleshoot problems.

In addition, ARS members conduct ongoing evaluations of all roses available for purchase—not only modern varieties but also species and old garden roses. The results are used to establish quality ratings on a scale of 1 to 10: Roses rated 9 and above are considered "outstanding," an 8 rating is "excellent," and any rose rated below 6 is deemed "of questionable value." The ratings, which factor in the same qualities judged by the AARS, are published annually in the society's *Handbook for Selecting Roses,* available for a small fee from the society. The ratings also appear in many other rose and gardening publications and are included in the encyclopedia entries at the back of this book.

Keep in mind, though, that the best strategy for choosing your roses is the simplest: Talk to your local rose society and to neighbors who grow them. Ratings and awards are only a guide; a high-rated rose might do poorly for you, while one with a mediocre rating might be a showstopper where you live. Another good source of information is your local Cooperative Extension Service, as well as any local experts, both amateur and professional, who know which roses do best in your area.

A Grading System for Roses

Both bare-root and container-grown roses are evaluated according to strict quality standards and then assigned a rating, or grade, based on the number and diameter of their canes, as well as on the general vitality of the plant. The grading system, established by the American Association of Nurserymen, a nonprofit trade organization, applies only to roses budded onto rootstock. Roses are graded from highest quality to lowest: 1, 1½, or 2. The grade is usually indicated on the plant's label or container; if you order by mail, you will generally find the grade in the nursery catalog.

Experts unanimously recommend buying Grade 1 plants. These roses will grow faster and produce more blooms in the first season than lower-grade roses. To be rated Grade 1, a bare-root plant must be 2 years old when taken from the field. Container-grown roses must have been growing in their container for at least 1 month during the growing season and have been in the container no more than two growing seasons. Both bare-root and container-grown roses must have at least three strong, healthy canes, pruned back to 6 inches or more above the bud union for bare-root plants and 4 inches or more for container-grown roses.

Grade 1 canes must measure at least ⅚₆ inch in diameter; canes of polyantha, shrub, and low-growing floribunda roses must have a diameter of ¼ inch or more. The canes should branch no higher than 3 inches above the bud union. Grade 1½ plants will grow well but will take longer to develop. These plants must have two or more strong canes, at least ⅚₆ inch in diameter and branched not higher than 3 inches from the bud union. The canes of polyantha, shrub, and low-growing floribunda roses must measure ¼ inch or more. Grade 2 plants must have at least two canes, one of which must be fully developed and at least ⅚₆ inch in diameter. The second cane must measure at least ¼ inch. For polyantha, shrub, and low-growing floribunda roses, one cane must be at least ¼ inch in diameter. Use these roses only for mass plantings.

Container-grown roses must also meet a minimum container size. Grade 1 roses must be potted in a container that is at least 7½ inches high, with a diameter of 7½ inches at the top and 6½ inches at the bottom. For Grades 1½ and 2, the pots must measure at least 6 inches high, with a diameter of 6 inches at the top and 5 inches at the bottom.

A Guide to Buying and Siting Roses

Once you've decided on the best roses for your site conditions, the next step is to buy them. You can purchase bare-root plants by mail or buy container-grown plants at a garden center or nursery.

Experts often suggest buying bare-root plants because they are less expensive, the choices are greater than with container-grown roses, and, most important, they usually have longer roots than their potted cousins. Bare-root plants are taken from the field when they are nearly dormant, stripped of their leaves, and wrapped in moisture-preserving peat moss and plastic. Held in cold storage until they are shipped, bare-root roses must be planted before warm weather starts them growing again or they will die.

When you buy a container-grown rose, on the other hand, the plant is actively growing rather than dormant. This gives you the advantage of being able to evaluate the quality and overall health of your plant before you take it home. Steer clear of a rose potted in a small container: The roots have likely been cut short or simply crammed into the pot. Always deal with a reputable nursery that pots its roses in containers large enough to accommodate long, healthy roots; these roses can happily remain in their pots for an entire growing season. At any time during that period, you can use them as additions or replacements in the garden.

Whether you choose bare-root or container-grown roses, try to make your purchases early in the season so you'll have the greatest possible selection to choose from. And to be sure you get the highest-quality plants, buy from reputable growers who specialize in roses or suppliers recommended to you by seasoned rose gardeners.

As soon as your bare-root plants arrive, unwrap them and look them over. A healthy, top-grade plant will have at least three strong canes and a sturdy root system proportionate to the top growth. The bark should be green and healthy, the pith white, and the canes smooth and plump, not dry or shriveled. The plant itself should be well shaped, with no obvious deformities or abnormal swelling, which would indicate disease. If your plant appears damaged, rotted, or diseased, return it for a refund.

If you decide to purchase container-grown roses, make sure that the nursery or garden center has kept its plants cool and moist. Inspect them for signs of damage or disease as you would with bare-root plants, and check the bottom of the container to be sure that the plant is not potbound.

When it comes to the conditions roses enjoy, it doesn't matter whether they are bare-root or container-grown. Most need at least 5 to 6 hours of sun a day to sustain vigorous, healthy growth. A south-facing site provides the best light, but an eastern exposure also has advantages: The morning sun dries the dew quickly, which is a plus since moisture promotes disease.

Good soil drainage is another must—roses will drown if their roots stand in water. To test how ef-

ficiently your soil drains, dig a hole 18 inches deep (the depth of the roots of most rosebushes), fill it with water, and record the time it takes for the hole to drain completely. If water remains after more than an hour, you will need to amend the soil before you plant *(pages 194-197)*. Test the soil again once you've enriched it.

Healthy roses also require good air circulation, since plants growing too close together are prone to mildew and other diseases. Allow adequate space between your rosebushes *(chart, page 205)*, as well as between your roses and other plants in the garden. Proper spacing will also help alleviate root competition with existing trees or shrubs and with some deep-rooted perennials, which can rob roses of much-needed water and nutrients.

As you consider spacing and air circulation, also think about exposure to harsh elements like wind. Roses love a breeze, but hot summer winds and cold winter gusts can dry them out. So avoid planting on high, exposed ground. Likewise, try to stay away from low-lying areas where air can become stagnant; still, moist air can lead to fungal diseases. Such spots also become frost pockets in winter, which can kill even the hardiest roses.

Obviously, you can change neither the climate or the fundamental lay of the land in your garden. But if you plant your roses along the south wall of your house, for example, they'll have the sunlight they need, some protection from hot afternoon sun, and a barrier against cold north winds. A hedge or a fence can also be a perfect windbreak.

Planted against a wood fence that offers protection from wind, this California garden fairly bursts with colorful blooms. 'White Delight' and orange-red 'Fragrant Cloud' roses harmonize with a profusion of deep pink phlox (left), white Shasta daisies, purple clematis, and the variegated foliage of geranium (foreground).

Designing with Roses

An arbor blanketed with 'Cl. First Prize' and 'Abraham Darby' serves as a threshold between rose beds with such beauties as deep red 'Chrysler Imperial' and a cutting garden beyond. The formality of the Long Island garden is emphasized by the straight lines of a trim yew hedge, low edgings of boxwood, and a wide brick walk.

With their multitude of colors, shapes, and sizes, roses exist for almost any garden situation. In choosing the plants that bring the most beauty into your garden, you'll be considering the hues of both flower and foliage, the texture of the leaves, and even the winter charm of hips. But it is the form of the plant that will help you decide how best to use it. Plump shrubs make sumptuous hedges, stiffly elegant bushes are for formal beds, tall climbers enliven a trellis or fence, and low growers blanket the ground—and these are only some of the ways to introduce roses into your landscape.

For many gardeners, the thought of a rose garden conjures up an image of upright bushes neatly arranged inside a formal, geometric frame of dense, clipped greenery. This stately, even spare, look can be magnificent, showcasing the beautiful long-stemmed blooms of hybrid teas such as the deep red 'Mister Lincoln' or the pale yellow 'Elina' and grandifloras such as the elegant pink 'Queen Elizabeth'. If growing roses for cutting and exhibiting in competitions is your goal, devote space solely to these showy types, and—because hybrid teas and grandifloras are typically scant on leaves—enclose the bed with a low hedge of yew, holly, or boxwood to contribute foliage to the overall picture. A protective barrier of greenery also creates a pleasant microclimate for roses, shielding them from strong winds and shading the soil to slow the rate of evaporation. Partial afternoon shade will help keep the blossoms looking their best longer and preserve their fragrance.

If you're planning a large traditional garden, plant a network of several rose beds, divided by paths of brick, stone, or turf grass. The straighter the paths and the more symmetrical their arrangement, the more formal your rose garden will look. And any number of special touches can be added. For variety in height, try planting climbers and ramblers, trained along arches and tripods *(page 154)*. Ornaments such as urns, a sundial, or statuary will give the garden a sense of whimsy, dignity—or whatever personality you wish to convey.

Hedges: Double-Duty Roses

Roses can also play a substantial role outside of the formal setting. Define the perimeter of your property with species roses; separate one area from another with teas and shrubs; edge a walkway with miniatures or clustering floribundas. The floribunda 'Betty Prior', for example, makes a lush yet tidy

hedge to guide visitors to your front door. Plant a single row of 'Betty Prior' 3 feet apart and keep the bushes trimmed to shorter than 5 feet. Unlike 'Betty Prior', modern shrub roses such as pink 'Bonica' and the snow white hybrid rugosa 'Blanc Double de Coubert' spread out and form a loosely cascading hedge. Use these shrubbier roses as a transition between the patio and the lawn or as a low screen to block the view of your neighbor's yard. Planted in staggered rows about 2½ feet apart, the shrubs create an impenetrable barrier of thorny canes and foliage. Roses suitable for both formal and informal hedges are listed on page 151. For information on planting rose hedges, see page 205.

Woody Shrubs and Roses

If you have room for only one hedge, try combining evergreen shrubs with roses. In moist, well-drained soil in the hot southeastern United States,

Upright and vase shaped in habit, the floribunda 'Iceberg' rises to 5 or 6 feet and spreads only slightly, making it an ideal rose for use as an open hedge. Its plush, pure white 3-inch flowers offer a textural contrast to this driveway of concrete pavers in southern California.

Roses and Herbs: Sharing a Gardening Heritage

Roses and herbs have made ideal garden companions for centuries. The oldest known gallica and the first rose known to be cultivated for medicine and perfume, *Rosa gallica officinalis*—'Apothecary's Rose'—shared a bed with fragrant herbs and, in time, with other roses in the enclosed walls of medieval monastery gardens. For hundreds of years, essences were distilled from the plants and combined into conserves, syrups, balms, and ointments that were used for treating ailments ranging from lung and liver disorders to headaches and hangovers. These mixtures contained the petals of gallicas and their citrus- and clove-scented damask descendants such as 'York and Lancaster' and 'Celsiana', vitamin-rich hips of rugosas, and such pungent herbs as lavender, chamomile, and fennel.

Today, a garden of herbs and roses is still an enticing blend of function and beauty. Herbs may be grown for their culinary and possible medicinal value, and their powerful aromas help keep insects and pests away from prized roses. In addition, the striking foliage of such plants as gray-green santolina, silvery artemisia, and lacy-textured tansy offers an ideal foil for roses' showy blooms. Bushy herbs like germander also have a place, forming short, dense hedges of tiny, glossy green leaves, which add a sober note to the heady tumble of color and fragrance. In planting roses and herbs together in your own garden, you can create anything from a casual cottage version, with roses spotted here and there, to a dramatic setting that echoes the walled gardens of the past, like the Atlanta, Georgia, garden shown at right.

Traditionally, roses were awarded the prime sites within a walled garden, surrounded by low, trimmed hedges outlining island beds in ornamental shapes. In the garden pictured here, the narrow, walled space is divided into three main diamond-shaped beds, each defined by a clipped hedge of true dwarf box and ground-hugging, yellow-green marjoram. A weeping standard of the polyantha 'The Fairy' adds a vertical dimension to the center of each bed, and underplantings of herbs and vegetables such as basil, chives, lettuce, and chard fill the areas inside the hedges. At left center, a potted standard lemon verbena and a rosemary topiary echo the upright form of the roses and relieve the strict symmetry of the patterns, creating a garden that is lush yet orderly, and a feast for the senses.

plant *Photinia* x *fraseri* (Fraser photinia), whose new foliage is tipped with red, and *Raphiolepis indica* 'Springtime' (Indian hawthorn), which forms stiff mounds of dark green foliage, behind 'Buff Beauty' and 'Mrs. Dudley Cross' to get a gorgeous living fence. 'Buff Beauty' is a fragrant hybrid musk with 2-inch pale apricot blooms that grows to 6 feet, and 'Mrs. Dudley Cross'—a 4-foot tea rose that does especially well in warm climates—has smaller, pink-tinged yellow flowers. The photinia grows quite straggly if left untamed and should be pruned to 6 feet, while the Indian hawthorn tops out at 6 feet and needs only occasional shaping.

Farther north, alternate cool-climate needled and broad-leaved evergreens with the hardy silvery pink rugosa 'Frau Dagmar Hartopp', pruned to 4

'Bonica'

Beside a trickling fountain in this garden in Vancouver, British Columbia, apricot 'Leander' blooms mingle gently with the off-white peony 'Coral Sunset'. The blue foliage of common rue, the pure green leaves of a pink shrub rose, and the glossy evergreen foliage of a cherry-laurel hedge bring the soft tints into sharper focus.

Recommended Roses for a Hedge

FORMAL HEDGES

UNDER 3 FEET
'Cécile Brunner'
'La Marne'
'Marie Pavié'
'Nearly Wild'
'White Pet'

3 TO 5 FEET
'Archduke Charles'
'Autumn Damask'
'Betty Prior'
'Carefree Beauty'
'Elina'
'French Lace'
'Iceberg'
'Old Blush'
'Olympiad'

TALLER THAN 5 FEET
'John Cabot'
'Penelope'
'Queen Elizabeth'

INFORMAL HEDGES

3 TO 5 FEET
'Ballerina'
'Belle Poitevine'
'Blanc Double de Coubert'
'Bonica'
'Erfurt'
'Hansa'
'Sea Foam'

TALLER THAN 5 FEET
'Belinda'
'Cl. Pinkie'
R. glauca
R. palustris
R. rugosa alba
'Simplicity'
'Will Scarlet'

feet in height and width. *Picea pungens* 'Montgomery', a spruce with a bluish cast that forms a dwarf pyramid, and *Ilex glabra* 'Compacta' (dwarf inkberry), with dark green foliage and black berries in fall, will complement the rugosa's flashy passage to winter as its foliage turns deep maroon, then golden yellow, and its large hips ripen to red.

Color Schemes for Beds and Borders

Get the most out of your roses' vibrant color display by placing them in beds and borders with other flowering plants. The opportunities to compose a stunning picture of color and form are in-

finite; just make certain that the companions you choose share the same cultural conditions required by most roses—fairly acid, well-drained, loamy soil, and plenty of sunlight and water.

Tall or spiky plants such as lilies, hollyhocks, and foxgloves complement the arching or rounded shapes of rosebushes. Low-growing plants, including annual 'Carpet of Snow' sweet alyssum and candytuft, conceal the bare, twiggy ankles of hybrid teas—and they produce white flowers that go with roses of any color. When combining roses with other colorful plants, keep in mind that pleasing arrangements are usually harmonious—composed of colors that are within the same color family—or contrasting—meaning that the colors are from the opposite side of the color spectrum. The

vivid magenta flowers of *Geranium psilostemon*, for example, harmonize well with the perfumed deep pink bourbon 'Madame Isaac Pereire'. As an added bonus, the rose acts as a brace for the tall geranium.

Since roses come in virtually every color except blue, try pairing them with perennials and annuals in tints or shades of blue or violet. The yellow-pink blooms of the hybrid tea 'Peace' or the bright pink trusses of the bourbon 'Louise Odier' rising above the pale blue, cloudlike flowers of *Nigella damascena* (love-in-a-mist)—a self-sowing annual—paints a portrait of soothing pastels. For more drama, plant the clear yellow shrub 'Graham Thomas' with deep violet 'Black Knight' delphiniums. If you want truly eye-popping color, pair 'Playboy'— whose blooms are splashed with orange, yellow, and scarlet—with blue-violet flower stalks of *Nepeta* x *faassenii* (catmint) and *Salvia* x *superba* 'May Night' (sage). If the combination seems too garish, add bright yellow 'Moonshine' achillea to temper the mix.

The Many Tones of White

White roses come in creamy tones tinged with yellow—the climbing tea 'Sombreuil' is one example—and blush tones flushed with the lightest tints of pink, such as 'Celestial', an alba. When placed amid delicate pastel flowers of pink and apricot, these near white roses seem to deepen the tints of their neighbors. And in a garden of hot colors—orange, scarlet, fiery red—a mass of pure white roses is a refreshing respite.

For a cool midsummer display, plant white 'Frau Karl Druschki', using a technique called pegging to create a low habit and encourage prolific blooms *(page 158)*. Back the rose with the sculpted foliage of sea kale and its lacy mounds of dainty white flowers, then let tall, steel blue spherical flower heads of *Eryngium* x *tripartitum* (three-lobed eryngium) lean on the sea kale for support.

The large floribunda 'Iceberg' helps make a gleaming white statement when it is combined with the almost translucent white cups of *Campanula persicifolia alba* (white bellflower) and a pure white cultivar of fireweed, *Epilobium angustifolium* 'Album'. In back of this trio— which will bloom from early summer through fall—plant a tall stand of the big-leaved foliage

Saucer-shaped semi-double pink blooms of the floribunda 'Simplicity' contrast merrily with sunny yellow bearded iris. At upper right, the deep blue spikes of rocket larkspur and white and lilac dame's rocket add a sedate note to the cheery scene.

The Whitest Roses

'Alba Semi-plena'	*R. rugosa alba*
'Blanc Double de Coubert'	'Sally Holmes'
	'Sea Foam'
'Boule de Neige'	'Silver Moon'
'Fair Bianca'	'Snow Bride'
'Frau Karl Druschki'	'Sombreuil'
'Iceberg'	'White Meidiland'
'Irresistible'	'White Pet'
'Lamarque'	
'Linville'	
'Madame Alfred Carrière'	
'Madame Hardy'	
'Madame Legras de St. Germain'	
'Madame Plantier'	
'Marie Pavié'	
'Nastarana'	
R. banksiae banksiae	

'Frau Karl Druschki'

152

of *Macleaya cordata* (plume poppy), which should reach at least 7 feet by July, lending an otherworldly quality to the luminous landscape.

Bicolored/Multicolored Roses

Not all rose blooms are one solid color. Apricot-and-salmon 'Party Girl' and yellow-and-red 'Rainbow's End', for instance, are blends, which means that varying degrees of each color merge in the blooms. A bloom can also be striped, blotched, or mottled with separate colors, or there may be an "eye" of a second color at its center. The oldest striped rose of record, 'Rosa Mundi', a sport of the gallica 'Apothecary's Rose', has pale pink blooms blotched with the vivid pink of its parent. Alternate plants of 'Rosa Mundi' and 'Apothecary's Rose' for an enchanting hedge or border.

'Camaïeux', with crimson, purple, and lilac stripes on a creamy background, is at home with solid-colored flowers such as the wine red and pink hybrids *Penstemon campanulatus* 'Garnet' and 'Evelyn'. The colors of the two penstemons match the rose's stripes, but the shape of their blooms is tubular, making for a pleasing contrast in form against the roundness of the rose. Add white foxglove to complement the red and pink.

TIPS FROM THE PROS

Companions Worth Cultivating

Pair roses and ornamental grasses for a sensational-looking garden, says Mike Shoup, founder of the Antique Rose Emporium in Brenham, Texas. Ornamental grasses come in many colors, to be combined with roses of all hues, and their graceful, linear growth habit—tufted, mounded, arching, and upright—offers a refreshing counterpoint to the more rounded shapes of rosebushes and their blooms. To delight the eye with a planting composed of varying forms, textures, and colors, try the following combinations:

- Tufted, fine-textured, icy blue *Festuca ovina* var. *glauca* 'Blaufuchs' with soft pastels such as light pink 'Old Blush' and 'Cécile Brunner', rose pink 'Duchesse de Brabant', and pink-apricot 'Perle d'Or'.

- Arching, burgundy-leaved *Pennisetum setaceum* 'Rubrum' (purple fountain grass) with yellow-pink 'Lafter', 'Dr. Eckener', and yellow 'Graham Thomas' for dramatic contrast.
- Metallic blue *Panicum virgatum* 'Heavy Metal' (switch grass) and *Elymus arenarius* 'Glaucus' (blue Lyme grass) with mauve 'Reine des Violettes' and 'Cardinal de Richelieu', bright pink 'Betty Prior', and rose pink 'Nearly Wild'.
- Tall *Miscanthus sinensis* 'Morning Light' (Japanese silver grass), whose slender green leaves have a narrow margin of clear white, with red shrub rose 'John Franklin' and in front of climbers such as bright pink 'Zéphirine Drouhin' and dark red, tiny-leaved 'Red Cascade'.

'Gruss an Aachen' and Helictotrichon sempervirens (blue oat grass)

Climbers and Ramblers: The Most Versatile of Roses

The robust rambler 'Albéric Barbier', whose creamy white double blooms emit the scent of apple blossoms, scales a wrought-iron four-legged support, while nearby fiery red 'Dortmund' festoons an identical quadropod. The contrasting towers of red and white emphatically divide the rose bed in this Portland, Oregon, garden from the flat green lawn.

Climbers and ramblers are perhaps the most dramatic roses for landscape use. They add color and movement up high, at eye level, and along the ground. Scaling a trellised wall, stiff-caned climbers can cover an expanse of gritty masonry with lush foliage and velvety petals from late spring until frost. Blanketing a fence or sprawling down a slope, long-limbed ramblers burst into a cascade of early-summer blooms that soften the rough edges of wood, warm up the cold glare of cast iron, and cushion rocky ground with mounds of color and texture. Trained up and over a tall arch, they invite a stroll beneath them to other parts of the garden, and viewed from beneath the open crossbeams of a pergola, a plush awning of blooming climbers and ramblers expands a garden skyward. These charming plants lend themselves to picturesque effects. On the following pages you will learn how to showcase their glorious blooms in your garden.

Growing Roses Upward

Most climbing and rambling roses combine the best qualities of their bushier cousins—abundant flowers, fragrance, and ruggedness—with the long, foliage-covered shoots and bloom clusters that characterize vines. But unlike true vines—such as Japanese wisteria, cup-and-saucer vine *(Cobaea scandens),* and climbing hydrangea, to name only a treasured few—these roses are shrubs that need a gardener's assistance to grow to great heights. Because roses do not possess the ability to wind around or cling to trellises and other vertical structures, their canes must be tied or otherwise fastened in place *(pages 160-162).*

Few vines, however, can match the spectacular floral display of climbing and rambling roses. 'Madame Alfred Carrière', whose pink buds open to white cups, 'Cl. Crimson Glory', with shocking

Supports for Roses That Climb

TRIPODS AND QUADROPODS
Three-legged tripods and four-legged quadropods —designed of metal or rot-resistant hardwoods, or homemade of poles lashed together—are effective when wrapped or braided with roses.

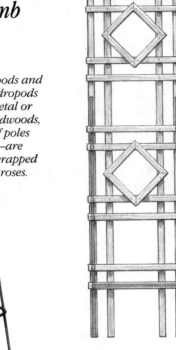

WIRE GRIDS
Climbers can be tied to wire grids installed in stone or masonry. Fanning over the wall, the foliage and blooms of the rose hide the network of wire.

CONTAINER ROSE SUPPORTS
Lengths of seasoned willow shoots, grapevines, and other pliable sapling branches twisted into various shapes add an attractive rustic element to an otherwise ordinary container.

TRELLISES
Freestanding as a screen or attached to a wall, a trellis made of geometrically patterned latticework or fashioned in a more casual freehand design is a versatile support for roses.

FENCES
Sturdy fences of natural or painted wood, wrought iron, and wire mesh ensure privacy, enclose spaces, and define boundaries while offering support for climbers and ramblers.

PERGOLAS
Wood, stone, or brick posts supporting an open-beam or latticework roof transform robust climbers and ramblers into a tunnel of blooms. These handsome garden structures capture a visitor's attention immediately and should be placed with care— leading to a different part of the garden, perhaps, or framing a favorite sitting area.

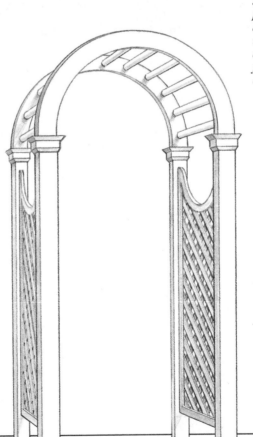

ARCHES
As an eye-pleasing gateway into or out of a garden, or outlining a view or defining a path, arches of treated wood or nylon-coated steel support vigorous climbers and ramblers.

The glossy dark green leaves and blush pink blooms of the climber 'New Dawn' tumble over a gray picket fence in southern California. 'New Dawn', a sport of the lusty climber 'Dr. W. Van Fleet', was awarded the first-ever U.S. plant patent in 1930. Unlike its parent, which blooms just once, 'New Dawn' flowers continuously throughout the growing season.

deep red blooms, and 'New Dawn', with a multitude of delicate apple-blossom pink flowers, are just a few examples of robust climbers that bloom over and over throughout the growing season. The prickly rambler 'Albertine' has so many large salmon pink blooms in early summer that its foliage is virtually hidden, while the robust and nearly thornless 'Veilchenblau' sports a profusion of semidouble violet-blue flowers that fade to a lovely gray-tinged mauve during a burst of glory that lasts up to 4 weeks.

Choosing between Climbers and Ramblers

When selecting a climber or rambler to cover a support, consider the differences between the two types of long-caned roses. Ramblers bloom only once per season, with smallish flowers borne in large clusters. Although some climbers also bloom just once, many others flower repeatedly

during the growing season, and their blooms can be quite large. Climbers also have larger leaves than do ramblers, but their canes are slower growing and generally stiffer and less pliable, making them more difficult to train.

Two traits make ramblers more labor-intensive than climbers. Because ramblers bloom only on new wood produced the previous growing season, they need extensive pruning after flowering. Climbers, on the other hand, need less pruning because even older canes produce the lateral shoots that bear flowers.

Second, although many climbers and ramblers are rugged specimens—winter-hardy to temperatures as low as -5°F—ramblers are prone to mildew, which is made worse by poor air movement. For this reason, ramblers are better suited for clambering up and over open, airy structures rather than walls. These vigorous roses quickly cover arches, pergolas, fences, and freestanding lattices as well as sparsely foliated, deciduous trees with foliage and flowers. Climbers, too, work well

Easy-Care Roses for Training

'Altissimo'
'America'
'Ballerina'
'Belinda'
'Blaze'
'Buff Beauty'
'Cl. Cécile Brunner'
'Céline Forestier'
'Cl. Crimson
    Glory'
'Dortmund'
'Dublin Bay'
'Handel'
'Joseph's Coat'
'Lamarque'
'Lavender Lassie'

'Madame Alfred
    Carrière'
'Marchioness
    of Londonderry'
'New Dawn'
'Cl. Pinkie'
'Prosperity'
'Rêve d'Or'
'Silver Moon'
'Sombreuil'
'Cl. Souvenir
    de la Malmaison'
'Cl. The Fairy'
'William Baffin'
'Will Scarlet'
'Zéphirine Drouhin'

on these supports, and they also tolerate situations where there is less air circulation, such as a trellis or wire grid attached to a wall.

Selecting Structural Supports

Covered with roses, a vertical structure adds a great deal of decoration to the garden. Fences, tripods, trellises, arches, and pergolas are just some of the many supports that can serve as major design features in your garden *(page 155),* shaping and defining space in much the same way that paths, walls, trees, and tall hedges do.

Drape a rose over a fence or train it up a freestanding lattice. Any way you use them, ramblers and climbers soften the hard edges of wood, timber, brick, stone, or metal fencing with their gentle curves. Even an ordinary chain-link or steel mesh fence at the perimeter of your property can be a breathtaking sight when it supports a mantle of rose foliage and flowers. Be sure, though, that whatever you choose to cover with roses is constructed of sturdy materials and solidly anchored. A vigorous rambler or climber will quickly burden a fence or lattice with weighty canes, causing a weak one to buckle and eventually collapse.

When you choose a rose to cover your fence or lattice, pick one that matches the support's texture and color. Yellow roses, for example, complement natural wood, whereas white blooms stand out against paints and stains of forest green. For pink and red roses, a whitewashed picket fence makes an especially cheerful background.

If you want quick coverage, keep in mind that ramblers generally grow faster than climbers. Try 'Tausendschön', whose 3-inch deep pink flowers

Weaving Roses and Vines Together

While slower-growing but more enduring roses make their way to the top of a support, annual and tender perennial vines shoot up quickly, offering nearly instant foliage and color. Once the sturdy rose canes are established, they supply even more support for vines of all sorts. *Lonicera heckrottii* (goldflame honeysuckle), for example, has gracefully coiled itself around a found rose on the leafy, bloom-laden Texas fence shown here.

A classic trio to cover a trellis or arbor includes roses, honeysuckle, and clematis, all of which come in a wide assortment of colors. White *Clematis* 'Alba Luxurians', the single vivid red flowers of *Rosa* 'Dortmund', and dusky yellow *Lonicera sempervirens* 'Sulphurea' create an arresting contrast of color and flower shape. Or combine orangy *Lonicera sempervirens* (trumpet honeysuckle) with the white climber 'Silver Moon' and the huge purple flowers of *Clematis* 'Gipsy Queen'. This grouping needs sun to bloom profusely, but be sure the roots of the clematis are shaded and thickly mulched.

How to Peg a Rose

Roses that aren't tall enough for trellises or arches but at the same time don't have a pretty, compact shape can achieve full glory in the garden by pegging. To peg a rose, simply arch the canes downward and anchor their tips close to the ground to form low mounds of flowers and foliage that radiate from a central point in half-moon, spiral, and spoke-shaped patterns. Plants with canes between 5 and 7 feet long—such as bourbons and hybrid perpetuals as well as some damasks and centifolias—are ideal candidates. Besides giving the plants an attractive shape, horizontally training their canes alters the distribution of nutrients so that roses bloom at every bud joint rather than just the top one—transforming a thicket of near bare canes into a dazzling sprawl of color.

Choose vigorous canes that bend easily, and remove any leaf buds at the tips. Arcing it downward, secure one cane to the ground with a 20-inch rustproof, U-shaped pegging staple or long metal hook positioned at a point a few inches from the cane's tip (inset). Keep the cane at least 2 inches above the soil to prevent it from taking root and to allow air to circulate. Peg the other canes in the same manner, arranging them in the desired pattern. Prune back any unpegged canes to the base of the shrub.

'John Hopper'

flecked with white grow on thornless canes that extend as far as 10 feet by early summer. There are some vigorous climbers, though, such as 'Altissimo'; this rose has dark gold stamens surrounded by a blood red collar of seven to 10 petals instead of the five petals typical of most single blooms. Another reliable climber for covering a fence or lattice is the popular hybrid tea 'Cl. Etoile de Hollande', whose deep crimson blooms are not only jumbo-sized but are also intensely fragrant.

Simple Supports

The simplest freestanding support is a tripod or quadropod. These three- and four-legged structures add a strong vertical dimension when situated at the rear of a bed or border. More than one tripod placed side by side or in various geometric configurations anchors a garden design and adds a sense of permanence to the planting. Sited by themselves—at the edge of a lawn, for instance—these roughly cone-shaped structures command immediate attention.

For an altogether spectacular effect, plant a different climber at the foot of each tripod leg. In a warm climate—or in a protected setting colder than Zone 6—grow the 4-inch daffodil yellow blooms of 'Golden Showers' up one leg; 'America', whose salmon buds open to coral pink, on the second; and multicolored 'Joseph's Coat' up the third. The latter's yellow blooms diffused with orange and pink will bring together the colors of all three roses in a medley of tints and contrasts.

Grand Supports

More elaborate structures such as arches and pergolas require thoughtful placement in your garden if they are to be used to best advantage. Arches can be used to mark an entranceway or top a gate; a series of them creates a living, leafy, flowering tunnel called an arbor. Pergolas—open structures with flat, peaked, or curved roofs —can create a shaded walkway or a sanctuary where you can sit and enjoy the color and scent.

Both arches and pergolas should be at least 8 feet tall and 5 feet wide so that two people can walk side by side through them without brushing against dangling blooms or wayward thorns.

Position these dramatic structures where they'll make the most impact—as an inviting threshold at a garden entrance, to span a seating area and cover it with lavish blooms, at the intersection of garden paths.

'American Pillar', a robust rambler with single bright pink white-centered blooms, and *Rosa banksiae lutea* (yellow Lady Banks' Rose), which grows rapidly to 25 feet and bears a wealth of 1-inch lemon yellow double flowers, will swiftly cover an arch or a pergola. If you decide to plant once-blooming ramblers on a pergola, you may want to alternate them with everblooming climbers to prolong the color display. Fast-growing climbers to ascend an arch or the columns of a pergola include the buff yellow 'Rêve d'Or', the sweetly perfumed, pale pink 'Cl. Cécile Brunner', and the buttery white 'Sombreuil', with puffy, cakelike petals arranged in near perfect symmetry.

Attached Supports

You can also send roses to new heights by blanketing the walls of your home or other buildings with climbers, using trelliswork and wire grids. Choose walls that face south or west and that bask in direct sunlight most of the day, and when you position the support, maintain as much as a foot of space between it and the wall to allow the good air circulation that all roses need.

To surround a window or doorway of a white or gray clapboard house with colorful blooms, choose the crimson-streaked white flowers of 'Variegata di Bologna' or the smoky red blooms of 'Don Juan'. Bedeck a brick wall with the clear yellow of 'Lawrence Johnston', the lemon-tinted white flowers of 'Lamarque', or the pale pink blossoms of disease-resistant 'Dr. W. Van Fleet', which blooms once but grows far more robustly than its silver-pink sport, the everblooming 'New Dawn'.

For a wall of big, voluptuous, ruffled blooms, the old-fashioned bourbon 'Zéphirine Drouhin' is hard to beat. Partner its blowzy pink flowers with rich purple *Clematis* x *jackmanii* (Jackman clematis) for a soothing color harmony. And peg a few of its thornless plum red canes to the ground in front of the wall to simulate a churning waterfall of pink and purple.

Roses to Carpet the Ground

Besides providing vertical interest, long-caned roses can do horizontal service in your landscape: Certain roses with long, trailing canes become graceful low mounds of flowers and foliage if allowed to sprawl over uneven ground and bare slopes. The single pink, yellow-eyed 'Max Graf', the single white, gold-centered 'Paulii Rosea', and the creamy white 'Sea Foam' form thorny mats with glossy foliage ideal for covering old tree stumps, hiding unsightly humps, and concealing drainage covers and utility lines. Their dense growth smothers weeds and helps control erosion because their canes frequently take root, producing new plants that can later be separated from the parent. Climbing miniatures can also lend their beauty to the landscape in less utilitarian ways. 'Red Cascade', for example, which hugs the ground with glossy foliage and 1-inch brilliant red flower clusters, or two-toned 'Jeanne Lajoie'—pink with a dark pink reverse—makes an ornate edging for a garden path.

The canes of 'White Meidiland' grow to 5 feet, spreading on the ground and forming mounds of large white blooms that sparkle in the sunlight at the edge of this Virginia lawn. Disease resistant and virtually maintenance free, the rose has thick canes that need little pruning and just the occasional deadheading of spent blooms to prolong its pristine beauty.

Training Climbers and Ramblers

Since roses will not naturally twist around a support or send out tendrils as do vines, your climbers or ramblers must be trained to accomplish this effect. The task can be as uncomplicated as coaxing the plants to drape over an existing fence or wall in your garden. Or you may choose to build a freestanding support—an arch, pergola, trellis, pillar, or tripod—and train your roses to grow around it.

Be sure to select a rose that will not only bloom when you want it to but will also be able to adapt to the kind of support you have in mind. Climbers have thick, sturdy canes; the canes of ramblers are more pliable and thus may be easier to train to some supports. But ramblers bloom only once a season and are vulnerable to mildew, whereas many climbers bloom all summer and rarely have mildew problems.

No matter what rose variety and type of support you decide on, remember that most rose canes that are left to grow upward produce flowers only at their tips. Canes that are bent to grow horizontally, however, will produce flowers all along their length. So when you arrange your twining roses, you can trick nature into producing the fullest possible display of blooms by training a number of canes to grow laterally.

Materials for Supports

Choose support structures made of hardwoods such as cedar, black locust, redwood, cypress, and hickory. Avoid softwoods, which will rot after a few years. Metal is also appropriate for most supports; it is more durable than wood and never requires painting. Just be sure you use sturdy, galvanized metal, which won't rust. Anchor the supports deeply and securely in the ground. You can provide stability for the wood by setting the bottoms of the supports in concrete below ground level or by inserting the ends into hollow metal pipes driven into the earth.

Securing the Canes

Plant the rose about 16 to 18 inches from the support, and begin training the canes right away. Use materials that stretch, such as green plastic stretch ties, vinyl gardener's tape, or nylon hosiery, to secure the canes. You can use raffia or soft twine, but if you do, check the ties periodically to see if they

The long, flexible canes of hybrid musk 'Bubble Bath' roses shimmy up the trunks of two dead cedar trees, which the owner of this walled garden in Charlotte, North Carolina, stripped of limbs and recycled as supports for a dramatic display of soft pink blooms. Although not officially classified as a climber, 'Bubble Bath's' cascading habit and its height—8 to 10 feet—make it a perfect choice for training to a pillar or other rose support.

Training Climbers on a Vertical Support

Beginning about 2 feet from the ground, hammer U-shaped construction staples partway into the wood at about 4-foot intervals along the support. Next, wrap the canes around the support in an ascending spiral pattern, keeping them in a horizontal position as much as possible so that they will produce a greater display of blooms than they would if kept in their natural, or upright, position. Tie the canes loosely to the staples as you come to them, using either a figure-eight loop or a double loop (page 162). Once the main shoots reach the top of the support, you can either secure them there with more staples or allow them to drape over the top.

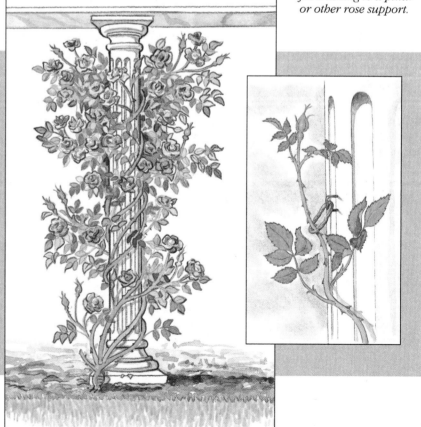

need loosening. Never use twist ties or any other form of wire—it will cut into the canes. Always secure canes loosely to their supports so that as they grow and thicken they won't be constricted.

To keep canes from rubbing and chafing against their supports in the wind, attach ties in a figure-eight or double-loop configuration *(below)* so that the tie, not the cane, is in contact with the support. Never weave canes in and out of narrow spaces in fences, lattices, or trellises; if you do, the canes will be nearly impossible to extricate for pruning or removal once they are fully grown.

Roses on Solid Surfaces

To train roses to grow on walls, you can either drive U-shaped construction staples into the mortar between bricks or stones and then tie the canes to them, or you can cover the wall with a wire grid made from strands of plastic-coated straining wire or 16-gauge utility wire. The wires fasten to brackets that hold them 4 to 12 inches away from the wall to allow for air circulation. Adjusting for the growth habit of your particular rose, space the brackets no more than 4 feet apart horizontally across the wall and about 1½ feet apart vertically to give adequate support to the grid and the roses. Attach the wire to the brackets and pull it taut.

Climbers and ramblers that grow 8 to 10 feet tall perform well on vertical wooden posts, tepees (three posts joined at the top), or tripods. When you plant the rose, tilt it toward the support to direct its growth, and wrap the canes in an upward spiral pattern *(page 160)*. For a fuller effect, you can wrap one plant clockwise and another counterclockwise on the same support. If you let the canes grow higher than the post, the roses will cascade from the top, creating an umbrella effect.

Training Roses to a Trellis

Begin training the rose by working with an outside cane near the bottom of the plant. Gently bend the cane into a horizontal position to encourage the best distribution of blossoms. Tie it loosely to the structure using either of the two loops shown at right. Continue positioning and tying the canes, working toward the center of the plant; then start on the other side and work inward to create a symmetrical design. Save the center canes for last.

 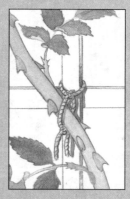

To create a figure-eight tie, loop vinyl gardener's tape or other material around the cane, cross the strands, then bring them around the support and tie the ends together, making sure the crossed section of the eight lies between the cane and the support (above, left). To make a double loop, first knot the tie around the support and then knot it around the cane (above, right). The knot between the support and the cane will keep the two from rubbing together excessively.

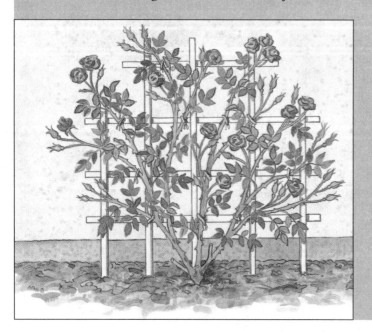

Plant Selection Guide for Roses

Organized by predominant flower color, this chart provides information needed to select roses that will thrive in the particular conditions of your garden. For additional information, refer to the encyclopedia section that begins on page 358.

WHITE		ZONE 3	ZONE 4	ZONE 5	ZONE 6	ZONE 7	ZONE 8	ZONE 9	ZONE 10	PARTIAL SHADE	DISEASES	HEAT	SEASIDE CONDITIONS	SPRING	SUMMER	FALL	SINGLE	SEMIDOUBLE	DOUBLE	VERY DOUBLE	MINIATURE	BUSH/SHRUB <3'	BUSH/SHRUB 3-6'	SHRUB >6'	CLIMBER/RAMBLER	FRAGRANCE	CUT FLOWERS	HIPS
	'ALBA SEMI-PLENA'		✓	✓	✓	✓	✓	✓		✓	✓				✓			✓						✓		✓		✓
	'BLANC DOUBLE DE COUBERT'	✓	✓	✓	✓	✓	✓	✓	✓		✓		✓	✓	✓	✓								✓			✓		✓
	'BOULE DE NEIGE'			✓	✓	✓	✓	✓		✓					✓	✓			✓					✓			✓	
	'CANDEUR LYONNAISE'			✓	✓	✓	✓	✓						✓	✓	✓			✓					✓				✓
	'CITY OF YORK'			✓	✓	✓	✓	✓	✓						✓			✓							✓	✓	
	'FAIR BIANCA'		✓	✓	✓	✓	✓	✓							✓	✓			✓	✓			✓					
	'FRENCH LACE'		✓	✓	✓	✓	✓	✓		✓					✓	✓			✓				✓				✓	
	'GREAT MAIDEN'S BLUSH'		✓	✓	✓	✓	✓	✓							✓				✓				✓			✓		
	'HANDEL'			✓	✓	✓	✓	✓		✓					✓	✓			✓						✓			
	'HENRY HUDSON'	✓	✓	✓	✓	✓	✓	✓	✓		✓		✓	✓	✓	✓		✓					✓			✓		
	'ICEBERG'		✓	✓	✓	✓	✓	✓		✓					✓	✓			✓				✓			✓	✓	
	'IRRESISTIBLE'			✓	✓	✓	✓	✓						✓	✓	✓			✓		✓						✓	✓
	'KORICOLE'			✓	✓	✓	✓	✓						✓	✓	✓			✓			✓						
	'LAMARQUE'				✓	✓	✓	✓			✓			✓	✓					✓					✓	✓	✓	
	'MADAME ALFRED CARRIERE'				✓	✓	✓	✓		✓		✓		✓	✓				✓						✓	✓		
	'MADAME HARDY'		✓	✓	✓	✓	✓					✓		✓	✓					✓			✓			✓	✓	
	'MADAME LEGRAS DE ST. GERMAIN'		✓	✓	✓	✓	✓	✓							✓					✓					✓	✓	✓	✓
	'MADAME PLANTIER'		✓	✓	✓	✓	✓	✓	✓						✓					✓				✓		✓		
	'NASTARANA'				✓	✓	✓	✓	✓		✓			✓	✓		✓							✓				
	'PRISTINE'			✓	✓	✓	✓	✓		✓					✓				✓				✓				✓	
	'PROSPERITY'				✓	✓	✓	✓	✓						✓	✓			✓				✓					
	ROSA BANKSIAE BANKSIAE					✓	✓	✓						✓	✓			✓							✓	✓		
	ROSA RUGOSA ALBA	✓	✓	✓	✓	✓	✓				✓		✓	✓		✓							✓			✓		✓
	'SALLY HOLMES'			✓	✓	✓	✓	✓		✓	✓	✓			✓	✓	✓						✓	✓		✓		
	'SEA FOAM'			✓	✓	✓	✓	✓							✓	✓			✓		✓			✓		✓		
	'SILVER MOON'				✓	✓	✓	✓	✓						✓			✓							✓	✓	✓	
	'SNOW BRIDE'			✓	✓	✓	✓	✓							✓	✓			✓		✓					✓		
	'SOMBREUIL'				✓	✓	✓	✓	✓			✓			✓	✓			✓						✓	✓	✓	

163

Column groups: **ZONES** (Zone 3–Zone 10) · **TOLERATES** (Diseases, Heat, Seaside Conditions) · **BLOOMING SEASON** (Spring, Summer, Fall) · **BLOOM TYPE** (Single, Semidouble, Double, Very Double) · **PLANT HABIT** (Miniature, Bush/Shrub <3', Bush/Shrub 3–6', Shrub >6', Climber/Rambler) · **NOTED FOR** (Fragrance, Cut Flowers, Hips)

Color	Variety	Z3	Z4	Z5	Z6	Z7	Z8	Z9	Z10	Partial Shade	Diseases	Heat	Seaside Cond.	Spring	Summer	Fall	Single	Semidouble	Double	Very Double	Miniature	Bush/Shrub <3'	Bush/Shrub 3–6'	Shrub >6'	Climber/Rambler	Fragrance	Cut Flowers	Hips
YELLOW	'WHITE MEIDILAND'		✓	✓	✓	✓	✓			✓				✓	✓				✓			✓						
	'WHITE PET'		✓	✓	✓	✓	✓						✓	✓	✓				✓		✓						✓	
	'ALBERIC BARBIER'		✓	✓	✓	✓	✓	✓		✓	✓	✓		✓		✓			✓						✓	✓		
	'ALCHYMIST'		✓	✓	✓	✓	✓	✓						✓					✓						✓	✓	✓	
	'CELINE FORESTIER'			✓	✓	✓	✓	✓				✓		✓	✓				✓						✓	✓		
	'ELINA'		✓	✓	✓	✓	✓	✓						✓	✓				✓				✓				✓	
	'GOLDEN SHOWERS'		✓	✓	✓	✓	✓	✓		✓	✓			✓	✓				✓						✓	✓	✓	
	'GOLDEN WINGS'	✓	✓	✓	✓	✓	✓	✓			✓	✓		✓	✓	✓	✓						✓			✓	✓	✓
	'GOLD MEDAL'		✓	✓	✓	✓	✓	✓		✓				✓	✓				✓				✓				✓	
	'GRAHAM THOMAS'	✓	✓	✓	✓	✓	✓	✓				✓		✓	✓				✓				✓			✓	✓	
	'GRANADA'		✓	✓	✓	✓	✓	✓						✓	✓				✓				✓			✓	✓	
	'LAFTER'		✓	✓	✓	✓	✓	✓		✓				✓	✓			✓					✓			✓		
	'MRS. DUDLEY CROSS'			✓	✓	✓	✓	✓			✓	✓		✓	✓	✓			✓				✓			✓	✓	
	'MUTABILIS'			✓	✓	✓	✓	✓				✓		✓	✓	✓	✓						✓	✓		✓		
	'PARTY GIRL'		✓	✓	✓	✓	✓	✓						✓	✓				✓	✓		✓						
	'PEACE'		✓	✓	✓	✓	✓	✓		✓				✓	✓				✓				✓				✓	
	'RAINBOW'S END'		✓	✓	✓	✓	✓	✓						✓	✓				✓	✓		✓						
	'REVE D'OR'			✓	✓	✓	✓	✓				✓		✓	✓	✓			✓						✓	✓		
	'RISE 'N' SHINE'		✓	✓	✓	✓	✓	✓		✓				✓	✓				✓	✓		✓						
	'SUN FLARE'	✓	✓	✓	✓	✓	✓	✓		✓				✓	✓				✓				✓			✓	✓	
	'SUNSPRITE'			✓	✓	✓	✓	✓					✓	✓	✓				✓				✓			✓	✓	
ORANGE/APRICOT	'ALBERTINE'		✓	✓	✓	✓	✓	✓						✓					✓					✓	✓	✓		
	'AMERICA'		✓	✓	✓	✓	✓	✓		✓				✓	✓				✓						✓	✓	✓	
	'APRICOT NECTAR'	✓	✓	✓	✓	✓	✓	✓						✓	✓				✓				✓			✓		
	'BUFF BEAUTY'			✓	✓	✓	✓	✓	✓					✓	✓				✓					✓		✓	✓	
	'CHERISH'	✓	✓	✓	✓	✓	✓			✓				✓	✓				✓			✓					✓	
	'FIRST EDITION'	✓	✓	✓	✓	✓	✓	✓		✓				✓	✓				✓				✓				✓	
	'FOLKLORE'		✓	✓	✓	✓	✓	✓						✓	✓				✓				✓			✓	✓	
	'JEAN KENNEALLY'			✓	✓	✓	✓	✓						✓	✓				✓	✓		✓						
	'JUST JOEY'			✓	✓	✓	✓	✓							✓				✓				✓			✓	✓	
	'LEANDER'	✓	✓	✓	✓	✓	✓	✓						✓	✓					✓				✓		✓		
	'LOVING TOUCH'		✓	✓	✓	✓	✓	✓						✓	✓	✓			✓		✓					✓	✓	

		ZONES								TOLERATES				BLOOMING SEASON			BLOOM TYPE				PLANT HABIT					NOTED FOR		
		Zone 3	Zone 4	Zone 5	Zone 6	Zone 7	Zone 8	Zone 9	Zone 10	Partial Shade	Diseases	Heat	Seaside Conditions	Spring	Summer	Fall	Single	Semidouble	Double	Very Double	Miniature	Bush/Shrub <3'	Bush/Shrub 3-6'	Shrub >6'	Climber/Rambler	Fragrance	Cut Flowers	Hips
ORANGE/APRICOT	'MARGO KOSTER'			✓	✓	✓	✓	✓		✓					✓	✓			✓		✓							
	'PIERRINE'			✓	✓	✓	✓	✓						✓	✓	✓		✓				✓				✓		✓
	'PLAYBOY'		✓	✓	✓	✓	✓	✓	✓	✓	✓			✓	✓	✓	✓						✓			✓	✓	✓
	ROSA FOETIDA BICOLOR			✓	✓	✓	✓							✓			✓						✓	✓				
	'STARINA'				✓	✓	✓	✓						✓	✓				✓		✓							
	'TOUCH OF CLASS'			✓	✓	✓	✓	✓						✓	✓				✓			✓					✓	
	'TROPICANA'			✓	✓	✓	✓	✓				✓		✓	✓				✓			✓				✓	✓	
PINK	'AQUARIUS'			✓	✓	✓	✓	✓			✓			✓	✓	✓			✓			✓						
	'AUTUMN DAMASK'		✓	✓	✓	✓	✓							✓	✓	✓			✓			✓				✓		
	'BALLERINA'			✓	✓	✓	✓	✓	✓	✓	✓				✓	✓	✓					✓	✓				✓	
	'BARONNE PREVOST'			✓	✓	✓	✓	✓			✓				✓	✓				✓		✓				✓		
	'BELINDA'			✓	✓	✓	✓	✓		✓	✓				✓	✓		✓				✓	✓	✓				
	'BELLE POITEVINE'	✓	✓	✓	✓	✓	✓	✓		✓		✓		✓	✓			✓				✓				✓		✓
	'BELLE STORY'		✓	✓	✓	✓	✓	✓						✓	✓			✓				✓				✓		
	'BETTY PRIOR'		✓	✓	✓	✓	✓	✓	✓		✓			✓	✓	✓	✓					✓				✓		
	'BONICA'		✓	✓	✓	✓	✓	✓		✓	✓			✓					✓			✓						✓
	'BRIDE'S DREAM'			✓	✓	✓	✓	✓						✓	✓				✓			✓					✓	
	'CAREFREE BEAUTY'		✓	✓	✓	✓	✓	✓			✓			✓	✓			✓				✓				✓		
	'CECILE BRUNNER'		✓	✓	✓	✓	✓			✓				✓	✓	✓			✓			✓				✓	✓	
	'CELESTIAL'		✓	✓	✓	✓	✓	✓	✓						✓				✓			✓				✓		
	'CELSIANA'		✓	✓	✓	✓	✓	✓		✓					✓			✓				✓				✓		
	'COMPLICATA'		✓	✓	✓	✓	✓					✓		✓		✓	✓						✓	✓	✓			✓
	'CONSTANCE SPRY'		✓	✓	✓	✓	✓								✓				✓					✓	✓	✓		
	'CRESTED MOSS'		✓	✓	✓	✓	✓			✓					✓					✓		✓						
	'DAINTY BESS'			✓	✓	✓	✓	✓		✓	✓			✓	✓		✓					✓				✓	✓	
	'DUCHESSE DE BRABANT'				✓	✓	✓	✓						✓	✓	✓			✓			✓				✓		
	'FELICITE PARMENTIER'		✓	✓	✓	✓	✓	✓	✓	✓	✓				✓					✓		✓				✓		
	'FRAU DAGMAR HARTOPP'	✓	✓	✓	✓	✓	✓	✓				✓	✓	✓	✓	✓	✓					✓				✓	✓	✓
	'GARTENDIREKTOR OTTO LINNE'			✓	✓	✓	✓	✓		✓					✓	✓			✓				✓		✓	✓		
	'GRUSS AN AACHEN'			✓	✓	✓	✓	✓	✓	✓	✓			✓	✓	✓			✓		✓	✓				✓	✓	
	'HERITAGE'			✓	✓	✓	✓	✓							✓				✓			✓				✓	✓	
	'ISPAHAN'		✓	✓	✓	✓	✓	✓		✓				✓	✓				✓			✓				✓	✓	

		Zone 3	Zone 4	Zone 5	Zone 6	Zone 7	Zone 8	Zone 9	Zone 10	Partial Shade	Diseases	Heat	Seaside Conditions	Spring	Summer	Fall	Single	Semidouble	Double	Very Double	Miniature	Bush/Shrub <3'	Bush/Shrub 3-6'	Shrub >6'	Climber/Rambler	Fragrance	Cut Flowers	Hips
PINK	'JEANNE LAJOIE'			✓	✓	✓	✓	✓						✓	✓	✓			✓					✓	✓			✓
	'JENS MUNK'	✓	✓	✓	✓	✓	✓	✓		✓		✓		✓	✓	✓			✓				✓			✓		
	'LA MARNE'			✓	✓	✓	✓	✓						✓	✓	✓	✓							✓				
	'LOUISE ODIER'			✓	✓	✓	✓					✓			✓	✓				✓				✓			✓	✓
	'MADAME ISAAC PEREIRE'			✓	✓	✓	✓								✓	✓				✓				✓	✓	✓	✓	✓
	'MARCHESA BOCCELLA'			✓	✓	✓	✓	✓						✓	✓					✓				✓			✓	
	'MINNIE PEARL'			✓	✓	✓	✓	✓				✓			✓	✓				✓		✓						✓
	'MRS. B. R. CANT'				✓	✓	✓	✓				✓		✓	✓	✓				✓				✓	✓		✓	✓
	'NEW DAWN'			✓	✓	✓	✓	✓	✓	✓	✓				✓					✓					✓	✓	✓	
	'OLD BLUSH'				✓	✓	✓	✓	✓			✓	✓		✓	✓				✓				✓				
	'PENELOPE'			✓	✓	✓	✓	✓	✓	✓	✓				✓	✓	✓		✓					✓			✓	
	'QUEEN ELIZABETH'		✓	✓	✓	✓	✓					✓			✓	✓				✓				✓			✓	
	ROSA GLAUCA		✓	✓	✓	✓	✓							✓	✓		✓							✓			✓	✓
	'ROSA MUNDI'		✓	✓	✓	✓	✓	✓			✓				✓			✓						✓			✓	✓	✓
	ROSA PALUSTRIS			✓	✓	✓	✓	✓	✓	✓		✓			✓		✓							✓	✓			✓
	'SOUVENIR DE LA MALMAISON'			✓	✓	✓	✓					✓			✓	✓					✓		✓				✓	
	'THE FAIRY'		✓	✓	✓	✓	✓					✓	✓		✓	✓				✓			✓				✓	
	'TIFFANY'			✓	✓	✓	✓	✓				✓			✓	✓				✓				✓			✓	✓
	'WILLIAM BAFFIN'	✓	✓	✓	✓	✓	✓	✓				✓			✓	✓			✓					✓	✓	✓		
	'ZEPHIRINE DROUHIN'			✓	✓	✓	✓	✓							✓	✓				✓					✓	✓		
RED	'ALTISSIMO'			✓	✓	✓	✓					✓	✓		✓	✓		✓						✓	✓			
	'ARCHDUKE CHARLES'			✓	✓	✓	✓	✓				✓			✓	✓				✓			✓					
	'BLAZE'			✓	✓	✓	✓	✓				✓			✓	✓	✓		✓						✓			
	'CHAMPLAIN'		✓	✓	✓	✓	✓	✓		✓					✓	✓				✓				✓				
	'CHRYSLER IMPERIAL'			✓	✓	✓	✓	✓				✓			✓	✓				✓				✓			✓	✓
	'COUNTRY DANCER'		✓	✓	✓	✓	✓	✓							✓	✓				✓			✓	✓			✓	
	'CRIMSON GLORY'			✓	✓	✓	✓	✓				✓			✓	✓				✓				✓			✓	
	'DON JUAN'			✓	✓	✓	✓	✓			✓				✓	✓	✓			✓					✓	✓	✓	
	'DORTMUND'		✓	✓	✓	✓	✓	✓		✓	✓				✓	✓	✓							✓	✓			✓
	'DOUBLE DELIGHT'			✓	✓	✓	✓	✓							✓	✓				✓			✓				✓	✓
	'DREAMGLO'			✓	✓	✓	✓	✓				✓			✓	✓				✓		✓						
	'DUBLIN BAY'			✓	✓	✓	✓	✓	✓			✓			✓	✓				✓					✓	✓	✓	

COLOR	Variety	ZONE 3	ZONE 4	ZONE 5	ZONE 6	ZONE 7	ZONE 8	ZONE 9	ZONE 10	PARTIAL SHADE	DISEASES	HEAT	SEASIDE CONDITIONS	SPRING	SUMMER	FALL	SINGLE	SEMIDOUBLE	DOUBLE	VERY DOUBLE	MINIATURE	BUSH/SHRUB <3'	BUSH/SHRUB 3-6'	SHRUB >6'	CLIMBER/RAMBLER	FRAGRANCE	CUT FLOWERS	HIPS
RED	'EUROPEANA'		✓	✓	✓	✓	✓	✓		✓					✓	✓			✓		✓	✓					✓	
	'F. J. GROOTENDORST'	✓	✓	✓	✓	✓	✓	✓	✓	✓		✓			✓	✓			✓			✓						
	'FRAGRANT CLOUD'			✓	✓	✓	✓	✓							✓	✓			✓			✓				✓	✓	
	'HANSA'	✓	✓	✓	✓	✓						✓	✓	✓	✓	✓			✓			✓				✓		✓
	'HURDY GURDY'			✓	✓	✓	✓	✓	✓			✓		✓	✓	✓			✓		✓	✓						
	'JOHN CABOT'	✓	✓	✓	✓	✓	✓	✓							✓	✓			✓						✓			
	'JOHN FRANKLIN'		✓	✓	✓	✓	✓	✓						✓	✓			✓				✓				✓		
	'LINDA CAMPBELL'	✓	✓	✓	✓	✓	✓			✓		✓			✓	✓		✓				✓						
	'LOUIS PHILIPPE'				✓	✓	✓	✓		✓				✓	✓	✓			✓			✓				✓		
	'MAGIC CARROUSEL'			✓	✓	✓	✓	✓	✓						✓	✓			✓		✓					✓		
	'MISTER LINCOLN'			✓	✓	✓	✓	✓		✓					✓				✓			✓				✓	✓	
	'OLYMPIAD'			✓	✓	✓	✓	✓							✓	✓			✓			✓				✓		
	'ROGER LAMBELIN'			✓	✓	✓	✓	✓						✓	✓	✓			✓			✓				✓		
	'ROSERAIE DE L'HAY'	✓	✓	✓	✓	✓	✓					✓	✓	✓	✓	✓	✓					✓				✓		
	'SHOWBIZ'			✓	✓	✓	✓	✓	✓						✓	✓			✓	✓		✓				✓		
	'THERESE BUGNET'	✓	✓	✓	✓	✓	✓					✓			✓				✓			✓				✓		
	'UNCLE JOE'			✓	✓	✓	✓	✓							✓	✓				✓		✓				✓	✓	
	'VARIEGATA DI BOLOGNA'			✓	✓	✓	✓								✓					✓		✓		✓	✓	✓		
	'WILL SCARLET'			✓	✓	✓	✓	✓	✓	✓					✓		✓		✓			✓			✓			✓
MAUVE/PURPLE	'ANGEL FACE'		✓	✓	✓	✓									✓	✓			✓			✓				✓	✓	
	'CAMAIEUX'		✓	✓	✓	✓	✓	✓				✓			✓				✓			✓				✓	✓	
	'CARDINAL DE RICHELIEU'		✓	✓	✓	✓	✓					✓			✓				✓			✓				✓		
	'CELINA'		✓	✓	✓	✓						✓			✓		✓					✓				✓		
	'DELICATA'	✓	✓	✓	✓	✓	✓	✓		✓		✓		✓	✓	✓		✓				✓				✓		✓
	'ESCAPADE'		✓	✓	✓	✓	✓	✓							✓	✓	✓					✓					✓	
	'LAVENDER LASSIE'			✓	✓	✓	✓	✓					✓		✓	✓			✓				✓	✓	✓			
	'PARADISE'			✓	✓	✓	✓	✓							✓	✓			✓			✓				✓	✓	
	'PLUM DANDY'			✓	✓	✓	✓	✓						✓	✓	✓				✓	✓					✓		
	'REINES DES VIOLETTES'		✓	✓	✓	✓									✓				✓			✓			✓	✓	✓	
	'RUGOSA MAGNIFICA'	✓	✓	✓	✓	✓	✓	✓					✓	✓	✓	✓	✓					✓				✓		✓
	'TUSCANY'		✓	✓	✓	✓	✓	✓				✓			✓			✓				✓				✓		--
	'VEILCHENBLAU'			✓	✓	✓	✓			✓					✓			✓		✓				✓	✓	✓	✓	

CHAPTER SIX

Shade Gardening

Shade falls on just about every property at some time, and a large amount of it can leave a gardener feeling unlucky. But don't despair. The virtues of shade far outweigh the few restrictions it imposes.

Whether it is cast by trees or by the walls of a house, shade can make a garden into a refreshing place—a haven from heat and harsh sunlight. Shaded spots need not be dark, dank places. Even a patch that sees only short periods of sun, or perhaps no direct sun at all, can still collect enough light to grow sun-loving plants, such as the pale blue delphinium nestled among violets, columbines, and enormous foxgloves in the partial shade of the California garden at right.

In this chapter you will find out how to use shade to best advantage, both for its practical benefits and as a design element. You will also learn ways of analyzing the light conditions on your property and, if necessary, altering them. And you will discover the large array of plants that not only survive but thrive in all types of shade.

The Nature of Shade

Whether you live on a small city plot that is hemmed in by fences and neighboring houses or on a suburban property where saplings planted decades ago have matured into sizable trees, you must, as a gardener, come to terms with shade. The best way to start is to understand the practical benefits it offers.

Shade can be a gardener's best ally in hot climates. Not only does it provide a cool retreat from the sun, it also, by moderating extremes of heat, broadens the range of plants you can grow. The temperature under a tree, for example, may be 15° cooler than out in the sun.

To survive in the South, all but the toughest plants need some relief from the intense summer heat. For example, the delicate petals of *Clematis lanuginosa* 'Nelly Moser' can fade from a dark pink to a bleached-out tinge of color if they are not protected from strong sunlight. And although plants tend to bear fewer flowers in the shade than they would if they were growing in full sun, the blossoms will last longer. Even sunloving annuals such as *Cleome* (spider plant) will have longer-lasting blooms when they are grown in partial shade.

Not just flower petals but also foliage may need the protection of shade. For example, the frosty blue leaves of *Hosta* 'Krossa Regal' (plantain lily) may turn brown in the direct sun of the South. *Cimicifuga* (bugbane) exposed to sun can collapse and wither away, even if the plant has been given plenty of water.

Another considerable benefit of shade is that no matter where you live, shade cuts down on maintenance chores. First, a shady garden needs less water. In the cool shelter of a tree or wall, moisture evaporates from the soil more slowly and needs replenishing less often.

Pruning becomes less of a chore as well. Plants that have evolved in the low light of the forest tend to grow more slowly and need less cutting back than sun lovers. If you choose plants that are conditioned to shade and grow them in adequate soil with ample space around each one, you should be able to leave them undisturbed for many years.

A shade garden will also have less of a struggle with certain pests—aphids, mites, and scale—although you may have to anticipate other pests and diseases that are partial to shade plants. Slugs and snails, for example, prefer cool shady areas.

Shade Foliage and Flowers

In addition to lightening a gardener's chores, shade also confers design benefits—in the types of plants you can grow and in the impact of shade itself on garden design.

Shade-tolerant species are among the most unusual and beautiful of all garden plants, producing leaves and flowers in a vast range of sizes, textures, and colors. In shade, you can grow the spectacular *Gunnera manicata* (giant rhubarb), with leaves that are sometimes as wide as 6 feet, and the minuscule *Soleirolia soleirolii* (baby's-tears), which carpets the ground with shiny green leaves that are as small as the nail on your little finger. You can also choose from an array of leaf textures and shapes ranging from the lacy brocades of ferns, astilbes, corydalis, and *Dicentra* (bleeding heart) to the broad masses of *Ligularia* (leopard plant), *Rodgersia,* hydrangea, and *Mahonia* (Oregon grape).

Much of the color in a shade garden will come from foliage, especially from variegated leaves. Varieties of hosta, *Pulmonaria* (lungwort), *Hedera* (ivy), *Elaeagnus* (oleaster), *Ilex* (holly), *Ajuga* (bugleweed), *Euonymus* (spindle tree), *Vinca* (periwinkle), and *Lamium* (dead nettle) are striped, speckled, or blotched with cream or white. Caladium, the ultimate shade foliage plant, is splashed with tones of cream, pink, purple, orange-red, or scarlet.

In addition to the marvels of shade foliage, you will also find a delightful assortment of flowers that are completely at home in shade. Some of the earliest-blooming plants in the garden do best when they are out of direct sunlight: perennials such as *Helleborus* (hellebore), lungwort, *Primula* (primrose), *Galanthus* (snowdrop), and *Scilla* (squill); the flowering shrubs *Hamamelis* (witch hazel), rhododendron, and *Corylopsis* (winter hazel); and the small trees *Cornus* (dogwood) and *Cercis* (redbud).

In the diffused light of shade, flower colors appear more saturated. Whites and pale yellows shine against the dark background of a shady spot and do not look faded, as they might in full sun. Yet strong contrasts among colors are toned down. Orange with blue, or yellow with purple, which might be eye-popping in strong light, become mellow in shade.

This Virginia garden sited between a sun-streaked lawn and a dappled woodland shows how plants with varying light requirements can be neighbors. Parts of the garden get enough light for such sun lovers as Achillea 'Moonshine', ornamental onion, Yucca filamentosa, variegated maiden grass, and roses. These coexist happily with such shade stalwarts as Hosta 'Gold Standard', ligularia, hardy geranium, and hellebore, planted to the left of the bed.

Analyzing Shade

To incorporate shade into a coherent garden design, you must first know what type of shade you have. You must understand what is casting the shade and how to track the shade footprint as it sweeps across your property from hour to hour and from season to season.

Shade comes mainly from two sources: structures and plants. A third, more temporary, shade maker is the atmosphere—clouds, fog, and even pollution, which can filter out substantial sunlight. This last source of shade is the reason cities generally receive less sun than dry, windy, and high-altitude areas.

Evaluating the light that reaches your plants is an inexact science. The common measures are duration and intensity, both of which vary by time of day, season, and latitude—the position of your garden relative to the equator *(pages 172-173)*.

Duration, or how long a spot is shaded, is easy to observe. Intensity, on the other hand, requires a bit more thought. Sunlight is least intense in the morning, for three reasons: The sun is low in the sky; the earth is cool from the hours without sun; and the humidity near the ground is high, scattering some of the light.

The sun is at its most intense at noon because that is when its rays travel almost straight down through the atmosphere with minimal deflection or dispersion; this is also the time when shadows are at their shortest. By afternoon, although the angle of the sun's rays is once again becoming acute, the sun remains intense because the day's heat has evaporated most of the moisture from the ground surface.

Categories of Shade

A useful way to make sense of these complexities is to organize shade into general types based on a combination of duration and intensity:

• **Partial shade.** This is the sunniest shade, in which an area receives up to 6 hours of direct sun, including 4 or more hours in the morning, but lies in shadow the rest of the day. Many plants listed as requiring full shade will tolerate partial shade if the soil is kept moist, especially in cooler climates. And many sun plants will adapt well to partial shade. Note, however, that if 4 or more of those 6 hours of sun occur in the afternoon instead of the morning, the area is considered to be in full sun.

• **Filtered or dappled shade.** The sun's light is screened through the open foliage of high-branched trees or through latticework structures. It shines in shifting patterns all day, thus striking with diminished intensity. Most plants will thrive in dappled shade, though sun lovers might produce fewer flowers than they would in full sun.

• **Full shade.** Direct sunlight never reaches an area in full shade. Some full shade may be deep and dense, and few plants will survive there. But an area in full shade can also experience considerable ambient or reflected light and sky shine. These conditions often occur on the north side of a building, fence, hedge, or tree. Shade-tolerant plants will grow in this kind of full shade if they have enough air circulation and moisture. By contrast, if trees are spaced too close together or include species with dense roots on or just below the surface, the soil will have little water or nutrients for other plants. This so-called dry shade condition is the worst kind of full shade for gardeners.

Planning a Shade Garden

As straightforward as these categories seem, probably no environmental condition on a property is as hard to quantify as shade. It not only shifts through the day and year but also deepens and spreads as trees mature and suddenly disappears when a tree dies or is removed. So give yourself as much time as possible to study the different types of shade on your property before doing anything irrevocable to change them. Look at the garden in winter, when it is least shaded, and in summer, when plants are in full leaf. Map out where the sunlight falls through the day and through the year. Look for indicators, such as the presence of moss, that might point out shadows in places where you simply never noticed them.

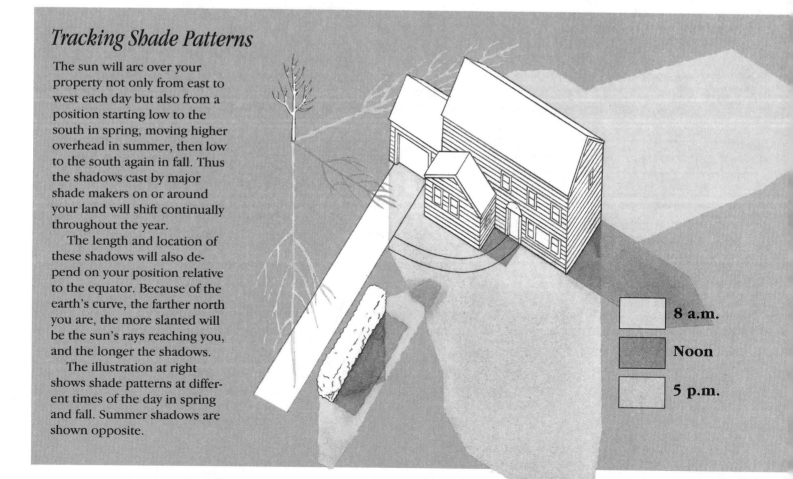

Tracking Shade Patterns

The sun will arc over your property not only from east to west each day but also from a position starting low to the south in spring, moving higher overhead in summer, then low to the south again in fall. Thus the shadows cast by major shade makers on or around your land will shift continually throughout the year.

The length and location of these shadows will also depend on your position relative to the equator. Because of the earth's curve, the farther north you are, the more slanted will be the sun's rays reaching you, and the longer the shadows.

The illustration at right shows shade patterns at different times of the day in spring and fall. Summer shadows are shown opposite.

8 a.m.

Noon

5 p.m.

If there are any high walls or large trees that substantially block out light, consider making some changes. You could paint a dark wall a pale color to reflect more light, or prune large trees to thin out the leafy canopy. A more drastic step is to remove a tree. Plan this action carefully, however—tree removal can be quite expensive and is, of course, permanent. Keep your best shade trees, especially those with deep roots and small leaves that don't block sun and rain. Those preferred for moderate climates are oak *(Quercus)*, Kentucky yellowwood *(Cladrastis lutea)*, and black tupelo *(Nyssa sylvatica)*; olive *(Olea)* and loblolly pine *(Pinus taeda)* are desirable in warm climates; and bald cypress *(Taxodium distichum)* works well in boggy soil.

The bane of the shade garden is shallow-rooted trees with dense leaf canopies that rob underlying plants not only of light but also of moisture and nourishment. The greediest types are beech *(Fagus)*, elm *(Ulmus)*, and the particularly troublesome Norway, sugar, and silver maples *(Acer platanoides, A. saccharum,* and *A. saccharinum,* respectively). Remove elms and silver maples and make do with the others by creating a raised bed around the tree or, as a last resort, by trimming the roots. Note, however, that trimmed tree roots may reinvade in a single season. In this case, containers filled with plants arranged around the base of the tree may be your best alternative.

Recognizing Shade Lovers

Shade plants have evolved to compete effectively for the limited light of a woodland or rain forest. Generally, their leaves, like those of this Hosta 'Frances Williams', are large, dark, and flat, enabling them to absorb the maximum possible light for photosynthesis. The surfaces also shed rainwater easily, which helps them resist disease. Shade plants conserve energy by producing fewer flowers and fruit.

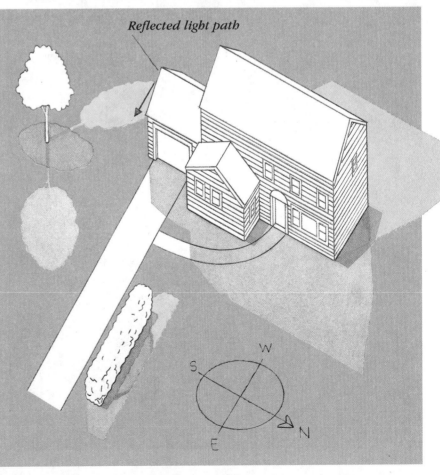

Reflected light path

In spring and fall (left), shadows are long. Both the house and the hedge on this property—located at latitude 38°N, which stretches from Washington, D.C., to San Francisco—throw a small patch of all-day shade along their northern side year round. But during these seasons, much larger shadows begin in the west in early morning (green shadows), shorten considerably at noon (red shadows), and lengthen to the east in the afternoon (blue shadows). With the sun low in the sky to the south at these times, the northern side of the house and the hedge stay chilly. The soil and the plants residing in their shadows are thus protected from cycles of freezing and thawing.

The same property in summer (right) receives far more sunlight, as the shadows shrink closer to house and hedge. Full shade still exists along the northern wall and on the north side of the hedge, where morning, noon, and afternoon shadows overlap. But south-facing vertical surfaces bear the brunt of unrelieved sunshine throughout the day and reflect it back to the ground. Thus the shade under the tree, though full, is quite bright. In the morning and afternoon, the sun's rays, striking at a slant, cast longer shadows than at noon. But with surface moisture dissipated by the afternoon, the sun burns hotter, and plants getting a western exposure need extra water.

Flowering Plants for Shade

Red- and white-flowering trillium, blooming amid native bleeding heart in this Portland garden, is a wide-ranging native. Over 30 trillium species grow wild in U.S. woodlands.

Shade plants were among the first flowering vegetation to appear on earth. Cousins of those primordial flowers flourish in shady gardens today in the form of rhododendron and magnolia species, and many other shade plants have since evolved in the shadows of taller neighbors. Nurseries now offer a steady stream of new shade-tolerant varieties.

Ornamental trees are the most prominent plants to display brilliant color in the shade. Many produce not only flowers but also colorful fruit. Dogwood *(Cornus)* trees, for example, bear flowerlike bracts in the spring and may display bright berries or tinted bark in the winter. *Stewartia* produces white flowers in summer and exhibits handsomely mottled bark throughout the winter.

Shrubs and Vines

At eye level come a host of shrubs that, like ornamental trees, bring sparkling color to the shade garden not only with flowers but also with berries in many hues. Rhododendron species—which include the azaleas—are mainstays for shady areas throughout much of North America. Their bloom times range from early spring into the summer, and flower colors run from white to deep purple. While most azaleas are deciduous shrubs, almost all other rhododendrons are evergreen, helping to maintain the garden's structure year round.

Hydrangea is another reliable shade shrub, with long-lasting summer blooms in white, pink, or blue. Soil chemistry governs color in some cultivars, with acid soil producing blue flowers and alkaline soil, pink. A climbing form, *H. anomala* var. *petiolaris,* winds along walls or around trees.

Less commonly grown, but handsome, shrubs for the shade garden include the evergreen *Mahonia* (Oregon grape), with cascades of yellow flowers in early spring and edible berries later. In late spring, *Gaultheria shallon* (salal) yields spikes of tiny white or pink flowers, followed by purple to black berries.

Strong performers for partial shade include *Chionanthus virginicus* (old-man's-beard), which produces fragrant white flowers in late spring, and mountain laurel *(Kalmia latifolia)*, which fares well in full shade but flowers best with some sun.

Most flowering vines are considered sun lovers, but a few, such as *Gelsemium sempervirens* 'Pride of Augusta', *Akebia quinata* (five-leaf akebia), and some species of clematis and *Lonicera* (honeysuckle), will bloom in partial shade, and some, such as *Aristolochia macrophylla* (Dutchman's-pipe) and x *Fatshedera lizei* (miracle plant) don't care for direct sun at all.

Herbaceous Bloomers

Shade-loving herbaceous perennials make up a long and colorful list. No perennial bed or border in shade need lack for variety and visual impact. But the story doesn't end there. Gardeners in the South can also use partially shaded sites to grow a large number of perennials that require full sun in northern zones. Indeed, no matter where you live, you may be able to grow perennial species and cultivars you never thought you could simply by understanding their origins and getting tips from other gardeners who have grown them.

Annuals, like flowering vines, are generally held to be sun plants, but many can bloom in dappled or partial shade. The beautiful, easy-care impatiens—a dependable favorite of shade gardeners—flowers freely in whites, pinks, reds, oranges, and a few blue-violets. Ageratum, a tidy little plant with blue, pink, or white flowers, tolerates partial shade and blooms for a long time without deadheading. Begonia flowers dependably from spring through to frost—or year round, in frost-free zones. Similarly, fuchsia blooms richly as an annual in hanging baskets in the shade, and hardy varieties survive the year in mild climates.

Wildflowers hold a special place in shade gardens: Shade-conditioned native plants can provide color and interest from earliest spring through late summer. Some, like jack-in-the-pulpit or dogtooth violet, grow, bloom, and disappear quickly. But others, including the dainty spray of Solomon's-seal, last for weeks, while a rare native, *Spigelia marilandica* (Indian pink), opens new blooms over a long period.

Bulbs are another good source of herbaceous flowers for the shade garden. About half of all bulb genera tolerate, prefer, or require a degree of shade. A few are comfortable even in full shade—for example, *Achimenes* (orchid pansy), *Arisaema* (dragonroot), *Begonia* x *tuberhybrida* (tuberous

The sprightly pale lavender blooms of the perennial Anemone nemorosa (wood anemone) spread a frothy carpet from which the compact forms of the evergreen Rhododendron yakusimanum emerge, bursting with bell-shaped pink flowers. Forming a backdrop to this cheerful Oregon garden is another, larger rhododendron and the pendulous brilliant yellow blossoms of a small Laburnum (bean tree).

begonia), dogtooth violet, *Hyacinthoides,* and *Ornithogalum nutans* (nodding star-of-Bethlehem).

Ground Covers

And finally, carpeting the shade-garden floor with blossoms are some of the most popular evergreen and deciduous ground covers, with flowers ranging from white to yellow to blue-purple. *Vinca* (periwinkle) sends evergreen strands across almost any type of soil and produces blossoms in white or violet, according to the cultivar. *Heuchera* displays beautifully veined foliage and red, pink, or greenish white flowers. And several types of *Epimedium* (bishop's hat), such as *E. perralderanum* and *E.* x *versicolor* 'Sulphureum', blanket the ground even in dry shade and produce lovely yellow blossoms.

Unique Traits of Shade Plants

Diverse though they are, flowering shade plants share many characteristics derived from the often difficult conditions in which they exist. Adapted to soil already congested by tree roots, for example, most shade-loving varieties have shallow roots. This makes planting them easy; even large rhododendrons have manageable rootballs.

Shade lovers are also highly sensitive to moisture levels in the soil. Many require a natural layer of leaf litter or an application of mulch to keep them from drying out. Paradoxically, this trait makes the shady flower garden a fairly low-maintenance proposition. In fall, you need remove only the heaviest drifts of fallen leaves from areas planted with flowering species, leaving in place a protective covering of leaf litter.

In the partial shade of this Pennsylvania cottage garden, a gold-tipped Chamaecyparis obtusa 'Crippsii' (Hinoki false cypress) and a white-blossomed viburnum anchor drifts of pale lavender-blue forget-me-not and snowy candytuft. Hybrid tulips provide splashes of pink.

Shade-flowering plants have a few other virtues that make life easier for the gardener. Many of them self-sow, meaning that if you don't tidy up too much, you'll get more seedlings to increase your stock of plants. And those plants pollinated by insects have a variety of ways to attract them. In shrubs such as *Chionanthus* (fringe tree), which blooms in spring, or those that flower in late winter, such as *Hamamelis* (witch hazel) and *Chimonanthus* (wintersweet), rich fragrance entices the pollinators. Color, too, plays a role. Foraging bees respond to blue and yellow above all other colors, and bright yellow is among the commonest flower colors in shade-blooming species. The vivid red of cardinal flower *(Lobelia cardinalis),* one of the few shade-blooming plants pollinated by birds, attracts hummingbirds to its languid blossoms.

The Effects of Color

Besides attracting pollinators, color contributes mightily to the mood of a garden. The glowing yellow of spring flowers warms us and draws us in; the heat of summer seems moderated by pastel flowers under trees, furthering the shade's actual cooling effect. Shadows tend to make colors look deeper and to heighten blue tones. White flowers appear brighter in shade; an all-white garden fairly glows in the low light.

In fact, the same blossom on a given plant may take on a color in shade that is markedly different from the one it wears in sun. And because shade softens contrasting flower colors, you can use bolder combinations than you might otherwise dare. Bear in mind, too, that a given flower color can strike different notes on different types of plants. A sprinkling of pink lily blooms is gentle and soothing, while the massed blossoms of one pink azalea can inflame an entire area.

Flowering dogwood glows in the dappled shade of spring in this St. Louis garden. The tree's fall foliage and bright berries will shine long after the bluebells and bleeding heart below it have retired, providing interest throughout the year.

TIPS FROM THE PROS
Choosing Flowers for Shade

Remember these tips when making your plant selections:

- Plants grow leggier in shade, so buy the bushiest, most compact specimens you can.
- Don't collect wildflowers from the wild. Learn what plants can be nursery propagated, and buy them only from sources certifying that the plants were propagated— not merely grown—in the nursery. Consult native-plant societies and local arboretums for suggestions about plants and other information.

- When buying plants that are marked shade-tolerant, pick varieties that bloom early, when deciduous trees still admit the light they need for their most active growth.
- If you like a certain sunloving plant but have only shade, try it there. Many sun plants appreciate afternoon shade; others adjust to dappled shade, especially in the South. Sun plants that originated in cool areas are good candidates for growing in partial shade in the South.

Planting for Year-Round Color

With careful planning, it's possible for shade gardens in many North American hardiness zones to have flowers or fruit displaying color all through the year. Milder climates favor flowery displays, of course, but even in snow country, a shade garden can be bright through the cold months.

Your greatest allies are trees and shrubs, which not only may produce berries and display colorful bark but also will provide shelter for other plants. Massed plantings of trees and shrubs cut the force of drying winds, both winter and summer. Even leafless bushes make a noticeable windbreak.

Sizing Up Your Site

One secret to achieving a garden with color the year round is to make use of microclimates. These areas, created both by shade and by the effects of various physical features, can allow you to grow plants you might otherwise not consider.

The shady north wall of your house, for example, may be the perfect place to set an early-blooming shrub, shielding it from sun that might encourage it to flower a little too early for its own good. And the same cover that gives your plants shade—be it wall, fence, or tree—also provides some protection from battering by hard rain, hail, or wind. Rocks, too, provide protection, not only from desiccating wind but also from sunscald, a kind of damage that can occur to bark low on the west side of tree trunks exposed to intense afternoon sun in winter. And large rocks not only cast shade but also absorb and store heat, creating microclimates around them.

Similarly, an exposed slope that looks frigid might actually warm up faster on winter mornings than a naturally enclosed "frost pocket" at the bottom of the hill. And a water feature—a stream, or even a small lily pond—has at least a modest tempering effect on cold or heat, letting temperature-sensitive plants flourish near it.

Choosing the Plants

When deciding on flowering plants to add to your shade garden, keep in mind the ideal of a succession of bloom. A sequence of flowers seen through more than one season is far more interesting than a great show of bloom all at once, followed by long stretches of green only. Mixing plants that bloom at different times also lets you use flower colors to alter your garden's moods dramatically during the year.

Spring's Explosion of Color

Spring is the peak time for flowering for most shade-tolerant genera, just as it is for sun lovers. In a secluded corner under a white-flowering dogwood, for instance, a brilliant splash of tulips can open the gardening season with pizzazz. As the tulips fade and their foliage becomes shabby, an early shade perennial like *Dicentra spectabilis* (common bleeding heart), with its arching lines of pink and white blossoms, can take over the area; for yellow blossoms, use *Corydalis lutea*.

Indeed, you can fill a bed with almost any color that suits you, including the blues, violets, and whites that so nicely light up a shaded area. Virginia bluebells or Siberian iris are good choices for

Sun-loving tulips and phlox adorn a wooded Alabama pathway in early spring, before the trees leaf out overhead. The blue Phlox divaricata (wild sweet William) will hide the dying tulip foliage later in the season, just as the blossom focus shifts to the massed azaleas at upper right and to other shade-loving species.

The rosy purple foliage of spring-blooming blue ajuga (below) forms a ground-cover mat beneath the hostas at left in this northeastern shade garden. Hydrangea contrasts with the wall of evergreen trees behind, echoing the pink in the spring-blooming irises.

most areas. You can also set out tender annuals after the last frost date: Impatiens, begonias, and ageratums cover most of the color families, with yellows best represented by tuberous begonias.

Ground covers can adorn your open spaces with flowers in shades of yellow *(Mahonia repens)*, white *(Pachysandra terminalis)*, or blue *(Vinca major)*. *Akebia quinata,* with its dark purple blooms, yellow-blossomed *Gelsemium sempervirens* 'Pride of Augusta', and white climbing hydrangea are among the vines that flower early. And spring is also the season when the great majority of flowering shrubs and trees for shade produce their blooms *(chart, page 180).*

Summer-Flowering Plants

Although the possibilities are not quite as broad as in spring, enough shade-loving perennials bloom in summer to allow you to plan for a wide range of colors—in fact, there is no spring color you cannot duplicate in your summer herbaceous shade bed or border. Possibilities for summer-flowering ground covers are fewer, but include white-blossomed *Ardisia japonica* (marlberry) and bright yellow *Hypericum calycinum* (creeping St.-John's-wort). For vines, choose *Aristo-*

lochia macrophylla, with purplish brown, yellow-throated flowers; bluish purple *Clematis* 'The President'; or *Jasminum officinale* 'Grandiflorum' (common white jasmine), whose blooms carry over into autumn.

Among shrubs, several hydrangea and kalmia cultivars, as well as white-blooming *Abelia* x *grandiflora* 'Prostrata', golden yellow *Hypericum* 'Hidcote', yellow-green *Laurus nobilis* (laurel), fragrant white sweet bay magnolia, and purple-and-orange *Stewartia ovata* var. *grandiflora* (mountain camellia) flower in summer. Summer-blossoming trees include *Stewartia pseudocamellia* (Japanese stewartia), with orange-and-white flowers, and *Styrax obassia* (fragrant snowbell), with flowers hanging in white racemes.

Autumn and Winter Bloomers

Fall-flowering herbaceous plants still offer a fair range of colors. If, for example, you add Japanese anemone to the mix of plants in your bed or border, you'll get late-summer flower heads in shades of red and pink that coordinate with the changing foliage of trees and shrubs. Some late-blooming hardy chrysanthemums tolerate light shade, too. Autumn crocus bulbs, concealed among tree

179

FLOWERING TIMES FOR SELECTED SHRUBS, VINES, AND TREES

Shade-flowering plants can be classified according to the conditions that allow them to bloom. Some flower when the weather is cold; others when nights are cold but days are warm, as in spring and autumn; still others in warm weather. Except where otherwise noted, all plants listed do well in both partial and dappled shade.

PLANT	TYPE	COMMENTS
Cold Climate (from below freezing to 60°F)		
Camellia oleifera and *C. sasanqua* (camellia)	Evergreen shrub	Blooms throughout winter, depending on cultivar.
Cornus mas (cornelian cherry)	Small deciduous tree	Produces berries for birds.
Corylopsis pauciflora (buttercup winter hazel)	Deciduous shrub	Tolerates alkaline soil.
Daphne odora (winter daphne)	Evergreen shrub	Tender in northern zones; very fragrant.
Hamamelis species (witch hazel)	Deciduous shrub	Fragrant.
Jasminum nudiflorum (winter jasmine)	Deciduous shrub	Fragrant; can be trained up walls or fences.
Lonicera fragrantissima (winter honeysuckle)	Semi-evergreen vine	Very fragrant; climbs walls or fences.
Mahonia bealei (leatherleaf mahonia)	Evergreen shrub	Fragrant; produces large berries; tolerates full shade.
Sarcococca (sweet box)	Evergreen shrub	Fragrant; tolerates dry and full shade.
Cool Nights/Warm Days (40° to 70°F)		
Amelanchier canadensis (shadblow serviceberry)	Deciduous shrub	Some have edible berries; tolerates full shade.
Calycanthus floridus (Carolina allspice)	Deciduous shrub	Fragrant.
Camellia japonica (common camellia)	Evergreen shrub	Blooms in early spring.
Cercis (redbud)	Small deciduous tree	
Cornus species (dogwood)	Small deciduous tree	
Cotoneaster (cotoneaster)	Shrub, ground cover	Some are evergreen; some have berries.
Fothergilla (fothergilla)	Deciduous shrub	Fragrant; bright autumn foliage.
Fuchsia (lady's-eardrops)	Shrub; vine	Tender to hardy; blooms throughout warm weather; tolerates full shade.
Gelsemium sempervirens (false jasmine)	Evergreen vine	
Halesia (silver bell)	Small deciduous tree	Tender to hardy, depending on cultivar
Jasminum mesnyi (Japanese jasmine)	Evergreen shrub or vine	Fragrant.
Kalmia (American laurel)	Shrub	Most evergreen; may flower early summer; tolerates full shade.

PLANT	TYPE	COMMENTS
Cool Nights/Warm Days (continued)		
Kerria japonica (Japanese rose)	Deciduous shrub	
Lonicera 'Serotina Florida' (woodbine)	Semi-evergreen vine	Fragrant; blooms from late summer into fall frosts.
Magnolia species (magnolia)	Evergreen or deciduous tree	Some species grow very large.
Malus species (apple)	Small deciduous tree	Produces edible fruit.
Nandina domestica (heavenly bamboo)	Evergreen shrub	Red winter foliage on some cultivars.
Osmanthus species (devilwood)	Small evergreen tree or shrub	White-bordered foliage on some cultivars.
Pieris (andromeda)	Evergreen shrub	White-bordered foliage on some cultivars.
Prunus (plum, cherry, peach)	Small deciduous tree	Most species flower in spring.
Rhododendron (azalea)	Deciduous or evergreen shrub	Bloom time varies by cultivar, early spring-late summer.
Skimmia japonica (Japanese skimmia)	Evergreen shrub	Male flowers are fragrant.
Warm Climate (above 60°F)		
Abelia (abelia)	Deciduous shrub	
Akebia quinata (five-leaf akebia)	Semi-deciduous vine	
Callicarpa (beautyberry)	Deciduous shrub	Late-summer berries persist to provide winter color.
Chionanthus virginicus (old-man's-beard)	Deciduous shrub	Fragrant.
Clematis (virgin's-bower)	Deciduous vine	Some spring/summer bloomers repeat in autumn.
Clethra alnifolia (sweet pepperbush)	Deciduous shrub	Fragrant; tolerates wet soil.
Hydrangea (hydrangea)	Deciduous shrub	Blooms change color through season on most cultivars.
Jasminum officinale (white jasmine)	Deciduous shrub	Fragrant; can be trained as climber.
Rhododendron (azalea)	Large-leaved evergreen shrub	Flowers late spring through summer, depending on cultivar; tolerates full shade.
Trachelospermum jasminoides (star jasmine)	Evergreen vine	Fragrant; tolerates moist soil and full shade.
Viburnum (arrowwood)	Deciduous shrub	Flowers on some varieties have unpleasant scent.

roots, send up lavish pink cups amid russet fallen leaves to startle and delight garden visitors.

In addition, you can expect a pretty spectrum of autumn blossom colors to emerge on the pale-green-flowered vine x *Fatshedera lizei;* shrubs such as lavender-pink *Camellia* 'Winter's Interlude', white *Fatsia japonica* (glossy-leaved paper plant), and white *Osmanthus heterophyllus* 'Variegatus' (holly olive); and the orange-flowered ornamental tree *Osmanthus fragrans* (sweet olive).

After a hiatus during the first part of winter, you can complete the year of shade perennials with late-winter-blooming plants such as white-flowering *Galanthus nivalis* 'Flore Pleno' (common snowdrop) and *Leucojum vernum* (spring snowflake), yellow *Eranthis hyemalis* (winter aconite), or purple *Viola odorata* 'Royal Robe' (sweet violet). The seed heads left standing on the Japanese anemones that flowered in late summer make a further contribution to the shade garden's winter look—they assume striking shapes when snow mounds on them.

A number of shrubs flower during this season, including *Camellia japonica* 'Berenice Boddy', with pink semidouble blooms; lavender *Daphne mezereum* (February daphne); rosy purple *D. odora* (winter daphne); reddish-brown-and-yellow *Hamamelis mollis* 'Goldcrest' (Chinese witch hazel); yellow to red *H. vernalis* (American witch hazel); yellow winter jasmine; and cream-colored *Sarcococca confusa* (sweet box).

Beyond Blooms

After their flowers are gone, some woody plants keep the color coming with berries, which come into their own as the leaves fall from deciduous shrubs and trees. On evergreen species, berries ripen to showy colors in autumn. Besides being decorative, many berries attract birds and other wildlife to your garden. Most of the berries are borne on shrubs—the fruits of the herbaceous perennial *Arum italicum* (Italian arum) and ornamental holly trees are exceptions. Reliable berry-growing shade species include red chokeberry, American holly, *I. verticillata* (winterberry), beautyberry, *Fatsia japonica, Gaultheria procumbens* (wintergreen), *G. shallon,* bayberry, heavenly bamboo, *Viburnum prunifolium* (black haw), and *V. dilatatum* (linden viburnum).

If you want to keep the berries on your bushes longer, put in cultivars that produce yellow or orange fruit; the birds go for the red ones first. Use the chart at left to help you choose shrubs that flower at different times.

A New Breed of Camellias for the Cold-Climate Shade Garden

Bearing glossy evergreen leaves and large, elegant flowers of white, pink, or red, shade-loving *Camellia* resembles rhododendron in its qualities and growing preferences. Both genera originated in mountain woodlands, which means they prefer shade and acid soil. Both often have shallow roots. Depending on species and cultivar, camellia blooms either in fall and early winter or in early to late spring. But unlike rhododendron, until lately it was too tender to grow in most of North America north of Zone 8. A breeding program begun at the National Arboretum in Washington, D.C., has developed crosses between a fall-blooming camellia, *C. oleifera,* from the People's Republic of China, and three other species, yielding plants hardy to -2° F. For a good performer in Zones 6-8, look for *C. oleifera* or *C. sasanqua.*

Plant the new hardy camellias where they will be protected from winter winds and morning sun, setting the base of the stem slightly higher than the surrounding soil. Water thoroughly once a week through the first season. Maintain 2 to 4 inches of mulch around the plant to keep the soil moist and stable through periods of freezing and thawing.

Plants for Problem Areas

Whether you are adding flowering species to an existing shade garden or are planning a new garden area, deciding which plants to put in requires some forethought. Impulse purchases at the local nursery can be fun, but may also result in a hodge-podge of plants. To create a garden that is visually exciting, you must think of it as a community of plants and choose its occupants according to how well they work together for the look you want. As you appraise plants that attract you, imagine them in the garden, in the company of existing plantings or of other potential plant choices.

Look for foliage shapes, textures, and colors that complement the leaves of nearby plants; choose flower colors that will mingle happily with those of neighboring blossoms. Make sure you have enough room for a new specimen at its mature size, so that it won't dominate the space and crowd out established plants. And remember, plants that tolerate both sun and shade tend to grow taller in shade.

Next, consider your soil, drainage, and light, and match your plants to your growing conditions. A plant may grow for you in the wrong situation, but it may or may not bloom there. Consult the encyclopedia *(pages 270-371)* for cultural information on a variety of flowering plants.

Building the Garden Structure

When planning for the addition of flowers to a shady space, think of the space in terms of horizontal layers—created by woody or herbaceous plants—and vertical planes—created by trees, tall shrubs, walls, or fences—that can mark a shade garden off into "rooms" filled with "furniture." For instance, in a yard where high shade is cast by tall trees underplanted only with grass, you can develop a more interesting design by first setting in a middle layer of flowering shrubs. Then add your favorite shade-loving perennials and annuals around and under the shrub framework. If your shade is cast mainly by tall, mature shrubs, or by a wall or fence, consider adding a flowering accent tree—say, a magnolia or dogwood—to break the horizontal line of the shade makers.

Above all, place plants so that they will appear to best advantage when in bloom. Oakleaf hydrangeas *(Hydrangea quercifolia),* for example,

are showy enough to be effective at a distance, so you can put them in the depths of the garden. But you might want to set low-growing, delicate-bloomed wildflowers like trout lilies along the path to the front door or at the edge of the patio, where they can be easily seen and admired.

Solving Shade Problems

While some gardeners enjoy the wonderful growing conditions that prevail in bright shade, many others have to deal with truly daunting situations: areas choked with tree roots; dry, deep shade where the soil is poor and thin; soggy patches where the soil is poorly drained; a strip of dense, all-day shade in a city lot. Proper plant selection is the key to converting problem shade into beautiful garden vistas, but a few tricks of the trade may also help in your own difficult site.

If your garden is shaded by trees with large, greedy roots, your choice of plants will be limited; most flowering shrubs and perennials languish in

Moisture-loving Ligularia 'Othello' sends up golden flowers between tall spears of iris and white-flowered bush honeysuckle in this tranquil poolside planting. During rainless spells, add water to a bog garden to keep it from drying out, and be ready to trim back enthusiastic colonizers that spread too fast and crowd their neighbors.

This New Jersey garden displays a clever use of containers in the arid soil beneath a shallow-rooted maple (center) and a dogwood (far right, not seen). Impatiens are planted in boxes, some angled around the tree trunks, others concealed in the ground covers and sunk into the mulch.

such conditions. You can try planting shallow-rooted ground covers—among the best are *Epimedium alpinum,* which creates a blanket of gray-and-yellow blossoms with red spots; white-blooming *E. grandiflorum;* and yellow *E. pinnatum* var. *colchicum.* But the prudent solution may be to surround the trees with container plants.

While they can be planted with everything from the tiniest flowers to shrubs and small trees, the most versatile containers are the ones you can move about—allowing you to vary the plants' effect or to give them more or less shade as the season progresses. Whatever their size, container plants will usually need more watering, feeding, and general care than the same plants set in the ground, so you may want to use them judiciously.

Match your containers first to the size and type of each plant. A shrub may need a half whiskey barrel, while a planting of impatiens will do fine in a 10-inch terra-cotta pot. Consider, too, your plants' growth habits—a sprawling fuchsia might look too casual in a formal stone urn but just right in a hanging rattan basket. Trailing species look best in hanging planters; tuberous begonias, with their large flowers in a wide range of colors, do particularly well in them. Swing the planters from the branches of shade-making trees or, with equally

good effect, from walls, fences, or the sides of buildings. For a rugged, natural look, plant small woodland genera like *Viola* (violet) or shallow-rooted ones like *Ajuga* (bugleweed) in hollowed logs scavenged from the woods. Or hide pots in soil or mulch, or among ground-cover plants.

Plants are more directly exposed to cold in containers than in the earth, so either choose hardy species or plan to move those that are borderline frost-tender into a sheltered porch or greenhouse for the cold weather. Shade-flowering plants that do well in containers include *Acanthus mollis* (common bear's-breech), anemone, *Bergenia,* camellia, *Convallaria* (lily-of-the-valley), fatsia, fuchsia, hosta, impatiens, holly, mahonia, daffodil, *Nicotiana* (flowering tobacco), rhododendron, *Saxifraga* (saxifrage), *Pieris,* thunbergia, *Myosotis* (forget-me-not), skimmia, *Thalictrum* (meadow rue), *Viola,* and periwinkle.

Planting in Dry, Deep Shade or Hot Shade

Dry shade, another challenging garden habitat, can occur under a tree whose canopy of leaf cover is so dense that it acts like an umbrella, diverting most

clude ajuga, *Aquilegia canadensis* (wild columbine), epimedium, heuchera, Japanese anemone, *Pulmonaria* (lungwort), *Scilla, Tradescantia,* and *Vinca.* Shrubs that bloom in these conditions include *Sarcococca,* kalmia, *Myrica cerifera* (wax myrtle), and some viburnum cultivars.

In parts of the West, where dry shade is accompanied by high heat and low humidity, plants that do well include begonia, *Enkianthus,* epimedium, *Gaultheria,* hellebore, heuchera, *Hosta lancifolia* (narrow-leaved plantain lily), hydrangea, saxifrage, skimmia, and yucca.

Boggy Shade and Poorly Drained Soil

At the other end of the soil spectrum lies the problem of wet ground. Muddy patches that persist even in dry weather or areas where rainwater regularly pools reveal poor drainage and a boglike condition that is deadly to many plant species. Planting bog-tolerant species is an easy-care solution, one that is far simpler than trying to change soil drainage patterns.

Some of the many flowering shade dwellers that flourish in boggy soil are *Calycanthus floridus* (Carolina allspice), *Clethra alnifolia* (sweet pepperbush), *Hemerocallis* (daylily), forget-me-not, hosta, winterberry, impatiens, lobelia, sweet bay magnolia, bayberry, *Primula* (primrose), species irises, and *Rhododendron viscosum* (swamp azalea).

In moist but drained soil at the edge of a bog, try *Astilbe, Dicentra* (bleeding heart), *Ligularia* (leopard plant), and *Fothergilla;* just be sure their crowns are above the wet soil.

Planting in City-Lot Shade

City gardens often have challenging environments. Many lots are narrow, squeezed between buildings or fences that produce dense shade where few plants can grow. Painting walls, fences, and even paving stones a light color, so that they reflect available light, helps considerably. Even a 1 percent increase in ambient light can greatly increase plant growth and blooming.

Flowering vines such as climbing hydrangea (*Hydrangea anomala* var. *petiolaris*) or shade-tolerant varieties of clematis can turn those same walls and fences from liabilities to assets. You might train a shrub or small tree as an espalier against a wall, or let clematis climb along a fence. Use small, open-structured trees to showcase

Making spectacular use of dappled vertical shade, this 30-year-old climbing hydrangea vine grows into the canopy of a large tulip poplar (Liriodendron tulipifera) in Delaware. The deciduous hydrangea blooms in mid-summer; later on, its elegant shape and exfoliating bark make a fine winter display.

rainfall to the soil outside its drip line. Few flowering shade plants thrive in dry, poor soil areas. Your best bet is to turn dry shade into moister shade.

Digging organic matter such as leaves, compost, or rotted manure into the soil will help. If direct soil amendment is too difficult, a 2- to 4-inch layer of organic mulch spread on the ground and under shrubs can begin the process. Renewed over several seasons, the mulch will enrich the soil and help hold what little water soaks in. You can also loop soaker hoses through the areas you want to plant. Cover them with a leaf-litter mulch and water slowly on a regular basis.

Flowering herbaceous plants for dry shade in-

climbing plants as well, letting their flowers peep out among the branches.

Flowering shrubs, trees, and herbaceous plants can do much to reconfigure a narrow lot; use them, in combination with foliage plants, as focal points and accents to lead the eye through the garden. And if your garden, because of a narrow, channel-like shape, suffers from a wind-tunnel effect, a well-placed row of a shrub such as Chinese witch hazel, *Kerria japonica* (Japanese rose), *Ligustrum obtusifolium* (border privet), or *Osmanthus heterophyllus* 'Variegatus' (holly olive) can dissipate the wind's force and slow it down.

City gardeners may also face compacted soil and pollution in soil and air. To improve the soil and make it more hospitable for your plants, double dig the beds and add humus, in the form of compost, well-rotted manure, or peat moss. In some areas, park departments or similar public agencies give away composted leaf humus; check with your local government.

As a last resort for badly polluted soil, plant in containers filled with potting mix. Container plants recommended for city conditions include dogwood, holly, *Andromeda* (bog rosemary), hydrangea, laurel, rhododendron, witch hazel, dicentra, corydalis, daylily, epimedium, hosta, begonia, and impatiens.

Artful design expands the visual size of a tiny urban shade garden nestled amid buildings. An oakleaf hydrangea, hostas, and ground covers flower copiously in the scant summer sun; vines and espaliers soften the enclosing walls; and a small pond and waterfall highlight the island plantings.

Gardening in a Shady Woodland

To successfully turn a woodland into a garden, your hand must be light enough not to disturb a carefully established natural balance, yet firm enough to build on the aesthetics of nature. You should try to create a beautiful setting and an ecologically stable habitat in which pests and plant-care requirements are kept to a manageable level.

Wherever you have a collection of trees, you can plant a woodland garden. The most extensive plantings will be at the farthest reaches of your property, in the outer zone, where cultivation gives way to wildness. If you have no such area, create one by planting a grove of small, fast-growing understory trees in company with large, slower-growing shade trees. The small trees will provide enough cover for woodland plants and will survive in the shade when the larger trees mature. Silver bell *(Halesia)*, dogwood, and Carolina cherry laurel *(Prunus caroliniana)* are excellent choices.

If your woodland is already in place, you must first decide where to locate your garden. The sunniest part of a wood is its perimeter. Or you may want to go into the deeper shade, selectively removing a tree here, pruning a branch there, and laying a winding path to make a woodland walk.

The area of transition between open lawn and woodland, or the space in a forest where a tree has fallen and created a small clearing, can sustain both sun- and shade-loving plants. Partly sheltered by trees, plants in a transitional space will be exposed to moderate degrees of both sun and shade. Here is where most flowering trees are found—low-growing species such as hawthorn, cherry, *Amelanchier* (serviceberry), witch hazel, dogwood, redbud, sumac, magnolia, camellia, and the "escaped" specimens of domestic fruit trees called wildings.

Stocking Your Woodland Garden

When shopping for woodland plants, choose native, unhybridized species when possible. Species rhododendrons and azaleas, for example, look more at home in a naturalized setting, and are less demanding, than their hybrid cousins. *Rhododendron viscosum* (swamp azalea), which grows from Maine to the Carolinas and as far west as Mississippi and the Great Smokies, can survive in soggy ground and has deliciously scented blossoms.

This colony of celandine poppies has spread around the feet of maples and a pair of hemlocks at the edge of a Pennsylvania hardwood forest. In moist woods like these, the poppies may bloom a second time in fall.

A mossy stone bench surrounded by Trillium ovatum (coast trillium) and T. sessile (toadshade) and overhung with blossoms of a Rhododendron yakusimanum 'Ken Janek' provides a spot to sit and contemplate this woodland walk in Oregon.

At ground level, spring-blooming plants start the season off, growing in full sun under a lattice-work of bare tree limbs. Naturalized bulbs like daffodils, species tulips, squill, and crocus, planted in wide swaths in the grass along the woodland margin, will reappear year after year, spreading into the woods. Once the foliage canopy has filled in for summer, shade-tolerant natives like *Lilium canadense* (Canada lily) and *L. philadelphicum* (wood lily) come into bloom.

Other spring flowers to try are such natives as columbine, dicentra, *Thalictrum* (meadow rue), Solomon's-seal, and *Tiarella* (foamflower). Pair these plants with some of the many native ferns, such as the maidenhair *(Adiantum)*, lady *(Athyrium filix-femina)*, hay-scented *(Dennstaedtia punctilobula)*, shield *(Dryopteris)*, and chain *(Woodwardia)* ferns.

As dependable and appropriate as native plants are, a woodland verge can accommodate exotics as well. Spice up the garden with plants imported from the flower bed—perennials like astilbe, hosta, hellebore, and *Rheum palmatum* (ornamental rhubarb); annuals like shimmery *Lunaria* (money plant), self-sowing forget-me-not, and fragrant nicotiana; and bright ground covers like lamium, *Ajuga reptans* 'Multicoloris', or, in warm regions, *Fittonia,* with its small yellow flowers, and the evergreen *Aspidistra* (cast-iron plant).

Remember to include some evergreen shrubs and trees to give the garden shape in winter, when deciduous trees are bare. Reliable performers include Oregon grape, daphne, holly, and hemlock.

Preparing the Site

As you plot your woodland garden, spend time observing how the wild vegetation on the site grows. In spring, at the height of summer, and in fall, catalog the plants and note how the light reaches them. Preserve some of the area's wild growth in a remote corner of the woodland as a source of food and shelter for wildlife, but clear out noxious or destructive plants like *Rhus radicans* (poison ivy), *Vitis labrusca* (fox grape), and *Convolvulus arvensis* (field bindweed).

If the shade is too dense, hire an arborist to help you take out trees and prune branches to create small clearings. For an additional fee, a professional will also take away the cut wood or provide you with a log splitter to make firewood. Rent an industrial-grade wood chipper to convert medium-sized branches and twigs into mulch. Branches pruned in winter, being bare, make cleaner, longer-lasting mulch.

Designing with Nature

The design of your woodland garden should be a collaboration between you and nature, which has created the conditions that exist in your woods.

Such an open-minded approach on your part will not only ensure the survival of your plants but will also produce a more pleasingly natural result.

After taking into account the shade conditions, determine the quality of your soil and choose suitable plants. Woodland soil, at its surface, is made up of decomposing leaves, which render it acidic. Plants that have evolved in the woods have developed a taste for this kind of soil and should do well with a light fertilizer and a generous covering of leaf mulch. Soil that is sandy and fast draining can be conditioned by adding leaf mold or humus, as can clayey and waterlogged earth.

Soil nutrients in a woodland setting are probably less of a problem than is aridity. In an environment where the soil is densely packed with thirsty roots and the area overhung with a canopy of rain-blocking leaves, soil can be surprisingly dry in the summer. You could install an irrigation system to water your woodland garden, but a more practical approach is to choose drought-tolerant plants.

Plotting a Woodland Path

A path enables you to get close to your woodland garden without trampling on the plants or getting your feet muddy. It should meander along inviting curves and be flanked with interesting plants, as in this Maine garden bursting with *Primula japonica* (Japanese primrose) and columbine.

For two people to walk abreast, a path should be 4 feet wide—or, at any rate, wide enough for a garden cart to pass. To keep weeds down, smother them with thick layers of newspaper, which will eventually decay to a mulch. Then cover the paper with materials natural to the woods. Woodchips from recycled tree cuttings are long-lasting. Pine needles make a silky, springy walking surface but can be slippery on an incline.

Achieving the Desired Look

Woodland plants do best, and also look most natural, when they are arranged in colonies or clusters. This applies to a stand of *Mertensia virginica* (Virginia bluebells) or *Podophyllum peltatum* (May apple) at ground level as much as to a group of hollies or a grove of hemlock. And since nature is constantly replenishing itself, saplings will grow alongside mature trees. To reinforce the natural look of your woodland shade garden, intersperse young plants among the older ones.

Large shrubs and trees can fill the interior of a woodland garden and cut off views to the woodland edge, giving an illusion of greater space. Place scented azaleas or witch hazel along the path, to sweeten the air and hide where the path is going.

A Rock Garden in the Woods

If you have a rock outcrop in your woods, use it as a focal point to provide texture, color, and a visual anchor for your garden. Rocks can act as a foil for small woodland plants that might get lost amid lush growth. A cluster of jewel-like *Primula vialii* (Littons primrose) or the dainty native *Aquilegia canadensis* (wild columbine) paired with delicate *Adiantum pedatum* (northern maidenhair fern) will stand out beautifully against a large granite or limestone rock.

Newly exposed rocks will lose their raw look and acquire the patina of age as moss and lichens build up on them in the shade. If your rock has a level or slightly concave top, cap it with a layer of transplanted moss installed atop an inch or two of soil. Keep the moss out of direct sun and water it well through the first summer to get it established.

A slope in the woods is a good place to establish a woodland rock garden, especially if you can lay a path up the slope to permit viewing of the plants up close. Grow smaller ferns and hostas, the hardy *Shortia*, natives such as violets, *Gaultheria*, and *Mitchella repens* (partridgeberry), and such ground-hugging plants as *Cornus canadensis* (bunchberry), wild ginger, and saxifrage. Be sure to cover the ground around the plants with a layer of leaf mulch to build up the soil and keep it moist and cool.

The widening of a pathway provides a sunny resting place among the trees of this shaded woodland garden in New Jersey. Close enough to the house for outdoor eating or for sitting in the evening, and paved with local flagstone to make a terrace, this retreat can be a destination in its own right or a stopping place before venturing deeper into the woods.

To speed drainage, dig the hole 4 inches deeper than twice the depth of the rootball and line the bottom with 4 inches of pebbles. Cover the pebble layer with 4 inches of soil mix made up of 1 part original soil, 4 parts compost or other humus, and 1 part pebbles. Set the crown of the plant slightly above the soil level and fill with soil mix. Tamp down firmly, water and tamp down again, then cover with mulch.

Planting amid Tree Roots

To grow herbaceous plants at the foot of a mature tree, the soil must be relatively free of roots—unless you are willing to cut away some roots, a method of last resort. To find out how thickly grown the roots are, push a shovel into the ground. If the blade is stopped by a mesh of roots, move to a new spot and try again until the shovel penetrates at least as deep as the length of the blade.

If your situation requires you to chop through a major root, take care not to overstress the tree. Don't cut away more than about 10 percent of the total root network, and have the crown pruned back a proportionate amount. After you finish digging, place landscape mesh around the perimeter of the hole to slow down encroachment by new root growth from the tree.

Drainage must always be checked in such soil. Dig a hole twice as wide and deep as the rootball you are planting and fill it with water. If the water doesn't drain away after 15 minutes, either improve the drainage *(above)* or put in plants that tolerate boggy conditions.

Planting Directly under Trees

It is possible to install flower beds under large shade trees without building a raised bed , but you'll have to take several factors into consideration: How much light and rain will the trees' canopy of leaves allow through? How thick and shallow are the tree roots? Even if enough light and rain reach the soil, shallow tree roots can be an almost prohibitive problem. Tree roots do not grow straight down into the earth, as is commonly believed. They grow in the top 18 inches of soil, spreading out far beyond the drip line. Roots can quickly invade flower beds and sap all the water and nutrients from them. Maples, sycamores, and beeches are among the worst offenders and planting beneath them is almost always disappointing. Some trees, however, such as oaks and conifers, have deeper-growing roots and can coexist well with other plantings. And beds planted beneath small trees, with a mature height of under 20 feet, typically do well since such trees have smaller, less invasive root systems.

If you find relatively root-free areas under trees where you can place a plant, you are in luck; some of the most beautiful landscape scenes are made up of lush plants in the shade of handsome trees.

'Hyperion' daylilies, bearing scented yellow blossoms from late spring to midsummer, bloom beneath a river birch in Charlottesville, Virginia. Hosta cultivars flank the tree at the rear and upper right.

For such a garden to thrive, consider thinning the tree crown to allow more dappled sunlight to shine through.

If your space is so limited that every square foot counts, you may be able to garden beneath shallow-rooted trees, but the method is a drastic one and will take some muscle power. You can create planting and growing room by exposing a large root near the trunk and cutting it out with an ax or hatchet. Since new tree roots will penetrate this bed within a season or two—even if you line the hole with landscaping mesh—limit your plantings to annuals, and reclear the bed each year.

Putting Your Plants into the Ground

Choose a time to plant when temperatures are not too high, such as in the late afternoon. Before placing a plant in a hole, loosen its rootball, splitting it in half at the bottom and spreading the halves. Cut back any discolored roots. The most important point to remember about shade plants is to set the plant's crown no deeper than it was in the container. Always err on the side of raising the crown. Shade plants are accustomed to light, airy humus and cannot tolerate being smothered under soil. Give the young plant extra water until it is established. If the soil has been prepared well, perennials and woody plants will not need additions of fertilizer the first year. Annuals can be fertilized halfway through the growing season.

TIPS FROM THE PROS
Letting Moss Have Its Way

If you want to keep some open space on your property but your attempts to cultivate a turf-grass lawn in the shade are being subverted by moss, give in to nature and let the moss take over. Moss thrives in the shade in moist clay soil with a pH of about 5.5. You can hurry up the conversion by spreading garden sulfur; 4 pounds per 100 square feet will lower the soil pH by about 1.5 points. Once the moss is established, it will spread steadily, covering the area with a green carpet that needs no mowing or fertilizing. To fill in bare spots in an established moss lawn, transplant small clumps of moss in early spring. First moisten the soil and loosen it with a hoe or three-pronged cultivator. Then lay the patches in the bare spots, patting them firmly into the soil so that no air spaces remain. Keep the area moist for a few weeks, covering it with wet burlap if the weather turns hot and dry.

CHAPTER SEVEN

Planting Guide

Savvy gardeners know that some of the most important work done in the garden is the effort that goes into preparing the soil to receive new plants. What it takes to grow robust bloomers—like the tea and hybrid tea roses and verbena filling the front yard of this Independence, Texas, home—is a fertile, loamy soil that supplies your plants with the air, water, and nutrients that keep them growing strong. Knowing how to enrich your soil will go a long way toward achieving your goal of a beautiful flower garden.

In addition to cultivating your soil, understanding how your plants should be placed in the ground will help ensure that they survive and thrive in the garden. Peonies, for example, perform best when their roots are planted with the buds only an inch or two below the soil's surface—shallow enough for them to experience a necessary period of chill, but not so shallow they might freeze. Whether you purchase your plants in containers or as bare roots will also determine how they should go into the ground. On the following pages, you'll learn how to plant a variety of garden flowers.

Readying New Ground to Receive Plants

The first steps toward creating a new flower garden—deciding on the site and settling on the design—take you only so far: After that it's time to go outdoors and mark off your plot *(below),* begin preparing the soil, and choose your plants.

Good soil preparation is the single most important factor in growing beautiful, healthy annuals, perennials, roses, and bulbs. To properly ready the soil in your garden you must first understand it. Does the soil drain well? Although some plants thrive in soil that remains continuously moist or is dry, most require good drainage. Look at the soil texture and color, and the health of plants that may already be growing in it. Is the soil heavy clay or loose sand? Is it poor or fertile? Adding organic amendments will condition the soil and fertilizer can replenish its nutrients.

Other factors, including light and exposure, will affect how your garden grows. For example, most perennials and roses prefer full sun, meaning at least 6 hours a day with 4 of those in the after-noon. But a lush garden is still possible even if your site has full or partial shade; it all depends on the plants you choose. The Plant Selection Guides that appear at the end of each plant chapter in this book and the Encyclopedia of Plants that begins on page 272 can help you select the plants best suited to your garden's conditions.

Investing some initial time and effort in cultivating and fertilizing the soil in your beds, improving areas of poor drainage, and choosing and siting your plants correctly will pay off handsomely later in vigorous growth and abundant blooms. Remember, your perennials are going to be in the ground for a long time, and there will never be another opportunity to start them out right.

Appraising Your Soil

Bringing your soil to the point where it's ready for planting means first knowing its present condi-

Outlining Your Garden Plot

For a plot with a curving edge, *use a garden hose to outline the perimeter, matching the bed's size to the dimensions shown on your garden plan. Then mark the perimeter with powdered lime or by cutting into the soil alongside the hose with a garden spade.*

For square corners, first stake off one side of the bed. *Then set a peg 3 feet from the first stake and tie a string to it; mark the string at a point 5 feet from the peg. Tie a string to the first stake and mark it at 4 feet from the stake. Cross the two strings at the marks. Set a third stake at that point, creating a right angle at the first stake.*

The 3:4:5 ratio used to find the right angle at left, which can be used with a garden plot of any size, demonstrates that a triangle with its three sides in the proper ratio will have a right angle opposite the longest side.

Preparing the Ground without Digging

Some professional gardeners have devised a way of preparing a plot of land for gardening virtually without turning a single spadeful of soil. The method, called smothering, holds obvious advantages for the home gardener who wants to cultivate a relatively large piece of ground, for which the labor of digging, or even using a power tiller, would be great.

Smothering consists simply of covering up unwanted vegetation to deprive it of light until the plants die—a period of about 3 months. Once the covering is in place and the process has begun, you don't even have to wait the full time before you plant. You can cut down through the cover—indeed, you need never remove it—to put in your plants, which will begin growing while the grass and most weeds around them are dying.

If your chosen garden plot is covered with sod, mow the grass as low as possible, then cover the area with sheets of old newspaper. But take care not to use papers with colored inks, which can deposit harmful chemicals in the soil. A covering three or four sheets thick should be enough to do the job; overlap the edges a few inches to ensure that all sunlight is blocked out. Then cover the newsprint with a layer of leaves or other organic mulch about 1 foot deep, which will weigh down the paper, improve the appearance of the plot, and eventually decompose and add humus to the soil.

Smothering woody plants and persistent weeds will require a heavier covering—perhaps a layer of cardboard or a thickness of 30 or so sheets of newspaper, followed by the mulch. Any weeds that are strong enough to survive smothering can be destroyed by digging them out.

---

tion. You should make at least a rough determination of the soil's texture—that is, the relative amounts of clay, silt, and sand particles that make up most of the mineral content of soil.

Soil with a high percentage of clay or silt is likely to be quite dense and compact, allowing little space for air and growing plant roots to penetrate and for water to slowly percolate and drain away. If you dig into these soils with a spade, they feel heavy; clay soil will also stick to the blade, making it difficult to turn and break up.

At the other end of the scale, sandy soil is so loose and porous that it cannot retain moisture or nutrients and offers plant roots little to grab onto. It feels coarse and gritty in your hand and does not clump together well.

The soil with the best texture is loam. A mixture containing roughly 20 percent clay and 40 percent each of silt and sand, loam is easy to work, holds water and nutrients well, and allows air to reach plant roots. Loam also has an ideal soil structure, which is determined by how well the soil particles cling together and in what shapes. The best structure is one in which the soil is friable—meaning that the particles form small, irregularly shaped, slightly moist clumps or crumbs that hold together well but will break up easily in your hand. Soil with this ideal structure contains countless small spaces that conduct air, water, and nutrients to plant roots.

Another factor you should take into account when analyzing your soil is its acidity or alkalinity—the pH level—which you can measure using an inexpensive tester available at garden shops and home centers. Most plants will flourish in soil ranging from somewhat acid—a pH of about 5.8—to slightly alkaline, or just above the neutral level of 7; it is in this range that soil nutrients become most available to the plants. Should the soil test excessively acid, you can raise its pH by working in a quantity of dolomitic limestone. If it is too alkaline, an application of sulfur will bring it to the desired level of acidity.

Soil Fertility

Three chemical elements are essential to plant growth—nitrogen, phosphorus, and potassium—and these all occur naturally in soil. Responsible for strong roots and healthy leaf, stem, flower, and fruit development, these elements, as well as traces of secondary elements, are the products of decaying organic matter. Compost, well-rotted cow manure, and leaf mold—soil made up chiefly of decayed vegetable matter, particularly leaves—are good sources of organic matter, and working them into the soil of a new flower garden may well provide all the fertilization the plot needs during its first year.

Soil Amendment of Choice

If you had to select one all-purpose soil amendment that would both improve soil structure and supply nutrient-rich organic matter, the choice would undoubtedly be compost. Compost is made up of rotted plant materials such as grass clippings and fallen leaves, fruit and vegetable scraps from the kitchen, aged livestock manure, sawdust, newsprint, and any number of other organic ingredients. It also contains a teeming population of living organisms and microorganisms, who did the work of breaking down the raw materials into the black, moist, crumbly humus.

Building a Compost Pile

A well-made compost pile is an ideal habitat for microorganisms, providing the food, water, air, and warmth they need to grow and reproduce at top speed. A thriving population quickly converts ordinary wastes from kitchen and garden into an invaluable fertilizer and soil conditioner.

The microorganisms need a balanced diet of carbon and nitrogen. Fibrous materials such as dry leaves, straw, and sawdust provide plenty of carbon, while nitrogen is furnished by green materials such as grass clippings, wastes from the vegetable garden or flower bed, and kitchen scraps (vegetable or fruit only).

To start a compost pile, spread a layer of brown fibrous material several inches deep and at least 3 feet wide and 3 feet across on bare soil. Add a layer of green material and

sprinkle it with soil or a commercial compost activator to introduce microorganisms. Water until the materials are sponge damp. Continue in this fashion until the layered pile is at least 3 feet high—the size necessary to generate sufficient heat. Turn the pile once or twice a week with a garden fork to aerate it and rid the center of excess moisture. Water as needed to keep the pile slightly moist. The compost is ready to use when it is dark and crumbly.

The three-bin composter shown below can produce a large, steady supply of compost. The decomposing pile in the center bin is flanked by a newly assembled pile *(right)* and a bin containing finished compost *(left)*. Wire mesh on three sides and the gaps between the slats on the bin's front help keep the pile aerated. The slats are removable, making it easy to turn the pile. Several smaller compost bins are shown on the next page.

Compost is almost a panacea for imperfect soils. If a soil is loose and sandy, generous additions of compost will pull it together and make it crumbly, so that water, nutrients, and plant roots can get a good foothold. If the soil is heavily compacted clay, compost will loosen and lighten it. As a fertilizer, finished compost provides a good balance of 2 parts nitrogen to 1 part each of phosphorus and potassium. And if it is made from a large variety of materials, compost will contain a healthy balance of trace elements as well. Even the best soil can benefit from periodic additions of compost to help maintain its structure and replenish its supply of nutrients.

Choosing a Fertilizer

Although compost adds nutrients to the soil, you may need to add fertilizer periodically to meet the needs of particular plants or to help replenish depleted nutrients. Fertilizers take two forms—organic and inorganic. Organic fertilizers are derived from animal or vegetable matter. Examples include compost, cottonseed meal, blood meal (from slaughtered cattle), and finely ground bone. Many gardeners prefer organic fertilizers because they are manufactured by environmentally friendly methods, don't harm important soil microbes,

Decomposing waste occupies one of the two cinder-block bins at left; the other stores finished compost. The spaces between the blocks allow air to circulate. You can mortar the blocks at the back and the sides of the bins, but leave the front blocks free so you can withdraw the compost.

A Compost Bin to Suit Your Needs

Even the simplest compost bin keeps decomposing wastes tidy and compact. And as long as you have the right mix of ingredients and enough of them, it will generate the heat needed to ensure speedy composting. For freestanding compost piles or those in open bins, you should start with a pile measuring 3 feet wide, deep, and high. For the ready-made bins available at garden and home centers, simply fill them according to the manufacturer's instructions.

Each of the composters shown here can be easily constructed or purchased for less than a hundred dollars. Some require manual forking and turning of the debris pile, while others need little or no attention from the gardener.

To create the bin at right, wrap a length of hardware cloth 4 feet wide and 12 feet long around two stakes hammered into the ground. Secure the ends of the hardware cloth with wires. To turn the compost pile, unfasten the cylinder, reposition the stakes adjacent to the loose pile, reassemble the cylinder, and fork in the pile.

The plastic barrel composter at left is designed to produce finished compost in a month or less. The barrel rests on rollers; turning a handle rotates the barrel and aerates the contents thoroughly. Finished compost is removed through a hinged door on the barrel; a finished batch must be removed before starting a new one.

A compact plastic compost bin like the one at left is an excellent choice where space is limited. Fresh waste material can be added continually to the top of the bin while older material is decaying to finished compost. Compost is retrieved from the pull-out drawer at the bottom of the bin. Enough air enters the pile through the large slots to supply the decay microorganisms completely, making it unnecessary to turn the pile.

Breaking Ground for the Garden

1. Shave off any sod with your garden spade, *cutting through the soil horizontally. Use the surplus sod to fill in bare spots on your lawn, or shake off the loose soil and save the remaining material for the compost pile. If your plot is large—and you're not in a hurry to plant—you may choose to smother the grass (page 195).*

2. To work the soil, drive your spade all the way into the soil at 4-inch intervals; *toss each slice of loosened soil forward and use the blade to break it up. Be careful not to step on the broken soil, which might compact it into a dense, unworkable mass.*

3. Use a spading fork to work amendments into the broken-up soil. *Choose from such amendments as compost, rotted cow manure, limestone, peat moss, and other materials as needed to ready the soil for your perennials.*

and don't leave chemical residues. They also work a little slower than their inorganic counterparts, lessening the chance of burning plant roots if you happen to overfertilize.

Inorganic fertilizers are products of the petrochemicals industry. On the plus side, they tend to be faster acting and easier to use. However, they can leach out of soils quickly, requiring repeated applications that over time can become expensive. The most significant disadvantage of chemical fertilizers is that they can damage the many beneficial microorganisms that live in the soil.

Either type of fertilizer may be sold as a so-called complete fertilizer, its packaging indicating the percentages of nitrogen, phosphorus, and potassium—always in that order—that it contains. The percentages may sometimes be labeled N-P-K, the chemical symbols for these elements. A 5-10-5 fertilizer, for example, contains 5 percent nitrogen, 10 percent phosphorus, and 5 percent potassium, plus small or trace amounts of other chemicals; the remainder is inert filler. A product labeled 10-10-10 is called a balanced fertilizer. One labeled 0-20-0 is a single-nutrient fertilizer, in this case an all-phosphorus product called a superphosphate.

As a rule, perennials need relatively little fertilizer compared with the amount needed by annuals and roses. But because perennials stay in the ground for so long, they may benefit from judicious applications of fertilizer from time to time. For more information on fertilizing particular types of plants, see pages 226-227.

Cultivating the Soil

Many professional gardeners recommend digging and amending the soil for a garden in the fall, covering it with a mulch to hold in moisture and prevent weeds, and then waiting until spring to begin planting. During the wait the soil will settle, and winter frosts and thaws will cause it to expand and contract, improving its structure by breaking it into smaller clumps.

In areas of the country where the summers are hot and dry, it is often best to work the soil in spring and let it lie until fall. If you are too impatient to let a growing season slip by, however, it is still important to give your cultivated plot at least several weeks to begin settling before you plant it.

Make sure the soil is slightly moist before you dig; otherwise you risk destroying the soil's structure. If the ground is too wet, digging will pack the soil into a dense mass that blocks the movement of water, air, and roots. If the ground is dry, the digging may cause it to disintegrate into a powder.

To determine if your soil is ready for digging, turn over a spadeful and break up a clod. If the clod comes apart easily, you can proceed. If it sticks stubbornly together or can be formed into a ball in your hand, it is too wet; wait a few rainless days and try again. If the clump of soil crumbles to dust, it is too dry; soak the entire plot, then let it drain for 3 or 4 days before you begin digging .

Reasons for Double Digging

The technique called double digging involves digging up and amending a layer of topsoil about 12 inches deep and then loosening and amending to an equal depth the layer of subsoil beneath it.

Professional gardeners differ on the importance of double digging. Some say it is unnecessary extra work, that you can have a fine garden without it. Others say it gives the plants plenty of loosened soil in which to sink their roots—which in the case of some perennials can grow to a depth of 24 inches. Still other gardeners don't even stop at conventional double digging. After removing the topsoil and amending it, they do not merely loosen the subsoil, they dig it up and amend it thoroughly, put the original topsoil back where the subsoil was, and put the former subsoil on top.

Personal preferences aside, many experts agree that if your soil is a heavy clay with poor drainage, it is important to double dig. If you have better soil, double digging may not be absolutely necessary but will probably return a dividend in more robust, more extravagantly blooming plants.

The Deluxe Treatment: Double Digging

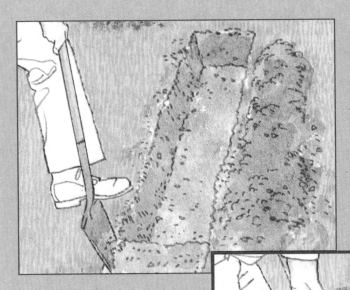

1. Beginning at one end of the garden plot you have laid out, remove any sod covering as shown opposite. Then dig a trench about 1 foot wide and as deep as the blade on your spade, running from one side of the plot to the other. Remove the topsoil and heap it in a cart or wheelbarrow. Thoroughly loosen the layer of exposed subsoil with a spading fork and work in the appropriate soil amendments. Do not remove the subsoil.

2. Dig out another trench next to the first one, moving the loosened topsoil over to cover the amended subsoil of the first trench. Work amendments into this topsoil. Then loosen and amend the subsoil in the second trench. Repeat the process for each succeeding trench until the last one. Then amend the topsoil reserved from the first trench and use it to fill the last one.

Planting Annuals

Annuals are good choices for any landscape, and if you're a novice gardener, they make for an easy and immediately gratifying introduction to gardening. Starting out can be as simple as sowing seeds directly into the ground and then watching what happens, or pushing aside some soil and setting in young bedding plants purchased from your local nursery or garden center.

If you're an experienced gardener who enjoys devoting more time and effort to a project, you can spend delightful hours poring over mail-order nursery catalogs, choosing between the countless beautiful varieties of annuals pictured and described there. You can also get seeds started indoors before spring arrives, then wait for the perfect day to transplant them to the garden. Here and on the next two pages, you'll learn all you need to know about the three techniques for getting your annual garden started—indoor sowing, transplanting, and direct-seeding.

Starting Seeds Indoors

Some annuals have tiny seeds that may be lost if sown outdoors. Others need a long time to grow before they flower. If you want annuals such as zinnias, geraniums, and verbena blooming in your garden as early as possible—and you want to ensure the highest rate of germination for your seeds—get them going in the protected, controlled environment of your home. Seeds can be started indoors in winter so that young plants will be ready to put into the ground in spring.

Purchase a soil mix that has been specifically formulated for starting seeds. Wet the mix completely and let it sit for a few minutes until the water is thoroughly absorbed; then fill seed flats to a depth of about 3 inches. If you don't want to use flats, you can also use individual plastic pots or even small plastic cups or cartons you may find around your house. Simply clean them well first and poke a few drain holes in the bottom.

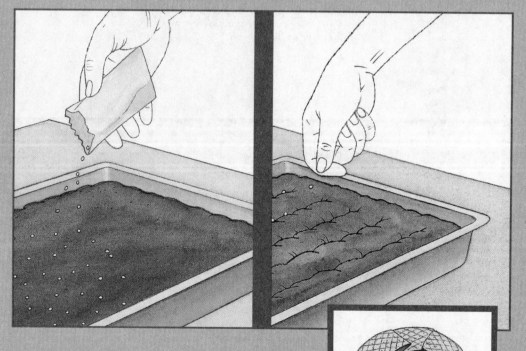

1. Scatter tiny seeds on top of the moistened soil mix (above); place larger seeds one by one in ¼-inch furrows, spaced ½ inch apart (above, right). If the seed-packet directions indicate, cover the seeds with a thin layer of soil. Alternatively, gently press the seeds into a wet peat pot as shown at right. Then set the flats or peat pots under grow lights on a warm, bright but indirectly lit window sill, or in a darkened setting, according to seed-packet instructions. All seedlings should be placed in a well-lit spot once they become visible.

2. Keep the soil mix moist by watering gently and then covering the flat with a clear, thin plastic bag supported by metal hoops (above). You can use clothes hangers for the hoops. Seal the bag with a twist tie to maintain high humidity. After the shoots are plainly visible, remove the plastic covering. Continue watering to keep the soil moist but not soaked; overwatering can cause damping-off, a disease that kills seedlings.

After sprouting in a well-lit greenhouse window, these flats of annual seedlings await transplanting to larger containers. The robust scarlet and yellow potted marigolds were started at an earlier date and are ready to be hardened off and planted in the garden.

Annuals to Start Indoors

Ageratum houstonianum
(flossflower)
***Asclepias* spp.**
(bloodflower)
Browallia speciosa
(browallia)
Cardiospermum halicacabum
(balloon vine)
Coleus* x *hybridus
(coleus)
***Dianthus* spp.**
(pink, sweet William)
Eustoma grandiflorum
(tulip gentian)
***Impatiens* spp.**
(impatiens)
Lagurus ovatus
(hare's-tail grass)
Petunia* x *hybrida
(petunia)
***Salvia* spp.**
(sage)
Torenia fournieri
(wishbone flower)

Note: The abbreviation "spp." stands for the plural of "species"; where used in lists it means that many, but not all, of the species in a genus meet the criterion of the list.

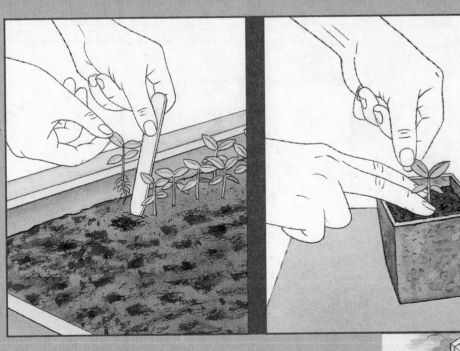

4. Two weeks before transplanting—which should be done once the danger of frost is past—*move your plants to a cold frame to acclimate them to outdoor conditions, a process known as hardening off. Open the frame during the day to maintain proper air circulation and to keep plants from getting too much heat under the glass; close it at night. If you don't have a cold frame, place the seedlings outside a few hours each day, gradually lengthening the exposure time.*

3. After the seedlings produce a second set of leaves *(their first true leaves), use a plant marker or similar instrument to separate and lift each one out of the flat (above, left). Hold each seedling by its leaf (it can grow a new leaf, but not a new stem) and place it in a peat pot or other container filled with moist, sterile potting soil. Position the seedling in a hole the size and depth of its tiny root system. Gently tamp the soil without injuring the stem (above, right). Place the pots on a tray to be set under grow lights or near a warm, sunny window. Keep the plants well watered.*

201

Transplanting Annuals

Before transplanting seedlings to your garden, take time to ready their new home. If you're preparing a new flower bed, dig in an inch or two of organic matter such as leaf mold or compost before planting. This will improve drainage and supply the young plants with nutrients. If you're adding annuals to an existing bed, use a hand cultivator to loosen the soil and add a slow-release dry fertilizer, using the amount recommended on the package. Transplant your annuals on a cool, cloudy day or in the late afternoon so that the flowers are not stressed by sun and heat.

1. With a trowel, dig a hole slightly larger and deeper than the plant's rootball. Water the plant thoroughly and allow the excess to drain away. Then gently remove the plant from its cell pack or other container by turning it upside down and easing the plant out. With a cell pack, support the plant with one hand, then gently press your thumb against the bottom of the pack to push the plant out (right).

2. Use your fingers to gently loosen the roots at the bottom and sides of the plant's rootball (right). If the plant is extremely root-bound, use a knife to slice partway into the root-ball, then fluff the roots apart. For plants in peat pots, gently tear off the lip or the top part of the pot (far right), then set the pot in the ground; this will help the pot's soil retain moisture.

3. Set the plant into the hole with the base of its stem slightly below the rim. Return the soil to the hole and firm it around the plant, creating a slight depression around the plant's stem to direct water there. Water thoroughly and mulch with an organic material such as shredded bark, making sure the mulch doesn't touch the stem.

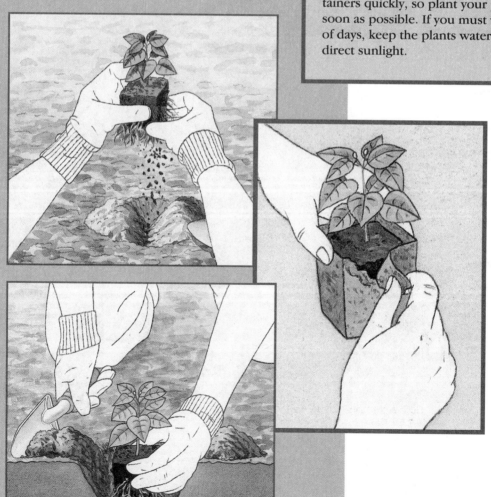

Direct-Seeding

The simplest way to start annuals is by sowing seeds directly into the soil of the garden—and there are, in fact, a number of annuals that prefer to be direct-seeded *(list, right)*. To prepare a seedbed, first clear all vegetation from a patch of ground and amend the soil to a depth of 8 inches with 1 to 2 inches of compost or other organic matter. Break up any soil clumps with a spading fork, and smooth the bed with a tined rake.

You can sow seeds in one of two ways. The easiest is to scatter them on the prepared bed; if planting small seeds, mix some sand in before scattering to prevent them from massing together. The second method, described below and used for a more controlled effect, involves only slightly more effort. With the handle of a rake, draw furrows in the seedbed that are 1 inch deep—or as deep as the seed packet instructs. Follow the packet's recommendation for spacing between furrows, which will vary depending on the species.

1. Sprinkle the seeds out of the packet evenly into the furrows, *sowing about four seeds for every plant you plan for. Cover the seeds with a thin layer of soil, if the seed packet calls for it. To sow very tiny seeds like basil (inset, below), line the furrow with white, unscented toilet paper so that you can easily see their number and distribution. The paper will disintegrate. Lightly tamp the seedbed's surface with a rake to press the seeds gently into the ground; mist or water lightly with an adjustable spray nozzle to dampen the bed, and water daily thereafter so that the ground does not dry out.*

2. After a week or 10 days, when the seedlings begin to crowd one another, *thin the crop by cutting off three out of four seedlings just above the stem's base. Cut out the weakest seedlings, retaining only those with the stoutest stems and the greenest leaves. When the seedlings are around 4 inches high, pinch back the plant's top growth with your thumb and index finger. This will encourage side branching of new stems and will stop the plant from growing too leggy in its first few weeks. Continue to keep the flower bed well watered, and put down an organic mulch after the annuals are well established, usually 6 to 8 weeks later.*

Planting Perennials

Perennials are long-lived plants that must be given room and time to grow and flourish. This means that a newly planted perennial bed or border may look somewhat skimpy its first year, even after the plants are established.

Achieving Flowers the First Year

Many perennials, especially first-year seedlings and those that were planted with bare roots, will not bloom until their second year in the garden. If you have your heart set on seeing abundant flowers the first year, however, you can do several things to make that happen while waiting for your fledgling perennials to mature.

One option is to plant annuals among the perennials. If you have left the proper amount of space between the young perennials, you will have plenty of room to interplant colorful annuals without disturbing the roots of the long-term inhabitants. Annuals that tend to reseed, such as marigolds and snapdragons, should be deadhead-ed as flowers fade to prevent unwanted seedlings the following year, to encourage abundant bloom, and to keep the plants tidy.

If you are willing to pay higher prices for your plants, you can buy container-grown perennials that are large enough to bloom the year you plant them. A third option is to plan your garden to include *Rudbeckia fulgida* 'Goldsturm', *Coreopsis verticillata* 'Moonbeam', *Hibiscus moscheutos* hybrids, or several other perennial varieties that bloom nicely their first year in the ground. If none of these flowers appeals to you, you can get your garden started with plants donated by friends who have divided their overgrown perennials and now have more healthy, mature plants than they know what to do with. These too will flower the year you plant them, if you can get them into the ground before their normal bloom time.

Finally, and perhaps most gratifying of all the possibilities, you can make sure that flowering perennials of all kinds show up in your garden the first year by filling the beds and borders with plants that you yourself have nurtured for a year or more in a separate nursery bed.

Planting Depths for Bare-Root Perennials

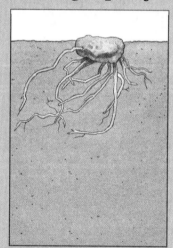

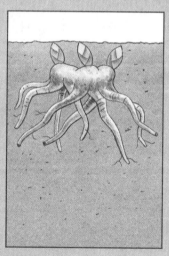

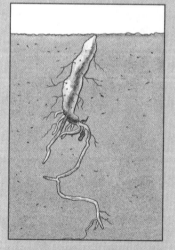

Perennials that grow from rhizomes, such as iris and bergenia, should be planted with the roots below ground and the rhizome's surface just emerging from the soil.

Plant peonies with the tips of the buds just below ground level if your area has mild winters, and up to 2 inches below the surface if you live in the North.

More than half of all perennials (including hostas, above) do best when planted so that the crown—where the roots and the stem meet—is flush with the soil surface.

Plant daylilies (Hemerocallis) and other plants with a fleshy main root or taproot with the taproot straight up and down and the bud just below ground level.

Planting Bare-Root Perennials

Unwrap the plant and check its roots, *clipping off any that are damaged or diseased (left). Place the plant in a bucket of water to keep the roots wet while you dig a hole as deep and as wide as the plant's longest roots. Form a cone of soil in the hole high enough to hold the plant at the proper level. Place the plant atop the cone, gently spreading out the roots (above). Fill in the rest of the soil, tamp down, water generously, and mulch.*

Planting a Nursery Bed

Setting aside a small plot of ground—perhaps a 10-by-10-foot area—for a nursery bed can pay dividends both in the quality and beauty of your perennial garden and in the money you save by raising your own stock. Almost any sunny spot will do for most perennials; a part of the vegetable garden or an out-of-the-way area behind the garage would be ideal. And the space can be compact because you can set the plants in neat rows and much closer together than you would in the garden. With a nursery bed you can buy one plant each of as many varieties as you are interested in and watch them grow and flower. In a year, stem cuttings *(pages 248-249)* can be taken from some perennials to propagate additional plants. In a few years, others can be divided to produce the number of new plants you want.

In the meantime, you will have a chance to learn the plants' behaviors—whether they spread too fast; require staking; respond well to your property's climate; demand little attention or much care; and, perhaps most important, produce flowers of the color, size, and shape you expected. You also can judge how the colors, flower shapes, and foliage types of different plants work next to each other before taking the trouble to establish them in your garden.

Planting Container-Grown Perennials

Dig a hole slightly larger than the plant's rootball. *Then tap the bottom of the pot to loosen the plant and slide it out. With your fingers, fluff out the roots. If the plant is severely root-bound, use a knife to cut an inch or two into the rootball from its base.*

Without disturbing the top of the rootball, *carefully pull apart the two lower sections and gently tease loose as many roots as possible with your fingertips. Take care not to break the rootball apart.*

Place the plant in the prepared hole, *spreading the roots out all around (left). Make sure the base of the plant is level with the surrounding soil. Fill the hole with soil, tamp it down, then water the plant thoroughly and mulch.*

205

Where and When to Plant

Even with a garden plan to guide you, there still remains the process of actually placing individual plants for best effect. To achieve a natural, unforced look, start with an area you have marked off for a single variety, and try to site the plants randomly rather than in a straight line or some other rigid formation. It also helps to work with an odd number of plants—three, five, or seven is best.

Allow enough space between the plants to afford them room to grow and to enjoy good air circulation—important for preventing lingering dampness in flowers and foliage, which can lead to disease. Perennials that are difficult to transplant successfully when mature, such as peonies and wild (false) indigo, should be given even more space to spread out than other plants.

As a rule, bare-root perennials should be planted at a time that will give them a chance to establish themselves before they have to face extremes of weather. This means, usually, in the spring or fall. Most larger, container-grown plants can be planted anytime during the growing season and into the fall.

Late-season bloomers such as asters, phlox, and chrysanthemums should be planted in the spring. They need time to become firmly rooted before they can direct their energy toward flowering later in the season. For the same reason, Oriental poppies, peonies, and other early-blooming perennials should be planted in the fall for flowering the following spring. Hostas, pachysandra, and other foliage plants can be planted anytime, because their flowers are not their main attraction.

In regions colder than Zone 6, limit the planting of bare-root perennials to the spring so that the plants will have the summer and fall to establish deep roots before cold weather sets in. Container-grown plants, however, will tolerate fall planting well if you follow up with a mulch of pine needles or salt hay to protect the roots from extreme cold over the winter.

Conversely, in the warmest zones it is best to plant bare-root perennials in the fall, giving them

Delphiniums and foxgloves give way to yellow chamomile, dahlias, and violet sage at the front of this new 7-by-20-foot Maine border. Planted in ready-to-bloom condition, these perennials were grown first in the gardener's own nursery bed. Annuals and biennials fill the bed's bare spots with color.

A member of a vast and hardy genus, this Hemerocallis 'Cherry Cheeks', with its 6-inch flowers on 28-inch stalks, will flourish in almost any soil. Daylilies are robust spreaders, but they are not invasive. To keep them in check, divide daylilies about every 3 years.

Holding Bare-Roots for Planting

Occasionally a spring shipment of bare-root plants arrives from the mail-order nursery before the soil has thawed and dried out enough to cultivate. If that happens, or if for some other reason you are unable to put the plants into the ground immediately, it is essential to keep their roots moist and covered. Even the best care won't preserve bare-root perennials out of the soil for more than about 2 weeks, however. If you are delayed in planting beyond that time, pot the plants temporarily in a good growing medium such as moist sawdust, moist finished compost, or leaf mold, and set them in a cool, shady spot. You won't need to worry about the plants' roots drying out, and, in addition, potting helps get growth under way.

Another method for holding plants until you are ready to plant them in the garden is "heeling in." An acclimatization process, heeling in is recommended only if the cold weather—and any chance of hard frost—has passed.

To heel in plants, you need to find a sheltered spot outdoors. Dig a narrow, shallow trench and lay the plants across it so that their crowns are at ground level and their roots are spread out in the trench. The plants can be placed side by side—spacing does not matter. After positioning the plants, water the roots, cover them with soil, and gently tamp the soil in place. This not only will keep your bare-root plants alive but will also give them a head start on becoming accustomed to outdoor living. Remember, though, that this is only a temporary procedure and that when the plants show signs of growing, you must dig them out and put them into the garden or nursery bed without delay.

Planting Tips

Planting can be hard work, but you need not do it all in one day. Have the soil ready for the plants before you dig the holes; to keep roots from drying out, unpot, unwrap, or unearth each perennial just before you place it in the hole. If you are cultivating a new bed, loosen and amend the soil as needed. When putting new plants into an existing bed, mix some fertilizer into the soil before digging planting holes. Use a product that blends organic ingredients such as dehydrated manure, blood meal, bone meal, and sunflower meal with minerals such as phosphate and potassium.

time to take hold before the heat of summer arrives. Container-grown plants will tolerate planting in the spring if they are protected by a good mulch, which will shield the roots from the effects of extreme heat by moderating ground temperatures. But to avoid rot, take care that the mulch does not touch the crown, stem, or any low-growing leaves of the plants.

Planting in midsummer is not recommended, but if you must do it, water the soil a few days before you dig so that it will be slightly moist. After planting, water the site well, apply mulch, and keep the plants shaded from the sun for the first few days. Whatever the season, your perennials will have an easier time of it if you plant them on an overcast day.

Planting Bulbs

When choosing a planting site for your bulbs, you first need to consider the area's light and temperature. Early-flowering bulbs such as snowdrop, winter aconite, spring snowflake, endymion, spring cyclamen, and crocus can be planted beneath deciduous trees and shrubs, whose bare branches in the first weeks of spring do not block the sun's rays. Areas that receive partial shade (3 to 4 hours of full sun) work well for wild and dwarf daffodils, snowflake, windflower, winter aconite, meadow saffron, and trout lily. The bulbs of late-flowering daffodils, Dutch hyacinths, and tulips take longer to mature and must be planted in full sun in northern regions.

Summer-blooming bulbs such as cannas and dahlias require at least 6 hours of full sun to develop strong stems and large blooms. When planting these bulbs in the spring, take care that they won't be in the shade cast by a building or under the dense canopy of a tree later in the season. And in southern states where the sun is very hot at noon, flowers that bloom from late spring through

DEPTH AND SPACING OF FALL-PLANTED BULBS

SOIL DEPTH

Plant spring-blooming bulbs and hardy summer-blooming bulbs in late summer to late fall, depending on the specific variety. This chart gives the recommended planting depth and spacing for a number of bulb varieties.

1"

Eranthis (winter aconite)
2-3 inches apart

2"

Crocus vernus (Dutch crocus)
2-3 inches apart

Anemone blanda (windflower)
2-3 inches apart

3"

Chionodoxa (glory-of-the-snow)
2-3 inches apart

Iris reticulata (dwarf iris)
2-3 inches apart

Muscari (grape hyacinth)
3 inches apart
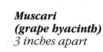

4"

5"

Allium aflatunense (ornamental onion)
4-6 inches apart

6"

Iris hollandica (Dutch iris)
6 inches apart

7"

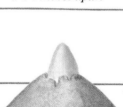
Tulipa (tulip)
6 inches apart

Narcissus (daffodil)
4-6 inches apart

8"

the summer months will last longer if they are planted in a part of the bed that receives filtered sun in the afternoon. Bulbs planted in a warm, protected southern exposure next to a building or wall will bloom earlier than those planted in an unprotected northern exposure.

Preparing the Soil

After you've decided on a spot for your bulbs, get to know your soil type. Most bulbs require soil that holds moisture—but not too much. Heavy clay is lethal to bulbs because it can become sodden and rot them. Be wary of sandy soils as well, since they can drain water away too fast. Loam, a crumbly combination of clay, sand, silt, and organic matter, is the ideal. (*Fritillaria meleagris* and several types of Siberian and Japanese iris are the exceptions to this rule—they prefer moist soil.)

If your soil has too much clay or sand to allow proper drainage, improve it by adding organic matter, such as compost, shredded leaves, or ground pine bark, or commercial composted sewage sludge. Peat moss will do the job, although it doesn't last as long. For heavy clay, add sand to the amendments to further loosen the soil.

Besides improving drainage, organic matter will add nutrients and help maintain a pH of 6.0 to 7.0, the slightly acid to neutral level preferred by most bulbs. If your soil's pH is below 5.9, you will also need to add lime. The amount needed will

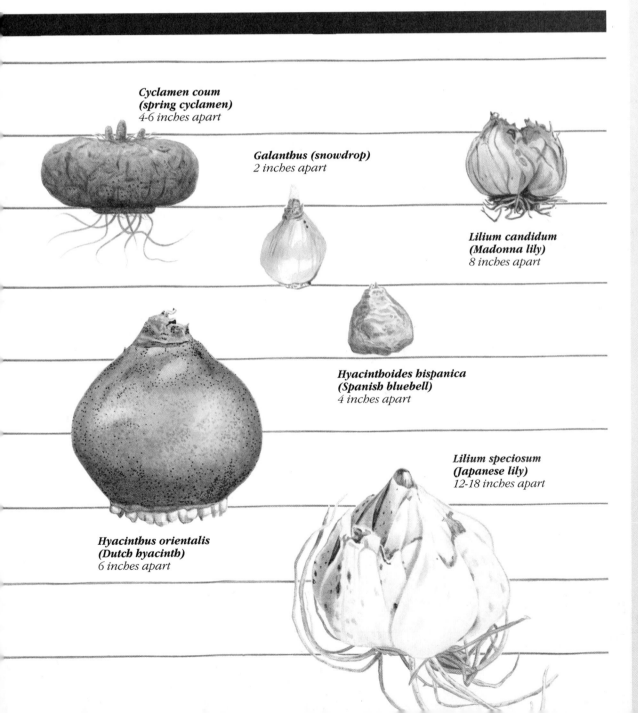

Cyclamen coum (spring cyclamen)
4-6 inches apart

Galanthus (snowdrop)
2 inches apart

Lilium candidum (Madonna lily)
8 inches apart

Hyacinthoides hispanica (Spanish bluebell)
4 inches apart

Hyacinthus orientalis (Dutch hyacinth)
6 inches apart

Lilium speciosum (Japanese lily)
12-18 inches apart

depend on your soil type and its pH reading.

Work the soil to a depth of 10 to 12 inches for large bulbs and 6 to 8 inches for smaller bulbs; remove rocks, old roots, and weed clumps. For soil that is in good condition, cover the bed with a 1-inch layer of organic matter; if major improvement is in order, spread several inches of organic matter over the plot and dig it into the soil.

If you are preparing the bed at least several weeks before planting, you can also dig in a slow-release fertilizer such as a 9-9-6 or a low-nitrogen 5-10-20; these chemical granules need time to break down or they will burn the bulbs. If you are planting at the same time you are preparing the bed, avoid fertilizer burn by enriching the soil with compost and an organic fertilizer rather than a synthetic one. Several organic formulas that are specially suited for bulbs are available at your local garden center. Refer to the package to determine the correct application rate. If a test of your soil indicates adequate phosphorus, you can get by with putting down a top dressing of compost and fertilizer rather than digging them in.

Planting Your Bulbs

A rule of thumb for planting most bulbs is to dig a hole 3 times as deep as the bulb is high. However, depth varies with soil type: In lighter soils, bulbs can be planted an inch or so deeper; in heavy soils, prepare a shallower hole and top with several

---

DEPTH AND SPACING OF SPRING- AND SUMMER-PLANTED BULBS

SOIL DEPTH

Plant tender summer-blooming bulbs in late spring to early summer, and hardy fall-blooming bulbs as soon as they are available in late summer. This chart gives the recommended planting depth and spacing for a number of bulb varieties.

1 "

Begonia x tuberhybrida (tuberous begonia)
10 inches apart

2 "

Ranunculus asiaticus (Persian buttercup)
4 inches apart

Crocosmia (montbretia)
6 inches apart

3 "

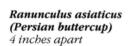

Gladiolus callianthus (Ethiopian gladiolus)
5 inches apart

Canna x generalis (canna lily)
16 inches apart

4 "

5 "

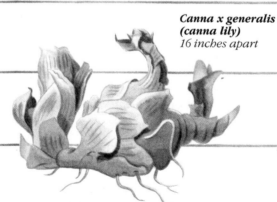

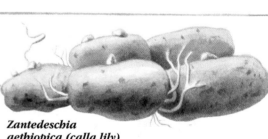

Zantedeschia aethiopica (calla lily)
10-12 inches apart

6 "

7 "

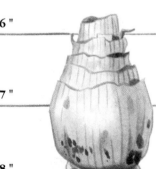

Galtonia candicans (summer hyacinth)
6-8 inches apart

8 "

inches of organic mulch. Exceptions include the Madonna lily, tuberous begonia, and *Hippeastrum* (amaryllis), which are always planted close to the surface. Refer to the charts below and on pages 208-209 for specific spacing and planting depths for the different bulb species.

When planting many bulbs in a new bed where the soil is loose and crumbly, a small trowel is the best tool for the job *(pages 212-213)*. If you're planting bulbs in an established bed among perennials and shrubs, use a shovel to loosen the soil in small areas and a trowel to dig individual planting holes. If the soil is not compacted, a hand-held hollow bulb planter *(page 213)* can be used to remove plugs of earth. Dig several inches below where the bulb will rest, and work in organic matter or a slow-release synthetic fertilizer at the rate of 1 tablespoon per square foot. If you use a synthetic, prevent damage to the bulbs by covering the fertilized layer with untreated soil up to planting depth before placing the bulbs in the holes. Position the bulbs with their pointed ends up; plant flat tubers of anemones and cyclamens sideways.

Cover the bulbs with soil, tamp it down, and water the planting thoroughly. Mulch the entire bed—new or established—with 2 to 4 inches of shredded pine bark, pine needles, or shredded leaves to control weed growth, retain moisture, and moderate soil temperature.

To keep track of the bulbs after they are planted and after the foliage has died back, you may want to mark their location. Metal labels have tabs that

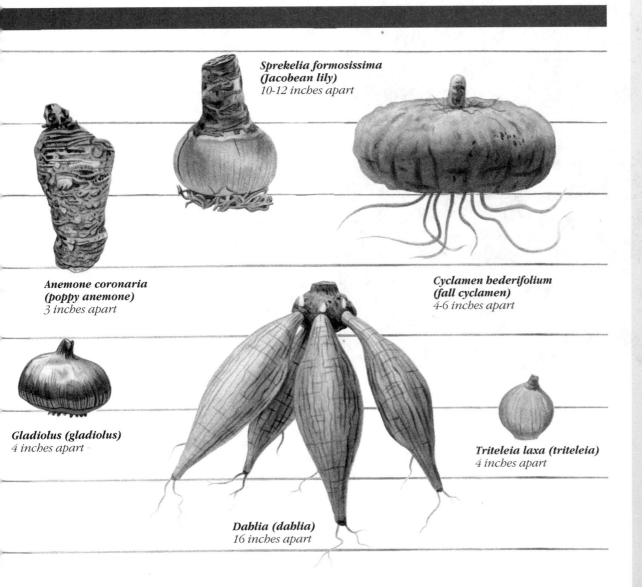

Sprekelia formosissima (Jacobean lily)
10-12 inches apart

Anemone coronaria (poppy anemone)
3 inches apart

Cyclamen hederifolium (fall cyclamen)
4-6 inches apart

Gladiolus (gladiolus)
4 inches apart

Triteleia laxa (triteleia)
4 inches apart

Dahlia (dahlia)
16 inches apart

Nestled among evergreens at the base of a fountain, purple Crocus speciosus 'Artabir' adds a pocket of color to a backyard Virginia garden. Plant the hardy autumn-flowering bulbs in late summer for blooms 6 to 8 weeks later.

southern areas, as late as December. Hardy summer-blooming bulbs are usually planted in the fall. They can be planted in late spring with other flowering perennials, but in the North they may not get established sufficiently to bloom the same year.

Tender summer-blooming bulbs can't be planted until the soil temperature reaches 65° to 70° F, because they will rot if planted in cold, wet earth. Some, such as caladium and tuberous begonia, should be started indoors in spring, 3 to 4 weeks before the last frost date, so they have several inches of growth before they're moved outdoors. Canna and dahlia benefit from being started indoors in northern areas where summers are short.

Use flats filled with an enriched potting mix containing peat moss. If you are starting caladium and begonia tubers, soak them in tepid water to remove the wax coating that is applied to prevent them from dehydrating during transit. If you are planting caladiums, encourage them to produce many leaves by breaking off the primary shoot.

Arrange the tubers in the potting mix, cover them with another inch of it, and place the flats in a sunny window. Water regularly to keep the mix barely moist, and feed the growing plants every 2 weeks with a diluted fish or seaweed liquid fertilizer. Plant the tubers outdoors when they have sprouted several inches of foliage and the soil temperature is 70° F.

For a continuous show of color over several weeks, combine bulbs that bloom at different times. If your combinations include both large and small bulbs, plant them in layers. First dig a rectangular hole 12 inches deep. Loosen the soil in the bottom of the hole, mix in a slow-release bulb food, and top with a layer of unfertilized soil to bring the depth of the prepared trench up to about 8 inches. Place large bulbs in the bottom and cover with 4 inches of soil. Next, set the smaller bulbs in the trench and fill to the top with soil. Tamp it down and water thoroughly, then cover with a layer of mulch.

Bulbs that can be layered include dwarf iris over early daffodils or early to midspring tulips, squill over late-spring ornamental onion, windflower over early to midspring daffodils, muscari over mid- to late-spring tulips, and crocus over early to midspring hyacinths.

If you're interplanting similar-size bulbs that bloom at different times in the spring, dig an area to the required depth and alternate the bulbs, placing them as close together as possible. Bulbs with sequential bloom times that can be planted at the same depth include late-blooming daffodils and ornamental onion, crocus and muscari, and dwarf iris and windflower.

can be marked with permanent ink, and their two pin legs keep them securely anchored in the ground. Vinyl markers are also good because they can be cut, are flexible, and won't break in the cold. Or you can use labels made of sturdy plastic, which are pointed at one end for insertion into soft earth.

When to Plant

Hardy spring-blooming bulbs require a chilling period and should be planted in early fall. This gives them time to develop a good root system before the ground freezes. In northern areas the best planting time may be as early as September; in

Tools for Planting Bulbs

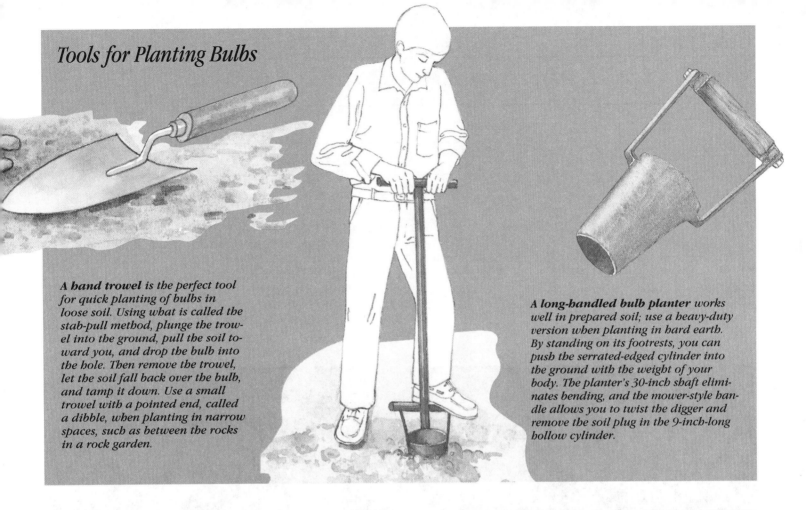

A hand trowel is the perfect tool for quick planting of bulbs in loose soil. Using what is called the stab-pull method, plunge the trowel into the ground, pull the soil toward you, and drop the bulb into the hole. Then remove the trowel, let the soil fall back over the bulb, and tamp it down. Use a small trowel with a pointed end, called a dibble, when planting in narrow spaces, such as between the rocks in a rock garden.

A long-handled bulb planter works well in prepared soil; use a heavy-duty version when planting in hard earth. By standing on its footrests, you can push the serrated-edged cylinder into the ground with the weight of your body. The planter's 30-inch shaft eliminates bending, and the mower-style handle allows you to twist the digger and remove the soil plug in the 9-inch-long hollow cylinder.

Protecting Bulbs from Animals

Many small rodents are fond of tulip and crocus bulbs. To outwit them, place chipped stones at the bottom of the planting hole, position the bulb, and sprinkle more stones around it to reach but not cover the pointed tip. Fill in with soil.

Larger rodents—chipmunks and squirrels among them—also find tulip and crocus bulbs a tasty treat and will dig them up before the ground freezes. In the West, gophers can quickly destroy entire plantings. One way to prevent such foraging when putting in bulb beds is to plant in wire baskets. Dig a trench and line the bottom and sides with metal hardware cloth. Lay the bulbs on top, cover with several inches of soil, and tamp down. A top dressing of well-aged cow manure or commercial composted sewage sludge will further repel pests. Bulbs not bothered by rodents include daffodils, squills, glory-of-the-snow, and snowdrops.

Planting Roses

Roses grow best in rich, loamy, well-drained, slightly acidic soil that holds water and nutrients well and allows air to reach plant roots. To achieve such a combination, you'll probably need to amend your soil with both organic and inorganic materials. If the overall quality and texture of your soil is generally inferior for growing roses, you'll want to work on the entire bed. If the soil is in good shape, you can focus your attention on the roses' planting holes. Either way, soil preparation takes time, but it can mean the difference between roses that limp along from year to year and those that are long-lived, with lush growth and opulent blossoms.

Using Soil Amendments

There is an array of organic and mineral amendments to help bring your soil to peak condition. To improve drainage in tightly compacted clay soil or help sandy soil retain moisture, incorporate organic materials such as peat moss, leaf mold, ground-bark mulch, well-rotted manure, or compost. As an added bonus, these amendments also provide plant roots with some of the nutrients they need and help keep soil pH in the slightly acid range preferred by roses. Just be sure that any organic

With their clusters of pink blossoms dancing at the tips of gently arching stems, 'Ballerina' hybrid musk roses create a lovely informal hedge in this Houston, Texas, garden. The plants are closely spaced to create a continuous line of color but allow enough room for maintenance.

matter you dig into the soil is well decomposed—it should be dark, crumbly, and earthy smelling.

Mineral amendments include gypsum, which helps to loosen heavy clay soils and lower the pH of alkaline soil. Coarse sand, perlite, vermiculite, and pumice are other mineral amendments that improve soil by adding bulk and changing texture. Do not use vermiculite in heavy clay, however, since it tends to absorb and retain water. The amount of mineral amendments you use will depend on your particular soil. Organic material, in any case, should make up about one-quarter of your total soil volume.

Roses prefer a pH level of around 6.5. To determine the pH level of your soil, you can pick up an inexpensive testing kit at any garden center. Or, for a more detailed analysis, take a soil sample to your local Cooperative Extension Service or to a private laboratory. Either way, aim to test and amend the soil a few months before putting your roses into the ground—in the late fall before spring planting, for example—so that the pH balance has a chance to adjust properly.

If your soil is too acidic, you can raise the pH by adding dolomitic limestone. Work it into the top 6 inches of soil and then water. Your soil type will dictate how much lime to apply—sandy soils generally require the least amount of lime to raise the pH level by one point; clayey soils need more. Since too much lime can burn tender roots, start out cautiously, digging in no more than 5 pounds of lime per 100 square feet of area. Then wait a month or so before retesting your soil and adding more lime, if needed.

To lower the pH of alkaline soil, dig in iron sulfate, ground sulfur, or gypsum, following package directions. Use a maximum of 2 pounds per 100 square feet per application, then wait a month and retest. Experts recommend lowering or raising your soil's pH level no more than one point per year. Since extremely alkaline soil can be difficult to alter, you may want to consider growing your roses in raised beds or containers as an alternative.

Spacing Between Roses	
Type of Rose	**Planting Distance**
Miniatures	1–1½ ft.
Hybrid Tea, Grandiflora, & Floribunda Bushes *Compact and average varieties*	2–2½ ft.
Hybrid Tea, Grandiflora, & Floribunda Bushes *Tall varieties*	2½–3 ft.
Low-Growing Shrubs	3–4 ft.
Standards	4 ft.
Shrubs	4–6 ft. or half of expected height
Climbers & Ramblers *Trained horizontally*	8–10 ft.

Preparing the Rose Bed

Gardeners once believed that planting new roses in a bed where other roses had grown would result in "rose sickness"—reduced vigor caused by the depletion of trace elements in the soil or vestiges of root diseases left in the soil by the old plants. Experts now agree that as long as the soil is amended to replenish nutrients or replaced if there has been disease in a particular spot, there's no reason to avoid repeated plantings in the same bed.

To ready a bed for planting, begin by removing any existing sod. Then, with a hoe, dig about 16 inches down into the soil, removing any large rocks. If you're willing to spend extra time with the soil, consider double digging *(page 199)*. Although this technique involves digging up and amending 24 inches of soil rather than the usual 12 inches, many rose gardeners think the added work is worth the payoff in more and larger blooms. Whether or not you double dig, add all of your amendments during the digging phase. This is also the best time to add bone meal or another source of phosphorus—at 3 to 4 pounds per 100 square feet—to promote healthy root growth. Unlike the other major nutrients, phosphorus is difficult to supply to roots once plants are established. You can also include a granular fertilizer if you are preparing the bed about a month before planting; the idle weeks before you plant will give the fertilizer time to blend with the soil.

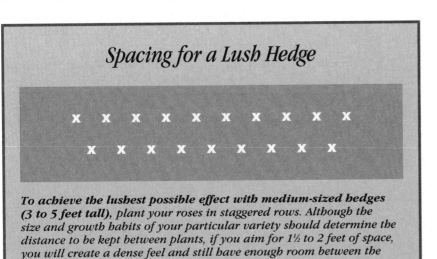

Spacing for a Lush Hedge

To achieve the lushest possible effect with medium-sized hedges (3 to 5 feet tall), plant your roses in staggered rows. Although the size and growth habits of your particular variety should determine the distance to be kept between plants, if you aim for 1½ to 2 feet of space, you will create a dense feel and still have enough room between the plants to perform maintenance chores.

Planting a Bare-Root Rose

Before planting your bare-root rose, do the following: Rinse the plant under a hard stream of water from a garden hose to clean off any bacteria or fungal spores. Then immerse the rose in a bucket of water for at least 1 hour and no more than 24 hours to replenish the plant's moisture. Never leave the rose soaking more than a day, or the plant may die. Using a pair of sharp shears, prune off any broken or injured roots just above the point of the injury, and cut back any canes that are damaged or are the diameter of a pencil or less. Set the plant aside, keeping it in water until you are ready to transfer it to the planting hole.

1. Dig a planting hole at least as wide and as deep as the spread of the plant's roots. If you haven't already prepared the soil, add the necessary amendments to the soil removed from the hole. Next, return enough of the improved soil to the hole to form a cone-shaped mound; this will serve as a support for the plant.

2. Lay a spade across the hole to mark ground level, then set the plant on top of the mound, spreading its roots out evenly all around. Allowing for changes as the soil settles, adjust the height of the mound so that the plant's bud union will be just above ground level in climates where temperatures do not drop below 20°F, or 1 to 2 inches below ground level in colder climates.

3. Fill the hole about halfway with soil and tamp it down gently with your hands; this removes air pockets around the roots. Fill the hole with water and allow it to drain. Then fill the hole to the top with soil and water once more. Check to see that the bud union remains at the proper level; if not, add or remove soil as necessary.

4. Mound additional soil around the bottom of the plant and up to within 3 inches of the tops of the canes; this will keep them from drying out while the plant is getting established. Check every 2 to 3 days for new growth. When buds sprout, usually after about 2 weeks, gradually and gently remove the soil mound with water from a garden hose or with your fingers. Loosen the plant's nametag so that it does not constrict the cane as it grows.

Planting a Container-Grown Rose

A container-grown rose can be planted any time from early spring to midfall, as long as the ground is not frozen or waterlogged and the plant has enough time to establish itself before frost occurs. Choose a day that is overcast, with no wind or direct sun to dry canes and roots. If you must plant on a sunny day, wait until late afternoon to spare the plant the midday sun. If the rose has been sitting in a sunny location while waiting its turn for planting, this precaution is unnecessary.

1. Dig a hole slightly wider than the container and, if your soil has been prepared, of equal depth. If the soil is unprepared, dig 6 inches deeper and add amendments to the removed soil; return about 6 inches of soil to the hole. Then loosen the plant from the sides of its container by gently inserting a trowel in a few places around the pot. Take care not to disturb the roots.

2. Support the plant at its base and invert the container to slide it out; if the plant won't slide out on its own, press on the bottom of the container, or carefully cut away the pot from around the plant. Keeping the soil intact and without disturbing the roots, position the plant in the hole.

3. Add or remove soil as necessary to be sure that the rose's bud union is at the correct position for your climate. Typically, the nursery establishes the correct position when it pots the plant; you should only have to keep the soil surface of the rootball flush with the edge of the planting hole. Fill in the hole, tamping soil around the roots to remove air pockets. Water the plant thoroughly, add more soil if necessary, and spread a layer of mulch around the plant. Keep the rose well watered until it is established.

Spacing Your Plants

Spacing between rose plants is determined by climate, growth habits, and the visual effect you want to achieve *(chart, page 215)*. However, a few rules always apply. Most important, never crowd your plants. Crowding hampers air circulation and makes it more difficult for you to move around between your plants to tend them. Second, arrange plants so you can avoid as much as possible having to step into the bed, since walking on the bed compacts the soil.

When to Plant

The climate in your area and whether your rose is bare-root or container grown will determine the best time for planting. Ideally, bare-root roses should be planted as soon as you receive them—in late winter in areas where temperatures remain above freezing year round; in early spring or late fall where winter temperatures remain above 0° F; and in midspring where winters are extremely cold. Before you plant, make sure all danger of hard frost has passed and that the ground is neither hard or frozen nor soggy and waterlogged. Container-grown roses may be planted anytime from early spring to midfall. If you plant during hot weather, however, be sure to keep the rose well watered for the first 6 weeks.

If you intend to plant your bare-root roses within a few days of receiving them, keep them wrapped in their shipping materials and place them in an unheated but frostproof location, such as a garage or shed. But if it will be 2 weeks or more before you plant, you must heel the roses in. To do this, dig a shallow V-shaped trench, lay the plants side by side in the trench, and add just enough moist soil to cover the roots. This will insulate the plants and keep them from becoming dehydrated. If you must wait awhile before planting container-grown roses, keep them in a warm, sunny spot out of the wind, and keep the soil moist.

Maintaining the Garden

If soil is properly prepared and planting is done correctly, a flower garden should require relatively little upkeep. The one shown at left, in Los Angeles, was designed with the region's dry climate in mind: It is filled with many heat- and drought-tolerant plants and is mulched with gravel to conserve water.

Watering, fertilizing, and mulching give plants the moisture and nutrients they need to blossom, while staking, pruning, and weeding keep a bed looking tidy. Dividing overgrown plants keeps them healthy and increases your stock, and checking your plants for pests and diseases can help keep trouble at bay (see the Troubleshooting Guide, pages 258-269, for descriptions of common pests and diseases).

In areas of the country where the ground alternately freezes and thaws, winter's approach calls for putting down a protective mulch. But whatever the winter weather, most perennials should be cut to the ground at the end of the growing season. Roses also benefit from pruning and winter protection (pages 236-241), while spent annuals can simply be discarded in the compost pile.

Mulching and Weeding

The work required to keep a garden well mulched pays off handsomely. Besides helping to create the best growing conditions for your plants, a mulch minimizes watering and weeding chores and gives beds and borders a finished look.

Organic Mulches versus Stone

Mulches best suited to a flower garden include numerous organic materials—shredded bark, cocoa shells, woodchips, and leaves, among others—and one inorganic material—stone. Stone mulch is available in different forms, most commonly as gravel, crushed rock, or stone chips. Another useful inorganic mulch is the long-lasting, porous synthetic material called landscape fabric. While it is an effective weed blocker, landscape fabric is unat-

tractive and should be covered with a decorative mulch (*opposite*) if used in a bed or border. If you use the fabric on a steep slope, however, don't cover it with another mulch—the loose pieces of mulch would likely be washed downhill by rain.

Both organic and stone mulches slow the evaporation of soil moisture and keep soil temperatures fairly cool and steady. Organic mulches are especially effective shields against heat—on a 100°F day, the soil beneath a 3-inch layer of mulch may be as much as 30°F cooler than the air above. Organic mulches also improve the soil as they decay, creating humus. Because they decompose, however, they have to be replenished regularly.

Stone mulches have the virtue of permanence. And only 1 inch of rock or gravel may be enough to cover the soil beneath your plants. But there are drawbacks. When spread under a deciduous tree, for example, the mulch makes fallen leaves

Unfit for brewing because they were roasted too long, these coffee beans were put to work as an eye-catching mulch in a Seattle, Washington, garden.

An expanse of fine stone chips provides a handsome setting for sand phlox, a spring-blooming native perennial that thrives in fast-draining sandy or rocky soil. The heat and light a stone mulch reflects help keep foliage dry, reducing the likelihood of crown rot in susceptible plants.

difficult to rake up. It can also become hot enough in bright sun to raise the air temperature by 10°F or more, and the stones themselves can burn any plant stems they touch. In addition, sunlight hitting pale-colored stones can produce an unpleasant glare. And finally, the very permanence of stone means that it doesn't improve soil structure.

Choosing and Applying a Mulch

Looks, longevity, site, and price are all factors to consider when selecting and using organic mulch. Using one type of mulch throughout the garden will give it a uniform appearance, but combining materials is also an option: A serviceable but unsightly layer of newspapers, ground corncobs, or ground sugarcane stalks can be concealed beneath a more appealing top dressing of chunks of bark or pine needles. Avoid using peat moss as a mulch, however. Although it's a good soil amendment, when placed on top of the soil peat moss blows around, is hard to rewet when it dries out, is a fire hazard, and is expensive to boot.

There are no hard-and-fast rules about how deeply you should mulch. Soil type must be taken into account; a loose, sandy soil, for instance, dries out more quickly than clay soil and consequently needs a thicker layer of mulch. The density of the mulch itself is important—the coarser and airier it is, the deeper you can apply it. Be careful, however, not to use a mulch so dense that little air and water can pass through it into the soil.

Whatever material you choose, lay it thickest between plants, tapering it down to soil level within an inch or two of the base of the plants. Avoid piling up mulch against trunks or stems lest it encourage pests and diseases. As a rule of thumb, use a 1- to 2-inch layer for a mulch with particles measuring ½ inch in diameter. Particles ranging from ½ inch to an inch or so should be spread at least 2 to 3 inches deep, and dry leaves, pine needles, and woodchips deeper still. If the woodchips are fresh, mix each cubic yard with 3 pounds of controlled-release nitrogen fertilizer before you lay down the mulch. Otherwise, microorganisms in the woodchips will draw nitrogen from the soil.

If weeds continue to appear, you've probably skimped on mulch and should add more. But if slugs and snails are a problem, additional mulch may draw still more of them. In such cases, it's better to use a combination of landscape fabric and a thin covering of mulch. Plan on renewing bark and leaf mulches annually. Woodchips can last 2 years and pine needles up to 3 years.

Laying Landscape Fabric in an Existing Bed

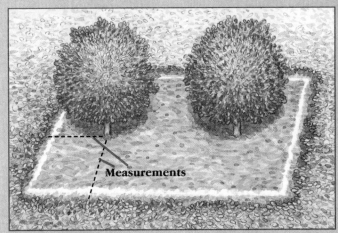
Measurements

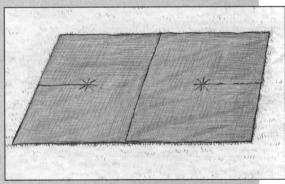

1. Use lime to outline the area that is to be mulched, then remove any weeds and debris from around the plants. Measure the bed's length and width to determine how many lengths of fabric to cut, allowing for a 4- to 6-inch overlap between adjoining sections. Correctly position the fabric in an area adjacent to the bed. Next, measure the distance from a plant's center to the two closest edges of the bed that form a right angle. Transfer this measurement to the fabric and mark the point where the two lines intersect.

2. Cut from one edge of the fabric to the point where the two lines intersect, then make a series of radiating cuts around it (above). The cuts should equal the radius of the plant's trunk or stem cluster, plus about 3 inches.

3. Slip the fabric around each plant, then fold the pie-shaped wedges under to make a neat circle. When all of the sections of fabric are in place, cover them with a decorative mulch such as woodchips or pine needles.

Using an Onion Hoe

A lightweight onion hoe that is well sharpened and properly wielded requires little effort to use. To sever a weed just below ground level, position the blade a few inches above the soil *(inset)* and pull it toward you in a shallow arc. In tight spots, turn the hoe sideways and use one of its narrow edges to slice off a weed. A blade used in rocky soil will need more frequent sharpening than one used in sandy soil. This chore is easily accomplished with a sharpening file called a bastard mill file, which you stroke over the blade.

Using a Dandelion Digger

Working when the soil is moist, thrust a long-handled dandelion digger into the ground deep enough to reach the tip of a weed's root (inset). Then push down on the tool's handle to pry the weed out. Examine the root; if it isn't intact, dig out the portions that broke off to prevent regrowth.

In those climates where the ground alternately freezes and thaws in winter, apply a winter mulch to newly planted beds after the soil has frozen to keep the temperature constant. The best choices are airy materials such as pine boughs, straw, and salt hay, laid down over what remains of the growing-season mulch.

When Weeds Appear

Although keeping soil mulched is an excellent preventive, no garden is completely free of weeds. Perennial weeds are a worse problem than annual ones. Their more extensive root systems are harder to dig out, and any fragments left behind may grow anew. Use a digging fork with ground ivy, Bermuda grass, and other perennial weeds that have wide-spreading runners; a narrow-bladed dandelion digger *(left)* is best for weeds with deep roots such as Canada thistle and dandelion. An onion hoe works well for cutting larger shallow-rooted annual weeds, including chickweed. For weeds in spots that are hard to get at with a digging tool, try pouring boiling water on them.

Working the garden with a hoe to destroy weeds is an art that becomes easier with practice. Hold the hoe so that the blade cuts through the soil in a shallow arc, going no deeper than about an inch below the surface. Avoid turning over soil clods; this may expose buried weed seeds and encourage resprouting. And above all, hoe regularly. Annual weeds may be killed quickly, but perennial weeds may take repeated cutting.

Watering and Fertilizing

Water droplets deposited by a sprinkler's low-pressure spray linger on this daylily blossom. Overhead watering has the advantage of rinsing plants clean of dust and pollutants, but soaker hoses can also be used in perennial beds. For optimum flowering, keep the plants well watered during the period that they are forming flower buds and are just starting to produce blooms.

Proper watering and fertilizing of your plants will keep them growing robust and strong. Plants are most demanding while they're becoming established—a year or so for perennials, twice as long for shrubs and trees. Give new plantings relatively light, frequent waterings and monitor for signs of stress, such as drooping or dull-looking leaves. The soil should dry out slightly between waterings so that oxygen can reach plant roots.

As plants mature, progressively deeper and less frequent watering is called for. This encourages the roots to penetrate far into the soil, where they can tap into moisture reserves and come through dry spells in good condition. Established plantings of drought-tolerant trees, shrubs, and perennials may need only minimal watering during such periods—or even none at all, depending on the soil's structure. A good rule of thumb, though, is to moisten soil to a depth of 12 inches two to three times a month for woody plants, and every 7 to 10 days for herbaceous plants. Roses need at least an inch of water each week during the growing season, and at the height of summer—when roses are in full flower and the days are at their hottest—

they may need an inch of water every other day. For bulbs, normal rainfall usually provides enough moisture. However, if you experience a long period of dry weather during the bulbs' active growth periods, give them at least 1 inch of water a week.

Even though plants in the shade do not face harsh, moisture-evaporating sun, rainfall may be prevented from reaching them by tree foliage or high walls, and the rain that does get through is often soaked up by competing tree roots. As a result, you can't assume that even ample rainfall has met your shade plants' moisture needs, so check the plants regularly. Water them as needed, making sure they receive about an inch of water every 7 to 10 days in a long, slow soaking.

The Best Watering Methods

Watering large areas with a hand-held, high-pressure hose is a waste of time because so much of the water runs off instead of sinking into the soil. Moving hoses and sprinklers from place to place is tedious work as well. For the best results with the least effort, consider a system of low-flow, low-pressure hoses and delivery devices that is custom tailored to your site. These systems can be installed above ground or buried, and not all of them require installation by a professional. Some can be easily put together by the homeowner from materials available in a local garden center (shown in the box at right) and can be ready to operate in just a few hours.

First off, there are two basic ways to apply water to your garden: by sprinkling or by soaking. Sprinkling works well with perennials and ground covers, especially those that thrive in a humid environment. The overhead action helps wash dust and pollutants from foliage, and it also discourages undesirable insects such as spider mites. Roses and bulbs—plants that are prone to fungus diseases—will benefit most from watering with a soaker hose, which supplies a slow, steady flow of water directly into the soil. Soaker hoses are also preferable for areas prone to summer drought such as California, Texas, and other arid spots, and for those flower beds too narrow to be sprinkled without a lot of waste.

Testing Soil Moisture

To determine how well a watering regimen delivers moisture to the root zone of your plants, use a soil auger *(below)* to collect a sample of earth. The auger, basically a hollow cylinder with a handle and a window cut in one side, is pushed into the ground vertically, twisted to free a core of soil, then pulled out at an angle, window side up. Feel the soil; if only the top few inches are moist, adjust your watering regimen to get deeper penetration.

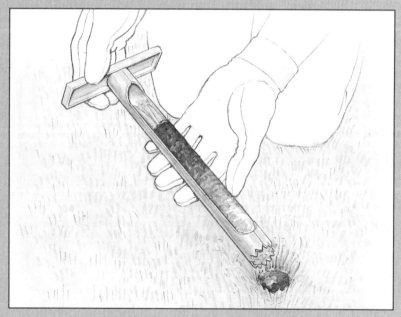

An Off-the-Shelf Irrigation System

At a very reasonable cost, you can put together an irrigation system using garden hoses, soaker hoses, sprinklers, timers, and other accessories widely available at garden centers and hardware stores. The property illustrated at right has a series of setups that are arranged to suit a variety of plantings in different parts of the garden. Except for two garden hoses that need to be moved into position when it is time to water, the irrigation system can be left in place year round.

The system uses two different kinds of soaker hose. One has metal fittings at each end that are identical to those of a conventional garden hose. The other kind allows the gardener maximum flexibility in customizing an irrigation system because it is cut to the lengths appropriate for particular areas.

The various pieces of the system are joined with specially designed tubular fittings. Virtually any layout can be assembled. In the example shown here, a timer—either electronic or mechanical—is attached to each of the three outdoor faucets supplying water to the garden.

The system supplies different areas as follows:
• The backyard lawn and most of the surrounding perennial border are irrigated simultaneously by a single impulse sprinkler, which is stored beside the house between waterings, along with the garden hose *(brown)* that supplies it. A soaker hose with brass fittings on its ends *(green)* is operated off the same faucet via a Y-connector and waters the back of the border, to the left of the lawn.
• Custom-cut lengths of soaker hose are placed in a ring around each of the trees planted behind the garage *(red)*, and are joined by tubular connectors to nonporous supply pipes *(blue)*.
• The garden hose *(brown)* running from the faucet beside the driveway does double duty, supplying the backyard trees and the hedge flanking the driveway. Two-part metal couplings at either end of the hose make the hose easy to connect and disconnect.
• A Y-connector attached to the faucet on the front of the house allows the sunny street-side perennial bed and the shrubs in the partly shaded side yard to be watered independently with soaker hoses *(green)*.

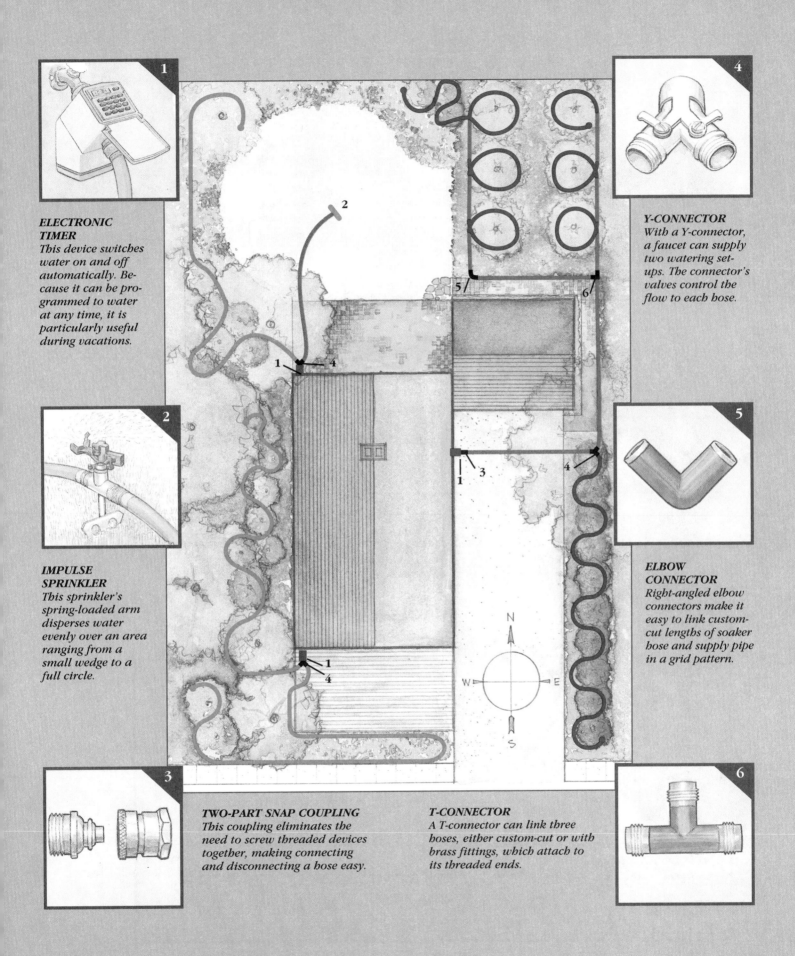

1

ELECTRONIC TIMER
This device switches water on and off automatically. Because it can be programmed to water at any time, it is particularly useful during vacations.

2

IMPULSE SPRINKLER
This sprinkler's spring-loaded arm disperses water evenly over an area ranging from a small wedge to a full circle.

3

TWO-PART SNAP COUPLING
This coupling eliminates the need to screw threaded devices together, making connecting and disconnecting a hose easy.

T-CONNECTOR
A T-connector can link three hoses, either custom-cut or with brass fittings, which attach to its threaded ends.

4

Y-CONNECTOR
With a Y-connector, a faucet can supply two watering set-ups. The connector's valves control the flow to each hose.

5

ELBOW CONNECTOR
Right-angled elbow connectors make it easy to link custom-cut lengths of soaker hose and supply pipe in a grid pattern.

6

In fact, a major disadvantage of sprinklers is that they can waste water, especially if the pressure isn't appropriate to the soil. For clay, where water runoff is a problem, pick a sprinkler that has a low—or slow—delivery rate. A sprinkler with a higher delivery rate suits a sandy soil, providing a fast soaking that minimizes evaporation.

Whatever the soil type, a sprinkler head should produce droplets rather than a fog or mist. (The easiest time to check a sprinkler's output is when it is illuminated by the low, slanting rays of an early-morning or late-afternoon sun.) In addition, the droplets should be emitted at a low angle; sprayed high into the air, water is more likely to drift out of range of the garden or evaporate. All told, as much as 50 percent of the output of an ill-chosen and ill-used sprinkler can go to waste.

Fertilizing for Best Results

In addition to regular moisture and the nutrient boost they gain from decaying organic mulch, your plants will likely benefit from a well-timed dose of fertilizer. For perennials, one application of organic fertilizer just before the growing season

begins will usually be enough. Supplement that with a second application in midsummer or early fall if plants show stunted growth, yellowing leaves, or small, sparse flowers. As an alternative to using a granular fertilizer on a flagging perennial, give the plant a quick, temporary boost by sprinkling or lightly spraying its leaves with a liquid infusion of seaweed or fish emulsion.

Fertilizing should be done with a light hand, especially in the case of chemical fertilizers, which can burn a plant's tender roots. In addition, a nitrogen-rich fertilizer, whether chemical or organic, can cause excess vegetative growth and, as a consequence, make staking necessary *(pages 228-229)*. Be especially sparing with chemical fertilizers late in the season, since a burst of growth then may not have time to mature and will be damaged by winter cold.

Giving Roses a Boost

The simplest way to boost a rose's diet is to use a commercial fertilizer sold as a "rose food." These dry, granular products contain a combination of natural organic materials, which provide nutrients

Watering a Slope

The chart at right shows how a garden's contours and its soil type—sandy, loamy, or clay—affect the rate of water absorption. A sandy, level area, for instance, can absorb up to 1.7 inches of water per hour. But on a sandy 10 percent slope—one whose elevation rises 1 foot for every 10 feet of run—only 1.02 inches are absorbed; the remainder runs off before it can soak into the ground. When the slope increases to 20 percent, the maximum amount of water absorbed in an hour falls still further, to 0.68 inch.

To give a slope a proper soaking without excessive runoff, apply water more slowly than on level ground. In addition, water the top of the slope more heavily than the bottom, since as much as half of that water may move downhill, either on the surface or underground. If you're using soaker hoses, minimize runoff by laying them across the slope.

SOIL TYPE	INCHES OF WATER ABSORBED PER HOUR ON THREE GRADES		
	LEVEL	*10% SLOPE*	*20% SLOPE*
SANDY	.5"-1.7"	.3"-1.02"	.2"-.68"
LOAMY	.25"-1.0"	.15"-.6"	.1"-.4"
CLAY	.1"-.2"	.06"-.12"	.04"-.08"

over a period of time, and inorganic chemicals, which deliver nutrients right away. In general, you'll want to feed your roses before they come out of dormancy in the early spring and again about 2 months before the first expected frost date *(see pages 270-271 for frost date maps)*. In warm climates where frost isn't a threat, though, you can feed your plants late in the season for a burst of autumn bloom.

Give roses that bloom repeatedly an additional dose of fertilizer after their first bloom cycle. If you want to grow the largest blooms possible on repeat-blooming modern roses, you may fertilize every month during the growing season, up to the frost cutoff date. Check the fertilizer label, however, for instructions on when and how often to apply a specific product.

Roses growing in containers need more frequent feeding than plants in the ground because the near daily watering they require tends to leach nutrients out of the soil. Your best bet with these plants is to cut the recommended dosage of rose food in half and apply it twice as often. You may also use an appropriate liquid fertilizer—a complete chemical formula mixed with water and typically applied every 2 weeks.

Fertilizing Bulbs

Although bulbs contain their own food supply for the next season's blooms, feeding them each year with commercial fertilizers ensures stellar performances. Fertilize established beds in mid- to late fall when the bulbs are sending out good root growth and before the ground starts to freeze. Use a 9-9-6 slow-release synthetic sprinkled over the ground at the rate of 1 pound per 100 square feet of surface area.

If your bulbs are in a mixed herbaceous bed that has been fertilized regularly, these additional feedings aren't necessary. Also, soils that have been amended with organic materials such as compost, shredded leaves, shredded bark, or aged manure don't need regular, additional fertilizing. Instead, layer compost around the plants in the spring and put down mulch in the fall. If the soil was not amended at planting time, periodic top-dressing with organic-rich materials will create nutrient-laden, moisture-retentive, loamy soils.

A Quick Plant Pick-Me-Up

To give your plants a quick temporary boost, spray a diluted liquid fertilizer, such as manure or com-post "tea" or fish emulsion, directly onto the plants' leaves, which will absorb the nutrients quickly. Or pour the fertilizer onto the soil so that it soaks down to the plants' roots.

To make manure or compost tea, first fill a bucket two-thirds full of water. Add manure or compost to bring the water level to the top of the container, and steep for a day or two. Alternatively, put the manure or compost in a cheesecloth or burlap bag and soak it in the water as you would a tea bag. Then, either removing the bag or leaving the solid material at the bottom of the bucket, pour off the liquid into another container and dilute it with more water to the color of weak tea. Never use manure tea full strength; it can burn your plants. (To use the tea in small amounts, dip off what you need and dilute it.) Pour about 1 pint of manure or compost tea around each plant, or pour it into a clean sprayer and spray the leaves thoroughly on both sides. Since manure and compost teas are good sources of nitrogen, this tonic will be especially welcomed by plants with leaves that are yellowing or turning bluish purple underneath or by those that are showing spindly or stunted growth. Plants that bloom throughout the season may benefit from a spritz of fertilizer every 2 weeks or so during flowering.

After globes of silver-lilac flowers have faded, the broad blue-green leaves of Allium kara-taviense (ornamental onion) will continue to add interest to this perennial border for several weeks. Properly fed, watered, and left undisturbed, clumps of ornamental onions will flower and multiply for 10 seasons or more.

Staking Plants to Add Support

The majority of plants have stems that are strong enough to remain erect when their blossoms open. Nevertheless, you may find that in some cases—with perennials in particular and with some bulbs—you will need to devise simple supports to keep your plants standing upright and the garden looking orderly.

Why Plants Fall Over

In general, plants over 2 feet in height are more likely to need staking for suppprt, especially those plants with large, heavy blossoms; bulbs such as dahlias, turberous begonias, and some gladiolus and lilies fall into this category. A severe thunderstorm can easily flatten such top-heavy plants to the ground and snap off the blooms. In addition, recently planted perennials that haven't had time to develop sturdy stems may need temporary support until they become established.

Sometimes, however, an apparent need for staking may actually indicate a separate problem. Weak stems, for example, may be a sign that the plants need better care. In the case of an old, overgrown clump of perennials, dividing the plants may be the best solution (pages 242-247). Other common sources of trouble include overwatering and a soil oversupplied with nitrogen and lacking in phosphorus and potassium.

Location plays a role as well. Plants exposed to wind will be more susceptible to toppling than those in a sheltered spot, and a sun-loving plant set in the shade may grow lanky and lean toward the light. In either case, transplanting when the plants are dormant should solve the problem.

Staking Methods

When staking is necessary, choose a method that is appropriate to the plant's growth habit. Use

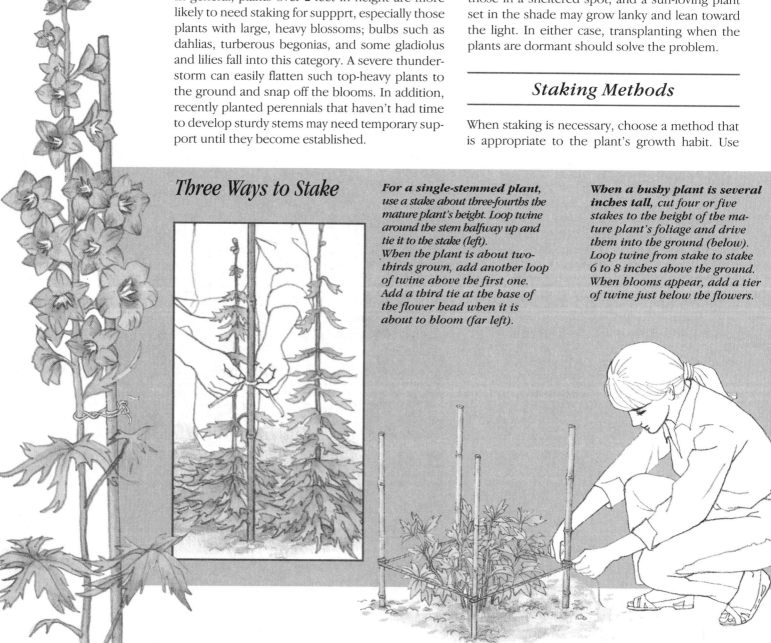

Three Ways to Stake

For a single-stemmed plant, use a stake about three-fourths the mature plant's height. Loop twine around the stem halfway up and tie it to the stake (left).
When the plant is about two-thirds grown, add another loop of twine above the first one. Add a third tie at the base of the flower head when it is about to bloom (far left).

When a bushy plant is several inches tall, cut four or five stakes to the height of the mature plant's foliage and drive them into the ground (below). Loop twine from stake to stake 6 to 8 inches above the ground. When blooms appear, add a tier of twine just below the flowers.

The foliage and blossoms of blue bellflowers and white feverfew hide the bamboo stakes that keep them from sprawling (left). In the photograph below, a framework of twiggy branches is barely visible beneath a stand of yellow yarrow.

To stake a fine-textured perennial such as baby's-breath (above), *choose several twiggy branches about 6 inches shorter than the plant's mature height and sharpen their ends. Push the branches into the ground around the plant, angling them toward its center.*

single stakes to brace the unbranched stems of tall perennials such as pompon, cushion, and decorative chrysanthemums and the delphinium illustrated on the following page. Single staking is also appropriate for gladiolus, dahlias, and other heavy-bloomed bulbs. Bamboo canes, a half-inch in diameter and painted green, are perfect for blending in with the foliage of a fully grown plant, although steel stakes, sometimes coated with dark green plastic, are also available.

Push the support gently into the ground beside the plant's stem; if the stem's natural inclination is to bend a little, angle the stake to follow it. For bulbs, place the stake in the planting hole next to the bulb when you are planting it. Use twine, which may be green or tan colored, to tie the plant's stem to its support—or you may use raffia fiber, paper- or plastic-coated thin wire, or green-tinted plastic gardening tape, which is slightly elastic. Knot the twine around the stake, securing it tightly, then loop the twine loosely around the plant so that it does not constrict the stem.

For dense, bushy perennials such as heliopsis, Shasta daisies, and peonies, you can buy wire hoops or frames at garden centers. These supports are circular, square, or rectangular in shape, with three or four long legs. When the clump of growing foliage is about a foot tall, place the support over the plant and push its legs several inches into the ground until the frame is at the height of the plant growth.

A homemade frame of twine and stakes *(page 228)* is just as effective and much less expensive than wire hoops. For groups of spiky plants such as delphiniums, you may choose to stake them on a frame rather than tie each stem individually. Simply use four or five canes that are about three-fourths as tall as you expect the plant to grow, and push them into the ground around each cluster. As flowers begin to bloom, tie twine to the stakes at height intervals of 12 inches and weave it among the stems.

For staking bushy plants and for baby's-breath and other fine-textured plants, try using twiggy branches *(page 229)*. Birch, oak, buddleia, and vitex are good choices.

When to Stake

The key to successful, unobtrusive staking is planning ahead. Put the stakes in place early in the season, while the plant is still growing upright and before flower buds appear. As the plant fills out, its foliage will hide the stakes *(page 229, top)*.

Perennials That Need Staking

TALL FLOWER STEMS:
Single Stakes

Chrysanthemum (pompon, cushion, decorative)
Delphinium (*elatum* hybrids)
Digitalis (foxglove)

BUSHY PLANTS:
Stakes and Twine or Twiggy Branches

Anchusa azurea 'Dropmore' (bugloss)
Aster novae-angliae (New England aster)
Campanula lactiflora (milky bell-flower)

Centaurea montana (cornflower)
Chrysanthemum maximum (Shasta daisy)
Chrysanthemum morifolium (florist's chrysanthemum)
Chrysanthemum nipponicum (Nippon daisy)
Chrysanthemum parthenium (feverfew)
Clematis heracleifolia 'Davidiana' (clematis)
Gaillardia x *grandiflora* (blanket-flower)
Helenium autumnale 'Bruno', 'Riverton Beauty' (sneezeweed)
Helianthus x *multiflorus* (sunflower)

Heliopsis (false sunflower)
Paeonia lactiflora (peony)
Salvia azurea ssp. *pitcheri* (sage)
Solidago (goldenrod)
Thalictrum delavayi (Yunnan meadow rue)
Thalictrum rochebrunianum (lavender mist meadow rue)
Thalictrum speciosissimum (dusty meadow rue)

FINE-TEXTURED PLANTS:
Twiggy Branches

Achillea millefolium (yarrow)

Clematis integrifolia 'Caerulea' (clematis)
Coreopsis grandiflora 'Badengold', 'Mayfield Giant' (tickseed)
Gypsophila paniculata 'Bristol Fairy', 'Perfecta' (baby's-breath)
Limonium (sea lavender, statice)
Linum (flax)
Physostegia (false dragonhead)
Veronica latifolia 'Crater Lake Blue' (speedwell)

'Fanfare' Delphinium

Enhancing the Bloom

Applying a handful of special pruning methods at the right time and to the right plant will increase the number of blooms or the size of the blooms your plants produce. Such techniques—including pinching, thinning, disbudding, deadheading, and cutting back—help keep a plant looking its best and direct energy that would otherwise be spent on seed production into creating more flowers.

Many plants benefit from a combination of the pruning methods. When delphiniums are in bloom, for example, deadheading, or removing faded blossoms, prolongs the display. When flowering stops, cutting back the stalks to the rosette of leaves at the base of each plant makes the plants look tidy and often stimulates a second flowering.

Why Deadhead?

Removing flowers as they begin to fade is an important garden chore, and not for appearance alone. Some perennials, such as pincushion flower and Stokes' aster, may stop blooming if they aren't attended to promptly, and a hybrid perennial allowed to go to seed may in time be crowded out by its less desirable offspring. Deadheading also stimulates some roses—hybrid teas, grandifloras, floribundas, and repeat-blooming climbers—to produce another round of flowers. Cut away the old blooms throughout the growing season, stopping several weeks before the first

Pinching Stem Tips

Using your fingers, pinch off emergent stem tips just above the topmost unfurled leaves. The net result will be three or four new branches, smaller but more plentiful flowers, and a stockier plant. This technique works well with plants that can develop numerous stems and buds, and that look attractive when bushy. Chrysanthemums can be pinched two or three times, up until the flower buds develop.

Deadheading Spent Flowers

For perennials with flowers at the tips of leafy stems, cut just below the fading flowers (right) to stimulate new buds. For plants with leafy flower stems and a rosette of leaves at the base of the plant, cut back to just above the topmost unopened bud. If there are no buds, cut the stem off just above the foliage rosette. For perennials with bare stems, cut off close to the ground to encourage new growth.

Deadheading Rhododendrons

The gorgeous blossoms of frothy pink Rhododendron 'Centennial Celebration' suggest the rewards that can be gained by a little tinkering with a plant's growth processes.

Pinching off spent rhododendron flowers can double or triple the number of blossoms next year as well as make the bush more compact. Remove dead blossoms and developing seed pods by bending the woody stem, just above where new buds are forming, and pulling gently until it snaps (below). With the seed pods gone, growth will be concentrated in the new buds. After a few weeks, when the buds have grown out about 4 inches, pinch off the last inch or so of that growth to encourage more shoots to sprout (bottom).

frost—you wouldn't want to promote any new growth that would be vulnerable to the cold.

Not all plants require deadheading. Species, antique, and shrub roses, as well as climbers that bloom once per season, don't need this treatment. And neither do the blossoms of linums, geraniums, and penstemons, which fall off by themselves. Other plants, such as rudbeckia and 'Autumn Joy' sedum, have ornamental seed heads that enliven a garden through the fall and provide interest into the cold months of winter.

Pinching Plants to Stimulate Blooming

Perennials that bloom in midsummer or later and annuals such as coleus and most vines benefit from having their stem tips pinched back early in the growing season. In response to pinching, a stem produces several new branches that together may yield double or even triple the number of blooms on an unpinched stem. The technique makes plants shorter and more compact—and, in the case of perennials, less likely to need staking.

Pinching done early in the growing season has little or no effect on a plant's blooming schedule. If, however, you want to delay a plant's flowering, pinching in midsummer is desirable. The technique is not appropriate for spring perennials, however, because these plants don't have enough time to form new flower buds before their blooming season comes to an end.

Thinning for Larger Flowers

If you'd prefer fewer but larger flowers to an abundance of smaller ones, you can prune away up to a third of a plant's stems, cutting them off at the base. Perennials that bloom in midsummer should be thinned in early spring, and fall bloomers in midsummer. As with pinching, this method isn't suitable for spring bloomers—it merely reduces the number of flowers, with no payoff in size.

Thinning is particularly useful for restoring the display of phlox, sunflower, and rudbeckia that are several seasons old and that, if left unattended, would likely produce a dense mass of stems with undersized blooms. And in addition to rejuvenating a plant's blooming, thinning improves its form, opens its center up to more light, and reduces the risk of disease by improving air circulation. When a plant is heavily thinned, it sends up more vigorous growth from its roots.

Disbudding for Showy Blooms

For peonies, chrysanthemums, and other perennials whose flower buds appear in groups, removing all but the central bud yields a single blue-ribbon blossom. However, this showy flower is likely to make the stem so top-heavy that staking is required *(pages 228-229)*. For a different effect, pinch off the central bud but leave the side buds, which will develop into a spray of flowers.

For exhibition-size blooms on hybrid tea roses and grandifloras, pinch off any buds that sprout below the top, or terminal, bud *(box, right)*. Do this when the buds are tiny, because later disbudding will leave black scars on the stem.

On floribundas and miniature roses, which produce clusters of blossoms, pinch off the terminal, or central, bud in a cluster. Ordinarily, the terminal bud blooms first, then fades and leaves a hole in the cluster just as the adjacent buds are opening up. For prettier sprays that bloom together, remove the terminal bud as early as possible. The other blooms will fill in the space and be more uniform in size. Disbudding is not necessary for antique (old garden) roses, shrub roses, species roses, climbers, and polyanthas.

Cutting Back for Better Shape and Bloom

Cutting back simply means shortening a stem or branch to stimulate new growth, usually from the vegetative bud located just below the point where the branch or stem was pruned. You can steer the new growth in a particular direction—from the center of the plant outward, for example—by choosing where to make your cuts.

This pruning technique may be undertaken at two different times in a perennial's growing cycle, and for different reasons. In both cases, all of the plant's stems should be reduced in height by one-third to one-half. Performed early in the growing season, cutting back results in shorter plants that bloom later than usual. Carried out later in the season, as soon as a plant stops flowering, the shearing stimulates the growth of new foliage and, in the case of catmint, bellflowers, and many other perennials, a second wave of bloom. Refer to the chart on pages 234-235 for more information on when and how to prune specific plants. For particulars on pruning roses, see pages 236-240.

Encouraging the Most Beautiful Blooms

By disbudding, deadheading, and fertilizing your roses, you can spur them to produce abundant blooms that are even more gorgeous than usual. Removing certain buds affects the size or proportion of remaining buds and the flowers that follow; deadheading stimulates the plant to bloom again sooner than it otherwise would. A good diet ensures that the plant has the nutrients it needs to put on a spectacular show.

DISBUDDING *Grasp the cane securely and with your fingers gently pinch off all buds that sprout on the sides of the cane (right). Do this as soon as these lateral buds appear. If the rose is a type that produces clusters of blooms, pinch off the terminal, or center, bud to get blooms of equal size in the spray.*

DEADHEADING *After a bloom has passed its peak, use a clean pair of pruning shears to cut the stem and remove the flower. Make the cut at a 45° angle on the cane, ¼ inch above the highest outward-facing leaf bearing five leaflets (left). The dormant bud seated on the cane at the base of the leaf will grow into a new shoot and produce a bloom within 6 weeks.*

FEEDING *Water the soil thoroughly around the plant. The next day, measure an appropriate fertilizer according to the package directions, pull the mulch away from the plant to expose the soil, and sprinkle the fertilizer around the drip line—the area beneath the outermost leaves. Use a trowel to dig the food into the top 2 inches of soil (right). Last, sprinkle the soil with water to dissolve the nutrients and start them seeping into the soil.*

The perennials, shrubs, and vines listed below can be trimmed or pruned at strategic times during the year to encourage more blooms and produce shapelier plants. Perennials are deadheaded, pinched back, or cut back at intervals during the growing season to discourage seed production and encourage reblooming. Shrubs and vines can be thinned, which involves cutting an old branch or stem back to where it started as a bud or to the ground, or you can give them a heading cut, which removes part of a branch back to a bud or leaf node. Some shrubs and vines benefit from deadheading, and can be encouraged to produce new, flower-bearing branches by cutting them back hard in early spring. In all cases, timing is crucial: Prune shrubs that flower in early spring after they finish blooming; shrubs that flower later, which bloom on new spring growth, should be pruned in late winter or early spring.

		BLOOM SEASON	WHEN TO PRUNE	THIN OUT	PINCH BACK	DEAD-HEAD	COMMENTS
PERENNIALS	*Achillea* (yarrow)	summer				✔	cut back for second flowering
	Anaphalis (pearly everlasting)	late summer to fall			✔		
	Anthemis (golden marguerite)	midsummer to early fall			✔	✔	cut back for second flowering
	Armeria (thrift)	spring to summer				✔	
	Aster x *frikartii* (Frikart's aster)	early summer to fall				✔	
	Boltonia (boltonia)	late summer to frost	early summer		✔		pinch back for compact growth
	Campanula (bellflower)	early to midsummer				✔	
	Centaurea (cornflower)	spring to summer			✔	✔	
	Centranthus (red valerian)	summer					cut back for second flowering
	Chrysanthemum x *morifolium* (florist's chrysanthemum)	late summer to frost	spring to midsummer		✔	✔	pinch back every 3 weeks to midsummer
	Chrysanthemum x *superbum* (Shasta daisy)	spring to fall			✔	✔	
	Delphinium (delphinium)	summer				✔	cut back for second flowering
	Dianthus (pink, carnation)	spring to summer				✔	shear mat-forming types to promote compact growth
	Digitalis (foxglove)	spring to summer				✔	
	Echinacea (coneflower)	summer		✔			
	Echinops (globe thistle)	summer				✔	cut back for second flowering
	Erigeron (fleabane)	summer		✔			
	Eupatorium (boneset)	summer			✔	✔	
	Gaillardia (blanket-flower)	summer to fall			✔	✔	
	Gillenia (bowman's root)	spring to summer					
	Heliopsis (false sunflower)	midsummer to fall			✔		
	Nepeta (catmint)	summer			✔	✔	cut back for second flowering

		BLOOM SEASON	WHEN TO PRUNE	THIN OUT	PINCH BACK	DEAD-HEAD	COMMENTS
PERENNIALS	*Penstemon* (cardinal flower)	spring to fall			✔	✔	cut back for second flowering
	Perovskia (Russian sage)	summer			✔		
	Phlox paniculata (summer phlox)	spring to fall			✔	✔	cut back for second flowering
	Platycodon (balloon flower)	summer			✔	✔	
	Scabiosa (pincushion flower)	summer				✔	
	Stokesia (Stokes' aster)	summer				✔	cut back for second flowering
	Veronica (speedwell)	spring to summer				✔	cut back for second flowering
SHRUBS	*Buddleia* (butterfly bush)	summer	early spring			✔	cut to 12 inches to rejuvenate
	Caryopteris (bluebeard)	summer to fall	early spring				cut to 12 inches to rejuvenate
	Forsythia (forsythia)	early spring	after flowering	✔			cut branches in winter for indoor forcing
	Halesia (silver bell)	midspring	after flowering				
	Hibiscus (rose of Sharon)	summer to fall	early spring				head back to 2 or 3 buds in spring for larger flowers
	Hydrangea (hydrangea)	summer	early spring	✔			head back in midsummer for second flowering
	Philadelphus (mock orange)	early summer	after flowering	✔			cut to 12 inches to rejuvenate
	Potentilla (bush cinquefoil)	summer to frost	late winter	✔			
	Rhododendron (rhododendron)	spring	after flowering		✔	✔	snap off spent blooms; pinch back new growth a few weeks later
	Spiraea (spirea)	spring to summer	after flowering	✔			cut to 8 inches to rejuvenate
	Syringa (lilac)	spring	after flowering	✔		✔	cut to 3 feet to rejuvenate
	Weigela (weigela)	spring	after flowering	✔			
VINES	*Campsis* (trumpet creeper)	late summer	spring				head back summer growth to 3 or 4 buds
	Clematis (spring-blooming clematis)	spring	after flowering				cut back old vines
	Clematis (fall-blooming clematis)	summer to fall	early spring				head back to 3 or 4 buds
	Lonicera japonica (Japanese honeysuckle)	summer	early spring				head back to 3 or 4 buds
	Wisteria (wisteria)	midspring	end of summer/ early spring				cut summer growth to 2 inches; cut end tips in spring

Pruning Roses

Pruning is a necessary chore for many plants, but roses above all others. Sooner or later, any unpruned rose—even a species or low-maintenance shrub rose—will grow lanky, and flower production will gradually diminish as older canes become exhausted. Neglected, unpruned roses are also more vulnerable to pests and diseases, and can eventually die if left untended. Pruning not only protects the plant's health, it also encourages strong root development and stimulates growth. Well-trimmed plants are attractively shaped, their flowers are bigger and more abundant, and their canes are stronger and more vigorous.

What to Prune Away

How and when roses are pruned varies according to the type of rose in your garden, the growth habits you hope to encourage, and where you live. But there are some general approaches to pruning you'll need to know before tackling your particular plants. First, you should examine the base of the rose for suckers—canes growing up from the rootstock, below the bud union. If left unchecked, these can overwhelm and eventually kill the grafted cultivar. Clipping them off at ground level is an exercise in frustration, however; they will only grow back. You must remove them as close to the bud union as possible.

Next, look for dead, diseased, and damaged canes; they will appear blackened and withered. Cut the canes back to healthy white or pale green pith, or back to the bud union if no healthy tissue is visible. It is also a good rule of thumb to remove any cane thinner than a pencil, including small, twiggy shoots with fewer than five leaves; if they appear too weak to support blossoms, remove them. Canes growing in awkward directions—into the center of the plant or into tangles where they will rub against each other and become damaged—are also candidates for pruning. Cutting

Roses That Need Little Pruning

'Ballerina'
'Belle Poitevine'
'Blanc Double
    de Coubert'
'Bonica'
'Boule de Neige'
'Erfurt'
'Frau Dagmar
    Hartopp'
'Gabrielle Privat'
'Hansa'
'Henry Hudson'
'Jens Munk'
'La Marne'
'Linda Campbell'
'Max Graf'
'Mrs. B. R. Cant'
'Nearly Wild'
'Nozomi'
'Pinkie'
'Red Cascade'
R. banksiae
    banksiae
R. palustris
'Roseraie de l'Hay'
'Sea Foam'
'The Fairy'
'Thérèse Bugnet'
'White Meidiland'

'Hansa'

Pruning a Hardy Rose

Hardy roses include such antique varieties as damasks, gallicas, centifolias, albas, and mosses, as well as shrub roses and some species roses. These tend to be robust plants that require less pruning and care in general. Nevertheless, all hardy roses benefit from a spring cleanup that includes trimming away dead, diseased, or damaged canes; canes too thin and weak to support flowers; and any crossing canes or canes growing into the center of the plant. Hardy roses benefit as well from an overall shaping to improve the appearance of the plant. Pruning all the longer canes back by one-third will give the bush a well-tended, healthy look; it will also promote outward growth and abundant blossoms. Make the cuts in late spring, after the rose has flowered.

A. Cut off dead canes and those more than 4 years old at the bud union (left). Cut back diseased or damaged canes to healthy wood ¼ inch above an outward-facing bud, or, if there is no healthy tissue, to the bud union. Use loppers for canes over ½ inch in diameter and make clean, angled cuts.

B. When two canes are entangled or rubbing against each other, cut away the smaller of the two. Prune below the point of contact and about ¼ inch above an outward-facing bud; this will direct new growth away from the center of the plant.

C. Cut spindly stems that are too weak to support blossoms—generally those thinner than a pencil—back to a junction with a larger, healthier cane.

D. To give the plant an overall full, rounded shape, cut off one-third of the overall length of the longer canes. Cut off the tips of all other canes to stimulate growth.

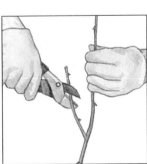

E. To increase plant fullness and encourage the production of more blossoms, cut lateral growth down to an outward-facing bud, pruning as much as one-third of the length of the cane.

237

How to Remove Suckers

Suckers—those canes that sprout from the rootstock below the bud union—are aptly named since they drain energy from the rootstock and can overcome and kill the cultivar if they are not removed. You can easily identify suckers: They are thinner and paler than the cultivar and display a different leaflet pattern. Do not cut suckers off at ground level, as this stimulates growth just as pruning does. Instead, dig gently down to where the sucker attaches to the rootstock and pull it away, taking care not to disturb the plant.

them away will not only improve the appearance of the rose and avoid further injury to canes, it will also open up the center of the plant to air and light, which will help prevent disease.

How Much to Prune

Once the initial pruning of unwanted wood is complete, further cuts are usually made to stimulate growth, or to give your rose an overall shaping. Shaping typically takes the form of light, moderate, or hard pruning.

Light pruning, usually performed on antique, species, and shrub roses, involves cutting back the ends of most canes by no more than one-third. In fact, some gardeners cut away just the tips of canes on species roses and low-maintenance shrubs. Grandifloras and floribundas should also receive this type of light pruning if abundant blooms are desired. But if your species and shrub

Pruning a Modern Rose

1. Cut off dead canes and those more than 4 years old at the bud union. *Cut back diseased or damaged canes to healthy white or pale green pith (inset), or, if no healthy tissue can be found, to the bud union. Next, remove canes that are crossed and those smaller than a pencil in diameter. Thin out any canes growing toward the center of the plant. Make all cuts at a 45° angle ¼ inch above an outward-facing bud.*

2. Decide whether you wish to do moderate or hard pruning. *If hard pruning is your goal, remove all but three or four healthy canes, leaving them no more than a foot long (below). This will yield large, show-type blooms. For moderate pruning, leave six to 12 canes at about one-third of their original height, or 1 to 2 feet. This will produce abundant, slightly smaller blooms and a fuller rosebush. In deciding how to prune, remember that modern roses with an upright habit look best if pruned to an urn shape, with canes growing evenly outward and upward.*

roses begin to grow leggy under this regimen, prune some of the main canes back by one-third and the rest back by about two-thirds to bring them back to a healthier, fuller shape.

Moderate pruning is generally practiced on modern roses with an upright habit and where a larger, fuller plant is desired. Remove all but six to 12 canes, and cut back the remaining canes to a length of 1 to 2 feet. Practice moderate pruning if you are inexperienced or unsure about the growth habits of your roses. Severe, or hard, pruning is practiced on hybrid teas and grandifloras when show-quality blooms are desired. In this case, all but two to four canes are removed; those left should be cut to a length of between 6 and 12 inches, or up to 18 inches with grandifloras. In northern climates, where roses can be badly damaged during the winter, plants may need hard pruning in spring. In milder climates, hard pruning may restore a weakened, neglected plant to health.

Making a Cut

Before making a cut, look for a healthy bud that is just beginning to swell and that faces in the direction in which you want the new shoot to grow. Generally this will be facing outward on the cane, but in some cases you may wish to encourage growth toward the center of a leggy, spreading plant. Make a clean, sharp cut at a 45° angle ¼ inch above, and in the same direction as, the bud. The angled cut ensures that rainwater will run off the stem rather than collect as it would in a flat cut. And some experts believe that such a cut, by exposing more of the cane to the air, will help it heal more quickly.

Tools for Pruning

You will need three cutting tools for pruning roses: pruning shears, long-handled loppers, and a pruning saw. Bypass pruning shears, which have curved, scissor-action blades, are the best for all-purpose work such as removing canes, flowers, and leaves. Avoid anvil shears, which have a straight blade that strikes against a blunt surface: They can crush delicate rose canes and leave them vulnerable to pests and diseases. Anvil shears should be used only on wood that is completely dead.

Long-handled loppers have short, heavy-duty blades useful for cutting canes that are too thick for pruning shears, or that are difficult to reach. For woody canes that are too thick even for lop-

Pruning Climbers and Ramblers

To prune ramblers and once-blooming climbers, wait till after they flower so as not to remove potential flowering buds. Cut off old, woody canes at the bud union (above), and remove all weak, diseased, or overlong canes. Cut flowering shoots back to four or five sets of leaves.

Prune repeat-blooming climbers while they are dormant, in late winter or early spring. Remove suckers; dead, diseased, or damaged canes; and weak new growth. Prune out the oldest canes, keeping three or four vigorous young canes; trim these back to promote even distribution of buds. If you tie long young canes horizontally to a support, pointing their ends downward, you will encourage lateral growth and more blooms.

pers, use a pruning saw with large teeth and a long, thin, curved blade.

Keep all of your pruning tools sharp and clean. Dull blades make jagged cuts and can even tear the canes, creating entry points for infestation. Disinfect pruning tools after each use with rubbing alcohol or a solution made from 1 part household bleach to 9 parts water.

As important as the right tools for the job are the right clothes. Be sure to wear gloves—thick leather ones are best—so that you can grasp thorny stems properly to make the cleanest cuts. And when you need to reach into the spiky interior of a plant, you'll appreciate having on long sleeves and pants.

The Right Time of Year to Prune

In general, the best time to prune is just as the plant's dormancy period ends—when you see buds beginning to swell on the plant but before active growth has begun. In mild climates, dormancy may end in late winter—as early as January—or in early spring; in locations with severely cold winters you may have to wait until April. In any event, you must be sure the threat of a late freeze has passed. Some gardeners wait to prune their roses until forsythia is in bloom.

The timing and extent of pruning is also determined by the type of roses in your garden. Hybrid tea roses, grandifloras, floribundas, miniatures, and standard roses should all receive a hard pruning in early spring before the onset of new growth. Since these roses bloom on new wood, pruning is necessary to stimulate the growth of new canes and ensure an abundance of blooms. Antique roses and shrub and species roses may require no more than a hygienic pruning in spring to remove dead, diseased, or damaged canes. If the plants have become unshapely, however, wait until after their flowers have faded to prune them back within bounds. There are exceptions to this rule: Hybrid perpetuals, hybrid musks, noisettes, Chinas, repeat-blooming damasks and portlands, old garden tea roses, and moss roses bloom on new wood, so if they require shaping up, it should be done in early spring.

Ramblers and once-flowering climbers bloom on growth from the previous year, so early-spring pruning should involve nothing more than the removal of dead wood. Wait until the plants have finished blooming to perform any shaping that needs to be done. Prune repeat-blooming climbers while they are dormant—in late winter or early spring.

After spring pruning is finished, keep your plants well watered. Pruning induces new growth, and water is crucial to maintaining it.

In summer, deadheading is all that's necessary. But if you are cutting roses for flower arrangements, make the same type of cut you use when pruning—angled, and ¼ inch above a bud. Stop deadheading and cutting blooms a month before the first expected frost to avoid winterkill of new growth.

Fall pruning is undesirable in most climates, except to cut back very long canes. But in areas where winter temperatures drop to between 10° and 15° F for as long as 2 weeks at a time, hybrid roses will need pruning after the first frost. Cut them down to three to six canes, and shorten each cane to 1 to 2 feet. Then protect the roses from the extreme cold (opposite).

Pruning a Standard Rose

Begin pruning a standard, or tree, rose by removing suckers, which in this case grow not only from the rootstock but along the trunk. Pull them from the rootstock, and cut them as close as possible to the trunk. Remove undesirable canes, twiggy stems, and canes that rub or grow into the plant center (right). Next, depending on the cultivar, trim to produce either a round, symmetrical shape or a loose, cascading one. Aim for even spacing and uniform cane length, leaving four to six canes pruned to about 12 inches (far right). Prune only to outward-facing buds.

240

Winter Protection

In late summer to midfall, reduce watering and stop dead-heading and applying nitrogen fertilizers, both of which spur new growth. Where temperatures drop to between 10° and 15°F for 2 weeks at a time, you can protect most roses by heaping material around the plant's base *(far right)*. Where temperatures drop below zero, bury the entire plant *(below);* this is especially important for tree roses. To insulate climbers, remove them from their support and tie the canes loosely with twine. Dig a trench, lay the canes in it, and cover with soil and organic mulch. Add more mulch after the ground freezes. Do not start winter protection too soon; the increased warmth may produce new growth that will be hurt by a sudden chill.

1. After the first frost, cut back all canes to 1 to 2 feet. *This helps the plant conserve energy and eliminates the parts that are the weakest and likeliest to suffer damage in a freeze. It also eliminates the possibility of injury caused by canes whipping against each other in the wind.*

2. In climates where winter temperatures drop periodically into the teens *or go as low as 10° to 15°F for 2 weeks at a stretch, surround rosebushes with imported soil, mulch, or leaves. Pile the insulating material up around the plant and between the canes to a height of 6 to 12 inches above the bud union. Then spread a layer of straw, loose leaves, peat moss, or ground bark over the mound.*

3. If winter temperatures regularly drop below 0°F, *or if extended frigid weather is predicted, mound soil around the base of the plant to a height of 6 to 12 inches above the bud union. Then form a cage from chicken wire or tar paper stapled together, and place it around your rose. To secure the cage, pack another few inches of earth around its base.*

4. Next, fill the cage to the top with leaves, straw, or ground bark. *Make sure not to pack the insulating material too tightly; wet, matted leaves can harbor disease. Avoid removing the cages too early at winter's end—a late-spring freeze can be fatal to a newly exposed rose. After the last freeze, gently remove the leaves or straw and carefully scrape away the earth mound covering the canes. Rinse the canes with a light spray of water.*

Propagating Perennials
by Division

Most herbaceous perennials enthusiastically colonize their surroundings, spreading new roots and shoots outward every year. Though their stems and leaves may die back each fall, the roots are dormant through the winter, then thrust out new growth in both roots and shoots every spring. Perennials are slow to mature, and generally spend more than one season growing roots and foliage before they bloom or propagate in any other way. This is the vital habit distinguishing them from the annuals, which throw their energy into growing fast, blooming, and scattering seed in the single season before they die.

Because nurseries have to work with nature's timing, the perennials they propagate and sell

The dusty pink blooms of Sedum telephium 'Autumn Joy' turn russet in the fall, then last through the winter as eye-catching seed heads. Trouble free if grown in well-drained soil, sedums are easy to propagate by division or from stem cuttings (pages 248-249).

must be carefully tended for a year or more before coming to market. This makes perennials a costly crop for nurseries—one reason they carry higher prices than annuals. If you are growing perennials in your garden, however, propagation is already taking place. To propagate your own plants, you have only to take charge of the process.

Dividing to Increase Plants

The simplest propagation practice in perennial gardens is division, which takes direct advantage of the plants' tendencies to spread. Division is simply separating young, already rooted offshoots from mature perennials and placing them elsewhere in the garden. The independent plants produced are called divisions, or slips. New plants created by this method develop the same growth traits and flower color as the originals, so you can confidently fill flower beds with your favorites. Another bonus from division is that most slips establish themselves quickly and bloom the same season or the following one.

Dividing for Healthy Plants

Division is also a means of maintaining your mature perennial plantings; many perennials look their best only when regularly divided. Gaillardias and chrysanthemums tend to deteriorate at their centers, while growing actively around the edges. You may wind up with unsightly, dead-looking patches in the midst of your lovely blooming clumps unless you dig the plants out, trim old growth away, and reset new growth in its place.

Other perennials, such as rudbeckia, outgrow their spaces, crowd their neighbors, and make the whole flower bed more susceptible to disease. Division of such plants thins the invaders, permits air to circulate through the bed once more, and lets you develop a colorful new border with your fledgling plants elsewhere in the garden.

Division is also the easiest way to keep some of the shorter-lived perennials growing in your garden year after year. Members of the genus Dianthus—sometimes called pinks—generally last only a few years. You must replace the plants with offspring if you want to keep these popular plants growing in your garden.

When to Divide

Although a few plants, like the globe thistle and the gas plant, will remain the same size in the same place for years, they are exceptions in the world of perennials. Most genera actively grow outward from their centers as they deplete soil nutrients there and develop new roots away from the plants' centers. This pattern produces a natural crisis, and when it arrives, perennials send out clear distress signals. These include a dead, woody portion at the center of the clump, fewer blooms, and fewer stems emerging in the spring. Crowns or rhizomes may be forced out above the surrounding soil, and a plant may grow so large that there is no air space around it in the bed. The remedy is division.

Perennials in need of division should be tackled while they are dormant or growing vegetatively, not when they are preparing to bloom. For most plants, this means early spring to early summer, as soon as the growing crowns can be seen. (Exceptions include plants like doronicum, primrose, iris, and other early-spring bloomers, which should be divided after flowering.) When performing any divisions, work on a cool, cloudy day—it helps keep the plants' roots moist while they are exposed to the air.

How to Begin

Division starts at the roots of the plant, since offshoots must have their own roots already formed if they are to live on their own. The root systems of perennials fall into several categories—fibrous, fleshy, and rhizomatous.

Most perennials have fibrous roots. These resemble slender, outspread fingers, and grow relatively close to the soil surface. A few plant types, most notably *Hemerocallis* (daylily), have thick, fleshy roots that can closely intertwine. Another handful of perennials, including iris, grow from rhizomes—hard, tuberous stems planted just below the soil's surface.

Choose your division method to match the root type of your plants *(list of plants, above; division methods, pages 244-247)*. For every method, the overall procedure is the same: Gather your tools and prepare replanting sites ahead of time; work fast; protect roots from drying out; and pamper the slips while they acclimate.

Plants Recommended for Division

FIBROUS ROOTS:		
Acanthus (bear's-breech)	(pinks)	*Pulmonaria* (lungwort)
Achillea (yarrow)	*Dicentra* (bleeding heart)	*Rudbeckia* (coneflower)
Ajuga (bugleweed)	*Doronicum* (leopard's-bane)	*Sedum* (stonecrop)
Alchemilla (lady's-mantle)	*Geranium* (cranesbill)	*Smilacina* (false Solomon's-seal)
Allium (flowering onion)	*Geum* (avens)	*Solidago* (goldenrod)
Amsonia (bluestar)	*Hosta* (plantain lily, funkia)	*Stachys* (lamb's ears)
Anchusa (bugloss)	*Iris sibirica* (Siberian iris)	*Stokesia* (Stokes' aster)
Anemone (windflower)	*Lamium* (dead nettle)	*Thalictrum* (meadow rue)
Arabis (rock cress)	*Ligularia* (golden-ray)	*Tricyrtis* (toad lily)
Arenaria (sandwort)	*Limonium* (sea lavender, statice)	*Trollius* (globeflower)
Armeria (thrift, sea pink)	*Lobelia* (cardinal flower)	*Veronica* (speedwell)
Artemisia (wormwood)	*Lychnis* (catchfly, campion)	*Viola* (violet)
Aruncus (goatsbeard)	*Monarda* (bee balm)	FLESHY ROOTS:
Astilbe (astilbe, false spirea)	*Nepeta* (catmint)	*Hemerocallis* (daylily)
Brunnera (brunnera)	*Oenothera* (sundrop, evening primrose)	*Kniphofia* (torch lily, tritoma)
Campanula (bellflower)	*Phlox paniculata* (summer phlox)	RHIZOMES:
Centaurea (knapweed)	*Polygonum* (smartweed, knotweed)	*Bergenia* (bergenia)
Delphinium (delphinium)	*Potentilla* (cinquefoil, five-finger)	*Iris* (iris)
Dianthus	*Primula* (primrose)	

***Regular division necessary for health of plants.**

Before beginning the actual work of dividing, consider both the parent plant and your intentions for the offspring. Do you want to populate the garden with many shoots, even if some will not bloom this year? Or do you want to turn last year's single clump into three distinct blooming plants? Or is your aim to rejuvenate the parent by maintenance division, whether or not you end up with more individual plants? Starting out knowing what you want will shorten the handling time for the plants—and the less time they're out of their natural element, the better.

Ready the soil in the area where you will put the new divisions, so that they can go into the ground immediately. Preparation should include adding a soil amendment such as compost, peat, or sand as necessary to ensure good drainage and improve soil structure *(pages 63-64)*. Judging by the size of the parent plant, allow plenty of space around the hole you dig for each new shoot, so that the plant will not be crowded when it is mature. If the ground is not wet from a recent watering or rain, water anything you plan to divide at least an hour before you start work.

Making the Cut

The simplest way to divide a perennial with a healthy center is to slice off the new growth from the sides with a spade or sharp knife, leaving the main clump undisturbed in the ground. This is also a good way to handle invasive plants that seem to have no recognizable center. Cut so that each section of new growth includes one or two visible growing crowns or shoots, and an intact portion of root. Daylilies, phlox, centaurea, and bleeding heart are among those you can divide this way. If a plant looks poorly at the center, or if you want many divisions, dig it out of the bed, using the technique shown below.

Both your new divisions and the parent plants require a little extra care after the main procedures are complete. Set the new divisions into prepared holes, spreading out the roots and positioning the crowns at ground level, not below. Press soil firmly over the roots, eliminating air pockets and giving the roots good contact with the soil. If you have lifted the parent plants from the soil, take this opportunity to work up the soil there, too, and add compost to the holes before resetting the plants in them.

If you are dividing in late summer or fall, when perennials have full complements of foliage, prune back the stems and leaves of plant divisions by about half after planting. This restores balance to the plant, giving the smaller root system less top growth to nourish and reducing water loss through respiration. If you are dividing in early spring, before the plants have developed much top growth, cutting back is unnecessary.

Water all your new plantings thoroughly and keep the soil moist for the next few days. Providing shade from full sun for a week also helps—an old lawn chair or pruned-off evergreen branches strategically placed can intercept the scorching

How to Divide Perennials with Fibrous Roots

While the main goals of division are to separate offshoots for distribution and to rejuvenate aging perennials, keeping all the plants healthy and growing afterward is a major concern. Give them the best chance to thrive by minimizing root damage, preserving a balance between the top growth and the roots, and treating new transplants tenderly after separation and moving.

The tools for division will vary with the type of plant you're working on, but you probably already have the equipment on hand. You'll need a spade or a shovel for digging large clumps and a trowel for small, shallow-rooted ones; a bucket of water or a hose for rinsing soil off the roots; and an old kitchen knife or cross-bladed shears. Wet burlap is useful to cover dug-up plants when you're not working on them.

Keep spades, knives, and shears sharp so you can make clean cuts. Having all the equipment at your fingertips before you start speeds the operation and spares the plants unnecessary stress.

1. Dig deeply around the plant with a sharp shovel or spade, along a line below the tips of the foliage. Don't use a fork for this job—it is too likely to sever roots. To test whether you have freed the root mass, grasp the foliage at its base and rock the plant gently. Dig deeper anywhere roots are still holding on.

2. Lift the plant carefully from the ground, supporting the roots with your hands (left). Shake and rinse off the soil until you can clearly see the roots and the crowns—where roots join stems. Cut out and discard any old, woody tissue, rotted soft tissue, or areas of insect damage on roots or foliage.

rays. Because the smaller root systems of divisions are especially vulnerable to drought in dry spells and to frost-heave damage in winter, protect them with ample mulch through their first seasons.

Divisions well established in their transplant locations will soon show new growth. When they do, they should share in your normal maintenance procedures, including fertilizing and pinching back to encourage bushy growth. If it's still early in the growing season, you may well see blooms this year on the newly divided plants of most genera.

Dividing Fleshy-Rooted Plants

Hemerocallis (daylily), *Kniphofia* (torch lily), and a few other perennials grow from fleshy rootstocks, which tangle together underground and can be more difficult to separate than fibrous roots. Where the plant clumps are large and unwieldy, some experts recommend dividing them as they stand in the flower bed *(page 246)*. This approach may cause some foliage and root damage, but daylilies bounce back very quickly; most divisions that have two or three fans of foliage will take hold and bloom happily the next season. To divide smaller clumps of daylilies, dig them up completely, as you would fibrous-rooted perennials. Wash and examine the roots before cutting them apart; slice off any soft, rotted tissue and discard it in the compost pile.

Replant your fleshy-rooted divisions in holes that you have prepared; spread the roots out horizontally and press the soil firmly around them. To minimize water loss through respiration, trim off half of the foliage on each fan. Keep the new plants well watered for the first few days while they adjust to their new spot.

Dividing Rhizomatous Perennials

Bearded iris and bergenia grow from rhizomes—stems that grow horizontally underground and

3. Separate the plants into smaller clumps. *Some roots—like those of primroses or Siberian iris—can be pulled apart by hand, as at left above. Some, like those of phlox, can be teased apart with a hand fork. For solid, tangled roots use a knife,* spade, or other sharp instrument to separate stubborn masses (above, right). Cut down among the roots to divide the various growing crowns and stems. Each division should have a growing crown or two and some fibrous roots attached. After *you have severed your divisions, examine each one again, removing any dead or rotted sections. It's a good idea to thin out matted roots; this will stimulate strong new root growth. Trim off broken or very long roots.*

Three Ways to Divide Daylilies

Daylilies—the most widely grown of the fleshy-rooted perennials and the most frequently divided—spread exuberantly from single, original plantings to form densely packed clumps. Although they keep blooming even when crowded, you'll have even more of a good thing after you divide them (below).

The best time to work on daylilies is in early fall, after flowering has finished for the season, but well before frost. Before digging up any plants, prepare holes in which to replant the divisions. Obviously, you will have to cut roots inside a clump, but as you dig to free the edges, keep clear of the roots by digging around the clump just outside the leaf tips. A sharp edge on your shovel or knife makes the job a bit easier on both you and the plant.

Large clumps of daylilies can be divided right in the ground. Plan your cuts so that each division will include one to three foliage fans and the root tissue below. Drive a sharp spade or shovel down firmly between the fans, cutting through the roots (below). Then dig up the sections, working from the outside of the clump toward the center.

To shave outer fans off the edges of a large clump without disturbing or replanting the lilies at the center, angle the spade as you drive it in between fans, keeping one to three fans in each group (below). Go deep enough to cut the roots, then dig around and under the cut sections and lift them away from the sides of the main clump.

To divide small clumps of daylilies, dig them out of the ground with a spade or shovel, digging in a wide circle just outside the foliage tips to avoid roots. Lift the entire clump from the hole, supporting the center of the clump as you lift. Rinse hardened soil from the roots, then cut them apart with a sharp knife, or divide them with your spade as they lie on the ground (below).

store nourishment that is drawn in through small feeder roots. Irises in particular show their need for division and renewal by diminished bloom. Really crowded specimens of both iris and bergenia will push their rhizomes up out of the soil, sometimes causing the plant to keel over, pulling exposed rhizomes completely out of the soil.

The best time to divide rhizomatous plants is after they have bloomed. Because rhizomes lie close to the surface, they are easy to dig up with a garden fork or spade, but you must loosen the soil thoroughly to minimize breakage of the feeder roots. Some rhizomes are prone to rot and to infestation by root maggots. Before you dig, sterilize your tools in a solution of 1 part chlorine bleach to 10 parts water; once you've dug up a rhizome, dip it in the bleach solution as well. Use a sharp knife to divide the rhizomes, and shears to trim the foliage. Replant the divisions in shallow, trenchlike holes that have soil mounded up in the center. Spread the feeder roots out evenly over the mounds of soil.

Layering to Form New Roots

Another strategy for dividing some perennials is to encourage a plant to form roots where none exist—along stems—and then separate the root-studded stem as a new plant. This is done by an old-fashioned technique called layering. Layering lets you create divisions during the growing season while leaving plants in place in their beds—even while they bloom. And it takes almost none of your valuable gardening time.

Plants that respond well to layering include

those with creeping stems or stems that are upright but flexible and long enough to be bent to the ground without breaking. *Dianthus, Geranium, Campanula, Arabis,* and *Phlox subulata* are all good candidates.

The best time to begin the rooting process is spring, as soon as stems have grown to several inches long. Start with a plant that has some space in the bed around it, since you will be staking the stems down on the soil. You may need to pin down the stems if they are too firm to stay down obediently; fence staples, hairpins, or a small rock will usually do the job.

Choose an outer stem and trim off all but the top few leaves. Bend the stem down to the soil surface so that the leafless part touches the ground. Loosen the soil there and bury the stem about 2 inches deep, pinning it in place if neces-sary. Keep the stem tip, with its remaining leaves, above the ground, staking it to hold it erect. Water the area thoroughly and mulch to help keep the moisture in. If you want more rooting stems, you can repeat this treatment all the way around the plant, if the plant and the surrounding space are large enough. Once you've positioned the stems, all you have to do is keep the layered area moist while you wait for roots to form along the buried section of stem.

How long the rooting takes will vary according to climate and the type of perennial you're layering. Even while stems are staked and buried, their tips may bloom for you. It is easiest to leave the whole setup alone, if you can, until the next spring. Then dig up the rooted stems, sever them below the roots, and plant the new individuals as you would any other rooted division.

Dividing and Planting Rhizomes

Since a rhizome is a specialized form of stem growing horizontally underground, it needs gentle uprooting and careful replanting. The technique is shown here with iris rhizomes.

Use these same steps to divide bergenia, but don't trim back its foliage, as shown in Step 3; instead, remove a couple of leaves entirely before replanting the rhizome.

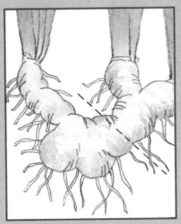

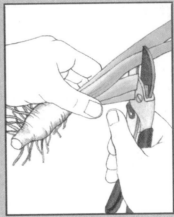

1. Loosen the soil thoroughly around the plants and lift the rhizomes with a garden fork (above) or shovel, taking care not to break tender feeder roots. Shake or rinse the soil off and examine the rhizomes for damage. If you find iris-borer holes, rotted spots, or dried-out hollows, cut off and discard these areas.

2. Separate the rhizomes, starting with those that split into sections naturally in your hand. Cut others apart with a sharp, clean knife, separating V-shaped pieces and preserving the feeder roots. Dip the divided rhizomes in the diluted bleach solution and let them dry briefly in the shade before you replant.

3. Trim the foliage fans to a third of their height, or about 4 inches long, to reduce respiration and water loss while the divisions adjust. You can give the plant a more natural look by angling the cuts and by making the outer leaves shorter than the center leaf. Remove any foliage that is withered or diseased.

4. Set divided rhizomes on soil mounded in the middle of prepared holes, with the fans parallel and the feeder roots spread over the mounds; the tops of the rhizomes should just peek through at the soil surface. Tamp 2 to 4 inches of soil firmly over the feeder roots and water the area well.

Propagating Perennials through Stem Cuttings

Dividing your perennials at the roots is not the only way to produce exact replicas of them. Cuttings taken from the stems or side shoots of a wide range of plants can be encouraged to form roots and become independent plants. These new plants almost always bloom in the very next growing season.

Stem cuttings are a good means of getting offspring from a plant that doesn't need dividing, from one that you don't want to dig up, or (with the owner's permission) from one that doesn't belong to you. And plants that are hard to divide because they grow from taproots, like lupines or wild indigo, are good candidates for stem-cutting propagation. Perhaps you want a great many more of some specimen. Dividing the roots of that special chrysanthemum might yield only four rooted pieces, whereas stem cuttings could give you perhaps 20 rooted sections to transplant.

Stem cutting is also a good fallback procedure for the gardener who missed the proper time to propagate perennials by division: Cuttings can be taken almost anytime the plants are growing strongly, although it's best to take them either before or after flowering.

Of course, like every other method, this one has its drawbacks as well as its advantages. It is more labor-intensive than propagation by simple division. Cuttings require lots of attention from you; in the early stages, you may need to check them several times daily. Stem cutting is also a long-term proposition—it may take several months from the time you cut stems to when you set the new perennials in their permanent beds. In addition, fungus disease flourishes among cuttings, lowering the success rate—in some batches, every one of your leafy babies may mysteriously wilt and die. But with care and attention to details, you can multiply your stock of a fine plant many times over by cultivating stem cuttings.

Preparations for Cutting

Before making your stem cuttings, there are a few things you'll need to do. Several hours ahead of time, water the plants well so the stem tissue will be firm. Then mix up a solution of 10 parts water to 1 part bleach and use it to wash a sharp cutting knife, a cutting board, your work surface, and the containers that will hold the stem cuttings. Flats can hold quite a few cuttings, as can dishpans, but you can also use individual plastic pots or even small plastic cups or cartons you may find around your house. Simply clean them well first and poke a few drain holes in the bottom. Next, fill the containers with a 4-inch layer of a sterile growing medium: A commercial blend or a 50/50 mix of perlite and vermiculite works well. Don't use houseplant potting soil or topsoil, and don't use soil brought in from the garden. Water the sterile medium until it is well moistened but not soggy.

Each container will need an incubator tent to cover the planting and keep in moisture, so have on hand plastic food wrap or large clear plastic bags. Also gather wooden or wire supports—pencils will do nicely—to insert at the rims of the containers; these will keep the plastic from resting on the cuttings.

Once you've gathered all the necessary materials, examine your plants for erect but bendable stems. As you snip off these stems, put them into a moistened plastic bag to keep them damp while you are working.

All-Important Follow-Up

Place your containers of cuttings in a bright but shaded location—under a large tree is a good place in the summer. Temperatures of 65° to 75°F are ideal. Cuttings taken late in the season may need bottom heat from an electric mat or cable, available at nurseries and garden centers, to encourage them to root.

Check the containers regularly, opening each plastic tent at least once a day for air flow. If large drops of water appear on the plastic, punch a few small air holes. If the surface of the planting medium feels dry or any cuttings shrivel, carefully add a little water without disturbing the cuttings. If any leaves drop, remove them immediately; they may be hosts for disease organisms. If an entire cutting dries up, remove it as well.

Roots should form in 3 to 4 weeks, or even sooner. New growth on the foliage tips indicates roots are developing, as does resistance to a gentle tug on the tops of the cuttings. When roots have formed, remove the plastic covers and allow the plants to harden off—become accustomed to the outdoor conditions—for several days before you transplant them.

Transplant rooted cuttings directly into flower beds if frost is still several weeks away. If the growing season has ended, leave small plants together in the container, but give them some shelter—a cold frame or a heavy mulch if your climate is mild. If the cuttings have grown large, separate them into individual pots before sheltering them. Rooted cuttings can safely be planted with other perennials the next spring.

How to Propagate from Stem Cuttings

1. Locate a number of strong plant stems. *Then, using a sharp, clean knife or cross-bladed plant shears, slice off a few 5- to 6-inch segments, making slanting cuts about ¼ inch below a leaf joint or node. Trim off the lower leaves, leaving a rosette of leaves at the top of each cutting. Place the cuttings in a moistened plastic bag.*

2. Pour some commercial rooting hormone powder onto a piece of paper. *Following the manufacturer's instructions, dip the cut end of each stem into the powder. Do not dip the stems into the container, as this could contaminate the powder. Tap off any excess and lay the stems aside.*

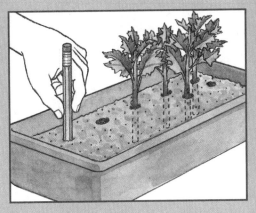

3. Use a pencil to make holes at least 3 inches deep in the planting medium; *space the holes far enough apart so the leaves of the cuttings won't touch. Set the cuttings in the holes, pressing soil around each stem so it stands upright. Add wooden or wire supports to the rim of your container, and wrap the pot with plastic sheeting to seal in humidity. Tape down the plastic or tuck it underneath the container. Make sure the plastic doesn't touch the cuttings or the soil surface.*

Perennials to Propagate from Stem Cuttings

Amsonia (bluestar)	(plumbago)	*Eupatorium* (boneset)	(lavender)	*Phlox paniculata* (summer phlox, garden phlox)
Anthemis (chamomile)	*Chrysanthemum* (chrysanthemum)	*Helenium* (sneezeweed)	*Linum* (flax)	*Physostegia* (false dragonhead)
Arabis (rock cress)	*Clematis* (clematis)	*Helianthus* (sunflower)	*Malva* (mallow)	*Salvia* (sage)
Aster (aster)	*Delphinium* (delphinium)	*Heliopsis* (false sunflower, oxeye)	*Monarda didyma* (bee balm)	*Sedum* (stonecrop)
Baptisia (wild indigo)	*Dianthus* (pinks)	*Iberis* (candytuft)	*Nepeta* (catmint)	*Verbena* (verbena, vervain)
Boltonia (boltonia)	*Echinops* (globe thistle)	*Lamium* (dead nettle)	*Perovskia* (Russian sage)	*Veronica* (speedwell)
Ceratostigma	*Erigeron* (fleabane)	*Lavandula*	*Phlox divaricata* (wild blue phlox)	

Propagating True Bulbs

Most gardeners are familiar with growing plants from seeds they order through catalogs or buy at the nursery and increasing their number of plants by sowing seeds gathered from the original stock. The process of creating new plants from seed is termed sexual propagation, because the seeds originate from reproductive plant parts that are fertilized through pollination.

Since true bulbs produce viable seed, they can be propagated by this method. But the wait for bulbs to grow to maturity from seed may require more patience than you—and many other gardeners—possess. Tulips and daffodils, for example, can take up to 4 or 5 years to flower from seed, and hyacinths may take even longer. Furthermore, cultivars and hybrids that have been propagated from seed are susceptible to reverting to earlier forms in their genealogy. The resulting plants may not give you the exact look you were expecting from your flowers.

Starting from Seed

If you can commit yourself to a long-term proposition, the best approach to propagating true bulbs from seed is to sow a different variety of seed every year. Although the first crop will take years to come into flower, after that your waiting will be over. Each year a different planting will add its blooms to the existing bulb show.

Despite the long wait, propagating by seed is the best choice for a few true bulb genera, including Scilla, simply because they don't easily lend themselves to other propagation methods. Planting scilla seed will give you flowers in 3 to 4 years.

Nevertheless, for most true bulbs it's far easier and more reliable to propagate asexually—by dividing the bulbs and then planting their offsets. Some bulbs, such as daffodils, have large offsets that will flower as early as the first season.

Separating True Bulbs

After the foliage has turned brown, dig the bulbs up in their naturally formed clumps. Taking care not do damage the roots, brush away clinging soil *(below, left)*. Discard any injured, diseased, or rotted bulbs. Ease the daughter bulbs away from the mother bulb *(below, right)*, making sure each one includes a portion of the basal plate. The smallest, youngest bulbs may still be firmly attached to the mother. If they do not separate easily, leave them in place and allow them to mature for another year or two. Dust the separated mother and daughter bulbs with a fungicide such as garden sulfur and replant.

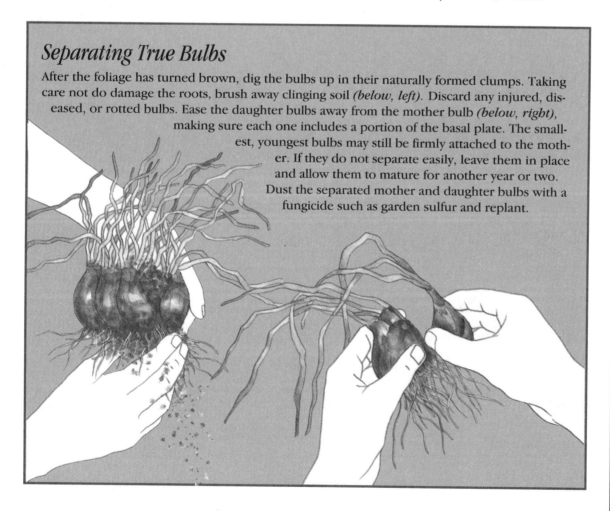

When and How to Divide Bulbs

The correct time for digging and dividing true bulbs depends on the growth habit of the plant. Most should be dug after their foliage has withered but while it still remains in place to show the location of the bulbs. If the foliage is not too far gone, it might even serve as a handle to help lift the bulbs. An exception is *Galanthus* (snowdrop), which should be dug immediately after flowering.

If you plan to propagate several varieties of bulbs, it's a good idea to mark the foliage with an indelible pen while the plants are still in flower. That way, you'll be able to identify the bulbs later when all the withered, brown leaves look more or less the same.

Choose only healthy, disease-free plants for propagation. Dig the bulbs carefully with a spading fork, making sure not to damage them; cuts and bruises can give rise to rot. Imbricate bulbs such as lily and fritillary, which have scales but no papery outer covering, are especially fragile and vulnerable to injury. Gently brush away any clinging soil and carefully separate the bulbs as shown in the box at far left.

Different Treatment for Different Bulbs

In general, hardy bulbs such as tulips and daffodils can be dug, divided, and replanted all in one operation. Tender summer bulbs, such as *Zephyranthes* (zephyr lily) and *Chlidanthus* (delicate lily), should be dug in fall, separated, stored over the winter, and planted in spring.

Once they are divided, sort the bulbs according to size—small, medium, or large. You can plant the largest ones in the garden to flower the following year. Medium-sized bulbs can also go directly into the garden, but they may or may not bloom the following year.

The smallest bulbs will need further growing before they are mature enough to bloom. It's best

Rising above tiny blue Myosotis sylvatica (forget-me-not) blossoms, these gloriously hued Dutch irises stand about 18 inches tall. One of the few irises that grow from bulbs, not rhizomes, the plants can be propagated by seed or by division.

Selected True Bulbs

Allium
(onion)
Amaryllis belladonna
(belladonna lily)
Calochortus
(mariposa lily)
Camassia
(camass)
Chionodoxa
(glory-of-the-snow)
Crinum
(spider lily)
Eucharis grandiflora
(Amazon lily)
Eucomis
(pineapple lily)
Fritillaria
(fritillary)
Galanthus
(snowdrop)
Galtonia
(summer hyacinth)
Habranthus
(habranthus)
Hippeastrum
(amaryllis)
Hyacinthoides
(hyacinthoides)
Hyacinthus
(hyacinth)
Hymenocallis
(spider lily)
Ipheion
(spring starflower)
Iris
(iris)
Lachenalia
(Cape cowslip)
Leucojum
(snowflake)
Lilium
(lily)
Lycoris
(spider lily)
Muscari
(grape hyacinth)
Narcissus
(daffodil)
Nerine
(nerine)
Ornithogalum
(star-of-Bethlehem)
Oxalis
(sorrel)
Puschkinia
(striped squill)
Scilla
(squill)
Sprekelia formosissima
(Jacobean lily)
Sternbergia
(winter daffodil)
Tulipa
(tulip)
Vallota
(Scarborough lily)
Zephyranthes
(zephyr lily)

to plant them in a nursery bed to allow them to develop a bit before planting them in the garden.

Lily bulblets and bulbils, too, should be planted out in a nursery bed to mature *(right)*. Separate the bulblets from the mother bulb and the bulbils from the stem in late summer, about 6 weeks after flowering, and then replant the mother bulb in the garden.

Nursery Beds

Immature bulbs, bulblets, and bulbils will do best in more carefully arranged growing conditions than you would use for full-sized bulbs. The prime consideration is good drainage. Another is freedom from competition with larger plants for moisture and nutrients. Still another is the need to grow in a situation where the baby bulbs' tiny, grasslike sprouts will not be mistaken for unwanted grass or weeds and pulled out.

The arrangement that meets all these needs perfectly is a nursery bed. Set aside a small, sunny, out-of-the-way piece of ground devoted exclusively to young plants. Here, without excessive effort, you can cultivate and amend the soil for ideal drainage and fertility.

Because the plants you start here will be transplanted as soon as they are mature enough, you can grow them relatively close together and in rows without worrying about aesthetics. And because you know that those wisps of vegetation that appear in the bed may well be something you planted, there's less danger you'll uproot them.

Water the bed amply to encourage good growth. Take pains to weed it carefully in the autumn, because when new shoots begin to emerge the following spring you may find it difficult to weed without jeopardizing them.

As soon as winter weather arrives, mulch the ground to moderate changes in the temperature of the soil. Otherwise, the expansion and contraction of earth that alternately freezes and thaws could heave the tiny bulbs out of the ground.

Allow the plants to grow for a year or two in the nursery bed; at the end of that time they should be ready to go into the garden. Dig them after the foliage dies back and plant where desired.

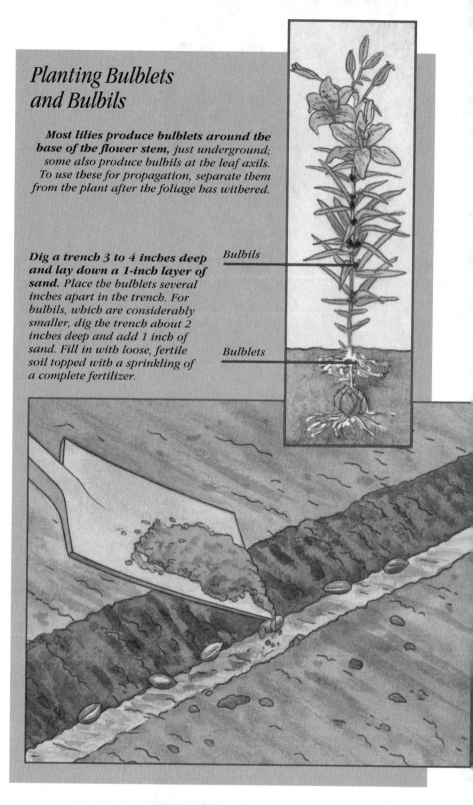

Planting Bulblets and Bulbils

Most lilies produce bulblets around the base of the flower stem, just underground; *some also produce bulbils at the leaf axils. To use these for propagation, separate them from the plant after the foliage has withered.*

Dig a trench 3 to 4 inches deep and lay down a 1-inch layer of sand. Place the bulblets several inches apart in the trench. For bulbils, which are considerably smaller, dig the trench about 2 inches deep and add 1 inch of sand. Fill in with loose, fertile soil topped with a sprinkling of a complete fertilizer.

Bulbils

Bulblets

Lilies That Produce Bulblets and Bulbils

BULBLETS:

Lilium auratum
(gold-banded lily)
L. henryi
(Henry lily)
L. lancifolium
(tiger lily)
L. longiflorum **hybrids**
(Easter lily)
L. regale
(regal lily)

L. speciosum
(showy Japanese lily)
L. **Asiatic hybrids**
(lily)
L. **Oriental hybrids**
(lily)
L. **trumpet hybrids**
(lily)

BULBILS:

L. lancifolium
(tiger lily)
L. **Asiatic hybrid
'Enchantment'**
(lily)

Scaling to Propagate Lilies

Most lily bulbs look something like artichokes, being made up of a series of overlapping fleshy scales that grow out in a spiral formation from a central, flowering axis. All of the scales are attached to the bulb's basal plate, but they grow in a loose configuration, and the outer ones can easily be removed without cutting and without harming the remaining bulb. This characteristic allows lilies and a few fritillaries—especially *Fritillaria imperialis*—to be propagated by a special technique called scaling. (Most fritillaries, which are composed of very few scales, may be destroyed in the process.)

Planted in a proper medium, at the right temperature, the scales will form bulblets at their base. These can be planted in turn, just like the bulblets from the underground portion of the stem of a growing lily bulb. Each scale will produce at least one bulblet, and each bulblet, potentially, will grow into a mature bulb. You can use scaling to supplement the bulblets and bulbils that grow naturally on lilies, particularly for varieties that produce few offsets. Scaling before you plant an expensive lily variety also helps ensure survival to the next generation—and protects your investment—should the original die during its first year, as sometimes happens.

How to Scale

Bulbs can be scaled at any time—even when you've just brought them home from the nursery. However, because lily and fritillary are hardy bulbs, meant to stay in the ground over winter, most bulblets produced by scaling will need to experience a period of chilling before they can begin to sprout. Therefore, the best time to scale is in late summer or early autumn, which will allow time for the bulblets to emerge and then be refrigerated for several months before you plant them out in the garden in the spring. Also, completing the operation by autumn will give the parent bulb time to reestablish itself after you replant it, before winter sets in.

Brightening a garden in Washington, D.C., orange Fritillaria imperialis (crown imperial) and its purple-hued cousin, F. persica, both can be propagated by growing bulblets on scales removed from the original bulbs.

Propagation by Scaling

Scales will produce bulblets quite readily, but there are some minimum requirements for success. The scales will do best planted in a flat containing coarse vermiculite or a combination of coarse sand and peat moss. Keep the medium moist and the temperature between 60° and 70°F. The top of the refrigerator or a warm cupboard is a good place to keep the flat; light does not matter. After the bulblets emerge and the necessary chilling has taken place, plant them, with scales attached, in a nursery bed. Place the scales upright so that the tips of the scales are about 1 inch below ground and 6 inches apart.

1. Dig the bulb and gently remove the soil, taking care not to damage the roots. Cut off the top growth to about 6 to 8 inches.

2. Carefully pull off several outer scales, discarding any that are unhealthy, broken, or otherwise damaged. Rinse them, let them dry on newspaper, and dip them—and the wounded areas of the bulb—in a fungicide. Replant the bulb immediately; it will bloom normally again the next spring.

3. Plant the scales upright, about half to two-thirds submerged, in a flat filled with a suitable medium. Slip the flat into a plastic bag propped up with small sticks to protect the scales. Inspect occasionally for adequate moisture or rot.

4. After 6 weeks, check one scale for bulblets with roots. Leaving the flat in plastic, chill over winter and plant the scales in spring.

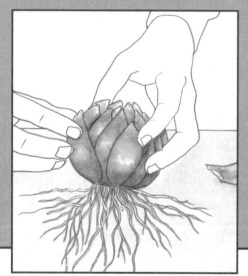

Choose the plants you'd like to scale, and mark them while they are still in flower. When the time is right, dig the bulbs carefully and remove and plant the scales as described above. Scales from most lilies will produce bulblets in 6 to 8 weeks; trumpet lilies will take about 12 weeks.

The newly emerged bulblets will be ready for chilling once they reach ¼ inch or more in height. You can accomplish the chilling in one of two ways. The first option is to do your initial planting of the scales in a cold frame in the garden, where the emerging bulblets will remain to be chilled over the winter, or, once the bulblets have reached the proper size, you can place them in your refrigerator. They should be kept at 35° to 40°F—the temperature range in most refrigerators—for 2 months or longer.

If you keep them in the refrigerator, wait until the proper spring planting time to set them out in the garden. Don't remove the bulblets from the withered scales, as the tiny bulbs are fragile and easily damaged; also, the scales can still provide some nourishment to the bulblets after they are in the ground. Allow the bulblets to grow over the summer, then dig them up and replant them the following fall; set them at a depth of 6 inches and about 4 to 6 inches apart.

Propagating Corms

Like other bulbs, cormous plants can be propagated from seed. Indeed, gladiolus produces abundant seed, is easy to grow from seed, and may bloom the first year. *Ixia, Sparaxis,* and *Tritonia* should bloom from seed within 2 years; *Babiana, Crocosmia, Tigridia,* and *Watsonia* within 3 years; *Crocus* and *Colchicum* in 3 or more years.

Still, unless you are growing only species, not cultivars or hybrids, the easiest and most reliable way to increase your stock of most cormous plants is to grow them from the corms and cormels they produce. For example, although hybrid gladiolus grows well from seed, the flowers that emerge may be throwbacks. Gladiolus also produces many cormels, however, which grow into clones of the original plant. So if you want your favorite gladiolus hybrids to reappear year after year, use this method to reproduce them.

Propagating from Cormels

Obtain cormels by lifting the desired plant when the foliage has withered but is still visible. Remove the cormels as illustrated at left and replant the mother corm in the garden.

In most climates, the cormels of gladiolus, freesia, and watsonia must be stored over the winter before being set out. And because their blooms will not appear until the second or third year, you will have to lift and store them once or twice more before they flower.

Prepare a shallow trench in a nursery bed and plant the cormels 1½ to 2 inches deep and 2 to 3 inches apart. In their first year, they will produce narrow, grasslike foliage. If need be at the end of the season, dig hardy corms such as crocus and replant them farther apart.

Separating Cormels

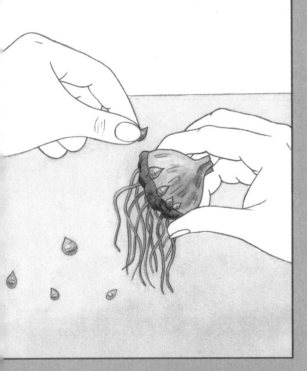

When propagating with cormels from a tender plant, such as the gladiolus hybrid above, wait until fall before digging. By then the mother corm has died, the daughter corm is fully mature, and cormels have emerged. Dry the new corm as quickly as possible, then gently pull off the cormels. Place the corm in a paper bag filled with dry peat moss and store over winter in a cool area such as a basement or garage. Sort the cormels by size and store them similarly. Plant them in a nursery bed in spring after all danger of frost has passed. If the plants you are propagating are hardy, you can simply lift them when the foliage has died, separate the cormels, and replant both corm and cormels immediately.

Crocus 'Snow Beauty'
(crocus)

***Note:** The abbreviation "spp." stands for the plural of "species"; where used in lists it means that many, but not all, of the species in a genus meet the criterion of the list.*

Propagating Tubers and Rhizomes

Some tuberous and rhizomatous plants can be started from seed. Seeds of dahlia and tuberous begonia, for example, are readily available through nursery catalogs. Or you can collect seeds from plants in your garden, though you run the risk of ending up with a different—and perhaps inferior—new generation. A tuber such as caladium, for example, grown solely for its strikingly colored foliage, may produce a good deal of undesirable variation when grown from seed.

Dahlia and tuberous begonia, if propagated from seed, require a long growing season to begin to flower. In all but the warmest regions, if the plants are to have time to flower the first year, the seeds must be started indoors in late winter, then planted out after the weather has warmed.

You will have a longer wait before you see flowers from other tubers and rhizomes started from seed. *Achimenes* (orchid pansy), anemone, begonia, belamcanda, corydalis, ranunculus, and *Zantedeschia* (calla lily), won't bloom until the second year, and *Gloriosa* may take even longer. If you don't want to wait that long, your alternative is asexual propagation techniques that are appro-priate to tubers and rhizomes, such as division or stem cutting.

Asexual Propagation

The need to lift and store tender plants such as canna, dahlia, and tuberous begonia offers a convenient opportunity to propagate them asexually, by division. However, the process is a bit more invasive than that of separating true bulbs or plucking bulblets or cormels.

Instead of producing neatly sectioned or self-contained offsets that practically come off in your hand, tubers and rhizomes must be separated by force. Some tubers do grow offsets, but even these are firmly attached to the main body. To divide them, you must cut them into pieces.

Nevertheless, division is a faster, easier, and more foolproof way to increase your stock of

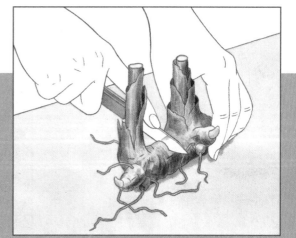

Dividing Tubers and Rhizomes

***In dividing a dahlia tuber (below),** cut it so that each section includes a portion of the root, a slice of the crown, and a growth bud. The buds, which are located around the crown, have been exaggerated for clarity in this illustration. Dip the cut surfaces in a fungicide and plant as described in Chapter 7.*

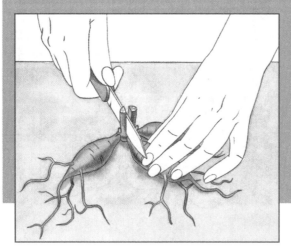

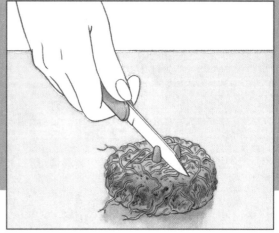

These striking blooms of the Dahlia cultivar 'Cherry Drop' demonstrate that asexual propagation from your own stock of tubers and rhizomes can be a reward for the eye as well as the pocketbook.

these plants than growing them from seed. The divided pieces usually will produce flowers their first year in the ground. And the offspring will be exact duplicates of the originals.

Dividing Tubers and Rhizomes

To propagate them successfully, you must make sure to cut the tuber or rhizome so that each piece contains one or more growth nodes. These will appear on the tops of tubers and along the tops or sides of rhizomes.

Use a sharp knife sterilized in a solution of 1 part household bleach to 10 parts warm water. Dip the knife in the solution after each cut. If you are dividing tender plants that were lifted and stored for the winter, do your cutting just before spring planting. Hardy plants should be dug when the foliage has died back, divided, and replanted.

Before replanting, allow the cut pieces to heal for 2 days in a warm place. During that time, a callus will form over the cut, protecting the tuber or rhizome from rot once it is planted in the soil.

Plant the divided pieces in the garden, following the planting instructions for different genera shown in Chapter 7. The pieces cut from tender

bulbs will bloom later that season; those cut from hardy bulbs will bloom the following year.

Propagating from Stem Cuttings

Both dahlia and tuberous begonia produce branching plants and can be propagated by stem cutting. Pick plants that are the best examples of the hybrids or cultivars you wish to reproduce. Tag your choices early in the growing season and switch to better ones should any originals falter.

There are two ways to obtain stems for rooting. One is to cut them directly from desired varieties in your garden when the plants are in full growth. Use a sterilized knife to cut 4 to 6 inches off the growing end of a stem, making sure that the cut piece has a terminal bud or growth node, for further vertical growth, and intact nodes in the axils of its lowest set of leaves, for root growth. Make your cut just below the lowest leaves. You can also take a cutting from farther down on a stem; just be certain that you include at least two sets of leaves with growth nodes in their axils.

Whether you cut from the tip of a stem or farther down, follow the instructions on pages 248-249 to root the stem cuttings.

Place tuberous begonias (left) in a warm, bright location to promote emergence of the eyes, or growth points. Cut a large tuber into 2 or 3 divisions, each of which must contain an eye. Dust the pieces with a fungicide and let them callus over for 2 days before planting.

Canna rhizomes, like the one at left, must be stored over winter from Zone 7 northward. In early spring, remove the rhizomes from storage and discard any withered or diseased ones. Cut so that each section contains a growth node and roots. Pot the sections or plant in the garden, depending on your climate.

Troubleshooting Guide

Even the best-tended gardens can fall prey to pests and diseases. To keep them in check, regularly inspect your plants for warning signs, remembering that lack of nutrients, improper pH levels, and other environmental conditions can cause symptoms like those typical of some diseases. If wilting or yellowing appears on neighboring plants, the source is probably environmental; pest and disease damage is usually more random.

This guide is intended to help you identify and solve most of your pest and disease problems. In general, good drainage and air circulation will help prevent infection, and the many insects, such as ladybugs and lacewings, that prey on pests should be encouraged. Natural solutions to garden problems are best, but if you must use chemicals, treat only the affected plant. Try to use horticultural oils, insecticidal soaps, and the botanical insecticide neem; these products are the least disruptive to beneficial insects and will not destroy the soil balance that is at the foundation of a healthy garden. If these solutions fail, remove and discard the infected plants. Do not compost them.

PESTS

PROBLEM: Insects appear on buds and other plant parts. Eventually, leaves curl, are distorted in shape, and may be sticky and have a black, sooty appearance. A clear, shiny substance often appears on stems and leaves. Buds and flowers are deformed; new growth is stunted, and leaves and flowers may drop.

CAUSE: Aphids are pear-shaped, semitransparent, wingless sucking insects, about ⅛ inch long; they may be green, yellow, red, pink, black, or gray in color. They suck sap and through feeding may spread viral diseases. Infestations are most severe in spring and early summer when pests cluster on tender new shoots, on undersides of leaves, and around flower buds. Winged forms appear when colonies become overcrowded. Aphids secrete honeydew, a sticky substance that fosters the growth of a black fungus called sooty mold.

SOLUTION: Aphids are fairly easy to control. Pick them off by hand, or early in the morning knock them off by spraying plants with a strong, steady stream of water from a garden hose. Ladybugs or green lacewings, which eat aphids, may be introduced into the garden. In severe cases, prune off infested areas, and use an insecticidal soap or a recommended insecticide. As a last resort, remove and discard the plant.
SUSCEPTIBLE PLANTS: VIRTUALLY ALL ANNUALS, MANY PERENNIALS, MOST BULBS, ROSES.

PROBLEM: Round or oblong holes are eaten in leaves, leaf edges, and flowers, especially those that are light colored. Leaves may be reduced to skeletons with only veins remaining.

CAUSE: Japanese beetles, iridescent blue-green with bronze wing covers, are one of the most destructive of a large family of hard-shelled chewing insects ranging in size from ¼ to 1 inch long. Other genera include Asiatic garden beetles, rose chafers, Fuller rose beetles, blister beetles, and goldsmith beetles. Adult beetles are voracious in the summer. Larvae, the white grubs, may feed on roots and are present from midsummer through the following spring, when they emerge as adults.

SOLUTION: In morning, when beetles are sluggish, handpick, placing them in a can filled with soapy water. Don't use Japanese beetle traps; they only lure more beetles into your garden. The larval stage of most beetles can be controlled with milky spore disease. For heavy infestations, call your local Cooperative Extension Service for information on registered pesticides and the best times to apply them in your region.
SUSCEPTIBLE PLANTS: MANY ANNUALS, PERENNIALS, AND ROSES.

PROBLEM: Rose canes, new growth, and leaves droop and wilt. Canes turn brown and die. The centers of pruned canes are hollowed out, or swollen areas appear on the surface of canes.

CAUSE: Cane borers, the larvae of several insects, penetrate rose canes through pruned ends or by puncturing their sides, and then hollow them by consuming the pith. The commonest borer, the larvae of the small carpenter bee, develops from eggs laid on top of unprotected cut stems.

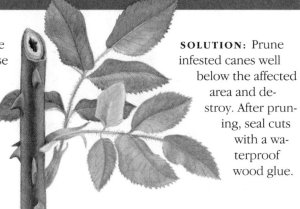

SOLUTION: Prune infested canes well below the affected area and destroy. After pruning, seal cuts with a waterproof wood glue.

PROBLEM: Holes appear in leaves, buds, and flowers; stems may also be eaten.

CAUSE: Caterpillars, the wormlike larvae of moths, butterflies, and sawflies, come in a variety of shapes and colors and can be smooth, hairy, or spiny. These voracious pests are found in gardens during the spring.
SUSCEPTIBLE PLANTS: MANY PERENNIALS, ESPECIALLY TENDER NEW SHOOTS.

SOLUTION: Handpick to control small populations. The organic pesticide *Bacillus thuringiensis* (Bt) kills many types without harming plants. If caterpillars return to your garden every spring, spray Bt as a preventive measure. Identify the caterpillar species to determine the control options and timing of spray applications. Several species are susceptible to sprays of insecticidal soap, which must directly hit the caterpillar. Keep the garden clear of debris and cultivate frequently. Deep spading in early spring can destroy many species that pupate underground. Destroy all visible cocoons and nests.

PROBLEM: Stems of emerging young plants are cut off near the ground; seedlings may be completely eaten. Leaves of older plants show ragged edges and chewed holes.

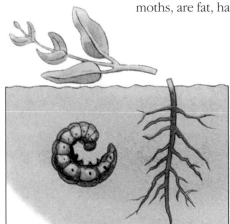

CAUSE: Cutworms, the larvae of various moths, are fat, hairless, and gray or dull brown in color. These 1- to 2-inch-long night feeders do the most damage in the spring. In the daytime, they curl up into a C shape and are found under debris or below the soil surface next to the plant stem.

SOLUTION: Place barriers called cutworm collars around the base of a plant. Force cutworms to the surface of the soil by flooding the area and then handpick them. To reduce hiding places, keep the area weeded and free of debris. Spade the soil in late summer and fall to expose and destroy cutworms. Apply *Bacillus thuringiensis* (Bt).
SUSCEPTIBLE PLANTS: VIRTUALLY ALL ANNUALS AND MANY PERENNIALS, PARTICULARLY YOUNG SEEDLINGS AND TRANSPLANTS.

PROBLEM: Iris leaves show pale brown irregular lines or tunnels burrowed down their length, and leaf edges are ragged. Leaves wilt and become discolored. The rhizomes may be rotten, foul smelling, and soft.

CAUSE: Iris borers, the most serious insect pest of the iris, are cream-colored chewing moth larvae that emerge in the spring from eggs laid the previous fall. They bore into new iris leaves and eat the soft interior tissue, migrating through leaves to flower stalks and buds. By late summer the larvae—fat and about 1½ inches long, and pink with brown heads—gradually work down into the rhizomes, where boring activity often results in foul-smelling bacterial soft rot.
SUSCEPTIBLE PLANTS: IRIS, ESPECIALLY BEARDED VARIETIES.

SOLUTION: After first frost, remove and destroy all damaged and dead foliage and stems to eliminate overwintering eggs. In spring, young borers are visible in the leaves and may be removed by hand. When new plant growth is 4 to 6 inches high, apply a labeled systemic insecticide—one that is intended for use on ornamental plants—to kill young larvae. In midsummer, apply beneficial nematodes in the soil at the base of stems to kill larvae. When irises are dug and divided in late summer, rhizomes that are heavily damaged should be destroyed.

PROBLEM: Leaves become stippled with white dots, then turn yellowish brown or have a burned look around the edges. Leaves and stems curl upward; young leaves become distorted. Plant growth may be stunted.

CAUSE: Leafhoppers are small (¼ inch long), yellow-green, cricket-like, wedge-shaped sucking insects with colorful spots or bands. They jump quickly into flight when disturbed. Most active in spring and summer, leafhoppers feed on the undersides of leaves and, like aphids, secrete a sticky honeydew that fosters sooty mold. Adult leafhoppers overwinter on host plants; in spring, the females insert eggs into leaf or stem tissue. Nymphs are smaller, often wingless, versions of adults.

SOLUTION: Spray with water to knock exposed leafhoppers off plants. Remove and destroy damaged foliage and heavily infested plants. Direct spraying with insecticidal soap will give short-term control, but leafhoppers migrate freely, so repeated applications may be necessary. A labeled systemic insecticide will provide the longest control.
SUSCEPTIBLE PLANTS: MANY PERENNIALS, INCLUDING BABY'S-BREATH, CATMINT, CHRYSANTHEMUM, COREOPSIS, AND ITALIAN BUGLOSS; ALSO ROSES

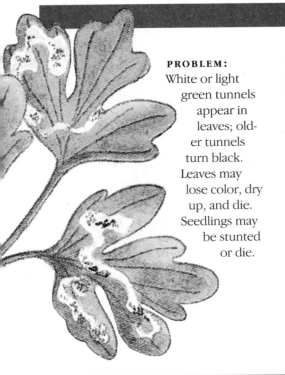

PROBLEM: White or light green tunnels appear in leaves; older tunnels turn black. Leaves may lose color, dry up, and die. Seedlings may be stunted or die.

CAUSE: Leaf miners—minute (1/16 to 1/8 inch long), translucent, pale green larvae of certain flies, moths, or beetles—are hatched from eggs laid on the leaves of plants. During spring and summer, the larvae eat the tender interior below the surface of the leaf, leaving behind serpentine trails of blistered tissue known as mines. *SUSCEPTIBLE PLANTS: MANY PERENNIALS, INCLUDING CHRYSANTHEMUM, COLUMBINE, DELPHINIUM, MONKSHOOD, PRIMROSE, AND SHASTA DAISY.*

SOLUTION: Damage may be unsightly but is usually not lethal. Pick off and destroy infested leaves as they appear. In the fall, cut the plant to the ground and discard stalks. Remove and destroy leaves with egg clusters. Keep the garden well weeded since organic waste attracts maggots. Use a systemic insecticide, timing applications at proper intervals, before leaf mining becomes extensive.

PROBLEM: Leaves become stippled or flecked with yellow. Often the entire leaf becomes yellow or bronzed and curled. Flowers and buds discolor or dry up, and fine webbing may be seen on the undersides of leaves and on new growth. Leaves may drop. Growth is stunted.

CAUSE: Mites, about the size of a grain of salt, are spiderlike sucking pests that can be reddish, green, yellow, or brown. These insects can become a major problem, especially in hot, dry weather, when several generations of mites may occur in a single season. Adults of some species hibernate over the winter in sod, in bark, and on weeds and plants that retain foliage.

SOLUTION: Keep plants watered and mulched. In the early morning, regularly spray a strong stream of water at the undersides of leaves, where mites feed and lay eggs. Introduce predators such as ladybugs, green lacewing larvae, and predatory mites. Horticultural oil can also be applied to leaf undersides. Insecticides destroy the beneficial insects that control mites. *SUSCEPTIBLE PLANTS: VIRTUALLY ALL ANNUALS; MANY PERENNIALS; ROSES.*

PROBLEM: Light-colored sunken brown spots appear on the upper surfaces of leaves. Foliage may wilt, discolor, and fall from the plant. Shoots may be distorted or blackened. Flower buds may be deformed.

CAUSE: Plant bugs include the four-lined plant bug, lygus bug, and tarnished plant bug. These 1/4-inch-long sucking insects are brown, black, green, yellow, or brightly colored with antennae and wings, and are active from early spring to early summer.

SOLUTION: In most cases, plants recover from the feeding injury, and control is often unnecessary. But if infestation is severe, eliminate debris that could be breeding ground. Spray plants with water or a diluted soap solution, or use an insecticidal soap to control nymphs. *SUSCEPTIBLE PLANTS: MANY PERENNIALS, INCLUDING CLEMATIS, CORAL BELLS, PURPLE CONEFLOWER.*

PROBLEM: On roses, foliage at the tips of new growth appears burned around the edges. Flowers are deformed. Tender foliage and buds may suddenly turn brown or black.

CAUSE: Tiny (⅒₅ inch) white larvae of the rose midge, a kind of fly, emerge from eggs laid in the sepals of flower buds or in opening leaf buds; they slash plant tissue with sickle-shaped mouth parts and suck the sap. The larvae drop to the ground to pupate; adults emerge within days. Numerous life cycles may be repeated throughout the growing season. Damage is particularly severe in the summer.

SOLUTION: Prune off and destroy affected leaves and buds promptly to break the life cycle. For severe infestations, spray a recommended insecticide. *SUSCEPTIBLE PLANTS: ROSES.*

PROBLEM: On roses, small holes are eaten out of leaves, or leaves are skeletonized.

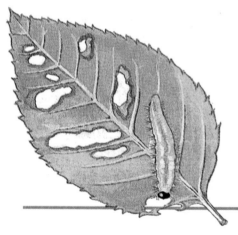

CAUSE: Rose slugs, which are not actual slugs but the larvae of three different sawflies, feed on rose leaves. The half-inch-long, pale green common rose slug skeletonizes the upper leaf surface in early spring. The bristly rose slug is pale green and slightly longer, its wormlike body covered with stiff hairs when mature. It feeds on the undersides of leaves, first skeletonizing them and later chewing large holes. The curled rose sawfly larva, ¾ inch long, consumes the leaves from a coiled position and burrows into pruned twigs to pupate, which opens twigs to fungal infection.

SOLUTION: Spray plants with a strong, steady stream of water to knock larvae off; most won't climb back up. Handpick to control small populations. Bristly rose slugs can irritate the skin, so wear gloves. In case of severe infestation, spray an insecticidal soap directly on the slugs. *SUSCEPTIBLE PLANTS: ROSES.*

PROBLEM: On roses, leaves discolor, wilt, and drop. Growth is stunted. Stems, canes, and leaves are covered with small, white, cottony patches or with rounded or oval shells in various colors. The problem occurs most often on climbers that have not been pruned yearly.

CAUSE: Scale insects have hard or soft shells, ⅒ to ⅜ inch long, that may be white, yellow, green, gray, red, brown, or black. They usually appear in clusters. Hard-shelled adult males and females and soft-shelled females appear on stems or leaves as bumps. Adult soft-shelled males are minute flying insects with yellow wings. The insects suck plant juices.

SOLUTION: Remove scales with a cotton swab or soft toothbrush dipped in soapy water or an alcohol-and-water solution. Prune off and destroy any canes that are severely infested. Spray roses with horticultural oil in early spring to smother eggs before plant growth begins. Insecticidal soaps are effective when eggs have just hatched. *SUSCEPTIBLE PLANTS: ROSES.*

PROBLEM: Ragged holes appear on leaves, especially those near the ground. New leaves and entire young seedlings may disappear. Telltale shiny silver streaks appear on leaves and garden paths.

CAUSE: Slugs or snails hide during the day and feed on low-hanging leaves at night or on overcast or rainy days. They prefer damp soil in a shady location and cause the most damage in summer, especially in wet regions or during rainy years.

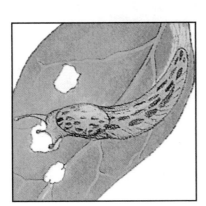

SOLUTION: Keep garden clean to minimize hiding places. Handpick slugs and snails or trap them by placing saucers of beer level with the soil surface near plants. Slugs will also collect under inverted grapefruit halves or melon rinds. Because slugs and snails find it difficult to crawl over rough surfaces, barrier strips of copper, wood ashes, coarse sand, cinders, or diatomaceous earth (DE) placed around plants will deter them. Introduce or encourage rove beetles, which prey on slugs. Turning the soil in spring often destroys dormant slugs and eggs.
SUSCEPTIBLE PLANTS: VIRTUALLY ALL PLANTS, ESPECIALLY THOSE WITH YOUNG OR TENDER FOLIAGE. HOSTA IS HIGHLY SUSCEPTIBLE.

PROBLEM: Buds open only partway or not at all. Flower petals turn brown at the edges, darken, or have brownish yellow or white streaks and small dark spots or bumps. Young growth may be deformed or mottled. The problem is most evident on light-colored roses.

CAUSE: Thrips are quick-moving sucking insects that are barely visible to the naked eye. They look like tiny slivers of yellow, black, or brown wood. Emerging in early spring, thrips are especially active in late spring and early summer, attacking sepals of buds and sucking juices from the petals. Adults are weak fliers but are easily dispersed by wind and can therefore travel great distances.

SOLUTION: Control of thrips is difficult, especially during a migratory period in early summer. Lacewings, ladybugs, pirate bugs, and several predaceous mites feed on them; late in the growing season such predators often check thrips populations. Remove and destroy damaged buds and flowers. In severe cases, spray plants with an insecticidal soap or systemic insecticide.
SUSCEPTIBLE PLANTS: ANNUALS; PERENNIALS, INCLUDING DAYLILY, FOXGLOVE, AND PEONY; BULBS, INCLUDING GLADIOLUS AND BULBS WITH WHITE OR PASTEL FLOWERS.

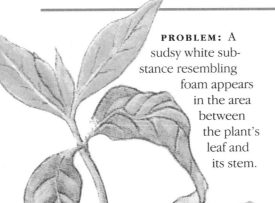

PROBLEM: A sudsy white substance resembling foam appears in the area between the plant's leaf and its stem.

CAUSE: Spittlebugs hatch from eggs in the spring, and young insects produce the foamy substance for protection while they feed on sap under tender leaves and stems.

SOLUTION: Although unsightly, spittlebugs and their residue are not serious. To control, wash off plants with water spray or a diluted soap solution.
SUSCEPTIBLE PLANTS: MANY PERENNIALS.

PROBLEM: Leaves turn yellow, and plants are stunted. When plants are shaken, a white cloud appears.

CAUSE: Whiteflies, sucking insects ¹⁄₁₆ inch long that look like tiny white moths, generally collect on the undersides of young leaves. Seedlings are especially susceptible. Found year round in warmer climates but only in summer in colder climates, they like warm, still air. Whiteflies are often brought home with greenhouse-raised plants and can carry viruses. They secrete honeydew, a substance that promotes sooty mold.

SOLUTION: Carefully inspect plants, especially the undersides of leaves, before purchasing. Spray plants frequently with a steady stream of water from a garden hose to knock whiteflies off plants and discourage them from returning. Set yellow sticky traps near infected plants. Introduce lacewings and parasitic wasps; apply pyrethrum. Keep the garden well weeded. In severe cases, spray with insecticidal soap or remove the plant from the garden and throw it away. *SUSCEPTIBLE PLANTS: VIRTUALLY ALL ANNUALS; MANY PERENNIALS, INCLUDING LUPINE.*

PROBLEM: Foliage develops irregular yellow to purplish brown spots that darken with age. These spots may also expand and join to cover the leaves. Purplish lesions form along the stem; plant growth is often stunted.

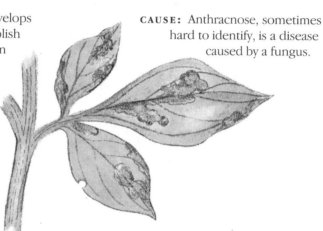

CAUSE: Anthracnose, sometimes hard to identify, is a disease caused by a fungus.

SOLUTION: Grow resistant plant varieties. Thin stems and tops to improve air circulation. Remove and destroy all shoots after first frost in the fall. If infection is severe, spray with a fungicide in early spring. *SUSCEPTIBLE PLANTS: PERENNIALS, PARTICULARLY HERBACEOUS TYPES, INCLUDING PEONY, HOLLYHOCKS, AND FOXGLOVES.*

PROBLEM: A slight yellowing along leaf veins occurs on young plants. As the disease progresses, the entire plant yellows. Flowers are small and have a yellow-green color. New root, flower, and leaf growth is distorted, and leaves are stunted. Plants wilt and die.

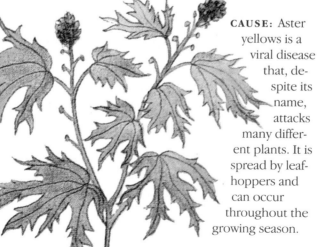

CAUSE: Aster yellows is a viral disease that, despite its name, attacks many different plants. It is spread by leafhoppers and can occur throughout the growing season.

SOLUTION: Remove and destroy infected plants. Do not plant annuals, especially China asters, in the same spot each year. Keep garden clean; remove perennial weeds in which leafhopper eggs often overwinter. Sterilize heavily infested soil through a process known as solarization: Fix a sheet of clear plastic over the soil and leave it in place 1 to 2 months. *SUSCEPTIBLE PLANTS: MANY ANNUALS, BUT PRIMARILY ASTER; PERENNIALS SUCH AS COREOPSIS, PURPLE CONEFLOWER, DELPHINIUM, AND BELLFLOWER.*

PROBLEM: On roses, circular black spots with fringed margins that are ⅟₁₆ to ½ inch in diameter appear on upper leaf surfaces. The spots enlarge and coalesce, and infected leaves turn yellow and drop. Raised dark reddish or black blotches appear on young canes.

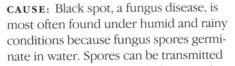

CAUSE: Black spot, a fungus disease, is most often found under humid and rainy conditions because fungus spores germinate in water. Spores can be transmitted by splashing water, clothing, garden tools, or hands. A severe infection can defoliate a rosebush. The fungus overwinters on infected canes, on fallen leaves, and inside leaf buds.

SOLUTION: Plant roses that are less susceptible in your area. Water early in the day and avoid splashing leaves. Prune canes of infected plants farther back than normal to eliminate fungus that survives over the winter, and apply a commercial lime-sulfur spray before leaves open. If symptoms appear, remove and destroy all infected leaves, including those on the ground. For light infestations, spray a solution of 1 tablespoon of baking soda and ¼ teaspoon of summer horticultural oil to 1 gallon of water every 5 to 7 days until symptoms disappear. For heavier infestation, remove the plant or spray with a fungicide to control fungus.
SUSCEPTIBLE PLANTS: ROSES.

PROBLEM: Small yellow to orange-brown or gray-brown spots appear on flowers, foliage, and stems, which may also look pinpricked or bruised. The spots then develop into blotches of fuzzy gray or brown mold. Flowers are distorted; buds may not open. Stem bases blacken and rot. Affected parts eventually turn brown and dry. Bulbs have dark, sunken areas and are covered with brown growth.

CAUSE: Botrytis blight, also known as gray mold, is a fungus disease that is most prevalent in damp spring-to-summer weather and often occurs if a plant has been stressed by a late freeze or frost or has suffered physical damage. The blight is spread by water and wind. It survives the winter as hard, black lumps in the soil or on dead plant parts.
SUSCEPTIBLE PLANTS: MANY PERENNIALS; MOST BULBS, ESPECIALLY TULIP; ROSES.

SOLUTION: Inspect bulbs for blight before purchase; use a pre-plant dip; plant in well-drained soil; water early in the day and avoid overhead watering; thin out plants to provide more light and air or transplant them to a drier location. Cut off and destroy all infected plant parts. Spray plants with fungicide in spring when shoots emerge to keep any disease from spreading.

PROBLEM: Brown, sunken spots with dark margins and lesions develop on rose canes and then encircle them. Leaves and flowers above the damaged area wilt and die.

CAUSE: Canker, a fungal disease, spreads in water and enters rose canes through cuts or wounds, especially those caused by pruning, cutting flowers too far from a bud, or canes rubbing against each other. One type of canker develops during cold weather when roses have been covered by winter protection.

SOLUTION: Prune infected canes ¼ inch above the node below the canker, disinfecting tools with alcohol after each cut. Removing infected canes promptly will help prevent the spread of the disease. There are no chemical preventives or cures. Choose hardy roses that don't need winter protection.
SUSCEPTIBLE PLANTS: ROSES.

PROBLEM: Corky growths, or galls, appear at the base of a rose, near the graft union, on roots, and occasionally on canes. Growths are white or light green at ground level when young and turn brown and woody as they age.

CAUSE: Crown gall is a disease caused by bacteria that live in the soil and enter a plant through wounds at the root area. The bacteria cause abnormal cell growth, which produces the galls, thus stunting the rose's normal growth.

SOLUTION: Inspect newly acquired plants for signs of gall and dispose of any diseased ones. Avoid wounding plants, especially near the soil line. Prune out and destroy galled canes, sterilizing the knife after each cut. Remove and destroy severely infected plants. Bacteria will remain in the soil for several years. *SUSCEPTIBLE PLANTS: ROSES.*

PROBLEM: Overnight, young seedlings suddenly topple over and die. Stems are rotted through at the soil line.

CAUSE: Damping-off is a disease caused by several soil fungi that infect seeds and the roots of seedlings at ground level. The problem often occurs in wet, poorly drained soil with a high nitrogen content.

SOLUTION: Use fresh or treated seeds. Plant in a sterile medium topped with a thin layer of sand or perlite to keep seedlings dry at the stem line. Plants in containers are more susceptible than those growing outdoors. Give them well-drained soil with plenty of light; avoid overcrowding. Do not overwater seed flats or seedbeds. *SUSCEPTIBLE PLANTS: VIRTUALLY ALL SEEDLINGS.*

PROBLEM: Leaves turn yellow. Angular pale green or yellow blotches appear on the leaf's upper surface, with gray or tan fuzzy growths that resemble tufts of cotton forming on the underside. Leaves wilt, turn brown, and die.

CAUSE: Downy mildew, caused by a fungus, thrives in cool, wet weather, often in late summer and early fall. *SUSCEPTIBLE PLANTS: PERENNIALS, INCLUDING ASTER, CINQUEFOIL, CRANESBILL, LUPINE, PURPLE CONEFLOWER; ROSES.*

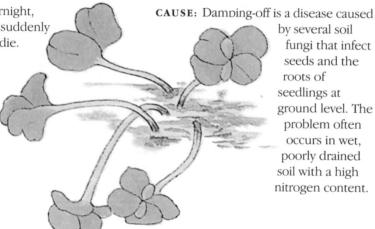

SOLUTION: Grow resistant species and cultivars. Promote dry conditions by not watering plants overhead after morning. Space plants and thin stems to encourage air circulation. Remove and destroy blighted plant parts or the entire plant if the infection is severe.

PROBLEM: Yellow blotches that progress to brown may appear on leaves. Damaged areas are bound by large leaf veins. Eventually the leaf dies and becomes brittle. Young foliage curls and twists; growth is stunted. Symptoms appear first on older leaves, then move up the plant. Flowers and buds may also be affected.

CAUSE: Foliar nematodes, microscopic worms, feed on the outside of young foliage and the inside of mature foliage, spending most of their time inside a leaf. They thrive in warm, wet summers. Wet conditons help them migrate on films of water to infect plants and soil.

SOLUTION: Remove and destroy infected plants. If plant is not severely infected, pull off affected leaves and their two closest healthy neighbors. In fall, cut plants to the ground and destroy stalks. Avoid watering foliage since splashing water can spread the disease. *SUSCEPTIBLE PLANTS: PERENNIALS, INCLUDING ALUMROOT, BERGENIA, CHRYSANTHEMUM, HOSTA, IRIS, LILY, PEONY, PHLOX, SOLOMON'S-SEAL, WINDFLOWER.*

PROBLEM: Leaves develop small yellow spots that gradually turn brown, frequently surrounded by a ring of yellow or brownish black tissue. Spots often join to produce large, irregular blotches. The leaf may turn yellow, wilt, and drop. Extensive defoliation can occur, weakening plant. The problem usually starts on lower leaves and moves up.

CAUSE: Leaf-spot diseases, caused by various fungi and bacteria, are spread by air currents and splashing water. Most prevalent from summer into fall, they thrive when humidity is high. *SUSCEPTIBLE PLANTS: VIRTUALLY ALL ANNUALS; PERENNIALS, INCLUDING ASTER, CARDINAL FLOWER, CHRYSANTHEMUM, CRANESBILL, DELPHINIUM, FOXGLOVE, MONKSHOOD, PHLOX, POPPY; IRIS.*

SOLUTION: Remove and destroy infected leaves as they appear; do not leave infected material in the garden over the winter. Water only in the morning. Thin plants to encourage good air circulation. A fungicide can protect healthy foliage but will not destroy fungus on infected leaves.

PROBLEM: White or pale gray powdery growth appears on upper leaves and is followed by leaf distortion, yellowing, withering, and leaf drop. The powdery growth may also be seen on stems, buds, and shoots.

CAUSE: Powdery mildew, a fungal disease, is especially noticeable in late summer and early fall when cool, humid nights follow warm days. Unlike most fungal diseases, powdery mildew does not spread readily under wet conditions. More unsightly than harmful, it rarely kills the plant.

SOLUTION: Grow mildew-resistant varieties. Place susceptible plants in areas with good air circulation, mist frequently, and spray with baking-soda solution or a fungicide. *SUSCEPTIBLE PLANTS: ANNUALS: ANNUAL PHLOX, BELLFLOWER, FUCHSIA, MONKEY FLOWER, SPIDER FLOWER, SWEET PEA, VERBENA, AND ZINNIA; PERENNIALS: ASTER, BLANKET-FLOWER, CHRYSANTHEMUM, COLUMBINE, DELPHINIUM, PEONY.*

PROBLEM: Leaves turn blue, red, or yellow, then wilt and die. Growth is stunted. Flowers do not develop. Bulbs are either soft and mushy with a bad smell, or hard and dried out. They may be covered with sunken lesions. White, pink, gray, or black mold may form on bulbs or on the stem near the soil line. Roots become dark and slimy.

CAUSE: Root rot and bulb rot—specifically, bacterial soft rot, fusarium basal rot, and pythium root rot—are fungal and bacterial diseases that may occur either while the bulb is in the ground or during storage. Cultivar susceptibility and stressful conditions such as water-logged soil are the major causes. Rot occurs most often in warm, wet soil when bulbs are not actively growing, a time when spores multiply rapidly.
SUSCEPTIBLE PLANTS: MOST BULBS.

SOLUTION: Discard infected bulbs and all the soil for 6 inches around them. Be careful not to cut or bruise bulbs when digging or handling them; bulbs naturally carry the spores on their surface, and damage makes them highly susceptible to invasion. Good drainage is essential. Store bulbs properly; immediately after digging and cleaning, dry thoroughly, then pack and store according to the requirements of each type. Examine bulbs for white mold or brown splotches near the basal plate and for overall softness. Choose resistant cultivars. Never put fertilizer in a hole immediately before planting a bulb; it will burn the roots and cause root rot.

PROBLEM: Upper leaf surfaces have pale yellow or white spots; undersides of leaves are covered with orange or yellow raised pustules. Leaves wilt and hang down along the stem. Pustules may become more numerous, destroying leaves and occasionally the entire plant. Plants may be stunted in severe cases.

CAUSE: Rust, a disease caused by a fungus, is a problem in the late summer and early fall, and is most prevalent when nights are cool and humid.

SOLUTION: Grow resistant varieties. Water early in the day; avoid wetting leaves. Remove and destroy infected leaves. In fall, cut infected plants to the ground and destroy stalks. Spray with sulfur or a garden fungicide.
SUSCEPTIBLE PLANTS: MANY PERENNIALS, INCLUDING ORNAMENTAL GRASSES, CLEMATIS, BEE BALM, CHRYSANTHEMUM, COLUMBINE, CONEFLOWER, COREOPSIS, DELPHINIUM, DIANTHUS, GAY-FEATHER, HOLLYHOCK, IRIS, LUPINE, PHLOX, SEA LAVENDER.

PROBLEM: Plant is wilted, yellowed, or stunted, and it may die. Sometimes roots have knots or galls.

CAUSE: Soil nematodes—colorless, microscopic worms that live in the soil and feed on roots—inhibit a plant's intake of nitrogen. Damage is at its worst in warm, sunlit, sandy soils that are moist.

SOLUTION: Only a lab test can detect nematodes. Be wary of swollen or stunted roots. There are no chemical controls; dispose of infected plants and the surrounding soil, or solarize the soil by fixing a sheet of clear plastic over the ground and leaving it in place 1 to 2 months. Grow resistant varieties; rotate or interplant with plants that repel nematodes, such as marigolds. Add nitrogen fertilizer.
SUSCEPTIBLE PLANTS: MOST PERENNIALS, ESPECIALLY CHRYSANTHEMUM, CLEMATIS, CRANESBILL, DAYLILY, GLADIOLUS, IRIS, PHLOX, AND VIOLET; ROSES.

PROBLEM: Leaves and stems turn yellow, wilt, rot, and die. Crowns may mold. Stems blacken and rot at base. White fibers and small tan lumps are visible at the base of the plant. Roots show signs of decay.

CAUSE: Southern blight, a disease caused by a fungus, enters the stems at soil level. It is most prevalent in hot weather.

SOLUTION: Remove and discard all infected plants and the soil that surrounds them. Thin out overcrowded plants, improve soil drainage, and avoid overwatering by letting soil dry out somewhat between waterings. Organic matter helps reduce disease. *SUSCEPTIBLE PLANTS: PERENNIALS: BALLOON FLOWER, BUGLEWEED, COLUMBINE, DELPHINIUM, HOSTA, IRIS, PURPLE CONEFLOWER, TORCH LILY.*

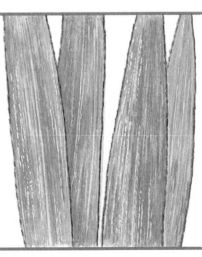

PROBLEM: Entire plant becomes yellow, wilts, fails to grow, and eventually dies. Symptoms usually appear first on the lower and outer plant parts. A cut made across the stem near the base reveals dark streaks or other discoloration on the tissue inside.

CAUSE: Vascular wilt caused by fusarium and verticillium fungi in the soil display similar symptoms. Fusarium wilt is more prevalent in hot weather, and verticillium wilt is found in cool weather.

SOLUTION: Remove and destroy infected plants; substitute wilt-resistant varieties. Wash hands and disinfect tools. There are no effective chemical controls. Fungus stays in the soil a long time, so transplant susceptible plants away from infected area. Solarize the soil by fixing a sheet of clear plastic over the ground and leaving it in place 1 to 2 months. *SUSCEPTIBLE PLANTS: ANNUALS, INCLUDING CAPE MARIGOLD, COLEUS, DAHLIA, IMPATIENS; PERENNIALS, INCLUD*

PROBLEM: Leaves become streaked with yellow to green, eventually turning completely yellow. Leaves may curl or become distorted. Flowers are smaller than normal and may be streaked or spotted with yellow, blue, or green. The plant may be stunted or cease to grow.

CAUSE: Infection by mosaic, yellows, ring spot, and tulip-breaking viruses.

SOLUTION: There are no chemical controls for viruses. Remove and destroy infected bulbs. Disinfect gardening tools with rubbing alcohol after working on infected plants. To help prevent virus, control aphids, which spread viral diseases. Plant virus-resistant species of lilies. *SUSCEPTIBLE PLANTS: MOST BULBS, ESPECIALLY DAFFODIL, LILY, AND TULIP.*

Zone and Frost Maps of the U. S.

To determine if a plant will flourish in your climate, first locate your zone on the map below and check it against the zone information given in the Plant Selection Guides that follow each chapter or in the Encyclopedia entries that begin on page 273. For annuals and biennials, planting dates depend on when frosts occur: Hardy annuals can be safely sown 6 weeks before the last spring frost, whereas tender annuals should be sown only after all danger of frost is past. Also, while cool-season annuals can withstand some frost, warm-season plants can be grown without protection only in the frost-free period between the last and first frosts. Used together, the zone map and the frost date maps shown opposite will help you select plants suited to your area and determine when to plant them. Frost dates vary widely within each region, however, so check with your weather service or Cooperative Extension Service for more precise figures, and record the temperatures in your own garden from year to year.

Zone 1: Below -50° F
Zone 2: -50° to -40°
Zone 3: -40° to -30°
Zone 4: -30° to -20°
Zone 5: -20° to -10°
Zone 6: -10° to 0°
Zone 7: 0° to 10°
Zone 8: 10° to 20°
Zone 9: 20° to 30°
Zone 10: 30° to 40°
Zone 11: Above 40°

AVERAGE DATES OF LAST SPRING FROST

JUNE
MAY
APRIL
MARCH
FEBRUARY
JANUARY

AVERAGE DATES OF FIRST FALL FROST

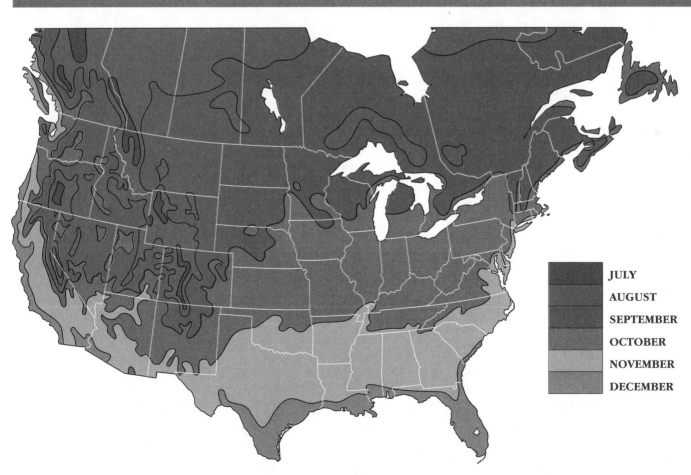

JULY
AUGUST
SEPTEMBER
OCTOBER
NOVEMBER
DECEMBER

Encyclopedia of Plants

Presented on the following pages is information on most of the plants mentioned in this volume. Each genus is listed alphabetically by its Latin botanical name, followed by a pronunciation of the Latin and the genus's common name. (If you know a plant only by its common name, see the index.) A botanical name consists of the genus and, usually, a species, both written in italics. Species often have common names of their own, which are given in parentheses in each entry, and many species have one or more cultivars, which are set off by single quotation marks.

Information is given for plant hardiness, flowering season, height, flower color, and soil and light needs. Selected species and varieties are discussed, as well as a plant's optimum growing conditions and maintenance requirements.

ANNUALS & BIENNIALS, pages 273-301

Entries designate these plants as either annuals, biennials, or tender perennials. Since the planting dates for most annuals and biennials depend on the dates of the last spring frost and the first fall frost, refer to the maps on page 271 to determine which plants will grow most successfully in your region.

PERENNIALS, pages 302-334

Perennials are likely to have a home in your garden for a long time to come, so use the information in the entries on the following pages to choose those plants that are the most compatible with your garden's conditions and fulfill your desires for a garden design.

BULBS, pages 335-357

In addition to identifying whether a plant is a true bulb, rhizome, corm, or tuber, the entries that follow designate some bulbs as "tender"; these bulbs are able to survive winter in the ground only in warm zones. Elsewhere, they must be dug up in fall and stored for the winter or grown in containers.

ROSES, pages 358-371

The roses presented in this section have been chosen for their enduring appeal, availability, bloom colors, and landscape uses. Many are notable for disease resistance, winter-hardiness, or low-maintenance requirements—and sometimes all three. The American Rose Society's (ARS) evaluation of overall quality is given for each rose that has received a rating. Winners of the coveted All-American Rose Selections (AARS) award are also identified.

Ageratum
(aj-er-AY-tum)
FLOSSFLOWER

Ageratum houstonianum 'Blue Horizon'

Plant type: *annual*

Height: *6 to 30 inches*

Interest: *flowers, foliage*

Soil: *moist, well-drained*

Light: *full sun*

A profusion of fluffy flowers with thread-like petals crown flossflower's clumps of heart-shaped leaves. With soft colors and a compact mounding habit, dwarf varieties create excellent garden edgings. Taller varieties combine well with other flowers in the middle or back of a border and are good candidates for indoor arrangements.

Selected species and varieties: *A. houstonianum* bears tiny blue or bluish purple flowers in dense, fuzzy clusters from summer through fall; white- and pink-flowered varieties are available; 'Blue Horizon' grows to 30 inches with deep blue flowers that are excellent for cutting; 'Capri' grows to a uniform 12 inches, producing bicolored flowers that are medium blue with white centers, and it is heat tolerant; 'Summer Snow' grows 6 to 8 inches tall with pure white flowers that begin early and continue to frost.

Growing conditions and maintenance: Sow seed indoors 6 to 8 weeks before the last expected frost. Space plants 6 to 12 inches apart. Pinching early growth will promote compactness, and removing spent blooms will encourage continuous production of flowers.

Agrostemma
(ag-roe-STEM-a)
CORN COCKLE

Agrostemma githago

Plant type: *annual or biennial*

Height: *1 to 4 feet*

Interest: *flowers, foliage*

Soil: *poor, well-drained*

Light: *full sun*

Corn cockles are troublefree plants from Europe that have naturalized throughout the eastern United States. They provide a long season of bright blooms for borders. Abundant 1- to 2-inch flowers in shades of pink, lilac, cherry red, or magenta top their stems throughout the summer. Their old-fashioned appearance is effective massed or in combination with other flowers in a cottage garden. Blooms are excellent for cutting.

Selected species and varieties: *A. githago* is a hardy annual with willowy stems up to 4 feet tall and narrow leaves covered with a silvery down; each flower has five petals that sport delicate stripes or spots seeming to radiate from the center; the black seeds are plentiful—and poisonous.

Growing conditions and maintenance: Corn cockle is easy to grow. Sow seed in place in late fall or early spring. Thin plants to stand 6 to 12 inches apart. They tolerate dry conditions and almost any soil. Deadhead to encourage reblooming and prevent excessive self-seeding.

Amaranthus
(am-a-RAN-thus)
AMARANTH

Amaranthus caudatus

Plant type: *annual*

Height: *18 inches to 6 feet*

Interest: *flowers, foliage*

Soil: *dry to well-drained*

Light: *full sun*

Amaranths are large, brilliantly colored plants that hail from the tropics of the Far East. They add a bold touch to borders with their long-lasting tasseled flowers and colorful leaves. Tall types are effective as accents, while shorter selections are suited to beds or containers. Flowers are suitable for both fresh and dried arrangements.

Selected species and varieties: *A. caudatus* (love-lies-bleeding) grows 3 to 5 feet tall with green or red leaves and huge drooping tassels of red flowers that may reach 2 feet in length; 'Viridis' grows 2 to 3½ feet with greenish yellow flower tassels. *A. cruentus* (purple amaranth, prince's-feather) produces huge 12-inch leaves along erect 6-foot stems, and drooping red or purple flower spikes. *A. tricolor* (Joseph's-coat amaranth, tampala) grows from 1½ to 5 feet tall with variegated leaves up to 6 inches long that sport shades of green, red, and gold.

Growing conditions and maintenance: Seed requires very warm temperatures and can be started indoors 4 to 6 weeks prior to the last frost. In warm areas sow seed directly. Thin to allow 1 to 2 feet between plants. Water sparingly.

Antirrhinum
(an-tir-RYE-num)
SNAPDRAGON

Antirrhinum majus 'White Sonnet'

Plant type: *tender perennial*
Height: *6 inches to 4 feet*
Interest: *flowers*
Soil: *well-drained, fertile*
Light: *full sun to partial shade*

Snapdragons, with their wide range of heights and flower colors and long season of bloom, have been cultivated since ancient times. Short varieties add color to rock gardens and edgings, while taller types are well suited to the middle and rear of mixed borders, where they provide a vertical accent. They are outstanding in fresh arrangements.

Selected species and varieties: *A. majus* bears terminal clusters of flowers that open from the bottom up. Each bloom has five lobes, divided into an upper and a lower lip. Varieties are classified by height: small (6-12 inches), intermediate (12-24 inches), and tall (2-4 feet); 'Black Prince' is 18 inches with deep crimson flowers and bronze foliage; 'Madame Butterfly' grows to 3 feet with flaring blossoms in a range of colors; 'White Sonnet' is 22 inches with white flowers that are superb for cutting.

Growing conditions and maintenance: Start seed indoors in late winter for transplanting in mid- to late spring. Space plants 6 to 18 inches apart. Deadhead to encourage continuous flowering. Taller types may need staking. Perennial in Zones 8 to 11.

Asclepias
(as-KLEE-pee-as)
MILKWEED

Asclepias curassavica

Plant type: *tender perennial*
Height: *2 to 6 feet*
Interest: *flowers, seedpods*
Soil: *moist to dry*
Light: *full sun*

Often referred to as weeds in South America, *Asclepias* species are suited to the rear of a herbaceous border, where their clusters of flowers put on a fine display from summer until frost. Flowers are followed by attractive seedpods that are useful in dried arrangements.

Selected species and varieties: *A. curassavica* (bloodflower) develops sturdy branched stems 2 to 4 feet tall and narrow 5-inch dark green leaves that clasp the stems in pairs. The 6-inch flower clusters arise from branch tips and axils and are made up of many tiny purplish red and orange flowers. Flowers are followed by 4-inch brown seedpods. *A. fruticosa* (gomphocarpus) grows 3 to 6 feet tall and bears creamy white flowers and spiny silvery green pods.

Growing conditions and maintenance: Start seed indoors in midwinter for transplanting to the garden after all danger of frost has past. Space plants 15 to 18 inches apart and pinch when they reach 4 to 6 inches to promote branching. Plants thrive in warm weather and can be grown as perennials from Zone 8 south.

Begonia
(be-GO-nee-a)
WAX BEGONIA

Begonia 'Cocktail Series'

Plant type: *tender perennial*
Height: *5 to 16 inches*
Interest: *flowers, foliage*
Soil: *moist, fertile*
Light: *partial shade to shade*

Wax begonias add color to the shady garden with both their perpetual clusters of delicate flowers and their glossy rounded leaves. Flowers range from white to pink to red, and leaves may be green, bronze, or variegated green and white. They are useful for edging, massing, and growing in containers both indoors and outside.

Selected species and varieties: *B.* x *semperflorens-cultorum* (bedding begonia) has a mounding habit and produces flowers nonstop from spring until frost. In Zones 9 and 10 they bloom almost year round. Selections vary in both flower and leaf color, flower size, and height; 'Cocktail Series' offers white, pink, rose, salmon, and red flowers on dwarf 5- to 6-inch plants with glossy bronze foliage; 'Pizzazz Mixed' grows to 10 inches with large red, pink, or white flowers and glossy green leaves.

Growing conditions and maintenance: Start seed 4 to 6 months prior to the last frost, or purchase bedding plants in spring. Plants can also be propagated by cuttings. Space 8 to 12 inches apart. Although the ideal site is filtered shade, plants will tolerate full sun if given sufficient water, especially in cooler regions.

Borago
(bor-RAY-go)
BORAGE

Borago officinalis

Plant type: *annual*

Height: *2 to 3 feet*

Interest: *flowers, foliage*

Soil: *well-drained*

Light: *full sun to light shade*

This European native makes an attractive addition to flower or herb gardens, fresh flower arrangements, and summer salads. Both leaves and flowers are edible, with a refreshing cucumber-like flavor, and can be used to garnish salads or fruit cups. It has a somewhat sprawling habit that is best suited to an informal garden, where its soft-textured leaves and sky blue flowers add a cool, gentle touch.

Selected species and varieties: *B. officinalis* (talewort, cool-tankard) is a hardy annual with a rounded, sprawling habit, bristly gray-green foliage, and succulent stems. Flowers are arranged in drooping clusters. Each is ¾ inch across and star shaped, with five petals. Though usually clear blue, they are sometimes light purple. Flower buds are covered with fine hairs.

Growing conditions and maintenance: Sow seed directly in the garden at monthly intervals beginning 2 to 3 weeks prior to the last frost for continuous summer bloom. Once established, plant will self-seed. Allow 12 to 18 inches between plants. Where summers are very hot, afternoon shade is recommended. Borage tolerates drought.

Brachycome
(bra-KIK-o-me)
SWAN RIVER DAISY

Brachycome iberidifolia

Plant type: *annual*

Height: *9 to 14 inches*

Interest: *flowers*

Soil: *moist, well-drained, fertile*

Light: *full sun*

The Swan River daisy is a tender annual from Australia with a neat, mounding habit and colorful daisylike flowers. Although small, the brightly colored flowers are produced in masses, making this plant a good choice for rock gardens, edgings, and containers, including hanging baskets.

Selected species and varieties: *B. iberidifolia* grows to 14 inches tall with a compact habit and a 12-inch spread. The delicate pale green leaves are 3 inches long and are borne on slender stems. Flowers are about 1 inch across and appear for 4 to 6 weeks in the summer, tapering off toward the end of the season. Colors include white, pink, lavender, and blue.

Growing conditions and maintenance: Start seed indoors 5 to 6 weeks prior to the last frost, or sow directly in the garden when the soil has warmed. Successive plantings will lengthen the flowering season. Allow 6 to 12 inches between plants. Water during dry spells.

Brassica
(BRASS-i-ka)
ORNAMENTAL CABBAGE

Brassica oleracea

Plant type: *biennial*

Height: *10 to 15 inches*

Interest: *foliage*

Soil: *moist, well-drained*

Light: *full sun*

This ornamental cousin of the familiar vegetable side dish is highly valued for the splash of color it provides in the fall and winter landscape. A biennial, it is grown as an annual for its brightly colored and intricately curled foliage, which grows in a flowerlike rosette.

Selected species and varieties: *B. oleracea,* Acephala group (ornamental kale) does not form heads but produces an open rosette of leaves that typically spreads 12 inches across. Foliage colors include lavender-blue, white, green, red, purple, pink, and assorted variegations. Color improves in cool weather. Leaves of 'Cherry Sundae' are a blend of carmine and cream; 'Color Up' displays a center of red, pink, cream, white, and green surrounded by green margins; 'Peacock' series has feathery notched and serrated leaves in a variety of colors.

Growing conditions and maintenance: For spring planting, start seed indoors 4 to 6 weeks prior to the last frost. For fall gardens, start seed 6 to 8 weeks prior to the first anticipated frost. Space plants 18 to 24 inches apart. Plants will last all winter in Zones 8 to 10.

Browallia
(bro-WALL-ee-a)
BUSH VIOLET

Browallia speciosa

Plant type: *tender perennial*

Height: *8 to 16 inches*

Interest: *flowers*

Soil: *moist, well-drained*

Light: *partial shade to shade*

A good choice for the shady border, bush violet bears clusters of blue, violet, or white flowers from early to late summer. It has a low-growing rounded habit that is well suited for use as an edging, and it's an outstanding choice for window boxes or hanging baskets, where it cascades gracefully over the edge. In fall, plants can be cut back severely and potted to be grown as flowering houseplants through the winter.

Selected species and varieties: *B. speciosa* has a rounded to sprawling habit with 1½- to 2-inch long-throated, star-shaped flowers; 'Blue Bells' bears blue-violet flowers with prominent white centers; 'Jingle Bells' bears flowers in a mixture of colors including shades of blue, white, and lavender; 'Silver Bells' bears large white blooms.

Growing conditions and maintenance: Start seeds indoors about 8 weeks prior to the last frost. Plant in the garden after all danger of frost is past, spacing plants 8 inches apart. Avoid overwatering and overfertilizing.

Calendula
(ka-LEN-dew-la)
POT MARIGOLD

Calendula officinalis

Plant type: *annual*

Height: *12 to 24 inches*

Interest: *flowers*

Soil: *moist, well-drained*

Light: *full sun*

The long-lasting blooms of pot marigolds are daisylike with flattened, wide-spreading rays ranging in color from deep orange to yellow or cream. They are a good choice for mixed beds, containers, or indoor arrangements. Native to the Mediterranean, this hardy annual has long been grown as an ornamental and used as a flavoring for puddings and cakes.

Selected species and varieties: *C. officinalis* has a neat, mounding habit and grows 1 to 2 feet tall with a similar spread. Leaves are 2 to 6 inches long, blue-green, and aromatic. The solitary 2½- to 4½-inch flower heads close at night; 'Bon-Bon' grows 12 inches tall with a compact, early-blooming habit and a mixture of flower colors.

Growing conditions and maintenance: Start seed indoors 6 to 8 weeks prior to the last frost, for transplanting to the garden after the last hard frost. In areas with mild winters it can be sown directly outdoors in fall or early spring. Space plants 12 to 18 inches apart. Deadhead to increase flowering. Calendulas thrive in cool conditions and tolerate poor soils if they have adequate water.

Canna
(CAN-ah)
CANNA

Canna x generalis 'Lerape'

Plant type: *tender perennial*

Height: *18 inches to 6 feet*

Interest: *flowers*

Soil: *moist, well-drained*

Light: *full sun*

Cannas produce 4- to 5-inch flowers with a tousled arrangement of petal-like stamens from summer through frost. Bold leaves provide a dramatic backdrop to the flowers. They are well suited to the back of borders and to massing. Grow dwarf cultivars as edgings or in patio containers.

Selected species and varieties: *C. x generalis* (canna lily) is available in standard varieties that grow 4 to 6 feet tall or dwarfs that are less than 3 feet. The flowers are carried on stiff, erect stems; colors include red, orange, salmon, yellow, pink, white, and bicolors. The broad leaves, up to 24 inches long, are usually a deep glossy green but are sometimes bronzy red or striped or veined in white or pink; 'Lerape' bears yellow flowers with bright orange spots; 'Seven Dwarfs Mixed' grows to 18 inches with a wide range of flower colors.

Growing conditions and maintenance: Soak seed prior to planting indoors in midwinter, or start rhizomes indoors 4 weeks before the last frost and move them to the garden when night temperatures reach 60° F. In Zones 9 and 10, plant directly in the garden in spring, spaced 1 to 2 feet apart.

Capsicum
(KAP-si-kum)
PEPPER

Capsicum annuum 'Treasure Red'

Plant type: *tender perennial*

Height: *6 to 20 inches*

Interest: *fruit*

Soil: *moist, well-drained, fertile*

Light: *full sun*

Bushy, rounded pepper plants produce brightly colored fruit that is well displayed against dark green leaves. In its native environment of tropical North and South America, peppers are woody perennials, but in temperate climates they are treated as annuals. Ornamental varieties make tidy and colorful edgings for beds and are superb for containers.

Selected species and varieties: *C. annuum* (ornamental pepper) has a bushy, compact habit with evergreen leaves from 1 to 5 inches long. Flowers are white and small. Fruit ranges from ¾ to 2 inches long and may be red, purple, yellow, green, black, cream, or variegated; 'Holiday Cheer' grows to 8 inches with round 1-inch fruit that turns from cream to red; 'Red Missile' grows to 10 inches with tapered 2-inch fruit; 'Treasure Red' grows 8 inches tall with conical fruit that turns from white to bright red.

Growing conditions and maintenance: Start seed indoors in late winter to transplant to the garden after all danger of frost has past. Space plants to stand 8 to 15 inches apart. Dig and pot plants in the fall to grow as houseplants; perennial in Zones 10 and 11.

Catharanthus
(kath-ah-RAN-thus)
PERIWINKLE

Catharanthus roseus

Plant type: *tender perennial*

Height: *3 to 18 inches*

Interest: *flowers, foliage*

Soil: *moist, well-drained*

Light: *sun to partial shade*

Periwinkle provides summer-to-fall color for temperate gardens. Its flowers resemble those of *Vinca,* and it is available in both creeping and upright varieties. Use it as a summer ground cover or in mass plantings, annual borders, or containers.

Selected species and varieties: *C. roseus* [sometimes listed as *Vinca rosea*] (Madagascar periwinkle) produces glossy oblong leaves, 1 to 3 inches long. Creeping varieties grow 3 inches tall, spreading 18 to 24 inches across. Erect strains grow 8 to 18 inches tall. Flowers are 1½ inches wide and cover the plant throughout the summer; colors range from shades of pink or mauve to white; 'Parasol' produces large 1½- to 2-inch white flowers with pink eyes on 12- to 18-inch plants; 'Tropicana' grows to 12 inches and produces flowers in several shades of pink from pale blush to deep rose, with contrasting eyes.

Growing conditions and maintenance: Start seed indoors 10 to 12 weeks prior to the last frost for late-spring transplanting to the garden; space 1 to 2 feet apart. Plants can also be started from cuttings. They thrive in warm, humid conditions and are perennial in Zones 9 to 11.

Celosia
(sel-OH-see-a)
CELOSIA

Celosia cristata 'Pink Tassels'

Plant type: *annual*

Height: *6 to 24 inches*

Interest: *flowers, foliage*

Soil: *moist to dry, well-drained*

Light: *full sun*

These vibrant annuals are native to the tropics of Asia. Their crested or plumed flowers are extremely long-lasting, making them ideal for bedding and cutting for both fresh and dried arrangements.

Selected species and varieties: *C. cristata* displays a range of heights and flower types. Leaves may be green, purple, or variegated. Flowers appear from midsummer to fall and are usually deep shades of red, orange, yellow, or gold. The species is divided according to flower type: Childsii group (crested cockscomb) produces crested or convoluted flower heads that resemble lumps of coral. Plumosa group (feather amaranth) bears feathery 6- to 12-inch flower heads. Spicata group bears flowers in slender spikes; 'Pink Tassels' bears long pale pink spikes with bright pink tips.

Growing conditions and maintenance: Start seed indoors 4 to 6 weeks before transplanting to the garden after all danger of frost has passed. In warm areas, sow directly outside. Space plants 6 to 18 inches apart. Celosias thrive in warm weather and tolerate dry soils. For use in winter arrangements, cut flowers at their peak and hang them upside down to dry.

Centaurea
(sen-TOR-ee-a)
KNAPWEED

Centaurea cyanus

Cheiranthus
(ky-RAN-thus)
WALLFLOWER

Cheiranthus cheiri 'Bowles' Mauve'

Chrysanthemum
(kri-SAN-the-mum)
CHRYSANTHEMUM

Chrysanthemum coronarium 'Primrose Gem'

Plant type: *annual*

Height: *1 to 6 feet*

Interest: *flowers*

Soil: *well-drained*

Light: *full sun*

Plant type: *tender perennial*

Height: *6 to 24 inches*

Interest: *flowers*

Soil: *well-drained, fertile*

Light: *full sun*

Plant type: *annual*

Height: *1 to 3 feet*

Interest: *flowers*

Soil: *well-drained*

Light: *full sun to partial shade*

The tufted blooms of these popular annuals come in shades of pink, blue, lavender, yellow, and white. Sprinkle them liberally in informal borders, wildflower gardens, and the cutting garden. They can be used for both fresh and dried arrangements.

Selected species and varieties: *C. americana* (basket flower) grows up to 6 feet tall with sturdy stems and 4- to 5-inch pink flowers with cream centers and a fringe of thistlelike bracts. *C. cyanus* (bachelor's-button, cornflower) produces gray-green leaves on erect stems to 3 feet; perky 1-inch flowers appear from early summer until frost and are available in many colors. *C. moschata* (sweet-sultan) grows 2 to 3 feet with 2- to 3-inch musk-scented flowers; the hybrid 'Imperialis' grows to 4 feet with pink, purple, or white flowers.

Growing conditions and maintenance: Sow seed in place in late winter or early spring; in areas with mild winters it can also be sown in fall. Space 6 to 12 inches apart. Once established plants often self-seed. For continuous bloom, make successive plantings 2 weeks apart throughout the season.

This Eurasian native bridges the flowering season between early bulbs and bedding plants. Fragrant 1-inch flowers are borne in clusters resembling stock; colors include deep shades of yellow, orange, red, purple, and brown. Dwarf varieties are perfect for rock gardens or growing in gaps of stone walls. Plant taller types in borders.

Selected species and varieties: *C. cheiri* (English wallflower) has a low, erect habit; dwarf varieties grow 6 to 9 inches, while tall varieties may reach 2 feet. Early-flowering strains often bloom their first year from seed, but most varieties are treated as biennials; 'Bowles' Mauve' produces large clusters of deep pink flowers.

Growing conditions and maintenance: Sow seed outdoors in spring or fall for bloom the following season. Provide winter protection in areas with severe winters. Early-flowering varieties can be started indoors in midwinter, hardened in a cold frame, and transplanted to the garden as soon as the soil can be worked in spring. Space plants about 12 inches apart. Wallflowers thrive in cool climates and do well in coastal and mountainous areas such as the Pacific Northwest.

Annual chrysanthemums, which hail from the Mediterranean region, supply the summer and fall border with a nonstop production of colorful daisylike flowers. They are also cheerful and dependable cut flowers.

Selected species and varieties: *C. carinatum* (tricolor chrysanthemum) grows 2 to 3 feet tall with dark green toothed leaves. It derives its common name from its 2½-inch flower heads that are white with a yellow band surrounding a purple or chocolate brown central disk; 'Court Jesters' produces red, pink, orange, yellow, maroon, and white flowers with red or orange bands. *C. coronarium* (crown daisy, garland chrysanthemum) grows 1 to 2½ feet tall with coarsely cut leaves and yellow and white flowers, 1 to 2 inches across, which may be single, semidouble, or double; 'Primrose Gem' bears semidouble soft yellow blooms with darker yellow centers.

Growing conditions and maintenance: These plants are easily grown from seed planted directly in the garden as soon as soil can be worked in the spring. Thin plants to stand 12 to 18 inches apart. Once established they will self-seed.

Clarkia
(KLAR-kee-a)
GODETIA

Clarkia amoena

Plant type: *annual*

Height: *1 to 3 feet*

Interest: *flowers*

Soil: *dry, sandy*

Light: *full sun to partial shade*

Clarkias are free-flowering annuals from the coastal ranges of the western United States. They are named after the explorer William Clark, who collected their seed during the Lewis and Clark expedition. These species are also listed under the genus *Godetia.*

Selected species and varieties: *C. amoena* (farewell-to-spring, satin-flower) grows 1 to 3 feet tall. Throughout summer, 2- to 4-inch cup-shaped flowers appear in the axils of the upper leaves. Petals number four and are pink to lavender with a bright red or pink splash at the base; the four sepals are red. *C. concinna* (red-ribbons) grows 1 to 2 feet tall and bears rose-purple flowers with deeply cut fan-shaped petals in late spring and early summer. *C. purpurea* grows to 3 feet tall with 1-inch flowers in shades of purple, lavender, red, and pink, often with a dark eye.

Growing conditions and maintenance: Sow seed outdoors in fall where winters are mild, and elsewhere in spring as soon as the soil can be worked. Sow fairly heavily since crowding will encourage flowering. Plants perform best where nights are cool.

Cleome
(klee-O-me)
SPIDER FLOWER

Cleome hasslerana 'Helen Campbell'

Plant type: *annual*

Height: *3 to 4 feet*

Interest: *flowers, seedpods*

Soil: *moist, well-drained*

Light: *full sun to light shade*

Enormous clusters of 1-inch flowers top the stems of cleome continuously from summer until frost. Pink, lavender, or white flower petals surround 2- to 3-inch-long stamens that protrude from the center, creating a spiderlike effect further enhanced by the slender, conspicuous seedpods that follow the flowers. Cleome makes a graceful summer hedge, accent, or border plant.

Selected species and varieties: *C. hasslerana* [also known as *C. spinosa*] has an erect habit with dark green palmately compound leaves and airy, ball-shaped flower heads. While flowers are short-lived, new ones are produced continuously at the top of the stem; 'Cherry Queen' bears rose red flowers; 'Helen Campbell' has white blooms; 'Pink Queen' bears clear pink blossoms; the flowers of 'Violet Queen' are purple, and leaves display a purple tint at their edges.

Growing conditions and maintenance: Start seed indoors 4 to 6 weeks prior to the last frost, or plant directly in the garden in early spring. Plants often self-seed. Space plants about 24 inches apart. Cleome thrives in warm weather and responds well to abundant moisture.

Consolida
(kon-SO-li-da)
LARKSPUR

Consolida ambigua

Plant type: *annual*

Height: *1 to 4 feet*

Interest: *flowers*

Soil: *well-drained, fertile*

Light: *full sun to light shade*

This native of southern Europe produces dense clusters of flowers upon stately, erect spikes. The flowers are available in shades of blue, lilac, pink, red, purple, and white and are quite long-lasting. Plant tall types toward the rear of a border, where they provide a graceful vertical accent and a fine source of fresh-cut flowers. Shorter varieties can be placed in the mid- or foreground of a mixed border.

Selected species and varieties: *C. ambigua* (rocket larkspur) produces lacy, deeply cut leaves. Spurred flowers in many pastel shades are borne in dense, graceful spikes throughout the summer; 'Imperial Blue Bell' grows to 4 feet with double blue flowers; 'Imperial White King' is similar with double white flowers.

Growing conditions and maintenance: Start seed indoors in peat pots 6 to 8 weeks prior to the last frost. Seed can be sown directly outdoors in fall from Zone 7 south and or in early spring elsewhere. Space plants to stand 8 to 15 inches apart. Tall varieties often require staking. Plants thrive in cool conditions, and where summers are warm will benefit from light shade. Keep soil evenly moist throughout the growing season.

Coreopsis
(ko-ree-OP-sis)
TICKSEED

Coreopsis tinctoria

Plant type: *annual*

Height: *2 to 3 feet*

Interest: *flowers*

Soil: *well-drained to dry*

Light: *full sun*

This easy-to-grow annual is native to the eastern United States and is a common component of wildflower mixtures. Daisylike flower heads are borne on wiry stems and appear throughout the summer to early fall. Colors include yellow, orange, red, mahogany, and bicolors. Plant them in mixed borders and wildflower gardens, and cut them for fresh indoor arrangements.

Selected species and varieties: *C. tinctoria* (calliopsis) produces wiry, multiply branched stems with opposite-lobed or dissected leaves. Flower heads may be solitary or appear in branched clusters. Ray flowers are notched and often banded, surrounding a dark red or purple center. Double-flowered and dwarf varieties are available.

Growing conditions and maintenance: Start seed indoors 6 to 8 weeks before the last frost or sow directly in the garden in early spring. Space plants 6 to 8 inches apart. Make a second sowing in midsummer for fall flowers. Deadhead to prolong flowering. Plants tolerate hot weather and drought.

Cosmos
(KOS-mos)
COSMOS

Cosmos bipinnatus 'Sonata White'

Plant type: *annual*

Height: *10 inches to 6 feet*

Interest: *flowers*

Soil: *well-drained to dry*

Light: *full sun to light shade*

Daisylike flowers crown the wiry stems of this tropical American native. Its showy, delicate blossoms appear singly or in long-stalked loose clusters from midsummer until frost. Cosmos makes a graceful addition to mixed borders, where it will attract numerous butterflies, and is an excellent source of long-lasting cut flowers.

Selected species and varieties: *C. bipinnatus* grows to 6 feet with delicate, finely cut leaves and flowers in shades of red, pink, and white; 'Candy Stripe' grows 30 inches tall with white flowers with crimson markings; 'Seashells Mixture' grows 3 to 3½ feet with fluted petals of white, pink, or crimson surrounding a yellow center; 'Sonata White' grows 24 inches tall with snowy white blooms; 'Versailles Pink' develops strong, tall stems and pink flowers and is recommended for cutting. *C. sulphureus* grows to 6 feet— and cultivars to 18 to 36 inches—with yellow, orange, or scarlet flowers.

Growing conditions and maintenance: Sow seed directly in the garden after the last frost in spring. Thin to allow 12 to 18 inches between plants. Do not fertilize. Taller types are subject to lodging and may need staking. Plants often self-seed.

Cynara
(SIN-ah-ra)
CYNARA

Cynara cardunculus

Plant type: *tender perennial*

Height: *4 to 6 feet*

Interest: *flowers, foliage*

Soil: *moist, well-drained, fertile*

Light: *full sun*

Related to the edible artichoke, this species forms clumps of thick stems lined with spiny, lacy silver-gray leaves with woolly undersides that provide a bold accent in a border or form a fast-growing summer hedge. Fuzzy thistle-like flower globes tip each stem from summer through fall. Both leaves and flowers are prized by floral designers for fresh and dried arrangements. It is native to southern Europe.

Selected species and varieties: *C. cardunculus* (cardoon) will grow 6 feet tall in warm climates, though it often reaches only 4 feet in cooler regions. Leaves grow to 3 feet long. Both the leafstalks and the roots are edible. Flower heads are purplish, up to 3 inches across, and are surrounded by spiny bracts.

Growing conditions and maintenance: Start seed indoors in late winter, transplanting to successively larger pots as needed before moving to the garden in midspring. Allow 3 feet between plants. Cardoon can be grown as a perennial from Zone 8 south.

Dahlia
(DAH-lee-a)
DAHLIA

Dahlia 'Audacity'

Plant type: *tender perennial*

Height: *12 inches to 8 feet*

Interest: *flowers*

Soil: *moist, well-drained, fertile*

Light: *full sun*

Dahlias brighten the border over a long season with diverse blooms whose sizes range from a few inches across to the diameter of a dinner plate. Their tightly packed disk flowers are surrounded by one or more rows of petal-like ray flowers that may be doubled, curved, twisted, cupped, or rolled into tiny tubes. Colors range widely; some are bicolored or variegated. The more than 20,000 cultivars available today descend from a few wild species cultivated by Aztec botanists. Dwarf dahlias are cultivated in beds or borders as low-growing bushy edgings; standard dahlias are grown as medium to tall fillers in beds and borders or as specimens. All make long-lasting cut flowers.

Selected species and varieties: *Anemone-flowered dahlias*—a central disk obscured by a fluffy ball of short, tubular petals and rimmed by one or more rows of longer, flat petals. *Ball dahlias*—cupped, doubled petals crowding spirally into round domes or slightly flattened globes. *Cactus dahlias*—straight or twisted petals rolled like quills or straws over half their length to a pointed tip. *Chrysanthemum-type dahlias*—double rows of petals curving inward and hiding the central disk. *Collarette dahlias*—central disks surrounded by a collar of short petals backed by a second collar of broader, flat petals; 'Mickey' bears neat yellow-centered blooms with red and yellow ruffles surrounded by red outer petals. *Formal decorative dahlias*—double rows of flat, evenly spaced petals covering the central disk; 'Audacity' produces lavender-pink petals that fade to white at the base. *Informal decorative dahlias*—double rows of randomly spaced flat petals hiding the central disk. *Peony-flowered dahlias*—two or three overlapping layers of ray petals surrounding a central disk. *Pompom dahlias*—small, round balls of tightly rolled petals less than 2 inches in diameter. *Semi-cactus dahlias*—flat petals curling over less than half their length into tubes at their tips. *Single dahlias*—one or two row of flat petals surrounding a flat central disk. *Star dahlias*—two or three rows of short petals curving inward. *Waterlily-flowered dahlias*—short petals tightly clasped over the central disk like a waterlily bud, surrounded by several rows of broad, flat petals. Dahlias are further categorized by flower size.

Growing conditions and maintenance: Start seed indoors in very early spring, or plant tubers directly in the garden in spring, spacing them 1 to 4 feet apart, depending on their type. Provide abundant water and mulch. Remove faded blooms to extend bloom period. Taller types require staking. Dahlias are perennial in Zones 9 to 11; elsewhere tubers may be dug up in fall and stored in a dry, cool location until planting time the next spring.

Datura
(da-TOOR-a)
ANGEL'S-TRUMPET

Datura inoxia

Plant type: *annual or tender perennial*

Height: *2 to 5 feet*

Interest: *flowers*

Soil: *moist, well-drained*

Light: *full sun to light shade*

Datura's large flower trumpets bloom above coarse, oval leaves on shrubby plants that are useful as fillers or as backdrops in a border. Each summer-blooming flower opens at sunset and lasts only a day. Though flowers are sometimes fragrant, the leaves are unpleasantly scented, and most plant parts are extremely poisonous. Plant them only in places where they are completely out of the reach of children and pets.

Selected species and varieties: *D. inoxia* (angel's-trumpet, thorn apple) grows to 3 feet with 10-inch leaves and pendant pink, white, or lavender flowers 8 inches long and 5 inches wide. *D. metel* (Hindu datura) grows 3 to 5 feet tall with 8-inch leaves and 7-inch white or yellow- or purple-tinged flowers. *D. stramonium* (jimson weed) grows to 5 feet with 8-inch leaves and white or purple 2- to 5-inch flowers; it is extremely poisonous.

Growing conditions and maintenance: Start seed indoors 6 to 8 weeks prior to moving outdoors to warmed soil. Space plants 1½ to 2 feet apart. Provide shelter from wind. *D. inoxia* may survive as a short-lived perennial in Zones 9 and 10.

Daucus
(DAW-kus)
DAUCUS

Daucus carota var. carota

Plant type: *biennial*

Height: *3 to 4 feet*

Interest: *flowers*

Soil: *average to poor, well-drained*

Light: *full sun*

This native of Eurasia has naturalized in the United States along roadsides and in abandoned fields. It is very closely related to the garden carrot but is grown for its dainty 4-inch flower heads, called umbels, which appear in late spring to midsummer. The flat-topped umbels consist of tiny white flowers with, often, a single dark red flower at the center. Its lacy appearance serves as a nice filler in a sunny border, and it naturalizes easily in wildflower meadows, attracting butterflies and bees. Flowers are valued for both fresh and dried arrangements.

Selected species and varieties: *D. carota* var. *carota* (Queen Anne's lace, Queen's lace, wild carrot) produces a prominent rosette of fernlike leaves in early spring, from which grows a 3- to 4-foot branched flowering stem. Each branch is topped by a 3- to 4-inch umbel.

Growing conditions and maintenance: Sow seed outdoors in late spring for flowers the following year. Once established, plant will vigorously self-seed. To prevent unwanted plants, remove flowers before seeds mature. Plants are easy to grow and thrive in nearly any well-drained soil.

Dianthus
(dy-AN-thus)
PINK

Dianthus chinensis 'Telestar Picotee'

Plant type: *annual, biennial, or tender perennial*

Height: *4 to 30 inches*

Interest: *flowers, foliage*

Soil: *moist, well-drained, slightly alkaline*

Light: *full sun to partial shade*

Pinks form mats of grassy foliage with white, pink, red, and bicolored flowers with fringed petals. Low-growing types make delightful edgings or rock-garden or container specimens, while taller selections are useful in the foreground or middle of a border, and as cut flowers.

Selected species and varieties: *D. barbatus* (sweet William) is a biennial that self-seeds freely; dwarf varieties grow 4 to 10 inches tall, while tall varieties may reach 2 feet. Flowers are borne in dense, flat-topped clusters from late spring to early summer. *D. chinensis* (China pink, rainbow pink) is an annual, biennial, or short-lived perennial that grows 6 to 30 inches tall with a dense, mounded habit; 1- to 2-inch flowers, often fragrant, are borne singly or in loose clusters from early summer to fall; 'Telestar Picotee' has a compact habit with deep pink flowers fringed with white.

Growing conditions and maintenance: Sow sweet William seed outdoors in late spring for flowers the following year. Start seed of China pinks indoors 6 to 8 weeks prior to the last frost for transplanting to the garden in midspring. Space plants 8 to 18 inches apart.

Digitalis
(di-ji-TAL-us)
FOXGLOVE

Digitalis purpurea 'Excelsior'

Plant type: *biennial*

Height: *2 to 6 feet*

Interest: *flowers, foliage*

Soil: *moist, well-drained, acid*

Light: *partial shade*

Foxglove's striking summer-blooming flower trumpets line the tips of stiff stalks above clumps of coarse, hairy leaves. Most are native to Europe and North Africa but have been grown in the Americas since Colonial times. They add an old-fashioned look and a vertical accent to borders. They also fit well into naturalized plantings such as a woodland garden, and bees love their flowers. Though most bloom their second season, some varieties flower the first year from seed. Because foxglove self-seeds easily, new plants appear each year, giving it a perennial quality. Leaves contain digitalis and are poisonous if eaten.

Selected species and varieties: *D. ferruginea* (rusty foxglove) produces a basal clump of narrow, deeply veined dark green leaves, each up to 9 inches long. A leafy 5- to 6-foot flower stalk rises from the clump, bearing dense clusters of small yellowish blooms that open from mid- to late summer. Each flower is ½ to 1¼ inches long, yellow-brown, and netted with a rusty red. Tiny hairs fringe the flower lip. *D. purpurea* (common foxglove) produces a broad clump of large rough-textured woolly leaves from which an erect flower stem with smaller leaves emerges in early summer. The flower stalk ranges in size from 2 to 5 feet. The 2- to 3-inch pendulous flowers are borne in a one-sided cluster up to 2 feet long. Their colors include purple, pink, white, rust, or yellow, and their throats are often spotted; 'Alba' grows to 4 feet with white flowers; 'Apricot' grows to 3½ feet with flowers ranging from pale pink to bold apricot; 'Excelsior' grows to 5 feet with blooms borne all around the stem rather than on one side, in colors of purple, pink, white, cream, and yellow; 'Foxy' grows 2½ to 3 feet with flowers in pastel shades from rose pink to white appearing the first year from seed; 'Giant Shirley' grows 5 feet or more, producing strong stems with large mottled blooms in shades of pink.

Growing conditions and maintenance: Start seed outdoors in spring or summer, thinning to stand 6 inches apart. Transplant seedlings to their flowering location in fall or early spring. Types that bloom their first year from seed should be started indoors about 10 weeks, and transplanted to the garden 2 weeks, before the last frost. Space plants 18 to 24 inches apart. Foxgloves thrive in a rich, loose soil and benefit from the addition of compost. Provide water during dry periods and mulch after the ground freezes in fall.

Dolichos
(DO-li-kos)
HYACINTH BEAN

Dolichos lablab

Plant type: *tender perennial*

Height: *10 to 20 feet*

Interest: *flowers, foliage, fruit*

Soil: *loose, well-drained*

Light: *full sun*

This lush, tropical twining vine produces purplish stems and purple-veined compound leaves. Attractive clusters of pink, purple, or white pea-like flowers appear in summer and are followed by showy red-purple seedpods. The seeds are edible and are an important food source in many parts of the world. As an ornamental, plants provide a colorful screen or covering for a fence, an arbor, or a trellis.

Selected species and varieties: *D. lablab* climbs to 20 feet in one season by twining stems. Leaves are composed of three heart-shaped leaflets, each 3 to 6 inches long. The loosely clustered flowers stand out against the deeply colored leaves. Pods are 1 to 3 inches long.

Growing conditions and maintenance: Start seed indoors in peat pots 4 to 6 weeks prior to the last frost, or sow directly in the garden after the soil has warmed. Space plants 12 to 24 inches apart and provide support for climbing. Hyacinth bean thrives in warm weather and is perennial in Zones 10 and 11.

Dyssodia
(dis-OH-dee-ah)
DAHLBERG DAISY

Dyssodia tenuiloba

Plant type: *annual or tender perennial*

Height: *4 to 8 inches*

Interest: *flowers, foliage*

Soil: *well-drained to dry*

Light: *full sun*

Their dainty blooms lavishly sprinkled on a dense carpet of finely divided foliage, Dahlberg daisies (also called golden-fleece) constantly flower throughout the summer. They are perfect for bedding and edging, in rock gardens, and in hanging baskets. They can be planted between steppingstones to add color to a sunny garden path.

Selected species and varieties: *D. tenuiloba* grows to 8 inches tall but spreads up to 18 inches wide. Its slender stems produce threadlike, bristle-tipped leaves that are aromatic. Flower heads are ½ to 1 inch across with orange-yellow ray flowers surrounding a yellow center.

Growing conditions and maintenance: Start seed indoors 6 to 8 weeks prior to the last frost to transplant to the garden after all danger of frost has passed. In warm areas they can be planted directly in the garden and will self-seed. Allow 6 to 12 inches between plants. Water sparingly and do not fertilize. Plants thrive in sunny, dry locations and tolerate heat, drought, and coastal conditions.

Echium
(EK-ee-um)
VIPER'S BUGLOSS

Echium candicans

Plant type: *biennial*

Height: *1 to 10 feet*

Interest: *flowers, foliage*

Soil: *dry, poor*

Light: *full sun*

These tropical natives provide a striking accent to borders and rock gardens with their brightly colored and closely packed tubular flowers, which appear from early to late summer. Plants often flower their first year from seed. They are especially useful in sunny, dry locations where the soil is poor.

Selected species and varieties: *E. candicans* (pride-of-Madeira) grows 3 to 6 feet tall with narrow gray-green leaves covered with silvery hairs and an erect 20-inch cluster of white or purple ½-inch flowers held well above the leaves. *E. lycopsis* (viper's bugloss) grows 1 to 3 feet tall with a bushy habit; flowers are blue, lavender, purple, pink, or white and appear on dense 10-inch spikes. *E. wildpretii* (tower-of-jewels) grows to a show-stopping 10 feet, with pale red blooms.

Growing conditions and maintenance: Start seed indoors 6 to 8 weeks before the last frost or outdoors as soon as soil can be worked in spring. In Zones 9 and south, seed can be sown in fall for earlier bloom. Space plants 12 to 18 inches apart. They thrive in poor soils and will produce few flowers on a fertile site. Water sparingly.

Eschscholzia
(es-SHOL-zee-a)
CALIFORNIA POPPY

Eschscholzia californica

Plant type: *annual or tender perennial*

Height: *4 to 24 inches*

Interest: *flowers*

Soil: *dry*

Light: *full sun*

This genus includes both annuals and tender perennials native to the grasslands of California and the Southwest. Flowers open during the day and close at night and in cloudy weather. They are effective for massing in beds and borders and compete well in wildflower meadows.

Selected species and varieties: *E. caespitosa* (tufted California poppy, pastel poppy) is an annual with pale yellow flowers on 4- to 12-inch stalks above finely cut basal foliage. *E. californica* is a 1- to 2-foot tender perennial from Zone 8 south but is grown as an annual elsewhere, with 1- to 3-inch yellow or orange flowers from spring to fall and feathery blue-green foliage; 'Aurantiaca' is an old variety with rich orange single blooms; 'Monarch Mixed' bears single and semi-double flowers in yellow, orange, red, and pink; 'Orange King' bears translucent orange flowers.

Growing conditions and maintenance: Plant seed outdoors in early spring; seedlings do not transplant well. Once established, plants self-seed freely. Space them 6 inches apart. Though they tolerate most soils, they prefer a poor, sandy one.

Euphorbia
(yew-FOR-bee-a)
EUPHORBIA

Euphorbia marginata

Plant type: *annual*

Height: *18 inches to 2 feet*

Interest: *flowers, foliage*

Soil: *dry to wet*

Light: *full sun*

This hardy annual is native to many parts of the United States and is grown as much for its neatly variegated leaves as for its tiny green flowers surrounded by white bracts. It is an effective accent for annual beds, especially planted in groups of three or five among plants with dark leaves or brightly colored flowers. The sap may cause skin irritation.

Selected species and varieties: *E. marginata* (snow-on-the-mountain, ghostweed) produces erect, stout, branched stems bearing gray-green oval leaves attractively striped and margined with white. Though the late-summer flowers are small, they are surrounded by showy white leaflike bracts.

Growing conditions and maintenance: Sow seed directly in the garden in late fall or early spring. Allow 10 to 12 inches between plants. Moisture is needed for seed to germinate and for the plants to become established, but they become very drought tolerant as they mature. They self-seed easily and may become invasive. Use gloves when handling stems to avoid contact with the sap.

Gazania
(ga-ZAY-nee-a)
GAZANIA

Gazania rigens 'Fiesta Red'

Plant type: *tender perennial*

Height: *6 to 16 inches*

Interest: *flowers*

Soil: *well-drained to dry*

Light: *full sun*

This tender perennial from South Africa produces daisylike flowers from midsummer to frost. Blossoms open when the sun is out, and close at night and on overcast days. They provide a colorful show in beds or containers.

Selected species and varieties: *G. linearis* grows to 16 inches with narrow leaves and 2¾-inch flower heads with golden rays and orange-brown disks. *G. rigens* (treasure flower) grows 6 to 12 inches tall with 3-inch flower heads, borne on long stalks, that may be yellow, orange, pink, or red; 'Chansonette' grows to 10 inches with a compact habit and flowers in a wide range of colors; 'Fiesta Red' bears deep burnt orange flowers with a dark ring surrounding a yellow disk; 'Harlequin Hybrids' bear flowers in many shades with a brown zone around the central disk; 'Sunshine' grows to 8 inches with 4-inch multicolored flowers.

Growing conditions and maintenance: Sow seeds indoors in early spring to transplant to the garden after all danger of frost has passed. Space plants 12 inches apart. Do not overwater. They thrive in sunny, dry locations, and tolerate wind and coastal conditions.

Gomphrena
(gom-FREE-na)
GLOBE AMARANTH

Gomphrena globosa

Plant type: *annual*

Height: *8 to 24 inches*

Interest: *flowers*

Soil: *well-drained*

Light: *full sun*

Colorful cloverlike flower heads of gomphrena top upright stems from summer to frost. A native of India, this half-hardy annual is easy to grow and imparts a cheerful, informal appearance to beds and borders. Plants perform well in patio planters and window boxes. Flowers, which have a papery texture even when fresh, are excellent for both fresh and dried arrangements.

Selected species and varieties: *G. globosa* produces erect, branched stems and somewhat coarse, hairy leaves. The globular flower heads are 1 inch long and may be pink, white, magenta, orange, or red.

Growing conditions and maintenance: Start seed indoors 8 to 10 weeks before the last frost and transplant outdoors after all danger of frost has passed. Seed can be sown directly outside in late spring. Allow 8 to 15 inches between plants. Though slow to start, plants are easy to grow once established, and they thrive in warm weather. To use in dried arrangements, cut before the flowers are fully open and hang them upside down in an airy room until dry.

Gypsophila
(jip-SOFF-il-a)
BABY'S-BREATH

Gypsophila elegans

Plant type: *annual*

Height: *8 to 24 inches*

Interest: *flowers*

Soil: *well-drained, alkaline*

Light: *full sun*

This hardy annual from Europe and northern Asia produces a cloud of delicate, tiny flowers on sprawling, branched stems from midspring to early fall. It is beautiful as a filler between more brightly colored and boldly textured plants in flower borders or rock gardens and in indoor arrangements both fresh and dried.

Selected species and varieties: *G. elegans* has a mounded habit with thin, multibranched stems bearing pairs of narrow gray-green leaves and airy clusters of white, pink, red, or purple flowers. Each flower is ¼ to ¾ inch across.

Growing conditions and maintenance: Sow seed directly in the garden in midspring. Supplement acid soils with limestone. Plants are short-lived, so make successive sowings every 2 to 3 weeks for continuous bloom. Thin plants to stand 9 to 12 inches apart. Taller varieties may need staking. In Zone 9 and south, provide afternoon shade.

Helianthus
(hee-lee-AN-thus)
SUNFLOWER

Helianthus annuus 'Inca Jewels'

Plant type: *annual*

Height: *2 to 10 feet*

Interest: *flowers*

Soil: *moist, well-drained*

Light: *full sun*

The sunflower's daisylike blooms in yellow, cream, mahogany, crimson, and assorted blends appear from midsummer to frost on erect stalks. The flowers make a bold statement in mixed borders, and a row of them makes a delightful temporary screen. Flowers are great for cutting. The seeds are a favorite food of many wild birds.

Selected species and varieties: *H. annuus* (common sunflower) has an erect habit and a coarse texture, producing sturdy stems with broad, bristly leaves and flowers composed of petal-like, often yellow rays surrounding brown or purple disk flowers; 'Inca Jewels' has a multibranched habit with yellow-tipped orange rays; 'Italian White' grows to 4 feet with multibranched stems and 4-inch cream-colored flowers with a brown center; 'Sunbeam' grows 5 feet tall with 5-inch pollenless flowers ideal for cutting; 'Teddy Bear' produces single and double yellow flowers on 2-foot plants.

Growing conditions and maintenance: Sow seed directly outdoors after the last frost. Thin seedlings to allow 1 to 2 feet between plants. Plants thrive in hot, dry weather conditions.

Helichrysum
(hel-i-KRY-sum)
EVERLASTING

Helichrysum bracteatum

Plant type: *tender perennial*

Height: *1 to 3 feet*

Interest: *flowers*

Soil: *light, well-drained*

Light: *full sun*

This Australian native, also known as immortelle, produces papery-textured flowers in shades of white, yellow, orange, salmon, red, and pink. What appear to be the flower's petals are actually colorful bracts; the true flowers are at the center of the flower head. Use dwarf types for adding color to a rock garden or the edge of a border. Taller varieties are highly valued for cutting, especially for winter arrangements. Flowers retain their colors very well when dried.

Selected species and varieties: *H. bracteatum* (strawflower) produces narrow, coarsely toothed leaves on wiry, branching stems. Flower heads appear from midsummer to early fall and are 1 to 2½ inches across.

Growing conditions and maintenance: Start seed indoors 6 to 8 weeks prior to the last frost. In warm climates, seed can be sown directly in the garden. Allow 12 inches between plants. Once established, plants thrive in dry soil and often self-seed. They do not perform well in areas with very high humidity. For winter arrangements, cut flowers when they are about half open and hang them upside down in an airy room to dry.

Heliotropium
(hee-lee-oh-TRO-pee-um)
HELIOTROPE

Heliotropium arborescens 'Marine'

Plant type: *tender perennial*

Height: *1 to 3 feet*

Interest: *flowers*

Soil: *well-drained, fertile*

Light: *full sun to partial shade*

Heliotrope is a tender perennial from Peru grown as an annual in temperate zones. Large clusters of summer flowers range from deep purple to white and bear a lovely vanilla fragrance. Site plants in the foreground of a mixed border; they are especially effective in groups located where their fragrance will be appreciated. They are ideal container plants, and flowers can be cut for fresh arrangements.

Selected species and varieties: *H. arborescens* (cherry pie) grows 1 to 3 feet in the garden, though plants grown in a greenhouse or in their native range may reach 6 feet. Foliage is dark green and wrinkled. Five-petaled flowers are ¼ inch across, occurring in clusters as large as a foot across; 'Marine', a compact variety reaching 2 feet, has large deep purple flowers and is excellent for bedding, although it lacks intense fragrance.

Growing conditions and maintenance: Start seed indoors 10 to 12 weeks prior to the last frost, or buy young plants in spring. Plants can also be started from cuttings. Do not transplant to the garden until soil has warmed, as plants are very frost sensitive. Allow 12 inches between plants and keep them well watered.

Hibiscus
(hy-BIS-kus)
MALLOW, ROSE MALLOW

Hibiscus acetosella

Plant type: *tender perennial*

Height: *18 inches to 8 feet*

Interest: *flowers, foliage*

Soil: *moist, well-drained*

Light: *full sun to light shade*

These shrubby tender perennials are attractively grown as annuals in many temperate gardens. Some are grown for their ornamental foliage, while others produce large funnel-shaped five-petaled flowers with prominent stamens that add a tropical flavor to a border. You will find many uses for these bold-textured plants. Plant them individually as specimens or in groups as a fast-growing summer hedge. Tall types are effective as a background for mixed borders or as the centerpiece of an island bed. Shorter ones are useful for fronting shrub borders or planting in the foreground of annual beds. Both large and small types are excellent choices for patio containers.

Selected species and varieties: *H. acetosella* hails from Africa and is grown primarily for its attractive foliage. Purple flowers form so late in the season in most areas that they fail to open before frost. The plant grows to 5 feet tall, with glossy red leaves and stems. Leaves may be smooth in outline or deeply lobed. This plant makes a bold accent mixed with other annuals, or a stunning summer hedge; the variety 'Red Shield' produces burgundy leaves with a metallic sheen that resemble maple leaves in shape. *H. moscheutos* (common rose mallow, swamp rose mallow, wild cotton) grows 3 to 8 feet tall with a shrubby habit. It is native to marshlands of the eastern United States and can be grown as a perennial in Zones 7 and south, but is often grown as a half-hardy annual. The large gray-green leaves provide a soft foil for the huge white, pink, rose, or red summer flowers that are often 8 inches across; 'Southern Belle' grows 4 to 6 feet tall with red, pink, or white flowers with a distinct red eye, up to 10 inches across. *H. trionum* (flower-of-an-hour) grows 18 to 36 inches with a bushy habit and dark green three- or five-lobed leaves. Flowers are 2 inches across and are creamy yellow with a deep maroon throat. Though flowers are short-lived, they appear in abundance from midsummer to late fall.

Growing conditions and maintenance: Start seed of *H. acetosella* and *H. moscheutos* indoors about 8 weeks prior to the last frost and transplant outdoors after all danger of frost has passed. Space *H. acetosella* 12 to 14 inches apart, *H. moscheutos* 3 feet apart. Because *H. trionum* is difficult to transplant, seed should be sown directly in the garden after all danger of frost has passed, allowing 12 inches between plants. Plants tolerate heat as long as abundant moisture is supplied.

Iberis
(eye-BEER-is)
CANDYTUFT

Iberis umbellata

Plant type: *annual*

Height: *6 to 18 inches*

Interest: *flowers*

Soil: *well-drained*

Light: *full sun*

These European wildflowers are easy to grow and free flowering. Like the perennial species *[I. sempervirens],* annual candytufts produce clusters of tiny four-petaled flowers above dark green leaves. They flower throughout the summer and are effective in rock gardens and borders, or as an edging or in a planter, where their sweet fragrance will be noticed.

Selected species and varieties: *I. amara* (rocket candytuft) grows 12 to 18 inches tall with fragrant white flowers in cone-shaped spikes that can be cut for fresh arrangements. *I. odorata* (fragrant candytuft) grows 6 to 12 inches with flat clusters of white flowers. *I. umbellata* (globe candytuft) grows 8 to 16 inches with clusters of pink, red, lilac, or violet flowers that are not fragrant.

Growing conditions and maintenance: Sow seed in the garden in fall or as soon as soil can be worked in the spring, thinning to allow 6 to 9 inches between seedlings. Make successive sowings to extend the flowering season. Cut back lightly after bloom to stimulate growth. Plants thrive in city conditions.

Impatiens
(im-PAY-shens)
BALSAM, JEWELWEED

Impatiens wallerana 'Super Elfin Twilight'

Plant type: *annual*

Height: *6 inches to 8 feet*

Interest: *flowers, foliage*

Soil: *moist, well-drained*

Light: *full sun to full shade*

Massed as edgings or ground covers, impatiens brighten a shady garden with flowers in jeweled hues from summer through frost. Low-growing types are ideal for planters and hanging baskets.

Selected species and varieties: *I. balsamina* (garden balsam, rose balsam) grows to 3 feet, producing 1- to 2-inch flowers in mixed colors. *I. glandulifera* (Himalayan jewelweed) grows to 8 feet with 2-inch purple, pink, or white flowers in mid- to late summer. *I.* x *New Guinea* (New Guinea impatiens) grows to 2 feet with showy, often variegated leaves with flowers up to 3 inches across. *I. wallerana* (busy Lizzie) grows 6 to 18 inches tall with a compact, mounded habit and 1- to 2-inch flat-faced flowers available in many colors; 'Super Elfin Twilight' bears deep pink flowers on spreading plants.

Growing conditions and maintenance: Plant *I. glandulifera* seed outdoors in fall. Start impatiens indoors 3 to 4 months prior to the last frost, or purchase bedding plants to transplant to the garden after all danger of frost has passed. Space *I. glandulifera* 2 feet apart, others 12 to 18 inches apart. Most species prefer some shade and abundant water.

Kochia
(KOE-kee-a)
BURNING BUSH

Kochia scoparia f. trichophylla

Plant type: *annual*

Height: *2 to 4 feet*

Interest: *foliage*

Soil: *moist, well-drained*

Light: *full sun*

This Eurasian annual has naturalized in some parts of the United States. Its fine-textured foliage and neat, symmetrical form make it an attractive summer hedge, screen, or background for a flower border.

Selected species and varieties: *K. scoparia f. trichophylla* (summer cypress, firebush) has an erect, uniform habit with dense, feathery foliage that is light green in summer, turning bright red in fall, while flowers are insignificant; 'Acapulco Silver' produces variegated silver-tipped leaves.

Growing conditions and maintenance: Start seed indoors in individual peat pots 6 to 8 weeks prior to the last frost or plant directly in the garden after all danger of frost has passed. Do not cover the seed; it needs light for germination. Plants often self-seed and may become invasive. Allow 1½ to 2 feet between plants. Plants can be sheared to maintain their shape or size, and they tolerate heat. Avoid overwatering. In windy locations, plants may require staking.

Lathyrus
(LATH-er-us)
LATHYRUS

Lathyrus odoratus

Plant type: *annual*

Height: *6 inches to 6 feet*

Interest: *flowers*

Soil: *moist, well-drained*

Light: *full sun to partial shade*

The sweet pea is a hardy annual from southern Europe that bears puffy flowers on branching flowering stalks. It can be used as a trailing ground cover, a climbing vine for a screen or backdrop, or a bushy accent among bulbs.

Selected species and varieties: *L. odoratus* (sweet pea) produces fragrant spring or summer flowers up to 2 inches wide on compact 6-inch- to 2½-foot-tall annual bushes, or on a twining vine 5 to 6 feet long. Flower colors include deep rose, blue, purple, scarlet, white, cream, salmon, pink, and bicolors; 'Bijou Mixed' is a bush type that grows to 12 inches with a full range of colors; 'Royal Family' is a vining type that comes in a wide range of colors, grows to 6 feet, and is heat resistant.

Growing conditions and maintenance: Sow seed 2 inches deep in well-prepared soil in late fall or early spring. Provide climbing types with support. Mulch to keep soil cool, and provide abundant water. Remove faded blooms to prolong flowering.

Lavatera
(lav-a-TEER-a)
TREE MALLOW

Lavatera trimestris

Plant type: *annual*

Height: *2 to 6 feet*

Interest: *flowers*

Soil: *well-drained*

Light: *full sun*

Native to the Mediterranean region, lavatera is a hardy annual with a bushy habit and cup-shaped summer flowers that resemble hollyhocks. Their long blooming season makes these plants a good choice for the mixed border. They are also useful as a summer hedge, and flowers can be cut for fresh arrangements.

Selected species and varieties: *L. trimestris* produces pale green rounded leaves on branched stems that may reach 6 feet, although most varieties are between 2 and 3 feet; both leaves and stems are hairy. Solitary 2½- to 4-inch flowers, each with five wide petals, are borne in great numbers throughout the summer. Colors include shades of pink, red, and white; 'Mont Blanc' grows only 2 feet tall and bears pure white flowers; 'Silver Cup' also grows to 2 feet, bearing salmon pink flowers with darker veins.

Growing conditions and maintenance: Sow seed outdoors in midspring, thinning to allow plants to stand 1½ to 2 feet apart. Young plants require abundant water and should be mulched. Once established, plants are drought resistant. Deadhead to prolong flowering.

Layia
(LAY-ee-ah)
TIDYTIPS

Layia platyglossa

Plant type: *annual*

Height: *1 to 2 feet*

Interest: *flowers*

Soil: *well-drained*

Light: *full sun*

Layia is a member of the sunflower family and is native to California, where it grows as a wildflower. Its common name refers to the showy white-tipped ray petals that surround a golden disk. It is a good choice for beds, borders, rock gardens, and sunny banks. Flowers are excellent for fresh arrangements.

Selected species and varieties: *L. platyglossa* has a neat habit and coarsely toothed gray-green leaves covered with dense hairs. Flowers appear from spring to early summer; they are bright yellow, single, 2 inches across, and daisylike. This species is often included in wildflower mixes.

Growing conditions and maintenance: Start seed indoors 6 to 8 weeks prior to the last frost, or sow outdoors in early spring. In Zone 9 and warmer, seed can be sown in fall. Space plants 9 to 12 inches apart, and provide abundant moisture to seedlings. Once plants are established, they are quite drought tolerant. Remove flowers as they fade to prolong blooming period.

Limonium
(ly-MO-nee-um)
STATICE

Limonium sinuatum

Plant type: *annual or biennial*

Height: *10 to 24 inches*

Interest: *flowers*

Soil: *well-drained, sandy, slightly alkaline*

Light: *full sun*

Statice, also called sea lavender, is native to the Mediterranean region and bears clusters of brightly colored flowers surrounded by a papery calyx that remains after the rest of the flower drops. This long-lasting display is useful both in beds and for cutting. Flowers dry easily and retain their color well so are often used in dried arrangements.

Selected species and varieties: *L. sinuatum* (notchleaf statice) grows 18 to 24 inches with a clump of 4- to 8-inch basal leaves and branched, winged flower stems. The papery-textured flowers are borne in short one-sided clusters; colors include pink, blue, lavender, yellow, and white. *L. suworowii* [also known as *Psylliostachys suworowii*] (Russian statice) grows 10 to 20 inches tall with large basal leaves and spikes of lavender and green flowers from summer to frost.

Growing conditions and maintenance: Start seed indoors in individual peat pots 8 weeks prior to the last frost, or sow directly outdoors in midspring in warm climates. Allow 9 to 18 inches between plants. They tolerate drought and seaside conditions but will rot in soil that remains wet.

Lobularia
(lob-yew-LAIR-ee-a)
SWEET ALYSSUM

Lobularia maritima

Plant type: *tender perennial*

Height: *4 to 12 inches*

Interest: *flowers*

Soil: *well-drained*

Light: *full sun to partial shade*

This Mediterranean native spreads to nearly twice its height, producing tiny fragrant flowers from late spring to frost. It makes a good choice for an edging, for a rock garden, along dry walls, or for window boxes. In the front of a mixed border, it neatly covers the dying foliage of spring-flowering bulbs.

Selected species and varieties: *L. maritima* is a fine-textured plant with alternate narrow leaves 1 to 2 inches long. It has a low-branching and spreading habit. Four-petaled flowers are borne in clusters and bear a honeylike scent; colors include white, lilac, pink, and purple.

Growing conditions and maintenance: Start seed indoors 6 to 8 weeks prior to the last frost, or sow directly in the garden in early spring. Avoid overwatering seedlings. Space plants 6 inches apart; they tolerate crowding. In warm areas, they will self-seed. They thrive in cool weather; flowering may stop in hot temperatures. Cutting back plants will encourage further flowering.

Lunaria
(loo-NAY-ree-a)
HONESTY, MONEY PLANT

Lunaria annua

Plant type: *biennial*

Height: *2 to 3 feet*

Interest: *fruit*

Soil: *well-drained*

Light: *full sun to partial shade*

This old-fashioned biennial is native to southern Europe. It is grown primarily for its fruit, a flat, oval, translucent seedpod. Plants are best suited to the cutting garden, an informal border, or a wildflower meadow. Their papery seedpods are highly valued for dried arrangements.

Selected species and varieties: *L. annua* (silver-dollar, bolbonac) has an erect habit with broad, coarsely toothed leaves and fragrant pink or purple flowers, each with four petals, borne in terminal clusters in late spring. Flowers are followed by the seedpods, which fall apart, revealing a thin, silvery white disk, 1 to 2 inches across, to which the seeds cling; 'Alba' produces white flowers well displayed when grown against a dark background.

Growing conditions and maintenance: Lunaria can be grown as an annual or a biennial. For flowers and seedpods the first year, sow seed outdoors in very early spring, or plant in midsummer to early fall for flowers and seedpods the following year. Once established they will reseed through Zone 4. Space plants 8 to 12 inches apart. They tolerate wet and dry conditions and are not fussy about soil quality, as long as it is well drained.

Matthiola
(ma-THY-o-la)
STOCK

Matthiola incana

Plant type: *annual or biennial*

Height: *12 to 30 inches*

Interest: *flowers*

Soil: *well-drained, fertile*

Light: *full sun to light shade*

The blossoms of stock perfume a garden throughout summer. Plant them in beds, window boxes, or patio containers where their fragrance can be appreciated. Flowers add a dainty appearance and sweet scent to fresh indoor arrangements.

Selected species and varieties: *M. bicornis* [also known as *M. longipetala* ssp. *bicornis*] (night-scented stock, evening stock, perfume plant) has a bushy habit and grows 12 to 18 inches tall. It bears single ¾-inch flowers in shades of lilac and pink that open at night from mid- to late summer and are extremely fragrant. *M. incana* (common stock, gillyflower) grows 12 to 30 inches with gray-green oblong leaves and terminal clusters of 1-inch-long flowers that may be single or double and bear a spicy fragrance; colors include pink, purple, white, and blue.

Growing conditions and maintenance: Start seed indoors 6 to 8 weeks prior to the last frost, or sow directly in the garden in early spring. Space plants to stand 6 to 12 inches apart; they tolerate crowding. Plants thrive in cool weather and may stop flowering when temperatures rise. *M. bicornis* will tolerate poorer soil and drier conditions than will *M. incana*.

Mimulus
(MIM-yew-lus)
MONKEY FLOWER

Mimulus x hybridus

Plant type: *tender perennial*

Height: *10 to 14 inches*

Interest: *flowers*

Soil: *moist, well-drained, fertile*

Light: *partial to full shade*

Blooming from midsummer to fall, this native of both North and South America provides bright color to shady beds and borders. It fits well alongside a garden pond or stream and also makes an attractive container plant. Funnel-shaped, two-lipped flowers are thought to resemble monkeys' faces.

Selected species and varieties: *M.* x *hybridus* has a mounded habit with glossy 2- to 2½-inch leaves and 2-inch tubular flowers in shades of red, yellow, orange, rose, and brown, usually with brown or maroon spotting or mottling.

Growing conditions and maintenance: Start seed indoors 10 to 12 weeks prior to the last frost for transplanting to the garden after all danger of frost has passed. Space plants 6 inches apart. Plants benefit from the addition of organic matter to the soil. They require some shade and ample moisture. In fall, plants can be dug and potted to continue flowering indoors over the winter.

Myosotis
(my-oh-SO-tis)
FORGET-ME-NOT

Myosotis sylvatica 'Ultramarine'

Plant type: *annual or biennial*

Height: *6 to 10 inches*

Interest: *flowers, foliage*

Soil: *moist, well-drained*

Light: *full sun to partial shade*

Airy clusters of dainty flowers with prominent eyes open above the forget-me-not's low mounds of delicate foliage. Forget-me-nots provide a soft filler or a delicate border edging. They are particularly attractive in combination with spring-flowering bulbs such as tulips.

Selected species and varieties: *M. sylvatica* (woodland forget-me-not, garden forget-me-not) produces 8- to 10-inch stems in clumps almost as wide, lined with soft, elongated leaves and tipped with loose clusters of ¼-inch yellow-centered blue flowers from spring through early summer; 'Ultramarine' is very dwarf, growing to 6 inches, with dark blue flowers; 'Victoria Blue' grows 6 to 8 inches, forming neat mounds and producing early flowers of gentian blue.

Growing conditions and maintenance: Start seed outdoors in late summer to early fall for flowers the following spring. Once established, forget-me-nots self-seed readily, performing like a perennial. Enrich the soil with organic matter. Allow 6 to 12 inches between plants, and water during dry periods.

Nemophila
(nem-OFF-i-la)
BABY-BLUE-EYES

Nemophila menziesii

Plant type: *annual*

Height: *6 to 10 inches*

Interest: *flowers*

Soil: *moist, well-drained*

Light: *full sun to partial shade*

Baby-blue-eyes hails from California and Oregon, where it grows as a wildflower. In the garden its low, mounded habit and dainty flowers make good edgings, rock-garden specimens, and companions for spring-flowering bulbs. They are also attractive when planted so that their trailing stems spill over the edge of a wall.

Selected species and varieties: *N. menziesii* produces trailing stems to form a mounding plant, usually about 6 inches tall and 12 inches across, with deeply cut light green leaves. Flowers are tubular, 1 to 1½ inches across, and sky blue in color with white centers; 'Pennie Black' has deep purple ¾-inch blooms edged with silvery white.

Growing conditions and maintenance: Sow seed directly in the garden in early spring, thinning the seedlings to stand 6 inches apart. Enrich the soil with organic matter and provide abundant moisture. Plants thrive in areas with cool summers and will self-seed under favorable conditions.

Nicotiana
(ni-ko-she-AN-a)
TOBACCO

Nicotiana sylvestris

Plant type: *annual*

Height: *1 to 6 feet*

Interest: *flowers, foliage*

Soil: *moist, well-drained*

Light: *full sun to partial shade*

Flowering tobacco produces clusters of fragrant, flat-faced flowers with elongated tubular throats growing at the tips of soft stems, and clumps of large leaves. Plants are useful as border fillers or specimens. Flowers of some varieties close in sunlight but open on cloudy days or in the evening. Leaf juices are poisonous.

Selected species and varieties: *N. alata* (jasmine tobacco) produces 1- to 2-foot-tall clumps with flowers that bloom from spring to fall; 'Domino Hybrids' have compact cushions of foliage to 15 inches and early-spring flowers in mixed colors; 'Nikki' grows to 18 inches tall with pink, red, white, yellow, or lime green flowers; 'Sensation Mixed' grows 2 to 2½ feet tall with red, pink, purple, white, and yellow blooms. *N. langsdorffii* produces nodding green flowers with turquoise anthers at the tips of 5-foot stems. *N. sylvestris* (woodland tobacco) produces drooping white flowers tinged pink or purple on branching plants 3 to 6 feet tall.

Growing conditions and maintenance: Start seed indoors 6 to 8 weeks prior to the last frost, or sow directly outdoors in late spring. Space plants about 12 inches apart. Deadhead spent blooms.

Nigella
(nye-JEL-a)
LOVE-IN-A-MIST

Nigella damascena

Plant type: *annual*

Height: *18 to 24 inches*

Interest: *flowers, seed heads*

Soil: *well-drained*

Light: *full sun*

Love-in-a-mist adds a delicate, fine texture to any border or flower arrangement in which it is used. Its fernlike leaves are light green, and solitary flowers are nestled in a mist of foliage at the ends of stems throughout the summer. Interesting seed capsules replace the flowers and are attractive in dried flower arrangements. This annual is native to southern Europe and North Africa.

Selected species and varieties: *N. damascena* has an erect multibranched habit with delicate leaves divided into threadlike segments. Flowers are 1 to 1½ inches across with blue, white, or pink notched petals. The papery 1-inch seed capsules are pale green with reddish brown markings.

Growing conditions and maintenance: Start seed directly outdoors in early spring, and make additional sowings every 2 or 3 weeks until early summer to extend the flowering season. Plants are not easily transplanted. Thin to allow 6 to 10 inches between plants. Water during dry periods. If pods are allowed to remain on plants, they will self-seed.

Oenothera
(ee-no-THEE-ra)
EVENING PRIMROSE

Oenothera biennis

Plant type: *biennial*

Height: *2 to 8 feet*

Interest: *flowers*

Soil: *well-drained to dry*

Light: *full sun to partial shade*

Among this genus of mostly perennial plants are a few hardy biennials that can be treated as annuals. Their pale yellow funnel-shaped blooms appear from early summer to midfall, opening in the evening atop tall, erect stems. They are suitable for massing at the rear of a border or for use in a wildflower garden.

Selected species and varieties: *O. biennis* produces a clump of coarse basal leaves from which a stout, erect flower stem rises. Stems may reach 6 feet and bear 1- to 2-inch flowers that open pale yellow and turn gold. *O. erythrosepala* [also called *O. glaziovinia*] grows 2 to 8 feet tall with yellow flowers that turn orange or red; 'Tina James' grows 3 to 4 feet with showy yellow flowers that burst open in 1 to 2 minutes and are pleasantly fragrant.

Growing conditions and maintenance: Start seed indoors 8 to 12 weeks prior to the last frost, or outdoors in early spring. Where winters are mild, seed can be sown outdoors in fall. Once established, plants will often self-seed, and may become invasive. Space plants 12 inches apart. They thrive in warm weather and tolerate poor soil.

Papaver
(pa-PAY-ver)
POPPY

Papaver nudicaule

Plant type: *annual or tender perennial*

Height: *1 to 4 feet*

Interest: *flowers*

Soil: *well-drained to dry*

Light: *full sun to light shade*

Poppy's showy spring flowers surround prominent centers above clumps of coarse, hairy, deeply lobed leaves. The brightly colored flower petals are extremely delicate in appearance, with a tissuelike texture. Flowers may be single, with four overlapping petals, or double, with many petals forming a rounded bloom. They are borne on solitary stems, and are suitable for mixed borders and good for cutting.

Selected species and varieties: *P. nudicaule* (Iceland poppy, Arctic poppy) produces a fernlike clump of 6-inch lobed gray-green leaves from which 12- to 18-inch leafless flower stems rise from spring to early summer. Flowers are fragrant, 2 to 4 inches across, and saucer shaped; colors include white, yellow, orange, salmon, pink, and scarlet. *P. rhoeas* (corn poppy, Flanders poppy, Shirley poppy, field poppy) grows to 3 feet with wiry, branching stems and pale green deeply lobed leaves. Flowers may be single or double, and are borne from late spring to early summer in colors of red, purple, pink, and white; 'Fairy Wings' produces flowers in soft shades of blue, lilac, dusty pink, and white with

faint blue margins; 'Mother of Pearl' bears flowers in shades of blue, lavender, pink, gray, white, and peach, and the flowers may be solid or speckled. *P. somniferum* (opium poppy) grows 3 to 4 feet tall with large white, red, pink, or mauve flowers that appear throughout summer and are often double or fringed; 'Alba' bears white blooms; 'Pink Chiffon' produces double bright pink flowers; 'White Cloud' bears large double white blooms on sturdy stems.

Papaver rhoeas

Growing conditions and maintenance: *P. nudicaule* can be started indoors 10 weeks prior to the last frost for transplanting in late spring. Handle seedlings carefully because they are difficult to transplant. You can also sow directly in the garden in late fall or early spring. Other species are so difficult to transplant that they are best sown in place. Papaver seed is very small and can be mixed with sand for easier handling. Thin *P. nudicaule* to stand 8 to 10 inches apart, *P. rhoeas* about 12 inches apart, and *P. somniferum* 4 to 8 inches apart. Double-flowered varieties of *P. somniferum* often require staking. Poppies will often self-seed. Deadhead plants to prolong flowering season. For use in indoor arrangements, cut the flowers as the buds straighten on their nodding stems but before the flowers actually open.

Perilla
(per-RILL-a)
BEEFSTEAK PLANT

Perilla frutescens 'Crispa'

Plant type: *annual*

Height: *2 to 3 feet*

Interest: *foliage*

Soil: *well-drained to dry*

Light: *full sun to partial shade*

This Asian native is grown for its attractive foliage, which resembles that of coleus or purple basil. Plants are useful as accents in borders, especially toward the back, where the dark leaves contrast well with brightly colored flowers. Leaves are used as a seasoning in oriental cooking.

Selected species and varieties: *P. frutescens* has an upright habit with the square stems and opposite leaves typical of the mint family. Leaves are up to 5 inches long, have a quilted texture, and are purple-bronze, green, or variegated in color; 'Crispa' develops bronze leaves with wrinkled margins; 'Atropurpurea' has very dark purple leaves.

Growing conditions and maintenance: Start seed indoors 6 weeks prior to the last frost, or sow directly in the garden after the soil has warmed. Space plants 15 to 18 inches apart. Once established, perilla will self-seed and may become invasive; to avoid this problem, remove flowers as they develop. Plants will tolerate poor soil.

Phaseolus
(faz-ee-OH-lus)
BEAN

Phaseolus coccineus

Plant type: *tender perennial*

Height: *6 to 10 feet*

Interest: *flowers, foliage, fruit*

Soil: *moist, well-drained, fertile*

Light: *full sun*

This tender perennial twining vine from tropical America produces abundant dark green leaves that are a perfect foil for its brilliant scarlet flowers. The vine will grow quickly to cover a trellis or fence, or climb up a porch railing. It also forms a dense and dramatic backdrop for a flower border. The flowers attract hummingbirds.

Selected species and varieties: *P. coccineus* (scarlet runner bean) produces twining stems with 5-inch dark green leaves composed of three leaflets. Flowers are bright red and pea-like and appear in large clusters from early to midsummer, followed by flat 4- to 12-inch pods filled with black-and-red mottled seeds. Both flowers and beans are edible.

Growing conditions and maintenance: Plant seed outdoors in spring after danger of frost has passed. Thin to allow 2 to 4 inches between plants. Provide support for climbing, and water when dry.

Phlox
(flox)
PHLOX

Phlox drummondii 'Palona Rose with Eye'

Plant type: *annual*

Height: *6 to 20 inches*

Interest: *flowers*

Soil: *dry, sandy*

Light: *full sun to partial shade*

This Texas native provides a long season of colorful blooms on low, spreading plants that are useful as edgings, in rock gardens, massed in beds, and in containers. Flowers are also good for cutting. Their colors include white, pink, red, purple, yellow, and bicolors.

Selected species and varieties: *P. drummondii* (annual phlox, Drummond phlox) grows to 20 inches with a spreading, mounded habit, hairy leaves and stems, and five-lobed flowers that are 1 inch across; 'Palona Rose with Eye' is compact, 6 to 8 inches tall, with rose flowers with contrasting white eyes; 'Petticoat' series are compact 6-inch plants that come in a mix of colors with good drought and heat tolerance; 'Twinkle' series are 8 inches with small, early, star-shaped flowers in mixed colors.

Growing conditions and maintenance: Start seed indoors 8 weeks prior to the last frost. In Zone 8 and warmer, seed can also be sown in fall. Remove spent flowers to extend bloom, and provide water when dry. Flowering often declines in midsummer but will resume in fall.

Rhodochiton
(ro-DOH-ki-ton)
RHODOCHITON

Rhodochiton atrosanguineum

Plant type: *tender perennial*

Height: *5 to 15 feet*

Interest: *flowers, foliage*

Soil: *well-drained, fertile*

Light: *full sun*

Native to Mexico, where it is a perennial, the purple bell vine is grown as an annual north of Zone 9. It climbs by twisting its long petioles around any nearby support. From summer to frost, tubular deep purple flowers hang from thin stalks and are surrounded by a four-pointed fuchsia calyx. Plants make an attractive cover for a fence or trellis, or can be allowed to cascade from a hanging basket.

Selected species and varieties: *R. atrosanguineum* [also called *R. volubile*] (purple bell vine) grows to 15 feet in its native habitat but usually reaches 5 to 8 feet in temperate zones. Its thick-textured, heart-shaped leaves are tipped with purple. Elongated bell-shaped flowers are about an inch in length.

Growing conditions and maintenance: Start seed indoors in individual peat pots 3 to 4 months prior to the last frost. Place several seeds in each pot because germination may be spotty. Cut out all but the strongest seedling. Transplant to the garden after soil has warmed, allowing 1 foot between plants. They thrive in warm weather. Fertilize and water regularly.

Rudbeckia
(rood-BEK-ee-a)
CONEFLOWER

Rudbeckia hirta 'Double Gold'

Plant type: *annual, biennial, or tender perennial*

Height: *1 to 3 feet*

Interest: *flowers*

Soil: *moist to dry, well-drained*

Light: *full sun to partial shade*

Rudbeckias have prominent dark centers fringed with petal-like ray flowers. The yellow summer flowers bloom on stems lined with large, hairy leaves. They are useful as a filler or backdrop in a border or sunny meadow garden.

Selected species and varieties: *R. hirta* (black-eyed Susan) may be an annual, a biennial, or a short-lived perennial with single or double 2- to 3-inch flower heads whose drooping yellow rays surround dark centers; 'Double Gold' produces spectacular double yellow blooms; 'Gloriosa Daisy' bears flowers in shades of yellow with mahogany centers, and other bicolors; 'Goldilocks' grows to 15 inches with 3- to 4-inch double flowers; 'Green Eyes' (also called 'Irish Eyes') grows to 30 inches and bears 5-inch flowers with golden rays around a green eye.

Growing conditions and maintenance: Start seed indoors 8 to 10 weeks prior to the last frost, or sow directly outdoors in fall or early spring. Allow 9 to 24 inches between plants. Once established they may self-seed. They tolerate a wide range of soils and drought.

Salpiglossis
(sal-pi-GLOSS-is)
PAINTED TONGUE

Salpiglossis sinuata 'Bolero'

Plant type: *annual*

Height: *2 to 3 feet*

Interest: *flowers*

Soil: *well-drained, fertile*

Light: *full sun*

The flowers of salpiglossis come in an incredible range of colors, including red, pink, purple, blue, white, yellow, and brown. Blooms are typically veined or spotted with a contrasting color. Plants add a cheerful accent to beds and borders, and are excellent for cutting.

Selected species and varieties: *S. sinuata* has an erect, bushy habit with narrow 4-inch leaves. Both leaves and stems are slightly hairy and sticky. Flowers resemble petunias, are 2 to 2½ inches wide, have a velvety texture, and appear in terminal clusters; 'Bolero' is 18 to 24 inches tall with flower colors that include gold, rose, red, and blue.

Growing conditions and maintenance: Start seed indoors 6 to 8 weeks prior to the last frost for transplanting to the garden after all danger of frost has passed, or plant directly outdoors in late spring. Space plants 10 to 12 inches apart. Prepare soil deeply to provide excellent drainage. Taller varieties may need staking. Plants thrive in cool weather and die in high heat and humidity.

Salvia
(SAL-vee-a)
SAGE

Salvia coccinea 'Lady in Red'

Plant type: *annual or tender perennial*

Height: *8 inches to 4 feet*

Interest: *flowers, foliage*

Soil: *sandy, dry to well-drained*

Light: *full sun to partial shade*

Whorled spikes of tiny hooded summer-to fall-blooming flowers line the tips of salvia's erect stems above soft, sometimes downy leaves. Salvias are particularly effective in masses that multiply the impact of their flowers. Tender perennial salvias that cannot withstand frost are grown as annuals in Zone 8 and colder.

Selected species and varieties: *S. argentea* (silver sage) produces branching clusters of white flowers tinged yellow or pink on 3-foot stems above rosettes of woolly gray-green 6- to 8-inch leaves. *S. coccinea* (Texas sage) produces heart-shaped leaves on 1- to 2-foot branching stems; 'Lady in Red' has slender clusters of bright red flowers. *S. farinacea* (mealycup sage) grows 2 to 3 feet tall with gray-green leaves and spikes of small blue flowers; 'Silver White' grows 18 to 20 inches tall with silvery white flowers; 'Strata' reaches 16 to 24 inches with 6- to 10-inch spikes of bicolored flowers in blue and white that are useful in both fresh and dried arrangements; 'Victoria' grows to 18 inches with a uniform habit and a 14-inch spread with violet-blue flowers. *S. greggii* (autumn sage) grows 2 to 4 feet tall with an erect, shrubby habit, medium green leaves, and red, pink, yellow, or white flowers that bloom from midsummer through fall and attract hummingbirds. *S. leucantha* (Mexican bush sage) grows 2 to 4 feet with gracefully arching stems, gray-green leaves, and arching spikes of purple and white flowers in summer and fall. *S. officinalis* (common sage, garden sage, culinary sage) bears whorls of tiny white, blue, or purple flowers above hairy, aromatic

Salvia farinacea 'Victoria'

gray-green leaves used for cooking; 'Icterina' grows 18 inches tall with variegated leaves of golden yellow and green; 'Tricolor' grows to 18 inches and produces leaves that are white and purple with pink margins. *S. splendens* (scarlet sage) grows 8 to 30 inches with bright green 2- to 4-inch leaves and terminal clusters of red, pink, purple, lavender, or white flowers up to 1½ inches long; 'Blaze of Fire' grows 12 to 14 inches with bright red blooms; 'Laser Purple' bears deep purple flowers that resist fading; 'Rodeo' grows to 10 inches with early red flowers. *S. viridis* (clary sage, painted sage) grows to 18 inches with white and blue flowers with showy pink to purple bracts throughout summer and fall, and is superb for fresh and dried arrangements.

Growing conditions and maintenance: Start seed indoors 6 to 8 weeks prior to the last frost. Space smaller types 12 to 18 inches apart, larger types 2 to 3 feet apart. Salvias are generally drought tolerant. Remove faded flowers to extend bloom.

Sanvitalia
(san-vi-TAY-lee-a)
CREEPING ZINNIA

Sanvitalia procumbens

Plant type:	*annual*
Height:	*5 to 6 inches*
Interest:	*flowers*
Soil:	*well-drained to dry*
Light:	*full sun*

This low-growing annual from Mexico produces a nonstop display of flowers from early summer to frost. Flowers resemble zinnias, but each head is only ¾ inch across. Sanvitalia makes a superb edging or ground cover, and it is well suited to a sunny rock garden.

Selected species and varieties: *S. procumbens* (trailing sanvitalia) grows to a height of 6 inches, although its trailing stems spread to 18 inches, with pointed, oval leaves that are ½ to 1 inch long. Flowers are composed of yellow or orange rays surrounding a dark purple center and may be single, semidouble, or double; 'Gold Braid' produces double yellow blooms; 'Mandarin Orange' bears semidouble orange flowers.

Growing conditions and maintenance: Start seed indoors 4 to 6 weeks prior to the last frost, or sow directly outdoors in late spring. Allow 6 to 12 inches between plants. Sanvitalia thrives in hot, humid weather and is drought tolerant.

Scabiosa
(skab-ee-O-sa)
SCABIOUS

Scabiosa atropurpurea

Plant type:	*annual*
Height:	*18 inches to 3 feet*
Interest:	*flowers*
Soil:	*well-drained, fertile*
Light:	*full sun*

Scabiosa is easy to grow and produces long-lasting flowers that are well suited to borders, massing, and both fresh and dried arrangements. Flower heads are 1 to 2 inches across with prominent stamens that resemble pins stuck in a pincushion; colors include lavender, pink, purple, maroon, red, and white.

Selected species and varieties: *S. atropurpurea* grows 2 to 3 feet tall with an erect habit and showy, domed flower heads on long stems. *S. stellata* (paper moon) grows 1½ to 2½ feet with pale blue flowers that become papery when dry and are highly valued for dry arrangements; 'Drumstick' bears faded blue flowers that quickly mature to bronze; 'Ping-Pong' bears white flowers on heads the size of a ping-pong ball.

Growing conditions and maintenance: Start seed indoors 4 to 6 weeks prior to the last frost and transplant to the garden after danger of frost has passed, or sow directly outdoors in late spring. Space plants 8 to 12 inches apart. Water during dry periods.

Schizanthus
(ski-ZAN-thus)
BUTTERFLY FLOWER

Schizanthus pinnatus

Plant type: *annual*

Height: *1 to 4 feet*

Interest: *flowers*

Soil: *moist, well-drained, fertile*

Light: *full sun to partial shade*

Schizanthus is a native of Chile that produces exotic flowers resembling orchids. Borne in loose clusters, the two-tone flowers, which come in many colors, are pleasantly displayed against fernlike foliage. They are useful in beds or containers and are excellent for cutting.

Selected species and varieties: *S. pinnatus* grows to 4 feet with light green finely cut leaves and 1½-inch flowers produced in open clusters from early summer to early fall. Flowers have a tropical appearance, and colors include pink, rose, salmon, vivid red, lavender, violet, and cream. Each displays contrasting markings on the throat.

Growing conditions and maintenance: Start seed indoors 8 weeks before the last frost, or plant directly outdoors in midspring. Make successive plantings to extend the blooming season. Space plants 12 inches apart. Provide abundant moisture in a soil with excellent drainage. Grow in light shade where summers are hot. Tall varieties require staking; shorter types are better for borders.

Silybum
(sil-LY-bum)
BLESSED THISTLE

Silybum marianum

Plant type: *annual or biennial*

Height: *to 4 feet*

Interest: *flowers, foliage*

Soil: *well-drained*

Light: *full sun*

Silybum is grown primarily for its spiny, glossy foliage, which is dark green with silvery white spots. The 12- to 14-inch deeply lobed basal leaves form an attractive wide-spreading rosette from which 2-inch thistlelike flowers rise in late summer. It is useful as a ground cover in dry, sunny sites. The roots, leaves, and flower heads can be eaten as a vegetable.

Selected species and varieties: *S. marianum* grows to 4 feet with coarse, prominently veined and spotted leaves and solitary nodding flower heads ranging in color from rose to purple. Flowers are surrounded by curved, spiny bracts.

Growing conditions and maintenance: Sow seed directly outdoors in early spring. Once established, plants often self-seed and may become weedy. Space plants 2 feet apart. They tolerate poor soil and dry conditions.

Tagetes
(ta-JEE-tez)
MARIGOLD

Tagetes erecta 'Primrose Lady'

Plant type: *annual or tender perennial*

Height: *6 inches to 3 feet*

Interest: *flowers, foliage*

Soil: *well-drained*

Light: *full sun*

Marigolds are among the most popular bedding plants in the United States. They are easy to grow, provide a reliable display, and are available in a wide range of heights. Their flowers typically range from pale yellow to bright orange and burgundy and are produced nonstop from early summer to frost in many varieties. Some species are grown for their fernlike foliage, which is often quite aromatic. Marigolds are suited to many uses, depending on their size: They can be placed in the background of a border, used as an edging, or massed in a bed. They are suitable for cutting for fresh arrangements and can be effectively grown in patio planters and window boxes. Despite some of their common names, marigolds are native to Mexico and Central and South America.

Selected species and varieties: *T. erecta* (American marigold, African marigold, Aztec marigold) has an erect to rounded habit and a wide range of heights, categorized as dwarf—10 to 14 inches, medium—15 to 20 inches, or tall—to 36 inches; flower heads are solitary, single to double, and 2 to 5 inches across; 'Primrose Lady' is 15 to 18 inches with a compact habit and double yellow carnationlike flowers. *T. filifolia* (Irish lace) is grown primarily for its finely divided fernlike foliage; it grows 6 to 12 inches tall and wide and produces small white blooms in late summer. *T. lucida* (Mexican tarragon, sweet-scented marigold) grows 2 to 2½ feet tall with dark green tarragon-scented leaves and small, single yellow flowers in clusters; it may be

Tagetes tenuifolia

perennial in warm climates. *T. patula* (French marigold, sweet mace) grows 6 to 18 inches tall with a neat, rounded habit and deeply serrated bright green leaves; flower heads are solitary, up to 2½ inches across, and may be single or double; double flowers often display a crest of raised petals at their center; colors include yellow, orange, maroon, and bicolors. *T. tenuifolia* (dwarf marigold, signet marigold) grows 6 to 12 inches tall with compact mounds of fernlike foliage and single yellow or orange 1-inch flowers that are so profuse they almost completely cover the leaves; excellent for edgings and window boxes.

Growing conditions and maintenance: Start seed indoors 6 to 8 weeks prior to the last frost, or sow directly outdoors 2 weeks before that date. Space plants 6 to 18 inches apart, depending on the variety, and pinch the seedlings to promote bushiness. Marigolds thrive in a moist, well-drained soil but tolerate dry conditions. Remove dead blossoms to encourage continuous flowering. Avoid overwatering.

Thunbergia
(thun-BER-jee-a)
CLOCK VINE

Thunbergia alata

Plant type: *tender perennial*

Height: *3 to 6 feet*

Interest: *flowers*

Soil: *moist, well-drained, fertile*

Light: *full sun to partial shade*

Thunbergia, native to South Africa, is a small climbing or trailing vine that produces a mass of neat, triangular leaves and trumpet-shaped flowers in shades of yellow, orange, and cream, usually with a very dark center, throughout the summer. Plants are attractive in window boxes and hanging baskets, and are excellent as a fast-growing screen on a trellis or fence.

Selected species and varieties: *T. alata* (black-eyed Susan vine) develops twining stems with 3-inch leaves with toothed margins and winged petioles. The solitary flowers are 1 to 2 inches across with 5 distinct, rounded petal segments, usually surrounding a black or dark purple center.

Growing conditions and maintenance: Start seed indoors 6 to 8 weeks prior to the last frost, or sow directly outdoors after danger of frost is past. Space plants 12 inches apart and provide support if you wish them to climb. Plants thrive where summer temperatures remain somewhat cool. Water during dry periods.

Tithonia
(ti-THO-nee-a)
MEXICAN SUNFLOWER

Tithonia rotundifolia

Plant type: *annual*

Height: *2 to 6 feet*

Interest: *flowers*

Soil: *well-drained*

Light: *full sun*

This native of Mexico and Central America is exceptional in its ability to withstand heat and dry conditions. Its daisylike flowers range in color from yellow to red and are borne atop erect stems with coarse-textured leaves. Plants are suitable for the background of borders and for cutting; they can also be used as a fast-growing summer screen.

Selected species and varieties: *T. rotundifolia* has a vigorous, erect habit with broadly oval, velvety, serrated leaves that may reach 10 inches in length. Flower heads consist of orange, yellow, or scarlet raylike petals surrounding an orange-yellow disk; 'Goldfinger' grows 2 to 3 feet with 3-inch orange-scarlet blooms.

Growing conditions and maintenance: Start seed indoors 6 to 8 weeks prior to the last frost, or sow directly outdoors after all danger of frost has passed. Do not cover seed. Space plants 24 to 30 inches apart. Plants tolerate poor soil, heat, and drought. When cutting flowers for indoor arrangements, cut in the bud stage and sear the stem.

Torenia
(to-REE-nee-a)
WISHBONE FLOWER

Torenia fournieri

Plant type: *annual*

Height: *6 to 12 inches*

Interest: *flowers*

Soil: *moist, well-drained*

Light: *partial to full shade*

The blossoms of wishbone flower, also called blued torenia, have upper and lower lobed lips and are borne above a mound of foliage from midsummer to early fall. Because they thrive in shady locations, they are the perfect choice for a woodland bed or shady border. They are also well suited to hanging baskets and patio planters.

Selected species and varieties: *T. fournieri* (bluewings) has a rounded, compact habit with neat, oval leaves 1½ to 2 inches long. The 1-inch flowers appear in stalked clusters; each bloom displays a pale violet tube with a yellow blotch and flaring lower petal edges marked with deep purple-blue. A pair of fused yellow stamens resemble a poultry wishbone, hence the common name.

Growing conditions and maintenance: Start seeds indoors 10 to 12 weeks prior to the last frost; in Zone 9 and warmer, seed can be sown directly outdoors in early spring. Space seedlings 6 to 8 inches apart. Plants thrive in humid areas, and they tolerate full sun only in cool climates.

Tropaeolum
(tro-PEE-o-lum)
NASTURTIUM

Tropaeolum majus

Plant type: *annual*

Height: *6 inches to 8 feet*

Interest: *flowers, foliage*

Soil: *poor, well-drained to dry*

Light: *full sun*

Nasturtiums' bright flowers and attractive shieldlike leaves make them excellent fast-growing screens or bedding plants. Blooms appear from summer through frost. Young leaves and flowers are edible, and flowers are ideal for cutting.

Selected species and varieties: *T. majus* (common nasturtium) may be bushy, about 1 foot tall and twice as wide, or climbing, reaching 6 to 8 feet; leaves are round, 2 to 7 inches across, with long stems, and the showy 2- to 3-inch flowers are red, yellow, white, or orange and may be spotted or streaked. *T. minus* (dwarf nasturtium) reaches 6 to 12 inches in height, with a bushy habit suitable for edgings or massing; 'Alaska Mixed' grows 8 to 15 inches with variegated leaves and a wide range of flower colors. *T. peregrinum* (canary creeper, canarybird vine) is a climbing vine up to 8 feet long with pale yellow fringed flowers and deeply lobed leaves that resemble those of a fig.

Growing conditions and maintenance: Sow seed directly outdoors after danger of frost has passed. Nasturtiums do not transplant well. Space dwarf types 12 inches apart, vines 2 to 3 feet apart. Do not fertilize.

Verbascum
(ver-BAS-cum)
MULLEIN

Verbascum bombyciferum

Plant type: *biennial*

Height: *2 to 8 feet*

Interest: *flowers, foliage*

Soil: *well-drained*

Light: *full sun*

Mulleins develop a rosette of coarse leaves and tall, sturdy spikes of long-lasting summer flowers followed by attractive dried seedpods. Plant them in the rear of a border or in a wildflower garden.

Selected species and varieties: *V. blattaria* (moth mullein) grows 2 to 6 feet with dark green glossy leaves and slender spikes of pale yellow flowers with a lavender throat. *V. bombyciferum* (silver mullein) produces rosettes of oval leaves covered with silvery, silky hairs and 4- to 6-foot spikes of sulfur yellow flowers; 'Arctic Summer' is a heavy-flowering form with powdery white stems and leaves; 'Silver Candelabra' grows to 8 feet, with silver leaves and pale yellow blooms; 'Silver Lining' produces cool yellow flowers and metallic silver leaves and stems. *V. thapsus* (flannel mullein) bears felt-textured leaves and 3-foot spikes of yellow flowers, and may be found growing wild along the roadside.

Growing conditions and maintenance: Sow seed directly outdoors in spring to bloom the following year. Established plants will self-seed. Space 1 to 2 feet apart. Plants tolerate dry conditions.

Verbena
(ver-BEE-na)
VERVAIN

Verbena bonariensis

Plant type: *annual or tender perennial*

Height: *6 inches to 4 feet*

Interest: *flowers*

Soil: *moist, well-drained*

Light: *full sun*

From summer through frost, small, vividly colored flowers bloom in clusters on wiry stems with soft green foliage. Verbenas are useful as ground covers or as fillers in a border; smaller types are a good choice for containers, while taller types are excellent for cutting.

Selected species and varieties: *V. bonariensis* (Brazilian verbena) grows to 4 feet tall with slender, multibranched stems; wrinkled, toothed leaves grow primarily on the lowest 12 inches of the stem so that the fragrant rosy violet flower clusters seem nearly to float in the air. *V. x hybrida* (garden verbena) grows 6 to 12 inches tall and spreads to 2 feet, with wrinkled leaves and small flowers in loose, rounded heads to 2 inches across in shades of pink, red, blue, purple, and white; 'Peaches and Cream' bears flowers in shades of apricot, orange, yellow, and cream; flowers of 'Silver Ann' open bright pink and fade to blended pink and white.

Growing conditions and maintenance: Start seed indoors 12 weeks prior to the last frost and transplant outdoors after all danger of frost has passed. Allow 12 inches between plants of common verbena and 2 feet between Brazilian verbenas.

Viola
(vy-O-la)
PANSY

Viola tricolor

Plant type: *annual*

Height: *3 to 12 inches*

Interest: *flowers*

Soil: *moist, well-drained, fertile*

Light: *full sun to partial shade*

Although many pansies are technically short-lived perennials, they are considered annuals because they bloom their first year from seed and their flowers decline in quality afterward, regardless of region. They may also be treated as biennials, sown in late summer for bloom early the following spring. Their vividly colored and interestingly marked flowers are borne over a long season, often beginning with the first signs of spring and lasting until the summer heat causes them to fade, although a bit of shade and water may encourage the blossoms to continue throughout most of the summer. The rounded flower petals overlap, and their patterns often resemble a face. Pansies are a good choice for planting with bulbs, combining well with the flower forms and providing cover for fading foliage. They are attractive when massed in beds and useful as edgings or combined with other annuals in patio planters or window boxes.

Selected species and varieties: *V. rafinesquii* (field pansy) is a true annual that is native to much of the United States and grows 3 to 12 inches tall. Its ½-inch flowers are pale blue to cream, often

with purple veins and a yellow throat. *V. tricolor* (Johnny-jump-up, miniature pansy) is a European native that has naturalized in much of the United States. It typically grows to 8 inches with a low, mounded habit and small, colorful flowers that have been favorites in the garden since Elizabethan times. The 1-inch flowers are fragrant, and colors include deep violet, blue, lavender, mauve, yellow, cream, white, and bicolors; flowers are edible and are often used as a garnish; 'Bowles' Black' bears blue-black flowers. *V.* x *wittrockiana* (common pansy)

Viola 'Melody Purple and White'

grows 4 to 8 inches tall and spreads to 12 inches. The 1- to 2-inch flowers are usually three-tone in shades of purple, blue, dark red, rose, pink, brown, yellow, and white. Many varieties are available; 'Melody Purple and White' bears flowers with white and purple petals marked with deep violet-blue.

Growing conditions and maintenance: Sow seed outdoors in late summer for earliest spring blooms or purchase transplants. Pansies started in late summer should be protected over the winter in a cold frame or by covering plants after the first hard frost with a light mulch or branches. They can also be started indoors in midwinter to transplant to the garden in midspring. Germination can be enhanced by moistening and chilling the seed (between 40° and 45° F) for 1 week prior to planting. Space plants about 4 inches apart. Pansies prefer a cool soil. Remove faded blooms and keep plants well watered to extend flowering.

Xeranthemum
(zer-RAN-the-mum)
EVERLASTING

Xeranthemum annuum

Plant type: *annual*

Height: *18 inches to 3 feet*

Interest: *flowers*

Soil: *moist, well-drained to average*

Light: *full sun*

Xeranthemum's fluffy flower heads in purple, pink, and white are displayed on long stems from summer to early fall. This Mediterranean native is a good choice for the midground of a mixed border and is exceptional for cutting, for both fresh and dried arrangements.

Selected species and varieties: *X. annuum* has an erect habit and gray-green leaves that are concentrated toward the bottom of the wiry stems. The 1½-inch flowers may be single or double, and they are surrounded by papery bracts that are the same color as the true flowers at the center of the head.

Growing conditions and maintenance: In colder zones, start seed indoors in individual peat pots 6 to 8 weeks prior to the last frost, but handle carefully because they are difficult to transplant. In warmer climates, sow seed directly in the garden in spring after all danger of frost has passed. Allow 6 to 9 inches between plants. They adapt to most soils. For use in winter arrangements, cut flowers when they are fully open and hang them upside down in a well-ventilated room until dry.

Zinnia
(ZIN-ee-a)
ZINNIA

Zinnia elegans

Plant type: *annual*

Height: *8 to 36 inches*

Interest: *flowers*

Soil: *well-drained*

Light: *full sun*

Zinnias brighten the border with pompom or daisylike blooms whose petal-like rays may be flat and rounded, rolled into fringes, or crowded around yellow or green centers that are actually the true flowers. Hues range from riotous yellows, oranges, and reds to subdued pinks, roses, salmons, and creams, and maroon and purple. Flowers bloom from summer through frost and are best massed for effect as edgings or in the border. Low, spreading types are at home in window boxes and patio planters, while taller forms are excellent for fresh summer arrangements.

Selected species and varieties: *Z. angustifolia* (narrowleaf zinnia) has a compact, spreading habit, grows 8 to 16 inches in height with narrow, pointed leaves and 1-inch wide single orange flowers, and is excellent as an edging or ground cover; 'White Star' bears abundant 2-inch flowers consisting of white rays surrounding orange-yellow centers. *Z. elegans* (common zinnia) grows 1 to 3 feet with an erect habit, rough-textured, clasping leaves up to 4 inches long, and showy flowers in many colors up to 6 inches across; 'Big Red' bears blood red 5- to 6-

inch blooms on vigorous plants that reach 3 feet in height; 'Cut and Come Again' is a mildew-resistant variety that grows 2 feet tall and bears abundant 2½-inch flowers in a wide range of colors on long, sturdy stems that are suitable for cutting; 'Peter Pan' is an early bloomer with a uniform habit reaching 10 to 12 inches tall and 3- to 4-inch flowers in a wide range of colors. *Z. haageana* (Mexican zinnia) grows 1 to 2 feet tall with narrow leaves and 1½- to 2½-inch single or double flowers in colors that include red, mahogany, yellow, orange, and bi-

Zinnia angustifolia 'White Star'

colors; 'Persian Carpet' has a bushy habit and 2-inch, mostly bicolored flowers with pointed petals and crested centers in shades from maroon through chocolate to gold and cream.

Growing conditions and maintenance: Zinnias are among the easiest annuals to grow. Start seed indoors 6 weeks prior to the last frost, or sow directly outdoors after all danger of frost has passed. Space seedlings 6 to 12 inches apart and pinch young plants to encourage bushiness. Remove spent blooms to keep plants attractive and to encourage flowering. Zinnias thrive in hot weather but benefit from regular watering. *Z. angustifolia* tolerates dry conditions.

Achillea
(ak-il-EE-a)
YARROW

Achillea 'Coronation Gold'

Hardiness: *Zones 4-8*

Flowering season: *summer*

Height: *6 inches to 4½ feet*

Flower color: *white, yellow, pink*

Soil: *well-drained, poor*

Light: *full sun*

Flat-topped flower clusters grown above green or gray-green fernlike foliage. Long-lasting when cut, the flowers also dry well.

Selected species and varieties: *A. filipendulina* (fernleaf yarrow)—yellow flower clusters up to 5 inches across; 'Gold Plate', 6-inch yellow flower heads on 4½-foot stems. *A.* 'Coronation Gold', a hybrid with 3-inch deep yellow flower clusters on 3-foot stems. *A. x lewisii* 'King Edward'—small yellow flowers on 4-inch stalks. *A. millefolium* (common yarrow)—2-inch white flowers with cultivars in shades from pink to red; 'Red Beauty' has broad crimson flower clusters.

Growing conditions and maintenance: Plant taller species 2 feet apart and dwarfs 1 foot apart. Propagate by division every 2 to 4 years in spring or fall or from midsummer stem cuttings.

Aeonium
(ee-OH-nee-um)
AEONIUM

Aeonium arboreum 'Schwartzkopf

Hardiness: *Zones 9-10*

Flowering season: *succulent perennial*

Height: *1 to 3 feet*

Flower color: *yellow*

Soil: *light, well-drained*

Light: *full sun*

Aeoniums bear fleshy leaves in attractive rosettes on succulent stems. Flowers in shades of yellow develop in terminal pyramidal clusters. Aeoniums are prized for their long season of interest in West Coast gardens, where they are often used as accents in rock gardens, dry borders, and containers.

Selected species and varieties: *A. arboreum* 'Schwartzkopf'—2 to 3 feet tall, upright and shrubby, with golden yellow flowers and dark, shiny, purple-black leaves appearing in 6- to 8-inch rosettes on branched stems. *A. tabuliforme*—12 inches, with leaves forming saucer-shaped, stemless rosettes 3 to 10 inches across and pale yellow flowers.

Growing conditions and maintenance: Aeoniums thrive in California coastal conditions, where their soil and light needs are best met and they enjoy high humidity and mild temperatures. They can be grown farther inland, but may require some shade for protection from midday heat. They do not tolerate frost.

Agapanthus
(ag-a-PAN-thus)
AFRICAN LILY

Agapanthus africanus

Hardiness: *Zones 8-10*

Flowering season: *summer*

Height: *3 to 5 feet*

Flower color: *blue, white*

Soil: *moist, well-drained, acid loam*

Light: *full sun*

Slender stems support loose clusters of 30 to 100 small, tubular flowers, which bloom for 2 months among narrow, glossy, dark green leaves. African lilies make good potted plants north of Zone 8; they are evergreen in warm winters.

Selected species and varieties: *A. africanus*—up to 30 eye-catching deep blue blossoms on 3-foot stems; leaves are 4 to 10 inches long. *A. orientalis*—5 feet tall with up to 100 blue flowers in each cluster; the leaves of the variety 'Variegatus' are striped white. 'Albidus' has white flowers.

Growing conditions and maintenance: Plant agapanthus 2 feet apart and water well during the growing season. Plants tolerate dryness while dormant. South-facing locations are preferable, as agapanthus leans toward light if not in full sun. In northern zones, grow in large containers for porch or patio.

Ajuga
(a-JOO-ga)
BUGLEWEED

Ajuga reptans

Hardiness: *Zones 3-9*

Flowering season: *late spring to summer*

Height: *to 12 inches*

Flower color: *white, pink, violet, blue*

Soil: *well-drained, acid loam*

Light: *full sun to light shade*

An excellent ground cover, ajuga spreads by stolons in or on top of the soil, creating dense mats of attractive foliage that suppress weeds; very vigorous and sometimes invasive. The foliage, growing in shades of green, deep purple, bronze, or creamy white mottled dark pink, is topped by whorled flowers.

Selected species and varieties: *A. genevensis* (Geneva bugleweed)—blue, pink, or white summer flowers on erect stems 6 to 12 inches tall; Zones 4-9. *A. pyramidalis* (upright bugleweed)—blue late-spring flowers on 4- to 6-inch spikes; less invasive than other species; Zones 3-9. *A. reptans* (common bugleweed)—violet flowers ¼ inch long in late spring on 3- to 6-inch prostrate stems. 'Alba' offers white flowers; 'Atropupurea' bronze leaves; 'Rubra' dark purple leaves; and 'Metallica Crispa' curled metallic leaves and blue flowers. Zones 3-9.

Growing conditions and maintenance: Grows equally well in sun or shade. Sow seeds in late summer or fall. Divide in spring or fall.

Allium
(AL-lee-um)
FLOWERING ONION

Allium sphaerocephalum

Hardiness: *Zones 3-9*

Flowering season: *late spring to early summer*

Height: *18 inches to 5 feet*

Flower color: *blue, purple, red, pink, white*

Soil: *well-drained, fertile loam*

Light: *full sun to partial shade*

Flowering onion bears unique globes of tiny blossoms on stiff stalks above leaf clumps that fade after bloom. They make excellent cut flowers.

Selected species and varieties: *A. aflatunense* (Persian onion)—4-inch lilac-purple flowers on 2- to 4-foot stems; Zones 3-8. *A. chris-tophii* (stars-of-Persia)—10-inch violet spheres on 24-inch stems; Zones 4-8. *A. giganteum* (giant onion)—6-inch reddish purple flower clusters on 5-foot stalks; Zones 5-8. *A. sphaerocephalum* (drumstick chives)—green to purple flower clusters atop 2- to 3-foot stalks; Zones 4-8.

Growing conditions and maintenance: Some species form bulbils; others form small bulbs at base of main bulb. Plant bulbs in the fall. Propagate by seed and division. Some species, including *A. aflatunense,* may take two years to germinate. Resistant to pests.

Amsonia
(am-SO-nee-a)
BLUESTAR

Amsonia tabernaemontana

Hardiness: *Zones 3-9*

Flowering season: *late spring to early summer*

Height: *2 to 3 feet*

Flower color: *blue*

Soil: *moderately fertile, well-drained*

Light: *full sun to partial shade*

Amsonia produces pale blue star-shaped blossoms. Blooming in late spring and early summer, they are particularly effective combined with more brightly colored flowers. Its densely mounded willowlike leaves remain attractive throughout the growing season, providing a lovely foil for later-blooming perennials.

Selected species and varieties: *A. tabernaemontana*—produces steel blue flowers in terminal clusters on 2- to 3-foot-tall stiff, erect stems with densely occurring leaves 3 to 6 inches long that turn yellow in fall; *A. t.* var. *salicifolia* has longer and thinner leaves and blooms slightly later than the species.

Growing conditions and maintenance: Amsonias grown in shade will have a more open habit than those grown in sun. In poor to moderately fertile soil, amsonia stems rarely need staking; avoid highly fertile soil, which produces rank, floppy growth. Other than for propagating, division is usually not necessary.

Anemone
(a-NEM-o-ne)
WINDFLOWER

Anemone pulsatilla

Hardiness: *Zones 2-9*

Flowering season: *spring through fall*

Height: *3 inches to 2 feet*

Flower color: *white, cream, red, purple, blue*

Soil: *well-drained, fertile loam*

Light: *partial shade to full sun*

This diverse genus carries sprightly 1- to 3-inch-wide flowers with single or double rows of petals shaped like shallow cups surrounding prominent stamens and pistils. The flowers are held on branched stems above mounds of handsome deeply cut foliage. Many species brighten the garden during periods when few other plants with similar flowers are in bloom. Native to North America, anemone species can be found in moist woodlands, meadows, and dry prairies.

Selected species and varieties: *A. canadensis* (meadow anemone)—1 to 2 feet tall with deeply lobed basal leaves and 1½-inch white flowers with golden centers on leafy flower stems in late spring; Zones 2-6. *A. caroliniana* (Carolina anemone)—6 to 12 inches tall with numerous 1½-inch white flowers with yellow centers in spring; Zones 6-8. *A.* x *hybrida* (Japanese anemone)—white or pink flowers with a silky sheen on their undersides above dark green foliage from late summer to midfall; Zones 6-8; 'Alba' cultivar grows 2 to 3 feet tall with large clear white flowers; 'Honorine Jobert' has white flowers with yellow centers on 3-foot stems; 'Prince Henry', deep rose flowers on 3-foot stems; 'Queen Charlotte', full, semidouble pink flowers; 'September Charm', single-petaled silvery pink flowers; 'September Sprite', single pink flowers on 15-inch stems. *A. magellanica*—cream-colored flowers bloom from late spring through summer atop 18-inch stems; Zones 2-8. *A. multifida* (early thimbleweed)—loose clump of silky-haired stems up to 20 inches tall with deeply divided leaves on long stalks; sepals of the ⅜-inch flowers that appear from late spring to summer are usually yellowish white but occasionally bright red; Zones 3-9. *A. pulsatilla* [also classified as *Pulsatilla vulgaris*] (pasqueflower)—2-inch-wide blue or purple bell-shaped spring flowers on 1-foot stems above hairy leaves; Zones 5-8. *A. sylvestris* 'Snowdrops' (snowdrops windflower)—1 to 1½ feet tall, with light green foliage topped by dainty, fragrant 2-inch spring flowers. *A. vitifolia* 'Robustissima' (grapeleaf anemone)—branching clusters of pink flowers from late summer to fall on 1- to 3-foot stalks; an invasive variety good for naturalizing; Zones 3-8.

Growing conditions and maintenance: Plant small anemones 1 foot apart, taller varieties 2 feet apart. The latter may require staking. Meadow anemone prefers a moist, sandy soil and needs frequent division to prevent overcrowding. Pasqueflowers need full sun and a neutral to alkaline soil in a cool location. Snowdrops windflowers prefer moist soil; grapeleaf anemones tolerate dry conditions. Protect all anemones from afternoon sun and do not allow to dry out completely. Propagate cultivars of Japanese anemone by root cuttings or division, others from seed. Divide Japanese and grapeleaf anemones in spring every 3 years to maintain robustness. Other species grow slowly and division is rarely needed.

Anthemis
(AN-them-is)
CHAMOMILE

Anthemis tinctoria

Hardiness: *Zones 3-8*

Flowering season: *midsummer through early fall*

Height: *2 to 3 feet*

Flower color: *yellow, orange*

Soil: *well-drained to dry, poor*

Light: *full sun*

Anthemis has daisylike blossoms 2 to 3 inches across. They grow amid shrubby, aromatic, gray-green foliage and are excellent as cut flowers.

Selected species and varieties: *A. sanctijohannis* (St. John's chamomile)—2-inch bright orange flowers on evergreen shrubs; Zones 5-8. *A. tinctoria* (golden marguerite)—2-inch, upturned gold-yellow flowers above finely cut, aromatic foliage; 'Kelwayi' has bright yellow flowers; 'Moonlight', pale yellow; 'E.C. Buxton', creamy white; Zones 3-8.

Growing conditions and maintenance: Plant anthemis 1½ feet apart. Remove spent flowers for continuous bloom over several months. Propagate by division every 2 years, from seed, or from stem cuttings in spring.

Aquilegia
(ak-wil-EE-jee-a)
COLUMBINE

Aquilegia canadensis

Hardiness: *Zones 3-9*

Flowering season: *spring to early summer*

Height: *8 inches to 3 feet*

Flower colors: *white, yellow, pink, red, blue*

Soil: *moist, well-drained, acid loam*

Light: *full sun to shade*

The flowers of this beautiful and delicate wildflower come in many colors and bi-colors, appearing in spring on erect stems; they are nodding or upright and consist of a short tube surrounded by five petals and backward-projecting spurs of varying lengths. The blue-green compound leaves fade early. Many species have a life span of only 3 to 4 years.

Selected species and varieties: *A. caerulea* (Rocky Mountain columbine)—2- to 3-inch blue-and-white flowers. *A. canadensis* (Canadian columbine)—1 to 3 feet tall, with nodding flowers consisting of yellow sepals, short red spurs, and yellow stamens that project below the sepals. *A. flabellata* 'Nana Alba' (fan columbine)—8 to 12 inches tall, with pure white nodding flowers 2 inches wide with spurs to 1 inch long. *A.* x *hybrida* 'Crimson Star'—30 to 36 inches tall, bearing bright red and white upright flowers with long spurs.

Growing conditions and maintenance: Columbines require good drainage; for heavy soils, work pebbles in before planting. Plant 1½ feet apart. Propagate from seed or by careful division in the fall.

Arenaria
(a-ren-AIR-ee-a)
SANDWORT

Arenaria montana

Hardiness: *Zones 5-9*

Flowering season: *spring*

Height: *2 to 8 inches*

Flower color: *white*

Soil: *moist but well-drained, sandy*

Light: *full sun to partial shade*

Sandwort forms mats of small, dainty evergreen foliage crowned with tiny white flowers. This low, spreading perennial is ideal tucked into wall crevices and between pavers.

Selected species and varieties: *A. montana*—trailing stems up to 12 inches long with grasslike leaves and topped by 1-inch star-shaped white flowers with yellow centers. *A. verna caespitosa* [now formally listed as *Minuartia verna* ssp. *caespitosa*] (Irish moss)—narrow mosslike leaves and ⅜-inch star-shaped white flowers in dainty 2-inch clumps that grow rapidly and withstand heavy foot traffic.

Growing conditions and maintenance: Plant sandwort 6 to 12 inches apart. Water well during dry spells in the growing season. Propagate by division in late summer or early fall.

Armeria
(ar-MEER-ee-a)
THRIFT, SEA PINK

Armeria maritima 'Laucheana'

Hardiness *Zones 3-8*

Flowering season: *spring or summer*

Height: *6 inches to 2 feet*

Flower color: *white, pink, rose*

Soil: *well-drained, sandy loam*

Light: *full sun*

Thrifts produce spherical clusters of flowers on stiff stems above tufts of grassy evergreen leaves.

Selected species and varieties: *A. alliacea* [also called *A. plantaginea*] (plantain thrift)—1¾-inch rosy pink or white flower clusters on 2-foot stems; 'Bee's Ruby' cultivar has intense ruby red flower clusters. *A. maritima* (common thrift)—white to deep pink flowers on 1-foot stems; 'Alba' is a dwarf cultivar with white flowers on 5-inch stems; 'Bloodstone' has brilliant bright red flowers on 9-inch stems; 'Laucheana', rose pink flowers on 6-inch stems.

Growing conditions and maintenance: Space thrifts 9 to 12 inches apart. Older clumps die out in the middle. Rejuvenate and propagate plants by division every 3 or 4 years.

Asclepias
(as-KLEE-pee-as)
MILKWEED

Asclepias tuberosa

Hardiness: *Zones 3-9*

Flowering season: *summer to fall*

Height: *2 to 4 feet*

Flower color: *rose, orange, yellow*

Soil: *well-drained sandy, or moist and deep*

Light: *full sun*

Milkweed's flower stalks bear brilliantly colored flower clusters followed by canoe-shaped pods, which burst to release silky seeds. The flowers are excellent for cutting, and the decorative pods dry well. Some species may be weedy.

Selected species and varieties: *A. incarnata* (swamp milkweed)—clusters of fragrant, pink to rose ¼-inch flowers on 2- to 4-foot stems. *A. tuberosa* (butterfly weed)—showy, vibrant orange flower clusters on 2- to 3-foot stems; the leaves and stems are poisonous.

Growing conditions and maintenance: Plant asclepias 12 inches apart. Swamp milkweed prefers moist conditions; butterfly weed does best in dry soils, where its long taproot makes plants drought tolerant. Propagate from seed sown in spring to blossom in 2 years.

Aster
(AS-ter)
ASTER

Aster novae-angliae 'Harrington's Pink'

Hardiness: *Zones 3-9*

Flowering season: *early summer to fall*

Height: *6 inches to 8 feet*

Flower color: *white, blue, purple, pink*

Soil: *moist, well-drained, fertile*

Light: *full sun*

Asters are prized for their large, showy, daisylike flowers that appear over weeks and even months. Most varieties are subject to mildew.

Selected species and varieties: *A. alpinus*—a low-growing species forming 6- to 12-inch-high clumps topped by violet-blue 1- to 3-inch flowers with yellow centers; 'Dark Beauty' produces deep blue flowers; 'Goliath' grows a few inches taller than the species, with pale blue flowers; 'Happy End' has semidouble lavender flowers. *A.* x *frikartii* (Frikart's aster)—2- to 3-foot-tall plants topped by fragrant 2½-inch lavender-blue flowers with yellow centers blooming in summer and lasting 2 months or longer; 'Monch' has profuse blue-mauve flowers and is resistant to mildew. *A. novae-angliae* (New England aster)—3 to 5 feet tall with 4- to 5-inch leaves and 2-inch violet-purple flowers; less important than its many cultivars, most of which are quite tall and require staking; 'Alma Potschke' has vivid rose-colored blossoms from late summer to fall; 'Harrington's Pink' grows to 4 feet tall with large salmon pink flowers in fall; 'Purple Dome' is a dwarf vari-

ety, growing 18 inches tall and spreading 3 feet wide, with profuse deep purple fall flowers. *A. novi-belgii* (New York aster, Michaelmas daisy)—cultivars from 10 inches to 4 feet tall, blooming in white, pink, red, blue, and purple-violet from late summer through fall; 'Eventide' has violet-blue semidouble flowers on 3-foot stems; 'Professor Kippenburg' is compact and bushy, 12 to 15 inches tall with lavender-blue flowers; 'Royal Ruby' is a compact cultivar with large crimson fall flowers; 'Winston S. Churchill' grows violet-red flowers on 2-foot stems.

Growing conditions and maintenance: Choose sites for asters carefully to avoid mildew problems. Good air circulation is essential; well-drained soils deter rot. Space dwarf asters 1 foot apart, taller ones 2 to 3 feet apart, and thin out young plants to improve air circulation. Taller varieties may require staking. Prompt deadheading encourages a second flowering in early summer bloomers. *A.* x *frikartii* in Zone 5 or colder must be mulched over the winter and should not be cut back or divided in fall; otherwise, divide asters in early spring or fall every 2 years or so when a plant's center be-

Aster x frikartii 'Mönch'

gins to die out. Asters can also be propagated by stem cuttings in spring and early summer. Cultivars seldom grow true from seed.

Astilbe
(a-STIL-bee)
PERENNIAL SPIREA

Astilbe chinensis var. taquetii 'Purple Lance'

Hardiness: *Zones 3-9*

Flowering season: *summer to early fall*

Height: *8 inches to 4 feet*

Flower colors: *white, pink, red, lavender*

Soil: *moist, well-drained, fertile*

Light: *bright full shade to full sun*

Feathery plumes in many colors make astilbe one of the treasures of a shade garden. Depending on variety, blooms appear through summer and into early fall atop 1- to 4-foot stalks. The 6- to 18-inch-high foliage, consisting of finely divided fernlike leaves, adds a medium-fine texture to the landscape. Some varieties are nearly as ornamental in seed as they are in flower. Astilbe can be used as a background accent to shorter perennials, or to grace water features. The dwarf forms work well tucked into rock gardens and border fronts.

Selected species and varieties: *A.* x *arendsii* (false spirea)—a hybrid group, 2 to 4 feet tall, with pink, salmon, red, white, and lavender varieties; 'Bridal Veil' blooms early, with elegant creamy white flower spikes to 30 inches; 'Fanal' has carmine red flowers on 2-foot stems with bronzy leaves in early to midsummer; 'Cattleya' has 36-inch rose flower spikes at midseason; 'Feuer' ('Fire') bears coral red flowers on 30-inch stems in late summer; 'Red Sentinel', 3-foot-tall brilliant red flowers and reddish green leaves in midsummer; 'White Gloria' ('Weisse Gloria'), with white plumes to 2 feet in late summer. *A. chinensis* (Chinese astilbe)—to 2 feet tall, with white, rose-tinged, or purplish blooms; 'Finale' grows 18 inches tall with light pink blooms; 'Pumila' (dwarf Chinese astilbe), a drought-tolerant variety that produces mauve-pink flowers in narrow plumes on 8- to 12-inch stems in late summer and spreads by stolons for a good ground cover; var. *taquetii* 'Purple Lance' ('Purpulanze') (fall astilbe) grows 4 feet tall

Astilbe chinensis 'Pumila'

with purple-red flowers; 'Superba', 3 to 4 feet tall with lavender-pink or reddish purple spikes that bloom from late summer to fall over bronze-green, somewhat coarse foliage. *A. simplicifolia* (star astilbe)—a compact species with simple leaves having several cultivars from 12 to 20 inches tall in white and several shades of pink; Zones 4-8. *A. thunbergii* 'Ostrich Plume' ('Straussenfeder')—salmon pink plumes to 3 feet in midsummer.

Growing conditions and maintenance: Plant astilbes 1½ to 2 feet apart. In hot climates, they require shade, where the soil does not dry out; in cooler climates, partial or full sun is acceptable if the soil is moisture retentive. Select an area that has good drainage, and enrich the soil with compost, peat moss, or leaf mold. Astilbe is a heavy feeder, so take care not to plant under shallow-rooted trees. Allow soil to dry out in the winter. Apply a high-phosphorus fertilizer such as 5-10-5 each spring. Plants will multiply quickly and lose vigor as they become crowded. Divide clumps every 2 or 3 years to rejuvenate. Leave dried flower spikes on plants through the winter for ornamental effect.

Aurinia
(o-RIN-ee-a)
BASKET-OF-GOLD

Aurinia saxatilis

Hardiness: *Zones 4-10*

Flowering season: *late spring to early summer*

Height: *6 to 12 inches*

Flower color: *yellow, gold*

Soil: *well-drained, sandy*

Light: *full sun*

One of the most widely used rock garden plants, basket-of-gold's tiny flowers mass in frothy clusters on low-growing mats of silver gray foliage.

Selected species and varieties: *A. saxatilis* [formerly listed as *Alyssum saxatile*]—golden yellow flowers in open clusters; 'Citrina' has pale yellow flowers and gray-green, hairy foliage; 'Compacta' is dense and slow spreading, with vivid yellow blossoms; 'Dudley Neville' grows light apricot blooms.

Growing conditions and maintenance: Space aurinia plants 9 to 12 inches apart. Plants become leggy if overfertilized. Cut plants back by a third after flowering. Remove and replace plants when they become woody after a few years. Propagate from seed sown in spring or fall or from cuttings. Aurinia plants grow and bloom best in full sun.

Baptisia
(bap-TIZ-ee-a)
WILD INDIGO

Baptisia australis

Hardiness: *Zones 3-9*

Flowering season: *midspring to early summer*

Height: *3 to 4 feet*

Flower color: *blue*

Soil: *well-drained to dry, sandy*

Light: *full sun*

Wild (false) indigo produces dainty blue pealike flowers from midspring to early summer. Its blue-green leaves are an attractive foil for both its own blooms and those of surrounding plants. The leaves remain handsome throughout the growing season. The plant is useful for the background of a border or as a specimen; its pods are often used in dried flower arrangements.

Selected species and varieties: *B. australis*—erect stems to 4 feet in height, producing compound leaves with three leaflets, each 1½ to 3 inches long, and indigo blue flowers in long, terminal racemes, good for cutting. *B. alba*—to 3 feet tall with white flowers; Zones 5-8.

Growing conditions and maintenance: Wild indigo adapts to almost any well-drained soil. It is slow growing and non-invasive. Tall selections may require staking. Remove faded flowers to extend the blooming season.

Begonia
(be-GO-nee-a)
HARDY BEGONIA

Begonia grandis

Hardiness: *Zones 6-9*

Flowering season: *early summer to frost*

Height: *2 feet*

Flower color: *pink, white*

Soil: *moist, rich loam*

Light: *full sun to partial shade*

The popular hardy begonia bears 1-inch flowers at the tips of reddish branched stems. Leaves are hairy, with red-tinted undersides and veins.

Selected species and varieties: *B. grandis*—the hardiest of the begonia genus, with sprays of pink flowers surrounded by heart-shaped leaves; the variety 'Alba' has white flowers.

Growing conditions and maintenance: Plant hardy begonias 1½ feet apart. They tolerate full sun in cooler climates but require partial shade where summers are hot and dry. Propagate by digging and transplanting the sprouts that emerge from the small bulbils that form in leaf junctions, then fall to the ground to root.

Bergenia
(ber-JEN-ee-a)
BERGENIA

Bergenia cordifolia 'Purpurea'

Hardiness: *Zones 3-8*

Flowering season: *spring*

Height: *12 to 18 inches*

Flower color: *white, pink, red, magenta*

Soil: *moist, well-drained, poor*

Light: *full sun to light shade*

Bergenia bears flowers resembling tiny open trumpets in clusters 3 to 6 inches across. Blooms are held above handsome fleshy leaves that are evergreen in milder climates.

Selected species and varieties: *B. cordifolia* (heartleaf bergenia)—pink flower clusters; 'Purpurea' has magenta flowers above leaves that turn purplish in winter. *B. crassifolia* (leather bergenia)—reddish pink blossoms above leaves turning bronze in winter. *B. hybrids*—'Abendglut' ('Evening Glow') has magenta flowers on 1½-foot stems; 'Bressingham White', early-spring white flowers maturing to pale pink; 'Sunningdale', crimson flowers.

Growing conditions and maintenance: Plant bergenias 1 foot apart. Propagate by division after flowering.

Brunnera
(BRUN-er-a)
BRUNNERA

Brunnera macrophylla

Hardiness: *Zones 4-9*

Flowering season: *spring*

Height: *1 to 2 feet*

Flower color: *blue*

Soil: *moist, well-drained loam*

Light: *full sun to light shade*

Brunnera produces airy sprays of dainty azure blue flowers resembling forget-me-nots above large dark green, heart-shaped foliage that grows in loose, spreading mounds. The plant's stems are slightly hairy.

Selected species and varieties: *B. macrophylla* (Siberian bugloss)—boldly textured leaves up to 8 inches across and dainty bright blue flowers; 'Hadspen Cream' has light green leaves edged in cream; 'Langtrees', spots of silvery gray in the center of the leaves; 'Variegata', striking creamy white leaf variegations.

Growing conditions and maintenance: Plant brunneras 1 foot apart. Propagate from seed, by transplanting the self-sown seedlings, or by division in spring.

Campanula
(cam-PAN-ew-la)
BELLFLOWER

Campanula glomerata

Hardiness: *Zones 3-9*

Flowering season: *early summer to late fall*

Height: *6 inches to 5 feet*

Flower color: *blue, violet, purple, white*

Soil: *well-drained loam*

Light: *full sun to light shade*

With spikes or clusters of showy, bell- or star-shaped flowers on stems rising from deep green foliage, bellflowers offer a long season of bloom. Dwarf and trailing varieties enhance a rock garden, wall, or border edge. Taller species form neat tufts or clumps in a perennial border or cutting garden.

Selected species and varieties: *C. carpatica* (Carpathian harebell)—2-inch-wide, bell-shaped, upturned blue flowers bloom on plants up to 1 foot tall; 'Blaue Clips' ('Blue Clips') has 3-inch-wide blue flowers on 6- to 8-inch stems; 'China Doll', lavender flowers on 8-inch stems; 'Wedgewood White' is compact, with white flowers; Zones 3-8. *C. glomerata* (clustered bellflower)—1- to 2-foot stems, with clusters of 1-inch white, blue, or purple flowers; 'Joan Elliott' grows deep violet blooms atop stems 18 inches tall; 'Schneekrone' ('Crown of Snow'), white flowers; 'Superba' grows to 2½ feet, with violet flowers; Zones 3-8. *C. latifolia* (great bellflower)—purplish blue flowers 1½ inches long on spikes, tipping 4- to 5-foot stems; 'Alba' is similar to the species but with white flowers; 'Brantwood' has

large violet-blue trumpet-shaped flowers; Zones 4-8. *C. persicifolia* (peachleaf bellflower)—spikes of 1½-inch blue or white cup-shaped blossoms on stems to 3 feet; 'Alba' has white flowers; 'Telham Beauty', 2- to 3-inch lavender-blue blooms lining the upper half of 4-foot flower stalks; Zones 3-7. *C. portenschlagiana* (Dalmatian bellflower)—a 6- to 8-inch dwarf species with blue flower clusters; Zones 5-7. *C. poscharskyana* (Serbian bellflower)—a mat-forming, creeping dwarf with abundant 1-inch lilac blossoms; Zones 3-8. *C. rotundifolia* (Scottish bluebell)—profuse, nodding, 1-inch-wide blue-violet blooms; 'Olympica' cultivar has bright blue flowers; Zones 3-7.

Growing conditions and maintenance: Plant small bellflowers 12 to 18 inches

Campanula portenschlagiana

apart, larger ones 2 feet apart. Clip faded flowers to encourage further bloom. 'Superba' and Serbian bellflower are heat tolerant. Great bellflower thrives in moist shade. Dalmatian and Serbian bellflowers do well in sandy or gritty soil. Dig up and divide every 3 or 4 years to maintain plant vigor. Propagate from seed or by division every 3 or 4 years.

Centaurea
(sen-TOR-ee-a)
KNAPWEED

Centaurea montana

Hardiness: *Zones 3-8*

Flowering season: *spring to summer*

Height: *1 to 3 feet*

Flower color: *lavender, pink, blue, yellow*

Soil: *well-drained loam*

Light: *full sun*

Excellent plants for a flower garden, centaurea's fringed, thistlelike flowers bloom at the tips of erect stems that are lined with distinctive gray-green foliage.

Selected species and varieties: *C. dealbata* (Persian centaurea)—feathery, lavender to pink 2-inch flowers on stems to 3 feet with coarsely cut, pinnately lobed leaves. *C. hypoleuca* 'John Coutts' (John Coutts' knapweed)—2- to 3-inch pink-and-white flowers on stems to 3 feet tall. *C. macrocephala* (globe centaurea)—yellow flowers up to 3 inches across on erect stems up to 4 feet tall. Globe centaurea is generally planted as a specimen, not in groups. *C. montana* (mountain bluet, cornflower)—2-inch deep cornflower-blue blooms on 1- to 2-foot stems; *C. ruthenica* (ruthenian centaurea)—2 inch pale yellow flowers on stems 3 feet tall with pinnately divided leaves.

Growing conditions and maintenance: Space centaureas 1 to 2 feet apart. Taller species will need staking. Propagate by transplanting self-sown seedlings, by division, or from seed.

Chrysanthemum
(kri-SAN-the-mum)
CHRYSANTHEMUM

Chrysanthemum morifolium 'Pink Daisy'

Hardiness: *Zones 4-10*

Flowering season: *spring to fall*

Height: *1 to 3 feet*

Flower color: *all colors but blue*

Soil: *well-drained, fertile loam*

Light: *full sun to partial shade*

Chrysanthemum flower forms vary widely but generally consist of tiny central disk flowers surrounded by petal-like ray flowers. Reliable performers in the garden, often blooming throughout summer, they are also valued as cut flowers.

Selected species and varieties: *C. coccineum* (painted daisy)—white, pink, lilac, crimson, and dark red single radiating flowers 2 to 4 inches wide, blooming from late spring to early summer on stems 2 to 3 feet tall; 'Eileen May Robinson' produces salmon pink flowers atop 30-inch stems; 'James Kelway', scarlet flowers with bright yellow centers on 18-inch stems; 'Robinson's Pink', 2-foot-tall plants with medium pink flowers; Zones 3-7. *C. frutescens* (marguerite)—single or double daisylike flowers in pink, white, or pale yellow colors throughout the summer on shrubby plants that grow up to 3 feet tall; perennial in Zones 9 and 10, annual elsewhere. *C. leucanthemum* (oxeye daisy)—solitary flowers 1½ inches across with white rays surrounding yellow disks on stems to 2 feet tall in spring and summer. *C. morifolium* (hardy chrysanthemum, florist's chrysanthe-

mum)—rounded plants up to 3 feet tall with aromatic gray-green lobed leaves and 1- to 6-inch flowers in all colors but blue and in a wide range of forms; button chrysanthemums are usually under 18 inches tall with small double flowers less than an inch across; cushion mums usually grow less than 20 inches tall in rounded, compact mounds with numerous double blossoms; daisy chrysanthemums have pronounced yellow centers surrounded by a single row of ray flowers on 2-foot stems, the 'Pink Daisy' cultivar having 2-inch rose pink flowers; decorative chrysanthemums have semidouble or double 2- to 4-inch flowers on loose, open plants to 3 feet tall; pompom chrysanthemums, ball-shaped flowers on 18-inch plants; spider chrysanthemums, rolled petals of irregular lengths; spoon chrysanthemums, petals rolled so that open tips resemble spoons. *C. nipponicum* (Nippon daisy)—solitary 1½- to 3½-inch blossoms with single white ray flowers and greenish yellow disk flowers in the fall on erect, branching stems to 2 feet tall over shrubby mounds. *C. parthenium* (feverfew)—pungently scented ¼-

Chrysanthemum nipponicum

inch white flower buttons with yellow centers, growing from early summer through fall on plants 1 to 3 feet tall; 'Golden Ball' is a dwarf cultivar with yellow flowers; 'White Star', a dwarf with white flowers. *C. x superbum* (Shasta daisy)—white flowers with yellow centers up to 3 inches across from early summer to frost on 3-foot stems with narrow, toothed leaves up to a foot long; 'Alaska' cultivar has large single pure white flowers on 2- to 3-foot stems; 'Little Miss Muffet' is a 12-inch dwarf with semidouble white flowers. Double varieties include 'Horace Read', with 4-inch, ball-like blooms if grown in a cool climate, and 'Marconi', with 6-inch blooms.

Growing conditions and maintenance: Space chrysanthemums 1 to 2 feet apart. Their shallow root systems demand frequent watering and fertilizing. In cooler climates, apply winter mulch to prevent frost heaving. Divide *C. morifolium* and *C.* x *superbum* every 2 years to prevent

Chrysanthemum x superbum

overcrowding, which can lead to disease and fewer flowers. Cut back *C. morifolium* and Nippon daisies two or three times in spring and early summer to develop compact, bushy plants and abundant flowers. Feverfew and oxeye daisies self-sow. Shasta, feverfew, and oxeye daisies are easily propagated from seed. Propagate all chrysanthemums by division or from spring cuttings.

Chrysogonum
(kris-AHG-o-num)
GOLDENSTAR

Chrysogonum virginianum var. virginianum

Hardiness:	*Zones 5-9*
Flowering season:	*late spring to summer*
Height:	*4 to 9 inches*
Flower color:	*yellow*
Soil:	*well-drained*
Light:	*full sun to full shade*

The deep green foliage of goldenstar provides a lush background for its bright yellow, star-shaped flowers, which appear from late spring into summer. Its low-growing, spreading habit makes it useful as a ground cover, for edging at the front of a border, or in a rock garden.

Selected species and varieties: *C. virginianum* var. *virginianum*—6 to 9 inches, with dark green leaves that are bluntly serrated along upright spreading stems and flowers 1½ inches across that bloom throughout the spring in warm areas, well into summer in cooler zones; var. *australe* is similar to var. *virginianum* but more prostrate.

Growing conditions and maintenance: Goldenstar grows well in most soils with average fertility. For use as a ground cover, space plants 12 inches apart. Divide every other year in spring.

Cimicifuga
(si-mi-SIFF-yew-ga)
BUGBANE

Cimicifuga ramosa 'Brunette'

Hardiness:	*Zones 3-8*
Flowering season:	*late summer to fall*
Height:	*3 to 7 feet*
Flower color:	*white*
Soil:	*moist, well-drained, fertile*
Light:	*full sun to partial shade*

Bugbane's lacy leaflets create airy columns of foliage topped by long wands of tiny, frilled flowers. Use it as an accent specimen, naturalized in a woodland garden, or massed at the edge of a stream or pond.

Selected species and varieties: *C. americana* (American bugbane)—dense spikes of creamy blossoms on branched 2- to 6-foot-tall flower stalks in late summer to fall. *C. ramosa* (branched bugbane)—3-foot wands of fragrant white flowers on reddish stalks in fall; 'Atropurpurea' grows to 7 feet with bronzy purple leaves; 'Brunette' has purplish black foliage and pink-tinged flowers on 3- to 4-foot stalks. *C. simplex* 'White Pearl'—2-foot wands of white flowers on branching, arched 3- to 4-foot flower stalks followed by round, lime green fruits.

Growing conditions and maintenance: Plant bugbane in cooler areas of the garden in soil enriched with organic matter. Propagate by division in spring.

Coreopsis
(ko-ree-OP-sis)
COREOPSIS, TICKSEED

Coreopsis grandiflora

Hardiness: *Zones 4-9*

Flowering season: *spring to summer*

Height: *6 inches to 3 feet*

Flower color: *yellow, orange, pink*

Soil: *well-drained loam*

Light: *full sun*

Coreopsis bears single- or double-petaled daisylike, predominantly yellow flowers on wiry, sometimes branching stems over a long season of bloom. The blossoms are excellent for indoor arrangements.

Selected species and varieties: *C. auriculata* (mouse-ear coreopsis)—bears 1- to 2-inch flowers in late spring and early summer above fuzzy leaves with lobed bases lining 1- to 2-foot stems; 'Nana' is a creeping variety 4 to 6 inches tall. *C. grandiflora*—yellow or orange single, semidouble, and double flowers 1 to 1½ inches across, blooming from early to late summer on 1- to 2-foot stems; 'Sunburst' grows to 2 feet tall, with large semidouble golden flowers; 'Sunray', 2 feet tall, with 2-inch double yellow flowers. *C. lanceolata* (lance coreopsis)—yellow flowers 1½ to 2½ inches across, with yellow or brown centers, blooming from late spring through summer on stems up to 3 feet tall; 'Brown Eyes' has maroon rings near the center of yellow flowers; 'Goldfink' is a 10- to 12-inch tall dwarf that blooms prolifically from summer to fall. *C. maritima* (sea dahlia)—

1- to 3-foot stems with long yellow-green leaves and yellow flowers 2½ to 4 inches wide from early spring to summer; suited to the hot, dry summers of southern California. *C. rosea* (pink coreopsis)—delicate pink flowers with yellow centers on stems 15 to 24 inches tall lined with needlelike leaves; can be invasive. *C. verticillata* (threadleaf coreopsis)—yellow flowers 1 to 2 inches across from late spring to late summer grow atop stems that are 2 to 3 feet tall lined with finely cut, delicate leaves 2 to 3 inches long to form dense clumps about 2 feet wide; 'Zagreb' is a 12- to 18-inch tall dwarf with bright yellow flowers; 'Moonbeam' is a warm-climate variety that grows 18 to 24 inches tall with a prolific output of

Coreopsis verticillata

creamy yellow flowers; 'Golden Showers', 2 to 3 feet tall with 2½-inch-wide star-shaped flowers.

Growing conditions and maintenance: Space coreopsis 12 to 18 inches apart. Remove spent flowers to extend bloom time. Transplant the self-sown seedlings of threadleaf coreopsis. Propagate *C. maritima* from seed, all other coreopsis from seed or by division in the spring.

Cynara
(SIN-ah-ra)
CYNARA

Cynara cardunculus

Hardiness: *Zones 8-9*

Flowering season: *summer to fall*

Height: *6 to 8 feet*

Flower color: *blue-violet*

Soil: *well-drained*

Light: *full sun*

Related to the edible globe artichoke, cynara forms clumps of thick stems lined with spiny, lacy, silver-gray leaves with woolly undersides that provide a bold accent in a border. Fuzzy, thistlelike flower globes tip each stem from summer through fall. Both leaves and flowers are prized by floral designers for fresh and dried arrangements.

Selected species and varieties: *C. cardunculus* (cardoon)—deep blue-violet flower heads at the tips of 6-foot stems lined with spiny leaves up to 3 feet long.

Growing conditions and maintenance: Plant cardoon in moist soil enriched with organic matter. Propagate from seed or by transplanting suckers that grow from the base of established clumps.

Dianthus
(dy-AN-thus)
PINKS, CARNATIONS

Dianthus gratianopolitanus 'Karlik'

Hardiness: *Zones 4-8*

Flowering season: *spring to summer*

Height: *3 inches to 2 feet*

Flower color: *pink, red, white*

Soil: *moist, well-drained, slightly alkaline loam*

Light: *full sun to partial shade*

Pinks are old-fashioned perennials whose fragrant flowers with fringed petals are borne singly or in clusters above attractive grassy foliage that is evergreen in mild climates.

Selected species and varieties: *D.* x *allwoodii* (Allwood pinks)—single or double flowers in a wide range of colors grow for 2 months above gray-green leaves in compact mounds 12 to 24 inches tall; 'Aqua' grows white double blooms atop 12-inch stems. *D.* x *a. alpinus* (Alpine pinks)—dwarf varieties of Allwood pinks; 'Doris' grows very fragrant, double salmon-colored flowers with darker pink centers on 12-inch stems; 'Robin', coral red flowers. *D. barbatus* (sweet William)—a biennial species that self-seeds so reliably that it performs like a perennial; unlike other pinks, it produces flowers in flat clusters and without fragrance; 'Harlequin' grows ball-shaped pink-and-white flowers; 'Indian Carpet', single flowers in a mix of colors on 10-inch stems. *D. deltoides* (maiden pinks)—¾-inch red or pink flowers on 12-inch stems above 6- to 12-inch high mats of small bright green leaves; 'Brilliant' has scarlet flowers; 'Flashing Light' ('Leuchtfunk'), ruby red flowers. *D. gratianopolitanus* (cheddar pinks)—1-inch-wide flowers in shades of pink and rose on compact mounds of blue-green foliage 9 to 12 inches high; 'Karlik' has deep pink, fringed, fragrant flowers; 'Tiny Rubies', dark pink double blooms on plants just 4 inches tall. *D. plumarius* (cottage pinks)—fragrant single or semidouble

Dianthus plumarius 'Essex Witch'

flowers 1½ inches across in shades of pink and white or bicolors above 12- to 18-inch-high mats of evergreen leaves; 'Essex Witch' produces fragrant salmon, pink, or white flowers.

Growing conditions and maintenance: Space pinks 12 to 18 inches apart. Cut stems back after bloom and shear mat-forming types in the fall to promote dense growth. Maintain vigor by division every 2 to 3 years. Propagate from seed, from cuttings taken in early summer, or by division in the spring.

Dicentra
(dy-SEN-tra)
BLEEDING HEART

Dicentra spectabilis

Hardiness: *Zones 3-8*

Flowering season: *spring to summer*

Height: *1 to 3 feet*

Flower color: *pink, white, purple*

Soil: *moist, well-drained loam*

Light: *partial shade*

Bleeding heart's unusual puffy, heart-shaped flowers dangle beneath arched stems above mounds of lacy leaves.

Selected species and varieties: *D. eximia* (fringed bleeding heart)—pink to purple flowers above 12-inch mounds of blue-green leaves; 'Alba' has white flowers. *D. formosa* (Pacific bleeding heart)—deep pink flowers on 12- to 18-inch stems; 'Luxuriant', cherry pink flowers; 'Sweetheart', white flowers on 12-inch stems. *D. spectabilis* (common bleeding heart)—pink, purple, or white flowers on arching 3-foot stems.

Growing conditions and maintenance: Space fringed and Pacific bleeding hearts 1 to 2 feet apart, common bleeding heart 2 to 3 feet. Propagate from seed or by division in the early spring.

Doronicum
(do-RON-i-kum)
LEOPARD'S-BANE

Doronicum cordatum

Echinacea
(ek-i-NAY-see-a)
PURPLE CONEFLOWER

Echinacea purpurea

Echinops
(EK-in-ops)
GLOBE THISTLE

Echinops ritro 'Taplow Blue'

Hardiness: *Zones 4-8*

Flowering season: *spring*

Height: *1½ to 2 feet*

Flower color: *yellow*

Soil: *moist loam*

Light: *full sun to partial shade*

Hardiness: *Zones 3-9*

Flowering season: *summer*

Height: *2 to 4 feet*

Flower color: *pink, purple, white*

Soil: *well-drained loam*

Light: *full sun to light shade*

Hardiness: *Zones 3-9*

Flowering season: *summer*

Height: *3 to 4 feet*

Flower color: *blue*

Soil: *well-drained, acid loam*

Light: *full sun*

The daisylike flowers of leopard's-bane stand brightly above mounds of heart-shaped dark green leaves.

Selected species and varieties: *D. cordatum* (Caucasian leopard's-bane)—yellow flowers 2 to 3 inches across on 12- to 18-inch stems above mounds of leaves up to 24 inches across. *D.* 'Miss Mason'—compact 18-inch-tall plants with long-lasting foliage. *D.* 'Spring Beauty'—double-petaled yellow flowers.

Growing conditions and maintenance: Space leopard's-bane 1 to 2 feet apart in full sun but in cool locations where its shallow roots will receive constant moisture. Foliage dies out after flowers bloom. Propagate from seed or by division every 2 to 3 years.

Drooping petals surrounding dark brown, cone-shaped centers bloom on purple coneflower's stiff stems over many weeks.

Selected species and varieties: *E. pallida* (pale coneflower)—rosy purple or creamy white flowers up to 3½ inches long on 3- to 4-foot stems. *E. purpurea*—pink, purple, or white flowers up to 3 inches in diameter on stems 2 to 4 feet tall; 'Bright Star' has rosy pink petals surrounding maroon centers; 'Robert Bloom', reddish purple blooms with orange centers on 2- to 3-foot stems; 'White Lustre', abundant white flowers with bronze centers.

Growing conditions and maintenance: Space plants 2 feet apart. Transplant self-sown seedlings or propagate from seeds or by division.

The round, spiny, steel blue flowers of globe thistle are held well above coarse, bristly foliage on stiff, erect stems. Several stout stems emerge from a thick, branching taproot. Flowers are excellent for both cutting and drying.

Selected species and varieties: *E. exaltatus* (Russian globe thistle)—spiny flowers grow on stems up to 5 feet tall above deep green foliage. *E. ritro* (small globe thistle)—bright blue flower globes up to 2 inches across on stems 3 to 4 feet tall; 'Taplow Blue' has medium blue flowers 3 inches in diameter.

Growing conditions and maintenance: Space globe thistles 2 feet apart. Once established, the plant is drought tolerant. Propagate from seed or by division in the spring.

Erigeron
(e-RIJ-er-on)
FLEABANE

Erigeron speciosus 'Pink Jewel'

Hardiness: *Zones 3-8*

Flowering season: *summer*

Height: *1½ to 2 feet*

Flower color: *blue, lavender, pink*

Soil: *well-drained loam*

Light: *full sun*

Fleabane's asterlike blossoms grow singly or in branched clusters with a fringe of petal-like ray flowers surrounding a yellow center. Flowers sit atop leafy stems above basal rosettes of fuzzy swordlike or oval leaves.

Selected species and varieties: *E. pulchellus* (Poor Robin's plantain)—pink, lavender, or white flowers 1½ inches across on plants up to 2 feet tall. *E. speciosus* (Oregon fleabane)—the most popular species in the genus, *E. speciosus* bears purple flowers 1 to 2 inches across on stems to 30 inches; 'Azure Fairy' has semidouble lavender flowers; 'Double Beauty', double blue-violet flowers; 'Foerster's Liebling', deep pink semidouble flowers; 'Pink Jewel', single lavender-pink flowers; 'Sincerity', single lavender flowers.

Growing conditions and maintenance: Plant fleabane 18 inches apart. Propagate by transplanting self-sown seedlings or by division in spring.

Eupatorium
(yew-pa-TOR-ee-um)
BONESET

Eupatorium coelestinum

Hardiness: *Zones 5-10*

Flowering season: *summer to frost*

Height: *1 to 6 feet*

Flower color: *blue, mauve, purple*

Soil: *moist, well-drained loam*

Light: *full sun to partial shade*

Boneset produces flat, dense clusters of fluffy, frizzy ½-inch flowers on erect stems lined with hairy, triangular leaves. The sturdy clumps will naturalize in marshy areas at the edges of meadows or in wild gardens. The flowers provide a fall foil for yellow or white flowers such as chrysanthemums and are excellent for cutting.

Selected species and varieties: *E. coelestinum* (mist flower, hardy ageratum, blue boneset)—bluish purple to violet ½-inch flowers crowded in clusters at the tips of 1- to 2-foot-tall stalks in late summer to fall. *E. fistulosum* (hollow Joe-Pye weed)—large flat clusters of mauve flowers on hollow purple stems to 6 feet in late summer through fall. *E. maculatum* (Joe-Pye weed, smokeweed)—large flattened clusters of reddish purple or white flowers on 6- 10-foot stems.

Growing conditions and maintenance: Plant boneset 18 to 24 inches apart (allow 3 feet between taller species) in soil enriched with organic matter. Cut foliage back several times through the summer for bushier plants. Propagate from seed or by division in spring.

Euphorbia
(yew-FOR-bee-a)
SPURGE

Euphorbia griffithii 'Fireglow'

Hardiness: *Zones 3-10*

Flowering season: *spring to late summer*

Height: *6 inches to 3 feet*

Flower color: *yellow-green*

Soil: *light, well-drained*

Light: *full sun to partial shade*

A large, diverse genus, *Euphorbia* includes many easy-care perennials. It produces small flowers that are surrounded by showy bracts. Many species produce attractive foliage with intense fall color.

Selected species and varieties: *E. corollata* (flowering spurge)—1 to 3 feet tall, with slender green leaves that turn red in the fall. In mid to late summer, bears clusters of flowers surrounded by small white bracts; Zones 3-10. *E. epithymoides* (cushion spurge)—forms a neat, symmetrical mound 12 to 18 inches high, with green leaves that turn dark red in fall. In spring it produces small green flowers surrounded by showy, chartreuse-yellow bracts; Zones 4-8. *E. griffithii* 'Fireglow'—2 to 3 feet tall, with brick red flower bracts in late spring and early summer; Zones 4-8.

Growing conditions and maintenance: Plant in a sunny, dry location and soil that is not too rich. In moist, fertile locations, growth may become rank, unattractive, and invasive. These plants do not like to be transplanted. Use gloves when handling them, as they exude a milky sap that can cause skin irritations.

Geranium
(jer-AY-nee-um)
CRANESBILL

Geranium endressii

Hardiness: *Zones 4-8*

Flowering season: *spring to summer*

Height: *4 inches to 4 feet*

Flower color: *pink, purple, blue, white*

Soil: *moist, well-drained loam*

Light: *full sun to partial shade*

Cranesbill is valued for both its dainty flat, five-petaled flowers and its neat mounds of lobed or toothed leaves that turn red or yellow in the fall. The plants are sometimes called hardy geraniums to distinguish them from annual geraniums, which belong to the genus *Pelargonium*.

Selected species and varieties: *G. cinereum* (grayleaf cranesbill)—summer-long pink flowers with reddish veins above 6- to 12-inch-high mounds of deeply lobed, dark green leaves with a whitish cast. *G. dalmaticum* (Dalmatian cranesbill)—clusters of rosy pink inch-wide spring flowers on 4- to 6-inch trailing stems. *G. endressii* (Pyrenean cranesbill)—pink flowers ½ inch across in spring and summer above spreading 12- to 18-inch-high mounds of sometimes evergreen leaves; 'A.T. Johnson' has silver-pink flowers; 'Wargrave Pink', deep pink flowers. *G.* 'Johnson's Blue'—1½- to 2-inch blue flowers from spring to summer on plants up to 18 inches tall. *G. macrorrhizum* (bigroot cranesbill)—clusters of magenta or pink flowers with prominent stamens in spring and summer on spreading mounds of aromatic leaves

turning red and yellow in fall; 'Ingwersen's Variety' has lilac-pink flowers; 'Spessart', pink flowers. *G. maculatum* (wild geranium)—loose clusters of rose-purple or lavender-pink flowers in spring on 1- to 2-foot stems. *G. psilostemon* (Armenian cranesbill)—vivid purplish red flowers up to 2 inches across with darker centers on plants 2 to 4 feet tall and equally wide. *G. sanguineum* (bloody cranesbill)—solitary magenta flowers 1 to 1½ inches across in spring and summer on 9- to 12-inch-high spreading mounds of leaves turning deep red in fall; 'Album'

Geranium psilostemon

has white flowers; *G. s.* var. *striatum* [also listed as var. *lancastriense*], with dark red veins tracing light pink flowers.

Growing conditions and maintenance: Space Dalmatian cranesbill 12 inches apart, Armenian cranesbill 3 to 4 feet apart, and other species about 1½ to 2 feet apart. Cranesbill grows in full sun to partial shade in cool areas but needs partial shade in warmer zones. Taller species may need staking. Propagate from seed, summer cuttings, or by division. Divide in spring when clumps show signs of crowding—approximately every 4 years.

Geum
(JEE-um)
GEUM, AVENS

Geum x borisii

Hardiness: *Zones 5-8*

Flowering season: *spring to summer*

Height: *8 to 30 inches*

Flower color: *red, orange, yellow*

Soil: *well-drained, fertile loam*

Light: *full sun to light shade*

Geums produce flat-faced flowers in single or double blooms. The flowers, which resemble wild roses with ruffled petals surrounding frilly centers and growing singly on slender stems, make excellent cut flowers. The bright green, hairy leaves, which are lobed and frilled at their edges, form attractive mounds of foliage ideal for the front of a border or for the rock garden.

Selected species and varieties: *G. coccineum* [also called *G. borisii*, which is different from *G.* x *borisii*, below] (scarlet avens)—early-summer-blooming ½-inch bright orange flowers ride above bright green toothed leaves on 12-inch-tall stems; 'Red Wings' has semidouble scarlet flowers atop 2-foot stems. *G. quellyon* (Chilean avens)—scarlet flowers 1 to 1½ inches wide on plants 18 to 24 inches tall; needs winter protection in the North. 'Fire Opal' grows reddish bronze flowers that are up to 3 inches across; 'Mrs. Bradshaw' bears semidouble red-orange blossoms; 'Lady Stratheden' produces semidouble deep yellow flowers; 'Princess Juliana', semidouble orange-bronze blooms; 'Starker's Magnificent', double-petaled deep orange flowers. *G. reptans* (creeping avens)—yellow or orange flowers on plants 6 to 9 inches tall that spread by runners; Zones 4-7. *G. rivale* (water avens)—tiny, nodding, bell-shaped pink flowers on 12-inch stems above low clumps of dark green, hairy leaves; 'Leonard's Variety' produces copper-rose flowers on slightly taller stems than the species; Zones 3-8. *G. triflorum* 'Prairie Smoke'—nodding purple to straw-colored flowers on 6- to 18-inch-tall plants; Zones 5-10. *G.* x *borisii*—orange-scarlet flowers on 12-inch plants. *G.* 'Georgenberg'—drooping orange flowers on 10- to 12-inch stems.

Growing conditions and maintenance: Space geums 12 to 18 inches apart in soil enriched with organic matter. They grow best in moist but well-drained sites in cooler climates and will not survive wet winter soil. Most species dislike high temperatures; protect the plants from hot afternoon sun in warmer zones. *G. reptans* requires full sun and alkaline soil. Keep geums robust by dividing annually. Propagate by division in late summer for plants that will be ready to flower the following year, or from seed sown outdoors in fall; *G. rivale* may be sown in early spring.

Gillenia
(gil-LEE-nee-a)
BOWMAN'S ROOT

Gillenia trifoliata

Hardiness: *Zones 4-8*

Flowering season: *spring to summer*

Height: *2 to 4 feet*

Flower color: *white*

Soil: *moist, well-drained loam*

Light: *light to moderate shade*

Gillenia is a tall, delicate, woodland perennial with white, star-shaped flowers, often blushed with pink. The flowers emerge from wine-colored sepals, which remain as ornament after the petals drop. It is native to the eastern U.S.

Selected species and varieties: *G. trifoliata* [formerly *Porteranthus trifoliata*] (bowman's root)—five-petaled flowers 1 inch wide, growing in loose, airy clusters on wiry, branching stems 2 to 4 feet tall above lacy leaves with toothed edges.

Growing conditions and maintenance: Space gillenia 2 to 3 feet apart in sites with abundant moisture and light to moderate shade. Incorporate organic matter into soil to help retain water. Plants often require staking. Propagate from seed or by division in spring or fall.

Helleborus
(hell-e-BOR-us)
HELLEBORE

Helleborus orientalis

Hardiness: *Zones 3-9*

Flowering season: *winter to spring*

Height: *1 to 3 feet*

Flower color: *white, green, purple, pink*

Soil: *moist, well-drained, fertile*

Light: *partial shade to bright full shade*

The cuplike flowers of hellebores offer such subtle variation in rich coloration that every plant carries a distinctive look. Most species are long-lived, consistent bloomers for borders and perennial beds. Depending on the species, they are stemmed or stemless plants with deeply lobed leaves that may remain evergreen if given winter protection. *Caution:* All parts of the plant are poisonous.

Selected species and varieties: *H. argutifolius* [also listed as *H. corsicus* and *H. lividus* ssp. *corsicus*] (Corsican hellebore)—shrubby growth 1 to 2 feet tall without rhizomes, with glossy, heavily toothed leaves having ivory veins and, sometimes, red margins and producing clusters of yellowish green cups in spring; Zones 6-8. *H. atrorubens*—produces dark red, brownish, or plum-colored flowers on 1½ foot stems in winter or early spring followed by deciduous leaves; hardy to Zone 6. *H. foetidus* (stinking hellebore)—2 feet tall and bearing small green bells edged with maroon over lobed, glossy black-green leaves that form rosettes around the flowers; some hybrids are well scented; hardy to Zone 6.

H. lividus—12 to 18 inches tall, similar to Corsican hellebore, but the 2-inch-wide greenish yellow cups are brushed with pink and gray and borne in clusters of 15 to 20 in spring over deeply toothed, purple-toned leaves; hardy to Zone 8. *H. niger* (Christmas rose)—highly variable in size and bloom time and color, but generally 12 to 15 inches tall, each stalk bearing a seminodding, white or pinkish green flower almost 3 inches

Helleborus niger

across in late fall to early spring; Zones 5-8; ssp. *macranthus* has unusually large flowers in winter and pale blue-green foliage; hardy to Zone 5. *H. orientalis* (Lenten rose)—bears cream, pale to deep pink, plum, brownish purple, chocolate brown, or nearly black flowers 2 inches wide in early to midspring on 18-inch plants; Zones 4-9.

Growing conditions and maintenance: Hellebores are adaptable to most garden soils, but they do best when leaf mold or peat moss has been added to the soil. Although near neutral or alkaline soils are considered ideal, many hellebores seem to do just as well under acid conditions. Space smaller species 1 foot apart, larger ones up to 2 feet apart. Hellebores form clumps and self-seed under suitable conditions. Most species develop rhizomes; the exception is Corsican hellebore, which cannot be cut back because of its unusual habit. Christmas rose appears to thrive and flower best when it receives ample water from spring to midsummer followed by a dry period in late summer. Stinking hellebores are especially tolerant of dry shade. Hellebore roots are brittle; take special care when dividing, which is best done in early summer.

Hemerocallis
(hem-er-o-KAL-lis)
DAYLILY

Hemerocallis 'Stella de Oro'

Hardiness:	*Zones 3-10*
Flowering season:	*summer to fall*
Height:	*1 to 4 feet*
Flower color:	*all shades but blue*
Soil:	*moist, well-drained loam*
Light:	*full sun to partial shade*

Daylilies produce dainty to bold flower trumpets with petals resembling those of true lilies. Their colors span the rainbow with the exception of blue and pure white, and blooms are often bi- or tricolored. Sometimes with ruffled edges or double or even triple rows of petals, and occasionally fragrant, the flowers rise above mounds of grasslike, arching leaves on branched stems called scapes. Each flower lasts only one day, but each scape supports many buds that continue to open in succession for weeks, even months. Daylilies have been extensively hybridized, offering a wide choice of plant sizes, flower colors and styles, and periods of bloom. In some hybrids, the normal number of chromosomes has been doubled, giving rise to tetraploid daylilies with larger, more substantial flowers on more robust plants. Miniature varieties with smaller flowers on shortened scapes have also been bred.

Selected species and varieties: *H. fulva* (tawny daylily)—the common orange daylily found along roadsides; 6 to 12 orange flower trumpets per scape on vigorous, robust plants in large clumps;

'Kwanso Variegata' is a larger plant than the species and produces double blooms; 'Rosea' has rose-colored flowers. *H. lilio-asphodelus* (lemon daylily) [also known as *H. flava*]—lemon yellow 4-inch flowers on 2- to 3-foot scapes over clumps of slender dark green leaves up to 2 feet long; spreads rapidly by rhizomatous roots; 'Major' grows taller than the species and produces larger, deep yellow flowers. *H.* hybrids—yellow-gold hybrids include 'Golden Chimes', a miniature variety with gold-yellow flowers; 'Stella de Oro', another yellow-gold miniature that blooms from late spring until frost; 'Happy Returns', a hybrid offspring of 'Stella de Oro' with abundant, ruffled lemon yellow blooms and a similarly long flowering season; 'Little Cherub', 3½-inch light yellow flowers on 22-inch scapes over evergreen foliage; 'Alice in Wonderland', with 5½-inch ruffled lemon yellow flowers on 3-foot scapes and beautiful deep green foliage; 'Bountiful Valley', with 6-inch yellow blooms sporting lime green throats; 'Hyperion', an older variety still very popular

Hemerocallis 'Grapeade'

for its fragrant, late-blooming yellow flowers on 4-foot scapes; 'Fall Glow', a shorter alternative with late, golden orange blooms.

Among red hybrids are 'Artist's Dream', a midseason tetraploid bearing red blooms with yellow midribs above a yellow-green throat; 'Anzac', true red blooms with yellow-green throats, 6 inches wide on 28-inch scapes; 'Cherry Cheeks', with cherry red petals lined by white midribs; 'Pardon Me', prolific producer of cerise flowers 2¾ inches across with green throats on 18-inch scapes;

'Autumn Red', sporting late-season red flowers with yellow-green throats.

Pink to purple hybrids include 'Country Club' and 'Peach Fairy', with pink-peach-flowers; 'Joyful Occasion', 6-inch medium pink flowers with green throats and ruffled petals over evergreen foliage; 'Flower Basket', with coral pink double flowers; 'Catherine Woodbury', with pale lilac-pink flowers; and 'Grapeade', with green-throated purple blossoms.

Growing conditions and maintenance: Daylilies are among the least demanding of perennials, providing spectacular results with minimal care. Planted in

Hemerocallis 'Artist's Dream'

groups, they spread to create a rugged ground cover that will suppress most weeds. Plant daylilies in spring or fall, spacing miniature varieties 18 to 24 inches apart, taller varieties 2 to 3 feet apart. Daylilies prefer sunny locations but adapt well to light shade. Light-colored flowers that fade in bright sun often show up better with some shade. Fertilize with an organic blend, if necessary, but do not overfeed, as this will cause rank growth and reduce flowering. Propagate by dividing clumps every 3 to 6 years.

Heuchera (HEW-ker-a) ALUMROOT

Heuchera sanguinea

Hardiness:	*Zones 4-8*
Flowering season:	*spring to summer*
Height:	*12 to 24 inches*
Flower color:	*white, pink, red*
Soil:	*moist, well-drained, rich loam*
Light:	*partial shade to full sun*

The delicate, bell-shaped flowers of alumroot line slender upright stalks held above neat mounds of attractive evergreen leaves that can be rounded, triangular, or heart-shaped.

Selected species and varieties: *H. micrantha* (small-flowered alumroot)—white flowers above gray-green heart-shaped leaves; 'Palace Purple' has dramatic, deep bronze leaves. *H. sanguinea* (coral bells)—the showiest of the genus, with red flowers persisting 4 to 8 weeks; 'Red Spangles' grows scarlet flowers on short stems; 'Chatterbox', rose pink flowers; 'Snowflakes', white flowers.

Growing conditions and maintenance: Space heuchera 1 to 1½ feet apart. Water well during dry spells. Plants tolerate full sun in cooler climates but prefer partial shade in warmer zones. Propagate from seed or by division every 3 years.

Hosta (HOS-ta) PLANTAIN LILY

Hosta 'Krossa Regal'

Hardiness:	*Zones 3-9*
Flowering season:	*summer*
Height:	*5 inches to 3 feet*
Flower color:	*fwhite, lavender, violet*
Soil:	*moist, rich, acid loam*
Light:	*partial to bright full shade*

Hostas are valued chiefly for their foliage—mounds of oval or heart-shaped green, blue, and gold leaves in a variety of sizes—but also produce tall, graceful spires of pale lilylike flowers during the summer. They are useful as edging or border plants, as ground covers, and in mass plantings. The variegated and light green forms make beautiful accent plants and brighten shady corners.

Selected species and varieties: *H. decorata* (blunt plantain lily)—1 to 2 feet tall, with white-edged leaves 3 to 8 inches long and dark blue flowers. *H. fortunei* (Fortune's hosta, giant plantain lily)—to 2 feet tall, with 5-inch-long oval leaves and pale lilac to violet flowers; 'Albo-marginata' forms a 15- to 24-inch-high clump with white margins on 5-inch leaves. *H. lancifolia* (narrow-leaved plantain lily)—a 2-foot-high cascading mound of 4- to 6-inch-long leaf blades and 1- to 1½-inch blue-purple flowers in late summer; hardy to Zone 3. *H. plantaginea* (fragrant plantain lily)—fragrant pure white flowers 2½ inches wide open in late summer on 2½-foot stems above bright green heart-shaped foliage; Zones 3-8. *H.*

sieboldiana (Siebold plantain lily)—2½ to 3 feet tall with 10- to 15-inch-long glaucous, gray to blue-green puckered leaves and lavender flowers that bloom amid the leaves in midsummer; hardy to Zone 3; 'Big Mama' has blue puckered leaves and pale lavender flowers; 'Blue Umbrellas' grows 3 feet tall and 5 feet wide, with blue to blue-green leaves; 'Frances Williams', 32 inches tall and 40 inches wide with round, puckered, blue-green leaves having wide, irregular gold margins; var. *elegans* [also classified as *H. s.* 'Elegans'], 36 inches tall with lavender-white flowers that barely clear the large, dark blue puckered leaves. *H. tardiflora* (autumn plantain lily)—glossy dark

Hosta 'Golden Tiara'

green medium-sized leaves and large purple flowers on 1-foot scapes in fall. *H. tokudama*—18 inches tall and 40 inches wide, with cupped, puckered bluish leaves and white flowers in midsummer; 'Flavo-circinalis' grows to 18 inches tall and 50 inches wide with round, heavily puckered blue-green leaves that have irregular cream-and-yellow margins and white flowers in early summer. *H. undulata* var. *univittata* [also classified as *H. u.* 'Univittata'] (wavy-leaf shade lily, snow feather funkia)—2 to 3 feet tall and 3 feet wide, with broad white centers in medium green leaves and lavender flowers. *H. venusta* (dwarf plantain lily, pretty plantain lily)—5 inches tall and 8 inches wide with medium green leaves and light purple flowers. *H. hybrids*—'August Moon', to 12 inches tall, with small yellow puckered leaves and midsummer white flowers; 'Fringe Benefit', 36 inches tall and 42 inches wide, with broad cream-colored margins on green heart-shaped leaves

and pale lavender flowers in early summer; 'Ginko Craig', an excellent ground cover, 10 inches tall with narrow, white-edged, dark green lance-shaped leaves and lavender flowers in midsummer;

Hosta sieboldiana 'Frances Williams'

hardy to Zone 4; 'Golden Tiara', a low, compact mound 6 inches high and 16 to 20 inches wide bearing yellow-edged medium green heart-shaped leaves and purple flowers on 15-inch scapes in midsummer; 'Gold Standard', 15 inches tall with dark green margins on greenish gold leaves and lavender flowers on 3-foot scapes in mid- to late summer; 'Halcyon', 12 inches tall and 16 inches wide, with grayish blue heart-shaped leaves having wavy margins and distinct parallel veins and lilac-blue flowers blooming in late summer; 'Honeybells', fragrant lavender flowers and light green leaves to 2 feet tall; 'Krossa Regal', to 3 feet tall, with silvery blue leaves and 2- to 3-inch-long lavender flowers in late summer on 5-foot scapes; hardy to Zone 4; 'Royal Standard', full-sun-tolerant plant with fragrant white flowers on 30-inch stems in late summer to early fall; 'Shade Fanfare', lavender blooms on 2-foot scapes in midsummer above leaves with broad cream-colored margins.

Growing conditions and maintenance: Plant smaller hostas 1 foot apart, larger species 2 to 3 feet apart, in a moist but well-drained soil; wet soil in winter often damages plants. Water during dry spells. The blue forms need bright shade in order to hold color. *H. plantaginea* is tender until established; in the northern part of its range, mulch or cover during the first winter. Once established, hostas are long-lasting and need little attention.

Iberis
(eye-BEER-is)
CANDYTUFT

Iberis sempervirens 'Snowmantle'

Hardiness: *Zones 4-8*

Flowering season: *spring*

Height: *6 to 12 inches*

Flower color: *white*

Soil: *moist, well-drained loam*

Light: *full sun*

The dark green leaves of candytuft are effective year round covering the ground before a perennial border, edging a walkway, or cascading over a stone wall. The delicate white flowers that cover the plant in spring are a delightful bonus.

Selected species and varieties: *I. sempervirens*—to 12 inches high and 24 inches wide, with a low, mounded habit, linear evergreen leaves 1 inch long, semiwoody stems, and very showy white flowers in dense clusters 1 inch across; 'Snowflake' grows 10 inches high, with 2- to 3-inch flower clusters; 'Snowmantle', 8 inches high, with a dense, compact habit.

Growing conditions and maintenance: Incorporate organic matter into the soil before planting candytuft. Space plants 12 to 15 inches apart. Protect the plant from severe winter weather with a loose mulch in colder zones. Cut it back at least 2 inches after it flowers to maintain vigorous growth.

Inula
(IN-yew-la)
INULA

Inula ensifolia

Hardiness *Zones 4-9*

Flowering season: *summer*

Height: *6 to 12 inches*

Flower color: *yellow*

Soil: *well-drained, average fertility*

Light: *full sun to partial shade*

Inula produces cheerful, bright yellow, daisylike flowers at the tips of wiry stems that form mounds.

Selected species and varieties: *I. acaulis* (stemless inula)—single yellow flowers borne on 6-inch stems in midsummer, over tufts of spatulate leaves 2 inches tall. *I. ensifolia* (swordleaf inula)—dense clumps, 12 inches tall and wide, of wiry, erect stems lined with narrow, pointed 4-inch leaves and tipped with 1- to 2-inch flowers. The blooms last 2 to 3 weeks in warmer zones, up to 6 weeks in cooler areas.

Growing conditions and maintenance: Space inulas 1 foot apart in massed plantings. Propagate from seed or by division in spring or fall.

Kirengeshoma
(ky-reng-esh-O-ma)
YELLOW WAXBELLS

Kirengeshoma palmata

Hardiness: *Zones 5-8*

Flowering season: *summer to fall*

Height: *3 to 4 feet*

Flower color: *yellow*

Soil: *moist, well-drained, acid, fertile*

Light: *bright full shade*

Kirengeshoma is an unusual, semiexotic shade plant that is not often seen in the landscape. Shrubby but a bit spindly in habit, it produces handsome maplelike leaves on dark purple, semiarching stems and upright clusters of nodding yellow flowers in summer and fall. It makes an interesting specimen plant for edgings or borders.

Selected species and varieties: *K. palmata*—nearly round, toothed leaves, each with up to 10 lobes, arise from opposite sides of the stems and give an almost platelike appearance beneath clusters of 1½-inch-long butter yellow bell-shaped flowers whose buds last for months before opening.

Growing conditions and maintenance: Kirengeshoma needs soil that has been liberally supplemented with compost, leaf mold, or peat moss and is lime-free. Water during dry spells, and mulch to retain moisture. Propagate by dividing.

Kniphofia
(ny-FO-fee-a)
TORCH LILY, TRITOMA

Kniphofia uvaria 'Robin Hood'

Hardiness: *Zones 5-9*

Flowering season: *summer to fall*

Height: *2 to 4 feet*

Flower color: *red, orange, yellow, cream*

Soil: *well-drained, sandy loam*

Light: *full sun*

Torch lily's stiff clusters of tubular flowers on bare stems held above tufts of stiff, gray-green leaves are a bold accent in a mixed border and a favorite visiting place of hummingbirds.

Selected species and varieties: *K. uvaria* (red-hot poker)—individual 1- to 2-inch flowers clustered along the top several inches of stem like a bristly bottle brush open a bright red then turn yellow as they mature.

Growing conditions and maintenance: Plant torch lilies 1½ to 2 feet apart in locations protected from strong winds. Propagate from seed, by division in spring, or by removing and transplanting the small offsets that develop at the base of plants. Plants grown from seed require 2 or 3 years to flower.

Lavandula
(lav-AN-dew-la)
LAVENDER

Lavandula stoechas

Hardiness: *Zones 5-9*

Flowering season: *summer*

Height: *1 to 3 feet*

Flower color: *lavender, purple, pink*

Soil: *well-drained loam*

Light: *full sun*

Lavender forms neat cushions of erect stems lined with fragrant, willowy, gray or gray-green leaves tipped with spikes of tiny flowers. Lavender's attractive evergreen foliage blends into rock gardens or at the edges of borders and can be clipped into a low hedge.

Selected species and varieties: *L. angustifolia* (true lavender, English lavender)—whorls of lavender-to-purple ¼-inch flowers in summer on compact, round plants 1 to 2 feet tall; 'Hidcote' produces deep violet-blue flowers and silvery gray foliage. *L. latifolia* (spike lavender)—branched stalks of lavender-to-purple summer flowers above broader leaves than true lavender on plants to 2 feet tall. *L. stoechas* (French lavender)—dense whorls of tufted purple flowers in summer on plants to 3 feet tall.

Growing conditions and maintenance: Plant lavender 12 to 18 inches apart in soil that is not overly rich. Cut stems back to 8 inches in early spring to encourage compact growth and to remove old woody stems that produce few flowers. Propagate from seed or by division.

Liatris
(ly-AY-tris)
SPIKE GAY-FEATHER

Liatris spicata 'Kobold'

Hardiness: *Zones 3-9*

Flowering season: *summer to fall*

Height: *18 inches to 5 feet*

Flower color: *purple, pink, lavender, white*

Soil: *sandy, well-drained*

Light: *full sun to light shade*

The flowers of spike gay-feather are borne on erect stems, and unlike most spike flowers the top buds open first and proceed downward. The effect is that of a feathery bottle brush. It provides a striking vertical accent in both the garden and indoor arrangements.

Selected species and varieties: *L. pycnostachya* (Kansas gay-feather)—bright purple flower spikes on 4- to 6-foot stems. *L. spicata*—usually 2 to 3 feet tall and 2 feet wide but may reach 5 feet tall. Leaves are narrow and tapered, up to 5 inches long, on erect, stout stems; flowers are purple or rose, borne closely along top of stem in mid to late summer; 'Kobold'—18- to 24-inch dwarf form, bright purple flowers, good for the front or middle of the herbaceous border.

Growing conditions and maintenance: Space gay-feathers 1 foot apart. Spike gay-feather prefers a light, well-drained soil and full sun but adapts to light shade and tolerates wet conditions better than other species of liatris. Tall types often need support; however, 'Kobold', with its stout habit, rarely requires staking.

Linum
(LY-num)
FLAX

Linum perenne

Hardiness: *Zones 5-9*

Flowering season: *spring to summer*

Height: *12 to 24 inches*

Flower color: *blue, white, yellow*

Soil: *well-drained, sandy loam*

Light: *full sun to light shade*

Delicate flax blooms prolifically with inch-wide, cup-shaped flowers held aloft on soft stems. Though blossoms last only one day, new buds open continuously for 6 weeks or more.

Selected species and varieties: *L. flavum* (golden flax)—bright yellow flowers on stems 1 to 1½ feet tall. *L. perenne* (perennial flax)—sky blue, saucer-shaped flowers on stems up to 2 feet tall; 'Diamant White' has abundant white blossoms on 12- to 18-inch stems.

Growing conditions and maintenance: Space flax plants 18 inches apart in groups of 6 or more for an effective display. Flax is a short-lived perennial but often reseeds itself. Propagate from seed or from stem cuttings taken in late spring or summer, after new growth hardens.

Lobelia
(lo-BEE-lee-a)
CARDINAL FLOWER

Lobelia cardinalis

Hardiness: *Zones 3-9*

Flowering season: *summer*

Height: *2 to 4 feet*

Flower color: *red, pink, white, blue*

Soil: *moist, fertile loam*

Light: *light shade*

Cardinal flower bears spires of intensely colored tubular blossoms with drooping lips on stiff stems rising from rosettes of dark green leaves. Opening in mid- to late summer, the flowers last 2 to 3 weeks; they are followed by button-shaped seed capsules

Selected species and varieties: *L. cardinalis* (red lobelia)—1½-inch scarlet blossoms on 3-foot-tall flower stalks; pink and white varieties available. *L. siphilitica* (great blue lobelia)—1-inch-long blue flowers persist a month or more. 'Alba' has white flowers.

Growing conditions and maintenance: Plant lobelia 12 inches apart in locations with adequate moisture and in soil with ample organic matter. Lobelia will grow in full sun with sufficient moisture. Though short-lived, it self-sows freely. It can also be propagated by division in early fall. Lobelias are suited to moist-soil gardens, and do well alongside ponds and streams.

Lupinus
(loo-PY-nus)
LUPINE

Lupinus densiflorus var. aureus

Hardiness: *Zones 3-10*

Flowering season: *spring, summer*

Height: *4 inches to 3 feet*

Flower color: *blue, purple, yellow, white, pink*

Soil: *moist to dry*

Light: *full sun to partial shade*

Lupines inhabit prairies, open woodlands, and dry mountain slopes and bear dense, showy terminal clusters of flowers in spring or summer. They have attractive palmately compound leaves.

Selected species: *L. palmeri* (Palmer's lupine)—1 to 2 feet in height with blue flowers in late spring; southwestern mountains; Zones 6-9. *L. perennis* (wild lupine)—up to 2 feet tall with elongated clusters of late-spring to early-summer flowers that are usually purplish blue but occasionally white or pink; Maine to Florida; Zones 4-8. *L. sericeus* (silky lupine)—1 to 2 feet tall with blue flowers throughout the summer and velvety leaves; California to British Columbia and northern Rockies; Zones 4-7.

Growing conditions and maintenance: Space lupines 2 feet apart. Most need full sun and dry soils with excellent drainage. *L. sericeus* also thrives in partial shade and is tolerant of both moist and dry soils. Lupines benefit from soil or seed inoculants containing nitrogen-fixing bacteria. Propagate from seed sown in fall or spring. Scarify the seed with sandpaper or by nicking the seed coat.

Miscanthus
(mis-KAN-thus)
EULALIA

Miscanthus sinensis

Hardiness: *Zones 5-9*

Flowering season: *summer*

Height: *3 to 10 feet*

Flower color: *pink, red, silver*

Soil: *well-drained loam*

Light: *full sun*

Eulalia produces feathery flower fans on tall stems above graceful clumps of arching leaves an inch wide. Both the flowers and the foliage remain attractive throughout the winter and are useful as specimens and screens.

Selected species and varieties: *M. sinensis*—5 to 10 feet tall, narrow leaves 3 to 4 feet long with prominent white midrib; flowers are feathery and fan-shaped. Varieties offer a selection of colors and blooming periods; 'Condensatus' has purple flowers; 'Gracillimus' (maiden grass), fall flowers above compact clumps of fine-textured leaves; 'Purpurascens', silvery pink summer flowers above red-tinted foliage; 'Strictus' (porcupine grass), upright leaves striped with horizontal yellow bands; 'Yaku Jima', a 3- to 4-foot dwarf; 'Zebrinus' (zebra grass) striped with yellow band.

Growing conditions and maintenance: Space clumps of miscanthus 3 feet apart. Cut plants back to 2 to 6 inches in late winter before new growth begins. Propagate by division in spring.

Monarda
(mo-NAR-da)
BEE BALM

Monarda didyma

Nepeta
(NEP-e-ta)
CATMINT

Nepeta mussinii 'Blue Wonder'

Oenothera
(ee-no-THEE-ra)
SUNDROP

Oenothera fruticosa

Hardiness: *Zones 4-9*

Flowering season: *summer*

Height: *2 to 4 feet*

Flower color: *red, purple, pink, white*

Soil: *moist or dry loam*

Light: *full sun to light shade*

Bee balm has fragrant leaves and shaggy clusters of tiny tubular flowers growing on square stems. Attractive to bees, butterflies, and hummingbirds, these plants are easily cultivated.

Selected species and varieties: *M. didyma*—scarlet flowers on 3- to 4-foot stems; 'Cambridge Scarlet', wine red flowers; 'Croftway Pink', rose pink; 'Mahogany', dark red; 'Marshall's Delight', mildew resistant, with pink flowers on 2-foot stems; 'Blue Stocking', violet-blue; 'Snow Queen', white. *M. fistulosa* (wild bergamot)—lilac to pink flower clusters on plants up to 4 feet tall. *M. punctata* (spotted bee balm)—yellow blossoms with purple spots.

Growing conditions and maintenance: Plant monarda 1½ to 2 feet apart. It thrives in moist areas, although wild bergamot and spotted bee balm tolerate dry conditions. Propagate from seed or from cuttings; divide every two to three years in the spring to maintain vigor. Thin plants occasionally for air circulation and to avoid mildew.

Hardiness: *Zones 3-9*

Flowering season: *summer*

Height: *1 to 3 feet*

Flower color: *lavender-blue, white*

Soil: *average, well-drained loam*

Light: *full sun*

Catmint forms loose cushions of fragrant stems lined with soft, oval, pointed leaves and tipped with spikes of tiny white, mauve, or blue flower whorls that form a haze of color above the foliage. The plant is effective massed as a dense ground cover.

Selected species and varieties: *N.* x *faassenii* (blue catmint)—18- to 36-inch-high mounds of silvery gray foliage with lavender-blue spring-to-summer-blooming flowers; 'Six Hills Giant' grows taller and is more robust than the species. *N. mussinii* (Persian catmint)—sprawling 1-foot-high mounds with lavender summer flowers; 'Blue Wonder' has deep blue blossoms on compact plants to 15 inches.

Growing conditions and maintenance: Plant catmint 1 to 1½ feet apart in any well-drained soil. It can be invasive. Shearing plants after flowering may produce a second season of bloom. Propagate blue catmint from cuttings, Persian catmint from seed, and either species by division.

Hardiness: *Zones 4-8*

Flowering season: *summer*

Height: *6 to 24 inches*

Flower color: *yellow, pink, white*

Soil: *well-drained loam*

Light: *full sun*

Showy, four-petaled, saucer-shaped flowers bloom on sundrops during the day and on evening primroses (night-blooming oenothera) at night.

Selected species and varieties: *O. fruticosa* (common sundrop)—prolific clusters of 1- to 2-inch bright yellow flowers at the tips of 18- to 24-inch stems. *O. missouriensis* (Ozark sundrop)—large 5-inch yellow flowers on 6- to 12-inch plants. *O. speciosa* (showy evening primrose)—white or pink blossoms on spreading stems that grow 6 to 18 inches tall. *O. tetragona*—yellow flowers similar to those of *O. fruticosa* but with young buds and stems tinted red.

Growing conditions and maintenance: Plant Ozark sundrops 2 feet apart, other species 12 to 18 inches apart. Propagate Ozark sundrops from seed, other species either from seed or by division.

Paeonia
(pee-O-nee-a)
PEONY

Paeonia lactiflora

Hardiness: *Zones 3-8*

Flowering season: *spring to summer*

Height: *18 to 36 inches*

Flower color: *white, pink, red*

Soil: *well-drained, fertile loam*

Light: *full sun to light shade*

Peonies are long-lived perennials beloved for their large, showy flowers and attractive foliage. Dramatic in the garden, they are stunning in bouquets. Peony flowers are classified by their form. Single-flower peonies have a single row of five or more petals surrounding a center of bright yellow stamens. Japanese and anemone peonies have a single row of petals surrounding modified stamens that resemble finely cut petals. Semidouble peonies have several rows of petals surrounding conspicuous stamens. Double-flowered peonies have multiple rows of petals crowded into ruffly hemispheres.

Selected species and varieties: *P. lactiflora* (garden or Chinese peony)—white, pink, or red flowers on 3-foot stems. *P. mlokosewitschii* (Caucasian peony)—very early blooming, 2-inch single lemon yellow flowers on 2-foot-tall stems with soft gray-green foliage. *P. officinalis* (common peony)—hundreds of varieties with 3- to 6-inch blooms in various forms and colors from red to light pink to white on 2-foot stems. *P. tenuifolia* (fern-leaf peony)—single deep red flowers and finely divided, fern-like leaves on 18- to 24-inch stems; 'Flore Pleno' has double flowers.

Hundreds of peony hybrids are available. 'Lobata' (red-pink), 'Lotus Bloom' (pink), and 'Krinkled White' are outstanding singles. 'Isani-Gidui' (white) and 'Nippon Beauty' (dark red) are lovely Japanese types. 'Gay Paree' (pink with white-blush center) grows anemone-type blossoms. Semidouble varieties include 'Ludovica' (salmon pink) and 'Lowell Thomas' (deep red). Among the double-flowered varieties, 'Festiva Maxima' (white with red marking), 'Red Charm' (deep true red, early blooming), 'Mons. Jules Elie' (early, pink), 'Karl Rosenfeld' (deep red), and 'Nick Shaylor' (blush pink) are all exceptional.

Growing conditions and maintenance: Plant peonies 3 feet apart in soil containing some organic matter. Set the buds (eyes) 2 inches below the soil surface;

Paeonia mlokosewitschii

setting them deeper delays flowering. Propagate by dividing clumps in late summer-early fall into sections containing three to five eyes each.

Papaver
(pap-AY-ver)
POPPY

Papaver orientale

Hardiness: *Zones 3-9*

Flowering season: *spring to summer*

Height: *12 inches to 4 feet*

Flower color: *red, pink, orange, yellow, white*

Soil: *well-drained loam*

Light: *full sun to partial shade*

Poppies bear large, brilliantly colored, silky-textured blossoms on wiry stems above finely cut leaves. The blooms, which last for several weeks, open from nodding buds.

Selected species and varieties: *P. nudicaule* (Iceland poppy)—fragrant flowers up to 3 inches across on 12- to 24-inch stems. *P. orientale* (Oriental poppy)—blossoms up to 8 inches across composed of tissue-thin petals on wiry stems rising from mounds of coarse, hairy leaves; 'Glowing Embers' has orange-red ruffled petals; 'Mrs. Perry', clear pink flowers; 'Beauty of Livermore', deep red petals spotted black at the base; 'Princess Victoria Louise', bright salmon-pink flowers.

Growing conditions and maintenance: Space poppies 1½ feet apart. Propagate Oriental poppies, which are tough, long-lived plants, from seed or from root cuttings. Grow Iceland poppies from seed to flower in their first year; sow in late summer in the North and in fall in southern climates.

Pennisetum
(pen-i-SEE-tum)
FOUNTAIN GRASS

Pennisetum alopecuroides

Perovskia
(per-OV-skee-a)
RUSSIAN SAGE

Perovskia atriplicifolia

Phlox
(flox)
PHLOX

Phlox divaricata 'Fuller's White'

Hardiness: *Zones 5-9*

Flowering season: *summer*

Height: *2 to 5 feet*

Flower color: *silvery mauve, white*

Soil: *well-drained loam*

Light: *full sun*

Fountain grass forms a spray of arching leaves with bottle-brush flower heads borne on thin, arching stems in summer and fall. Stunning in masses, fountain grass graces borders, rock gardens, water features, and fall-blooming perennial beds. It is also useful as an accent plant.

Selected species and varieties: *P. alopecuroides* (Chinese pennisetum, perennial fountain grass)—silvery mauve 5- to 7-inch blooms on erect stems up to 5 feet tall above a mound of arching 2- to 3-foot leaves that turn a bright almond color in winter.; 'Hameln' (dwarf fountain grass) grows only 1 to 2 feet tall; 'National Arboretum', to 2 feet with a dark brown inflorescence; Zones 7-9. *P. caudatum* (white flowering fountain grass)—silvery white bloom spikes 4 to 5 feet tall.

Growing conditions and maintenance: Space plants 2 to 3 feet apart. Cut back to 6 inches before growth begins in the spring. Propagate the species from seed or by division, varieties by division. Divide every 5 to 10 years to prevent the center from falling open. Fountain grass tolerates wind and coastal conditions.

Hardiness: *Zones 5-9*

Flowering season: *summer*

Height: *3 to 4 feet*

Flower color: *lavender-blue*

Soil: *well-drained loam*

Light: *full sun*

Russian sage's shrubby mounds of fine-textured, deeply toothed aromatic gray foliage are an effective filler in the border and remain attractive through winter. In summer, spires of tiny lavender flowers tip each stem. They combine particularly well with ornamental grasses. Planted in a mass, Russian sage develops into a summer hedge, and the stems remain attractive through the winter.

Selected species and varieties: *P. atriplicifolia* (azure sage)—tubular, two-lipped lavender flowers growing in whorls, spaced along 12-inch flower spikes above downy gray, finely divided leaves. Clumps of woody stems grow to 4 feet tall and as wide. 'Blue Spire' is upright with violet-blue flowers.

Growing conditions and maintenance: Plant Russian sage 2 to 3 feet apart in full sun; shade causes floppy, sprawling growth. Soil should not be overly rich. Cut woody stems to the ground in spring before new growth begins. Propagate by seed or from summer cuttings.

Hardiness: *Zones 3-9*

Flowering season: *spring, summer, or fall*

Height: *3 inches to 4 feet*

Flower color: *pink, purple, red, blue, white*

Soil: *sandy and dry to moist, fertile loam*

Light: *full sun to full shade*

Versatile phlox produces flat, five-petaled flowers, either singly or in clusters, many with a conspicuous eye at the center. There is a species suitable for nearly every combination of soil and light, as well as for nearly any landscape use, from 3-inch creepers to upright border plants growing 4 feet tall.

Selected species and varieties: *P. divaricata* (wild blue phlox)—blue blossoms on 12-inch-tall creepers; 'Fuller's White' has creamy white flowers. *P. maculata* (wild sweet William)—elegant, cylindrical flower heads in shades of pink to white on 3-foot plants; 'Miss Lingard' [sometimes listed as a variety of *P. carolina*] has 6-inch trusses of pure white blossoms; 'Omega', white petals surrounding a lilac-colored eye; 'Alpha', rose pink petals around a darker pink eye. *P. paniculata* (summer phlox, garden phlox)—magnificent pyramidal clusters of white, pink, red, lavender, or purple flowers on 2- to 4-foot stems; 'Fujiyama' has white flower heads 12 to 15 inches long; 'Bright Eyes', pale pink petals surrounding a crimson eye; 'Orange Perfection', salmon orange blossoms; 'Starfire', cherry red. *P. stolonifera* (creeping phlox)—blue, white, or pink flowers on creeping 6- to 12-inch stems with evergreen leaves that form a dense ground cover; 'Blue Ridge' produces clear blue flowers; 'Bruce's White', white flowers with yellow eyes. *P. subulata* (moss phlox, moss pink)—white, pink, blue, lavender, or red flowers above dense clumps of evergreen foliage 3 to 6 inches tall and 2 feet wide.

Phlox subulata

Growing conditions and maintenance: Space lower-growing phlox 1 to 1½ feet apart, taller species up to 2 feet apart. Wild blue phlox grows well in shady, moist sites; moss phlox thrives in sunny, dry spots. Creeping phlox grows in sun or shade. Both moss phlox and creeping phlox form lush mats of evergreen foliage and made wonderful ground covers. Wild sweet William and summer phlox thrive in full sun, provided they receive ample moisture during the growing season. Space summer phlox for good air circulation to avoid powdery mildew. Propagate phlox by division. Promote dense growth and reblooming by cutting plants back after flowering.

Physostegia
(fy-so-STEE-gee-a)
FALSE DRAGONHEAD

Physostegia virginiana

Hardiness: *Zones 4-8*

Flowering season: *late summer to fall*

Height: *2 to 4 feet*

Flower color: *pink, purple, white*

Soil: *moist or dry acid loam*

Light: *full sun to partial shade*

False dragonhead produces unusual 8- to 10-inch flower spikes with four evenly spaced vertical rows of blossoms resembling snapdragons.

Selected species and varieties: *P. virginiana*—pink flowers tipping each stem in clumps of 4-foot stalks; 'Variegata' has pink flowers above green-and-white variegated leaves; 'Vivid', rosy pink blossoms on compact plants only 20 inches tall; 'Summer Snow', early-blooming white flowers.

Growing conditions and maintenance: Plant false dragonhead 1½ to 2 feet apart. It is so tolerant of varying growing conditions that it can become invasive. Propagate the plants from seed or by division every 2 years.

Platycodon
(plat-i-KO-don)
BALLOON FLOWER

Platycodon grandiflorus

Hardiness *Zones 4-9*

Flowering season: *summer*

Height: *10 to 36 inches*

Flower color: *blue, white, pink*

Soil: *well-drained, acid loam*

Light: *full sun to partial shade*

The balloon flower derives its common name from the fat, inflated flower buds it produces. These pop open into spectacular cup-shaped 2- to 3-inch-wide blossoms with pointed petals.

Selected species and varieties: *P. grandiflorus*—deep blue flowers on slender stems above neat clumps of blue-green leaves; 'Album' has white flowers; 'Shell Pink', pale pink flowers; 'Mariesii' is a compact variety 18 inches tall with bright blue flowers. 'Double Blue' has bright-blue double flowers on 2-foot stems.

Growing conditions and maintenance: Space balloon flowers 18 inches apart. Pink varieties develop the best color when grown in partial shade. Propagate from seed to flower the second year or by division.

Polygonum
(po-LIG-o-num)
SMARTWEED, KNOTWEED

Polygonum bistorta 'Superbum'

Hardiness: *Zones 4-9*

Flowering season: *summer*

Height: *6 inches to 3 feet*

Flower color: *pink, white, red*

Soil: *moist loam*

Light: *full sun to light shade*

Although the genus *Polygonum* contains many weeds familiar to gardeners, it also boasts a few highly ornamental species with colorful flower spikes held above neat mats of foliage.

Selected species and varieties: *P. affine* (Himalayan fleeceflower)—spikes of rose pink flowers 6 to 9 inches tall above dark green leaves turning bronze in fall; 'Superbum' produces crimson flowers. *P. bistorta* (snakeweed)—pink flowers like bottle brushes on 2-foot stems above striking clumps of 4- to 6-inch-long wavy green leaves with a white mid-rib; 'Superbum' grows to 3 feet.

Growing conditions and maintenance: Space polygonums 1 foot apart. Himalayan fleeceflower thrives in full sun; snakeweed prefers some shade. Propagate by division in spring. Use *P. bistorta* wherever you need a spreading ground cover; plant *P. affine* alongside a path or at the front of a border.

Potentilla
(po-ten-TILL-a)
CINQUEFOIL

Potentilla nepalensis 'Miss Wilmott'

Hardiness: *Zones 5-8*

Flowering season: *spring to summer*

Height: *2 to 18 inches*

Flower color: *white, yellow, pink, red*

Soil: *well-drained, sandy loam*

Light: *full sun to light shade*

Cinquefoil's neat, compound leaves, with three to five leaflets arranged like fingers on a hand, grow in spreading clumps of foliage. The open-faced flowers, which have five petals arranged around a ring of fuzzy stamens, resemble wild roses. Cinquefoils are effective creeping between stones in the rock garden and as a ground cover on dry slopes.

Selected species and varieties: *P. atrosanguinea* (Himalayan or ruby cinquefoil)—dark red 1-inch-wide flowers and five-fingered 8-inch green leaves with silvery undersides on plants 12 to 18 inches tall; 'Fire Dance' flowers have a scarlet center and a yellow border on 15-inch stems; 'Gibson's Scarlet' has bright scarlet flowers on 15-inch stems; 'William Rollinson' grows to 18 inches with deep orange and yellow semidouble flowers; 'Yellow Queen' grows bright yellow flowers with a red center on 12-inch stems above silvery foliage. *P. nepalensis* (Nepal cinquefoil)—a bushy species with cup-shaped flowers in shades of salmon, rose, red, orange, and purple, often flowering throughout the summer; 'Miss Wilmott' is a dwarf variety 10 to 12 inches

tall with cherry red flowers; 'Roxana' has coppery orange petals surrounding red centers on 15-inch stems. *P. x tonguei* (staghorn cinquefoil)—apricot-colored flowers with red centers on trailing stems 8 to 12 inches long above evergreen foliage. *P. tridentata* (wineleaf cinquefoil) [also classified as *Sibbaldiopsis tridentata*]—clusters of tiny white flowers blooming late spring to midsummer on 2- to 6-inch plants with shiny, leathery evergreen leaves that turn wine red in the fall; 'Minima' is a low-growing cultivar (3 inches high) that performs well as a ground cover. *P. verna* (spring cinquefoil)—a prostrate, fast-spreading plant that grows 2 to 3 inches high and produces golden yellow flowers ½ inch wide; 'Nana' has larger flowers than the species and grows slightly higher.

Growing conditions and maintenance: Plant smaller cinquefoils 1 foot apart and larger species 2 feet apart. Potentillas prefer a poor soil; they will produce excess leafy growth if raised in fertile soil. Wineleaf cinquefoil develops its best fall color in acid soils. Cinquefoils are generally short-lived perennials and grow best in areas with mild winters and summers. *P. verna* can be invasive; its stems may root, forming a broad mat. Propagate from seed or by division every 3 years in spring or fall.

Primula
(PRIM-yew-la)
PRIMROSE

Primula japonica 'Postford White'

Hardiness: *Zones 3-8*

Flowering season: *spring*

Height: *2 to 24 inches*

Flower color: *wide spectrum*

Soil: *moist loam*

Light: *partial shade*

Neat, colorful primroses produce clusters of five-petaled blossoms on leafless stems above rosettes of tongue-shaped leaves, which are evergreen in milder climates. More than 400 species of primroses in nearly every color of the rainbow offer the gardener a multitude of choices in height and hardiness.

Selected species and varieties: *P. auricula* (auricula primrose)—fragrant, bell-shaped flowers in yellow, white, or other hues on plants 2 to 8 inches tall; hardy to Zone 3. *P. denticulata* (Himalayan primrose)—globe-shaped clusters of purple flowers with a yellow eye on 8- to 12-inch stalks; varieties are available in strong red, pink, and white flower tones; to Zone 6. *P. helodoxa* (amber primrose)—soft yellow flowers on 24-inch stems; to Zone 6. *P. japonica* (Japanese primrose)—whorls of white, red, pink, or purple flowers on 2-foot stalks; 'Miller's Crimson' has deep red blossoms; 'Postford White', white flowers; to Zone 6. *P. x polyantha* (polyanthus primrose)—flowers singly or in clusters on 6- to 12-inch stems in a wide choice of colors; to Zone 4. *P. sieboldii* (Japanese

star primrose)—nodding heads of pink, purple, or white flowers on 12-inch stalks. *P. vulgaris* (English primrose)—fragrant single flowers in yellow and other colors on 6- to 9-inch stems.

Growing conditions and maintenance: Space primroses 1 foot apart in moisture-retentive soil. Water deeply during dry periods. Himalayan, amber, and Japanese primroses require a boglike soil. English and polyanthus primroses tolerate drier conditions, while other species mentioned fall somewhere in between. Polyanthus primroses are short-lived and often treated as annuals. Japanese star primroses go dormant after flowering. Propagate primroses from

Primula x polyantha

seed or by division every 3 to 4 years in spring. Auricula and Japanese star primroses can also be propagated from stem cuttings, Himalayan primroses from root cuttings. Plant primroses in masses with spring bulbs, or use as border plants.

Rudbeckia
(rood-BEK-ee-a)
CONEFLOWER

Rudbeckia hirta

Hardiness: *Zones 3-9*

Flowering season: *summer*

Height: *1 to 4 feet*

Flower color: *yellow*

Soil: *moist to dry*

Light: *full sun to partial shade*

Rudbeckias are annuals, biennials, and perennials from open woodlands and meadows throughout most of the United States. Their gay yellow daisylike flowers, with a fringe of narrow petals surrounding a prominent center, are favorites among wildflower gardeners. These plants bloom prolifically on wiry stems above vigorous clumps of deeply cut foliage.

Selected species: *R. fulgida* 'Goldstrum'—bright yellow flowers with brown centers, growing from midsummer to frost on compact 2-foot plants. *R. grandiflora* (large coneflower)—1½ to 3 feet tall. Flowers up to 6 inches or more across have drooping petals and a brown cone-shaped center. *R. nitida*—bright yellow petals surrounding extremely large 2-inch centers on 2- to 7-foot stems. *R. subtomentosa* (sweet coneflower)—1 to 4 feet tall with 3-inch flowers with dark centers.

Growing conditions and maintenance: Plant coneflowers 1½ to 2 feet apart. Propagate from seed or by division every 2 years in spring. Coneflowers are a good choice for southern gardens.

Salvia
(SAL-vee-a)
SAGE

Salvia coccinea 'Lady in Red'

Hardiness: *Zones 4-10 or tender*

Flowering season: *spring to fall*

Height: *1 to 6 feet*

Flower color: *blue, purple, white, red*

Soil: *well-drained loam*

Light: *full sun*

Whorled spikes of tiny, hooded, summer-to-fall-blooming flowers line the tips of salvia's erect stems above soft, sometimes downy leaves. Salvias are particularly effective in masses that multiply the impact of their flowers. Tender perennial salvias that cannot withstand frost are grown as annuals in Zone 8 and colder.

Selected species and varieties: *S. argentea* (silver sage)—branching clusters of white flowers tinged yellow or pink on 3-foot stems above rosettes of woolly, gray-green, 8-inch leaves. *S. azurea* ssp. *pitcheri* var. *grandiflora* (blue sage)—large, deep blue flowers on stems to 5 feet lined with gray-green leaves. *S. farinacea* (mealy-cup sage)—violet-blue or white flowers from midsummer to frost on 2- to 3-foot stems; 'Blue Bedder' has deep blue flowers on 8-inch clusters on compact plants to 2 feet tall. *S. haematodes* (meadow sage)—airy sprays of lavender-blue flowers from early to midsummer on plants to 3 feet tall. *S. jurisicii* (Jurisici's sage)—dangling lilac or white flowers on stems 12 to 18 inches tall. *S. officinalis* (common sage)—whorls of tiny white, blue, or purple flowers above wrinkled, hairy, aromatic gray-green leaves, which can be used as a seasoning for food; 'Purpurascens' has purple-tinged leaves; 'Tricolor', leaf veins turning from cream to pink and red as foliage ages. *S. sclarea* 'Turkestanica' [also called *S. s.* var. *turkestana* or var. *turkestaniana*]—rosy pink flower spikes tipping 3-foot stems above wrinkled, hairy leaves. *S. x superba* (perennial salvia)—violet-purple flowers in dense whorls around 4- to 8-inch spikes from late spring to early summer on rounded plants to 3 feet tall; 'Blue Queen' grows 18 to 24 inches tall; 'East Friesland' has deep purple blossoms on 18- to 24-inch plants; 'May Night' grows to 24 inches with intense violet-blue flowers.

Salvia officinalis 'Purpurascens'

Growing conditions and maintenance: Sage grows best in dry soils; its roots should not stay wet over winter. Because they vary in hardiness, particular care must be given to selection of species. Garden sage is hardy to Zone 4; Pitcher's salvia and perennial salvia, to Zone 5; meadow sage and Jurisici's sage, to Zone 6; mealy-cup sage, to Zone 8 and evergreen in Zone 9. Plant smaller salvia varieties 18 inches apart, larger ones 2 to 3 feet apart. Removing spent flowers encourages reblooming. Propagate by division in spring or fall, from cuttings, or, except for perennial salvia, from seed.

Santolina
(san-to-LEE-na)
LAVENDER COTTON

Santolina chamaecyparissus

Hardiness: *Zones 6-8*

Flowering season: *summer*

Height: *18 to 24 inches*

Flower color: *yellow*

Soil: *well-drained to dry loam*

Light: *full sun*

Santolina forms a broad, spreading clump of aromatic leaves, with slender stems topped by tiny yellow flower buttons. The foliage makes an attractive edging for a bed or walkway, or can be used as a low-growing specimen in a rock garden. It can also be sheared into a tight, low hedge.

Selected species and varieties: *S. chamaecyparissus*—up to 24 inches tall with equal or greater spread, forms a broad, cushionlike, evergreen mound. Leaves are silvery gray-green and ½ to 1½ inches long; yellow flowers bloom in summer and are often removed to maintain clipped hedge. *S. virens*—green toothed-edged leaves in dense 18-inch clumps.

Growing conditions and maintenance: Lavender cotten is a tough plant, well suited to adverse conditions such as drought and salt spray. It prefers dry soils of low fertility and becomes unattractive and open in fertile soils. Avoid excess moisture, especially in winter. Space plants 18 to 24 inches apart. Prune after flowering to promote dense growth, or shear anytime for a formal, low hedge. Propagate from seed or from stem cuttings taken in early summer.

Saxifraga
(saks-IF-ra-ga)
SAXIFRAGE, ROCKFOIL

Saxifraga umbrosa

Hardiness: *Zones 7-9*

Flowering season: *late spring to early summer*

Height: *4 to 24 inches*

Flower color: *white, pink, rose, bicolored*

Soil: *moist, well-drained, neutral, fertile*

Light: *full to dappled shade*

An ideal plant for rock gardens, saxifrage's rosettes of leaves form a mat from which runners or stolons spread. The red threadlike runners of strawberry geranium, which is also grown as a houseplant, produce baby plants. Delicate flowers rise above foliage in spring.

Selected species and varieties: *S. stolonifera* (strawberry geranium, beefsteak geranium)—18- to 24-inch branched stems bearing 1-inch-wide white flowers above 4-inch-tall clumps of round, hairy leaves with white veins and red undersides, up to 4 inches wide. *S. umbrosa* (London-pride)—18-inch-high clumps of 2-inch-long oval leaves, pea green above and red beneath, with white, pink, rose, or bicolored flower sprays on 6-inch stems from late spring to early summer.

Growing conditions and maintenance: Saxifrages grow best in neutral, rocky soil but will tolerate other soils as long as they are very well drained but evenly moist. Generously enrich the soil with leaf mold or peat moss. Plant 8 to 10 inches apart in spring, and mulch lightly to overwinter. Apply an all-purpose fertilizer in spring. Propagate by dividing after flowering.

Sedum
(SEE-dum)
STONECROP

Sedum 'Autumn Joy'

Hardiness: *Zones 3-10*

Flowering season: *spring to fall*

Height: *3 inches to 2 feet*

Flower color: *white, yellow, orange, red, pink*

Soil: *well-drained loam*

Light: *full sun to light shade*

Stonecrops are valued for both their flowers and their foliage, which add color and rich texture to a garden over a long season. Their thick, succulent leaves vary in color from bright green to blue-green to reddish green. Individual flowers are small and star-shaped, with 5 petals. Generally borne in dense clusters that cover the plant, they attract butterflies to the garden. The blooming season varies among species from spring to fall, with some flowers even persisting into winter. Sedums are easy to grow and tolerate drought, making them well suited to rock gardens and dry borders. They can be used as individual specimens, in groupings of three or more, or massed as a succulent ground cover.

Selected species and varieties: *S. aizoon* (Aizoon stonecrop)—yellow flowers above bright green leaves on stems 12 to 18 inches tall, blooming from spring to summer; 'Auranticum' has deep yellow flowers and red-tinted stems. *S.* 'Autumn Joy'—rosy pink flower buds that form above gray-green leaves on 2-foot stems in mid-summer, turn red before opening bronze-red in fall, and turn golden

brown if left in place for the winter. *S. kamtschaticum* (orange stonecrop)—6 to 9 inches tall with a wide-spreading habit, excellent for rock gardens, grows small orange-yellow flowers in summer; 'Variegatum' produces deep orange flowers and green leaves with a broad white margin blushed with pink. *S. maximum* (great stonecrop)—greenish yellow, star-shaped flowers in late summer above oval, gray-green leaves on stems up to 2 feet tall; 'Atropurpureum' has red flowers and maroon leaves. *S. rosea* (roseroot)—tiny yellow or purple flowers atop clumps of 12-inch stems with small toothed leaves; *S. r. integrifolium* has pink to red-purple flowers. *S.* 'Ruby Glow'—ruby red fall flowers above purple-gray foliage on compact plants 8 inches tall; a good choice for the front of a border. *S. sieboldii* (Siebold stonecrop)—dense heads of pink flowers effective throughout fall above nearly triangular blue-gray leaves on 6- to 9-inch somewhat trailing stems. *S. spectabile* (showy stonecrop)—a heat-tolerant

Sedum kamtschaticum

species with bright pink flowers that bloom from late summer till frost on 18-inch stems; 'Brilliant' has raspberry red flowers; 'Carmen', rose pink flowers; 'Variegatum', bright pink flowers atop leaves variegated yellow and green; 'Meteor', large wine red blooms; 'Stardust', white flowers that stand out against blue-green leaves; 'Variegatum', bright pink blooms above variegated foliage; Zones 3-10. *S. spurium* (two-row stonecrop)—pink, red, or white summer flowers on vigorously spreading evergreen stems 3 to 6 inches tall that make a tough evergreen ground cover; 'Bronze Carpet' has pink flowers and red-brown foliage; 'Coccineum' has scarlet blooms; 'Dragon's Blood' produces purple-bronze leaves and deep crimson star-shaped flowers; 'Red Carpet' has bronze leaves and red flowers; 'Variegatum', green leaves with creamy pink margins. S. 'Vera Jameson'—a slightly larger hybrid of S. 'Ruby Glow' at 12 inches tall, with

Sedum spurium

bronze foliage and magenta flowers.

Growing conditions and maintenance: Stonecrops are tough plants that spread without becoming invasive. Space *S. sieboldii* 1 foot apart, other species 1½ to 2 feet apart. They tolerate almost any well-drained soil, even if it is dry and sterile. Stonecrops can be left undivided for many years, but can be propagated by division in spring or from stem cuttings taken in summer.

Silene
(sy-LEE-ne)
CAMPION, CATCHFLY

Silene schafta

Hardiness:	*Zones 4-8*
Flowering season:	*summer to fall*
Height:	*4 inches to 2 feet*
Flower color:	*white, pink, red*
Soil:	*well-drained, sandy loam*
Light:	*full sun to light shade*

Campions produce star-shaped, five-petaled flowers on branching stems for several weeks during the growing season. The plant's tufts of low-growing, narrow foliage sometimes spread.

Selected species and varieties: *S. schafta* (moss campion)—rose pink or purple flowers on 12-inch stems above 6-inch rosettes of hairy, oblong, light green leaves. *S.* 'Robin's White Breast'—white flower bells above dense 8-inch mounds of silvery gray leaves. *S. virginica* (fire-pink catchfly)—clusters of pink to red flowers on sticky 2-foot stems above flat rosettes of evergreen leaves.

Growing conditions and maintenance: Space campions 12 inches apart. Propagate from seed or by division in spring.

Solidago
(sol-i-DAY-go)
GOLDENROD

Solidago canadensis

Hardiness:	*Zones 3-10*
Flowering season:	*summer, fall*
Height:	*1 to 10 feet*
Flower color:	*yellow*
Soil:	*moist, well-drained to dry*
Light:	*full sun to partial shade*

The upright stems of goldenrods are tipped with eye-catching clusters of yellow flowers in summer and fall. These tough, dependable perennials are native to meadows and prairies in Canada and throughout most of the United States. They make excellent cut flowers, and butterflies feed on their nectar.

Selected species: *S. caesia* (blue-stemmed goldenrod, wreath goldenrod)—slender blue- or purple-tinged stems 1 to 3 feet with small arching sprays of yellow flowers in late summer and fall; Zones 4-8. *S. canadensis* (Canada goldenrod)—2 to 4 feet tall with branching flower clusters in late summer; Zones 3-10. *S. juncea* (early goldenrod)—up to 6 feet or more in height with arching clusters of flowers from mid- to late summer; Zones 3-7. *S. missouriensis* (Missouri goldenrod)—an early-blooming goldenrod with nodding flower clusters on reddish stems 1 to 2 feet tall from mid- to late summer; Zones 4-8. *S. nemoralis* (gray goldenrod)—up to 2 feet high with plume-shaped flower clusters in late summer and fall; Zones 3-9. *S. odora* (sweet goldenrod)—2 to 5 feet tall with large flower clusters from midsummer through fall and neat, bright green foliage that smells like anise when crushed; Zones 3-9. *S. rugosa* (rough-leaved goldenrod)—2 to 5 feet tall with flower sprays composed of thin, arching stems for 3 to 4 weeks in fall; Zones 3-8. *S. sempervirens* (seaside goldenrod)—large branching clusters of flowers on stems to 8 feet tall

Solidago odora

in late summer and fall above a clump of narrow evergreen leaves up to 16 inches long; Zones 4-8.

Growing conditions and maintenance: Space goldenrods 18 to 24 inches apart. These plants thrive in full sun in soils of average fertility. *S. caesia* also tolerates partial shade. *S. sempervirens* tolerates salt spray and can be pinched in early summer to encourage compact growth. Most goldenrods are aggressive growers and may need dividing every 2 to 3 years. *S. caesia, S. odora,* and *S. sempervirens* are less vigorous growers than the others and easier to keep within bounds. Propagate goldenrods by seed or division. Propagate hybrids by division.

Stokesia
(sto-KEE-zi-a)
STOKES' ASTER

Stokesia laevis 'Blue Danube'

Hardiness: *Zones 5-9*

Flowering season: *summer*

Height: *12 to 18 inches*

Flower color: *lavender, blue, white*

Soil: *well-drained, sandy loam*

Light: *full sun*

The showy, fringed flowers of Stokes' aster bloom on branched flowerstalks rising from neat rosettes of shiny, narrow, straplike leathery leaves that are evergreen in warmer climates. Stokes' aster is excellent in bouquets.

Selected species and varieties: *S. laevis*—solitary flower heads 2 to 5 inches across, blooming over a 4-week season in summer; 'Blue Danube' has 5-inch clear blue flowers; 'Blue Moon', lilac flowers; 'Jelitto' has 4-inch deep blue blossoms; 'Silver Moon' blooms white.

Growing conditions and maintenance: Space *Stokesia* 18 inches apart. Mulch over winter in colder climates. Propagate the species from seed, and the species and its hybrids by division in the spring.

Verbena
(ver-BEE-na)
VERBENA, VERVAIN

Verbena canadensis 'Rosea'

Hardiness: *Zones 6-8*

Flowering season: *summer to fall*

Height: *4 inches to 5 feet*

Flower color: *pink, red, purple*

Soil: *well-drained loam*

Light: *full sun*

Verbena's tiny flowers bloom in flat, dainty clusters on wiry stems.

Selected species and varieties: *V. bonariensis* (Brazilian verbena)—fragrant purple flowers on stems to 5 feet. *V. canadensis* (rose verbena)—rose pink blossoms in rounded clusters on dense mats of creeping stems 6 inches tall; 'Rosea' produces fragrant rose-purple flowers blooming almost continuously. *V. peruviana* (Peruvian verbena)—crimson flowers on trailing stems 4 inches high. *V. tenuisecta* (moss verbena)—lavender flower clusters on 1-foot stems.

Growing conditions and maintenance: Space Brazilian verbena plants 2 feet apart, smaller forms 1 foot apart. Rose verbena is hardy to Zone 6, other species to Zone 8. Propagate from seed or from cuttings taken in the late summer.

Veronica
(ve-RON-i-ka)
SPEEDWELL

Veronica 'Sunny Border Blue'

Hardiness: *Zones 4-8*

Flowering season: *spring to summer*

Height: *6 inches to 4 feet*

Flower color: *blue, pink, white*

Soil: *well-drained loam*

Light: *full sun to light shade*

Clumps of spreading stems lined with soft-textured, narrow leaves and tipped with long spikes of tiny spring-to-summer flowers make speedwell a good choice for fillers or naturalizing.

Selected species and varieties: *V.* x hybrids—plants 12 to 24 inches tall; 'Sunny Border Blue' produces blue flowers. *V. incana* (silver speedwell, woolly speedwell)—pale lilac-blue flowers above low clumps of silver-gray foliage; 'Minuet' has pink flowers and gray-green leaves; 'Saraband', 12- to 18-inch plants with violet-blue flowers. *V. longifolia* (longleaf speedwell)—plants to 4 feet; 'Icicle' has white flowers; var. *subsessilis,* lilac blooms. *V. spicata* (spike speedwell)—18-inch plants; 'Blue Fox' has lavender-blue flower spikes; 'Red Fox', rose-to-pink blooms. *V. teucrium* [also called *V. austriaca* ssp. *teucrium*] 'Crater Lake Blue'—compact 12- to 18-inch plants with wide spikes of deep blue flowers.

Growing conditions and maintenance: Plant speedwell 1 to 2 feet apart. Remove spent flowers to extend bloom. Propagate from seed or cuttings or by division in spring or fall.

Veronicastrum
(ve-ro-ni-KAS-trum)
CULVER'S ROOT

Veronicastrum virginicum

Hardiness: *Zones 4-8*

Flowering season: *summer*

Height: *3 to 6 feet*

Flower color: *white, pale lavender, pink*

Soil: *well-drained, acid loam*

Light: *full sun to partial shade*

Veronicastrum produces branched clusters of tiny flower spikes on tall, erect stems. Its leaves are arranged in tiered whorls that ascend the stem.

Selected species and varieties: *V. virginicum* (blackroot)—tiny tubular flowers packed densely along 6- to 9-inch flower spikes on stems 6 feet tall in clumps 18 to 24 inches wide; 'Roseum' grows pink flowers; 'Album', white flowers. Veroniscastrum is a good background plant for the garden.

Growing conditions and maintenance: Space veronicastrum 18 to 24 inches apart in moderately acid soil. Plants that are grown in shade may require staking for support. Propagate plants by division in the fall.

Viola
(Vy-O-la)
VIOLET

Viola canadensis var. rugulosa

Hardiness: *Zones 3-9*

Flowering season: *spring and fall*

Height: *3 to 12 inches*

Flower color: *yellow, white, rose, violet*

Soil: *moist, well-drained loam*

Light: *partial shade*

Violets produce dainty blossoms that have 2 upper petals and 3 lower petals joined into a short spur on thin stems. Leaves are heart-shaped.

Selected species and varieties: *V. canadensis* (Canada violet)—white flowers with a yellow eye; *V. canadensis* var. *rugulosa* has narrower, wrinkled leaves with hairy undersides. *V. cornuta* (horned violet)—pansylike flowers on plants with evergreen leaves; 'Lord Nelson' has deep violet flowers. *V. cucullata* (marsh blue violet)—white flowers with purple veins; 'Royal Robe' has deep blue flowers. *V. odorata* (sweet violet)—fragrant flowers in shades of violet, rose, and white; 'Alba' has white blossoms; 'Czar', deep violet flowers. *V. tricolor* (Johnny-jump-up)—tricolored violet-blue-and-yellow flowers.

Growing conditions and maintenance: Space violets 8 to 12 inches apart. Propagate from seed or by division.

Agapanthus
(ag-a-PAN-thus)
LILY-OF-THE-NILE

Agapanthus africanus

Hardiness: *tender or Zones 8-10*

Type of bulb: *rhizome*

Flowering season: *summer*

Height: *18 inches to 5 feet*

Soil: *moist, well-drained*

Light: *full sun*

Domed clusters of five-petaled, star-shaped flowers with prominent stamens rise on leafless, hollow stalks from graceful clumps of straplike evergreen leaves that persist after the flowers fade. Agapanthus makes dramatic border specimens or pot plants and can be used as long-lasting cut flowers. Its seed pods add interest to dried arrangements.

Selected species and varieties: *A. africanus* 'Albus' (African lily)—clusters of 30 or more 1½-inch white flower stars on stems to 3 feet tall. *A. praecox* ssp. *orientalis* (Oriental agapanthus)—up to 100 white or blue flowers clustered on stems to 5 feet tall above 3-foot-long leaves that are up to 3 inches wide and sometimes striped yellow; 'Peter Pan' is an 18-inch dwarf cultivar with blue blossoms.

Growing conditions and maintenance: Plant rhizomes 24 inches apart in spring for summer bloom, setting the tops of the bulbs just below the soil line. In colder areas, grow plants in pots, moving them indoors before frost. They bloom best when slightly potbound. Cut stems back after flowers fade. Propagate by dividing rhizomes every 4 or 5 years in spring.

Allium
(AL-lee-um)
FLOWERING ONION

Allium cernuum

Hardiness: *Zones 3-9*

Type of bulb: *true bulb*

Flowering season: *spring to summer*

Height: *6 inches to 5 feet*

Soil: *moist, well-drained, sandy*

Light: *full sun to partial shade*

Related to edible culinary species, flowering onions produce showy 2- to 12-inch flower clusters, usually in dense spheres or ovals composed of hundreds of tiny blooms packed tightly together, but sometimes in loose, dangling or upright airy domes of larger flowers. Each stout, leafless hollow stem holds a single flower well above a low rosette of grassy or straplike leaves that die back after the bulbs produce their blooms. Many species smell faintly like onion or garlic when cut or bruised, but a few are sweetly fragrant. Mass alliums for effect in spring or summer beds or borders; strategically site larger flowering onions as dramatic garden accents; and interplant smaller species with ground covers or in a rock garden. Alliums are striking as cut flowers or in dried bouquets. Some flowering onion species will naturalize, and a few are suitable for forcing. Rodent pests find flowering onion bulbs unappealing.

Selected species and varieties: *A. aflatunense* (ornamental onion, Persian onion)—4-inch purple flower globes in late spring on 2- to 4-foot-tall stems above 4-inch-wide foliage; Zones 4-8. *A. atrop-urpureum*—2-inch wine red spheres on 2- to 3-foot stems in late spring above narrow 18-inch leaves; Zones 3-9. *A. caeruleum* (blue garlic, blue globe onion)—deep blue blossoms in dense 2-inch globes on 2-foot stems in late spring above narrow 10- to 18-inch leaves; Zones 3-9. *A. carinatum* ssp. *pulchellum* (keeled garlic)—carmine flower clusters on stems to 2 feet in summer; 'Album' has white flowers; Zones 3-9. *A. cernuum* (nodding wild onion)—loose clusters of 30 to 40 delicate pink flowers dangle atop 8- to 18-inch stems in late spring above rosettes of grassy 10-inch leaves; Zones 3-9. *A. christophii* (stars-of-Persia)—spidery late spring flowers with a metallic luster growing in lacy clusters up to 10 inches across on stout stems to 2 feet growing from rosettes of inch-wide leaves up to 20 inches long; Zones 4-8.

Allium christophii

A. flavum (small yellow onion)—dangling 2-inch clusters of yellow bell-shaped flowers on 1-foot stems in summer; Zones 4-9. *A. giganteum* (giant ornamental onion, giant garlic)—lilac-colored summer flower globes 6 inches across on stems to 5 feet rising from clumps of leaves 2 inches wide and up to 30 inches long; Zones 5-8. *A. jesdianum*—dense clusters of deep violet flowers; Zones 4-9. *A. karataviense* (Turkestan onion)—pale rose 3-inch or larger flower clusters on 10-inch stems above broad straps of attractive, spreading blue-green foliage in late spring; Zones 4-9. *A. macleanii*—red-violet blossoms clustered at the tips of 3-foot stems in late spring above broad, shiny foliage; Zones 4-9. *A. moly* (lily leek, golden onion)—flat clusters of ¾- to 1-inch flowers; 'Jeannine' has long-lasting 2- to 3-inch vivid yellow flowers on 12-inch stems in summer above blue-green leaves with a metallic sheen; Zones 3-9. *A. neapolitanum* 'Grandiflorum' (daffodil garlic, Naples garlic)—loose, open 3-inch clusters of up to 30 fragrant 1-inch white flower stars on 12- to 18-inch stems in late spring; Zones 6-9. *A. nigrum*—white spring flowers touched with gray on 2-foot stems; Zones 4-9. *A. oreophilum*—open clusters of fragrant 2-inch rosy pink blossoms on 4-inch stems in late spring; Zones 4-9. *A. rosenbachianum* 'Album'—silvery white 4-inch

Allium sphaerocephalum

flower clusters on stems to 3 feet in late spring above 2-inch-wide leaves up to 20 inches long; Zones 5-9. *A. roseum* 'Grandiflorum' (bigflower rosy onion, rosy garlic)—3-inch pinkish white flower globes in late spring on stems to 15 inches, frequently with tiny bulbils appearing after the flowers fade; Zones 5-9. *A. schubertii*—spidery pink-violet flowers in clusters up to a foot or more across on 1- to 2-foot stems in summer above distinctively wavy, inch-wide foliage; Zones 4-9. *A. sphaerocephalum* (drumstick chive, roundheaded leek, roundheaded garlic)—densely packed 2-inch oval heads of deep purple, bell-shaped summer flowers on 3-foot stems rising from clumps of hollow cylindrical leaves up to 24 inches long; Zones 4-8. *A. stipitatum* 'Album'—6-inch spheres of white flowers on stems to 4 feet in late spring above 2-inch-wide leaves; Zones 4-9. *A. triquetrum* (three-cornered leek, triangle onion)—dangling white flowers striped with green on unusual triangular 18-inch stems rising from clumps of deep green leaves 10 to 15 inches long throughout spring; Zones 4-

9. *A. unifolium*—rose flowers on 12- to 18-inch stems in late spring; Zones 4-9. *A. ursinum* (bear's garlic, ramsons, wood garlic)—2½-inch flat-topped clusters of white flowers with a strong garlicky odor on 12- to 15-inch stems in late spring; Zones 4-9. *A. zebdanense*—white blossoms clustered on 12-inch stems in late spring; Zones 4-9. *A. hybrids*—'Globemaster' has durable large purple blooms on 2- to 3-foot stems; 'Lucy Ball', deep lilac clusters on stems to 4 feet in summer; 'Purple Sensation', purple flowers on 30-inch stems in spring; Zones 4-9.

Growing conditions and maintenance: Plant flowering onions in fall in northern zones, in spring or fall in warmer areas. Set bulbs at a depth two to three times their diameter, spacing smaller bulbs 4 to 6 inches apart, larger ones 12 to 18 inches. Alliums suitable for naturalizing include *A. aflatunense*, *A. karataviense*, *A. moly*, *A. neapolitanum*, *A. oreophilum*, *A. sphaerocephalum*, and *A. triquetrum*, although *A. triquetrum* can be invasive. Alliums may be left undisturbed in the garden for years until diminished bloom signals that bulbs are overcrowded. Both pleasantly scented *A. neapolitanum* and low-growing *A. schubertii* are suitable for forcing; plant several bulbs per 6-inch pot or bulb pan. Cut stems back after flowers fade, but allow foliage to die back before removing it. Protect bulbs with winter mulch north of Zone 5. Propagate by separating and replanting tiny bulblets that develop at the base of parent bulbs, by potting tiny bulbils that appear amid flower clusters, or by sowing seed, which will grow blooming-size bulbs in 2 years.

Anemone
(a-NEM-o-nee)
WINDFLOWER

Anemone coronaria

Hardiness:	*Zones 3-9*
Type of bulb:	*tuber or rhizome*
Flowering season:	*spring*
Height:	*3 to 18 inches*
Soil:	*moist, well-drained*
Light:	*full sun to light shade*

Windflowers carpet a border with drifts of daisylike flowers held above whorls of attractively divided leaves resembling flat parsley. Single or double rows of petals surround a prominent cushion of anthers in a contrasting color, often with a halo of cream or white separating it from the main petal color. Mass windflowers for a tapestry of color beneath spring-flowering shrubs and trees or allow them to naturalize in woodland gardens. Anemones can be forced as houseplants, and the taller ones make good cut flowers.

Selected species and varieties: *A. apennina* 'Alba' (Apennine windflower)—inch-wide white flowers tinged blue on 6- to 12-inch stems; Zones 6-9. *A. blanda* (Grecian windflower)—2-inch single- or double-petaled flowers with prominent yellow centers on 3- to 8-inch stems; 'Blue Star' has light blue flowers; 'Blue Shades', light to dark blue blooms; 'Charmer', deep pink flowers; 'Pink Star', very large pink blossoms; 'Radar', reddish purple flowers with a white center; 'Rosea', rosy pink blooms; 'Violet Star', violet flowers with a white center; 'White Splendor', long-lasting, large white flowers; Zones 5-8. *A. coronaria* (poppy anemone)—'de Caen' hybrids grow 18 inches tall with single rows of petals; 'Mr. Fokker' has blue flowers; 'Sylphide', deep violet blooms; 'The Bride', pure white flowers. St. Brigid hybrids produce semidouble rows of petals; 'Lord Lieutenant' has bright blue flowers; 'Mt. Everest', white flowers; 'The Admiral', red-violet blooms; 'The Governor', deep scarlet flowers. 'Hollandia' has bright red flowers; Zones 6-9. *A. nemorosa* (wood anemone)—inch-wide white flowers tinged pink with yellow centers

Anemone blanda

on 6- to 10-inch stems; 'Alba Plena' has double petals; Zones 4-8. *A. ranunculoides* (buttercup anemone)—yellow blossoms on 6-inch stems; 'Flore Pleno' has semidouble yellow petals giving a ruffled appearance; 'Superba', large flowers above bronzy foliage; Zones 3-9.

Growing conditions and maintenance: Plant windflowers in the fall, massing them for best effect. Soak tubers overnight before setting them out 2 inches deep and 3 to 6 inches apart. *A. apennina* and Grecian windflower can be grown north of Zone 6 by setting tubers out in spring, then lifting them for storage in fall. *A. apennina*, Grecian windflower, and poppy anemone can be forced for houseplants. *A. apennina*, Grecian windflower, wood anemone, and buttercup anemone all naturalize well, although the latter two can be invasive. Anemones need constant moisture, though not soggy conditions, to bloom at their best. Propagate windflowers from seed or by division in late summer after foliage fades.

Arisaema
(a-ris-EE-ma)
DRAGONROOT

Arisaema triphyllum

Hardiness:	*Zones 4-9*
Type of bulb:	*tuber*
Flowering season:	*spring*
Height:	*1 to 3 feet*
Soil:	*moist, acid*
Light:	*partial to full shade*

Arisaemas produce a fleshy spike called a spadix nestled within an outer leaflike spathe, which folds over the spadix like a hood. Glossy, three-lobed leaves taller than the spathe and spadix persist throughout the summer. The spadix ripens to a cluster of attractive red fruit in fall. Use arisaemas in wildflower or woodland gardens or along stream banks, where they will slowly spread out and naturalize.

Selected species and varieties: *A. dracontium* (green-dragon)—green spathe enfolding a 4- to 10-inch green or yellowish green spadix on 1-foot stems. *A. sikokianum*—ivory spadix within a spathe that is deep maroon banded in green on the outside and ivory at its base on the inside, on 1-foot stems. *A. triphyllum* (jack-in-the-pulpit, Indian turnip)—green to purple spadix within a green to purple spathe striped purple, green, white, or maroon inside on 1- to 2-foot stems.

Growing conditions and maintenance: Plant arisaemas in fall, setting tubers 4 inches deep and 1 foot apart in soil that is constantly moist but not soggy. Propagate by division in early fall.

Arum
(A-rum)
ARUM

Arum italicum

Hardiness:	*Zones 6-9*
Type of bulb:	*tuber*
Flowering season:	*spring*
Height:	*12 to 18 inches*
Soil:	*moist, acid*
Light:	*partial shade*

Italian arum *(Arum italicum)* is noteworthy for its attractively marbled, arrow-shaped leaves, which appear in fall and persist through the winter. Inconspicuous flowers appear in spring, lining a fleshy, fingerlike spadix enfolded by a leaflike hood called a spathe, which rises to a sharp point. Most gardeners grow arum for the plump cluster of glossy, brightly colored berries that follows the flowers in summer. Arum will naturalize in moist woodland or wildflower gardens.

Selected species and varieties: *A. italicum* 'Marmoratum' [also called 'Pictum'] (Italian arum)—narrow, waxy leaves veined in cream or silver followed by a creamy yellow or yellow-green spadix and thick clusters of brilliant orange berries.

Growing conditions and maintenance: Plant Italian arum in late summer, setting tubers 3 inches deep and 1 foot apart in soil that is moist but not soggy. Propagate from seed or by division in late summer. Caution: Both the foliage and berries of Italian arum are poisonous and must be kept out of the reach of children.

Babiana
(bab-ee-AH-na)
BABOON FLOWER

Babiana stricta

Hardiness: *tender or Zones 9-11*

Type of bulb: *corm*

Flowering season: *spring*

Height: *8 to 12 inches*

Soil: *moist, well-drained*

Light: *full sun*

Baboon flowers produce 1½-inch fragrant flowers with pointed petals surrounding a contrasting eye; the blooms last as long as 5 weeks in the garden. Flowers grow in clusters on stems rising from stiff, sword-shaped leaves. Use baboon flowers in borders or grow them in containers as patio specimens.

Selected species and varieties: *B. stricta*—flowers in shades of cream, blue, lilac, and crimson; 'Purple Sensation' produces white-throated purple flowers; 'White King', white petals streaked blue on their undersides surrounding a deep blue eye; 'Zwanenburg Glory', lavender to violet petals splashed with white.

Growing conditions and maintenance: Plant baboon flowers in fall, setting corms 6 inches deep and 6 inches apart. North of Zone 9, plant corms in spring and lift after foliage fades in fall for replanting the following spring. Propagate from seed or by removing and planting the cormels that develop around parent bulbs every 3 to 4 years.

Caladium
(ka-LAY-dee-um)
ANGEL-WINGS

Caladium bicolor 'Aaron'

Hardiness: *tender or Zones 10-11*

Type of bulb: *tuber*

Flowering season: *summer*

Height: *1 to 2 feet*

Soil: *moist, well-drained*

Light: *partial shade to shade*

Exotic caladiums form clumps of intricately patterned translucent leaves that eclipse their insignificant flowers. The arrow-shaped leaves, rising continuously throughout summer, are vividly marbled, shaded, slashed, veined, and flecked in contrasting colors to brighten shady borders or decorate indoor gardens.

Selected species and varieties: *C. bicolor* [formerly *C.* x *hortulanum*]—foot-long arrow- or heart-shaped leaves; 'Aaron' has green edges feathering into creamy centers; 'Candidum' is white with green veining; 'Fannie Munson', pink veined red edged in green; 'Festiva', rose veined green; 'Irene Dank', light green edged in deeper green; 'June Bride', greenish white edged in deep green; 'Pink Beauty', a pink dwarf spattered with green; 'White Christmas', white with green veining.

Growing conditions and maintenance: Plant in spring when night temperatures remain above 60°F, setting the tubers 2 inches deep and 8 to 12 inches apart. North of Zone 10, lift and dry tubers in fall to replant the next spring. Provide high humidity and temperatures of 60°F or more. Propagate by division in spring.

Camassia
(ka-MA-see-a)
CAMASS, QUAMASH

Camassia quamash

Hardiness: *Zones 5-9*

Type of bulb: *true bulb*

Flowering season: *spring*

Height: *1 to 4 feet*

Soil: *moist, well-drained, sandy*

Light: *full sun to light shade*

Camass's spires of inch-wide flowers like tiny stars with a fringe of narrow, pointed, sometimes double petals open from bottom to top over several weeks. Naturalize camass in damp wildflower gardens, alongside streams or ponds, or among other spring-blooming bulbs.

Selected species and varieties: *C. cusickii* (Cusick quamash)—up to 300 flowers on stalks 3 to 4 feet tall; 'Zwanenburg' has horizontal stalks upturned at their ends. *C. leichtlinii* (Leichtlin quamash)—up to 40 flowers on stems to 4 feet; 'Alba' produces white blossoms; 'Blue Danube', very dark blue; 'Sempiplena', double-petaled creamy white to yellow. *C. quamash* (common camass)—foot-long spires on 2-foot stems; 'Orion' is very deep blue. *C. scilloides* (Atlantic camass, eastern camass, wild hyacinth)—blue or white ½-inch flowers on 2½-foot stems.

Growing conditions and maintenance: Plant camass bulbs in fall, setting them 4 inches deep and 6 to 9 inches apart. Provide shade where summers are dry. Bulbs can be lifted to remove offsets but are best left undisturbed unless flowering declines. Otherwise, propagate from seed.

Canna
(KAN-ah)
CANNA

Canna 'Brandywine'

Hardiness: *tender or Zones 8-11*

Type of bulb: *rhizome*

Flowering season: *summer to fall*

Height: *18 inches to 6 feet*

Soil: *moist, well-drained*

Light: *full sun*

Cannas produce a continuous show of bold 4- to 5-inch flowers with a tousled arrangement of petal-like stamens in strong colors from summer through frost. The flowers, which are sometimes bicolored, are carried on clumps of stiff, erect stems. The broad, bold leaves, up to 24 inches long, are usually a deep, glossy green but are sometimes bronzy red or striped or veined in white or pink. They line the stems to provide a dramatic backdrop to the flowers. Mass these coarse-textured plants at the back of borders in casual groupings or formal patterns, or grow dwarf cultivars as edgings or in patio containers.

Selected species and varieties: *C.* x *generalis* (canna lily)—standard varieties grow 4 to 6 feet tall; 'Black Knight' has deep velvet red flowers and bronze foliage; 'City of Portland', rosy salmon flowers above green leaves; 'Gaiety', yellow flowers edged in orange; 'Los Angeles', coral pink blooms above green foliage; 'The President', bright red flowers and deep green leaves; 'Red King Humbert', red flowers above bronzy foliage on very tall stems; 'Richard Wallace', canary yellow blossoms and green foliage; 'Rosamund Cole', red-and-gold bicolored blossoms; 'Stadt Fellbach', peach flowers with yellow throats fading to pink; 'Wyoming', rugged red-orange flowers and reddish bronze leaves. Dwarf varieties of this species grow to less than 3 feet tall; 'Ambrosia' has pinky orange blossoms on 18-inch stems; 'Brandywine', scarlet flowers on 3-foot stems; 'Pfitzer's Chinese Coral', rich coral pink blossoms; 'Pfitzer's Crimson Beauty', bright red flowers on 18-inch stems; 'Pfitzer's Primrose Yellow', soft yellow blooms; 'Pfitzer's Salmon', unusually large salmon pink flowers; 'Pretoria', yellow-orange flowers above deep green leaves striped with cream.

Growing conditions and maintenance: In Zones 9 and 10, set cannas out as bedding plants in spring, planting the rhizomes 4 to 6 inches deep; space standard cultivars 2 feet apart, dwarf cultivars 1 foot apart. Provide ample moisture and high humidity during the growing season. Cannas can remain in the ground year round in frost-free areas; in Zone 8, provide a protective winter mulch. North of Zone 8, start cannas for beds or containers indoors 4 weeks before night temperatures reach 60°F; in fall, cut foliage back to 6 inches and lift rhizomes for winter storage. Pinch each container-grown rhizome back to a single shoot for largest flowers. Propagate cannas from seed, soaking seeds for 48 hours before planting to loosen their tough outer coats; or by division in spring, sectioning to allow no more than two buds per piece.

Crinum
(KREE-num)
SPIDER LILY

Crinum x powellii

Hardiness: *tender or Zones 7-11*

Type of bulb: *true bulb*

Flowering season: *spring, summer, fall*

Height: *2 to 4 feet*

Soil: *moist, well-drained, fertile*

Light: *full sun to light shade*

Crinums produce whorls of lilylike flowers with a spicy fragrance over a long season of bloom. Each cluster blooms atop a stout stem rising from a clump of deep green, sword-shaped, evergreen or deciduous leaves. The blossoms are either funnel shaped with thick, ridged petals curving backward, or lacy and spidery with narrow, straplike petals. Crinum's unusual bulbs, about the size of a grapefruit, have elongated necks up to a foot long and bloom best when they are crowded. In warmer areas, plant them where they can remain undisturbed for several years. They do especially well at the edges of ponds and streams where there is constant moisture, slowly naturalizing into large clumps. In northern areas, sink bulbs in tubs, which can be moved indoors to a greenhouse or conservatory for the winter.

Selected species and varieties: *C. americanum* (Florida swamp lily)—up to 6 white flower funnels in late spring or summer on 2-foot stems before leaves appear. *C. asiaticum* (grand crinum, poison bulb)—up to 50 heavily scented white flowers with straplike petals and pink stamens in summer on stalks to 4 feet. *C. bulbispermum* (Orange River lily)—a dozen or more pink or white flower trumpets with rose-striped petals in fall on 3-foot stems above deciduous foliage. *C. moorei* (Cape Coast lily, longneck swamp lily)—10 to 20 rose red flower funnels in summer on 4-foot stalks rising from bold evergreen leaves. *C.* x *powellii* (Powell's swamp lily)—six to eight red flower trumpets touched with green at their base on 2-foot stalks rising from evergreen leaves up to 4 feet long; 'Album' has white flowers. *C.* 'Cecil Houdyshel'—profuse pink flowers. *C.* 'Ellen Bosanquet'—wine red summer flowers above evergreen foliage.

Growing conditions and maintenance: Outdoors, plant crinums so that the necks of the bulbs remain above ground and the bulbs are 2 to 3 feet apart. Keep constantly moist for best bloom. In tubs, allow no more than 1 or 2 inches of soil space between the sides of the bulbs and their container. With southern exposure and heavy mulching to protect them from frost, *C. bulbispermum* and *C.* x *powellii* sometimes thrive in Zones 7-8. *C. moorei* and *C.* 'Ellen Bosanquet' make excellent tub specimens. Propagate species from seeds, which sometimes begin forming roots while still on plants. Remove seeds as soon as they ripen and sow immediately to reach flowering-size bulbs in 3 years; hybrids may revert to their parent forms. Both species and hybrids can be propagated by removing and replanting the small offsets growing alongside mature bulbs in spring.

Crocus
(KRO-kus)
CROCUS

Crocus chrysanthus 'Cream Beauty'

Hardiness:	*Zones 3-8*
Type of bulb:	*corm*
Flowering season:	*winter, spring, fall*
Height:	*2 to 8 inches*
Soil:	*well-drained*
Light:	*full sun*

Delicate bowls of color in an otherwise drab landscape, crocus flowers hug the ground on short stems from late winter through midspring. There are also fall-blooming species, not to be confused with the flowers commonly known as autumn crocus, which are actually *Colchicum*. Narrow, grassy crocus leaves are sometimes attractively banded down their centers in gray-green or white and may appear before, at the same time as, or after several flowers rise from each small corm. They last several weeks before dying back. Some are fragrant. Each flower has six wide petals that open into a deep, oval cup shape, then relax into a round, open bowl. Crocuses are available in a broad range of hues, and are often striped, streaked, or tinged with more than one color. Prominent yellow or orange stigmas decorate the center of each blossom. Those of *C. sativus* are the source of saffron for many culinary uses; it takes more than 4,000 flowers to produce an ounce of the precious herb. Mass crocuses for best effect in beds, borders, and rock gardens. They naturalize easily and are often planted as edgings and allowed to ramble in lawns. Force them for indoor winter display.

Selected species and varieties: *C. ancyrensis* 'Golden Bunch'—winter-to-spring-blooming flowers that are yellow outside, orange fading to yellow inside, on 2-inch stems above 12-inch leaves; Zones 6-8. *C. angustifolius* 'Minor' (cloth-of-gold crocus)—deep yellow flower cups flushed with mahogany outside on stems 2 inches or less in winter to spring; Zones 5-8. *C. biflorus* (Scotch crocus)—white or lilac flowers veined or tinged purple with yellow throats on 4-inch stems in winter to spring; ssp. *alexandri* is white feathered with purple; ssp. *weldenii* 'Fairy', white with purple blotches; Zones 5-8. *C. chrysanthus* (snow crocus)—late winter flowers

Crocus ancyrensis

bloom on 4-inch stems before the 12-inch leaves appear; 'Advance' produces peachy yellow flowers touched with violet; 'Ard Schenk', long-lasting white blooms; 'Blue Bird', blooms that are blue violet outside, creamy inside; 'Blue Pearl', petals that are lavender outside touched with bronze at their base, white inside blending to a yellow throat; 'Cream Beauty', long-lasting creamy yellow blooms; 'Dorothy', long-lasting yellow flowers feathered with bronze; 'Gipsy Girl', profuse, long-lasting yellow flowers streaked reddish brown; 'Ladykiller', petals violet-purple outside, creamy white inside; 'Miss Vain', pure white blossoms with lemon yellow throats; 'Prins Claus' is a dwarf cultivar with long-lasting white flowers blotched in blue; 'Snow Bunting' has white flowers with lilac streaking and yellow throats; 'Zwanenburg Bronze', reddish brown petals striped with yellow; Zones 4-8. *C. etruscus* 'Zwanenburg'—lilac flowers veined with deep purple appearing the same time as the white-striped leaves in winter to spring; Zones 3-8. *C. flavus*—yellow to orange flowers appearing on 7-inch stems at the same time as the grassy foliage in winter to spring; 'Golden Yellow' [formerly *C. vernus* 'Yel-

Crocus chrysanthus 'Zwanenburg Bronze'

low Giant'] has rich yellow blossoms; Zones 4-8. *C. kotschyanus* [formerly *C. zonatus*]—rose-lilac flowers splashed with orange in fall; Zones 5-8. *C. medius*—lilac to purple flowers with deep purple veining on stems to 10 inches in fall; Zones 6-7. *C. minimus*—pale violet to white flowers with prominent red-orange stigmas on 2- to 3-inch stems in spring; Zones 5-8. *C. ochroleucus*—white to pale cream petals tinged with orange on 3- to 6-inch stems in fall; Zones 5-8. *C. pulchellus*—bright lilac blossoms with yellow interiors appearing the same time as the leaves in fall; 'Zephyr' is pure white; Zones 6-8. *C. sativus* (saffron crocus)—lilac or white fall flowers on 2-inch stems with prominent stamens that are dried and used for flavoring and coloring in cooking; Zones 6-8. *C. serotinus* ssp. *clusii*—fragrant, purple-veined pale lilac flowers with creamy throats on 3- to 4-inch stems appearing at the same time as sparse foliage in fall; ssp. *salzmannii* is similar but with sparser leaves and no fragrance; Zones 6-8. *C. sieberi* (Sieber crocus)—fragrant late-winter-to-spring flowers; ssp. *atticus* has white flowers streaked with purple on 2- to 3-inch stems; ssp. *sublimis* 'Tricolor', lilac blue flowers with white banding at the edge of a yellow

throat; 'Firefly', white flowers touched with violet; 'Hubert Edelsten', deep purple to soft lilac flowers on 4-inch stems; 'Violet Queen', deep violet blooms on 3-inch stems; Zones 7-8. *C. speciosus*—light blue fall flowers with darker blue veining and prominent orange stigmas on 3- to 6-inch stems; 'Artabir' grows fragrant light blue flowers with conspicuous veining; 'Cassiope', lavender-blue blooms with creamy yellow throats; 'Conqueror', clear blue flowers; var. *aitchisonii*, pale lilac flowers veined with deeper lilac, the largest of all crocus blossoms; Zones 5-8. *C. tomasinianus*—lilac to purple flowers appearing at the same time as leaves in late winter to spring, reputed to be rodent resistant; 'Barr's Purple' yields large royal purple flowers; 'Ruby Giant', large violet blooms; 'Whitewell Purple' is reddish purple; Zones 5-9. *C. vernus* (Dutch crocus, common crocus)—large flowers on stems to 8 inches tall appearing at the

Crocus tomasinianus

same time as leaves in late winter to spring; 'Flower Record' is deep purple; 'Jeanne d'Arc', white; 'Paulus Potter', shiny reddish purple; 'Pickwick', white striped with lilac and splashed with purple at its base; 'Remembrance', bluish purple; 'Striped Beauty', lilac striped with white. *C. versicolor* 'Picturatus'—white flowers striped in purple with yellow throats on 5½-inch stems in late winter to spring; Zones 5-8.

Growing conditions and maintenance: Plant corms 3 to 4 inches deep and 4 to 5 inches apart in groups. They are not fussy about soil, but good drainage is essential. Space more closely in pots for forcing, allowing six to eight corms per 6-inch pot

or shallow bulb pan, and setting the corms 1 inch deep. Hold potted corms at 40°F until roots form, then bring indoors at 65°F for flowering. Crocuses can also be forced in colorful bulb vases designed especially for the purpose with a pinched

Crocus vernus 'Jeanne d'Arc'

waist to suspend the corm just above the water line; when roots fill the vase, bring the corm into sunlight in a warm room for blooming. After forcing, allow foliage to die back, then plant corms out in the garden for reflowering the following spring. Cultivars of Dutch crocus are especially recommended for forcing. *C. ancyrensis* 'Golden Bunch', *C. speciosus* cultivars, and *C. vernus* 'Pickwick' are among the easiest crocuses to naturalize. To plant crocuses in lawns, cut and lift small patches of grass, place the corms, then replace the sod. Plant spring-flowering varieties from September to November, fall-flowering ones no later than August. Where crocuses have established themselves in lawns, avoid mowing in spring until the foliage of spring-flowering crocuses dies back; in fall, postpone mowing once the buds of fall-blooming species have broken through the ground until their flowers fade and foliage withers. Crocuses are easily grown from seed and self-sow freely, a characteristic that somewhat offsets the attractiveness of the corms to mice, chipmunks, and squirrels. Otherwise, propagate by lifting and dividing crowded clumps after foliage dies back, removing and replanting the smaller cormels that develop alongside mature corms. Buy *C. kotschyanus* only from reputable dealers who propagate their own bulbs, as collection in the wild has endangered this species.

Cyclamen
(SIK-la-men)
PERSIAN VIOLET

Cyclamen persicum

Hardiness: *Zones 6-9*

Type of bulb: *tuber*

Flowering season: *fall, winter, spring*

Height: *3 to 12 inches*

Soil: *moist, well-drained, fertile*

Light: *light shade*

Cyclamen's unusual, sometimes fragrant, flowers have petals swept back from a prominent center or eye. The petals are sometimes twisted, double, ruffled, shredded, or ridged, giving the delicate, inch-long blossoms the appearance of exotic birds or butterflies. Each flower rises on a slender stem from a clump of long-lasting heart- or kidney-shaped leaves that are sometimes marbled green and gray above or reddish underneath. Multiple flower stalks appear over a long season of bloom. While the florist's cyclamen, popular as a houseplant, is a tender pot plant, other cyclamens are hardy species that will spread in wildflower gardens, rock gardens, and shady borders, naturalizing into low ground covers beneath both deciduous and evergreen plantings.

Selected species and varieties: *C. africanum*—rose to carmine fall flowers above large, fleshy 6-inch leaves with wavy edges; Zones 8-9. *C. cilicium* (Sicily cyclamen)—twisted pink or light rose blossoms with a dark rose eye on 3-inch stems in fall above leaves with silver centers; Zones 7-8. *C. coum*—white to carmine flowers with purple blotches blooming from winter to spring on 3- to 6-inch stems above green or marbled leaves with reddish undersides; 'Album' is white; 'Roseum', pale pink. *C. graecum*—fall-blooming rose flowers with a deep carmine eye, sometimes scented; Zones 7-9. *C. hederifolium* [also called *C. neopolitanum*] (baby cyclamen, ivy-leaved cyclamen)—pink or white, sometimes fragrant, flowers with a crimson eye on 3- to 6-inch stems blooming from summer to fall above marbled leaves; 'Album' is white; Zones 6-9. *C. persicum* (florist's cyclamen, common cyclamen)—rose, pink, or white, sometimes fragrant flowers, with dark eyes on 6- to 12-inch stems above marbled leaves with toothed edges in winter; Zone 9.

Cyclamen repandum

Growing conditions and maintenance: Plant cyclamen's flat, cormlike tubers in summer or fall, setting them ½-inch deep and 4 to 6 inches apart in soil that has a neutral to alkaline pH. Provide an annual top dressing of leaf mold. Pot florist's cyclamen's large tuber-corms individually in pots and maintain plants at temperatures of 60° to 65°F throughout the blooming period. Cyclamens do not produce offsets, but plants self-sow seed freely. Propagate from seed to reach blooming size in 3 years or by transplanting the self-sown seedlings in summer or fall.

Dahlia
(DAH-lee-a)
DAHLIA

Dahlia 'Tamjoh'

Hardiness: *tender or Zones 9-11*

Type of bulb: *tuber*

Flowering season: *summer to fall*

Height: *12 inches to 8 feet*

Soil: *moist, well-drained, fertile*

Light: *full sun*

Dahlias reliably brighten the flower border over a long season of bloom with highly diverse blossoms varying from flat-faced, single-petaled types to round, dense mounds of petals. Dahlia sizes are as variable as petal forms, with some flowers only a few inches across and others the diameter of a dinner plate. Related to daisies, dahlias have a central disk of tightly packed disk flowers surrounded by one or more rows of petal-like ray flowers that are sometimes doubled, curved inward, twisted, cupped, or rolled into tiny tubes. Colors range widely, and some dahlias are bicolored or variegated, with petals tipped, streaked, or backed with contrasting color. The more than 20,000 cultivars available to modern gardeners descend from a few wild species cultivated by Aztec botanists. For the garden trade, dahlias are classified by the shape and arrangement of their ray flowers and coded according to flower size. Dwarf dahlias are cultivated in sunny beds or borders as low-growing bushy edgings, standard dahlias as medium to tall fillers or as exhibition-size specimens. The largest dahlias are diffilcult to use in the home garden simply because of their size—those with the largest blooms can have stems the thickness of broom sticks. Thus, the plants with smaller flowers are easier to work into a bed or border design. Regardless of their size, all dahlias make long-lasting cut flowers.

Selected species and varieties: *Single dahlias*—one or two rows of flat petals surrounding a flat, central disk; 'Bambino White' is a dwarf cultivar with 1-inch flowers on 14-inch bushes. *Anemone-flowered dahlias*—a central disk obscured by a fluffy ball of short, tubular petals and rimmed by one or more rows of longer, flat petals; 'Siemen Doorenbosch' has flat lavender petals surrounding a creamy central pincushion on 20-inch plants. *Collarette dahlias*—central disks surrounded by a collar of short, often ruffled or cupped petals, backed by a second collar of broader, flat petals; 'Jack O'Lantern' has an inner collar streaked

Dahlia 'Hullins Carnival'

yellow and orange and deep orange outer petals on 4-foot plants; 'Mickey' has a yellow inner collar backed by deep red outer ray flowers on 3-foot bushes. *Peony-flowered dahlias*—two or three overlapping layers of ray petals, often twisted or curled, surrounding a central disk; 'Japanese Bishop' grows dark orange flowers on 3-foot plants; 'Jescott Julie' has petals that are orange above, burgundy below, on 3-foot stems. *Formal decorative dahlias*—double rows of flat, evenly spaced petals covering the central disk; 'Duet' has crimson petals tipped with white on 3-foot plants; 'Orange Julius', orange petals edged in yellow on 4-foot stems. *Informal decorative dahlias*—double rows of randomly

spaced flat petals hiding the central disk; 'Gay Princess' is pink with creamy centers on 4-foot plants. *Ball dahlias*—cupped, doubled petals crowding spirally into round domes or slightly flattened globes; 'Nijinsky' has purple flowers on 4-foot stems; 'Rothsay Superb', red blooms on 3-foot plants. *Pompom dahlias*—small round balls of tightly rolled petals less than 2 inches in diameter; 'Amber Queen' is golden amber to bronze on 4-foot stems; 'Chick-a-dee', wine red touched with pink on 3-foot plants. *Cactus dahlias*—straight or twisted petals rolled like quills or straws over half their length to a pointed tip; 'Border Princess' is apricot-bronze to yellow on 2-foot stems; 'Brookside Cheri', salmon pink on 4-foot plants; 'Juanita', ruby red on 4-foot stems. *Semicactus dahlias*—flat petals curling over less than half their length into tubes at their tips; 'Amanda Jarvis' produces rose flowers on 3-foot stems; 'Bella Bimba', apricot pink blooms on 4-foot plants. *Star dahlias*—two or three rows of short petals curving inward. *Chrysanthemum-type dahlias*—double rows of petals curving inward and hiding the central disk. *Waterlily-flowered dahlias*—short petals tightly clasped over the central disk like a water lily bud, surrounded by several rows of broad, flat petals; 'Lauren Michelle' has petals that are rosy lavender above, purple below on 4½-foot stems; 'Gerry Hoek', shell pink flowers on 4-foot plants.

Within each of these classifications, dahlias are also coded by size: Giant or AA dahlias have flowers more than 10 inches wide; large or A, 8- to 10-inch flowers; medium or B, 6- to 8-inch flowers; small or BB, 4- to 6-inch blooms; miniature or M, flowers up to 4 inches across; pompom or P, blossoms under 2 inches.

Growing conditions and maintenance: Plant dahlia tubers in spring, placing those of taller cultivars in a hole 6 to 8 inches deep and covering them with 2 to 3 inches of soil. Space the holes 3 to 4 feet apart. As shoots develop and extend above ground level, remove all but one or two and add soil to fill the hole. Plant tubers of shorter cultivars 2 to 3 inches deep and 1 to 2 feet apart. In transplanting potted seedlings, position them 2

inches deeper than the depth of their pot. Stake all but dwarfs, pompoms, and miniatures. Dahlias bloom 2½ to 4 months after planting. To keep plants blooming continuously, give them at least an inch of water weekly while blooming, and mulch with 2 to 3 inches of manure, compost, or ground peat moss to retain moisture and provide nutrients. To produce bushy plants, pinch out terminal leaf buds when leaves first appear and again when the first lateral branches emerge. To develop large, exhibition-size blossoms, prune all lateral side shoots and remove all but the center bud when flower buds appear. Remove faded flowers before they go to seed to prolong blooming period. For long-lasting cut flowers, pick dahlias while it is cool and stand cut stems in hot water, 100° to 160°F, in a cool, shaded location for several hours before arranging. Propagate dahlias from seed started indoors in very early spring to flower that season, from stem cuttings, or by dividing tubers in spring.

Eranthis
(e-RAN-this)
WINTER ACONITE

Eranthis hyemalis

Hardiness: *Zones 4-7*

Type of bulb: *tuber*

Flowering season: *late winter to spring*

Height: *2 to 4 inches*

Soil: *moist, well-drained, fertile*

Light: *full sun to light shade*

Often blooming before the snow has melted, winter aconites produce cheery buttercup-like flowers composed of waxy, curved petals cradling a loose pompom of frilly stamens. Each almost stemless blossom opens above a tiny ruff of oval, pointed leaves. The blossoms close tightly to protect themselves during cold nights, then reopen the next day with the sun's warmth. Winter aconites readily naturalize into golden ground covers in woodland or rock gardens.

Selected species and varieties: *E. cilicica* (Cilician winter aconite)—1½-inch-deep yellow flowers on 2½-inch stems with bronzy foliage. *E. hyemalis*—inch-wide yellow flowers on 2- to 4-inch stems.

Growing conditions and maintenance: Plant winter aconite tubers in late summer or very early fall to allow roots time to establish themselves for late-winter blooming. Soak the brittle roots overnight, then set tubers 2 to 3 inches deep and 3 inches apart where they will receive sufficient moisture. Winter aconites self-sow readily. Propagate from seed or by dividing the tiny tubers in late summer.

Erythronium
(eh-rith-RONE-ee-um)
DOGTOOTH VIOLET

Erythronium 'Kondo'

Hardiness: *Zones 3-8*

Type of bulb: *corm*

Flowering season: *spring*

Height: *6 inches to 2 feet*

Soil: *moist, well-drained, fertile*

Light: *partial to full shade*

Native woodland wildflowers, dogtooth violets produce delicate, nodding lilylike blooms with petals curved back to reveal prominent stamens and anthers either singly or in small clusters. The flowers rise from pairs of oval, pointed leaves that are often marbled or mottled in gray, brown, or bronze. Mass dogtooth violets in woodland gardens or as a spring ground cover beneath deciduous shrubs, where they will naturalize into colonies.

Selected species and varieties: *E. citrinum*—clusters of 1½-inch white or cream flowers with pale lemon throats on 10- to 12-inch stems; Zones 6-8. *E. dens-canis* (dogtooth fawn lily, European dogtooth violet)—single white to pink or purple flowers 2 inches across with blue or purple anthers on 6- to 12-inch stems above leaves marbled brown and bluish green; 'Charmer' produces pure white flowers touched with brown at their base above leaves mottled with brown; 'Frans Hals', royal purple blooms with a green throat; 'Lilac Wonder' is soft lilac with a brownish base; 'Pink Perfection', bright pink; 'Purple King', reddish purple with a white throat above brown-

spotted leaves; 'Rose Queen', rosy pink; 'Snowflake', pure white; var. *japonicum* is a miniature only 4 to 6 inches tall with violet flowers tinged purple at the base; var. *niveus* is pale pink; Zones 3-8. *E. grandiflorum* (glacier lily, avalanche lily)—golden yellow flowers with red anthers in clusters on 1- to 2-foot stems. *E. revolutum* (mahogany fawn lily, coast fawn lily)—1½-inch white to pale lavender flowers aging to purple on 16-inch stems; 'White Beauty' is a dwarf producing 2- to 3-inch white flowers with yellow throats on 7-inch stems above leaves veined in white; Zones 3-8. *E. tuolumnense* (Tuolumne fawn lily)—1¼-inch

Erythronium grandiflorum

yellow flowers touched with green at the base on 12-inch stems above bright green 12-inch leaves; Zones 3-8. *E.* hybrids—'Citronella' yields lemon yellow flowers on 10-inch stems; 'Jeannine', sulfur yellow blooms; 'Kondo', greenish yellow blossoms touched with brown at the base; 'Pagoda', pale yellow flowers with a deeper yellow throat on 10-inch stems.

Growing conditions and maintenance: Plant dogtooth violets in summer or fall, placing the corms 2 to 3 inches deep and 4 to 6 inches apart. Dogtooth violets often take a year to become established before blooming. Provide adequate moisture in summer after flowers and foliage fade. Propagate from seed to bloom in 3 to 4 years or by removing and immediately replanting the small cormels that develop at the base of mature corms in late summer or fall.

Fritillaria
(fri-ti-LAH-ree-a)
FRITILLARY

Fritillaria imperialis

Hardiness:	*Zones 3-8*
Type of bulb:	*true bulb*
Flowering season:	*spring*
Height:	*6 inches to 2½ feet*
Soil:	*moist, well-drained, sandy*
Light:	*full sun to light shade*

From the imposing, musky-scented crown imperial bearing a garland of blossoms aloft on stout stalks to small, dainty woodland species with single blooms on wiry stems, fritillaries produce nodding flower bells in unusual colors and patterns in a variety of forms to accent spring gardens. The flowers have prominent, colorful stamens and are often striped, speckled, or checkered in a wide range of hues. Touching the petals sometimes produces a small "tear" from reservoirs of nectar at the base of each petal. The often glossy leaves are highly variable, sometimes appearing in whorls extending halfway up the flower stalk, sometimes alternating from one side of the stem to the other throughout its length, occasionally growing in a tuft at the stem's base. Mass fritillaries in wildflower gardens, rock gardens, or perennial borders where other plants will fill in when their foliage dies down in early summer.

Selected species and varieties: *F. acmopetala*—purple-striped olive green flower bells tinged lighter green inside on 18-inch stalks; Zones 3-8. *F. assyriaca*—lime green-and-violet blossoms on 12- to 20-inch stems; Zones 3-8. *F. biflora* 'Martha Roderick' (mission bells, black fritillary)—four to six brownish orange flower bells with white spots in their centers on 15-inch stems; Zones 3-8. *F. camschatcensis* (Kamchatka lily, black sarana)—one to six 1-inch purple-brown-and-black flower bells on wiry 2-

Fritillaria meleagris

foot stems; Zones 3-8. *F. davisii*—plum purple blossoms on dainty plants 6 to 10 inches tall; Zones 3-8. *F. imperialis* (crown imperial)—bold 30-inch stalks, the lower half lined with whorls of glossy, pointed leaves, the tip crowned by a tuft of shorter leaves with a ring of large, 2-inch flower bells with dangling yellow stamens below it; 'Maxima Lutea' is lemon yellow; 'Rubra Maxima', dark red; Zones 4-7. *F. meleagris* (snake's-head fritillary, checkered lily, guinea hen tulip, leper lily)—1½-inch flower bells checkered dark maroon and white on 8- to 10-inch stems; 'Alba' is pure white; Zones 3-8. *F. michailovskyi*—up to five deep purplish red-and-yellow flower bells with their tips flipped daintily outward on 4- to 8-inch stems; Zones 5-8. *F. pallidiflora*—up to a dozen pale yellow and green 1- to 1½-inch flower bells flecked with brown and red, borne in the upper leaf joints along arching 18-inch stems; Zones 3-8. *F. persica*—up to 30 velvety purple blossoms lining 30-inch stems; 'Adiyaman' yields inch-wide plum flowers; Zones 4-8. *F. pudica* (yellow fritillary, yellow bell)—¾-inch yellow-orange flowers tinged purple in clusters of three on 9-inch stems; Zones 4-8. *F. purdyi* 'Tinkerbell'—six or seven dainty white flower bells striped rusty brown on the outside and spotted red inside on 6-inch stems above a low rosette of 6-inch leaves; Zones 5-8. *F. uva-vulpis*—solitary purplish gray flower bells edged in yellow on 12- to 18-inch stems; Zones 3-8. *F. verticillata*—1¼-inch cup-shaped pale yellow blossoms flecked with green outside and spotted purple inside lining 2-foot stems, the tips of the upper leaves elongating into tendrils; Zones 6-8.

Growing conditions and maintenance: Plant fritillaries in late summer or fall, setting large bulbs 4 inches deep and 12 inches apart, smaller bulbs 2 inches deep and 8 inches apart. Bulbs may take a year to become established in new locations before they flower. Most fritillaries like full sun and very well drained soil, but *F. camschatcensis*, *F. meleagris*, and *F. pallidiflora* prefer light shade and moist soil. For all fritillaries, avoid sites with cold, wet soils, and reduce watering once

Fritillaria pudica

foliage dies back. Both *F. imperialis* 'Rubra Maxima' and *F. persica* are endangered in the wild; buy bulbs from reputable growers selling stock propagated by themselves or other growers rather than purchased from collectors. The skunklike odor of crown imperial is said to repel mice, chipmunks, and other rodents. Propagate fritillaries by removing and replanting bulb offsets in late summer or early fall to reach flowering size in 3 to 4 years; or by removing and planting bulb scales to produce bulblets.

Galanthus
(ga-LANTH-us)
SNOWDROP

Galanthus nivalis

Gladiolus
(glad-ee-O-lus)
CORN FLAG

Gladiolus communis ssp. byzantinus

Hardiness: *Zones 3-8*

Type of bulb: *true bulb*

Flowering season: *winter to spring*

Height: *6 to 12 inches*

Soil: *moist, well-drained, sandy*

Light: *full sun to light shade*

Snowdrops produce small white flowers that often bloom before the last snow melts. Each winged blossom is composed of three longer petals almost concealing three shorter, inner petals tipped with green. A single flower dangles from a slender stem above two to three grassy leaves. Snowdrops rapidly naturalize under deciduous shrubs or on lawns, in rock gardens, and in woodland borders. They can also be potted as houseplants.

Selected species and varieties: *G. elwesii* (giant snowdrop)—1½-inch blossoms on flower stalks to 12 inches above blue-green leaves. *G. nivalis* (common snowdrop)—1-inch blooms on 4- to 6-inch stems; 'Flore Pleno' produces double flowers; 'Sam Arnott', large, fragrant blossoms; 'Viridi-apice' has both its outer and inner petals tipped with green.

Growing conditions and maintenance: Plant bulbs 3 inches deep and 3 inches apart in late summer or fall. For indoor bloom, pot bulbs in fall, placing four to six bulbs an inch deep in each 4-inch pot. Snowdrops self-sow readily and can be propagated from seed or by lifting and dividing the clumps of bulbs that form.

Hardiness: *tender or Zones 4-11*

Type of bulb: *corm*

Flowering season: *spring to fall*

Height: *1 to 7 feet*

Soil: *well-drained, fertile*

Light: *full sun*

Gladiolus produce showy spikes of 1½- to 5½-inch flowers above fans of stiff, sword-shaped leaves. The closely spaced flowers open from bottom to top on alternate sides of the stiff flower stems. Abundant, sometimes fragrant, flowers open one at a time to provide several weeks of bloom. Use tall gladiolus in groups at the back of a border, shorter species in rock gardens or mixed in borders with spring bulbs. Gladiolus make long-lasting cut flowers; shorter species can be forced for indoor bloom.

Selected species and varieties: *G. callianthus* [formerly classified as *Acidanthera bicolor*] 'Murielae'—fragrant 2- to 3-inch white flowers with purple throats on 2-foot stems in summer; Zones 7-11. *G. carneus* (painted lady)—white, cream, mauve, or pink blossoms flecked purple on 2-foot stems, blooming spring to summer; Zones 9-11. *G.* x *colvillei* (Coronado hybrid)—2-inch scarlet flowers blotched yellow on branching 2-foot stems in spring; Zones 7-11. *G. communis* ssp. *byzantinus* (Byzantine gladiolus)—white-streaked burgundy flowers on 2-foot stems in spring to summer;

Zones 5-11. *G.* hybrids—ruffled, waved, crimped, or frilled flowers in shades of white, yellow, red, purple, blue, or green, sometimes bicolored or multicolored, on stems to 7 feet in summer through fall; 'Nova Lux' is pure velvety yellow; 'Red Bird', flaming red; 'Priscilla', white-feathered pink with a yellow throat; 'Royal Blush' has deep rose red petals edged in white; 'White Knight' is pure white; tender. *G. nanus* [also classified as *Babiana nana*]—spring-to-summer-blooming dwarf plants 1 to 2 feet tall; 'Amanda Mahy' is salmon with violet splotches; 'Desire', cream; 'Guernsey Glory' has pink to purple petals with red edges and cream blotches; 'Impressive' is pinkish white splotched deep rose; 'Prins Claus', ivory with purple spotting; Zones 4-11.

Growing conditions and maintenance: Work well-rotted manure or other organic matter deeply into the soil a year before planting. North of Zone 8, plant hardy gladiolus in fall, tender ones in spring. Set large corms 4 to 6 inches deep and 6 to 9 inches apart, smaller ones 3 to 4 inches deep and 4 to 6 inches apart. Provide ample water while growing and blooming. North of Zone 8, tender gladiolus should be dug in fall for replanting in spring. Early-blooming hybrids flower 90 days after planting, midseason varieties in 110 days, and late midseason ones in 120 days. To avoid fungus problems, do not plant gladiolus in the same location from year to year. Pick for cut flowers as the first bloom begins to open, leaving four to five leaves to feed the corm. Propagate by removing the cormels that develop around mature corms.

Haemanthus
(heem-ANTH-us)
BLOOD LILY

Haemanthus katherinae

Hardiness: *tender or Zones 9-11*

Type of bulb: *true bulb*

Flowering season: *summer*

Height: *12 to 18 inches*

Soil: *moist, well-drained*

Light: *full sun to light shade*

Blood lilies produce frothy clusters of tubular flowers with colorful protruding stamens cradled within broad, petal-like bracts or in spherical clusters atop stout, leafless stems. While sometimes grown outdoors in warm zones, they bloom best as root-bound container specimens.

Selected species and varieties: *H. albiflos* (white paintbrush)—2-inch flower clusters with yellow-orange stamens within greenish white bracts on 12- to 18-inch stems. *H. coccineus* (Cape tulip)—3-inch clusters of 1-inch flowers with golden stamens within red bracts on 12-inch stems. *H. katherinae* [also known as *Scadoxus multiflorus* ssp. *katherinae*] (Catherine-wheel)—over 200 small 2½-inch pink-red flowers in 9-inch globes on 18-inch stems. *H. multiflorus* (salmon blood lily)—up to 200 inch-long coral red flowers with spiky stamens in 3- to 6-inch spheres on 18-inch stems.

Growing conditions and maintenance: Plant 6 to 8 inches apart outdoors or in pots, with the tip of the bulb at the soil surface. Start potted lilies in spring, then dry off and store over winter. Propagate from seed or from bulb offsets.

Hippeastrum
(hip-ee-AS-trum)
AMARYLLIS

Hippeastrum 'Bold Leader'

Hardiness: *tender or Zones 9-11*

Type of bulb: *true bulb*

Flowering season: *spring*

Height: *1 to 2 feet*

Soil: *moist, well-drained, sandy*

Light: *full sun*

Spectacular amaryllis, with its flowers that can be as large as 8 inches across, is sometimes grown in sunny borders in warmer zones but is most renowned as a pot plant for indoor forcing.

Selected species and varieties: *H.* hybrids—'Apple Blossom' is cherry pink flushed white; 'Bold Leader', signal red; 'Double Record' has double white flowers veined and tipped red; 'Lady Jane', deep salmon orange double flowers; 'Orange Sovereign', bright orange blooms; 'Picotee', white petals rimmed red; 'Red Lion', velvety red flowers; 'Scarlet Baby' is a red miniature with two to three flower stems; 'White Christmas' is white.

Growing conditions and maintenance: Outdoors in Zones 10-11, plant in fall or spring, setting bulbs 6 inches deep and 1 foot apart. Indoors, plant the bulb with its top third out of the soil in a pot 2 inches wider than the bulb. Pot from late fall through winter; blooms in 5 to 8 weeks. Keep bulb barely moist until growth starts. After flowering, remove stem and fertilize until foliage dies. Dry bulb off for repotting. Propagate by separating offsets after foliage dies or from seed.

Hyacinthus
(by-a-SIN-thus)
HYACINTH

Hyacinthus 'Blue Jacket'

Hardiness: *Zones 3-7*

Type of bulb: *true bulb*

Flowering season: *spring*

Height: *4 to 12 inches*

Soil: *well-drained, fertile*

Light: *full sun*

With their heady fragrance, hyacinths are a classic bulb in the spring border. When first planted, most produce a single stiff, cylindrical cluster of inch-wide flower stars crowded on all sides of formally erect stems. Petal tips curve backward gracefully, giving the dense clusters a frilly appearance, an effect that is heightened when flowers are shaded in two tones of the same color. In subsequent years, flower stems grow longer and clusters become looser and more informal. The blooms last up to 2 weeks in the garden above straplike leaves at the base of the flower stalks. There are doubled cultivars with whorls of petals in graduated sizes engulfing each tiny blossom, and multiflora cultivars that produce several flower stems with widely spaced blossoms from each bulb. Mingle hyacinths with other spring bulbs in beds and borders, or force them indoors in pots or special glass hyacinth vases. They last almost a week as cut flowers.

Selected species and varieties: *H. orientalis* (Dutch hyacinth, common hyacinth, garden hyacinth)—clusters of star-shaped blossoms in an array of colors above foot-long leaves; 'Anne Marie' is pastel pink aging to salmon; 'Blue Giant' has large pastel blue clusters; 'Blue Jacket' is deep purple with paler petal edges; 'Blue Magic', purple-blue with a white throat; 'Carnegie', elegant pure white; 'City of Harlem', pastel lemon yellow; 'Delft Blue', porcelain blue with paler edges; 'French Roman Blue' is a multiflora cultivar with blue blooms; 'Gipsy Queen', yellow-tinged clear orange; 'Hollyhock' has flowers with double red petals on 4-inch stalks; 'Jan Bos' is clear candy-apple red in slender spikes; 'Lady Derby', rosy pink; 'Lord Balfour' has loose clusters of rose-purple blossoms; 'Oranje Boven' is salmon; 'Pe-

Hyacinthus 'Anne Marie'

ter Stuyvesant', deep purple-blue; 'Pink Pearl', deep luminescent pink; 'Snow White' is a white multiflora variety; 'Violet Pearl' is lilac-rose aging to silver.

Growing conditions and maintenance: Outdoors, plant bulbs in fall, setting them 4 to 6 inches deep and 6 to 8 inches apart. Indoors, allow 4 or 5 bulbs per 6-inch pot. Plant indoor bulbs in fall as well; specially prechilled bulbs will bloom earlier than ordinary bulbs. Keep potted bulbs damp in a dark location below 50° F for about 12 weeks or until roots fill the pot and bulbs show 2 inches of leaf growth. Then move the pots into filtered sunlight at a temperature no higher than 65° F. If using special hyacinth vases, suspend bulb above (but not touching) the water and treat the same as potted bulbs. 'Anne Marie' and 'Blue Jacket' are particularly good cultivars for forcing. Hyacinths are hard to propagate but sometimes form offsets alongside mature bulbs that can take up to 6 years to reach blooming size.

Ipheion
(IF-ee-on)
IPHEION

Ipheion uniflorum

Hardiness: *Zones 5-10*

Type of bulb: *true bulb*

Flowering season: *spring*

Height: *4 to 6 inches*

Soil: *acid well-drained loam*

Light: *full sun to light shade*

An ipheion bulb sends up several flowering stalks, each flower rising on a single stem from clumps of grassy leaves, for a long period of bloom. The flowers have tiny pointed petals surrounding a cluster of bright orange stamens. They are faintly mint scented, whereas the leaves give off an onion odor when bruised. The leaves appear in fall, and persist all winter and through the blooming period until the bulbs go dormant in summer. Plant ipheion in woodland or rock gardens, in meadows, or among paving stones, where it will rapidly naturalize. It can also be forced indoors for midwinter bloom.

Selected species and varieties: *I. uniflorum* [formerly *Brodiaea uniflora* and *Tritilea uniflora*] (spring starflower)— 1-inch white flowers tinged blue; 'Wisley Blue' is light blue with a white center; 'Rolf Fiedler', deep electric blue.

Growing conditions and maintenance: Plant ipheion in late summer or fall, setting bulbs 3 inches deep and 3 to 6 inches apart. Provide winter mulch in Zones 5-6. Pot bulbs 1 inch deep for forcing. Propagate spring starflowers by dividing clumps of bulb offsets.

Iris
(EYE-ris)
FLAG, FLEUR-DE-LIS

Iris reticulata 'Harmony'

Hardiness: *Zones 5-9*

Type of bulb: *rhizome; true bulb*

Flowering season: *spring or summer*

Height: *4 to 24 inches*

Soil: *well-drained, sandy*

Light: *full sun*

Most irises, including the dramatic, tall bearded types, grow from rhizomes—although a few species, including the delicate *I. reticulata,* are bulbous. Dwarf irises, which are sometimes scented, bloom on short stems before their grassy leaves have fully emerged. The leaves continue to grow to their full length after flowers fade. Bokara and Dutch iris emerge simultaneously with their leaves and produce their flowers on tall, erect stems. All irises have complex flowers composed of three drooping outer petals known as falls and three erect inner petals called standards. The falls are marked with contrasting color at their bases and are sometimes crested with a raised ridge or punctuated by a pair of small protrusions called horns. The shorter standards, appearing in a complementary or contrasting color, may be curved, frilled, or wavy. Flowers last 1 to 3 weeks in the garden. Dwarf irises are ideal in rock gardens and at the edge of borders. Dutch irises, some of which are fragrant, naturalize easily, rapidly forming large clumps in sunny beds. Both Bokara and Dutch irises make excellent cut flowers lasting up to 2 weeks. Irises can also be forced for indoor bloom.

Selected species and varieties: Rhizomatous bearded iris hybrids are classified according to plant height as dwarf, intermediate, and tall, and are then further subdivided by flower size and season.

Dwarf bearded iris hybrids derive many of their characteristics from the parent species, *I. pumila* and *I. chamaeiris*. Miniature dwarf bearded iris—less than 10 inches tall with 1½- to 2½-inch flowers in midspring; 'Already' has wine red flowers; 'Angel Eyes', white flowers with blue spots on falls; 'Sky Baby', ruffled blue blooms. Standard dwarf bearded iris—10 to 15 inches tall with 1½- to 2½-inch blossoms that appear a week later than those of miniatures; 'Baby Snowflake' has white flowers; 'Bingo', velvety purple flowers; 'Early Sunshine', yellow

Iris cristata

flowers; 'Red Dandy', wine red flowers.

Intermediate and border bearded iris—2- to 4-inch flowers on plants 15 to 28 inches tall, with intermediates blooming in midspring, borders in late spring to early summer; 'Little 'Angel' has white flowers; 'Lemonade', white falls on yellow blossoms.

Tall bearded iris—plants that grow upwards of 28 inches tall with flowers to 8 inches across in late spring to summer; 'Cindy' has red-bearded white flowers; 'Charade', ruffled medium blue flowers; 'May Magic', light pink blossoms.

Reblooming bearded iris—many heights and flowers sizes, blossoming in spring and again any time from midsummer to fall; 'Autumn Bugler' has violet flowers with dark purple falls.

I. cristata (crested iris)—blue or white

Iris pseudacorus

flowers with yellow or white crested ridges on 6- to 9-inch plants in early to mid-spring; 'Shenandoah Sky' grows pale blue flowers; 'Summer Storm', deep blue. *I. sibirica* (Siberian iris)—deep blue, violet, or white flowers 2 inches wide on stems to 4 feet tall in late spring.

Bulbous irises: *I. bucharica* (Bokara iris)—2- to 2½-inch-wide spring flowers with yellow falls touched with white on 18-inch stems; Zones 5-9. *I. danfordiae* (Danford iris)—a dwarf iris producing fragrant, spring-blooming, 4-inch single flowers with bristlelike canary yellow standards, falls splotched green and orange, and leaves growing to 12 inches; Zones 5-9. *I. histroides*—dwarfs to 9 inches tall with blue spring flowers and leaves up to 20 inches long; 'George' has plum purple falls touched with white; Zones 5-9. *I. hollandica* (Dutch iris)—fragrant 4-inch spring-to-summer flowers growing singly or in pairs on 15- to 24-inch stems; 'Angel's Wings' has pale blue standards and royal blue falls with white-rimmed yellow blotches; 'Blue Ideal', sky blue blooms on 20-inch stems; 'Blue Magic', deep blue-purple falls; 'Golden Harvest' is golden yellow shading to orange; 'Ideal' has dusty gray-blue falls blotched orange; 'Purple Sensation', deep violet falls with yellow blotches rimmed by royal blue; 'White Wedgewood' is pure white; Zones 6-9. *I. reticulata*—very fragrant, spring-blooming 3- to 9-inch dwarf plants, violet purple with white-bordered orange crests on falls and leaves to 18 inches; 'Cantab' is pale turquoise blue with white-rimmed orange blotches on its falls; 'Edward', dark blue spotted in orange; 'Gordon', medium blue with yellow-ridged falls; 'Har-

mony', pale blue standards and royal blue falls with white-rimmed yellow splotches; 'Ida', light blue falls marked in yellow; 'Joyce', lavender-blue standards and deep sky blue falls touched with yellow and green; 'J. S. Dijt', fragrant, rich purple standards and blue falls marked with yellow; 'Natashcha', snow white tinged blue with orange splashes on falls; 'Pauline', violet standards and dark purple falls marked with a blue-and-white variegated blotch; 'Purple Gem', deep violet standards and rich plum purple falls; 'Spring Time', pale blue standards and deep violet falls spotted purple and yellow and tipped with white; Zones 5-9.

Growing conditions and maintenance: Space dwarf bearded and crested irises

Iris sibirica 'Harpswell Haze'

1 foot apart. Allow 1½ feet between taller types. Most irises grow best in full sun, but crested iris prefers partial shade. Bearded irises thrive in a well-drained neutral loam. Siberian irises need constant moisture and a soil high in organic matter. Propagate by dividing the rhizomes or clumps after flowering. Plant bulbous dwarf irises in spring, Dutch irises in spring or fall, setting bulbs 4 inches deep and 3 to 6 inches apart and massing them for best effect. *I. reticulata* prefers slightly alkaline soil. North of Zone 8, place Dutch irises in sites protected from wind and cover with winter mulch. Allow foliage to mature through summer. Both dwarf and Dutch irises do best when allowed to form thick clumps over 3 to 5 years, after which flowering will probably diminish. Lift while dormant and propagate by removing and replanting the quantities of small offsets that form alongside mature bulbs in fall.

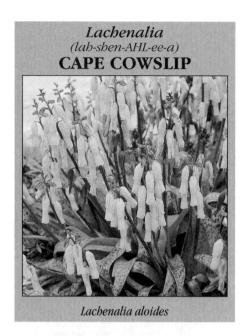

Lachenalia
(lah-shen-AHL-ee-a)
CAPE COWSLIP

Lachenalia aloides

Hardiness: *tender or Zones 9-10*

Type of bulb: *true bulb*

Flowering season: *spring*

Height: *6 to 12 inches*

Soil: *moist, well-drained, sandy*

Light: *full sun*

Cape cowslips bear long spikes of drooping, tubular flowers above broad, oval, pointed leaves. The waxy, inch-long flowers are often tinged and tipped in multiple colors, and the fleshy leaves and stems are marbled purple. Cape cowslips are rock-garden plants where winters are warm and are grown as container specimens elsewhere. They make long-lasting cut flowers.

Selected species and varieties: *L. aloides* (tricolored Cape cowslip)—yellow petals tinged green and touched with red; 'Pearsonii' is golden yellow with maroon tips; 'Aurea', bright yellow-orange. *L. bulbifera* (nodding Cape cowslip)—coral pink to red, tipped with green and purple.

Growing conditions and maintenance: Plant Cape cowslips outdoors in fall, setting bulbs 1 inch deep and 2 inches apart. Indoors, set five to six bulbs 1 inch deep in a 6-inch pot. Propagate by removing the bulblets that grow alongside mature bulbs or, for *L. bulbifera,* potting the small bulbils that develop in the plant's leaf joints.

Lilium
(LIL-ee-um)
LILY

Lilium columbianum

Hardiness: *Zones 3-9*

Type of bulb: *true bulb*

Flowering season: *late spring to fall*

Height: *2 to 8 feet*

Soil: *moist, well-drained, fertile*

Light: *full sun to light shade*

Funnel-shaped lily flowers are composed of six overlapping pointed petals called tepals. Sometimes smooth, sometimes wavy or frilled, the tepals are flecked with raised spots, often in a contrasting shade. The flowers curve backward to varying degrees from almost flat or bowl-shaped faces to flaring trumpets to tightly rolled tiny turbans. Curling stamens carry anthers dusted with pollen in vivid colors. Lilies offer a wide range of colors and color combinations, with tepals flushed or striped in contrasting hues in addition to their spots. They bloom on flower stalks, either singly or in clusters, at the tips of stiff, erect stems lined with short, grassy leaves. Flowers may face upward or outward or may nod from arching stalks. Up to 50 often highly fragrant flowers may appear on a single stem. The wide range of choices allows fanciers to plant lilies for continuous bloom throughout the summer. Lilies attract attention when planted in borders, where they quickly develop into spreading clumps. They can also be grown in patio containers, forced for indoor bloom, or used as long-lasting cut flowers.

Selected species and varieties: *L.* hybrids—thousands of hybrids grouped into divisions of plants with similar flower size, height, form, and bloom time. *Division 1. Asiatic hybrids:* Early-summer-flowering compact lilies, usually 2 to 4 feet tall, divided into up-facing, outward-facing, and pendent subgroups based on the form of their 4- to 6-inch flowers, which are borne singly or in clusters; 'Avignon' is mellow orange; 'Connecticut

Lilium 'Avignon'

King' has flat-faced, upright yellow blossoms with gold throats; 'Enchantment King', upright red-orange blooms with black spotting; 'Grand Cru' is yellow with tepal centers flushed maroon; 'Melon Time' has apricot-orange upright flowers; 'Mona' is clear yellow with yellow spots; 'Montreux', lightly spotted dusty rose; 'Roma', deep cream with few spots; 'Rosefire', clear reddish gold without spotting. *Division 2. Martagon hybrids:* Late-spring-flowering plants 3 to 6 feet tall with 3- to 4-inch nodding flowers like tiny turbans; 'Mrs. R. O. Backhouse' produces yellow-orange flowers flushed with rose; 'Paisley hybrids' are yellow-orange spotted maroon. *Division 3. Candidum hybrids:* 3- to 4-foot-tall or taller plants flowering from late spring to early summer with tiered clusters of 3- to 4-inch tiny turbans; 'Cascade Strain' produces fragrant pure white flowers. *Division 4. American hybrids:* Lilies to 7 or 8 feet, flowering from late spring to midsummer with tiers of up to 30 or more tiny Turk's caps; 'Bellingham Hybrids' are 3- to 4-inch midsummer-blooming flowers in shades of yellow, orange, and red. *Division 5. Longiflorum hybrids:* Fragrant, outward-facing flower trumpets blooming in midsummer, though the familiar Easter lily is often forced for earlier bloom; 'Casa Rosa' has 6-inch pink blossoms. *Division 6. Trumpet hybrids* [also called *Aurelian hybrids*]: Summer-flowering lilies 4 to 6 feet tall with large 6- to 10-inch flowers that are either trumpet shaped, sunburst shaped, bowl shaped, or nodding; 'Black Dragon' yields creamy 6-inch white flower trumpets flushed with purple on the outside; 'Golden Splendor', fragrant golden yellow trumpets flushed copper outside; 'Pink Perfection', large deep pink trumpets. *Division 7. Oriental hybrids:* Mid- to late-summer-blooming garden favorites from 2 to 8 feet tall bearing trumpet-shaped, flat-faced, or bowl-shaped flowers up to 12 inches across or trusses of smaller turban-shaped flowers; 'Casa Blanca' has pure white trumpets with orange anthers; 'Imperial Crimson', fragrant flat-faced white flowers blushed with pink; 'Imperial Gold', fragrant, flat-faced white flowers banded with yellow and spotted in crimson; 'Star Gazer', erect, deep carmine flowers up to 8 inches across with wavy tepals spotted dark red and rimmed in white on compact stems; 'White Mountain', upward-facing white trumpets with golden throats.

Lilium 'Rosefire'

Division 8. Miscellaneous hybrids: Reserved for future hybrids not fitting any previous division. *Division 9. Species lilies: L. auratum* (gold-banded lily, gold-rayed lily, mountain lily)—up to 30 bowl-shaped, fragrant 10-inch-wide white flowers with tepals banded in gold down their centers and spotted with crimson on 4- to 6-foot stems blooming in mid- to late summer. *L. canadense* (Canada lily,

meadow lily, yellow lily)—3-inch dangling, bowl-shaped yellow to red-orange flowers spotted with crimson on stems to 6 feet in early to midsummer. *L. candidum* (Madonna lily, white lily)—fragrant trusses of shimmering white trum-

Lilium candidum

pets with yellow throats on 2- to 4-foot stems in early summer. *L. columbianum* (Columbia lily, Columbia tiger lily, Oregon lily)—tiered clusters of nodding 2-inch yellow to red turbans spotted maroon on 5-foot stalks in summer. *L. hansonii* (Japanese Turk's-cap)—loose spikes of 2½-inch yellow-orange turbans spotted purple on 2- to 5-foot stems in early summer. *L. henryi*—20 or more dangling light orange turbans with green throats on stems to 8 feet in late summer. *L. lancifolium* [also called *L. tigrinum*] (devil lily, tiger lily)—up to 25 nodding 5-inch orange or red Turk's caps spotted with purple on 6-foot plants in midsummer. *L. martagon* (Martagon lily, Turk's-cap lily, turban lily)—tiered clusters of up to 50 nodding light purple-rose flower turbans spotted with dark purple and unpleasantly scented on stems to 6 feet in midsummer; 'Album' is a pure ivory. *L. monadelphum* (Caucasian lily)—bell-shaped 5-inch yellow flowers tinged and spotted purple on 4- to 5-foot stems in early summer. *L. pumilum* (coral lily)—up to two dozen inch-wide, lacquer red nodding Turk's caps on compact 1- to 2-foot plants in early summer. *L. regale* (regal lily, royal lily)—fragrant, outward-facing white flower trumpets flushed purple outside with gold throats inside, clustered like a crown atop 3- to 5-foot stems in midsummer. *L. speciosum* (showy Japanese lily)—fragrant, nodding Turk's

caps rimmed in white on 4- to 5-foot stems in late summer to early fall; 'Album' is pure white; 'Rubrum', white blushed and spotted with crimson; 'Uchida', deep reddish pink with a white throat and crimson spots. *L. superbum* (American Turk's-cap lily, swamp lily, lily royal)—deep yellow-orange 3-inch flowers with maroon spots nodding in trusses on 5- to 8-foot stems in midsummer. *L.* x *testaceum* (Nankeen lily)—nodding 3-inch apricot turbans spotted red on 4- to 6-foot plants in midsummer.

Growing conditions and maintenance: With the exception of *L. candidum* and its *Division 3* hybrids, plant lilies in spring or fall, setting bulbs 2 to 3 times deeper than their diameter. Space bulbs 1 foot apart. Plant *L. candidum* and its hybrids with bulb tips an inch below the surface in fall. Mulch lilies to keep roots cool and moist in summer, protected from frost in winter. *L. auratum* and *L. speciosum* will not tolerate lime in the soil. *L. auratum, L. canadense,* and *L. speciosum* are susceptible to the lily mosaic virus. *L. lancifolium* is a carrier of the virus, which does not harm it but is spread to other lilies by aphids; buy only disease-free stock and plant far from other lilies. Stake taller lilies for support. For pots and patio containers, choose compact lilies and set bulbs deep enough to allow space for stem roots. Propagate lilies by removing and replanting the small bulblets that grow along the underground stem or by removing and potting the tiny black bulbils that appear in the leaf joints of some species.

Mertensia
(mer-TENZ-ee-a)
BLUEBELLS, LUNGWORT

Mertensia virginica

Hardiness: *Zones 3-8*

Type of bulb: *rhizome*

Flowering season: *spring*

Height: *18 to 24 inches*

Soil: *moist, well-drained, fertile*

Light: *light shade to full sun*

Mertensia produces loose clusters of nodding flower bells over several weeks. The blossoms dangle near the top of stems lined with oval, pointed, soft green leaves. Foliage dies back by midsummer. Bluebells will slowly grow into large clumps in woodland borders, rock gardens, and wildflower gardens, and provide textural contrast when interplanted with spring bulbs such as narcissus and tulip.

Selected species and varieties: *M. virginica*—(Virginia bluebells, Virginia cowslip, Roanoke bells)—inch-long pale dusty blue flowers with tiny curling crests at the tip of each petal.

Growing conditions and maintenance: Plant Virginia bluebells in fall, setting the tips of crowns just at the soil surface with buds facing up. Space crown sections 1½ to 3 feet apart. When purchasing Virginia bluebells, look for nursery-propagated crowns; refuse plants collected in the wild. To propagate, divide crowns in fall, making sure each section has at least one bud.

Narcissus
(nar-SIS-us)
DAFFODIL

Narcissus 'Dutch Master'

Hardiness: *Zones 3-10*

Type of bulb: *true bulb*

Flowering season: *late winter to late spring*

Height: *4 to 18 inches*

Soil: *well-drained*

Light: *full sun to shade*

Daffodil flowers, growing either singly or in small clusters, bloom atop stout, hollow stems above clumps of narrow, glossy, grasslike leaves. Mature bulbs produce two or more stems. The 1- to 4-inch-wide flowers sometimes face upward or arch downward but most often face out. Each bloom consists of an outer ring of six petals called the perianth and a raised center called a corona, which may be an almost flat small cup, a large cup of medium length, or, when it is very long, a trumpet. The edges of the corona may be ruffled, fringed, flared, frilled, or split. The petals of the perianth may be pointed or round, overlapping or separate. Colors range the spectrum. Species narcissus are renowned for their sweet, intense fragrance. Hybrids of the species number in the thousands, and the genus is grouped into 12 divisions for identification. There are miniature cultivars within almost every division. Group them in borders, beds, and woodland or rock gardens, or scatter them to naturalize on lawns and in meadows. All narcissus make excellent cut flowers, and all, particularly some of the species,

are excellent for forcing. All parts of narcissus are poisonous.

Selected species and varieties: The 12 divisions are based on the shape of the corona, its size relationship to the perianth, and, sometimes, the species from which the plants originated. *Division 1. Trumpet daffodils:* One flower per 16- to 20-inch stem, with the corona a trumpet as long as or longer than the perianth petals; 'Arctic Gold' is deep yellow; 'Bravoure' has white petals and a yellow cup; 'Dutch Master' is all yellow, good for forcing; 'Las Vegas' has giant white petals and a yellow corona; 'Little Beauty' is a 6-inch miniature with white petals and a golden yellow trumpet; 'Little Gem' is an all-yellow miniature; 'Lunar Sea' has soft yellow petals and a white cup; 'Mount

Narcissus 'Gigantic Star'

Hood', white petals with a cream trumpet; 'Spellbinder', yellow-green flowers with a corona aging white; 'Unsurpassable' is golden yellow with extremely large trumpets. *Division 2. Large-cup daffodils:* One flower on each 12- to 20-inch stem, the corona ranging in size from one-third the length of the petals to almost their length; 'Accent' has white petals and a pink corona; 'Ambergate', red corona and orange petals blushed red; 'Camelot' is a long-lasting golden yellow bloom; 'Carlton' has two shades of yellow and is vanilla scented; 'Ceylon' has yellow petals and an orange cup and grows vigorously; 'Daydream' is translucent yellow with a cup maturing to white; 'Flower Record' has white petals and a yellow corona rimmed red; 'Gigantic Star' is an extremely large pale yellow orange bloom with a vanilla scent; 'Ice Follies' has creamy white petals and a flat yellow cup aging white; 'Kissproof', copper yellow petals, a red-orange cup; 'Pink Charm', white petals, a corona banded salmon; 'Redhill', ivory petals, a deep red-orange corona; 'Salome', ivory petals, a pale yellow corona aging to salmon pink;

Narcissus 'Ice Follies'

'St. Keverne' is all yellow; 'St. Patrick's Day', bright yellow with a flat white corona; 'White Plume', pure white. *Division 3. Small-cup daffodils:* One flower per 10- to 20-inch stem, with the corona less than a third the length of the perianth petals; 'Barrett Browning' is early flowering with a white perianth and an orange to red corona; 'Birma' has deep yellow petals with a red cup. *Division 4. Double daffodils:* One or more flowers per 12- to 16-inch stem, with either the perianth petals or the corona or both doubled, the corona sometimes a tuft of tousled petals almost as wide as the perianth instead of a cup; 'Bridal Crown' has cream petals, deep red-orange centers; 'Cheerfulness' is a single white bloom flecked yellow; 'Erlicheer' yields eight or more fragrant, white-petaled flowers with yellow-tinged centers on each stem; 'Flower Drift' is ivory with a ruffled yellow-orange center; 'Pencrebar' is a bright orange miniature cultivar less than 6 inches tall; 'Sir Winston Churchill' has fragrant white petals with orange centers; 'Tahiti' is deep yellow with a red center; 'Unique', ivory white with an extremely frilled golden center. *Division 5. Triandus hybrid daffodils:* Two or more drooping flowers per 10- to 12-inch stem, with the perianth petals flared backwards; 'Hawera' is less than 6 inches tall with clusters of tiny yellow bells; 'Liberty Bells' is soft yellow; 'Petrel' produces up to 7 fragrant white

flowers per stem; 'Thalia' grows two or more fragrant white flowers resembling orchids per stem. *Division 6. Cyclamineus hybrid daffodils:* One flower on each short stem—under 8 inches—with a trumpet-shaped corona and perianth petals swept backwards; 'February Gold' is yellow; 'Jack Snipe' has rounded white petals and a fringed yellow cup; 'Jenny' is pure white; 'Jet Fire' has red-orange petals with yellow cups; 'Jumblie' is a miniature, under 6 inches, with yellow petals swept back from a pencil-thin yellow-orange corolla; 'Peeping Tom' is lemon yellow; 'Tête-à-Tête' is a miniature under 6 inches with buttery yellow petals and a corona flushed orange. *Division 7.*

Narcissus 'Jack Snipe'

Jonquilla hybrid daffodils: Three to 6 fragrant flowers on a round 10- to 14-inch stem with small cups; 'Baby Moon' is a miniature, under 6 inches, with fragrant yellow blooms; 'Bell Song' is fragrant, with white petals and a pink corona; 'Pip-it', fragrant, with pale yellow petals and a white corona; 'Quail' is orangey yellow; 'Sun Disk', a yellow miniature, under 6 inches, with very rounded petals; 'Suzy' is fragrant, with yellow petals and a deep red-orange corona; 'Trevithian' has curled yellow petals and a frilled corona and is very fragrant. *Division 8. Tazetta hybrid daffodils:* Three to 20 fragrant flowers with almost flat coronas per 6- to 14-inch stem; 'Avalanche' has a perianth crowded with doubled white petals and a yellow corona; 'Geranium', fragrant white petals and a yellow-orange cup; 'Minnow', a miniature under 6 inches, has white petals and a bright yellow cup; 'Scarlet Gem', yellow-orange petals enfolding a deep red-orange corona with

frilled edges. *Division 9. Poeticus hybrid daffodils:* One fragrant flower per 12- to 16-inch stem with rounded pure white perianth petals and a tiny, brilliantly colored, disk-shaped, flat corona; 'Actaea' has brilliant white petals with deep green

Narcissus 'Minnow'

stamens tucked within a deep orange disk rimmed red. *Division 10. Species and wild forms:* N. *bulbocodium* var. *conspicuus* (hoop-petticoat daffodil)—petals reduced to tiny pointed projections around smooth, flaring yellow coronas like ladies' hoop skirts on 6- to 10-inch stems. N. *jonquilla* (jonquil)—2-inch golden yellow flowers with flat coronas in clusters on 12-inch stems. N. *papyraceus* (paper-white narcissus)—clusters of up to a dozen very fragrant flowers on 16-inch stems, excellent for forcing; 'Galilee' has pure white late blooms; 'Israel', creamy yellow petals and a deep yellow corona; 'Jerusalem' is pure white; 'Ziva', a very early white. N. *poeticus* var. *recurvus* (pheasant's-eye narcissus)—1½- to 3-inch blossoms with back-swept white petals and a flat, disk-shaped yellow to red corona on 8- to 16-inch stems. N. *pseudonarcissus* ssp. *obvallaris* (Tenby daffodil)—rich deep yellow 2- to 3-inch flowers with ruffled and flared trumpets on 10-inch stems. N. *tazetta* (bunch-flowered narcissus, polyanthus narcissus)—4 to 8 fragrant blooms with a white perianth and yellow corona; 'Canaliculatus' has very fragrant blossoms with backswept white petals ringing a yellow cup on 6-inch stems; 'Grand Soleil d'Or', a deep yellow perianth and bright orange cup on 12-inch stems. *Division 11. Split-corona daffodils:* One upward-facing flower with a flattened corona split one-third or more of its length on each 14- to 20-inch stem; 'Cassata' has white petals and a ruffled lemon yellow cup aging to white; 'Colbanc' is pure white with an "eye" of deep green stamens; 'Mondragon' is golden yellow and deep orange; 'Palmares' has white petals and pink ruffled centers; 'Tricollet', white petals around an orange corolla. Plants in the Division 11 subdivision *Papillion daffodils* resemble floral butterflies; 'Sorbet' is an ivory butterfly type with a sunny yellow center. *Division 12. Miscellaneous daffodils:* All daffodils not belonging to any of the previous divisions.

Growing conditions and maintenance: Plant narcissus in fall, setting the bulbs, which can range from ¼ to 2 inches in diameter, into the ground at a depth three

Narcissus bulbocodium

times the width of the bulb and spacing them 1 to 3 inches apart, depending on their size and the effect desired in the garden. Allow foliage to sprawl and to die back for at least 6 weeks in early summer before removing it. Fragrant *N. tazetta* and its hybrids are hardy only in Zones 9 and 10 but are among the choicest daffodils for forcing because they require no chilling. To force plants into bloom, buy prechilled bulbs or chill all daffodil bulbs except those of *N. tazetta* and its hybrids before potting them 1 inch deep in containers. Propagate narcissus by removing and immediately replanting the small bulblets that develop at the base of mature bulbs as soon as foliage withers, or dry the bulbs and hold them for replanting in fall. Bulblets take several years to grow to blooming size.

Puschkinia
(push-KIN-ee-a)
PUSCHKINIA

Puschkinia scilloides var. libanotica 'Alba'

Hardiness:	*Zones 4-9*
Type of bulb:	*true bulb*
Flowering season:	*spring*
Height:	*4 to 6 inches*
Soil:	*moist, well-drained*
Light:	*full sun to light shade*

Puschkinia's wands of tight, oval buds open first into loose clusters of tiny flower bells and finally into small stars on slender stems rising from tufts of narrow leaves like those of daffodils. The plants naturalize easily into drifts of blooms to carpet rockeries or beds and make an attractive border edging.

Selected species and varieties: *P. scilloides* var. *libanotica* (striped squill)—½-inch bluish white flowers striped darker blue above 6-inch leaves; 'Alba' is pure white.

Growing conditions and maintenance: Plant bulbs in fall, setting them 2 inches deep and 6 inches apart. Group them in small colonies for best effect. They bloom best when left undisturbed. Propagate by removing the small bulblets that grow alongside mature bulbs.

Ranunculus
(ra-NUN-kew-lus)
BUTTERCUP, CROWFOOT

Ranunculus asiaticus

Hardiness:	*tender or Zones 9-11*
Type of bulb:	*tuber*
Flowering season:	*spring and summer*
Height:	*10 to 18 inches*
Soil:	*moist, very well drained, sandy*
Light:	*full sun*

Buttercups produce quantities of saucer-shaped flowers over a long season of bloom. There are many hybrids, so thickly doubled that flowers become colorful domes of whorled overlapping petals. Each tuber may produce five or six dozen flowers up to four at a time throughout the season on stems lined with ferny leaflets. Buttercups can be used in borders and rock gardens, and they excel as cut flowers.

Selected species and varieties: *R. asiaticus* 'Tecolote Giants' (Persian buttercup)—flowers up to 5 inches across in pastel shades of pink, rose, yellow, tangerine, and white, with bi- and tricolors.

Growing conditions and maintenance: Plant Persian buttercups in fall, soaking the tubers overnight then setting them in the soil with the claws down with the tops 1½ inches deep. Space them 8 inches apart. Crowns are subject to rot, so sites with fast drainage are essential for success. Tubers go dormant in summer. North of Zone 9, treat plants as annuals, setting them out in spring and lifting them in fall for winter storage. Propagate from seed or by dividing tubers.

Rhodohypoxis
(ro-do-hi-POKS-is)
RHODOHYPOXIS

Rhodohypoxis baurii

Hardiness: *Zones 6-10*

Type of bulb: *rhizome*

Flowering season: *summer*

Height: *3 to 4 inches*

Soil: *well-drained, sandy*

Light: *full sun*

Rhodohypoxis sends up tufts of 3-inch, stiff, grassy leaves covered with downy hairs in spring, followed by dainty, flat-faced blossoms that appear throughout the season. Each blossom sits atop a slender stem; the plants produce several flowering stems at a time. Dwarf rhodohypoxis are excellent planted among paving stones and will form colonies in rock gardens or borders. They can also be grown as container specimens.

Selected species and varieties: *R. baurii* (red star)—1- to 1½-inch white, pink, rose, or red flowers with petals crowded closely together at the center, obscuring the stamens.

Growing conditions and maintenance: Plant rhodohypoxis in fall, setting rhizomes 1 to 2 inches deep and 2 to 3 inches apart. Protect rhizomes with winter mulch in Zones 5 and 6. North of Zone 6, treat rhodohypoxis as an annual, planting in spring and lifting in fall, or grow it in shallow containers, allowing 4 or 5 rhizomes per 6-inch bulb pan. They are best left undisturbed, but clumps of rhizomes can be lifted and separated for propagation in spring as leaves begin to show.

Sanguinaria
(sang-gwi-NAR-ee-a)
BLOODROOT

Sanguinaria canadensis

Hardiness: *Zones 3-9*

Type of bulb: *rhizome*

Flowering season: *spring*

Height: *6 to 14 inches*

Soil: *moist, well-drained, rich*

Light: *partial shade*

Bloodroot is one of the loveliest spring-blooming woodland wildflowers native to eastern North America, and its large round blue-green leaves make an attractive ground cover. The plant is named for its red sap, root, and stems.

Selected species: *S. canadensis* (bloodroot, red puccoon)—solitary white flower to 1½ inches across with gold stamens on a 6- to 10-inch stalk. Each flower bud is surrounded by a furled leaf when it emerges. When fully expanded, the leaves are up to 1 foot across and have five or more lobes whose edges curl slightly upward.

Growing conditions and maintenance: Bloodroot thrives in rich, moist soil and benefits from added organic matter. It does best when planted beneath deciduous trees, where it receives bright sunshine before the trees leaf out and partial shade for the rest of the growing season. Mulch lightly with deciduous leaves in winter. Propagate by seed planted immediately after collection, or by dividing rhizomes in fall or early spring.

Tulipa
(TOO-lip-a)
TULIP

Tulipa 'Plaisir'

Hardiness: *Zones 2-8*

Type of bulb: *true bulb*

Flowering season: *spring*

Height: *6 to 28 inches*

Soil: *well-drained, sandy, fertile*

Light: *full sun*

Synonymous with spring to many gardeners, tulips' egg-shaped buds unfold into a profusion of forms ranging from inverted bells to flat saucers, stars, urns, deep cups, and lilylike shapes, sometimes with the petals reduced to mere ribbons. Petals may be smooth, curled, frilled, crisped, ruffled, flared, doubled, or waved. Tulips come in every color except true blue and are often striped, edged, flecked, flushed with contrasting color, or "flamed" in a zigzag variegated pattern. The hundreds of tulip species and thousands of hybrids are sorted by botanists into groups with similar origins, shapes, and bloom times. Species tulips, also called wild tulips or botanical tulips, generally have very early flowers on strong, sturdy stems, and are the parents of the taller hybrids, which bloom at various times throughout spring. The botanical *Kaufmanniana*, *Fosteriana*, and *Greigii* tulips merited their own divisions in the latest shuffling of botanical nomenclature. Low-growing species tulips can be grown in rock gardens or as edgings for beds or borders and may naturalize where conditions are right for their growth. Plant taller hybrids in informal groupings or formal patterns where they will produce blooms for several years before requiring renewal. Tulips can be forced for indoor bloom and make excellent cut flowers.

Selected species and varieties: Hybrids and species tulips are organized into 15 divisions used in the garden trade. *Division 1. Single early tulips:* Among the

Tulipa 'Apricot Beauty'

first to flower, in very early spring, on 6- to 14-inch stems with smooth petals in neat cups; 'Apricot Beauty' is salmon edged in apricot; 'Princess Irene', orange-splashed purple. *Division 2. Double early tulips:* Bowls of ruffled, doubled petals up to 4 inches across on 12-inch stems in early spring; 'Monte Carlo' is deep, clear yellow; 'Peach Blossom' has honey-scented soft rose petals edged with cream. *Division 3. Triumph tulips:* Satiny-smooth flowers in midspring on 18- to 24-inch stems; 'Attila' is pale purple-violet; 'New Design', cream flushed pink and apricot with leaves edged pinky cream. *Division 4. Darwin hybrid tulips:* Large, smooth-petaled ovals opening into flat cups up to 7 inches across in midspring on stems to 36 inches; 'Daydream' has yellow petals aging to apricot-flushed orange; 'Golden Parade', bright yellow petals edged in red; 'Pink Impression', purplish pink. *Division 5. Single late tulips* [includes Cottage and Darwin tulips]: Distinctly rectangular flower cups, some with pointed petals, in late spring on stems to 30 inches; 'Blushing Beauty' is yellow to apricot-blushed rose; 'Georgette' has clusters of butter yellow blooms with the edges aging to red; 'Halcro' is raspberry with a

yellow base; 'Maureen', cool white; 'Mrs. J. T. Scheepers', pure yellow; 'Queen of the Night', deep maroon, almost black. *Division 6. Lily-flowering tulips:* Urn-shaped buds open in late spring into lily-like flowers with curved, pointed petals on 24-inch stems; 'Red Shine' is deep ruby red with blue center; 'White Triumphator', pure white. *Division 7. Fringed tulips:* Late-spring flowers with very finely fringed petals on 14- to 24-inch stems; 'Burgundy Lace' is deep wine; 'Fringed Elegance', yellow flecked with pink. *Division 8. Viridiflora green tulips:* Late-spring flowers with petals in varying degrees of green on 18-inch stems; 'Spring Green' is ivory white with the center of the petals slashed green. *Division 9. Rembrandt tulips:* Petal color is "broken," or variegated, with elaborately patterned stripes and blotches on 18- to 30-inch stems in midspring; 'Cordell Hull' is white streaked with red. *Division 10. Parrot tulips:* Tousled petals, exotically fringed, waved, crisped, and flared, on flowers blooming in late spring on stems to 24 inches; 'Flaming Parrot' is deep yellow flamed with crimson. *Division 11. Double late tulips* [also

Tulipa dasystemon

called *peony-flowered tulips*]: Bowls of doubled petals in late spring on 16- to 24-inch stems; 'Angelique' is deep pink shading to pale pink; 'Miranda', two shades of red with a yellow base. *Division 12. Kaufmanniana tulips:* Urn-shaped buds opening into large flowers with curved petals on stems under 12 inches in very early spring; 'Ancila' is soft rosy pink outside, white inside; 'Show Winner', deep scarlet. *Division 13. Fosteriana tulips:* Enormous blossoms in

early spring on stems to 18 inches; 'Juan' is orange with a yellow base. *Division 14. Greigii tulips:* Flowers on strong, 8- to 16-inch stems above attractively purple-mottled foliage; 'Czar Peter' is red rimmed with white; 'Red Riding Hood', deep red-orange with a black base. *Division 15. Species tulips:* T. bakeri 'Lilac Wonder'—rosy purple cups with yellow bases on 6-inch stems; Zones 5-9. *T. batalinii* 'Bright Gem'—yellow cups of pointed petals flushed orange, 6 inches tall; Zones 3-8. *T. clusiana* var. *chrysantha* (golden lady tulip)—deep saucers, yellow inside, crimson edged with yellow outside, 12 inches tall; Zones 3-9. *T. dasystemon* (Kuen Lun tulip)—clusters of white flower stars tinged bronze and green, 4 inches tall; Zones 4-8. *T. linifolia* (slimleaf tulip)—curled, pointed electric red petals and red-rimmed leaves, 6 inches tall; Zones 4-8. *T. pulchella* 'Violacea' (red crocus tulip)—tiny purple-red ovals tinged green at bases, 3½ inches tall; Zones 5-8. *T. turkestanica*—clusters of white flower stars tinged violet, 5 inches tall; Zones 5-8.

Growing conditions and maintenance: Plant tulips in late fall, at a depth equal to three times their diameter. Space according to bulb size. Plant up to 40 hybrid bulbs per square yard or up to 60 smaller species bulbs per square yard. Note, however, that the famous variegation of Rembrandt tulips is caused by a virus that does not hurt them but can be harmful if spread to lilies and other tulips by aphids. Site Rembrandts far from susceptible plants. In Zones 9 and 10, tulips must be prechilled. Buy them in that condition or prechill them yourself by placing them in a vented paper bag in the refrigerator at 40° F for 9 to 12 weeks before setting them out; in modern frost-free refrigerators, however, you run the risk of drying them out. *T. bakeri* 'Lilac Wonder', *T. clusiana* var. *chrysantha*, and the hybrids 'Burgundy Lace', 'Flaming Parrot', 'Golden Parade', 'Halcro', 'Maureen', 'Menton', and 'Mrs. J. T. Scheepers' require no prechilling and may naturalize in warm zones. Allow foliage to ripen before mowing or removing it. Tulips tend to disappear over time; either treat them as annuals or dig and replant bulbs every 2 to 3 years as flowering diminishes.

Veltheimia
(vel-TY-mee-a)
RED-HOT POKER

Veltheimia bracteata

Hardiness: *tender or Zones 10-11*

Type of bulb: *true bulb*

Flowering season: *late winter to spring*

Height: *15 to 20 inches*

Soil: *well-drained, sandy*

Light: *full sun*

Red-hot poker's oval clusters of up to 50 flower buds open from bottom to top into long, drooping funnels with curled lips. Clusters are carried on sturdy stems above attractive rosettes of glossy green leaves with wavy edges. Both leaves and stems are attractively mottled. Use red-hot poker outdoors in warm climates; grow as a pot plant elsewhere.

Selected species and varieties: *V. bracteata*—2-inch pink-red or pink-purple blossoms with green-and-white flecked lips above foliage and stems marbled green and purple.

Growing conditions and maintenance: Outdoors in Zones 10 and 11, plant red-hot poker bulbs 1 inch deep and 6 to 10 inches apart in fall. In pots, group several of the large, 6-inch bulbs together in large bulb pans for best effect. Plant them 4 to 6 inches apart with the top third of the bulb exposed and allow bulbs to dry off during summer dormancy. Propagate by removing bulb offsets after foliage withers.

Zantedeschia
(zan-tee-DES-ki-a)
CALLA LILY

Zantedeschia aethiopica

Hardiness: *tender or Zones 9-10*

Type of bulb: *rhizome*

Flowering season: *summer or fall*

Height: *2 to 3 feet*

Soil: *moist to well-drained*

Light: *full sun to partial shade*

Calla lily's gracefully curved and sculpted flowers have a cool, formal elegance few other blooms can match. Petal-like spathes curl into elongated trumpets with a flared lip pulled to a point. The waxy spathe curls around a colorful, sometimes fragrant, fingerlike spadix bearing the true flowers, which are tiny and inconspicuous. Up to 12 or more blossoms bloom at the same time amid broad, stalked, arrow-shaped leaves with wavy edges that are often heavily flecked and spotted with white for added interest. In warm zones, calla lilies are eye-catching specimens for beds or borders and will naturalize where conditions suit them. Elsewhere they are grown as annuals or as pot plants for patio or indoor use. Callas are prized as cut flowers.

Selected species and varieties: *Z. aethiopica* (common calla, giant white calla, arum lily, trumpet lily)—fragrant, snowy white flowers 10 inches long on 2-foot plants; 'Perle Von Stuttgart' is somewhat smaller than the species, with abundant blossoms. *Z. albomaculata* (spotted calla, black-throated calla)—

5-inch white flowers with purple throats on 2-foot plants. *Z. elliottiana* (golden calla, yellow calla)—6-inch golden yellow flowers, tinged greenish yellow on the outside, on 2½-foot plants. *Z. rehmannii* (red calla, pink calla)—3-inch pink flowers on 18- to 24-inch plants. *Z.* hybrids—'Black-Eyed Beauty' produces creamy white blossoms veined green, with a black throat or eye rimming the spadix; 'Black Magic' is yellow with a black eye; 'Cameo', salmon; 'Harvest Moon' is yellow with a red eye; 'Pink Persuasion', purple-pink; 'Solfatare' is a creamy pale yellow with a black eye.

Zantedeschia rehmannii

Growing conditions and maintenance: Outdoors in Zones 8-10, plant calla lilies in spring or fall, setting rhizomes 1 to 4 inches deep and spacing them 1 to 2 feet apart. Calla lilies tolerate boggy conditions and can be grown with their roots in water at the edges of ponds. North of Zone 8, start them indoors in early spring and transplant them outside after all danger of frost has passed for blooming in summer. Lift rhizomes in fall after foliage withers and store for winter. For pot culture, set growing tips of rhizomes at soil level and allow one root per 6-inch pot. Callas bloom about 2 months after planting. Golden calla lily can be propagated from seed. Propagate all calla lilies by dividing their rhizomes in spring or fall.

'ALBA SEMI-PLENA'

Classification: *alba*

Bloom period: *summer*

Height: *6 to 8 feet*

Hardiness: *Zones 4-10*

ARS rating: *8.6*

Date introduced: *prior to 1600*

'Alba Semi-plena' is also known as the White Rose of York. Its semidouble white flowers are 2½ inches across with prominent golden stamens, and they produce a powerful old garden fragrance. Borne in clusters, flowers appear in midseason and do not repeat. Elongated orange-red hips appear in late summer and fall. The foliage is gray-green.

With sturdy, arching canes that develop a vase-shaped form, 'Alba Semi-plena' can be grown as a freestanding shrub for a specimen or for use in borders, or it can be trained as a climber on a wall, a trellis, or a fence. Like other alba roses, it tolerates some shade and is quite hardy and disease resistant.

'AMERICAN PILLAR'

Classification: *rambler*

Bloom period: *summer*

Height: *15 to 20 feet*

Hardiness: *Zones 5-10*

ARS rating: *7.5*

Date introduced: *1902*

The five-petaled single blossoms of 'American Pillar' are carmine-pink with white centers and golden stamens. Erupting once in midsummer, they are produced in large clusters that almost cover the entire plant. Flowers have no scent. Leaves are leathery, large, and dark green; canes are green and prickly.

The plant is very vigorous, growing to 20 feet, and is best used for climbing on a fence or arbor. Like other ramblers, it may be subject to mildew.

'BARONNE PREVOST'

Classification: *hybrid perpetual*

Bloom period: *summer to fall*

Height: *4 to 6 feet*

Hardiness: *Zones 5-10*

ARS rating: *8.5*

Date introduced: *1842*

The elegant 3- to 4-inch blooms of 'Baronne Prévost' are very double, with 100 petals that quarter and fold back on a green button-eyed center. Ranging from pale pink to deep rose pink, the recurring blooms are extremely fragrant. Buds are globular, leaves are medium green, and canes are very prickly.

Best grown as a freestanding shrub, 'Baronne Prévost' grows between 4 and 6 feet high with an approximately equal spread. The plant is vigorous, and it has a less awkward form than do most hybrid perpetuals. Also, the foliage is more attractive and disease resistant than that of most of the class.

'BETTY PRIOR'

Classification: *floribunda*

Bloom period: *summer to fall*

Height: *4 to 5 feet*

Hardiness: *Zones 4-10*

ARS rating: *8.2*

Date introduced: *1935*

The carmine-pink buds of 'Betty Prior' open to 2- to 3-inch cupped single blossoms that flatten with age and bear a light, spicy fragrance. Blossoms occur in large clusters so profuse that they can cover the entire bush. In cool weather, flowers remain carmine-pink, but as temperatures rise they become medium pink. The five petals surround yellow stamens that darken to brown. Foliage is medium green and semiglossy.

Plants are vigorous and bushy with a rounded form. One of the most popular floribundas ever, this rose is effectively used for mass plantings and hedges, in small groups, and singly in a bed. It is also very winter hardy and exceptionally resistant to black spot, but less so to mildew.

'BLAZE'

Classification: *large-flowered climber*

Bloom period: *spring to fall*

Height: *12 to 15 feet*

Hardiness: *Zones 5-10*

ARS rating: *7.4*

Date introduced: *1932*

Clusters of cup-shaped scarlet blossoms occur on both old and new wood of 'Blaze' throughout the growing season. Flowers are semidouble, 2 to 3 inches across, lightly fragrant, and nonfading, even in hot weather. Early flowers are somewhat larger than those produced later in the season. Dark green leathery foliage contrasts nicely with the continuous show of blooms.

This easy-to-grow rose has a vigorous, upright habit, and its canes are quick to reach their height of 12 to 15 feet, making it a good choice for fences, arbors, pillars, and porches. It is quite hardy but is somewhat susceptible to powdery mildew.

'BONICA'

Classification: *shrub*

Bloom period: *summer*

Height: *3 to 5 feet*

Hardiness: *Zones 4-9*

ARS rating: *9.1*

Date introduced: *1981*

'Bonica' (also called 'Meidomonac') is free flowering and easy to grow. Large, loose clusters of up to 20 flowers appear throughout the summer. Each spiraled bud opens to reveal a 2½- to 3½-inch double blossom with soft pink ruffled petals. The foliage is dark green and glossy. Bright orange hips appear in fall and remain attractive all winter.

The plant has a spreading habit with arching stems spanning 5 to 6 feet. This rose is not fussy about pruning; it can be maintained as a compact hedge or lightly tip pruned for a more informal appearance. 'Bonica' is an excellent choice for beds or borders, for massing, or for use as a hedge along a walk or drive. It is highly disease resistant, exceptionally hardy, and tolerant of harsh climates. This is the first shrub rose to win the AARS award.

'BRIDE'S DREAM'

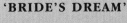

Classification: *hybrid tea*

Bloom period: *summer to fall*

Height: *3 to 4 feet*

Hardiness: *Zones 5-10*

ARS rating: *8.0*

Date introduced: *1985*

The large double flowers of 'Bride's Dream' are pale pink, high centered, and lightly fragrant. They usually occur singly on the stem and appear in great abundance throughout the growing season. Foliage is dark green, and stems bear brown prickles.

The plant is a strong grower with a tall, upright habit. It can be situated in beds or borders, and its flowers are excellent for cutting and exhibition. 'Bride's Dream' is judged by some growers to be the best hybrid tea in its color class.

'BUFF BEAUTY'

Classification: *hybrid musk*

Bloom period: *summer to fall*

Height: *5 to 6 feet*

Hardiness: *Zones 5-10*

ARS rating: *8.3*

Date introduced: *1939*

The color of the 3- to 4-inch double flowers of 'Buff Beauty' ranges from buff yellow to deep apricot, depending on weather conditions. Richly fragrant, flattened blossoms are borne in clusters. The abundant foliage emerges bronze-red, turning a glossy dark green as it matures. Canes are smooth and brown.

This rose is a very attractive plant with a graceful, arching habit and is often broader than it is tall. It requires a lot of space but makes a lovely specimen. It can also be trained to a pillar or wall, or can be used as a ground cover on banks.

'CAREFREE BEAUTY'

Classification: *shrub*

Bloom period: *summer to fall*

Height: *4 to 5 feet*

Hardiness: *Zones 4-10*

ARS rating: *8.5*

Date introduced: *1977*

The long, pointed buds of 'Carefree Beauty' open to semidouble medium pink flowers. Each blossom has 15 to 20 petals and bears a rich, fruity fragrance. Flowers appear in clusters of three to 20 and are produced freely all season. Foliage is a bright apple green.

This rose has a vigorous, bushy, spreading habit. It is easy to grow, as its name implies, and makes an excellent flowering hedge or garden shrub. Space plants 18 inches apart to form a dense hedge. A Dr. Buck rose, it is both disease resistant and very hardy.

'CATHERINE MERMET'

Classification: *tea*

Bloom period: *summer*

Height: *3 to 4 feet*

Hardiness: *Zones 7-10*

ARS rating: *8.1*

Date introduced: *1869*

Flowers of 'Catherine Mermet' open a blush pink with lilac edges and change to soft beige as they mature. Inner petals often display yellow at the base. The double blossoms are 3 inches across and are borne singly or in small clusters on graceful stems. Their fragrance is strong and spicy. Leaves are copper colored when young, maturing to a medium green.

This rose is somewhat delicate, requiring nothing less than a warm, sunny spot and rich, well-drained soil. It is quite tender and is frequently grown in greenhouses. With an upright, arching habit, it is well suited for beds, borders, and specimen plantings. Flowers are excellent for cutting. Pruning should be restricted to removal of dead and weak, spindly canes. It is moderately disease resistant and heat tolerant.

'CELSIANA'

Classification: *damask*

Bloom period: *summer*

Height: *4 to 5 feet*

Hardiness: *Zones 4-10*

ARS rating: *8.8*

Date introduced: *prior to 1750*

The semidouble, gently nodding blooms of 'Celsiana' are 3½ to 4 inches across, cup shaped, and deliciously scented. Borne in clusters, the flowers open a clear pink and fade to a soft blush as they age. Petals are silky textured and surround bright yellow stamens. The flower colors are complemented perfectly by gray-green foliage.

The plant has an upright habit with gracefully arching canes and makes a fine choice for a bed or border, where it can put on a midseason display of color. 'Celsiana' is disease resistant and very hardy.

'CHERISH'

Classification: *floribunda*

Bloom period: *summer to fall*

Height: *3 feet*

Hardiness: *Zones 4-9*

ARS rating: *8.3*

Date introduced: *1980*

The 3- to 4-inch double blossoms of 'Cherish' put out a light cinnamon fragrance and appear over a lengthy season. Borne both singly and in clusters of up to 20, the high-centered flowers are coral-apricot with a creamy white base. The spiraled buds open slowly, and the flowers are extremely long-lasting. New leaves are bronze red, turning very dark green and glossy with age.

The compact, symmetrical habit of the bush is somewhat spreading, making 'Cherish' an appropriate choice for beds and borders. It can also be used as a low hedge. Flowers are exceptional for cutting. Added to the long list of the rose's virtues are good disease resistance and hardiness. It is an AARS winner.

'COMMUNIS'

Classification: *moss*

Bloom period: *summer*

Height: *4 feet*

Hardiness: *Zones 4-10*

ARS rating: *7.7*

Date introduced: *late 1600s*

Considered by many to be the best moss rose, 'Communis' (also called 'Common Moss') produces mossy growths on its sepals, buds, and stems. Buds are rose pink, opening to pale pink, intensely fragrant double flowers that are 2 to 3 inches wide. Reflexed petals surround a green button eye. The abundant foliage is medium green.

'Communis' plants are moderate growers with an arching habit; they are usually slightly taller than they are broad. The rose is well suited to beds and borders, and is both disease resistant and hardy.

'CONSTANCE SPRY'

Classification: *shrub*

Bloom period: *midsummer*

Height: *6 to 15 feet*

Hardiness: *Zones 4-10*

ARS rating: *7.8*

Date introduced: *1961*

The light pink double or very double flowers of 'Constance Spry' resemble peonies. This rose blooms only once each year, but the display is dramatic, producing a wealth of 3½- to 5-inch flowers bearing a rich, myrrhlike fragrance. The flowers appear in clusters, showing up well against abundant dark green foliage. Canes bear lots of bright red prickles.

A very vigorous plant, 'Constance Spry' can either be pruned to maintain a large, rounded shrub or be trained to climb a fence, wall, tripod, or pillar, where it can grow as high as 15 feet.

'COUNTRY DANCER'

Classification: *shrub*

Bloom period: *summer to fall*

Height: *2 to 4 feet*

Hardiness: *Zones 4-10*

ARS rating: *7.5*

Date introduced: *1973*

The high-centered buds of 'Country Dancer', a Dr. Buck rose, open to large, flat, double flowers that are somewhere between deep pink and rosy red in color—and quite fragrant. The petals are slightly yellow toward their base, and they surround golden stamens. Flowers occur in clusters throughout the growing season. Foliage is dark green.

This rose is usually grown as a low, spreading shrub. It can also be used as a hedge. Canes can be trained to a pillar or fence but should be trained horizontally to obtain the best flowering display; canes that grow vertically will produce all of their flowers at the tips. Although it's extremely hardy, 'Country Dancer' is somewhat susceptible to black spot.

'DOUBLE DELIGHT'

Classification: *hybrid tea*

Bloom period: *summer to fall*

Height: *4 feet*

Hardiness: *Zones 5-10*

ARS rating: *8.9*

Date introduced: *1977*

Each blossom of 'Double Delight' is a uniquely colored combination of red and creamy white. The exact coloration depends on light and temperature, but generally the red begins at the petal tips and diffuses to a creamy center. The double flowers are 5½ inches across, borne singly on stems, and have a strong, spicy fragrance. Leaves are a medium matte green.

Its bushy form and free-flowering habit make this rose a fine choice for beds and borders. It is a superb cut flower, prized for its form, color, fragrance, and long vase life. 'Double Delight' is fairly disease resistant but is somewhat tender. It is an AARS winner.

'ESCAPADE'	'EUROPEANA'	'FANTIN-LATOUR'	'FELICITE PARMENTIER'

Classification: *floribunda*
Bloom period: *summer to fall*
Height: *2½ to 3 feet*
Hardiness: *Zones 4-10*
ARS rating: *8.8*
Date introduced: *1967*

Classification: *floribunda*
Bloom period: *summer to fall*
Height: *2 to 3 feet*
Hardiness: *Zones 4-10*
ARS rating: *9.0*
Date introduced: *1968*

Classification: *centifolia*
Bloom period: *late spring*
Height: *4 to 6 feet*
Hardiness: *Zones 4-10*
ARS rating: *8.2*
Date introduced: *unknown*

Classification: *alba*
Bloom period: *early summer*
Height: *4 to 5 feet*
Hardiness: *Zones 4-10*
ARS rating: *8.6*
Date introduced: *1834*

The 3-inch semidouble flowers of 'Escapade' are light mauve-pink or lilac to rosy violet with creamy white centers. They are borne in both large and small clusters, and each bloom has about 12 petals that surround amber stamens. Blooms commence in midseason, repeating consistently until a hard frost. The blooms are lightly fragrant. Leaves are light green and glossy.

'Escapade' plants have an upright, bushy habit and are vigorous growers. They are useful in beds and borders and can also be planted as a low hedge. The flowers are excellent for cutting.

Borne in large clusters, the double blooms of 'Europeana' are 3 inches across and cup shaped. Petals are deep crimson and have a velvety texture. Beginning in midseason, flowering continues prolifically until the fall. Leaves emerge bronze red, maturing to deep, glossy green with reddish tints.

This bush is quite robust. Its enormous flower clusters can cause the stems to bend under their weight, so it should be grouped with plants that will provide support for the flower-laden stems. Because it has a bushy, spreading habit, 'Europeana' is suitable for beds, borders, and low hedges. Flowers are good for cutting, and the plants are disease resistant and very hardy. This rose is an AARS winner.

Although 'Fantin-Latour' has a relatively short bloom period and does not repeat, the quality of the blossoms makes up for their short season. Each 2- to 3-inch very double flower is composed of 200 petals, giving it the full appearance typical of centifolia roses. When it first opens, the pale blush pink bloom is cupped; it then flattens as it matures. The blossoms emit a delicate fragrance. Leaves are dark green, and canes are nearly smooth.

'Fantin-Latour' plants produce arching canes that usually reach 5 feet in height and a little less in spread. They perform well in a bed or border where their late-spring flower display is breathtaking. This is a very hardy rose, but its disease resistance is only moderate.

The pale blush pink, very double blooms of 'Félicité Parmentier' open flat, then reflex to form a ball. As the 2- to 2½-inch flowers age, the tightly quartered petals fade to creamy white at their outer edges. Flowers are borne in clusters in profusion in early summer, but they do not repeat. Their fragrance is heady. Leaves are gray-green, and the abundant prickles are dark.

This rose has a bushy, compact habit, reaching 4 to 5 feet in height and 4 feet in width, and is less upright than most albas. The tidy form requires little pruning. It tolerates poor soil, partial shade, and climatic extremes, and is resistant to disease.

'FIRST EDITION'

Classification: *floribunda*

Bloom period: *summer to fall*

Height: *3½ feet*

Hardiness: *Zones 4-10*

ARS rating: *8.6*

Date introduced: *1976*

The pointed coral-orange buds of 'First Edition' open to luminous coral-rose blossoms with orange tints. The petals surround yellow anthers. Flowers are double, 2 to 2½ inches across, and lightly fragrant, and they are borne in flat-topped clusters. Their color deepens in cool weather. Foliage is glossy and medium green.

The bushes are vigorous and upright. They are suited to many uses, including beds and borders, low hedges, and containers. Flowers are excellent for cutting and exhibition, and the plants have good disease resistance. 'First Edition' is an AARS winner.

'FRAU KARL DRUSCHKI'

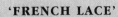

Classification: *hybrid perpetual*

Bloom period: *early summer and fall*

Height: *4 to 7 feet*

Hardiness: *Zones 5-10*

ARS rating: *7.8*

Date introduced: *1901*

This rose produces a great abundance of double blossoms from high-centered buds in early summer and repeats the show in fall. The elegant white flower is 4 to 4½ inches across with 30 to 35 rolled petals that display a touch of lemon yellow at their base. Canes are nearly smooth, supporting leathery, coarse, light green foliage.

The plant is vigorous and erect, with stout branches and long, strong stems. The color and form of its flower makes it useful in combination with other roses, both in beds and in indoor arrangements. Buds are reluctant to open in damp weather, and leaves are susceptible to mildew.

'FRENCH LACE'

Classification: *floribunda*

Bloom period: *summer to fall*

Height: *3½ feet*

Hardiness: *Zones 4-9*

ARS rating: *8.2*

Date introduced: *1981*

Flowers of 'French Lace' are borne singly or in clusters of up to 12 and bloom continuously from early summer to frost. Buds are pointed, opening to flat, 3- to 4-inch double blossoms that are ivory with apricot tones and emit a light tea fragrance. The thorny canes produce small, dark green hollylike leaves.

Plants are well branched, bushy, and upright. Their attractive form and abundant flowering potential recommend them for use as a low hedge or in a bed or border. Flowers are long-lasting and beautiful in indoor arrangements. To top off its list of virtues, 'French Lace' is highly resistant to disease. It is an AARS winner.

'GRUSS AN AACHEN'

Classification: *floribunda*

Bloom period: *spring to fall*

Height: *2 to 3 feet*

Hardiness: *Zones 4-10*

ARS rating: *8.3*

Date introduced: *1909*

Buds of 'Gruss an Aachen' are tinted with red-orange and yellow but open to reveal pale apricot-pink blooms that fade to creamy white. The flowers, reminiscent of old garden roses, are 3 inches across, double, and cup shaped, with a rich fragrance. They are borne in clusters throughout the season. Leaves are rich green and leathery.

This rose has a low growing, bushy habit and is very free blooming, even in partial shade. It is a good choice for a bed or low hedge. The plants are quite hardy and disease resistant.

'HANNAH GORDON'

Classification: *floribunda*

Bloom period: *spring to fall*

Height: *3 feet*

Hardiness: *Zones 4-10*

ARS rating: *8.2*

Date introduced: *1983*

'HERITAGE'

Classification: *shrub*

Bloom period: *summer*

Height: *4 to 5 feet*

Hardiness: *Zones 4-10*

ARS rating: *8.7*

Date introduced: *1984*

'ICEBERG'

Classification: *floribunda*

Bloom period: *summer to fall*

Height: *3 to 4½ feet*

Hardiness: *Zones 4-9*

ARS rating: *8.7*

Date introduced: *1958*

'ISPAHAN'

Classification: *damask*

Bloom period: *spring to summer*

Height: *4 to 6 feet*

Hardiness: *Zones 4-10*

ARS rating: *8.7*

Date introduced: *prior to 1832*

The large double flowers of 'Hannah Gordon' are white with bold cerise-pink markings and petal edges. Each bloom has about 35 petals and a light fragrance. Flowers appear continuously throughout the season. The foliage is large, medium green, and semiglossy.

Plants are upright, compact, and bushy. They are useful in beds and borders, can be very effective when massed, and also do nicely when used as a low hedge.

The blush pink double flowers of this David Austin rose are colored a bit deeper toward their centers. Their form is exquisite, with the outer petals forming a deep cup around precisely arranged and folded inner petals. Profusely borne in clusters throughout the summer, they create a cloud of rich scent that is a blend of myrrh and lemon. Foliage is dark green and semiglossy. The canes have few thorns.

The plant is a robust grower with a bushy, upright habit. It is a fine addition to beds or borders, makes a wonderful hedge, and provides a long season of cut flowers. Plants are fairly disease resistant but may be susceptible to rust.

Throughout summer, 'Iceberg' produces large clusters with up to a dozen pure white blossoms that stand out beautifully against small, light green, glossy foliage. Buds are long and pointed with high centers. Each double flower is 2 to 4 inches across, somewhat flat, and sweetly scented.

'Iceberg' is an all-purpose rose in that the vigorous plant can be grown as a hedge or a border or as a container specimen, trained as a tree rose, or used for cutting flowers for indoor arrangements. It is bushy and well branched and is easily trained. A climbing version is also available, rated 8.8 by the ARS. Both forms are disease resistant.

The very fragrant, double blooms of 'Ispahan' (also called 'Pompon des Princes') appear in profusion over a 2-month period in early and midseason, but they do not repeat. Borne in clusters, the bright clear pink flowers are 2½ to 3 inches across, cup shaped, and loosely reflexing. They are long-lasting, holding both their shape and their color well. Foliage is small with a blue-green cast.

This rose is bushy and upright. With a flowering season that is remarkably long for a damask, it is valued both as a garden shrub and for cut flowers. The plant is vigorous, disease resistant, and quite hardy.

'JEANNE LAJOIE'

Classification: *climbing miniature*

Bloom period: *spring to fall*

Height: *8 feet*

Hardiness: *Zones 5-10*

ARS rating: *9.2*

Date introduced: *1975*

'Jeanne Lajoie' produces long, pointed buds that open to miniature two-toned pink flowers. Usually borne in clusters, the flowers are most abundant during cool weather. The high-centered blooms have 20 to 25 pointed petals and are lightly fragrant. In fall, this rose produces small orange hips. Foliage is lush, glossy, and dark.

A very vigorous grower, 'Jeanne Lajoie' is upright and bushy. It can be trained as a climber, or used as a freestanding shrub or hedge rose. Deadheading after its first flush of blooms will significantly increase later flowering. Plants are disease resistant and hardy.

'JOSEPH'S COAT'

Classification: *large-flowered climber*

Bloom period: *summer to fall*

Height: *8 to 10 feet*

Hardiness: *Zones 6-9*

ARS rating: *7.6*

Date introduced: *1964*

The clusters of double blossoms of 'Joseph's Coat' create an amazing riot of color, with yellows, pinks, oranges, and reds all present at the same time. The red and orange tones become more prominent in autumn. Buds are urn shaped, and unlike those of many climbers they occur on new wood. Flowers are 3-inch cups that are lightly fragrant, leaves are dark green and glossy, and canes are prickly.

The plant is tall and upright. It can be trained as a climber on a pillar, fence, or trellis or, because it is not very robust, can be allowed to grow as a loose, freestanding shrub. It is somewhat tender and prone to powdery mildew.

'JUST JOEY'

Classification: *hybrid tea*

Bloom period: *summer*

Height: *3 feet*

Hardiness: *Zones 5-10*

ARS rating: *7.7*

Date introduced: *1972*

Blossoms of 'Just Joey' are 4 to 6 inches across, composed of 30 exceptionally large petals with interestingly frilly edges. Buds are large, elegantly pointed, and brandy colored, opening to double apricot blooms that lighten as they mature. Flowers bear a deep fruity scent. Both the flowers and their fragrance are long-lasting. Leaves are large and glossy, and stems are prickly.

Plants are rather squat and spreading, with a moderate growth rate. They are fairly disease resistant. The flowers are particularly outstanding for indoor arrangements because of their large size and long vase life.

'LA MARNE'

Classification: *polyantha*

Bloom period: *spring to fall*

Height: *2 to 4 feet*

Hardiness: *Zones 5-10*

ARS rating: *8.3*

Date introduced: *1915*

The delicately fragrant, cup-shaped blooms of 'La Marne' appear continuously throughout the season; it is one of the most profusely blooming roses grown. Semidouble flowers are borne in loose clusters and are blush white with a vivid pink edge; their color deepens in cool weather. Foliage is dense and glossy.

This bushy, vigorous rose is tall for a polyantha. It is happiest in sunny, open locations. The luxuriant foliage and nonstop blooming ability make it a superb choice for a hedge or garden shrub, and it is a fine container specimen as well.

'LEANDER'

Classification: *shrub*
Bloom period: *spring to summer*
Height: *6 to 8 feet*
Hardiness: *Zones 4-10*
ARS rating: *8.3*
Date introduced: *1982*

'MARCHESA BOCCELLA'

Classification: *hybrid perpetual*
Bloom period: *spring to fall*
Height: *4 to 5 feet*
Hardiness: *Zones 5-10*
ARS rating: *8.9*
Date introduced: *1842*

'MUTABILIS'

Classification: *China*
Bloom period: *summer to fall*
Height: *3 to 8 feet*
Hardiness: *Zones 7-10*
ARS rating: *8.2*
Date introduced: *prior to 1894*

'NASTARANA'

Classification: *noisette*
Bloom period: *summer to fall*
Height: *3 to 4 feet*
Hardiness: *Zones 6-10*
ARS rating: *8.3*
Date introduced: *1879*

'Leander', a David Austin rose, produces a dizzying profusion of deep-apricot-colored flowers in spring and early summer. Borne in clusters, the blooms are small and very double, and have a fruity fragrance. Although the rose is not considered a repeat bloomer, flowers may reappear later in the season. Semiglossy leaves are medium in both size and color.

This rose has a full habit, growing nearly as wide as it is tall, and makes a fine large garden shrub. It is among the most disease resistant of the English roses.

'Marchesa Boccella' (also known as 'Jacques Cartier') produces large, full flowers in repeat flushes throughout the growing season. Each very double bloom is delicate pink with blush edges. Borne in tight clusters on short, stiff stems, they are very fragrant. The petals are more numerous but smaller than those of most hybrid perpetuals. Foliage is dense and bright green.

One of the finest of the class, this rose is a robust grower with a medium to tall erect form and is somewhat spreading. Its recurring flowering habit and lush foliage are suited to large beds and borders.

The pointed orange buds of 'Mutabilis' open to single blooms that start out sulfur yellow, change to coppery pink, and then deepen to crimson. All three colors can be present on a bush at the same time. Irregularly shaped flowers resemble butterflies, earning the plant the nickname butterfly rose. The flowers are very fragrant. Leaves emerge in an attractive shade of bronze.

If grown beneath the protection of a wall, these vigorous, robust plants are capable of reaching 8 feet in height with a 6 foot spread. In a more open site, plants usually reach only 3 feet. They benefit from regular feeding and abundant watering. 'Mutabilis' tolerates slightly alkaline soil and summer heat and humidity but is fairly tender.

The semidouble blooms of 'Nastarana' are white tinged with pink and appear in large clusters on new wood. Each flower is about 2 inches across and bears a pleasant tea rose fragrance. Flowering repeats well throughout the season. Leaves are smooth, oval, and medium green.

Plants are very vigorous, with an upright habit. They prefer an open, sunny site but are tolerant of partial shade. They also tolerate poor soils, summer heat, and humidity, but may require winter protection. They may be susceptible to mildew and black spot.

'NEARLY WILD'

Classification: *floribunda*
Bloom period: *spring to summer*
Height: *2 to 4 feet*
Hardiness: *Zones 4-10*
ARS rating: *7.6*
Date introduced: *1941*

The small, tapered buds of 'Nearly Wild' open to rose pink blooms that have five petals and are very fragrant. The flowers occur prolifically along the length of each stem. The main flowering season is spring, but some blooms appear through summer.

Plants are compact and bushy, and are often wider than tall. This rose makes an excellent ground cover for sunny banks; space plants 2½ to 3 feet apart. It can also be planted to cascade down a wall or trained to climb a low fence. Placed in front of taller shrubs, it provides good foreground color, and it makes a fine container specimen. 'Nearly Wild' tolerates slightly alkaline soil and is very hardy.

'PARTY GIRL'

Classification: *miniature*
Bloom period: *summer to fall*
Height: *12 to 15 inches*
Hardiness: *Zones 5-10*
ARS rating: *9.0*
Date introduced: *1979*

'Party Girl' produces long, pointed buds that open into soft apricot-yellow high-centered blooms. Borne singly or in clusters, each flower is 1 to 1½ inches across and bears a pleasant, spicy fragrance. Leaves are dark green and glossy.

This miniature is bushy and compact—and very versatile. It makes a lovely potted plant, indoors or out, and it's well suited for mixing into perennial borders or for edging a rose or shrub garden. The flowers are outstanding for cutting and exhibition. Plants are hardy and disease resistant.

'PAUL NEYRON'

Classification: *hybrid perpetual*
Bloom period: *spring and fall*
Height: *3 to 6 feet*
Hardiness: *Zones 5-10*
ARS rating: *8.1*
Date introduced: *1869*

The huge, very double blossoms of 'Paul Neyron' are the size of small plates, measuring 4½ to 7 inches across. They are colored pink to rose pink with lilac shading, and the petals are intricately swirled. Flowers are very fragrant and appear in spring and repeat in fall. Foliage is large and matte green, and canes are nearly smooth.

This hybrid perpetual is a strong, vigorous grower with an upright habit. It's a nice choice for beds or borders, and its spectacular blooms are exceptional in indoor arrangements. 'Paul Neyron' is significantly more disease resistant than other roses in this class.

'PLAYBOY'

Classification: *floribunda*
Bloom period: *spring to fall*
Height: *3 feet*
Hardiness: *Zones 4-10*
ARS rating: *8.1*
Date introduced: *1976*

The burgundy-bronze buds of 'Playboy' open to display large flowers that are a vivid blend of orange, yellow, and scarlet. Each 3½-inch bloom has seven to 10 petals and a yellow eye. Borne in clusters, the flowers are delightfully fragrant and appear all season. In fall, spent blooms produce attractive hips. Foliage is dark and glossy.

'Playboy' is aggressive and easy to grow. The bushes are useful in beds and borders, and the long-stemmed flower sprays are long-lasting both in the garden and when cut for indoor arrangements. This rose is disease resistant and tolerates partial shade.

'QUEEN ELIZABETH'

Classification: *grandiflora*

Bloom period: *summer to fall*

Height: *4 to 7 feet*

Hardiness: *Zones 4-9*

ARS rating: *9.0*

Date introduced: *1954*

The 3½- to 4-inch double flowers of 'Queen Elizabeth' appear in a variety of soft pink shades in great abundance from summer to fall. They are borne singly or in clusters on extremely long stems, opening from pointed buds to lightly scented, cupped flowers. This was the first grandiflora rose introduced, and many consider it to be still the finest. Leaves are leathery, dark green, and glossy; stems are purplish brown and nearly thornless.

The tall, upright, vigorous plant is easy to grow and should not be overpruned. It can be effective planted either alone or in groups in beds or borders, or it may be used as a tall flowering hedge. The long-stemmed flowers are ideal for cutting and exhibition. Plants are disease resistant. This rose is an AARS winner.

'RISE 'N' SHINE'

Classification: *miniature*

Bloom period: *summer to fall*

Height: *12 to 16 inches*

Hardiness: *Zones 5-10*

ARS rating: *9.1*

Date introduced: *1977*

The 1½- to 2-inch blossoms of 'Rise 'n' Shine' are a bright, clear yellow, providing a dramatic contrast with foliage that is dark and glossy. The buds are long and pointed and open to high-centered flowers with 35 petals. Blossoms are borne singly or in clusters continuously throughout the summer, with a good repeat. They bear little fragrance.

Plants are upright and well branched, forming a short, rounded bush. They are perfect for edgings and containers and can easily be incorporated into beds or borders. They are easy to grow and disease resistant.

ROSA BANKSIAE BANKSIAE

Classification: *species*

Bloom period: *spring to early summer*

Height: *12 to 25 feet*

Hardiness: *Zones 8-10*

ARS rating: *8.6*

Date introduced: *1807*

The double white flowers of *R. banksiae banksiae* appear in profusion in spring and continue for up to 6 weeks. The flowers cover the plant during this period. Each blossom is less than 1 inch across, pure white, and extremely fragrant with the scent of violets. Leaves are long, light green, and shiny, and the canes are nearly thornless.

Where it is hardy, this rose is a fast, vigorous grower and is quite long-lived. It grows well on a tree, wall, or trellis but may become rampant where the growth is not controlled. The related variety *R. banksiae lutea* bears pale to deep yellow double flowers and is slightly hardier and less fragrant; its ARS rating is 8.8. Both varieties are known as the Lady Banks' Rose.

ROSA EGLANTERIA

Classification: *species*

Bloom period: *late spring*

Height: *8 to 14 feet*

Hardiness: *Zones 5-10*

ARS rating: *8.6*

Date introduced: *prior to 1551*

R. eglanteria is commonly called the sweetbrier or eglantine rose. Its single blush pink flowers are 2 inches across, with petals surrounding golden stamens. They appear singly or in small clusters in late spring. Bright red hips follow the flowers. The leaves are tough and dark green and are distinctly apple scented, while flowers are sweetly fragrant. Canes bear abundant prickles.

This is a large, vigorous rose with a rambling habit. It has become naturalized in North America and can be found growing in pastures. In the garden, plants should be heavily pruned to contain them and to encourage new growth, which is especially fragrant.

'ROSA MUNDI'

Classification: *gallica*

Bloom period: *summer*

Height: *3 to 4 feet*

Hardiness: *Zones 4-10*

ARS rating: *8.6*

Date introduced: *prior to 1581*

'Rosa Mundi' *(R. gallica versicolor)* is a sport of 'Apothecary's Rose' *(R. gallica officinalis).* Its 2- to 3-inch semidouble flowers are spectacularly striped crimson, pink, and deep pink over blush white. Borne singly or in small sprays, the very fragrant flowers open to wide and flattened cups. An occasional branch will revert to the deep-pink-colored flowers of its parent. Red hips appear in late summer. Leaves are a dark matte green, and stems are nearly smooth.

This upright, bushy rose is very hardy and tolerates summer heat and humidity. It is useful in beds or borders, and its flowers can be used for indoor arrangements and potpourri. This rose is somewhat prone to mildew.

'RUGOSA MAGNIFICA'

Classification: *hybrid rugosa*

Bloom period: *spring to fall*

Height: *4 to 6 feet*

Hardiness: *Zones 3-9*

ARS rating: *8.3*

Date introduced: *1905*

The deep red-purple to lavender petals of repeat-blooming 'Rugosa Magnifica' surround golden yellow stamens. The fragrant blooms are double and are followed by abundant large orange-red hips. Foliage is dense.

This shrub is a very vigorous grower with a wide-spreading habit. It is good in mixed-shrub plantings, as a specimen, or as a hedge. Like other hybrid rugosas, it is extremely hardy and disease resistant, adapts to a wide range of soils, and tolerates seaside conditions.

'SEXY REXY'

Classification: *floribunda*

Bloom period: *spring to fall*

Height: *3 feet*

Hardiness: *Zones 4-10*

ARS rating: *9.0*

Date introduced: *1984*

The 2½- to 3½-inch double flowers of 'Sexy Rexy' are carried in large clusters throughout the season. Each mildly fragrant blossom is composed of 40 or more medium to light pink petals. Flowers flatten as they mature. The abundant small leaves are light green and glossy.

This free-flowering rose is vigorous and bushy. It is effective in beds with perennials or in front of taller roses, where it can cover leggy stems. It also makes an attractive low hedge. Plants are very disease resistant.

'SHOWBIZ'

Classification: *floribunda*

Bloom period: *summer to fall*

Height: *2½ to 3 feet*

Hardiness: *Zones 4-10*

ARS rating: *8.6*

Date introduced: *1981*

The short, pointed buds of 'Showbiz' open to 2½- to 3-inch scarlet flowers. Blooming in large sprays, they are double and loosely cupped, with ruffled petals and bright yellow stamens, and have a slight fragrance. The abundant leaves are dark green and glossy.

This rose is bushy, low, and compact. A fine contribution to beds and borders with its boldly colored blooms and rich foliage, it also can be planted in numbers as an attractive low hedge or mass planting. The flowers are good for cutting, and plants are disease resistant. 'Showbiz' is an AARS winner.

'SIMPLICITY'	'SOUVENIR DE LA MALMAISON'	'SUN FLARE'	'SUNSPRITE'

Classification: *floribunda*

Bloom period: *summer to fall*

Height: *3 to 6 feet*

Hardiness: *Zones 4-10*

ARS rating: *8.1*

Date introduced: *1979*

The 3- to 4-inch semidouble flowers of 'Simplicity' are borne in clusters. Each blossom is cupped or flattened, with 18 medium pink petals surrounding yellow stamens that darken with age. Flowers bear little fragrance. Foliage is a fresh light to medium green and is semiglossy.

Bushy and dense with graceful, arching canes, 'Simplicity' is an excellent choice for a hedge; when first introduced it was even marketed as a "living fence." It also works well in beds and borders, and the flowers are good for cutting. Plants are disease resistant.

Classification: *bourbon*

Bloom period: *summer to fall*

Height: *3 feet*

Hardiness: *Zones 5-9*

ARS rating: *8.4*

Date introduced: *1843*

The delicate blush pink blossoms of 'Souvenir de la Malmaison' are slightly darker toward the center. They are cupped when they first open but gradually flatten into flowers that are 4 or 5 inches across. As the blooms age they fade slightly to almost white. Flowers are double and quartered, with a rich, spicy fragrance. Foliage is medium green and glossy.

This rose is a bit of a challenge to grow. It thrives in hot, dry weather but does poorly during wet periods, when buds may refuse to open. Dwarf, bushy, and rounded, it is lovely in beds and borders. A climbing form, rated 8.2 by the ARS, reaches 6 to 8 feet and is well suited to growing up a pillar.

Classification: *floribunda*

Bloom period: *summer to fall*

Height: *2 to 3 feet*

Hardiness: *Zones 4-10*

ARS rating: *8.1*

Date introduced: *1983*

The small, pointed buds of 'Sun Flare' open to 3-inch flat, double blossoms. Colored bright lemon yellow, the flowers have 25 to 30 petals and a licorice fragrance. They are borne freely, mostly in large clusters but sometimes singly. The leaves are very glossy and deep green, providing a dramatic foil for the blooms.

Plants are vigorous, with a round, somewhat spreading habit. Attractive landscape plants, they are well suited to many purposes, including beds, borders, and hedges. Flowers are good for cutting. 'Sun Flare' is highly disease resistant, a rare trait in a yellow rose. It's an AARS winner.

Classification: *floribunda*

Bloom period: *spring to fall*

Height: *2½ to 3 feet*

Hardiness: *Zones 5-10*

ARS rating: *8.7*

Date introduced: *1977*

The high-centered oval buds of 'Sunsprite' open to deep yellow flowers. Appearing in clusters of five or more, the blossoms are double, each with about 28 petals, and are richly scented. Flowers are borne continuously throughout the season. Foliage is light green and glossy.

This rose has a compact, upright habit. It is suitable for use in beds and borders, where its low growth neatly covers the base of taller, leggier plants. Its flowers are excellent for cutting and exhibition. It is disease resistant.

'TOUCH OF CLASS'

Classification: *hybrid tea*

Bloom period: *summer to fall*

Height: *4 feet*

Hardiness: *Zones 5-10*

ARS rating: *9.5*

Date introduced: *1984*

'Touch of Class' produces spiraled orange buds whose color takes on coral and cream shading as they open and eventually evolves to pink. Flowers are 4½ to 5½ inches across and double. They have little or no fragrance. Usually borne singly on long stems, the blooms are attractively set off against dark green, semiglossy foliage.

This rose has a tall, upright, bushy habit. It is well suited to beds and borders, where it produces its flowers over a lengthy season. The long-stemmed blooms are long-lasting in indoor arrangements. Foliage is prone to mildew. 'Touch of Class' is an AARS winner.

'TUSCANY'

Classification: *gallica*

Bloom period: *spring*

Height: *3 to 4 feet*

Hardiness: *Zones 4-10*

ARS rating: *7.7*

Date introduced: *prior to 1820*

The large semidouble flowers of 'Tuscany' are dark crimson to deep purple with a velvety texture. Petals are flat and are arranged around prominent yellow stamens, creating a dramatic contrast. Although very fragrant, the flowers are not as heavily scented as some gallicas. They appear in abundance in spring and do not repeat. Leaves are small and dark green.

The vigorous plants have a tidy, rounded form and are well suited to small gardens. The intense colors of the flowers make them spectacular in bloom. They are winter-hardy and tolerant of summer heat and humidity.

'UNCLE JOE'

Classification: *hybrid tea*

Bloom period: *summer to fall*

Height: *5 feet*

Hardiness: *Zones 5-10*

ARS rating: *7.7*

Date introduced: *1971*

'Uncle Joe' (sometimes listed as 'Toro') bears its 6-inch double blooms singly on long stems. The buds open slowly to become high-centered medium to dark red flowers with a strong fragrance. The large, leathery leaves are a glossy dark green.

Plants are vigorous growers with a tall, upright habit. Their stems are quite strong and amply able to hold up the huge blossoms. This rose is suitable for beds and borders and is excellent for cutting. Cool, damp weather may stunt the production of flowers.

'VARIEGATA DI BOLOGNA'

Classification: *bourbon*

Bloom period: *summer*

Height: *5 to 8 feet*

Hardiness: *Zones 5-9*

ARS rating: *7.6*

Date introduced: *1909*

No two flowers of 'Variegata di Bologna' are exactly alike in coloration: Petals are white and individually striped with various shades of crimson and purple. The very double blooms are 3 to 4 inches across and globular, flattening and quartering with age. Borne in clusters of three to five, the blossoms bear a strong and long-lasting fragrance. They appear in abundance in midseason but repeat sparsely, if at all. Leaves are narrow and glossy; canes are nearly smooth.

The bushes are vigorous, upright, and slender, and are versatile in the landscape. Their long, flexible canes are easily trained to climb a fence, trellis, or pillar, or can be pegged. Heavy pruning will produce a more compact, 4- to 5-foot shrub suitable for borders. Flowers are good for cutting.

Picture Credits

Index

Time-Life Books is a division of **TIME LIFE INC.**

TIME LIFE INC.

President and CEO: George Artandi

TIME-LIFE BOOKS

President: Stephen R. Frary

TIME-LIFE CUSTOM PUBLISHING

Vice President and Publisher: Terry Newell
Vice President of Sales and Marketing: Neil Levin
Director of Special Markets: Liz Ziehl
Managing Editor: Donia Ann Steele
Production Manager: Carolyn Mills Bounds
Quality Assurance Manager: James D. King

Editorial Staff for
***The Encyclopedia of Flower Gardening &
Landscaping***

Editor: Janet Cave
Administrative Editor: Roxie France-Nuriddin
Art Directors: Kathleen D. Mallow, Alan Pitts, Sue Pratt
Picture Editors: Jane Jordan, Jane A. Martin
Text Editors: Sarah Brash, Darcie Conner Johnston,
Paul Mathless
Associate Editors/Research and Writing: Megan
Barnett, Sharon Kurtz, Katya Sharpe, Robert Speziale,
Karen Sweet, Mary-Sherman Willis
Senior Copyeditor: Anne Farr
Picture Coordinators: David A. Herod, Betty H.
Weatherley
Editorial Assistant: Donna Fountain
Special Contributors: Jennifer Clark, Catherine Harper
Parrott (picture research); Vilasini Balakrishnan, Linda
Bellamy, Cyndi Bemel, Susan S. Blair, Dena Crosson,
Meg Dennison, Catriona Tudor Erler, Catherine Hackett,
Adrian Higgins, Marie Hofer, Ann Kelsall, Jocelyn G.
Lindsay, Carole Ottesen, Rita Pelczar, Ann Perry,
Roseanne Scott, Marianna Tait-Durbin, Margaret
Stevens, Susan Gregory Thomas, Olwen Woodier (re-
search and writing); Margery duMond, Marfé Ferguson-
Delano, Bonnie Kreitler, Gerry Shremp, Lynn Yorke
(editing); John Drummond (art); Judie McLane (index)

Correspondents: Christine Hinze (London), Christina
Lieberman (New York). Valuable assistance was also
provided by Liz Brown (New York).

ISBN 0-7835-5330-7

Library of Congress Cataloging-in-Publication Data
available upon application:

Librarian, Time-Life Books
2000 Duke Street
Alexandria, VA 22314